PENGUIN CLASSICS

WILLIAM SHAKESPEARE: FOUR TRAGEDIES

WILLIAM SHAKESPEARE

Four Tragedies

HAMLET
edited by T. J. B. SPENCER
with an Introduction by ANNE BARTON

OTHELLO
edited by KENNETH MUIR

KING LEAR
edited by G. K. HUNTER

MACBETH
edited by G. K. HUNTER

PENGUIN BOOKS

PENGUIN BOOKS

Published by the Penguin Group
Penguin Books Ltd, 27 Wrights Lane, London W8 5TZ, England
Penguin Books USA Inc., 375 Hudson Street, New York, New York 10014, USA
Penguin Books Australia Ltd, Ringwood, Victoria, Australia
Penguin Books Canada Ltd, 10 Alcorn Avenue, Toronto, Ontario, Canada M4V 3B2
Penguin Books (NZ) Ltd, 182–190 Wairau Road, Auckland 10, New Zealand

Penguin Books Ltd, Registered Offices: Harmondsworth, Middlesex, England

This edition of *Hamlet* first published in the New Penguin Shakespeare 1980
This edition of *Othello* first published in the New Penguin Shakespeare 1968
This edition of *King Lear* first published in the New Penguin Shakespeare 1972
This edition of *Macbeth* first published in the New Penguin Shakespeare 1967
This collection first published 1994
5 7 9 10 8 6 4

Introduction to *Hamlet* copyright © Anne Barton, 1980
Notes to *Hamlet* copyright © the Estate of T. J. B. Spencer, 1980
Introduction and notes to *Othello* copyright © Kenneth Muir, 1968, 1996
This edition copyright © Penguin Books, 1968, 1980, 1994
All rights reserved

Except for the Introduction, the edition of *Hamlet* in this volume was almost complete at the
time of Professor T. J. B. Spencer's death in March 1978. His typescript was edited and seen
through the press by Dr Stanley Wells, with the help of Mrs Katherine Spencer.

Set in 10.5/12.5 pt Garamond Monophoto
Typeset by Datix International Limited, Bungay, Suffolk
Printed in England by Clays Ltd, St Ives plc

Contents

HAMLET

Introduction   3
Further Reading   44
An Account of the Text   47
HAMLET   73

OTHELLO

Introduction   303
Further Reading   337
An Account of the Text   339
The Songs   358
OTHELLO   361

KING LEAR

Introduction   515
Further Reading   555
An Account of the Text   559
Words for Music in *King Lear*   583
KING LEAR   591

MACBETH

Introduction   787
Further Reading   822
An Account of the Text   826
Words for the Songs in *Macbeth*   838
MACBETH   841

These plays and the accompanying editorial apparatus are faithful reproductions of the original New Penguin Shakespeare editions. The text has been reset, with the textual notes placed at the bottom of the page for ease of reference, but the text itself is unchanged.

HAMLET

Introduction

Towards the end of the twelfth century, a Danish chronicler collecting information about his country's past wrote down the story of Amleth, Prince of Jutland. Although Saxo Grammaticus, the author of the *Historiae Danicae*, obviously shaped and elaborated his material, he did not invent it. Amleth's revenge upon Feng, the uncle who had treacherously murdered Amleth's father and married his mother, was part of Saxo's Northern inheritance. Probably he also remembered the Roman legend, retold by Livy at the end of the first century BC, of Lucius Junius Brutus, a forebear of the Brutus in Shakespeare's *Julius Caesar*. Ironically, considering that they were later to become attached to two of Shakespeare's most cerebral and meditative characters, the names 'Hamlet' and 'Brutus' both signify 'the stupid one'. Neither Amleth, however, nor the original Brutus was really witless. Both escaped death after the murder of their fathers only because they cunningly pretended to be fools, boys not worth killing. They concealed their true natures behind an antic disposition, a madness that had method in it, and in time avenged themselves.

Even in Saxo's Latin, Amleth's story has the universality, the capacity at once to satisfy and disturb, of the great world myths. The primal sins of fratricide and incest, hints of a seasonal or vegetation rite, sexual initiation, the emergence of a dark wisdom from riddles and apparent folly, a son's revenge for his dead father, and the cleansing of a polluted house: these potent and dangerous elements were all gifts from the myth to Shakespeare's play. They persist there in subtly altered forms, as do many of the characters and incidents of the old Icelandic legend. Equivalents, not only for Hamlet himself, but for Claudius, Gertrude, Polonius, Horatio, Ophelia, even Rosencrantz and Guildenstern, appear in Saxo. There are no ghosts – nor any need for one, because it is public knowledge that Feng slew his brother – no travelling entertainers, no Laertes or Fortinbras. There are also no pirates. After killing a spying councillor in his mother's chamber, Amleth completes his enforced voyage to England. He delivers the forged royal commission which seals the fate of his false companions, coolly collects blood-money by pretending to be outraged by their deaths, and then marries the king's daughter. A year later, the time at last being right, he returns home, resumes his feigned idiocy, and with the help of his repentant mother not only kills Feng but fires his palace, having trapped all the members of the court inside. No one, not even Saxo, seems to disapprove. Amleth has come of age. After explaining his actions to the people, he is elected ruler of Jutland. He dies in battle some years later, not because his actions necessitate any moral retribution, but simply because he has incurred the enmity of a neighbouring and more powerful king.

As told by Saxo, the story of Amleth is simple, irrational, and obscurely gratifying – like some savage stone, wave-worn but intact, cast up anonymously from the sea. There are no questions to be asked, or at least none that cannot be answered in their own terms, which are those of a primitive but consistent world of craft and heroic individualism. Some four hundred years later, however, when François de Belleforest set himself to retell it as part of his collection of *Histoires tragiques*, Saxo's tale had become altogether more problematic and refractory. Belleforest was obviously both fascinated and made uneasy by what his early-seventeenth-century English translator (1608) was to call *The History of Hamblet*. He felt obliged to make excuses for it on the grounds that it all happened long ago, in a cruel and barbarous age, before Denmark became Christian. Baffled to discover anything in Saxo that might be described as a moral purpose, Belleforest tries desperately to introduce one by way of a prolonged and quite gratuitous assault upon the worthlessness and deceit of women. Hamblet's mother, who in Saxo had been the innocent victim of her brother-in-law's ambition and lust, becomes in Belleforest an adulteress all too willing to marry the lover who assassinated her first husband. Saxo's Ophelia figure, loosed to Amleth in the forest as part of a ruse to test the supposed imbecility of her foster brother, remained scrupulously loyal to him afterwards, despite having been dragged off by the Prince, and virtually raped, in the middle of a fen. Her equivalent in *The History of Hamblet* is positively eager to be seduced and, Belleforest manages to hint, disappointed of her wish. When Hamblet finally does yield to what the translator terms 'concupiscence', it proves to be his undoing. The Prince of Jutland becomes a bigamist in both accounts but it was Belleforest who imagined, characteristically, that Hamblet's new and beloved Scottish wife not only callously married Wiglerus, after this rival king had killed Hamblet, but conspired with him before and during the battle. Wiglerus was another of Hamblet's uncles, on the maternal side, so that in this reading of the myth it almost seems as though Claudius ultimately was revenged.

Belleforest's misogyny, shrill and unattractive in itself, is also puzzling in the way that it deliberately seems to divert attention from what, in a late-sixteenth-century Christian writer, might seem to be a much more obvious and expected centre of moral blame: the revenge code itself. Belleforest is clearly aware, as Saxo appears not to have been, that Hamblet's actions need defending. The Prince may be admirable in his constancy of purpose, courage, and invention. He has trespassed nonetheless against the biblical injunction forbidding private revenge: 'Vengeance is mine, I will repay, saith the Lord'. Belleforest's nervousness emerges in his claim that 'if vengeance ever seemed to have any show of justice, it is then, when piety and affection constraineth us to remember our fathers unjustly murdered'. This is special and emotional pleading. He also brands Hamblet's uncle as a tyrant, and invokes the authority of both

the Old Testament and ancient Athenian law for the idea
that 'where the prince or country is interested, the desire of
revenge cannot by any means (how small soever) bear the title
of condemnation, but is rather commendable and worthy of
praise'. This last argument, inappropriate to the saga world of
the original Hamlet story, is also highly questionable in Christian terms. It was, however, essentially that of the 1584 Bond of
Association, a document which thousands of pious and con-
servative Englishmen signed. In doing so, they pledged themselves 'to take the uttermost revenge' on all persons conspiring
to overthrow Elizabeth I, and also upon any monarch succeeding to her throne by such means. As Helen Gardner has
pointed out, this vow made before 'the eternal and ever-living
God' violates one of the most explicit commandments received
from that God. To ask how it was that so many of Elizabeth's
subjects could put their names to such a document is to
confront an enigma. It is also to penetrate to the heart of that
contradiction in attitude towards private revenge upon which a
number of plays in the period, including *Hamlet*, are built.

As a structural and thematic centre for tragedy, revenge has
much to recommend it. It is not mere coincidence that the first
truly great tragedies which have survived from ancient Athens
and from Elizabethan England – the *Oresteia* of Aeschylus and
Hamlet – should be revenge plays. It is unlikely that Shakespeare
knew Aeschylus in any form, although he was certainly
acquainted with the complex of tragic myths upon which the
Oresteia draws. Analogies between Greek and Shakespearean
tragedy are notoriously treacherous. There is, nonetheless, an
uncanny resemblance between the opening of *Hamlet* and of
the *Agamemnon* (458 BC), the first play in the Aeschylean
trilogy. In both, an apprehensive and mysteriously dispirited
sentinel, a watchman on the roof of a royal palace in which
there is something obscurely but terribly wrong, scans the
night sky for a portent. This sign, when it comes, serves to
unleash the pent-up violence of the past upon the present. Both
tragedies involve the shameful killing of a great king and the

adultery of his consort. Both impose upon the son of the dead man a task which either way (if he fulfils it, or if he does not) will cost him dear. Like Hamlet after him, Agamemnon's son Orestes is both a passionate and a decidedly reluctant avenger: a man who needs to be spurred on at the last moment by the command of Apollo. His hesitation is entirely understandable. Although Hamlet may feel tempted to kill his mother as well as her lover (III.2.399–406), this is never, for him, an obligation. For Orestes it is, and the consequences are grim.

Most important of all, *Hamlet* and the *Oresteia* are alike in the way they juxtapose a primitive ethos in which personal retaliation for injuries is not only acceptable but mandatory, with a rival code in which 'civilized' considerations complicate what was once a relatively straightforward issue. Matricide is a terrible action, but the uncertainty of Aeschylus's hero also reflects the anguish of his position in a kind of no-man's-land, poised between the old, family-based law of blood vengeance and a new, essentially civic, order. The *Oresteia* is, among other things, about how an impersonal court of law, the Areopagus, finally superseded the claims of private revenge in historical Athens. It remembers a time, long before Aeschylus's birth, of transition and conflict between contradictory systems. But what Francis Bacon was later to call the 'wild justice' of personal vengeance can never really be legislated out of existence. When Euripides, in his tragedy *Orestes* (408 BC), retold the story of the revenge for Agamemnon, he imagined that the official court to try homicides which emerges only at the end of the *Oresteia* was already in existence at the time Agamemnon was killed. His Orestes has simply ignored the means of legal redress available to him, for reasons which have something to do with the kind of person he is, but also with the ineradicable belief of human beings that only the man who actually suffers in a situation has the right to deal with that situation: that the very impersonality which, in certain respects, constitutes the strength of criminal law renders that law emotionally inadequate.

In Elizabethan England, too, the conviction that retaliation for murder was solely the prerogative of the state and its legal institutions clashed with an irrational but powerful feeling that private individuals cannot be blamed for taking vengeance into their own hands, for ensuring that the punishment truly answers the crime. This response, arguably always latent in criminal cases, was likely to become especially forceful when, as sometimes happens, the law proved impotent or else too corrupt to pass sentence. As Bacon conceded, 'the most tolerable sort of revenge is for those wrongs which there is no law to punish; else a man's enemy is still before hand, and it is two for one'. Reasoning of this kind presumably gave the 1584 Bond of Association what shaky justification it had. It was also likely to generate clandestine sympathy for avengers who found themselves in the position of Shakespeare's Hamlet: unable to obtain legal justice for the premeditated killing of a parent, sibling, or child because of lack of circumstantial evidence and/ or of a court prepared to deal with the culprit.

For Shakespeare at the turn of the century, when he addressed himself to the Hamlet story, contradiction and ambiguity of attitude towards revenge would have been part of the air he breathed. He must also have been familiar with a considerable body of literature, much of it dramatic, in which revenge was a central preoccupation and motif. Aeschylus, and possibly Euripides, were not known to him, but the revenge plays of Seneca certainly were. By 1600 there was a considerable accumulation of native English tragedies dominated by the idea of 'paying back' an injury or a death. Some of them were imitations of Seneca. In others, such as Sackville and Norton's *Gorboduc* (1562) or Pickering's *Horestes* (1567), classical elements mingled with an indigenous Morality play tradition. *Horestes* is especially interesting because its recasting of the archetypal story of Orestes' revenge for the murder of his father provides a virtual diagram of the Elizabethan perplexity about vengeance. Pickering was careful to personify Revenge as an agent of hell, a Vice figure tempting Horestes to an unnatural and forbidden deed. At the end, this villainous seducer is ritually cast out of an ordered society which has formed itself around Horestes as king. Revenge is clearly wrong. But the revenger himself can be exonerated. Horestes does not have to shoulder moral responsibility for his actions, let alone be punished for them.

Although it is certainly ingenious, Pickering's formula in *Horestes* was too special and evasive to be of use to other dramatists. It also happens to be fundamentally anti-tragic. Revenge for merely social injuries can and often does motivate comedy plots – as in *The Merchant of Venice*, *The Merry Wives of Windsor*, *Twelfth Night*, *The Tempest*, or Marston's *The Malcontent*. Retaliation for an actual death, however, is never a laughing matter. It is inherently tragic, not only because blood will have blood, but because of what it usually does to the life and personality of the virtuous avenger: a man cruelly isolated from society by the nature of the task he has undertaken. The revenger's position, necessarily secretive, solitary, and extreme, is conducive to introspection. It encourages meditation on the anomalies of justice, both human and divine, on past time, and on the value of life and human relationships. Many revengers become bitter satirists of the society from which they have severed themselves. Some slip into madness, not simply because the dramatist needed to spin out and delay the revenge action, but because the strains imposed upon them by the period of lonely preparation and waiting become psychologically intolerable. When Pickering (who probably had a political axe to grind) chose to use the Vice as a scapegoat and allow Horestes to emerge from his ordeal unscathed, he rejected tragedy. His response was unusual. For most Elizabethan dramatists, the attraction of revenge plots lay precisely in their tragic potentiality.

There is no evidence to suggest that Shakespeare had read about Hamlet in Saxo, and only a remote possibility that he was familiar with Belleforest. His principal source, almost certainly, was a lost Elizabethan play – the so-called *Ur-Hamlet*

– probably derived from Belleforest, and quite possibly the work of Thomas Kyd. Little is known about this work except that it was in existence by 1589, was still being performed in the 1590s, and that it added a ghost to the story. In 1596, Thomas Lodge referred to 'the ghost which cried so miserably at the theatre, like an oyster-wife, "Hamlet, revenge"'. Further speculation as to the nature and quality of the *Ur-Hamlet* depends in part upon certain features of the 1603, or 'bad', quarto of Shakespeare's play. This first, unauthorized, edition incorporates material which seems to come from another and older tragedy on the same subject. The same may be true of a debased German text of 1710, *Der Bestrafte Brudermord*, or *Fratricide Punished*. This seems to have been a legacy from English actors performing a version of Shakespeare's *Hamlet* on the Continent early in the seventeenth century. Most import-ant of all – especially if Kyd, as his contemporary Nashe implied, was the author of the *Ur-Hamlet* – there is the evidence supplied by Kyd's extant and immensely successful revenge play, *The Spanish Tragedy* (1587).

A brilliantly inventive piece of theatre, *The Spanish Tragedy* was still being remembered and paid the tribute of parody well into the Jacobean period. The play is remarkable on a number of counts, but not least for its prophetic awareness of the dimensions of revenge as a tragic theme. Although Kyd's hero Hieronymo is himself a magistrate, he cannot obtain justice for the murder of his only son. Slowly, he retreats from the corrupt daylight world of the Spanish court into introspection and darkness, a questioning of the meaning of existence, mad-ness, and at last into a frenzy of retributive killing crowned by his own suicide. In 1601 someone (perhaps Ben Jonson) added to the original text a series of passages elaborating Hieronymo's psychological anguish and frustration. These impressive addi-tions may or may not have been the work of a man who had seen Shakespeare's *Hamlet*. What matters is that they take up and extend themes and preoccupations already present in Kyd's play. On a far more majestic scale, this may have been what

Shakespeare did as well when he transformed another, and now lost, revenge play by Kyd into *The Tragedy of Hamlet, Prince of Denmark*. In doing so, he created the first tragedy for over two thousand years which invites and also can support comparison with the *Oresteia*.

Hamlet is, by a significant margin, the longest of Shakespeare's plays. The two authoritative texts, that of the second Quarto (1604) and of the 1623 Folio, differ from one another in a multitude of individual readings. Each text also contains a substantial amount of material not present in the other. In terms of stage performance, even the shorter Folio version remains formidably long. The entire tragedy, on the rare occasions when it is attempted in the theatre, is likely to constitute an endurance test for performers and audience alike. Probably Shakespeare knew at an early stage that what he was writing would inevitably require playhouse abbreviation. Even if Elizabethan actors delivered their lines at what would seem to us break-neck speed, it would still seem impossible during much of the year to fit an uncut *Hamlet* into the number of daylight playing hours available during an ordinary afternoon at the Globe.

The impractical length of *Hamlet*, together with the existence of varying authoritative versions, suggests a protracted period of composition. Shakespeare may have added to the tragedy over a period of time. Certainly *Hamlet* has always registered as a mysteriously personal play: the sort of work an author composes primarily to please himself. For hundreds of years, readers have been recognizing themselves in the Prince of Denmark, as they do not in Lear, Othello, Brutus, Romeo, or Macbeth. But they have also been tempted to identify Shakespeare. T. S. Eliot went so far as to claim that the tragedy represented an unsuccessful attempt on Shakespeare's part to drag material deeply submerged in his own unconscious to light. Neither Eliot's idea that Hamlet is an artistic failure, nor his theory of the 'objective correlative', developed in an effort to characterize that failure, has worn particularly well. (Eliot's notion that Hamlet's emotional disturbance is insufficiently motivated by his circumstances has been brilliantly parodied by Tom Stoppard in the first act of *Rosencrantz and Guildenstern are Dead*.) Yet Hamlet himself, partly because of his obviously Oedipal situation, partly because he is a character about whom we are told so much yet understand so little, continues to be subjected to Freudian analysis. Such investigations tend to begin with the fiction and end with a diagnosis of the psychological problems of its creator. They have not proved very fruitful.

Like the *Essays* of Montaigne, with which it has other features in common, *Hamlet* marks a cultural and historical watershed: the moment when 'modern' man – sceptical, complex, self-lacerating, uncertain of his relationships with other people and with a possibly bogus world of heroic action – achieved artistic embodiment. This may or may not imply a self-portrait. What does seem clear is that the play occupied a special and important place in Shakespeare's artistic development: a new departure that was also a culmination. Certainly it seems more than any other play he wrote to provide a kind of retrospect on his previous work, gathering to itself many of the themes and preoccupations of the tragedies, histories, and comedies he had already produced. There is a sense in which they, quite as much as the *Ur-Hamlet*, provided a basis for Shakespeare's *Hamlet*.

Chronologically the first of what it has become customary to refer to as Shakespeare's 'great tragedies', *Hamlet* must have been written shortly after *Julius Caesar* (1599), another if very different revenge play. At two significant moments in *Hamlet* (I.I.113–20 and III.2.112–13) the killing of Caesar is remembered. *Julius Caesar* had contained a vengeful ghost. It also adumbrated, existing between Caesar and his protégé Brutus (and, in another form, between Caesar and Mark Antony), a troubled father-son relationship which, for some reason, seems to have occupied Shakespeare's imagination to a considerable extent around the turn of the century. (His own father died in September 1601.) This is a theme worked out in the second sequence of English histories as well, by way of Henry IV, Northumberland, and Falstaff, and their 'sons' Hotspur and Prince Hal. *Hamlet* complicates the motif by directing attention to three linked father-and-son pairs: old Hamlet and the prince who has inherited his name but not his kingdom, old Fortinbras and a son (again a namesake) whose situation parallels that of Hamlet but whose character is very different, Polonius and Laertes. All three fathers die by violence. All three sons feel it incumbent upon them to exact a revenge, but the response of each to his task is wholly individual.

Although the character of Brutus has attracted what is perhaps a disproportionate amount of attention, *Julius Caesar* might plausibly be sub-titled 'or The Revenge of Mark Antony'. It seems to have been the third tragedy Shakespeare wrote, at least according to the groupings established by Heminges and Condell in the first Folio. Its two predecessors, *Titus Andronicus* and *Romeo and Juliet*, were also revenge plays. In the early *Titus Andronicus* (c. 1594) Shakespeare had experimented successfully with the type of play made popular by Kyd: classicizing, rhetorical, beautifully patterned in terms of stage action, and coolly horrible. Titus himself, a father with two dead sons and a raped and mutilated daughter to avenge, produces many of the reactions of Hieronymo. He demands justice both from men and from the gods, and gets no response from either. Genuinely and incapacitatingly deranged during much of Acts III and IV, he is essentially mad in craft at the end, when he takes advantage of a 'play' devised by his enemy Tamora and her children (they visit him disguised as characters called Revenge, Rapine, and Murder) to destroy his persecutors at the cost of his own life. *Romeo and Juliet* (1595) may seem to push the revenge theme, in the form of the senseless vendetta between the Montagues and the Capulets, into the background. It is, nonetheless, the cause of the tragedy. The exceptional love which unites the children of the two warring houses does what all the threats and legislation of Verona's prince have failed to accomplish. It begins by over-riding Romeo's and Juliet's hereditary responses to incidents in the feud. Then, by way of their tragic fate, a calamity which accuses Montagues and Capulets alike, it puts an end to what Greek dramatists liked to describe as the virtually unbreakable chain of violence, retribution, and fresh violence in the city.

These three early revenge plays obviously prepared the way for Shakespeare's full-scale consideration of the revenge dilemma in *Hamlet*. But the English histories that he was writing throughout the 1590s also seem to have left their mark. The contrast between the reign of Richard Coeur-de-Lion and his younger brother John, between Richard II and his pragmatic successor Henry IV, or between Hotspur and the Machiavellian Prince John of Gaultree Forest, reappears in the distinction drawn between the vanished, chivalric world of the elder Hamlet and Fortinbras and the hard-headed, unglamorous court of Claudius. In the Denmark to which Prince Hamlet returns from his studies in Wittenberg, hired Swiss mercenaries guard a king more renowned for his drinking exploits than for any heroic achievement. International disputes are no longer settled by single combat but through the medium of ambassadors. Even the gentlemanly exercise of fencing (itself a trivialization of something the old Hamlet had done in earnest) is brushed aside by the new King as an accomplishment 'Of the unworthiest siege ... A very riband in the cap of youth' (IV.7.74–6).

At the end of *Richard II* (1595), Shakespeare had made it apparent that the medieval world of heraldry, honour, gages, oaths, and ceremonial combat within which the action began was now obsolete and even faintly absurd. Prince Hal's threat to appear in the lists at Oxford wearing a whore's glove as a favour may scandalize his father: it reflects his characteristically shrewd understanding of the change of climate in the new reign. In *Hamlet* too the new reigns in Norway and Denmark appear to have closed the door on a heroic past. Despite

Ophelia's encomium on his 'courtier's, soldier's, scholar's, eye, tongue, sword' (III.1.152), the Prince himself, as he ruefully admits, is no Hercules (1.2.153). But his father apparently was. There is more than mere filial loyalty and pride in Hamlet's comparison of the former King to Mars and Hyperion, or his sad recognition that 'I shall not look upon his like again' (1.2.188). For other people as well, the dead Hamlet is already becoming a legendary and distant figure. In *Julius Caesar* Antony began the mythologizing of the dead conqueror by identifying a mantle as the one he put on, new, 'on a summer's evening in his tent, | That day he overcame the Nervii' (III.2.173–4). Horatio creates the same kind of icon, a curious combination of the epic and the minutely personal, when he recalls the frown of the warrior king long ago when, 'in an angry parle' (1.1.62), he smote his weighted battle-axe on the ice.

Although he may seem to approximate to this vanished heroic past more closely than Claudius, Hamlet, or his own 'impotent and bedrid' uncle (1.2.29), young Fortinbras is really no substitute for it. The son of the king killed by Hamlet's father in single combat, he seems to have been nudged aside from the succession in Norway much as Hamlet has in Denmark (although, presumably, he was younger than Hamlet at the time). At the beginning of the play, Fortinbras has 'Sharked up' (1.1.98) a band of lawless and irregular soldiers. He hopes to recover by force the disputed lands his father surrendered to Denmark by agreement, as a result of his defeat. Significantly, young Fortinbras has waited for the death of King Hamlet before making this attempt. When Claudius's ambassadors complain to old Norway, Fortinbras, rebuked like a naughty boy, has to abandon his project. To keep him out of mischief, his uncle then gives him an annuity of three thousand crowns and packs him off to harass the unfortunate Poles – who seem to have done nothing whatever to provoke such hostility. The enterprise itself, as one of Fortinbras's own captains volunteers, is completely pointless:

> *We go to gain a little patch of ground*
> *That hath in it no profit but the name.*
> *To pay five ducats, five, I would not farm it;*
> *Nor will it yield to Norway or the Pole*
> *A ranker rate, should it be sold in fee.*   IV.4.18–22

It is characteristic of Hamlet that he should punish himself by transforming Fortinbras's activities into something they are not, and the Norwegian prince he is fated never to meet into a 'spirit, with divine ambition puffed' (IV.4.49). In his dialogue with the Norwegian captain only seconds before, Hamlet had matched the soldier's cynicism with his own. He assessed the Polish expedition then, quite accurately, as the symptom of a disease: 'th'imposthume of much wealth and peace, | That inward breaks, and shows no cause without | Why the man dies' (IV.4.27–9). Only when he is left alone does he invent a Fortinbras who is a type of honour, a man whose ability to find quarrel in a straw rebukes his own inaction. The exercise is dubious, but also familiar. Hamlet did something like this in Act II, with the Player whose tears for a purely fictional Hecuba seemed to inform against him as the procrastinating son of an actual murdered father. Fortinbras, although doubtless competent enough to pick up the pieces in Denmark after the final holocaust, is neither the idealized Renaissance prince of Hamlet's panegyric, nor a genuine reincarnation of the lost heroic past. He stands to the world of Hamlet's father much as the bastard Faulconbridge had to that of Coeur-de-Lion, the dead crusader king in *King John*. A kind of Henry V, he too conceals hard-headed opportunism beneath the chivalric surface of a military adventure which, in large measure, represents a politic distraction.

Behind *Hamlet* there lie, not only three revenge plays and the English histories, but at least nine of Shakespeare's comedies. *Twelfth Night* (1600), with its revenge sub-plot involving Malvolio, seems to have been composed at about the same time as *Hamlet*. *All's Well That Ends Well* (*c.* 1602?) and *Measure For Measure* (1604) probably succeeded it. The other nine plays which critics agree to call comedies (as opposed to 'romances') were all written before *Hamlet*, and their legacy can be felt in that play to an extent unmatched in the later tragedies. On the most basic level, *Hamlet* contains many more comic characters and episodes than *Othello*, *Lear*, *Macbeth*, and their successors. The elder statesman Polonius, garrulous, self-important, and fussy, is funny in a way that makes his death behind the arras doubly shocking: this is not the kind of fate that normally overtakes characters of his type. Rosencrantz and Guildenstern, Osrick, and the gravedigger are all creators of a somewhat sinister comedy, while Hamlet himself seems to be the only one of Shakespeare's tragic protagonists (apart from Cleopatra and her Antony) who possesses – and demonstrates – a sense of humour. Like the witty characters of the comedies, he likes to play games with language, to parody other characters' verbal styles, and he has a predilection for puns, bawdy double entendres, and sophisticated badinage which links him with figures like Petruchio, Berowne, Benedick, or even Touchstone and Feste.

Hamlet's situation at the beginning of the tragedy seems, to the other members of Claudius's court, to be like that of the Countess Olivia at the opening of *Twelfth Night*. Wilfully persisting in what Claudius denigrates as 'obstinate condolement', 'unmanly grief' (1.2.93–4), he refuses to bury the memory of his dead father. Olivia had done exactly this when she imposed seven years of deprivation and mourning upon herself in the effort to keep a dead brother's love 'fresh | And lasting, in her sad remembrance' (1.1.32–3). The impulse itself is not foolish or contemptible (Henry James handled it with great poignance and sensitivity in his story *The Altar of the Dead*), but it is something to which comedy, whether that of *Twelfth Night* or Chapman's *The Widow's Tears* (1605), has always been a mortal foe. Comedy insists that life must go on, that the dead must be forgotten, and the means is always the same: sexual love. In comic terms, it is quite right – although it is also a little sad – that Cesario/Sebastian should oust the dead brother from his place in Olivia's heart. The process itself is inevitably somewhat shaming and undignified (comedy admits this), but there is never any doubt as to its fundamental rightness and excusability.

Apart from *Timon of Athens*, where the issue never arises, and *Romeo and Juliet*, where, ironically, it precipitates the catastrophe, *Hamlet* is the only Shakespearian tragedy whose hero is unmarried and eligible. The play advances comedy's usual solution in the form of Polonius's daughter, Ophelia. Ophelia dutifully informs her father that the Prince has 'of late made many tenders | Of his affection to me' (1.3.99–100). The phrase 'of late' can only mean since the death of the old King and Hamlet's return from Wittenberg. During this period of about a month, he has written her love letters, given her presents, and tried to use her youth and beauty as a way of surmounting death and loss. The attempt has failed, for a number of reasons. In the first place, although her situation is potentially that of a comedy heroine, Ophelia herself is no Julia, Rosalind, Portia, or Helena – let alone a Juliet or a Desdemona. Naive, passive, and dependent, she accepts without demur what her father has to say about Hamlet's intentions, and her brother Laertes's stress on disparity of rank. She is wrong to do so, not only because, as Gertrude later reveals (v.1.240), there would in fact have been no objection to this alliance, but because comedy heroines worth their salt have always remembered that King Cophetua married the beggar maid. Even more important, her childish obedience to her family prevents her from giving Hamlet the kind of loyalty which even Miranda in *The Tempest* – who has never seen a man except her father – instantly gives young Ferdinand. Miranda disobeys Prospero and seeks Ferdinand out. Ophelia, by contrast, docilely returns the Prince's letters and refuses to speak to him. When a distracted Hamlet finally forces his way into her presence, she apparently sits staring at him in terrified silence, and then runs immediately to tell Polonius. In the third act she will allow herself, without asking any questions, to be used as a pawn against him.

Exactly why Hamlet should have intruded upon Ophelia in her closet, and paraded before her all the conventional symptoms of love melancholy, is one of the unresolved problems of the play. It is linked to the question of his madness: is his lunacy real, like that of Titus and Kyd's Hieronymo, feigned, or a mixture of the two? If, however, his appearance did constitute some kind of appeal, Ophelia was unable to rise to it. Later, when she is loosed to Hamlet by pre-arrangement in the lobby, she can think of nothing better to do than to blame him for a separation which she and her family have enforced. With feeble coquetry, she insists upon returning his love tokens: 'For to the noble mind | Rich gifts wax poor when givers prove unkind' (III.1.100–101). The trite little couplet is recognizably Polonian. It is also rather baffling: what unkindness there has been in this relationship so far has certainly not emanated from Hamlet. It is true that he is about to even the account, violently, but a modicum of exasperation might well be forgiven him.

When her father is killed, and hastily interred, Ophelia's quiet world crumbles around her. Unable to endure her situation, even for the time it takes Laertes to hasten back from France, she disintegrates into a plangent and gentle madness. Her involuntary disclosure, at this point, that she has secretly committed to memory the words of a rude song about how young men behave themselves on St Valentine's day (IV.5.48–67) seems especially pathetic. It offers a sad testimony to her hidden curiosity about precisely those areas of adult sexuality from which Polonius would protect her – not to mention her brother, who is convinced that 'The chariest maid is prodigal enough | If she unmask her beauty to the moon' (I.3.36–7). Characteristically, when Ophelia falls into the stream by accident, she makes no attempt to cry out for help, or save herself: she simply yields to the current, as she has always done in her life. This is why both the Clowns and holy Church suspect suicide. Long before that happens, Hamlet has outgrown his youthful attachment, much as he learns to put away the adolescent jests and persiflage of his university days. Ophelia's death shocks him, briefly, but it seems significant that he can respond to it by producing a wild parody of Laertes's histrionic grief: he does not offer her anything of his own, nor does he mention her again.

Even if the love between Ophelia and Hamlet had been made of stronger stuff, and he had not spoken with the Ghost, another powerful factor in the play must have militated against comedy's normal solution for cases of obstinate sorrow. This, of course, is the fact that Gertrude herself, after only one month of widowhood, has already embraced that solution with a precipitant haste that degrades comedy's process of natural healing to ugly farce: creating that askew and distorted face which Claudius smoothly conjures up, with one laughing and one weeping eye, 'With mirth in funeral and with dirge in marriage' (1.2.12). Gertrude's plea to her son to abandon his black clothes and his dejection –

> Do not for ever with thy vailèd lids
> Seek for thy noble father in the dust.
> Thou knowest 'tis common. All that lives must die,
> Passing through nature to eternity –   1.2.70–73

is, in itself, the counsel of comedy and, as such, unimpeachable. Unfortunately, she has contaminated it, not only by the unseemly and callous speed of her remarriage, but because of the suggestions both of incest and of adultery implicit in her union with Claudius. Hamlet is presumably thinking of Ophelia when he accuses his mother of having done something that 'takes off the rose | From the fair forehead of an innocent love | And sets a blister there' (III.4.43–5). For him, the words 'frailty' and 'woman' have become synonymous (1.2.146). In this equation, the wretched Ophelia inevitably comes to bear the burden of Gertrude's inadequacies, as well as her own.

Shakespeare had often, in the plays he wrote before *Hamlet*, considered the nature of poetry, the imagination, and the actor's art. *Love's Labour's Lost* and *A Midsummer Night's Dream* are both self-conscious in this way. In *Julius Caesar* the actors who played Brutus and Cassius were made to speculate in mock innocence how the 'lofty scene' of Caesar's murder might appear on the stage 'In states unborn, and accents yet unknown' (III.1.111–16). *Hamlet*, however, is unique in the density and pervasiveness of its theatrical self-reference. The glaringly topical and, in some ways, uncharacteristic passage about the 'little eyases' and the 1601 War of the Theatres which embroiled the adult companies with the children's troupes (II.2.338–61) is acceptable in this play as it would not be in another precisely because *Hamlet* as a whole is so concerned to question and cross the boundaries which normally separate dramatic representation from real life.

Those tragedians of the city who arrive so opportunely at Elsinore in Act II provide a focus for extended disquisitions upon acting, and for two inset plays. Kyd's *Spanish Tragedy* had also relied upon plays within the play, although the actors there were all amateurs. There seems no way of knowing whether the travelling players were present in the *Ur-Hamlet*, or whether they derive from the troupe which so perplexed Christopher Sly in Shakespeare's own early comedy *The Taming of the Shrew* (*c.* 1594). The stage imagery of *Hamlet*, however, exists independently of the professional actors who appear in Acts II and III. It is there from the beginning, and it remains important in the final movement of the tragedy. The ghost of Hamlet's father comes in the 'shape' or 'form' of the buried majesty of Denmark, as though he were an actor in a doubtful part. Alarmingly, this may be exactly what he is: an agent of hell impersonating the dead King. Hamlet himself, after having contemptuously repudiated those 'actions that a man might play' on his first appearance (1.2.84), confronts this ambiguous ghost, decides that henceforth he will play the part of madman, and proceeds to devise a lethal little dramatic entertainment in which to 'catch the conscience of the King' (II.2.603). Later, on the voyage to England, Rosencrantz and Guildenstern are sent

to death by way of a stratagem which Hamlet can identify as
that of a revenge tragedy (v.2.29–31). He is conscious again of
the playlike character of events when, at the very end, he
addresses the silent and horrified court of Denmark as 'mutes
or audience to this act' (v.2.329).

There are a number of reasons why the Prince should deal
obsessively in images of the theatre, and why the chance visit
of some strolling players should have consequences so far-
reaching. Polonius, it seems, like many an Elizabethan school-
boy, was an amateur actor in his youth. He played Julius
Caesar and, prophetically, was stabbed to death in the Capitol.
Hamlet is a devotee of the newer, professional stage. As a
university student in Wittenberg, he memorized speeches from
his favourite plays. He can give a creditable recitation, without
book, of Aeneas's speech to Dido, addresses the First Player
familiarly as 'old friend' (II.2.421), and chaffs the company's
youngest actor because he is demonstrably outgrowing his
childish line in female parts. A connoisseur as it seems of
revenge plays, well acquainted with their conventions and
character types, Hamlet is adept at parodying the melodramatic
excesses of the genre: 'Come; the croaking raven doth bellow
for revenge' (III.2.262–3). It is only natural, when he finds
himself swept against his will into a real-life revenge action,
that he should remember his fictional experience of such situations, and turn to the stage for assistance. Illusions perhaps can
be penetrated by counter-illusions. For Hamlet, the theatre
becomes a means of deciphering a treacherous world in which
Claudius can 'smile, and smile, and be a villain' (I.5.108), and
everyone, except Horatio, may be acting a part.

When the First Player weeps real tears for the fictional
sorrows of Hecuba, Hamlet is reminded by them of how thin
the dividing line can be between life and art. The speech for
which he has asked, a rhetorical and highly wrought account of
Pyrrhus's vengeance upon Priam for the death of Pyrrhus's
father Achilles, comments on Hamlet's immediate situation in
ways that go beyond a common concern with the slaying of

fathers. Although he has raged like a tiger through the burning streets of Troy, Pyrrhus hesitates strangely before letting his sword fall on the defenceless old man before him: 'So as a painted tyrant Pyrrhus stood, | And like a neutral to his will and matter | Did nothing' (II.2.478–80). Hamlet will later lecture the players on the importance of a naturalistic acting style, one capable of showing 'virtue her own feature, scorn her own image, and the very age and body of the time his form and pressure' (III.2.22–4). His strictures are obviously governed to some extent by anxiety lest *The Murder of Gonzago*, in performance, prove too bombastic and artificial to probe Claudius's guilt. The aesthetic principle itself, however, is a Renaissance commonplace – and essentially didactic. Sir Philip Sidney had justified comedy and tragedy in his *Apology for Poetry* (before 1586) in similar terms. What Hamlet does not reveal to the players is his private, and more unorthodox, understanding of how art may acquire a temporary and unpredictable dominion over life: how dramatic fictions can comment upon the situations in which individual members of the audience find themselves in ways far more complex and disturbing than any mere exemplary tale.

The momentary indecision of Pyrrhus, a vividly realized fact, in itself neither bad nor good, presents Hamlet with an image of his own, mysterious inactivity. Then, in the next instant, Pyrrhus decides. Priam falls, and Hecuba runs wild in a tragic grief which, unlike that of Gertrude, cannot be doubted or assuaged. For Hamlet, the speech has acquired new and alarming resonances since he heard it last, back in that vanished world of his university studies, when old Hamlet was still alive, and Gertrude apparently innocent. In Philip Sidney's sonnet sequence *Astrophil and Stella*, Astrophil relates how Stella, although unmoved by her lover's real anguish, has wept bitterly over a fable 'of lovers never known' and non-existent. He concludes wryly by imploring her to respond to him as though he were a character in a tragedy: 'I am not I: pity the tale of me' (Sonnet XLV). Like Astrophil, Hamlet broods on the complex and disturbing ways in which art and life may invade each other's territory. Because he himself has become 'the son of a dear father murdered' (II.2.581), the familiar account of Pyrrhus's revenge upon Priam suddenly looks different. The speech becomes an uncanny gloss on his own situation. The emotion it generates is compounded when he notices how, as with Stella, a purely fictional sorrow has brought real tears into the eyes of the First Player. These inexplicable and disproportionate tears seem to accuse Hamlet, by comparison, of producing only a meagre response to his father's actual murder. He stands condemned, in his own eyes, as 'a rogue and peasant slave' (II.2.547). But they also remind him of related, and potentially useful, ways in which art and life can exchange places.

Guilty creatures sitting at a play, so he has heard, have sometimes been forced to confess their hidden crimes through the power of theatrical suggestion. This might happen to Claudius. If it did, Hamlet would have something more substantial than a mere ghost story on which to base his revenge. Indeed, the killing of Claudius would transform itself from a wild and dubious thing to a judicial and open necessity. Accordingly, Hamlet arranges for a special performance of *The Murder of Gonzago*, another favourite from his theatre-going past that he remembers now with a difference. Unfortunately, although this tragedy shadows the facts of the situation at Elsinore more closely than Aeneas's tale to Dido, its effect upon Claudius and his court is inconclusive. This, of course, is the problem with using works of art as didactic instruments: unless they are very simple indeed, their interpretation must be conditioned to a considerable extent by the personal experience and predilections of the audience. Polonius, Rosencrantz, Guildenstern, and the city actors had all listened with Hamlet to the tale of Priam's slaughter. But it was only for the Prince that Hecuba, the 'mobled Queen' whose husband lies murdered, both was and was not Gertrude, the cruel Pyrrhus an avatar of Claudius the fratricide, and Pyrrhus's indecision (strangely) Hamlet's own. *The Mousetrap* turns out to be similarly private and enigmatic.

There is no way of knowing how the original Claudius at the Globe spoke the crucial line 'Give me some light. Away!' (III.2.278) and broke up the inset play. Subsequent actors have run the gamut between hysteria and controlled disgust. Hamlet announces, after the King and Queen have retired, that he would 'take the ghost's word for a thousand pound' (III.2.295–6), but even Horatio – who has seen the Ghost, and been admitted into Hamlet's confidence – is non-committal in response to the Prince's excited appeals. He offers no corroboration that the King's guilt has indeed unkennelled itself. For the rest of the Danish court, it seems only that this exasperating and tactless young man has carried resentment at his mother's second marriage to a socially unpardonable extreme. Given that Lucianus, the villain and poisoner of *The Murder of Gonzago*, is the nephew, not the brother, of the man he kills, the play is likely to be regarded by an ignorant court (and in some measure even by Claudius himself) as Hamlet's scandalous threat to the life of an innocent and long-suffering uncle.

Claudius, of course, is guilty. The moral blow registered in that heart-struck aside earlier in the act, a reaction to Polonius's comment upon man's ability to 'sugar o'er | The devil' (III.1.48–9), is exacerbated by this mysterious re-enactment of his crime. Left alone afterwards, he struggles vainly to repent and pray. It is important, however, to remember that both the King's incriminating aside and his subsequent soliloquy in III.3 are available only to the theatre audience: not until Hamlet unseals the royal commission entrusted to Rosencrantz and Guildenstern, on the voyage to England, does he or anybody else in the play have positive proof of his uncle's villainy. This is the evidence which finally persuades Horatio to exclaim: 'Why, what a king is this!' (V.2.62). But for the greater part of the tragedy Hamlet possesses only the word of a possibly unreliable ghost, plus his own instinctive dislike of Gertrude's second husband, as a basis for revenge. It is not much justification for suddenly stabbing a man in the back as he kneels at his devotions. Hamlet's excuse for sparing the King at prayers –

that Claudius's soul, released under such pious circumstances, would be likely to go straight to heaven – is characteristically devious and opaque. As with his encomium later on Fortinbras, it is difficult to believe that he really means what he says, as opposed to concocting the argument as a means of rationalizing his perfectly natural hesitation. It is true that Brutus, in *Julius Caesar*, persuaded himself to kill a head of state on similarly intangible and slippery evidence – but, significantly, the decision there was a mistake.

Hamlet has pursued his university studies in Wittenberg, the city where Luther nailed his ninety-five heretical theses to the church door. His father's ghost, however, comes from a surprisingly detailed and specific Catholic purgatory. Deprived by Claudius of the last rites of the Church, 'Unhouseled, disappointed, unaneled' (1.5.77), it haunts the earth by night and fasts in fire during the day until the sins committed during its lifetime have been 'burnt and purged away' (1.5.13). Just exactly what this supposedly penitent and suffering spirit is doing when it enjoins its only son to undertake a revenge action for which the orthodox theological punishment would be not purgatory, but an eternity of hell, never becomes clear in the play. All four of the characters who actually see the Ghost (Hamlet, Horatio, Barnardo, and Marcellus) have doubts as to its purpose and credentials. Hamlet himself is intelligently aware that demons can assume pleasing shapes, that the Ghost may be an infernal tempter playing upon his depression and his loathing of Claudius in order to lead him into mortal sin. During the oath-taking which concludes Act 1, he shouts to it under the stage with a hysterical levity more appropriate to a nervous conjuror than to a bereaved son miraculously in touch with his father beyond the grave. Confronting the apparition in the Queen's closet, on the other hand, Hamlet is reverent and tender. Yet neither he nor Horatio ever formulates the question which seems implicit in the situation: if the Ghost really is the repentant soul it claims to be, how can it ask the Prince to usurp God's prerogative and kill Claudius?

Critics have sometimes argued that the inconsistency between the Ghost's account of its eschatological state and its very un-Christian injunction to Hamlet confirms its diabolic origin. But this reading seems untrue to the complexity of the play. It does not, in any case, explain why Hamlet – for whom the situation of 'a father killed, a mother stained' (IV.4.57) prompts the most extraordinary, various, and far-reaching series of intellectual speculations – never articulates this particular, and glaring, problem. Perplexingly, he altogether avoids the issue of God's prohibition of revenge, although he has a good deal to say about what there may be in the afterlife, and about the Christian sanction against suicide. This silence seems odd in a play where even the unreflective Laertes admits that to exact revenge for a father's death is to 'dare damnation' (IV.5.135). But it must be intentional. In *The Spanish Tragedy* Hieronymo had explicitly weighed the biblical text forbidding private revenge against his own extremity and frustration before deciding to act. There is no way of telling how the issue was handled in the *Ur-Hamlet*. It seems likely, however, on the evidence of other Elizabethan revenge plays, that the original Prince Hamlet paid at least some attention to the question. After all, even in the non-Christian Rome of *Titus Andronicus*, in an alien society where human sacrifice appears to be accepted quite as a matter of course by everyone except the victim himself and his mother, the idea that vengeance belongs to heaven and that Titus ought to wait patiently for divine retribution was painstakingly expressed (IV.1.129–30).

In general, it is true of revenge tragedy as a form that the virtuous revenger (as opposed to villainous Machiavels like Iago or Marlowe's Barabas) attracts audience sympathy up to the point at which he resolves his predicament and actually kills. A sense of dissociation then supplants the earlier feeling of involvement. This distancing of audience from hero springs from the fact that the avenger, however sorely tried in the earlier sections of the play, almost inevitably becomes the deed's creature in accomplishing his vengeance. He may turn

bloodthirsty and berserk, like Hieronymo and Titus. Or, like
Vindice in Tourneur's (or Middleton's) *The Revenger's Tragedy*
(1606), he may metamorphose slowly into a man who takes a
suspect delight in the mechanics of murder. Even in *Antonio's
Revenge* (1600), a tragedy singularly tolerant of blood vengeance,
Marston makes it plain at the end that his hero has become so
warped and abnormal that he cannot continue to live in the
very society his vengeance has helped to purge. Only in Shakespeare's *Hamlet* does the audience retain sympathy for the hero
from beginning to end. This was no mean dramaturgical feat,
considering that Hamlet is responsible, either directly or indirectly, for the deaths of at least five other characters in the
tragedy before he finally kills Claudius.

There is no equivalent in Shakespeare's play to that moment
characteristic of other revenge tragedies when we realize that
the hero ought now to turn back, committing his cause to
God, to the state, or to a political revolution like the one
Titus's son Lucius plans to unleash upon Rome. As one of the
senators in *Timon of Athens* (1607) puts it, 'To revenge is no
valour, but to bear' (III.5.40). This position will be vindicated
in the end, regardless of the provocation, or the seemingly
intolerable nature of the revenger's situation. Elizabethan dramatists enlisted powerful emotional support for the virtuous
avenger, up to a point, but they almost invariably turned on
him in Act v. In doing so, they acknowledged that the man
who persists and actually does the deed must be contaminated
by it, that he cannot really be approved of or saved. It was an
ingenious way of dealing with the contemporary ambiguity of
attitude towards private revenge. Shakespeare adopted it himself in *Titus Andronicus*. *Hamlet*, however, creates a complex
variation on the pattern, deliberately shifting attention away
from an expected centre.

At the heart of *Hamlet* lie a number of riddling and important
silences. The nature of the Ghost remains impenetrable. The
Christian prohibition of revenge is never explicitly discussed.
The Ghost's injunction 'Taint not thy mind' (1.5.85) resounds

oddly, given that this, almost by definition, is what Elizabethan revengers always do. Arguably, Hamlet's mind was already tainted by melancholy and suspicion even before he met the Ghost and shouldered the burden of revenge. Ophelia's ideal Renaissance prince and courtier died with old Hamlet, and with Gertrude's remarriage. His subsequent destructiveness, however, is not that of the usual revenge hero obsessed and coarsened by his decision to kill. It derives, instead, from Hamlet's inability either to abandon the idea of revenge upon Claudius, or to carry it out. This dilemma is less easy to define than that of Aeschylus's Orestes, in part because the metaphysical structure of Shakespeare's play is so deliberately ambiguous, but it is as tragically irresolvable. For reasons which both Shakespeare and Hamlet himself refuse to make explicit, but about which they throw out a number of hints, the Prince cannot act in the brutal, uncomplicated way Amleth and Hamblet had acted in the older versions of the story. He is not that kind of person. But it is also impossible for him to ignore the Ghost's command and, like the exemplary but inhuman hero of Tourneur's *The Atheist's Tragedy, or the Honest Man's Revenge* (1609), simply sit still. He is not that kind of character either. Hamlet's problem is handed to the theatre audience shorn of any implied authorial solution, any intimation as to what the hero *ought* to have done.

Although critics have often pretended otherwise, the Prince of Denmark is almost the only one of Shakespeare's tragic protagonists to whom it is impossible to give advice. The situation with the others is relatively clear-cut, or at least it appears to be so from the special vantage-point of the study or the theatre. Titus ought to have waited until Lucius returned to Rome with his army. Romeo ought not to have sought out the apothecary with such haste. Brutus and Macbeth ought not to have killed. Othello should not have listened to Iago, Lear should never have banished Cordelia, Coriolanus ought to have trusted his instincts and refused to stand for consul, and Timon would have been saved by heeding his steward. Only the

Antony of *Antony and Cleopatra* resembles Hamlet, his fellow-humorist, in that no counsel given to this man so complexly torn between the rival worlds of Rome and Egypt could be other than an impertinence. Isolated actions may invite censure – Antony's flight from Actium, Hamlet's impulsive killing of Polonius – but even they are made difficult through their dependence upon a central situation in which there is no right course of action. Antony cannot opt for either Rome or Egypt without stifling a positive and vital half of himself. Even so, Hamlet can neither kill Claudius in cold blood nor decide to ignore his father's injunction without violating something in his innermost nature. The dilemma which torments both men is not really of their own making. Worse, it admits of no positive solution. To step either to the left or to the right is to commit an act of culpable self-maiming. Under circumstances like these, attempts to temporize are not only understandable but inevitable. They are also doomed. Ultimately, the situation forbids compromise, either psychologically or in terms of external pressures.

Claudius has prevented Hamlet from succeeding to the throne of Denmark, contracted a scandalous marriage with Hamlet's mother, and accomplished both these things through the secret murder of the father Hamlet loved. By insisting that the Prince remain at court, rather than returning to university at Wittenberg, he forces him to confront these enormities daily. The situation is one that no realistically conceived human being, however pious and right-thinking, could possibly tolerate. Hamlet himself makes it plain throughout that he is baffled and exasperated by his inability to behave like the revenge heroes of the plays he has seen. He accuses himself of being a peasant, a coward, an unnatural and unfeeling son. In Act IV, he confesses despairingly that

> *I do not know*
> *Why yet I live to say 'This thing's to do',*
> *Sith I have cause, and will, and strength, and means*
> *To do't.*   IV.4.43–6

In the end, Hamlet goads himself into cutting Claudius down in a moment of fury, much as he killed Polonius, that intrusive but scarcely vicious meddler, two acts before. By this point in the play, Hamlet not only has multiple proof of the King's guilt, he knows that he himself is dying. But had Claudius not taken the initiative by arranging the treacherous fencing match, would Hamlet ever have accomplished his revenge? Although he asks Horatio at the beginning of Act v whether it would not be 'perfect conscience' to kill such a king, and damnation to spare him (v.2.67), he puts forward no plan of action. His references in this very scene to the 'divinity that shapes our ends', determining even the sparrow's fall, are strikingly fatalistic. They scarcely suggest that he has committed himself now to the kind of active course embraced with such ease by Laertes, in which 'a man's life's no more than to say "one"' (v.2.74).

Hamlet never says why it is that he should remain unable to do the obvious: collect his friends about him, confront Claudius, accuse him, and then draw his sword and run him through. It is true that, until Act IV, he lacks real evidence of his uncle's villainy. This fact matters more than some commentators on the play have allowed. But it cannot be the whole explanation for Hamlet's delay, if only because Hamlet's tortured self-accusations make it clear that it is not. His four major soliloquies after encountering the Ghost, complex and probing though they are, are much more evasive as delineations of his perplexity and state of mind than the equivalent speeches of an Othello or a Macbeth. Meditations generated by a central but mysteriously inexpressible problem, they seem to describe circles around that problem without ever confronting it head-on. There are areas in which Hamlet's reason either cannot or refuses to operate, inhibiting factors more potent than mere doubt of the Ghost's veracity. Because he never articulates them even to himself, the audience is impelled to draw conclusions – necessarily tentative – from his speech and behaviour, as though he were not a dramatic character but someone known in real life.

Acting on impulse, it seems, Hamlet can kill an invisible foe like Polonius. He can annihilate Rosencrantz and Guildenstern, at even greater distance, by signing a paper. This, as Hamlet himself recognizes, is the moment when his behaviour approximates most closely to that of the conventional stage revenger. (His judicious friend Horatio, significantly, is shaken when he learns how 'Guildenstern and Rosencrantz go to't': v.2.56.) What the Prince apparently cannot do is the thing Hieronymo, Titus, Antonio, Vindice, and the other revenge protagonists all manage before the end. He cannot look at the face of an individual human being, however criminal, and then deliberately take his life. At least two reasons for this redeeming inability are suggested in the play. It is clear that for Hamlet a man's life – even that of a 'satyr', a 'vice of kings' like Claudius – is something equivocal and strange, a riddling compound of the bestial and angelic. However dutifully he may try to work himself into a more primitive state of mind, as soon as he thinks about it, murder becomes much more 'than to say "one"'. Currents of intention turn awry and lose the name of action. Secondly, Hamlet is too intelligent to be able to deceive himself into Laertes's belief that revenge can constitute a real answer, a meaningful redress of the situation. Stabbing Claudius might relieve his feelings temporarily and gratify the Ghost. It cannot bring back the past: restore old Hamlet, the warrior king, to life, render Gertrude innocent again, or cancel out the effects of what the Prince describes bitterly as 'Excitements of my reason and my blood' (iv.4.58). Claudius has changed Hamlet's world irretrievably. Killing him can never reanimate what he has destroyed. Hamlet knows this, and the knowledge exposes the fundamental futility of the revenge code.

Experienced theatre-goer though he is, Hamlet finds that in real life he cannot reduce his own complexity and awareness to that of the conventional stage revenger. Nor can he make himself think that the world would be any less of an unweeded garden, stale, flat, and unprofitable, if he did. This is why he ends up killing Claudius almost accidentally. It is also why, unlike Hieronymo, Titus, Antonio, or Vindice, he never becomes an object of condescension, alienated from the theatre audience. Claudius interrupts *The Murder of Gonzago* in the middle of Act I, before the revenge for the Player-King – the action which must have occupied the bulk of the inset play – can begin. We are told, however, that like Gertrude and the old Hamlet, the Player-King and Queen have been married for some thirty years, long enough for them to have a son Hamlet's age. Hamlet himself indicates that he is familiar with the source for *The Murder of Gonzago*: 'The story is extant, and written in very choice Italian' (III.2.271–2). This may be one of Shakespeare's jokes. It is possible that he drew upon an account, now lost, of the murder of Francesco Maria della Rovere, Duke of Urbino. The Duke died in 1538. Poison had been poured into his ears, and suspicion fell upon his kinsman, Luigi Gonzaga. The avenger's task was taken up by Guidobaldo, the Duke's son. No one, however, has been able to discover either an account of this incident that Shakespeare might have read, or an original for the inset play.

Only the tragedians of the city and Hamlet himself, who already know the story, could provide a detailed description of how *The Murder of Gonzago* developed, and how it was meant to end. But the second dumb show must have introduced the Player-King's son as revenger. Judging from what happens in other revenge plays of the period, this mimic double of Hamlet would gradually have begun to doubt, suspect, and question. Finally, he would have killed Lucianus, avenging his father but condemning himself in the process. Because Claudius exits abruptly, calling for lights, the play within the play merely points towards, without delineating, this conventional revenge pattern. But the sense of the unrealized paradigm is strong: both in *The Mousetrap* itself, and at Elsinore. *The Murder of Gonzago* breaks off – with the King dead and the murderer in possession of his victim's estate and Queen – precisely where the tragedy of *Hamlet* began. The Prince might finish the story in the traditional manner, allowing the fiction he has used to

threaten Claudius to control the facts of his own situation. The
pressure upon him is strong to do this, in effect to merge the
inset play with its frame, continuing the action Claudius interrupted. Part of him desires nothing better. The rest repudiates
the revenger's role, without understanding just why. Certainly
it does not seem to be either God's prohibition or what might
happen to his own personality that checks Hamlet. The situation
is more vexed and disturbing than that. In exploring it, Shakespeare created a character of a complexity unknown in previous
dramatic literature. He also extended to the limit the already
considerable potentialities of the revenge play as a means of
inquiring into the nature of the self, and into man's position in
society.

In the soliloquy which constitutes the most vehement of his
self-accusations, 'O, what a rogue and peasant slave am I'
(II.2.547–603), Hamlet reviews his circumstances and finds that
he is 'unpregnant of my cause, | And can say nothing'. He has
just been contemplating the Player's over-reaction to the
Hecuba speech, but his choice of the verb *say* as opposed to the
expected *do* is still peculiar and revealing. The discrepancy
between words and deeds is a familiar preoccupation of tragedy,
indeed of drama generally. Laertes's caution to Ophelia to
believe Hamlet's love-suit only so far as 'he in his particular act
and place | May give his saying deed' (1.3.26–7), Claudius's
despair over the relationship of 'my deed to my most painted
word' (III.1.53), and Ophelia's suspicion that her brother may
be a puritanical counsellor who 'recks not his own rede'
(1.3.51) are all well-tried versions of the antithesis. Hamlet's
inactivity, however, an inactivity coupled with febrile and
incessant verbalizing, gives the theme a special meaning and
significance. Claudius asks Laertes what he would do to 'show
yourself in deed your father's son | More than in words'
(IV.7.124–5), and is assured that Laertes would willingly cut
Hamlet's throat in a church. The attitude, brisk and unlovely,
forms an obvious contrast with Hamlet's uncertainty. A convinc-

ing demonstration that he is his father's son in deed more than mere word is precisely what the Prince spends most of the play thinking he ought to accomplish and failing to achieve. The example of Fortinbras is especially humiliating. The Norwegian Prince, after all, has converted a mere word – the name of a profitless and insignificant patch of Polish ground – into a fact so tangible and consequential that soldiers are prepared to die for it. Hamlet, on the other hand, dissipates the accusing facts of 'a father killed, a mother stained' (IV.4.57) into a series of verbal inquiries. He becomes, in the process, a character far more interesting and sympathetic than either Fortinbras or Laertes, but the price he pays is heavy.

Whatever his deficiencies as a revenge hero, as a parodist Hamlet is unrivalled. He can imitate the windy circumlocutions of Polonius, the state rhetoric of Claudius, full of ponderous 'as' clauses and diplomatic excuses for murder, the ranting grief of Laertes at Ophelia's grave, or the preciosity of Osrick. His ventriloquism, an art he practises throughout the play, goes beyond simple mockery. It seems to be part of a private investigation into how other people structure their experience in words. At other moments, Hamlet displays a relentless literal-mindedness, an insistence upon using puns or irrelevant secondary meanings as a way of reducing language to its most basic and non-metaphoric level. In this mood he wilfully misinterprets single words – Claudius's 'clouds' or 'fares', Gertrude's 'seems', Polonius's 'matter', Guildenstern's 'distempered' – or deflects an inquiry as to what he is reading with the mock-innocent reply 'Words, words, words' (II.2.193). The technique itself is familiar from Shakespeare's comedies. The women of France, in *Love's Labour's Lost*, engaged in it habitually as a way of deflating their lovers, and it is part of the stock in trade of jesters and witty servants. When Hamlet employs it, often under cover of his antic disposition, he usually succeeds in his intention to baffle and disconcert. But there is one other character in the play who defeats the Prince at his own game.

Like the cobbler in the opening scene of *Julius Caesar*, the

gravedigger in *Hamlet* has no proper name. He is identified in
both the Quarto and the Folio texts simply as 'clown'. He
shares with the anonymous cobbler of the preceding play what
amounts to an occupational obsession. Just as the cobbler
reduces all the variety of the world to a matter of shoes and
shoe-making, so the gravedigger in a far more sinister fashion
is interested only in death and burial. His riddles, his jokes, his
small talk, and even his songs all end in the same place: a hole
in the ground. Hamlet's first reaction to him is shock at the
incongruous cheerfulness with which the gravedigger goes
about his business. Time and habit, as Horatio points out, have
rendered his employment quite matter-of-fact and impersonal.
It is yet another example of something Hamlet has seen all too
much of: the fragility and impermanence of all human feeling.
Not only sympathy and a sense of the macabre, but friendship,
fidelity, even the passions of love and hate, fall victim to time.
After thirty years at his job, the gravedigger has become
death's familiar, almost his spokesman. He took up his occupation on the day old Hamlet overcame King Fortinbras. This
was also the day of young Hamlet's birth. He will, presumably, complete the circle by interring the Prince at the end
of the play. Meanwhile he proceeds with devastating effective-
ness to treat Hamlet linguistically as Hamlet himself has treated
others.

As the gravedigger unearths the tongueless skulls of men
who may once have been lawyers, politicians, and courtiers,
Hamlet fantasizes, characteristically, about their vanished exist-
ences as epitomized by the language they used. These chop-
fallen bones could once sing, as the sexton does now. The
politician used words to circumvent religion, the courtier flattered his way into preferment, and the lawyer was a compound
of verbal quiddities and quillets, cases, tenures, and tricks.
Then they died, and the rest was silence. From these sombre
reflections on the vanity of ambition, as embodied in the arts of
language, Hamlet turns to address the gravedigger for the first
time. And discovers that he has met his match.

HAMLET *Whose grave's this, sirrah?*
FIRST CLOWN *Mine, sir . . .*
HAMLET *What man dost thou dig it for?*
FIRST CLOWN *For no man, sir.*
HAMLET *What woman then?*
FIRST CLOWN *For none neither.*
HAMLET *Who is to be buried in't?*
FIRST CLOWN *One that was a woman, sir. But, rest her soul, she's
    dead.*   V.I.115–34

Asked how Prince Hamlet came to be mad, the gravedigger
retorts: 'Faith, e'en with losing his wits'. Perseverance gets
Hamlet nothing in the way of a more satisfactory reply. His
further query, 'Upon what ground?' is wilfully misunderstood
too, producing the non-answer 'Why, here in Denmark'.

There can be no arguing, nor even any dialogue, with a
literal-mindedness so absolute and perverse. In the face of
death, the wings of language are clipped. Hamlet's own verbal
trick played back on him declares itself for what it is: a
revelation of the essential meaninglessness, the nonsense of
human existence beneath its metaphoric dress. Abruptly, the
Prince abandons the contest in favour of the sort of question
the gravedigger takes seriously, and to which he is willing to
give a direct response: 'How long will a man lie i'th'earth ere
he rot?' (v.i.161). Always delighted to expatiate on the history
and secrets of his profession, the sexton obligingly produces
one skull to which a name can still be attached. Yorick, the old
King's jester, was a man defined twenty-three years before by
his verbal inventiveness and wit. There is nothing to laugh at
now. Hamlet, who lacks the gravedigger's familiarity with such
metamorphoses, looks at what remains of his childhood friend
and finds revulsion in his heart where once there was affection.

In the previous act, the Prince had confronted Claudius with
a calculatedly malicious description of 'how a king may go a
progress through the guts of a beggar' (IV.3.29–30). Now, as
he traces the dust of Alexander stopping a bung-hole, or the

earth which was once 'Imperious Caesar' plastering the chink in a cottage wall, he is attacking no one. These speculations, reproved gently by Horatio, have more of despair in them than wit. The gravedigger has brought Hamlet face to face with the ultimate reality. Before it, language fails and revenge becomes a bad joke. When Ophelia, the latest tenant of poor Yorick's grave, is brought in on her bier, the Prince may well feel that his whole world is slipping silently into the earth. His subsequent assault upon Laertes is complexly motivated: a mixture of shock, distaste for Laertes's futile rhetoric, and (surely) a sense of guilt engendered not only by remorse for his share in Ophelia's sufferings, but for the more basic human crime of having already forgotten about her.

Hamlet's physical grapple with Laertes in the graveyard, halted by Claudius, Gertrude, and the members of a shocked court, anticipates the ritualized combat of the final scene. By the time Shakespeare came to write *Hamlet*, the practice of ending revenge plays with some kind of play or show seems already to have become a convention. In *The Spanish Tragedy* Hieronymo and his accomplice Bel-Imperia stage *Soliman and Perseda* before the assembled court, and stab their fellow-actors in earnest, not in jest. Tamora and her sons in *Titus Andronicus* impersonate Revenge, Rapine, and Murder, only to find that Titus appropriates the entertainment for his own purposes, with lethal results. In *Antonio's Revenge* the conspirators kill Piero in a masque, a device also employed in *The Revenger's Tragedy* and in Middleton's *Women Beware Women* (1621) to bring about the final holocaust. A version of *The Murder of Gonzago* may or may not have appeared midway through the *Ur-Hamlet*. The evidence, however, of other revenge plays argues strongly for some equivalent at the end of the source play to the fencing match in Shakespeare's tragedy: a 'fictional' action, performed by selected characters before an unsuspecting on-stage audience, which explodes without warning into real, as opposed to mimic, destruction.

It is impossible to say how conscious sixteenth- and early-

seventeenth-century dramatists were of their reasons for presenting the culminating revenge action in this particular form.
Interestingly, Aeschylus seems to have felt the impulse too. His
Agamemnon, the first play in the Oresteian trilogy, moves to its
conclusion as Clytemnestra persuades her husband Agamemnon
to enact his triumphal return as king of Argos by walking into
the palace along a path strewn with rich, woven cloth. She,
Cassandra, and the Chorus become an audience to this ceremonial action. Inside the palace, however, lie the shambles: the
axe and the encircling net. Ritual collapses into chaos as
Clytemnestra accomplishes her revenge. Classical scholars have
often, on slender evidence, tried to explain Agamemnon's
formalized entry into his ancestral house as an example of
hubris, and almost a justification for his killing. It seems more
likely that the episode represents an ancient version of the
'play' scenes favoured by so many Elizabethan and Jacobean
revenge dramatists, and that it fulfils a similar theatrical and
emotional purpose.

It is in the nature of revenge plots, whether Greek or
Renaissance, to involve a significant amount of hypocrisy and
dissembling. Both the avenger and his adversaries have usually
indulged in a good deal of real-life play-acting before they
reach the final scene. When some of them agree openly to
adopt roles, while others watch as passive members of an
audience, all of this earlier duplicity takes on a new, and
superficially less dangerous, aspect. It is out in the open,
formalized, and apparently controlled. Masques and revels,
amateur theatricals of various kinds, barriers at court, and
fencing matches all show a society at play: relaxed, confident,
and secure. The very staging of many of these play scenes
constitutes a statement of social order, assembling a courtly
audience according to rank and function. Often, as in the case
of the *Agamemnon*, the spectacle itself is intended as a glorifica-
tion of that society, an image of its stability. When it disinteg-
rates into violence, into something horrifying and wild, it is
as though all the hidden corruption and ugliness masked by the

unacknowledged play-acting of the preceding acts has suddenly erupted into view.

The fencing match at the end of *Hamlet* is a mimic action of this kind. For the third and last time in the tragedy the entire court of Denmark – now a little depleted – assembles at the King's command. The wager itself, which pits the Prince against Laertes, is supposedly a polite show: a playful and artificial version of the kind of mortal combat in which old Hamlet and the elder Fortinbras once engaged. Like *The Murder of Gonzago* earlier, it constitutes 'poison in jest. No offence i'th'world' (III.2.244–5). This time, however, the actors are not disengaged professionals adhering to a script. Any bout of swordplay involving Hamlet and Laertes is bound to be something more than a fiction, given what Hamlet has done to the family of Polonius. This would be true even if Laertes had not conspired with Claudius, and did not intend to play what Hamlet calls 'this brothers' wager' (v.2.247) with an unbated and envenomed rapier. Hamlet's phrase here is unfortunate. Laertes is really brother to only one person: the crazed Ophelia, now buried in earth; and her wrongs guide his sword. However well intended, Hamlet's attempt to create another and spurious fraternity rings hollow. So does his excuse to Laertes that madness was responsible for all the damage he had inflicted: a madness, he suggests, as ruinous to himself as it has proved to be for Polonius and Ophelia.

Hamlet's situation, of course, is impossible. The Prince cannot – in a complex and double sense – explain. He has to fabricate a fiction in order to gesture at something which is emotionally, although not literally, true. He never meant to hurt Laertes. The fiction Laertes counters him with is far more reprehensible: a calculated and treacherous lie, not a despairing evasion. There is nothing real at all in Laertes's assurance that, personally, he bears no grudge. His reference to lingering scruples about points of honour, to be settled by the adjudication of some elderly Osrick at a later day, is wholly dishonest. Both men are conscious performers in a staged ritual of reconciliation, to be followed by a 'show', but Hamlet characteristically seeks something genuine in the episode, even if it is only partial, where Laertes yields himself to the King's travesty of a punctilious and chivalric court – the drums, the trumpets, and the cannon, the mimic gallantry, the pearl in the cup, and the royal wager – and embroiders on it freely.

The end of *Hamlet*, with its four violent deaths tearing through what was meant to be an innocent entertainment, is something with which the tragedians of the city would have been perfectly familiar. That the revenge hero, his task accomplished at last, should be one of the four who dies would also have seemed natural. The extraordinary thing, however, about this conventional conclusion is its irrelevance to most of the central issues of the tragedy. The ending of *Hamlet* resolves nothing that really matters. The nature of the Ghost, the question of what Hamlet ought to have done, the enigma of his delay and his own inability to explain it, the validity of action in a world where all achievement, all relationships, are mocked by death: these issues, of far more consequence than the killing of Claudius, are left untouched by that killing. They are still there, confronting us, when the play is done. This is not true, to any comparable extent, of other revenge tragedies.

The cool and rational Horatio behaves surprisingly at the end. His passionate and unexpected impulse towards suicide is thwarted by a Hamlet eager that his friend should live to 'tell my story' (v.2.343). When Fortinbras arrives, after the Prince is dead, Horatio obediently sketches out his version of that story. The account itself, for anyone who has just read or watched *Hamlet*, is startling:

> *So shall you hear*
> *Of carnal, bloody, and unnatural acts,*
> *Of accidental judgements, casual slaughters,*
> *Of deaths put on by cunning and forced cause,*
> *And, in this upshot, purposes mistook*
> *Fallen on th' inventors' heads. All this can I*
> *Truly deliver.*   v.2.374–80

This sounds like the prologue to a conventional revenge tragedy. It means to whet the appetite of its potential audience by emphasizing intrigue and sensational event, Machiavellian scheming, and fatal miscalculation. It might be the world of Shakespeare's twice-removed source material, of Saxo Grammaticus and Belleforest. As an account of *The Spanish Tragedy*, *The Revenger's Tragedy*, Marlowe's *The Jew of Malta* – or *The Murder of Gonzago* – it is (just) acceptable. As a description of Shakespeare's *Hamlet*, it is not. Horatio astonishes us by leaving out everything that seems important, reducing all that is distinctive about this play to a plot stereotype. Although his tale is, on one level, accurate enough, it is certainly not Hamlet's 'story'.

Horatio speaks, of course, from a knowledge much inferior to that accorded the theatre audience. Equally important, he is addressing Fortinbras, the 'delicate and tender prince' of Hamlet's fourth-act panegyric. This dangerous young Norwegian, who seems over a long period to have been moving closer and closer to the kingdom he covets, is about to become ruler of Denmark. The ghost of old Fortinbras, if such a spirit exists, must be overwhelmed with joy. Young Fortinbras himself is clearly not the kind of man who would be tempted to speculate over-curiously in a graveyard. He seems to find the 'feast of Death' upon which he stumbles at Elsinore acceptable in itself, although inappropriate to the place: 'Such a sight as this | Becomes the field, but here shows much amiss' (v.2.395–6). A practical spirit, not much interested in moral dilemmas or elaborate explanations, he will doubtless regard Horatio's reductive narration as entirely satisfactory. Meanwhile he inaugurates his authority by decreeing for Hamlet precisely the kind of soldier's funeral he would want for himself.

When Hamlet caught sight of Ophelia's funeral procession, he was struck by the pathetic and 'maimèd rites' accorded her. The play as a whole has been characterized by maimed rites. Old Hamlet's funeral was truncated and derided by its juxtaposition with the festivities accompanying the precipitate second marriage of his widow. Claudius's all-night wassails trivialized and debased the outward signs of royal authority into a matter of drunken clamour. Like Ophelia, the murdered Polonius was shoved into the earth 'In hugger-mugger' (IV.5.85), and neither *The Murder of Gonzago* nor the fencing match was allowed to run its ceremonious course. Hamlet's funeral looks like being the first ritual seen in this court for a long time that will be conducted with dignity and without interruption.

Not knowing what else to do, Fortinbras treats the dead Prince as himself. He proposes to bury a Hamlet he has never met according to his own lights and understanding. There is a certain rough grace and magnanimity in this, even though 'The soldiers' music and the rites of war' (V.2.393) constitute a painful simplification. They can speak only imperfectly for Hamlet, whatever they might do for Fortinbras himself. But then even Horatio, who has known and loved the Prince, seems unable to do anything more than 'Report' him and his 'cause aright' (V.2.333). He cannot tell his 'story'. That task was left to the tragedians of the city, the true custodians and interpreters of matter so complicated. And to their dramatist: a man well acquainted with the assumptions and conventions of revenge tragedy, who could see beyond them to a different kind of play. This play is the one Hamlet himself gestures towards in his last moments, when he addresses 'You that look pale and tremble at this chance, | That are but mutes or audience to this act' (V.2.328–9). It is part of the dizzying but creative self-consciousness of *Hamlet* that, as the Prince speaks these words, one should become aware that, in fact, the tragedy he wistfully perceives is the one Shakespeare has written.

Anne Barton

1979

Further Reading

The Text

Facsimiles of the first Quarto (1603) and the second Quarto (1604) with introductions by W. W. Greg were published for the Shakespeare Association in 1951 and 1940 respectively. The best facsimile of the first Folio is *The Norton Facsimile. The First Folio of Shakespeare* (edited by Charlton Hinman, New York, 1968). The textual problems are outlined by E. K. Chambers in *William Shakespeare: A Study of Facts and Problems* (2 vols., Oxford, 1930) and by W. W. Greg in *The Editorial Problem in Shakespeare* (Oxford, 1942; 2nd edition 1951) and *The Shakespeare First Folio* (Oxford, 1955). A detailed study of great value is J. Dover Wilson's *The Manuscript of Shakespeare's 'Hamlet' and the Problems of its Transmission* (2 vols., Cambridge, 1934). Dover Wilson's edition (The New Shakespeare, Cambridge, 1934) remains the most thorough attempt at a practical application of textual theory. Later textual studies include G. I. Duthie's *The 'Bad' Quarto of 'Hamlet'* (Cambridge, 1941); 'The Textual Problem of *Hamlet*: A Reconsideration', by Alice Walker (*Review of English Studies* 1951, pages 328–38); and several articles in *Studies in Bibliography* VII (1955).

The play's songs are discussed, and their music reprinted, in F. W. Sternfeld's *Music in Shakespearean Tragedy* (London, 1963).

Sources and Date

Sources and analogues are reprinted and discussed in Volume VII (1975) of Geoffrey Bullough's *Narrative and Dramatic Sources of Shakespeare* (8 vols., London, 1957–75). A concise survey is offered in Kenneth Muir's *The Sources of Shakespeare's Plays*

(London, 1977). The play's date is investigated by E. A. J. Honigmann in *Shakespeare Survey 9* (Cambridge, 1956).

Criticism

Hamlet has probably provoked more criticism than any other work of literature. There are judicious surveys by Clifford Leech and Harold Jenkins in *Aspects of 'Hamlet'* (edited by Kenneth Muir and Stanley Wells, Cambridge, 1979). A convenient anthology is *Shakespeare, 'Hamlet': A Casebook* (edited by J. D. Jump, London, 1968).

The comments of early critics can be read in *Dr Johnson on Shakespeare* (edited by W. K. Wimsatt, New York, 1960; London, 1969), *Coleridge on Shakespeare* (edited by Terence Hawkes, New York, 1959; London, 1969), and William Hazlitt's *The Characters of Shakespear's Plays* (1817, much reprinted). Later criticism often takes as its starting-point the chapters on the play in A. C. Bradley's *Shakespearean Tragedy* (London, 1904).

Book-length studies include J. Dover Wilson's *What Happens in 'Hamlet'* (Cambridge, 1935); Harley Granville-Barker's *Preface* (London, 1937); Ernest Jones's *Hamlet and Oedipus* (London, 1949); Peter Alexander's *Hamlet, Father and Son* (London, 1955); Harry Levin's *The Question of 'Hamlet'* (New York, 1959); L. C. Knights's *An Approach to 'Hamlet'* (London, 1960); *Hamlet* (Stratford-upon-Avon Studies 5, edited by J. R. Brown and B. Harris, London, 1963); Kenneth Muir's *Shakespeare: 'Hamlet'* (Arnold's Studies in English Literature, London, 1963); Morris Weitz's *'Hamlet' and the Philosophy of Literary Criticism* (Chicago, 1964); Eleanor Prosser's *Hamlet and Revenge* (Stanford, 1967); Maurice Charney's *Style in 'Hamlet'* (Princeton, N.J., 1969); Harold Fisch's *Hamlet and the Word* (New York, 1971); and Nigel Alexander's *Poison, Play, and Duel* (London, 1971).

Individual essays, and books containing studies of *Hamlet*, include T. S. Eliot's *Selected Essays, 1917–1932* (London, 1932); G. Wilson Knight's *The Wheel of Fire* (London, 1930; revised edition 1947); C. S. Lewis's *'Hamlet': The Prince or the Poem* (British Academy Lecture, London, 1942); H. B. Charlton's *Shakespearian Tragedy* (Cambridge, 1948); Francis Fergusson's *The Idea of a Theater* (Princeton, N.J., 1949); W. H. Clemen's *The Development of Shakespeare's Imagery* (London, 1951); D. G. James's *The Dream of Learning* (Oxford, 1951); Maynard Mack's 'The World of *Hamlet*' (1952, reprinted in, for example, the *Casebook* mentioned above); H. D. F. Kitto's *Form and Meaning in Drama* (London, 1956); Helen Gardner's *The Business of Criticism* (Oxford, 1959); John Holloway's *The Story of the Night* (London, 1961); Nicholas Brooke's *Shakespeare's Early Tragedies* (London, 1968); Stephen Booth's 'On the Value of *Hamlet*', in *Reinterpretations of Elizabethan Drama* (edited by Norman Rabkin, New York, 1969); Bridget Gellert Lyons's *The Voices of Melancholy* (London, 1971); Rosalie L. Colie's *Shakespeare's Living Art* (Princeton, N.J., 1974); E. A. J. Honigmann's *Shakespeare: Seven Tragedies* (London, 1976); and Inga-Stina Ewbank's '*Hamlet* and the Power of Words', in *Shakespeare Survey 30* (Cambridge, 1977).

An Account of the Text

Hamlet was entered in the Register of the Stationers' Company on 26 July 1602 to James Roberts as 'A booke called the Revenge of Hamlett Prince Denmarke as yt was latelie Acted by the Lo: Chamberleyn his servantes'. But it first appeared in print from the press of Valentine Simmes, in 1603. It was then described on the title-page as *The Tragicall Historie of Hamlet Prince of Denmarke By William Shake-speare*, and was said to be 'As it hath beene diuerse times acted by his Highnesse seruants in the Cittie of London: as also in the two Vniuersities of Cambridge and Oxford, and elsewhere'. This edition, printed in quarto (that is, on sheets of paper folded twice), is an unauthorized text which appears to derive not from Shakespeare's manuscript, or even from a good copy of it, but from a manuscript reconstructed from memory by one or more of the actors of Shakespeare's company. The performer of Marcellus, whose role is exceptionally well reported, is particularly open to suspicion.

The text of the first, or 'bad', quarto (hereafter referred to as 'Q1') is seriously corrupt. It contains only about 2200 lines, whereas there are about 3800 in the good quarto. The reporter's memory is often imperfect, as may be seen from his garbling of part of 'To be, or not to be' (III.1.56–88):

> To be, or not to be, I there's the point,
> To Die, to sleepe, is that all? I all:
> No, to sleepe, to dreame, I mary there it goes,
> For in that dreame of death, when wee awake,
> And borne before an euerlasting Iudge,

> From whence no passenger euer retur'nd,
> The vndiscouered country, at whose sight
> The happy smile, and the accursed damn'd.

At other times the reporter remembered little more than the dramatic situation, and seems to have composed his own verse, with occasional echoes of the original wording, as in Hamlet's 'pictures' speech (III.4.54–89):

>   . . . behold this picture,
> It is the portraiture, of your deceased husband,
> See here a face, to outface *Mars* himselfe,
> An eye, at which his foes did tremble at,
> A front wherin all vertues are set downe
> For to adorne a king, and guild his crowne,
> Whose heart went hand in hand euen with that vow,
> He made to you in marriage, and he is dead.
> Murdred, damnably murdred, this was your husband,
> Looke you now, here is your husband,
> With a face like *Vulcan*.
> A looke fit for a murder and a rape,
> A dull dead hanging looke, and a hell-bred eie,
> To affright children and amaze the world.

Other plays by Shakespeare, such as *Romeo and Juliet*, *Henry V*, and *The Merry Wives of Windsor*, also exist in 'bad' quartos; and Q1 of *Hamlet* shares some of their characteristics. But also, and more puzzlingly, it shows signs of deriving from a version of the play significantly different from that which we know today. Polonius is called Corambis; Reynaldo, Montano. Hamlet's madness is much more pronounced, and the Queen's innocence of her husband's murder much more explicitly stated. (In these respects, the earlier play corresponds more closely with the original story.) The Queen is represented as concerting and actively co-operating with Hamlet against the King's life. And there are structural differences; the 'nunnery' scene (III.1.56–150) comes earlier than in the accepted text, and a scene in which Horatio tells the Queen of Hamlet's return to Denmark from England replaces those in which Horatio receives Hamlet's letter (iv.6) and the episode in which Hamlet and Horatio discuss the events of the voyage (v.2.1–74). The 'bad' quarto, then, arouses suspicions that the play may have been performed soon after it was written in a text that has otherwise not come down to us, possibly an earlier version, possibly a shortened form of what we now regard as the authentic text, made conceivably for a touring company.

For all its faults, Q1 is occasionally useful to the editor. Once or twice, it is the only source of what seems an authentic reading (as at iii.2.261; see the Commentary). It provides supporting evidence for other readings. Its stage directions, scanty though they are, are of exceptional interest, since they give us information about the early staging of the play which is not available elsewhere (the more interesting of them are given in collations list 7 below). And it reports an expansion of Hamlet's comments to the First Player on 'those that play your clowns' which may well derive from Shakespeare's own theatre, and perhaps from his pen. Our edition is the first to include this passage in the text (iii.2.43–55).

The entry of *Hamlet* to James Roberts in 1602, mentioned above, was probably what is known as a 'staying entry', designed, that is, to prevent unauthorized publication. The players may well have wished to keep the play out of print while it was one of their main assets. If so, they failed, but after Q1 was published they appear to have authorized the play's publication; it is pleasant to think that this may have been in an attempt to redeem Shakespeare's reputation. James Roberts was the printer (though not the publisher) of the second quarto ('Q2'), which appeared late in 1604 (some copies are dated 1605), described on the title-page as 'The Tragicall Historie of Hamlet, Prince of Denmarke. By William Shakespeare. Newly imprinted and enlarged to almost as much againe as it was, according to the true and perfect Coppie'. This is the longest single version that we have. The enlargement is mainly in the contemplative and imaginative parts, little being added in the way of action and incident. The play appears to have been printed largely from Shakespeare's own manuscript, with some use of Q1. Unfortunately it is badly printed, with many obvious misprints and errors of omission, transposition, and so on, probably because the manuscript was difficult to read. And the punctuation is chaotic. Moreover, Q2 does not include passages totalling about 95 lines which were later printed in the first Folio ('F'). The two main omissions are II.2.239–69 and 336–61, and slight awkwardnesses in the surrounding dialogue suggest that they were cuts in Q2, rather than later rewritings. Although Q2 is the best single surviving text, it does not tell us all that we need to know.

The good quarto was reprinted several times, without authoritative alteration. The only other early text of the play of importance to an editor is the one included in the collected edition of Shakespeare's plays, known as the first Folio, which appeared in 1623. Here, as at the beginning of the text of Q2, it is called *The Tragedie of Hamlet, Prince of Denmarke*. Again the situation is not straightforward. The printers seem sometimes to have consulted a copy of Q2, but to have taken as their primary source either the prompt copy, or a transcript of it, which bore witness to changes made in the theatre, whether with or without Shakespeare's help and approval. Their text (which, on the whole, is well printed) omits about 230 lines that are found in Q2; most of these are in Hamlet's role, and they include one of his soliloquies ('How all occasions . . .', IV.4.32–66). A few of the omissions are clearly accidental, but most are deliberate cuts, made presumably to lighten the actor's task. The stage directions are rather more explicitly theatrical than those of Q2, especially in the final scene. And the text includes additions and repetitions of words and phrases unnecessary to the sense, along with indications for sounds 'within', that may be theatrical in origin. There are, then, good grounds for belief that the Folio comes closer than Q2 to representing the play as it was performed by Shakespeare's company. But in some respects it also offers a more carefully prepared, 'literary' version, correcting lacking concord between subject and verb (II.2.20; IV.5.99), regularizing the logic (II.2.216), and correcting words interpreted as being erroneous ('sulleyes' for 'sallies', II.1.39).

The modern editor, then, is faced with three different versions of the play. How can he best provide a single text which will not betray Shakespeare's intentions? When variants are indifferent, Q2 may claim superior authority as the text that is closest to Shakespeare's manuscript. Other variants have to be judged on their intrinsic merits (which usually means literary merits) in the light of all the information available. The Folio has its own kind of authority, both because it corrects many obvious errors in Q2, and because it represents the practice of the playhouse for which Shakespeare wrote. In this edition, changes made in F are admitted into the text when they seem to represent a genuine amendment of a probable error in Q2. When the changes are merely a 'modernization' of grammar or of the form of a word, the Q2 reading is usually retained. The longer passages contained in F but not printed in Q2 are included. So also are many of the repetitions in Hamlet's speech not found in Q2 (for example 'well, well, well' at III.1.92, where Q2 has only 'well'). Although these have sometimes been regarded by recent editors as 'actors' interpolations' and therefore denied a place in Shakespeare's 'authentic text', there is no need to take so derogatory a view of them. *Hamlet* was performed by the company to which Shakespeare belonged, and presumably he acted in it (there is a tradition that he played the Ghost). So changes in the Folio text may represent his own minor improvements to help the actors. We have reason to respect the modifications made in the acting versions of his plays; indeed, a director of the play might find it convenient to use some of F's slightly more theatrical readings that an editor feels obliged to exclude; and he could do so with the confidence that there is a good chance that they indicate Shakespeare's second thoughts.

Few additions have been made to the stage directions; usually the stage business that can be deduced from the text or derived from theatre traditions is discussed in the Commentary. The number of elisions of vowels has been reduced. The practice of the printers in the early texts is inconsistent and unreliable, and any relation to the pronunciation of words on the stage is not known. It seems likely that the scansion of the verse line demands the weakening of syllables, and that the vowels were pronounced lightly, retaining the rhythm of the line, rather than suppressed entirely and so causing uncouth consonant clusters.

In both Q1 and Q2, the play is printed continuously, without division into acts and scenes. In F, only a perfunctory attempt at division occurs, extending no further than II.2. In this edition the traditional division is followed.

COLLATIONS

The collation lists are *selective*. They are arranged as follows: (1) readings of this text derived from F, not Q2; (2) readings derived from Q1, not Q2 or F; (3) readings not derived from Q1, Q2, or F; (4) alterations of Q2's stage directions; (5) readings of F and Q1 not accepted in this text; (6) passages found in Q2 but omitted in F; (7) stage directions in Q1.

Quotations from early editions are unmodernized, except that 'long s' (ſ) is replaced by 's'.

I

The following readings in the present text of *Hamlet* derive from F, not from Q2. F's reading (as given in this edition) is followed by the Q2 form, unmodernized. The list includes passages found in F only, totalling about 95 lines. In general,

F's adoption of more familiar variant spellings and its correction of obvious misprints are not noted here.

1.1.	16	soldier] souldiers
	21	MARCELLUS] *Hora.*
	44	harrows] horrowes
	63	sledded] sleaded
	73	why] with
		cast] cost
	91	returned] returne
	93	covenant] comart
	139	you] your
	176	conveniently] conuenient
1.2.	58	He hath] Hath
	67	Not so] Not so much
	77	good] coold
	83	denote] deuote
	96	a] or
	132	self] seale
	133	weary] wary
	137	to this] thus
	143	would] should
	149	even she] *not in* Q2
	175	to drink deep] for to drinke
	178	see] *not in* Q2
	224	Indeed, indeed] Indeede
	237	Very like, very like] Very like
	257	Foul] fonde
1.3.	3	convoy is] conuay, in
	12	bulk] bulkes
	18	For . . . birth] *not in* Q2
	49	like] *not in* Q2
	68	thine] thy
	74	Are] Or
	75	be] boy
	76	loan] loue

	83	invites you. Go.] inuests you goe,
	125	tether] tider
	131	beguile] beguide
I.4.	2	a] *not in* Q2
	71	beetles] bettles
I.5.	20	fretful] fearefull
	47	a] *not in* Q2
	55	lust] but
	56	sate] sort
	68	posset] possesse
	95	stiffly] swiftly
	116	bird] and
	122	my lord] *not in* Q2
II.1.	28	no] *not in* Q2
	38	warrant] wit
	39	sullies] sallies
	40	i'th'] with
	52–3	at 'friend' . . . 'gentleman'] *not in* Q2
	63	takes] take
	105	passion] passions
	112	quoted] coted
II.2.	43	Assure you,] I assure
	57	o'erhasty] hastie
	73	three] threescore
	90	since] *not in* Q2
	126	above] about
	137	winking] working
	143	his] her
	148	watch] wath
	149	a] *not in* Q2
	151	'tis] *not in* Q2
	189	far gone, far gone] farre gone
	210	sanity] sanctity
	212–13	and suddenly . . . between him] *not in* Q2
	213	honourable] *not in* Q2
	214	most humbly] *not in* Q2

215	sir] *not in* Q2
224	excellent] extent
228	over-happy] euer happy
229	cap] lap
236	that] *not in* Q2
239–69	Let me . . . dreadfully attended] *not in* Q2
272	even] euer
278	Why] *not in* Q2
303	What a piece] What peece
305	moving how] moouing, how
	admirable, in] admirable in
306	angel, in] Angell in
309	woman] women
320	of] on
323–4	the clown . . . o'th'sere] *not in* Q2
325	blank] black
336–61	How comes . . . load too] *not in* Q2
363	mows] mouths
372	lest my] let me
397–8	tragical-historical, tragical-comical-historical-pastoral] *not in* Q2
424	By'r] by
428	French falconers] friendly Fankners
442	affectation] affection
445	tale] talke
472	Then senseless Ilium] *not in* Q2
477	reverend] reuerent
479	And] *not in* Q2
502	'Mobled Queen' is good] *not in* Q2
512	husband's] husband
537	ha't] hate
551	his] the
558	the cue] that
579	O, vengeance!] *not in* Q2
597	devil . . . devil] deale . . . deale
III.1. 1	And] an

28	too] two
32	lawful espials] *not in* Q2
46	loneliness] lowlines
55	Let's] *not in* Q2
83	of us all] *not in* Q2
85	sicklied] sickled
92	well, well, well] well
99	the] these
107	your honesty] you
121	to] *not in* Q2
129	all] *not in* Q2
138	Go] *not in* Q2
142	O] *not in* Q2
143	too] *not in* Q2
145	lisp] list
146–7	your ignorance] ignorance
153	expectancy] expectation
157	music] musickt
158	that] what
160	feature] stature
189	unwatched] vnmatcht
III.2. 10	tatters] totters
22	own] *not in* Q2
25	make] makes
26	of the which] of which
29	praise] praysd
36	sir] *not in* Q2
99	detecting] detected
123–4	HAMLET I . . . lord] *not in* Q2
144	*very lovingly*] *not in* Q2
	She kneels, and makes show of protestation unto him] *not in* Q2
146	is miching] munching
151	counsel] *not in* Q2
165	orbèd] orb'd the
173	your] our

	178	In neither] Eyther none, in neither
	179	love] Lord
	200	like] the
	209	joys] joy
	233	If, once a widow, ever I be wife] If once I be a widdow, euer I be a wife
	262	Pox] *not in* Q2
	265	Confederate] Considerat
	275	HAMLET What, frighted with false fire?] *not in* Q2
	285	two] *not in* Q2
	287	sir] *not in* Q2
	317	start] stare
	326	of my] of
	366	thumb] the vmber
	375	the top of] *not in* Q2
	379	can fret me] fret me not
	393–4	POLONIUS I will say so. HAMLET 'By and by' is easily said. *Exit Polonius* Leave me, friends.] Leaue me friends.	I will, say so. By and by is easily said,
	396	breathes] breakes
	398	bitter business as the day] busines as the bitter day
	403	daggers] dagger
III.3.	19	huge] hough
	22	ruin] raine
	23	with] *not in* Q2
	50	pardoned] pardon
	58	shove] showe
	73	pat] but
	79	hire and salary] base and silly
	89	drunk] drunke,
III.4.	5	with him] *not in* Q2
	6	HAMLET . . . mother] *not in* Q2
	7	warrant] wait
	21	inmost] most
	50	Yea] Ore
	53	That . . . index] *spoken by Hamlet*

	60	heaven-kissing] heaue, a kissing
	89	panders] pardons
	90	mine] my very
		very] *not in* Q2
	91	grainèd] greeued
	92	not leave] leaue there
	96	mine] my
	98	tithe] kyth
	140	Ecstasy?] *not in* Q2
	144	I] *not in* Q2
	159	live] leaue
	166	Refrain tonight] to refraine night
	187	ravel] rouell
	216	foolish] most foolish
IV.2.	2	GENTLEMEN (*within*) Hamlet! Lord Hamlet!] *not i*. Q2
	6	Compounded] Compound
30–31		Hide fox, and all after] *not in* Q2
IV.3.	42	With fiery quickness] *not in* Q2
	54	and so] so
	70	were . . . begun] will . . . begin
IV.5.	9	aim] yawne
	42	God] good
	57	la] *not in* Q2
	83	their] *not in* Q2
	90	his] this
	98	QUEEN Alack . . . this?] *not in* Q2
	108	They] The
	159	Till] Tell
	162	an old] a poore
163–5		Nature . . . loves] *not in* Q2
	167	Hey . . . nony] *not in* Q2
	183	O, you must] you may
	196	All] *not in* Q2
	200	Christian] Christians
		I pray God] *not in* Q2

	201	see] *not in* Q2
IV.6.	9	an't] (and't); and
	21	*good*] *not in* Q2
	25	*bore*] bord
	29	*He*] So
	31	give] *not in* Q2
IV.7.	6	proceeded] proceede
	14	conjunctive] concliue
	22	loud a wind] loued Arm'd
	24	And] But
		had] haue
	36	How . . . news] *not in* Q2
		Letters . . . Hamlet] *not in* Q2
	45	*your pardon*] you pardon
	46	*and more strange*] *not in* Q2
	47	*Hamlet*] *not in* Q2
	55	shall] *not in* Q2
	56	didest] didst
	61	checking] the King
	87	my] me
	133	on] ore
	139	that] *not in* Q2
	155	ha't] hate
	162	How, sweet Queen] *not in* Q2
	167	hoar] horry
	171	cold] cull-cold
	177	tunes] laudes
V.1.	9	*se offendendo*] so offended
	12	and to perform. Argal,] to performe, or all;
	34–7	SECOND CLOWN Why . . . arms?] *not in* Q2
	43	frame] *not in* Q2
	60	stoup] soope
	84	meant] went
	88	mazzard] massene
	104–5	Is . . . recoveries] *not in* Q2
	106	his vouchers] vouchers

107	double ones too] doubles
118	O] or
119	For . . . meet] *not in* Q2
141	*all*] *not in* Q2
163	nowadays] *not in* Q2
170–71	three-and-twenty] 23
181	Let me see] *not in* Q2
204	as thus] *not in* Q2
212	winter's] waters
222, 231	PRIEST] *Doct.*
225	have] been
227	Shards] *not in* Q2
257	and] *not in* Q2
273	thou] *not in* Q2
281	thus] this
294	shortly] thereby
v.2. 6	bilboes] bilbo
9	pall] fall
17	unseal] vnfold
43	as's] (Assis); as sir
52	Subscribed] Subscribe
57	Why . . . employment] *not in* Q2
68–80	To quit . . . here] *not in* Q2
93	Put] *not in* Q2
98	sultry] sully
	for] or
101	But] *not in* Q2
148	hangers] hanger
154	carriages] carriage
160	impawned, as] (impon'd as); *not in* Q2
175	re-deliver] deliuer
	e'en] *not in* Q2
179–80	Yours, yours. He] Yours
184	comply] so
185	bevy] breede
187	yeasty] histy

189	winnowed] trennowed
203	this wager] *not in* Q2
206	But] *not in* Q2
209–10	gaingiving] gamgiuing
214	now, 'tis] tis
234	Sir, in this audience] *not in* Q2
244	keep] *not in* Q2
	till] all
248	Come on] *not in* Q2
257	bettered] better
266	union] Onixe
280	A touch, a touch] *not in* Q2
293	afeard] sure
307	Hamlet. Hamlet,] *Hamlet*,
310	thy] my
319	murderous] *not in* Q2
320	thy union] the Onixe
345	the] th'
358	proud] prou'd
373	th'] *not in* Q2
377	forced] for no
386	on] no
393	rites] right

2

The following readings in the present text derive from Q1, and not from Q2 or F. Q1's reading (as given in this edition) is followed by the Q2 and F forms, unmodernized.

I.2.	209	Where, as] Whereas Q2, F
III.2.	43–55	And then you . . . Well] *not in* Q2, F
	261	must take] mistake Q2, F

3

The following readings in the present text are emendations of
the words found in Q1 (for III.2.45), Q2, or F (which are
printed, unmodernized, after the reading of this edition, with
where appropriate the forms found in other early texts). A few
of these alterations were made in the later quartos or folios.
Most of the other emendations were made by the eighteenth-
century editors.

THE CHARACTERS IN THE PLAY] *not in* Q2, F

I.I.	94	designed] desseigne Q2; designe F
	121	feared] feare Q2
I.2.	82	shapes] chapes Q2; she wes F
	129	sullied] sallied Q2; solid F
I.3.	109	Running] Wrong Q2; Roaming F
	130	bawds] bonds Q2, F
I.4.	27	the] their Q2
	36	evil] eale Q2
	70	summit] somnet Q2; Sonnet F
I.5.	43	wit] wits Q2, F
II.2.	324	tickle] tickled F
	341	berattle] be-ratled F
	348	most like] like most F
	493	fellies] follies Q2; Fallies F
	517	whe'er] where Q2, F
	581	father] *not in* Q2, F
III.2.	45	quote] quotes
	229	An] And Q2
III.3.	6	near us] neer's Q2; dangerous F
	17	or 'tis] or it is Q2; It is F
III.4.	170	master] *not in* Q2
IV.1.	40	So haply slander] *not in* Q2, F
IV.2.	17–	like an ape an apple] like an apple Q2; like an
	18	Ape F

IV.5. 16   QUEEN Let her come in] *spoken by Horatio in Q2;*
              printed in italic as part of a stage direction in F

       121   brows] browe Q2; brow F

       144   swoopstake] soopstake Q2; Soop-stake F

       154   VOICES (*within*) Let her come in] *spoken by Laertes*
              in Q2; F substitutes the stage direction 'A noise within.
              Let her come in.'

IV.7. 121   spendthrift] spend thirfts Q2

V.1.   272   eisel] Esill Q2; *Esile* F

V.2.   19   Ah] A Q2; Oh F

       29   villainies] villaines Q2, F

       73   interim is] *interim's* F

       78   court] count F

       109   feelingly] sellingly Q2

       140   his] this Q2

       141   them, in his meed he's] them in his meed, hee's Q2

       189   fanned] prophane Q2; fond F

       217   knows of aught he leaves,] of ought he leaues,
              knowes Q2; ha's ought of what he leaues. F

4

The directions in this edition are based on those of Q2, with
some additions from F. The original directions have been
normalized and clarified. Further directions have been added
where necessary to clarify the action. There are no directions
for speeches to be spoken aside or addressed to a particular
character in Q2 or F, except that Hamlet's interjections in the
play scene (III.2.191 and 234) are printed to the right of the
dialogue in Q2, as if to indicate their special nature. Below are
listed some of the more important additions and alterations to
Q2's directions. When these derive in whole or part from F,
this is noted. The list also includes the more interesting F
directions not accepted in this edition. Minor alterations to Q2,
such as the addition of a character's name to *Exit*, the change

of *Exit* to *Exeunt* or *Song* to *sings*, the normalization of character
names, and the provision of exits and entrances where these are
obviously required, are not listed here.

I.I.   127   *He spreads his arms*] It spreads his armes. Q2; *not in* F

I.2.   0   *Flourish. Enter Claudius, King of Denmark, Gertrua*
the Queen, and the Council, including Polonius with hi
son Laertes, Hamlet, Voltemand, Cornelius, and attena
ants] Florish. Enter Claudius, King of Denmarke, Ger
trad the Queene, Counsaile: as Polonius, and his Sonn
Laertes, Hamlet, Cum Alijs. Q2; Enter Claudiu
King of Denmarke, Gertrude the Queene, Hamlet, Polon
ius, Laertes, and his Sister Ophelia, Lords Attendant. l
(F directs Voltemand and Cornelius to enter after line 25

II.I.   0   *Enter Polonius, with his man Reynaldo*] Enter ol.
Polonius, with his man or two. Q2; Enter Polonius, an.
Reynoldo. F

II.2.   76   *He gives a paper to the King*] not in Q2, F

        167   *Enter Hamlet*] Q2; Enter Hamlet reading on a Booke
F

        170   *Exeunt the King and Queen*] Exit King and Queene. Q
(*after line 169*); Exit King & Queen. F (*after* 'Il
boord him presently')

III.I.   42   *Exit the Queen*] not in Q2, F

III.2.   0   *Enter Hamlet and the Players*] Enter Hamlet, and thre
of the Players. Q2; Enter Hamlet, and two or three o
the Players. F

        101   *Danish march. Flourish. Trumpets and kettledrums*
Enter the King and Queen, Polonius, Ophelia, Rosen
crantz, Guildenstern, and other lords attendant, with th
guard carrying torches] Enter Trumpets and Ketti
Drummes, King, Queene, Polonius, Ophelia. Q2; Ente
King, Queene, Polonius, Ophelia, Rosincrance, Guilden
sterne, and other Lords attendant, with his Guard carry
ing Torches. Danish March. Sound a Flourish. F

        144   *The trumpets sound*] Q2; Hoboyes play. F

	269	*He pours the poison in the King's ears*] *not in* Q2; *Powres the poyson in his eares.* F
	352	*Enter a Player with recorders*] *Enter the Players with Recorders.* Q2; *Enter one with a Recorder.* F
III.4.	8	*Polonius hides behind the arras*] *not in* Q2, F
	25	*He makes a thrust through the arras and kills Polonius*] *not in* Q2; *Killes Polonius.* F
	31	*He sees Polonius*] *not in* Q2, F
	218	*Exeunt Hamlet, tugging in Polonius, and the Queen*] *Exit.* Q2; *Exit Hamlet tugging in Polonius.* F
IV.2.	4	*Guildenstern*] *not in* Q2
IV.3.	11	*Guildenstern*] *not in* Q2
IV.6.	0	*Enter Horatio and a Gentleman*] *Enter Horatio and others.* Q2; *Enter Horatio, with an Attendant.* F
	4	*Exit the Gentleman*] *not in* Q2, F
V.1.	64	*Enter Hamlet and Horatio*] Q2; *Enter Hamlet and Horatio a farre off.* F (*after line 55*)
	74	*He throws up a skull*] *not in* Q2, F
	95	*He throws up another skull*] *not in* Q2, F
	213	*Enter the King and Queen, Laertes, and the corpse of Ophelia, with lords attendant and a Priest*] *Enter K. Q. Laertes and the corse.* Q2; *Enter King, Queene, Laertes, and a Coffin, with Lords attendant.* F; *Enter King and Queene, Leartes, and other lordes, with a Priest after the coffin.* Q1
	218	*He withdraws with Horatio*] *not in* Q2, F
	239	*She scatters flowers*] *not in* Q2, F
	246	*He leaps in the grave*] *not in* Q2; *Leaps in the graue.* F
V.2.	80	*Enter Osrick*] *Enter a Courtier.* Q2; *Enter young Osricke.* F
	104	*He invites Osrick to put on his hat*] *not in* Q2, F
	218	*Trumpets and drums. A table prepared, with flagons of wine on it. Enter officers with cushions, and other attendants with foils, daggers, and gauntlets. Enter the King and Queen, Osrick, Laertes, and all the state*] *A table prepard, Trumpets, Drums and officers with Cushions,*

King, Queene, and all the state, Foiles, daggers, an,
Laertes. Q2; Enter King, Queene, Laertes and Lords
with other Attendants with Foyles, and Gauntlets,
Table and Flagons of Wine on it. F

219 He puts Laertes's hand into Hamlet's] not in Q2, F

260 They prepare to play] not in Q2; Prepare to play. I
  (after line 259)

274 They play] F; not in Q2

275 Drum, trumpets, and shot. Flourish. A piece goe
  off] Q2; Trumpets sound, and shot goes off. F (afte
  line 277)

279 They play] not in Q2, F

285 She drinks] Q1; not in Q2, F

294 They play] not in Q2; Play. F

296 In scuffling they change rapiers, and both are wounde
  with the poisoned weapon] not in Q2; In scuffling the
  change Rapiers. F

297 The Queen falls] not in Q2, F

304 She dies] not in Q2, F

316 He wounds the King] not in Q2; Hurts the King. F

320 He forces the King to drink] not in Q2, F

321 The King dies] not in Q2; King Dyes. F

325 He dies] not in Q2; Dyes. F

343 A march afar off, and shout within] A march a farr
  off. Q2; March afarre off, and shout within. F

352 He dies] not in Q2; Dyes F

354 March within] not in Q2, F

355 Enter Fortinbras, with the Ambassadors and with hi.
  train of drum, colours, and attendants] Enter Forten
  brasse, with the Embassadors. Q2; Enter Fortinbra.
  and English Ambassador, with Drumme, Colours, an
  Attendants. F

397 Exeunt marching; after the which a peal of ordnance i.
  shot off] F; Exeunt. Q2

5

The following are some of the variant readings and forms of words more commonly found in other editions (especially nineteeth-century ones). The reading of this edition, with its origin, is given first, followed by the rejected variant. (Emendations proposed by other editors but not adopted here are discussed in the Commentary to 1.4.33, 11.2.255, III.3.7, III.4.4, 122, 163, and 170, IV.4.25–6, IV.5.39, and v.2.42 and 281.)

1.1	33	have two nights] Q2; two Nights haue F
	87	heraldy] Q2; Heraldrie F
	88	these] Q2; those F
	141	strike] Q2; strike at F
	162	stir] Q2; walke F
1.2	11	an . . .a] Q2; one . . . one F
	24	bands] Q2; Bonds F
	50	My dread lord] Q2; Dread my Lord F
	85	passes] Q2; passeth F
	127	heaven] Q2; Heauens F
	198	waste] Q2, F; vast Q1
	213	watch] Q2; watcht F
1.3.	26	particular act and place] Q2; peculiar Sect and force F
	63	unto] Q2; to F
	65	courage] Q2; Comrade F
	77	dulleth] Q2; dulls the F
	123	parle] Q2; parley F
1.4.	49	interred] Q2; enurn'd F
1.5.	33	roots] Q2; rots F
	62	hebona] Q2; Hebenon F
	112–13	*Enter Horatio and Marcellus* HORATIO My lord, my lord!] Q2; *Hor. & Mar. within.* My Lord, my Lord. | *Enter Horatio and Marcellus.* F
	132	I will] Q2; Looke you, Ile F

II.2.	20	is] Q2; are F
	97	he's] Q2; he is F
	142	prescripts] Q2; Precepts F
	203	yourself] Q2; you your selfe F
	203–4	shall grow] Q2; should be F
	216	will not] Q2; will F
	278	anything but] Q2; any thing. But F
	446	when] Q2; where F
	454	heraldy] Q2; Heraldry F
	522	abstract] Q2; Abstracts F
	556	her] Q2; *Hecuba* F
	585	stallion] Q2; Scullion F
III.1.	1	conference] Q2; circumstance F
	19	are here] Q2; are F
	33	We'll] Q2; Will F
	72	despised] Q2; dispriz'd F
	145	and amble] Q2; you amble F
	148	marriage] Q2; Marriages F
	159	time] Q2; tune F
III.2.	79	commeddled] Q2; co-mingled F
	191	That's wormwood] Q2; Wormwood, Wormwooc F
	328	ROSENCRANTZ] Q2; *Guild.* F
III.3.	15	cess] Q2; cease F
	25	about] Q2; vpon F
III.4.	23	Help] Q2; Helpe, helpe F
	24	Help] Q2; helpe, helpe, helpe F
	38	brassed] Q2 (brasd); braz'd F
	51	heated] Q2; tristfull F
	180	This] Q2; Thus F
IV.3.	15	Ho! Bring in the] Q2; Hoa *Guildensterne?* Bring ir my F
	66	congruing] Q2; coniuring F
IV.5.	39	ground] Q2; *graue* F
	99	is] Q2; are F
	158	paid with] Q2; payed by F

	201	O God] Q2; you Gods F
IV.7.	7	criminal] Q2; crimefull F
	8	safety, greatness,] Q2; Safety, F
	20	Work] Q2; Would F
	52	devise] Q2; aduise F
	91	Lamord] Q2; *Lamound* F
	104	you] Q2; him F
	124	in deed your father's son] Q2; your Fathers sonne indeed F
	158	preferred] Q2 (prefard); prepar'd F
	166	askant] Q2; aslant F
	168	Therewith . . . make] Q2; There with . . . come F
	191	drowns] Q2; doubts F
V.1.	60	in] Q2; to *Yaughan* F
	65	'A] Q2; that he F
	73	into] Q2; *intill* F
	86–7	chopless] Q2; Chaplesse F
	170	now hath lien you] Q2; now: this Scul, has laine F
	183	bore] Q2; borne F
	190	table] Q2; Chamber F
	233	a] Q2; sage F
	243	double] Q2; trebble F
	259	wisdom] Q2; wisenesse F
V.2.	63	think] Q2; thinkst F
	105	my ease] Q2; mine ease F
	187	out of an] Q2; outward F
	339	I leave] Q2; liue F
	352	silence.] Q2; silence. O, o, o, o. F

6

The following are the more important passages found in Q2 but omitted in F. They total about 230 lines. Odd words and insignificant phrases are not included here.

I.I. 108–25   BARNARDO I think . . . countrymen
I.2.   58–60   wrung . . . consent
I.4.   17–38   This heavy-headed . . . scandal
        75–8   The very . . . beneath
II.2.   17   Whether . . . thus
       443–4   as wholesome . . . fine
         463   So, proceed you
III.2. 176–7   women fear . . . And
        181–2   Where love . . . there
        228–9   To desperation . . . scope
III.4.   72–7   Sense sure . . . difference
         79–82 Eyes without . . . mope
        162–6   That monster . . . put on
        168–71 the next . . . potency
           181 One word more, good lady
        203–11 There's letters . . . meet
IV.1.   4   Bestow . . . while
         41–4   Whose whisper . . . air
IV.3.   25–7   KING Alas . . . that worm
IV.4.   9–66   Enter Hamlet . . . worth
IV.7. 67–80   LAERTES My lord . . . graveness
        99–101 the scrimers . . . opposed them
       113–22   There lives . . . ulcer
V.2.106–41   Sir, here is . . . unfellowed (replaced by 'Sir, you
                are not ignorant of what excellence Laertes is at
                his weapon')
        152–3   HORATIO . . . I knew . . . done
       190–202 Enter a Lord . . . Exit the Lord
           218 Let be

7

The following are the more interesting of the stage directions in
Q1. Some of them probably indicate impressions drawn from a

contemporary performance of the play. The line references are
to this edition.

I.I.	o	*Enter two Centinels.*
I.2.	o	*Enter King, Queene, Hamlet, Leartes, Corambis, and the two Ambassadors, with Attendants.*
I.5.	149	*The Gost under the stage.*
II.I.	o	*Enter Corambis, and Montano.*
II.2.	o	*Enter King and Queene, Rossencraft, and Gilderstone.*
	39	*Enter Corambis and Ofelia.*
	378	*The Trumpets sound, Enter Corambis.*
III.2.	144	*Enter in a Dumbe Shew, the King and Queene, he sits downe in an Arbor, she leaues him: Then enters Lucianus with poyson in a Viall, and powres it in his eares, and goes away: Then the Queene commeth and findes him dead: and goes away with the other.*
	163	*Enter the Duke and Dutchesse.*
III.3.	72	*hee kneeles. enters Hamlet*
III.4.	103	*Enter the ghost in his night gowne.*
	218	*Exit Hamlet with the dead body.*
IV.4.	o	*Enter Fortenbrasse, Drumme and Souldiers.*
IV.5.	20	*Enter Ofelia playing on a Lute, and her haire downe singing.*
	155	*Enter Ofelia as before.*
V.I.	o	*enter Clowne and an other.*
	213	*Enter King and Queene, Leartes, and other lordes, with a Priest after the coffin.*
	246	*Leartes leapes into the graue.*
	253	*Hamlet leapes in after Leartes*
V.2.	80	*Enter a Bragart Gentleman.*
	296	*They catch one anothers Rapiers, and both are wounded, Leartes falles downe, the Queene falles downe and dies.*
	355	*Enter Voltemar and the Ambassadors from England. enter Fortenbrasse with his traine.*

THE TRAGEDY OF HAMLET, PRINCE OF DENMARK
The Characters in the Play

GHOST of Hamlet, lately King of Denmark
Claudius, his brother, now KING of Denmark
Gertrude, QUEEN of Denmark, widow of the late King and
    now wife of his brother Claudius
HAMLET, son of the late King Hamlet and of Gertrude

POLONIUS, counsellor to the King
LAERTES, son of Polonius
OPHELIA, daughter of Polonius
REYNALDO, servant of Polonius

HORATIO, friend of Prince Hamlet

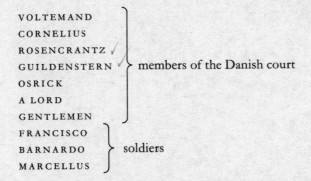

VOLTEMAND
CORNELIUS
ROSENCRANTZ
GUILDENSTERN   } members of the Danish court
OSRICK
A LORD
GENTLEMEN
FRANCISCO
BARNARDO   } soldiers
MARCELLUS

Throughout the notes, the abbreviation 'Q1' is used for the first ('bad') quarto (1603), 'Q2' for the second ('good') quarto (1604) and 'F' for the first Folio (1623). Biblical quotations are given, with modernized spelling and punctuation, from the Bishops' Bible (1568 etc.), the version probably most familiar to Shakespeare.

TWO MESSENGERS
A SAILOR
TWO CLOWNS, a gravedigger and his companion
A PRIEST

FORTINBRAS, Prince of Norway
A CAPTAIN, a Norwegian

English AMBASSADORS

FIRST PLAYER, who leads the troupe and takes the part of a
    king
SECOND PLAYER, who takes the part of a queen
THIRD PLAYER, who takes the part of Lucianus, nephew of
    the king
FOURTH PLAYER, who speaks a Prologue

Lords, attendants, players, guards, soldiers, followers of
Laertes, sailors

BARNARDO Who's there?

FRANCISCO Nay, answer me. Stand and unfold yourself.

BARNARDO Long live the King!

FRANCISCO Barnardo?

BARNARDO He.

FRANCISCO

You come most carefully upon your hour.

BARNARDO

'Tis now struck twelve. Get thee to bed, Francisco.

FRANCISCO

For this relief much thanks. 'Tis bitter cold,
And I am sick at heart.

1.1 The action of the scene takes place on a *platform* (1.2.213) – a level place for mounting guns – of the Danish royal castle at Elsinore. Historically, the castle included a gun-platform where batteries commanded the narrow entrance to the Baltic Sea between Denmark and (modern) Sweden, exacting tolls from ships passing through. It was well known to British voyagers.

(stage direction) *Enter Francisco and Barnardo, two sentinels.* Francisco is on duty, presumably pacing up and down. Barnardo enters to relieve him.

1 *Who's there?* Perhaps he fancies he sees the Ghost.

2 *Nay, answer me. Stand and unfold yourself.* The emphasis is on *me* and (perhaps)

yourself. Francisco is the sentinel at his post, and it is his duty, not Barnardo's, to challenge anyone who approaches. By putting the challenge in the mouth of the new arrival, Shakespeare creates a feeling of tension. *unfold* identify

6 *carefully upon your hour* considerately on time

7 *twelve* (when ghosts begin to walk; this prepares for 1.4.3–6: compare III.2.395–7)

8 *'Tis bitter cold.* Shakespeare carefully establishes the winter night, of which we are reminded at 1.4.1–2.

9 *I am sick at heart.* This, from an unimportant soldier, contributes to the emotional atmosphere and prepares for the Prince's heart-sickness at

BARNARDO

Have you had quiet guard?

10   FRANCISCO   Not a mouse stirring.

BARNARDO

Well, good night.

If you do meet Horatio and Marcellus,

The rivals of my watch, bid them make haste.

Enter Horatio and Marcellus

FRANCISCO

I think I hear them. Stand ho! Who is there?

HORATIO

Friends to this ground.

MARCELLUS   And liegemen to the Dane.

FRANCISCO

Give you good night.

MARCELLUS   O, farewell, honest soldier.

Who hath relieved you?

FRANCISCO   Barnardo hath my place.

Give you good night.   *Exit*

MARCELLUS   Holla, Barnardo!

BARNARDO   Say –

What, is Horatio there?

HORATIO   A piece of him.

1.2.129–59. It oddly contrasts with
the disciplined military scene.

10 *Have you had quiet guard?* Francisco's *I
am sick at heart* prompts Barnardo to
think of the apparition and so to ask
his vague question.

Not a mouse stirring. The ordinary
image gives a sense of reality to the
soldiers' language, preparing us to
accept the supernatural happenings.
It also implies the silence and acute-
ness of perception which anticipate
the coming awareness of the Ghost.

13 *rivals* partners
bid them make haste. Barnardo does
not want to be left alone now that it

is time for the feared appearance of
the Ghost.

15 *this ground* (the land of Denmark)
liegemen. The soldiers in this scene
seem to be nationals, not like the *Switzers* (IV.5.99), who are the King's personal bodyguard and imply a tyrant's
reliance on foreign mercenaries.
the Dane the King of Denmark

16, 18 *Give you good night* may God give
you good night. The repetition suggests Francisco's effort to get away
as soon as he can.

19 *What, is Horatio there?* This adds to
the impression that we are witnessing
a night scene.

BARNARDO

Welcome, Horatio. Welcome, good Marcellus.   20

MARCELLUS

What, has this thing appeared again tonight?

BARNARDO

I have seen nothing.

MARCELLUS

Horatio says 'tis but our fantasy,
And will not let belief take hold of him
Touching this dreaded sight twice seen of us.
Therefore I have entreated him along
With us to watch the minutes of this night,
That, if again this apparition come,
He may approve our eyes and speak to it.

HORATIO

Tush, tush, 'twill not appear.

BARNARDO   Sit down awhile,   30
And let us once again assail your ears,
That are so fortified against our story,
What we have two nights seen.

HORATIO   Well, sit we down,
And let us hear Barnardo speak of this.

BARNARDO

Last night of all,
When yond same star that's westward from the pole

---

21 *What . . . tonight?* Marcellus at once
asks the question which is uppermost
in their minds. The phrase *this thing*
indicates his puzzled awe. The line is
attributed to Horatio in Q2, but to
Marcellus in Q1 (a good authority in
this scene) and in F. It seems to
come more naturally from Marcellus
in view of Barnardo's promptly
understanding reply and of Horatio's
disbelief.

29 *approve our eyes* corroborate the existence of what we have seen

speak to it. See the note to line 42.

30–33 *Sit . . . sit* (referring to Horatio
and Marcellus, not Barnardo, who is
at his post)

31 *assail your ears* try to overcome your
incredulity by narrating to you. The
military imagery is appropriate in a
soldier's speech.

34 *let us hear Barnardo.* He has already
heard the story from Marcellus.

36 *yond same star.* Barnardo presumably
points to the sky at one side of
the stage, guiding the eyes of the

Had made his course t'illume that part of heaven
Where now it burns, Marcellus and myself,
The bell then beating one –
          Enter the Ghost

MARCELLUS

40   Peace, break thee off. Look where it comes again.

BARNARDO

In the same figure like the King that's dead.

MARCELLUS

Thou art a scholar. Speak to it, Horatio.

BARNARDO

Looks 'a not like the King? Mark it, Horatio.

HORATIO

Most like. It harrows me with fear and wonder.

audience away from where the Ghost will enter. A soldier on night duty notices the stars and their changing positions as the hours pass; and Shakespeare throughout the scene gives an impression of a clear, frosty, starlit sky.

the pole (the point where the Pole Star shines)

37 Had made his course. This, together with the strong words *illume* and *burns*, seems to imply that the *star* is a planet.

39 (stage direction) *Enter the Ghost*. It passes close to them (*Within his truncheon's length* (1.2.204), that is, only a few feet), and so can be imagined as seen clearly in the dim light. It is in full armour, carries a truncheon, and walks in military fashion, as is frequently iterated (lines 47, 60, and 110; 1.2.200–204, 226–30, and 255; 1.4.52). Further visual details are given at 1.2.231–4 and 242. On the Elizabethan stage it would almost certainly have emerged from a trap-door and have descended by the same

means. This is appropriate, for it later *cries under the stage* (1.5.148) and is called *this fellow in the cellarage* (1.5.151).

41 *like the King that's dead*. The likeness, insisted on (lines 43–4, 47–9, and 58–63), helps the watchers to believe that it is really King Hamlet's spirit, not a demon.

42 *Thou art a scholar. Speak to it.* Horatio was a fellow-student of Hamlet, and would therefore know Latin, in which language ghosts were conventionally addressed (though theatrical convention permitted English), and the correct form of words for exorcism. Hamlet in fact uses a Latin phrase in addressing the Ghost at 1.5.156.

42, 45 *Speak to it . . . It would be spoke to.* Ghosts could not initiate conversation. See lines 128–39 and III.4.105–10.

43 *'a* (the weakened, unstressed form of 'he')

44 *harrows* distresses

BARNARDO
   It would be spoke to.

MARCELLUS   Speak to it, Horatio.

HORATIO
   What art thou that usurpest this time of night,
   Together with that fair and warlike form
   In which the majesty of buried Denmark
   Did sometimes march? By heaven I charge thee, speak.

MARCELLUS
   It is offended.

BARNARDO   See, it stalks away.   50

HORATIO
   Stay. Speak, speak. I charge thee, speak.

                             Exit the Ghost

MARCELLUS
   'Tis gone and will not answer.

BARNARDO
   How now, Horatio? You tremble and look pale.
   Is not this something more than fantasy?
   What think you on't?

HORATIO
   Before my God, I might not this believe
   Without the sensible and true avouch
   Of mine own eyes.

MARCELLUS   Is it not like the King?

HORATIO
   As thou art to thyself.
   Such was the very armour he had on   60

45 *would be* wants to be
46 *usurpest* (because this is not a time when human beings are expected to be out walking, and because you are bearing the form of one we know to be dead and buried)
48 *buried Denmark* the dead King of Denmark
49 *sometimes* formerly
50 *It is offended* (presumably by Horatio's *usurpest*)
54 *fantasy.* See line 23.
57 *sensible* affecting my senses
   avouch assurance

When he the ambitious Norway combated.
So frowned he once when, in an angry parle,
He smote the sledded poleaxe on the ice.
'Tis strange.

MARCELLUS

Thus twice before, and jump at this dead hour,
With martial stalk hath he gone by our watch.

HORATIO

In what particular thought to work I know not.
But, in the gross and scope of mine opinion,
This bodes some strange eruption to our state.

MARCELLUS

70   Good now, sit down, and tell me he that knows

61 *he the ambitious Norway combated.* The episode is described later (lines 80–95). Horatio seems to speak from personal observation of the occasion, which we learn at v.1.141–60 was thirty years ago. But such details are not to be pressed as evidence for a time-scheme or as indications of Horatio's age.
ambitious. The word was generally derogatory; Hamlet describes himself as *very proud, revengeful, ambitious* (III.1.124–5). At 1.1.83 this King of Norway is described as *pricked on by a most emulate pride.*
Norway the King of Norway

62 *So frowned he.* Presumably this connects with Marcellus's *It is offended,* and refers only to that moment; when Hamlet later asks *looked he frowningly?,* Horatio replies *A countenance more in sorrow than in anger* (1.2.231–2), apparently describing the Ghost's usual expression.
parle (one syllable) parley

63 *sledded poleaxe* long military axe, weighted with lead (like a 'sledgehammer'): a favourite Scandinavian weapon. Q2 (and Q1) reads 'sleaded pollax', and F 'sledded Pollax'. Later

in the play an inhabitant of Poland is called a *Polack* (II.2.63 etc.), as well as *Pole* (IV.4.21). It has therefore often been supposed that the phrase should be 'sledded Polacks', that is, 'Poles on their sleighs', referring to a different military episode from the quarrel with the King of Norway. But the King is said to have been frowning during heated verbal negotiations (*angry parle*), and this does not seem an appropriate moment for his raining blows upon the enemy Poles, mounted on their sledges, during a battle on a frozen lake or river. In *Love's Labour's Lost,* v.2.571, the word 'poleaxe' is spelt 'Polax' by Q1 (1598) and 'Pollax' by F and by Q2 (1631).

65 *jump* exactly

67 *thought to work* train of thinking to act upon

68 *in the gross and scope of mine opinion* so far as I can make a general surmise without going into details

69 *strange eruption to our state* startling disturbance in the affairs of our country

70 *Good now* if you please

Why this same strict and most observant watch
So nightly toils the subject of the land,
And why such daily cast of brazen cannon
And foreign mart for implements of war,
Why such impress of shipwrights, whose sore task
Does not divide the Sunday from the week.
What might be toward that this sweaty haste
Doth make the night joint-labourer with the day?
Who is't that can inform me?

HORATIO   That can I.
At least the whisper goes so. Our last King,   80
Whose image even but now appeared to us,
Was, as you know, by Fortinbras of Norway,
Thereto pricked on by a most emulate pride,
Dared to the combat; in which our valiant Hamlet —

71 *watch* (literally, keeping awake; both the military night-watch and the night labours of the citizens in manufacturing armaments and building ships)

72 *toils* causes to toil
subject subjects

73 *cast* casting in a foundry

74 *foreign mart for implements of war* seeking foreign trade in armaments

75 *impress* conscription, forced enrolment

75–6, 78 *whose sore task | Does not divide the Sunday from the week | . . . the night joint-labourer with the day* They are working on Sundays and night shifts.

77 *toward* impending

79 *That can I.* Horatio provides the information needed by the audience to understand the situation. But in the next scene (1.2.164–9) he has recently arrived from Wittenberg, ignorant of events, and 1.4.12 he has to be informed about a local Danish custom. Later he becomes Hamlet's

confidant and often receives from him the information the audience requires. He is clearly *a Dane* at v.2.335. There is consistency in his character, but not in his role in the play.

80 *whisper* rumour

80–95 The account of the Danish successes against Norway emphasizes the strength of Denmark under the late King Hamlet and, potentially, under his successor. This impression is increased by the success of the diplomatic pressure put on the King of Norway at 1.2.17–39 and 11.2.60–80, and the reference to Danish power in England at IV.3.60–64.

81 *even but* only just

83 *emulate* (a strong word) emulous, full of jealous rivalry

84 *our valiant Hamlet.* This is the first mention of the family name, identifying *the majesty of buried Denmark* (line 48) and *Our last King* (line 80). Throughout, old Hamlet's virtue, dignity, valour, physical prowess, and personal beauty are strongly em-

For so this side of our known world esteemed him –
Did slay this Fortinbras; who, by a sealed compact
Well ratified by law and heraldy,
Did forfeit, with his life, all these his lands
Which he stood seised of, to the conqueror;

90   Against the which a moiety competent
Was gagèd by our King, which had returned
To the inheritance of Fortinbras,
Had he been vanquisher, as, by the same covenant
And carriage of the article designed,
His fell to Hamlet. Now, sir, young Fortinbras,

phasized. It is in the shadow of his worth that Hamlet has to reveal himself to us, and to act.

85 *so* (that is, *valiant*)
this side of our known world (all Europe, or the western hemisphere)

86–7 This personal combat between King Hamlet and King Fortinbras, authorized by *heraldy* and so on, seems to belong to a different and older world from that of King Claudius, who is a modern politician and works through his ambassadors.

86 *sealed compact* certified agreement

87 *heraldy* (an alternative form of 'heraldry') chivalric formalities

89 *stood seised* was possessed (*stood* is an emphatic auxiliary). The pronunciation of *seised* is the same as 'seized'. What Fortinbras offered as a wager was his personal possessions of land. The fate of the two kingdoms was, of course, not involved in this personal wager.

90 *moiety competent* equivalent portion of land

91 *gagèd* wagered
returned passed (not necessarily 'passed back again')

92 *inheritance* subsequent possession (not

necessarily with the notion of heirship)

93 *covenant*. This is F's reading (spelt 'Cou'nant'). It is intelligible, but metrically clumsy. Q2 has 'comart', which is a possible word ('co-mart', presumably meaning 'mutual bargain'), but there is no adequate evidence of its existence.

94 *carriage of the article designed* fulfilment of the article or clause in the prearranged compact

95 *sir*. Horatio seems to be addressing only Marcellus here, though it is Barnardo who next comments.
young Fortinbras. The parallel between the fathers and sons, Fortinbras and Hamlet, is deliberate. It becomes clear from 1.2.30 and 11.2.62 and 70 that in Norway, as in Denmark, a brother has succeeded to the throne in preference to the late monarch's son. Just as a remarkable contrast between old and young Hamlet is given us (see the note to line 84), so a difference of personality between old and young Fortinbras is implied. Old Fortinbras was a worthy opponent of old Hamlet. They met in personal combat. But young Fortin-

Of unimprovèd mettle hot and full,
Hath in the skirts of Norway here and there
Sharked up a list of lawless resolutes
For food and diet to some enterprise
That hath a stomach in't; which is no other,   100
As it doth well appear unto our state,
But to recover of us by strong hand
And terms compulsatory those foresaid lands
So by his father lost. And this, I take it,
Is the main motive of our preparations,
The source of this our watch, and the chief head
Of this posthaste and romage in the land.

BARNARDO

I think it be no other but e'en so.
Well may it sort that this portentous figure
Comes armèd through our watch so like the King   110

---

bras acts by a different code of conduct: he seeks by *terms compulsatory*, with *a list of lawless resolutes*, to wrest back what his father had honourably lost.

96 *unimprovèd mettle* vigour of mind and body uncultivated and unchastened by experience

97 *skirts* outskirts or borders (less in the control of the King's government)

98 *Sharked up* (presumably) recruited indiscriminately, like a shark seizing its prey at haphazard
list (perhaps disparagingly) collection, mere catalogue (but compare 1.2.32)
lawless resolutes determined and desperate characters, with nothing to lose because they have rejected the obligations and protection of the law. But when Fortinbras and his army appear in IV.4, they do not correspond to this derogatory description. The reading *lawless* comes from Q2 and is

supported by Q1. But F's 'Landlesse' might be preferred on the grounds that Fortinbras was himself one who had lost his inheritance of lands.

99 *For* (acting) in return for
diet daily pay

100 *stomach* exercise of stubborn courage (with a quibble on *food*). The *lawless resolutes* appreciate an enterprise with the excitement of danger.

101 *our state* (the government of Denmark)

102 *of* from

103 *compulsatory* (accented on the second syllable, and with a weakened fourth syllable) involving compulsion

106 *head* fountain-head

107 *romage* commotion

109–11 There is no hint in this scene of suspicion that the late King has met his death by foul play. See the note to lines 128–40.

109 *sort* be appropriate

That was and is the question of these wars.

HORATIO

A mote it is to trouble the mind's eye.
In the most high and palmy state of Rome,
A little ere the mightiest Julius fell,
The graves stood tenantless and the sheeted dead
Did squeak and gibber in the Roman streets –
As stars with trains of fire and dews of blood,
Disasters in the sun; and the moist star
Upon whose influence Neptune's empire stands
120   Was sick almost to Doomsday with eclipse.

111 *question* cause
112 *A mote it is to trouble the mind's eye.*
(The apparition is, after all, a trifle.
Yet a speck of dust can be trouble-
some in the eye, and so this apparition troubles our mental vision.)
113–20 This passage on the portents
which preceded Caesar's murder
recalls 1.3 and 11.2 of *Julius Caesar*,
probably written shortly before
Hamlet. Both derive from Plutarch's
Life of Julius Caesar in Sir Thomas
North's translation (1579 etc.). Horatio, a *scholar* (line 42), discourses
impressively to the two soldiers from
his reading of Roman history. Perhaps he also shows an unexpectedly
superstitious side.
113 *the most high and palmy state of Rome.*
Julius Caesar was regarded as the
first Roman emperor and his rule as
the high point of Roman prosperity
(ordained by Divine Providence to
produce a world at peace in readiness
for the birth of Christ). But Horatio
means simply 'in ancient Rome,
whose glories we all know about'.
palmy flourishing
state government
115 *sheeted* wearing their shrouds
116 *gibber* (pronounced with hard 'g' as
in 'give'). The shrill, weak, piping

cries of the souls of the dead are a
detail from classical poetry.
117 The syntax here is much broken;
probably a line or two have been
lost between 116 and 117, to the
effect that 'there were prodigies visible in the heavens as well as on
earth, for example . . .'. An alternative explanation is that some lines
have been misplaced: to insert 121–5
between 116 and 117 makes good
sense.
stars with trains of fire comets (rather
than shooting stars)
dews of blood. The phenomenon of
'red dews' is now known to be
caused by insects.
118 *Disasters* (an astrological word) unfa-
vourable appearances: here probably
eclipses or sun-spots
the moist star the moon (*moist* because of its relation to the tides).
The *influence* of its movements upon
marine tides was well known and
accurately calculated in Shakespeare's
time; but the cause of the relation
between the moon and the oceans
was not known.
119 *Neptune's empire* the sea
120 *sick almost to Doomsday.* On the Day
of Judgement, it was prophesied, the
second coming of Christ would be

And even the like precurse of feared events,
As harbingers preceding still the fates
And prologue to the omen coming on,
Have heaven and earth together demonstrated
Unto our climatures and countrymen.

    Enter the Ghost

But soft, behold, lo where it comes again!
I'll cross it, though it blast me.

    He spreads his arms

Stay, illusion.
If thou hast any sound or use of voice,
Speak to me.   130

accompanied by eclipses of the sun and moon. Scriptural language colours this whole passage; see especially Matthew 24.29, Luke 21.25–6, and Revelation 6.12–13.

121 *precurse* forerunner
    feared. Q2 reads 'feare', which could easily be a misreading of 'feard'.

122 *still* always

123 *prologue*. This is the first instance of the theatrical language which becomes prominent in the play.
    omen ominous event, calamity

125 *our*. The word is emphasized: such prodigies have occurred not only in ancient Roman times but also in the history of our own people. English history, as read by the Elizabethans, contained a good many supernatural warnings, and in recent years several eclipses had occurred, which superstitious persons (like Gloucester in *King Lear*, 1.2.103–4) regarded with anxiety.
    climatures regions of the earth

127 *cross it* stand in its path and so attempt to halt it. This was a dangerous action.

(stage direction) *He spreads his arms*. Q2 has the direction '*It spreads his armes.*'

This would seem to refer to an action by the Ghost. But the stage business required is that Horatio, with arms outstretched, should *cross* the Ghost, and '*It*' is usually regarded as an error for 'He'. Horatio thus also resembles the Cross, which would repel the spirit if it were of diabolical origin.

128 *illusion*. Presumably Horatio retains his scepticism about the Ghost's true nature.

128–40 Horatio interrogates the Ghost and suggests, one by one, the usual explanations for its walking: (a) it needs something to be done (for example, burial of its body) to give it rest; (b) it is a warning spirit (a *harbinger* of *feared events*, such as was discussed in lines 122–5); (c) it has buried treasure on its conscience. Horatio does not reach, before the cock crows, the fourth possible explanation – the true one: (d) a demand of revenge for murder.

130–133, 136 *Speak to me . . . O, speak!* The short lines no doubt indicate pauses while Horatio awaits an answer.

If there be any good thing to be done
That may to thee do ease and grace to me,
Speak to me.
If thou art privy to thy country's fate,
Which happily foreknowing may avoid,
O, speak!
Or if thou hast uphoarded in thy life
Extorted treasure in the womb of earth,
For which, they say, you spirits oft walk in death,
Speak of it.
                    The cock crows
140   Stay and speak. Stop it, Marcellus.
MARCELLUS
Shall I strike it with my partisan?
HORATIO
Do, if it will not stand.
BARNARDO   'Tis here.
HORATIO   'Tis here.
                                        Exit the Ghost
MARCELLUS
'Tis gone.
We do it wrong, being so majestical,
To offer it the show of violence,
For it is as the air invulnerable,
And our vain blows malicious mockery.
BARNARDO
It was about to speak when the cock crew.
HORATIO
And then it started, like a guilty thing
150 Upon a fearful summons. I have heard

---

135 *happily* haply (and perhaps also 'fortunately')
138 *Extorted* ill-gotten
141 *partisan* a pike with a broad head and (sometimes) a side projection
142 *stand* stop
144 *being* since it is
145–6 *offer it the show of violence,* | *For* offer it violence – which is only a show of violence, because

The cock, that is the trumpet to the morn,
Doth with his lofty and shrill-sounding throat
Awake the god of day, and at his warning,
Whether in sea or fire, in earth or air,
Th'extravagant and erring spirit hies
To his confine. And of the truth herein
This present object made probation.

MARCELLUS
It faded on the crowing of the cock.
Some say that ever 'gainst that season comes
Wherein our Saviour's birth is celebrated,   160
This bird of dawning singeth all night long.
And then, they say, no spirit dare stir abroad;
The nights are wholesome; then no planets strike;
No fairy takes; nor witch hath power to charm.
So hallowed and so gracious is that time.

HORATIO
So have I heard and do in part believe it.

151 *trumpet* trumpeter
152 *his* its
   shrill-sounding high-pitched (not necessarily unpleasant)
153 *god of day* (sun-god, Phoebus Apollo)
   his (the cock's)
155 *extravagant* vagrant outside its legitimate boundaries
   erring wandering
   hies hastens
156 *confine* place of confinement
157 *This present object made probation* the Ghost that has just appeared affords a proof
158–76 From the spectral terrors of this night, the mood of the scene now changes to the contemplation of the health and grace of Christmas nights, and then to the dawn of the new day with a revival of courage and determination.

159–65 This belief is not recorded elsewhere. Perhaps Shakespeare invented it for his theatrical purpose. Brilliantly written, it is also made plausible by Horatio's response (line 166).
159 *'gainst that season comes* in expectation of that season
162 *stir*. This is the Q2 reading; but 'walk' in Q1 and F is the more appropriate word for a ghost.
163 *The nights are wholesome*. The night air was proverbially bad for the health at ordinary times.
   strike exert their malign influence (presumably upon night travellers)
164 *takes* bewitches (not 'takes away')
   charm work magic
165 *gracious* full of divine grace

But look, the morn in russet mantle clad
Walks o'er the dew of yon high eastward hill.
Break we our watch up. And by my advice
170   Let us impart what we have seen tonight
Unto young Hamlet. For, upon my life,
This spirit, dumb to us, will speak to him.
Do you consent we shall acquaint him with it,
As needful in our loves, fitting our duty?

MARCELLUS

Let's do't, I pray. And I this morning know
Where we shall find him most conveniently.   *Exeunt*

I.2   *Flourish*
Enter Claudius, King of Denmark, Gertrude the
Queen, and the Council, including Polonius with his son
Laertes, Hamlet, Voltemand, Cornelius, and
attendants

167–8 *the morn . . . hill*. The rising sun is personified as a countryman appearing on the horizon at the break of day.

167 *the morn*. The period of time between midnight (line 7) and dawn has been shortened for dramatic purposes.

russet. The word can mean either 'grey' or 'reddish'. Either meaning would be suitable here; perhaps Shakespeare intended both. The light and colour replace the darkness and shadow of the early part of this episode.

171 *young Hamlet*. The first reference to the hero. The epithet, doubtless intended to differentiate him from the late King Hamlet, is the first indication of his youthfulness, emphasized in the early part of the play. Towards the end, he is felt to be older than the university student he was at the beginning. This does not mean that the time-scheme need include the passage of an equivalent amount of time. Shakespeare gives clear indications that Hamlet has matured, knowing that we shall not notice or protest that time has been inadequate.

I.2 It is not stated when exactly the marriage of Claudius and Gertrude, and their coronation, took place. This scene seems to be the first formal gathering after these events. We are perhaps given the impression that the Ghost began to walk three nights before, at the same time as the festivities commenced.

(stage direction) *Flourish*. This royal trumpet call would have been very prominent in production.

KING

    Though yet of Hamlet our dear brother's death
    The memory be green, and that it us befitted
    To bear our hearts in grief, and our whole kingdom
    To be contracted in one brow of woe,
    Yet so far hath discretion fought with nature
    That we with wisest sorrow think on him
    Together with remembrance of ourselves.
    Therefore our sometime sister, now our Queen,
    Th'imperial jointress to this warlike state,
    Have we, as 'twere with a defeated joy,   10
    With an auspicious and a dropping eye,
    With mirth in funeral and with dirge in marriage,
    In equal scale weighing delight and dole,
    Taken to wife. Nor have we herein barred

1 *our*. The King uses the 'royal plural', but sometimes in this speech *we*, *us*, and *our* refer to the Danish nation.

2 *that* (a substitute for *Though* in the previous line)

4 *contracted* drawn together (like the *brow* in a frown)
in one brow of woe with unanimous sorrow

5 *so far hath discretion fought with nature* to such an extent has our prudence struggled against our natural affection. This is also the theme of the King's speech to Hamlet at lines 87–106.

7 *Together with remembrance of ourselves*. This goes closely with *think on him* and explains *wisest*.

8 *our sometime sister, now our Queen*. The reprehensible nature of the relation between the King and his Queen (his former sister-in-law) is at once emphasized. Such a marriage was explicitly forbidden by the 'Table of Kindred and Affinity, wherein whosoever are related are forbidden in scripture and our laws to marry together', first printed in 1563 and incorporated into the Book of Common Prayer.
sometime former

9 *jointress* joint heretrix. No explanation is given of how Claudius's claim to the throne could be strengthened by his marriage to the late King's widow. It is not mentioned again.
this warlike state. This reminds us of the condition of vigorous military preparedness initiated by King Claudius, already described at 1.1.71–8.

10 *defeated* overcome (by its enemy, sorrow)

11 *With an auspicious and a dropping eye*. The comic or repulsive image (one eye smiling, the other weeping) is stronger in the F reading: 'With one Auspicious, and one Dropping eye'.

13 *In equal scale weighing* weighing out an equal quantity of
dole grief

14 *barred* kept out (of the discussion and the decision)

Your better wisdoms, which have freely gone
With this affair along. For all, our thanks.
Now follows that you know. Young Fortinbras,
Holding a weak supposal of our worth,
Or thinking by our late dear brother's death
20   Our state to be disjoint and out of frame,
Colleaguèd with this dream of his advantage,
He hath not failed to pester us with message
Importing the surrender of those lands
Lost by his father, with all bands of law,
To our most valiant brother. So much for him.
Now for ourself and for this time of meeting.
Thus much the business is: we have here writ
To Norway, uncle of young Fortinbras –
Who, impotent and bedrid, scarcely hears
30   Of this his nephew's purpose – to suppress
His further gait herein, in that the levies,
The lists, and full proportions are all made
Out of his subject. And we here dispatch

15–16 *Your better wisdoms . . . this affair along.* Claudius is shown as prudently consulting his Council of State and not as acting tyrannically; compare IV.1.38–40.

17 *Now follows that you know* the next matter for us to consider is something you know about already

18 *weak supposal* low estimate

20 *Our state to be disjoint and out of frame* (a curious anticipation (and refutation) of Hamlet's later *The time is out of joint*, I.5.188)
frame order

21 *Colleaguèd with* having as an (imaginary) ally and supporter. But perhaps this is the main verb (*Young Fortinbras* being the subject), with a full stop after advantage.
dream of his advantage fanciful estimate of his superiority

23 *Importing* concerning

25 *our most valiant brother.* Claudius tactfully praises the late King, in the same way as he had shown his affection for *our dear brother* (lines 1 and 19). Compare Horatio's *our valiant Hamlet* (I.1.84).
F gives the entry of Voltemand and Cornelius at this point. It probably means that they come forward, to kneel and to receive the King's letter and their commission (line 38) from his hands.

28 *Norway* the King of Norway

29 *impotent* helpless

31 *gait* proceedings
in that because

32 *lists* enlistments
full proportions supporting forces and supplies

33 *his subject* those subject to him

You, good Cornelius, and you, Voltemand,
For bearers of this greeting to old Norway,
Giving to you no further personal power
To business with the King, more than the scope
Of these delated articles allow.
Farewell; and let your haste commend your duty.

VOLTEMAND *and* CORNELIUS

In that, and all things, will we show our duty.   40

KING

We doubt it nothing. Heartily farewell.

Exeunt Voltemand and Cornelius

And now, Laertes, what's the news with you?
You told us of some suit. What is't, Laertes?
You cannot speak of reason to the Dane
And lose your voice. What wouldst thou beg, Laertes,
That shall not be my offer, not thy asking?
The head is not more native to the heart,
The hand more instrumental to the mouth,
Than is the throne of Denmark to thy father.
What wouldst thou have, Laertes?

LAERTES   My dread lord,   50

35 *greeting* (perhaps to be spoken ironically)
36–8 *no further . . . allow*. They are not plenipotentiaries but are to negotiate only in accordance with the limits laid down in Claudius's instructions.
38 *delated* set out in detail
allow. The plural form is used after *scope* because influenced by *articles*.
39 *let your haste commend your duty* show by your haste your high sense of duty
42 *Laertes* (accented on the second syllable: lay-ér-tees)
43 *suit* formal request
44 *speak of reason* make any reasonable request
Dane King of Denmark

45 *lose your voice* ask to no purpose
thou. The King shifts to the singular form and further softens to *my* (not 'our') *offer* in line 46.
46 *That shall not be my offer, not thy asking* ('Whenever they call, I will answer them; while they are yet but thinking how to speak, I will hear them', Isaiah 65.24)
47 *native* by its very nature closely related
48 *instrumental* serviceable
49 *the throne of Denmark*. The King tactfully generalizes Polonius's personal services to him into a devotion to the whole royal family.
50 *dread* revered

Your leave and favour to return to France,
From whence though willingly I came to Denmark
To show my duty in your coronation,
Yet now I must confess, that duty done,
My thoughts and wishes bend again toward France
And bow them to your gracious leave and pardon.

KING

Have you your father's leave? What says Polonius?

POLONIUS

He hath, my lord, wrung from me my slow leave
By laboursome petition, and at last
60   Upon his will I sealed my hard consent.
I do beseech you give him leave to go.

KING

Take thy fair hour, Laertes. Time be thine;
And thy best graces spend it at thy will.

---

51 *leave and favour* kind permission
return to France (to Paris: II.1.7).
Shakespeare carefully builds up
Laertes as a *foil* (v.2.249) to Hamlet,
by sending one to Paris, the other to
Wittenberg.

53 *To show my duty in your coronation.*
Laertes, as a loyal subject and the
son of the principal minister, returned to swear fealty to the new
King. Horatio says (line 176) that he
has returned to see King Hamlet's
funeral.

56 *bow* (as in entreaty)
pardon permission to depart

57 *Polonius* (pronounced with the first
'o' short and the second 'o' (accented) long). This is Latin for 'of
Poland': a surprising choice for the
name of the principal minister of
Denmark in a play which involves
the conquest of part of the adjacent
kingdom of Poland. In real life, there
is no reason why someone who hap-

pened to be named Mr Britain should
not be President of the United States,
or a M. Langlais Minister of Defence
in France. But in fiction we expect
things to be more carefully arranged.

58–61 *He hath ... go.* Polonius's first
speech is characterful: he takes thirty–
three words to say 'yes'.

58 *slow* reluctantly given

60 *will* (perhaps punning on the sense
'testament', which needs to have a
seal impressed upon it)
hard obtained with difficulty

62 *Take thy fair hour* enjoy your time of
youth
Time be thine (presumably) stay away
as long as you please. The King
grants Laertes's request and dis-
misses him. But it would presumably
be a violation of court etiquette to
insert an exit for Laertes: he withdraws to the side, and can watch
Hamlet, in preparation for his talk to
Ophelia in the next scene.

But now, my cousin Hamlet, and my son –

HAMLET (*aside*)

A little more than kin, and less than kind!

KING

How is it that the clouds still hang on you?

HAMLET

Not so, my lord. I am too much in the sun.

QUEEN

Good Hamlet, cast thy nighted colour off,

And let thine eye look like a friend on Denmark.

Do not for ever with thy vailèd lids   70

Seek for thy noble father in the dust.

Thou knowest 'tis common. All that lives must die,

Passing through nature to eternity.

HAMLET

Ay, madam, it is common.

QUEEN   If it be,

Why seems it so particular with thee?

64 *my cousin Hamlet, and my son.* Perhaps Claudius keeps his stepson (*son*) waiting while he dispatches other business; thus Hamlet is kept in his place. Certainly Claudius's refusal to permit Hamlet's return to Wittenberg contrasts with his treatment of Laertes.

65 *A little more than kin, and less than kind!* This must be spoken aside, as it interrupts Claudius's sentence. Hamlet's first words are, characteristically, a sardonic and cryptic pun. As Claudius's nephew he is more than a *cousin*, but he resents being called *son*, for any natural relationship (*kind*), such as a father and son feel, is impossible between them. Perhaps *kind* also means 'kindly' but we see no action of the King towards Hamlet which is not, at least on the surface, affectionate.

66 *the clouds still hang on you.* Hamlet's disaffection and melancholy, evident in his costume, are stressed after we have seen the King deal efficiently with state business.

67 *too much in the sun.* Another cryptic pun: presumably Hamlet refers to Claudius's *my son* (line 64) as well as to his being in the sunshine of court favour. He insinuates his resentment at having been deprived of the succession and at his new position of Claudius's stepson.

68 *nighted colour* (his black mourning garments and his melancholy)

69 *Denmark* the King of Denmark

70 *vailèd lids* downcast eyelids

75 *particular* personal

HAMLET
'Seems', madam? Nay, it is. I know not 'seems'.
'Tis not alone my inky cloak, good mother,
Nor customary suits of solemn black,
Nor windy suspiration of forced breath,
80   No, nor the fruitful river in the eye,
Nor the dejected 'haviour of the visage,
Together with all forms, moods, shapes of grief,
That can denote me truly. These indeed 'seem';
For they are actions that a man might play.
But I have that within which passes show –
These but the trappings and the suits of woe.

KING
'Tis sweet and commendable in your nature, Hamlet,
To give these mourning duties to your father.
But you must know your father lost a father;
90   That father lost, lost his; and the survivor bound
In filial obligation for some term
To do obsequious sorrow. But to persever
In obstinate condolement is a course
Of impious stubbornness. 'Tis unmanly grief.
It shows a will most incorrect to heaven,
A heart unfortified, a mind impatient,

78 *customary* (either 'following the conventions of society in wearing mourning for several months' or 'having now become usual with me')
79 *windy suspiration of forced breath* (an elaborate phrase for 'uncontrollable sighs')
80 *fruitful* flowing copiously
82 *moods* modes, appearances
shapes (in theatrical language, 'assumed roles')
83 *denote* portray
84 *play* (like an actor)
85 *passes* surpasses, goes beyond
86 *These* (both his clothes and his general behaviour)
87 *commendable* (accented on the first syllable)
90 *That father* (your grandfather)
bound was bound
92 *obsequious* dutifully mourning in a way appropriate to his obsequies
persever (accented on the second syllable)
93 *condolement* sorrowing
95 *incorrect to heaven* behaving contrary to piety
96 *unfortified* (against the inevitable misfortunes of life)
impatient lacking in the important Christian virtue of patience

An understanding simple and unschooled.
For what we know must be, and is as common
As any the most vulgar thing to sense,   *vulgar (common; universal)*
Why should we in our peevish opposition   100
Take it to heart? Fie, 'tis a fault to heaven,
A fault against the dead, a fault to nature,
To reason most absurd, whose common theme
Is death of fathers, and who still hath cried,
From the first corse till he that died today,
'This must be so'. We pray you throw to earth
This unprevailing woe, and think of us
As of a father. For, let the world take note,
You are the most immediate to our throne;
And with no less nobility of love   110
Than that which dearest father bears his son
Do I impart toward you. For your intent

99 *any the most vulgar thing to sense* (death is as common as) the most familiar experience we could have through our senses

100 *peevish* obstinate, foolish

103–4 *whose . . . who* (reason)

104 *still* always

105 *the first corse*. Actually the first *corse* ('corpse') in the world's history was a son and brother (Abel), not a father (Genesis 4.8). Further allusions to the biblical fratricide are at III.3.37–8 and v.1.77.

107 *unprevailing* unavailing

109 *the most immediate* closest in succession. Hamlet's position as heir under a quasi-elective system is strong. Ophelia testifies to his courtly qualities (III.1.151–5) and Claudius to his being loved by the people (IV.3.4 and IV.7.18). Claudius seeks to placate Hamlet with the expectation that his succession to the throne has been merely postponed. But with this public declaration he loses some of his power: by taking a secret revenge, Hamlet could now easily achieve the throne. It is only when Hamlet's disaffection shows him to be apparently irresponsible and dangerous and (eventually) to know about the fratricide that Claudius changes his intention about the succession. Shakespeare shows Claudius not as a usurper, but as duly elected. Later, facing death, Hamlet himself supports the election of Fortinbras, and Horatio thinks that this recommendation will win Fortinbras more votes (v.2.349–50 and 382–6).

112 *I*. Claudius adopts the singular pronoun when he addresses Hamlet as a *father* to a *son*.
impart toward bestow (my affection) upon. The syntax seems awkward; *with* in line 110 expects a different verb.
For as for

In going back to school in Wittenberg,
It is most retrograde to our desire;
And, we beseech you, bend you to remain
Here in the cheer and comfort of our eye,
Our chiefest courtier, cousin, and our son.

QUEEN

Let not thy mother lose her prayers, Hamlet.
I pray thee stay with us. Go not to Wittenberg.

HAMLET

120   I shall in all my best obey you, madam.

KING

Why, 'tis a loving and a fair reply.
Be as ourself in Denmark. Madam, come.
This gentle and unforced accord of Hamlet
Sits smiling to my heart; in grace whereof
No jocund health that Denmark drinks today
But the great cannon to the clouds shall tell,
And the King's rouse the heaven shall bruit again,
Re-speaking earthly thunder. Come away.

       Flourish   *Exeunt all but Hamlet*

HAMLET

In class.   O that this too too sullied flesh would melt,

---

113 *school* university. Wittenberg was famous as Luther's university (founded in 1502), where in 1517 he nailed up his ninety-five theses. Elizabethan audiences also knew it as Dr Faustus's university, from Marlowe's play.

114 *retrograde* contrary

115 *bend you* incline yourself (imperative)

117 *cousin* (probably a vocative)

120 *I shall ... obey you, madam.* Hamlet pointedly accedes to his mother's appeal to his affection, not to the King's ingratiating plea. But the King, with skilful tact, appropriates Hamlet's compliance as a *loving and a fair reply.*

in all my best in so far as I can

127 *rouse* bumper of wine
bruit echo

129–59 The importance of this soliloquy lies in its establishing Hamlet's personality and revealing his mental condition. The syntax is abrupt; the sentences progress by increments and interruptions; exclamations are followed by clarifications, questions, and imperatives.

129 *sullied.* Q2 reads 'sallied' (which could be a spelling of | *sullied*). F reads 'solid', which contrasts well with *melt,* | *Thaw, and resolve itself* ... and until the twentieth century was generally preferred by editors.

Thaw, and resolve itself into a dew;   130
Or that the Everlasting had not fixed
His canon 'gainst self-slaughter. O God, God,
How weary, stale, flat, and unprofitable
Seem to me all the uses of this world!
Fie on't, ah, fie, 'tis an unweeded garden
That grows to seed. Things rank and gross in nature
Possess it merely. That it should come to this –
But two months dead, nay, not so much, not two!
So excellent a king, that was to this
Hyperion to a satyr; so loving to my mother   140
That he might not beteem the winds of heaven
Visit her face too roughly. Heaven and earth,
Must I remember? Why, she would hang on him
As if increase of appetite had grown

But it may have an unpleasantly comic effect, especially if Richard Burbage, the actor who first played Hamlet, were putting on weight (compare *He's fat and scant of breath*, v.2.281). *Sullied* fits well into the feeling of contamination expressed by Hamlet; and for sullies (F 'sulleyes') at II.1.39 Q2 has the spelling 'sallies'.

130 *resolve* dissolve

132 *His canon 'gainst self-slaughter*. The sixth commandment, 'Thou shalt not kill' (Exodus 20.13), was generally regarded as a sufficient condemnation of suicide.

canon religious law

134 *all the uses* the whole routine of affairs

136 *rank* coarsely luxuriant

137 *merely* completely

139, 140 *to this . . . to a satyr* compared to this . . . compared to a satyr

140 *Hyperion to a satyr*. Hamlet's insistence (here and at III.4.65–103) on Claudius's unworthiness for the Kingship is not corroborated by what

Claudius does before the eyes of the audience, at any rate in the first half of the play. We are doubtless expected to feel that Hamlet is exaggerating Claudius's incompetence, while we share his moral indignation at the homicide and incest.

Hyperion (the sun-god). See also III.4.57. From his scansion here and in other plays it is clear that Shakespeare thought the accent was on the second syllable. Owing to the influence of these two famous passages in *Hamlet* and to false analogy with such names as Tiberius and Valerius, the customary pronunciation has become 'high-peer-i-on', and more 'correct' pronunciations – 'hipper-eye-on' or 'highper-eye-on' – would be intolerable.

satyr (pronounced 'satter'). In classical mythology, a satyr had a goat's legs, tail, ears, and budding horns, the rest of his form being human.

141 *beteem* permit

By what it fed on. And yet within a month –
Let me not think on't. Frailty, thy name is woman.
A little month, or e'er those shoes were old
With which she followed my poor father's body
Like Niobe, all tears, why she, even she –
150   O God, a beast that wants discourse of reason
Would have mourned longer – married with my uncle,
My father's brother, but no more like my father
Than I to Hercules. Within a month,
Ere yet the salt of most unrighteous tears
Had left the flushing in her gallèd eyes,
She married. O, most wicked speed, to post
With such dexterity to incestuous sheets!
It is not, nor it cannot come to good.
But break, my heart, for I must hold my tongue.
              Enter Horatio, Marcellus, and Barnardo

HORATIO
Hail to your lordship!

160   HAMLET   I am glad to see you well.

146 *Frailty, thy name is woman.* Shakespeare early establishes Hamlet's generalizing frame of mind.
147 *or e'er* before. Compare line 183
below. Probably Shakespeare and his
contemporaries supposed the second
word to be 'ever'. In fact both *or* and
e'er (or *ere*) are forms of the same
word, meaning 'before'.
149 *Niobe.* She was the type of the grieving mother – her seven sons and
seven daughters were slain by Apollo
and Diana – who shed so many tears
that she was turned into stone.
150 *wants discourse of reason* lacks the
(human) faculty of reason
153 *Hercules.* The amount of classical
allusion (*Hyperion, satyr, Niobe,
Hercules*) by the university-educated
Hamlet is doubtless intended to be a
character-indication.

154 *unrighteous* impiously insincere
155 *Had left the flushing in her gallèd eyes*
had had time to cause redness in her
eyes, that her salt tears had made
sore; or, perhaps, 'had left off causing redness . . .' Here *flushing* means
'reddening', not 'filling with water'.
156 *post* hasten
157 *dexterity* facility
159 *break, my heart.* A powerful phrase
which derived its currency from its
use in the Bible: 'The Lord is nigh
unto them that are of a broken heart',
Psalm 34.17 (also 51.17, 69.21, and
147.3; Isaiah 61.1; Luke 4.16–21).
Compare *Now cracks a noble heart*
(v.2.353). The modern use of the
phrase as referring sentimentally to
amorous disappointment came much
later.
160 *I am glad to see you well.* At first,

Horatio – or I do forget myself.

HORATIO

The same, my lord, and your poor servant ever.

HAMLET

Sir, my good friend. I'll change that name with you.
And what make you from Wittenberg, Horatio?
Marcellus?

MARCELLUS

My good lord!

HAMLET

I am very glad to see you. (*To Barnardo*) Good even, sir.
(*To Horatio*)
But what, in faith, make you from Wittenberg?

HORATIO

A truant disposition, good my lord.

HAMLET

I would not hear your enemy say so,   170
Nor shall you do my ear that violence
To make it truster of your own report
Against yourself. I know you are no truant.
But what is your affair in Elsinore?
We'll teach you to drink deep ere you depart.

HORATIO

My lord, I came to see your father's funeral.

HAMLET

I prithee do not mock me, fellow-student.

Hamlet merely gives a polite reply; then he recognizes Horatio.

163 *I'll change that name with you* I will be your *servant*, instead of your being mine

164 *make you from* are you doing away from

165 *Marcellus?* Presumably Hamlet recognizes Marcellus. He greets Barnardo formally as if not previously known to him, though Barnardo seems to

be of the same military rank as Marcellus. Horatio refers to them as *gentlemen* (lines 194 and 196).

169 *A truant disposition* a disposition to play truant (from his university studies)

175 *teach you to drink deep* (probably ironical, perhaps prompted by a piece of stage business such as the passing of a drink-laden servant or a burst of drunken hilarity off stage)

I think it was to see my mother's wedding.

HORATIO

Indeed, my lord, it followed hard upon.

HAMLET

180   Thrift, thrift, Horatio. The funeral baked meats
Did coldly furnish forth the marriage tables.
Would I had met my dearest foe in heaven
Or ever I had seen that day, Horatio!
My father – methinks I see my father.

HORATIO

Where, my lord?

HAMLET   In my mind's eye, Horatio.

HORATIO

I saw him once. 'A was a goodly king.

HAMLET

'A was a man. Take him for all in all,
I shall not look upon his like again.

HORATIO

My lord, I think I saw him yesternight.

HAMLET

190   Saw? Who?

---

180 *Thrift, thrift.* The repetition of words is soon felt to be characteristic of Hamlet. Compare lines 224 and 237 below. But these are more common in F than in Q2; so they may be due to an actor's affectation of a trick of speech.

180–81 *The funeral baked meats | Did coldly furnish forth the marriage tables.* Hamlet's bitter jest seems to derive from the King's remark about *mirth in funeral* and *dirge in marriage* (line 12). There was of course *A little month* (line 147) between the ceremonies.

180 *baked meats* pies

181 *coldly* as cold dishes

182 *dearest* (closest, and therefore deadliest)

185 *Where, my lord?* Horatio, who has come to give the news of the Ghost, is momentarily startled by the thought that Hamlet is himself seeing an apparition.

186 *once.* This seems inconsistent with 1.1.59–63 (which implies that Horatio was thoroughly familiar with King Hamlet's appearance) and with lines 211–12 and 241 below.

187 *'A was a man.* Hamlet has a view of moral worth largely based on stoical ideals. This is elaborated in his description of Horatio in III.2.75–81.

HORATIO
My lord, the King your father.

HAMLET   The King my father?

HORATIO
Season your admiration for a while
With an attent ear till I may deliver
Upon the witness of these gentlemen
This marvel to you.

HAMLET   For God's love, let me hear!

HORATIO
Two nights together had these gentlemen,
Marcellus and Barnardo, on their watch
In the dead waste and middle of the night
Been thus encountered: a figure like your father,
Armèd at point exactly, cap-a-pe,   200
Appears before them and with solemn march
Goes slow and stately by them. Thrice he walked
By their oppressed and fear-surprisèd eyes
Within his truncheon's length, whilst they, distilled
Almost to jelly with the act of fear,
Stand dumb and speak not to him. This to me
In dreadful secrecy impart they did,
And I with them the third night kept the watch,
Where, as they had delivered, both in time,
Form of the thing, each word made true and good,   210
The apparition comes. I knew your father.

192 *Season your admiration* control your   200 *at point* (as if) in readiness
    amazement   *cap-a-pe* from head to foot
193 *attent* attentive   203 *oppressed* distressed, troubled
    deliver report   204 *truncheon* military baton
198 *dead waste* desolate time (of night),   *distilled* melted
    as still as death. Q1 reads 'dead vast', 205 *act* effect
    which many editors have found   207 *dreadful* full of dread
    attractive.

These hands are not more like.

HAMLET   But where was this?

MARCELLUS

My lord, upon the platform where we watch.

HAMLET

Did you not speak to it?

HORATIO   My lord, I did,

But answer made it none. Yet once methought

It lifted up it head and did address

Itself to motion like as it would speak.

But even then the morning cock crew loud,

And at the sound it shrunk in haste away

And vanished from our sight.

220   HAMLET   'Tis very strange.

HORATIO

As I do live, my honoured lord, 'tis true.

And we did think it writ down in our duty

To let you know of it.

HAMLET

Indeed, indeed, sirs. But this troubles me.

Hold you the watch tonight?

ALL   We do, my lord.

HAMLET

Armed, say you?

ALL

Armed, my lord.

HAMLET

From top to toe?

ALL   My lord, from head to foot.

---

212 *These hands are not more like* (each
other than the Ghost was like your
father). An expressive gesture for the
actor.

216 *it* its

216–17 *address . . . would* begin to move as
if it were about to

222 *writ down* prescribed

HAMLET
 Then saw you not his face?
HORATIO
 O, yes, my lord. He wore his beaver up.   230
HAMLET
 What, looked he frowningly?
HORATIO
 A countenance more in sorrow than in anger.
HAMLET
 Pale or red?
HORATIO
 Nay, very pale.
HAMLET   And fixed his eyes upon you?
HORATIO
 Most constantly.
HAMLET   I would I had been there.
HORATIO
 It would have much amazed you.
HAMLET
 Very like, very like. Stayed it long?
HORATIO
 While one with moderate haste might tell a hundred.
MARCELLUS *and* BARNARDO
 Longer, longer.
HORATIO
 Not when I saw't.
HAMLET   His beard was grizzled, no?   240
HORATIO
 It was as I have seen it in his life,

---

229 *Then saw you not his face?* Hamlet is testing his informants. This may be a question, or a statement of inference which throws doubt upon their story of recognizing the late King Hamlet.
230 *beaver* visor of a helmet (the movable upper part which could be drawn down over the face for protection but was normally kept in the lifted position except when fighting)
235 *constantly* unchangingly, fixedly
236 *amazed* (a strong word) confounded
238 *tell* count
240 *grizzled* grey

A sable silvered.

HAMLET   I will watch tonight.
Perchance 'twill walk again.

HORATIO   I warrant it will.

HAMLET
If it assume my noble father's person,
I'll speak to it though hell itself should gape
And bid me hold my peace. I pray you all,
If you have hitherto concealed this sight,
Let it be tenable in your silence still.
And whatsomever else shall hap tonight,
250   Give it an understanding but no tongue.
I will requite your loves. So fare you well.
Upon the platform 'twixt eleven and twelve
I'll visit you.

ALL   Our duty to your honour.

HAMLET
Your loves, as mine to you. Farewell.

Exeunt all but Hamlet

My father's spirit! In arms! All is not well.
I doubt some foul play. Would the night were come!
Till then sit still, my soul. Foul deeds will rise,
Though all the earth o'erwhelm them, to men's eyes.

Exit

---

242 *A sable silvered* black streaked with
white
watch keep the watch (with you). But
the everyday meaning of *watch* was
'stay awake'.
243 *warrant* guarantee
248 *tenable in your silence* kept secret
249 *whatsomever* whatsoever
251 *requite your loves* reward your affectionate behaviour

254 *loves* (not merely *duty*)
256 *doubt* suspect. Hamlet is already suspicious of the cause of his father's
death, and the Ghost's revelations
confirm his *prophetic soul* (I.5.40).
257–8 *Foul deeds . . . men's eyes.* Compare
II.2.591–2.

Enter Laertes and Ophelia   I.3

LAERTES
My necessaries are embarked. Farewell.
And, sister, as the winds give benefit
And convoy is assistant, do not sleep
But let me hear from you.

OPHELIA   Do you doubt that?

LAERTES
For Hamlet, and the trifling of his favour,
Hold it a fashion and a toy in blood,
A violet in the youth of primy nature,
Forward, not permanent, sweet, not lasting,
The perfume and suppliance of a minute,
No more.

OPHELIA No more but so?

LAERTES   Think it no more.   10
For nature crescent does not grow alone

1.3. This scene informs the audience of the strong family feeling in Polonius's family. Laertes's love for his sister Ophelia, whom we see for the first time, and their regard for their father, in spite of his foibles, prepare for the violence of Laertes's impulses to revenge later. There is nothing to show that Laertes and Ophelia are contemptuous of Polonius's long-windedness.

1 *necessaries* personal baggage for the journey

2-3 *as the minds give benefit | And convoy is assistant* whenever the wind is favourable for the sailing of a ship to France and whenever any other means of sending a letter is available

5 *For Hamlet, and the trifling of his favour.* This remark introduces the love affair between Hamlet and Ophelia. Both Polonius and Laertes suppose that Hamlet has only a passing interest in the girl and that, since they see no hope of a royal marriage for their family, she will be either jilted or seduced. Yet she is the second lady in the land and might seem eligible.

6 *fashion* modish way of behaving
  a toy in blood mere whim of amorous passion

7 *violet.* It was proverbial for transient existence, as well as being associated with love.
  the youth of primy nature its spring-like prime

8 *Forward* blossoming precociously early

9 *suppliance* pastime

11 *crescent* increasing by the passage of time
   alone only

In thews and bulk, but as this temple waxes
The inward service of the mind and soul
Grows wide withal. Perhaps he loves you now,
And now no soil nor cautel doth besmirch
The virtue of his will. But you must fear,
His greatness weighed, his will is not his own.
For he himself is subject to his birth.
He may not, as unvalued persons do,
20   Carve for himself. For on his choice depends
The safety and health of this whole state.
And therefore must his choice be circumscribed
Unto the voice and yielding of that body
Whereof he is the head. Then, if he says he loves you,
It fits your wisdom so far to believe it
As he in his particular act and place
May give his saying deed; which is no further

12 *thews* muscles, bodily strength
this temple the human body that each
of us possesses (a biblical phrase: 'ye
are the temple of God', 1 Corinthians
3.16 etc.)

13 *inward service* faculties which are not
visible in our physical exterior

14 *withal* also. Laertes is suggesting that
Hamlet will soon grow out of his
shallow love for Ophelia. These lines
suggest Hamlet's youth.

15 *soil* blemish
cautel deceitfulness

16 *will* (sexual impulse, as well as 'intentions'; and Laertes continues the
complex meanings of *will* by using it
in line 17 as 'faculty of making
decisions')
fear be anxious about the fact that

17 *His greatness weighed* if you take into
account his high rank

18 *he himself is subject to his birth* he may
be a member of the royal family and

we his subjects, but he too is *subject*
to the princely rank into which he
was born. This line was omitted from
Q2, presumably by accident.

19 *unvalued persons* those whose social
and political position is of no
importance

20 *Carve for himself* make his own choice
of a royal consort (like one who
chooses to take his own slice of meat
at the dinner table)
choice (of a wife)

23 *voice* declared opinion (or approval)
yielding compliance
body nation (the 'body politic')

26 *he in his particular act and place* one
who is in his personal position (as a
prince). But the text may be wrong,
for F reads the even more difficult
phrase 'he in his peculiar Sect and
force'.

27 *give his saying deed* fulfil by his actions
what his words promise

Than the main voice of Denmark goes withal.
Then weigh what loss your honour may sustain
If with too credent ear you list his songs,   30
Or lose your heart, or your chaste treasure open
To his unmastered importunity.
Fear it, Ophelia, fear it, my dear sister.
And keep you in the rear of your affection,
Out of the shot and danger of desire.
The chariest maid is prodigal enough
If she unmask her beauty to the moon.
Virtue itself 'scapes not calumnious strokes.
The canker galls the infants of the spring
Too oft before their buttons be disclosed;   40
And in the morn and liquid dew of youth
Contagious blastments are most imminent.
Be wary then. Best safety lies in fear.
Youth to itself rebels, though none else near.

28 *main voice* majority opinion
    withal along with
30 *credent* trustful
    list listen to
    songs seductive avowals of love
32 *unmastered* uncontrolled
34 *keep you in the rear of your affection* do
    not go as far as your feelings would
    lead you
35 *shot.* Feelings of love were often imag-
    ined as provoked by Cupid's arrows.
    But here perhaps the image is from
    gunshot.
36 *chariest* most cautious
    prodigal enough quite sufficiently
    prodigal (if she does no more than
    unmask her beauty merely *to the* chaste
    moon, whose pale light will show little
    of it)
39 *canker* canker-worm or caterpillar
    galls injures
    infants of the spring young spring-time
    plants

40 *buttons* flower-buds
    disclosed opened out
41–2 *in the morn ... most imminent.* It is
    in the moist air of the morning that
    infectious diseases are most likely to
    strike. Similarly, it is young people
    who are especially vulnerable.
42 *blastments* blights
43 *Best safety lies in fear* to be afraid of
    doing something dangerous is the
    best way of keeping safe
44 *Youth to itself rebels, though none else near.*
    Young people are both frightened
    and adventurous. Their fearfulness is
    in conflict with their adventurous-
    ness, and may keep them safe when
    no other help is available. Or per-
    haps: the passions of youth lead to
    instinctive rebellion against self-
    restraint, even though no temptation
    is near.

OPHELIA

I shall the effect of this good lesson keep
As watchman to my heart. But, good my brother,
Do not, as some ungracious pastors do,
Show me the steep and thorny way to heaven
Whiles like a puffed and reckless libertine
Himself the primrose path of dalliance treads
And recks not his own rede.

LAERTES   O, fear me not.

I stay too long.

Enter Polonius

But here my father comes.
A double blessing is a double grace.
Occasion smiles upon a second leave.

POLONIUS

Yet here, Laertes? Aboard, aboard, for shame!
The wind sits in the shoulder of your sail,
And you are stayed for. There – my blessing with thee.
And these few precepts in thy memory
Look thou character. Give thy thoughts no tongue,

47 *ungracious* without grace
pastors. The word is carefully chosen. The 'good shepherd', unlike the *ungracious pastor*, will 'put forth his own sheep; he goeth before them, and the sheep follow him' (John 10.4).

48 *the steep and thorny way to heaven*. This, and *the primrose path of dalliance* (line 50), seem to derive from Matthew 7.13–14: 'Wide is the gate and broad is the way that leadeth to destruction ... Strait is the gate and narrow is the way which leadeth unto life.'

49 *puffed* swollen with pride (or exccess)

50 *primrose path of dalliance*. Similar phrases are used in *All's Well That Ends Well*, IV.5.51–3: 'the flowery way that leads to the broad gate and

the great fire', and by the Porter in *Macbeth*, II.3.18: 'the primrose way to the everlasting bonfire'.

51 *recks not his own rede* disregards his own advice
fear me not don't worry about me

53 *A double blessing*. Laertes has already once said goodbye to his father and received his blessing.

54 *Occasion smiles upon a second leave* it is a lucky chance when there is a second leave-taking

56 *sits in the shoulder of your sail* (an elaborate way of saying 'is favourable')

57 *There*. Polonius places his hand on the head of the kneeling Laertes.

59 *Look* be sure that
character (accented on the second syllable) inscribe

Nor any unproportioned thought his act.   60
Be thou familiar, but by no means vulgar.
Those friends thou hast, and their adoption tried,
Grapple them unto thy soul with hoops of steel.
But do not dull thy palm with entertainment
Of each new-hatched, unfledged courage. Beware
Of entrance to a quarrel. But, being in,
Bear't that th'opposèd may beware of thee.
Give every man thine ear, but few thy voice.
Take each man's censure, but reserve thy judgement.
Costly thy habit as thy purse can buy,   70
But not expressed in fancy; rich, not gaudy;
For the apparel oft proclaims the man,
And they in France of the best rank and station
Are of a most select and generous chief in that.
Neither a borrower nor a lender be,
For loan oft loses both itself and friend,
And borrowing dulleth edge of husbandry.
This above all: to thine own self be true,
And it must follow, as the night the day,
Thou canst not then be false to any man.   80

60 *unproportioned* inappropriate to the
circumstances (or perhaps 'badly
calculated' and so 'reckless')
his its
61 *Be thou familiar, but by no means vulgar*
be affable in dealing with others, but
don't make yourself cheap among
the common people
62 *and their adoption tried* once their association in friendship with you has
been tested
64 *do not dull thy palm* (so that your
handshake becomes meaningless, or
so that you lose your power of discrimination among true friends)
65 *courage* young man of bravado. F
reads 'Comrade'.

67 *Bear't* sustain it, carry it through
68 *voice* spoken opinion, support
69 *Take each man's censure* take notice of
the opinions expressed by other
people (on any matter)
71 *expressed in fancy* designed in some
peculiar and fanciful way
74 *Are of a most select and generous* (perhaps) show their refined and well-
bred taste. But the line is difficult to
interpret, and its twelve syllables suggest an error in the text.
chief in that especially in that respect
(of good taste in clothes)
77 *husbandry* thrift

Farewell. My blessing season this in thee!

LAERTES
Most humbly do I take my leave, my lord.

POLONIUS
The time invites you. Go. Your servants tend.

LAERTES
Farewell, Ophelia; and remember well
What I have said to you.

OPHELIA   'Tis in my memory locked,
And you yourself shall keep the key of it.

LAERTES
Farewell.   *Exit*

POLONIUS
What is't, Ophelia, he hath said to you?

OPHELIA
So please you, something touching the Lord Hamlet.

POLONIUS
90   Marry, well bethought.
'Tis told me he hath very oft of late
Given private time to you, and you yourself
Have of your audience been most free and bounteous.
If it be so – as so 'tis put on me,
And that in way of caution – I must tell you
You do not understand yourself so clearly
As it behoves my daughter and your honour.
What is between you? Give me up the truth.

OPHELIA
He hath, my lord, of late made many tenders
100   Of his affection to me.

---

81 *season this in thee* in due season bring
my good advice to fruition in you
(or 'make it palatable')

83 *invites you* requests your presence
tend attend you

90 *Marry* (a mild oath: 'by the Virgin
Mary')

well bethought well remembered ('I am
glad you reminded me'; or perhaps
'That was a good idea of his')

93 *audience* attention (to what Hamlet has
said)

94 *put on me* impressed upon me

POLONIUS

    Affection? Pooh! You speak like a green girl,
    Unsifted in such perilous circumstance.
    Do you believe his tenders, as you call them?

OPHELIA

    I do not know, my lord, what I should think.

POLONIUS

    Marry, I will teach you. Think yourself a baby
    That you have ta'en these tenders for true pay
    Which are not sterling. Tender yourself more dearly,
    Or – not to crack the wind of the poor phrase,
    Running it thus – you'll tender me a fool.

OPHELIA

    My lord, he hath importuned me with love   110
    In honourable fashion.

POLONIUS

    Ay, 'fashion' you may call it. Go to, go to.

OPHELIA

    And hath given countenance to his speech, my lord,
    With almost all the holy vows of heaven.

POLONIUS

    Ay, springes to catch woodcocks. I do know,

---

101 *green* inexperienced

102 *Unsifted* untried

107 *Tender*. Polonius puns on *tenders* meaning 'offers' (lines 103 and 106, and line 99) and to *Tender* (line 107) meaning 'look after' or 'have a proper esteem for'.

108 *crack the wind*. The image is from the excessive galloping of a horse or over-exertion of a hound, which will get the stitch.

109 *tender me a fool* (as the father of a girl who is intriguing with the heir to the throne, or who has been seduced; or perhaps 'exhibit yourself to me as a fool, a girl who has been seduced'.

Ophelia's reply shows that she understands her father to think she might be seduced.)

111 *fashion*. Ophelia uses the word simply as 'manner', but Polonius interprets it like Laertes in line 6 above.

112 *Go to* (an interjection of impatience)

113 *countenance* support, favourable appearance

115 *springes to catch woodcocks*. Proverbially the woodcock was a foolish bird which easily fell into snares (*springes*, pronounced to rhyme with 'hinges'). Compare *as a woodcock to mine own springe* (V.2.300).

When the blood burns, how prodigal the soul
Lends the tongue vows. These blazes, daughter,
Giving more light than heat, extinct in both
Even in their promise, as it is a-making,
120   You must not take for fire. From this time
Be something scanter of your maiden presence.
Set your entreatments at a higher rate
Than a command to parle. For Lord Hamlet,
Believe so much in him that he is young,
And with a larger tether may he walk
Than may be given you. In few, Ophelia,
Do not believe his vows. For they are brokers,
Not of that dye which their investments show,
But mere implorators of unholy suits,
130   Breathing like sanctified and pious bawds,
The better to beguile. This is for all:
I would not, in plain terms, from this time forth
Have you so slander any moment leisure
As to give words or talk with the Lord Hamlet.
Look to't, I charge you. Come your ways.

OPHELIA
   I shall obey, my lord.   *Exeunt*

116 *prodigal* prodigally
118 *extinct in both* both the light and
     heat of which are extinguished
121 *something* somewhat
122 *your entreatments* his solicitations of
     your favour
123 *a command to parle* an invitation to
     carry on a love conversation with
     him. Polonius sees the relationship
     between Hamlet and Ophelia as a
     siege of her chastity.
125 *with a larger tether* with a longer
     tethering-rope (and so with less
     control)
126 *In few* in brief

127 *brokers* go-betweens
128 *investments* garments (especially of a
     religious or otherwise imposing
     kind)
129 *implorators* solicitors
130 *Breathing* speaking persuasively
     bawds. This is an emendation of
     'bonds' (Q2 and F), which has been
     defended as meaning 'marriage
     bonds'.
131 *beguile* cheat
     This is for all to sum up
133 *slander* misuse
     moment moment's
135 *Come your ways* come away

Enter Hamlet, Horatio, and Marcellus   I.4

HAMLET
The air bites shrewdly. It is very cold.

HORATIO
It is a nipping and an eager air.

HAMLET
What hour now?

HORATIO   I think it lacks of twelve.

MARCELLUS
No, it is struck.

HORATIO
Indeed? I heard it not. It then draws near the season
Wherein the spirit held his wont to walk.

> *A flourish of trumpets, and two pieces of ordnance go*
> *off*

What does this mean, my lord?

HAMLET
The King doth wake tonight and takes his rouse,
Keeps wassail, and the swaggering upspring reels.
And as he drains his draughts of Rhenish down   10

1.4 (stage direction) Barnardo is not now
included in the group, though from
1.2.225 and 253 we are led to expect
him. As a sentinel, he could not abandon his post; and it would be awkward to leave him on stage when
Horatio and Marcellus rush off after
Hamlet.

1 *shrewdly* 'wickedly', sharply

2 *eager* biting

3 *lacks of* is a little before

5 *season* time of day

6 (stage direction) *pieces of ordnance*. The
gun-salutes honour Hamlet's *gentle
and unforced accord* (1.2.123), so cele-
brate a kind of triumph of the King
over Hamlet.

8 *The King doth wake tonight* . . . Compare
1.2.124–8.
doth wake stays awake, holds a late-
night revel
rouse bumper of wine

9 *Keeps wassail* gives a drinking-party
swaggering upspring reels. Probably the
rare noun *upspring* indicates some
kind of Teutonic dance which Shakespeare introduces as local colour.

10 *Rhenish* Rhineland wine (imported in
large quantities into England in
Shakespeare's time)

The kettledrum and trumpet thus bray out
The triumph of his pledge.

HORATIO   Is it a custom?

HAMLET

Ay, marry, is't.
But to my mind, though I am native here
And to the manner born, it is a custom
More honoured in the breach than the observance.
This heavy-headed revel east and west
Makes us traduced and taxed of other nations.
They clepe us drunkards and with swinish phrase
20 Soil our addition; and indeed it takes
From our achievements, though performed at height,
The pith and marrow of our attribute.
So oft it chances in particular men
That — for some vicious mole of nature in them,
As in their birth, wherein they are not guilty,
Since nature cannot choose his origin —

12 *The triumph of his pledge* his glorious
achievement as a drinker of toasts
(usually that of drinking a vessel of
wine down at one draught)
15 *to the manner born* habituated to it
from my birth
16 *More honoured in the breach than the
observance* which it is more honourable to disregard than to keep
17–38 *This heavy-headed . . . scandal.* This
passage about the drunkenness of the
Danes is not in F. Probably it seemed
tactless after the accession of James
VI of Scotland to the English throne,
with his Danish consort, Anne.
17 *heavy-headed.* Presumably the *revel*
causes heavy heads, rather than being
characterized by them.
east and west (presumably) throughout
the length and breadth of Denmark
(but perhaps the phrase goes with

Makes us traduced and means 'throughout Europe')
18 *Makes us traduced and taxed of* causes
us to be calumniated and to have
faults imputed to us by
19 *clepe us* describe us as
with swinish phrase in comparing us to
pigs
20 *Soil* blemish
addition honorary title (and so 'good
name')
it (the Danish custom of drunkenness)
21 *though performed at height* though they
are the summit of our endeavour
22 *our attribute* the reputation attributed
to us by others
23 *particular men* individuals
24 *vicious mole of nature* natural blemish
25 *As* for instance
26 *his* its

By the o'ergrowth of some complexion,
Oft breaking down the pales and forts of reason,
Or by some habit that too much o'er-leavens
The form of plausive manners – that these men,   30
Carrying, I say, the stamp of one defect,
Being nature's livery or fortune's star,
His virtues else, be they as pure as grace,
As infinite as man may undergo,
Shall in the general censure take corruption
From that particular fault. The dram of evil
Doth all the noble substance of a doubt,
To his own scandal –

> *Enter the Ghost*

HORATIO   Look, my lord, it comes.

HAMLET
Angels and ministers of grace defend us!

---

27 *o'ergrowth of some complexion* over-development of some natural trait
28 *pales* fences
29 *habit* acquired habit
too much o'er-leavens has too strong an effect upon (like something damaged by excessive fermentation)
30 *form of plausive* behaviour resulting from pleasing
32 *Being nature's livery or fortune's star* which is due either to their subservience to nature or to the influence of ill fortune (the *defect* is either natural or accidental)
33 *His.* So Q2, and probably the shift from plural to singular is Shakespeare's; but some editors emend to 'Their'.
virtues else other qualities
34 *may undergo* can support
35 *general censure* overall opinion of him
35–6 *take corruption | From* be falsely esteemed because of. Hamlet means

that a man may have many virtues and one fault, but this one fault will so damage his reputation that his virtues will be misjudged.
36–8 *The dram of evil . . . scandal.* These words do not make grammatical sense. It seems best to take the rather complicated sentence as broken off in the middle by the Ghost's appearance.
36 *dram* tiny quantity
evil. Q2 prints 'eale' (Q1 and F omit this passage), perhaps a misreading of 'evil'.
37 *of a doubt.* Plausible emendations are 'oft adulter' ('often adulterate or corrupt') and 'often dout' ('often efface')
38 *his* that man's
scandal shame
39 *ministers of grace* messengers from God

40 Be thou a spirit of health or goblin damned,
    Bring with thee airs from heaven or blasts from hell,
    Be thy intents wicked or charitable,
    Thou comest in such a questionable shape
    That I will speak to thee. I'll call thee Hamlet,
    King, father, royal Dane. O, answer me!
    Let me not burst in ignorance. But tell
    Why thy canonized bones, hearsèd in death,
    Have burst their cerements; why the sepulchre
    Wherein we saw thee quietly interred
50 Hath oped his ponderous and marble jaws
    To cast thee up again. What may this mean
    That thou, dead corse, again in complete steel,
    Revisits thus the glimpses of the moon,
    Making night hideous, and we fools of nature
    So horridly to shake our disposition

40–41 *Be thou . . . from hell.* Hamlet has initial doubts about the Ghost, but these are soon displaced by his (and the audience's) conviction that it is a veritable vision of his father. On two later occasions Hamlet suspects that *The spirit that I have seen | May be a devil,* which *Abuses me to damn me* (II.2.596–601 and III.2.92).

40 *Be thou* whether you are
   spirit of health benevolent spirit (or possibly 'saved soul')
   goblin damned evil spirit that has suffered damnation

41 *Bring* whether you bring

42 *Be thy intents* whether your intentions are

43 *questionable* inviting interrogation by me (since you appear like my father)

44 *call thee* invoke you by the name of

47 *thy canonized bones, hearsèd in death.* Hamlet's father had been properly buried with all due religious rites (see the note to I.1.128–40).

canonized (accented on the second syllable) consecrated by Christian burial
hearsèd coffined

48 *cerements* (two syllables, pronounced 'seer-') waxed shroud

49 *interred.* F's reading, 'enurn'd', is attractive, although the Roman-style obsequies of placing ashes in an urn would be inconsistent with the Christian burial of the shrouded body (the *canonized bones* in their *cerements*). Possibly 'enurn'd' merely means 'put into a coffin'.

52 *complete steel* full armour
   complete (accented on the first syllable)

53 *the glimpses of the moon* the earth illuminated by the uncertain light of the moon

54 *fools of nature* weak creatures limited by nature (but now having to face experience of the supernatural)

55 *horridly* (probably with the notion of 'making our hair stand on end')
   disposition composure of feelings

With thoughts beyond the reaches of our souls?
Say, why is this? Wherefore? What should we do?

The Ghost beckons him

HORATIO

It beckons you to go away with it,
As if it some impartment did desire
To you alone.

MARCELLUS   Look with what courteous action   60
It waves you to a more removèd ground.
But do not go with it.

HORATIO   No, by no means.

HAMLET

It will not speak. Then I will follow it.

HORATIO

Do not, my lord.

HAMLET   Why, what should be the fear?
I do not set my life at a pin's fee.
And for my soul, what can it do to that,
Being a thing immortal as itself?
It waves me forth again. I'll follow it.

HORATIO

What if it tempt you toward the flood, my lord,
Or to the dreadful summit of the cliff   70
That beetles o'er his base into the sea,
And there assume some other, horrible form,
Which might deprive your sovereignty of reason
And draw you into madness? Think of it.
The very place puts toys of desperation,
Without more motive, into every brain
That looks so many fathoms to the sea

56 *reaches* capacity
59 *impartment* communication
65 *a pin's fee* the value of a trifle
69 *flood* sea
71 *beetles* projects

73 *your sovereignty of reason* your reason of
its control over you
75 *toys of desperation* fanciful impulses
leading to despair (and suicide)

And hears it roar beneath.

HAMLET   It waves me still. –
Go on. I'll follow thee.

MARCELLUS
You shall not go, my lord.

80   HAMLET   Hold off your hands.

HORATIO
Be ruled. You shall not go.

HAMLET   My fate cries out
And makes each petty artere in this body
As hardy as the Nemean lion's nerve.
Still am I called. Unhand me, gentlemen.
By heaven, I'll make a ghost of him that lets me!
I say, away! Go on. I'll follow thee.

Exeunt the Ghost and Hamlet

HORATIO
He waxes desperate with imagination.

MARCELLUS
Let's follow. 'Tis not fit thus to obey him.

HORATIO
Have after. To what issue will this come?

MARCELLUS
90   Something is rotten in the state of Denmark.

HORATIO
Heaven will direct it.

MARCELLUS   Nay, let's follow him.

Exeunt

---

82 *petty* (relatively) weak
   artere (two syllables: an alternative
   form of 'artery') channel through
   which flowed the 'vital spirits' (not
   the blood)
83 *Nemean lion.* The killing of the terrible lion of Nemea was one of the
   twelve labours of Hercules.

Nemean (accented on the first syllable, which is short: 'nemm-ee-an')
85 *lets* hinders
87 *waxes* becomes increasingly
89 *Have after* I will follow
91 *Nay* (a mild contradiction to *Heaven
   will direct it*, implying that they themselves can do something)

Enter the Ghost and Hamlet   1.5

HAMLET
Whither wilt thou lead me? Speak. I'll go no further.
GHOST
Mark me.
HAMLET   I will.
GHOST   My hour is almost come,
When I to sulphurous and tormenting flames
Must render up myself.
HAMLET   Alas, poor ghost!
GHOST
Pity me not, but lend thy serious hearing
To what I shall unfold.
HAMLET   Speak. I am bound to hear.
GHOST
So art thou to revenge, when thou shalt hear.
HAMLET
What?
GHOST
I am thy father's spirit,
Doomed for a certain term to walk the night,   10
And for the day confined to fast in fires,
Till the foul crimes done in my days of nature
Are burnt and purged away. But that I am forbid
To tell the secrets of my prison house,
I could a tale unfold whose lightest word
Would harrow up thy soul, freeze thy young blood,

1.5.3 *sulphurous and tormenting flames*. This sounds more like hell than the purgatory referred to in lines 9–13 below.
6 *bound* ready (but the Ghost takes it to mean 'obliged')
11 *fast* do penance

12 *foul crimes*. The Ghost does not necessarily imply that he has been particularly wicked, but refers to the common situation of a sinner in this mortal life.
my days of nature this mortal life

Make thy two eyes like stars start from their spheres,
Thy knotted and combinèd locks to part,
And each particular hair to stand an end
20 Like quills upon the fretful porpentine.
But this eternal blazon must not be
To ears of flesh and blood. List, list, O, list!
If thou didst ever thy dear father love –

HAMLET
O God!

GHOST
Revenge his foul and most unnatural murder.

HAMLET
Murder?

GHOST
Murder most foul, as in the best it is,
But this most foul, strange, and unnatural.

HAMLET
Haste me to know't, that I, with wings as swift
30 As meditation or the thoughts of love,
May sweep to my revenge.

GHOST   I find thee apt,
And duller shouldst thou be than the fat weed
That roots itself in ease on Lethe wharf,
Wouldst thou not stir in this. Now, Hamlet, hear.

---

17 *spheres* (in which the heavenly bodies normally moved: see the note to IV.7.15)
19 *an* on
20 *fretful porpentine* porcupine when it has become angry. Q2 has 'fearefull' ('timid') for F's 'fretfull'.
21 *eternal blazon* revelation about what has been appointed for all eternity
25, 28 *unnatural* (because contrary to family feeling)
27 *in the best* even at best
30 *meditation* thought
32 *shouldst thou be* you would have to be
32–3 *the fat weed | That roots itself in ease*

on Lethe wharf. Lethe is a river of Hades: according to the classical poets, it caused oblivion in those who drank it. The word *wharf* is used because the spirits were supposed to embark on Charon's boat in order to cross the river. As *the fat weed* Shakespeare may have had in mind asphodel, which grew in the fields of Hades.
33 *roots.* F reads 'rots', which perhaps gives a more expressive meaning and is supported by *Antony and Cleopatra*, I.4.45–7.

'Tis given out that, sleeping in my orchard,
A serpent stung me. So the whole ear of Denmark
Is by a forgèd process of my death
Rankly abused. But know, thou noble youth,
The serpent that did sting thy father's life
Now wears his crown.

HAMLET   O my prophetic soul!   40
My uncle?

GHOST

Ay, that incestuous, that adulterate beast,
With witchcraft of his wit, with traitorous gifts –
O wicked wit and gifts, that have the power
So to seduce! – won to his shameful lust
The will of my most seeming-virtuous Queen.
O Hamlet, what a falling off was there,
From me, whose love was of that dignity
That it went hand in hand even with the vow
I made to her in marriage; and to decline   50
Upon a wretch whose natural gifts were poor
To those of mine!
But virtue as it never will be moved,

---

35 *orchard* garden (as at III.2.270)
36-8 *the whole ear of Denmark . . . abused.*
Old Hamlet's anticipation of his
account of his own poisoned ear
(lines 63-4; see also III.2.144, stage
direction) is almost like one of his
son's characteristic puns. The many
allusions in the play to ears (especially damaged ones) – e.g. 1.1.31,
1.2.171, II.2.475 and 560, III.2.10,
III.4.65 and 96, and IV.5.91 – produce
a half-conscious reminder of the circumstances of the murder.
37 *forgèd process* fabricated official report
38 *abused* deceived
40 *prophetic soul.* See I.2.255-8.
42 *adulterate.* This word, and the whole

passage 42-57, seem to imply that
Claudius had seduced Gertrude
before her husband's death. But nothing in the rest of the play supports
this, except perhaps Hamlet's *whored
my mother* (v.2.64) and, conceivably,
Horatio's words *carnal . . . acts*
(v.2.375). In the play of *The Murder
of Gonzago* the wooing definitely
takes place after the poisoning
(III.2.144, stage direction, and 270-
73).
47 *falling off* (both 'decline in moral
standards' and 'desertion')
50-51 *decline | Upon* sink to the level of
52 *To* in comparison with
53 *virtue as it* as virtue

Though lewdness court it in a shape of heaven,
So lust, though to a radiant angel linked,
Will sate itself in a celestial bed
And prey on garbage.
But soft, methinks I scent the morning air.
Brief let me be. Sleeping within my orchard,
60   My custom always of the afternoon,
Upon my secure hour thy uncle stole
With juice of cursèd hebona in a vial,
And in the porches of my ears did pour
The leperous distilment; whose effect
Holds such an enmity with blood of man
That swift as quicksilver it courses through
The natural gates and alleys of the body,
And with a sudden vigour it doth posset
And curd, like eager droppings into milk,
70   The thin and wholesome blood. So did it mine.
And a most instant tetter barked about,
Most lazar-like, with vile and loathsome crust

54 *lewdness* lust
   a shape of heaven a physical appearance of angelic attractiveness
56 *sate itself in a celestial bed* grow weary of sexual union with a lawful and virtuous partner. The F and Q1 reading *sate* seems to be required, against Q2's 'sort' ('separate'), which gives only a strained meaning.
57 *garbage* (originally) the offal and entrails of animals
61 *secure* (accented on the first syllable) thoughtlessly unguarded
62 *juice of cursèd hebona.* It is doubtful what precisely Shakespeare and his contemporaries meant by this poison. F uses the form 'Hebenon'. The word is related to 'ebony', but here it seems to be combined with some of the qualities of henbane.
63 *porches of mine ears.* Poisoning through

the ears was a legendary Italian method; but according to medical authority it could not be effective.
64 *leperous distilment* distillation causing a disease like leprosy (still fairly common in Shakespeare's England)
67 *gates and alleys.* The body is represented under the image of a city.
68 *sudden* rapid in action
   vigour power, efficacy
   posset curdle (so that the blood is clotted). A posset was a drink made from milk curdled with wine or ale.
69 *eager* sharp, sour (and so curdling the milk)
70 *thin* (not curdled into clots)
71 *tetter* scurf
   barked about (coated with a *crust*)
72 *lazar-like* like leprosy (the disease usually attributed to the beggar Lazarus in Luke 16.20)

All my smooth body.
Thus was I sleeping by a brother's hand
Of life, of crown, of queen at once dispatched,
Cut off even in the blossoms of my sin,
Unhouseled, disappointed, unaneled,
No reckoning made, but sent to my account
With all my imperfections on my head.
O, horrible! O, horrible! Most horrible!   80
If thou hast nature in thee, bear it not.
Let not the royal bed of Denmark be
A couch for luxury and damned incest.
But howsomever thou pursues this act,
Taint not thy mind, nor let thy soul contrive
Against thy mother aught. Leave her to heaven
And to those thorns that in her bosom lodge
To prick and sting her. Fare thee well at once.
The glow-worm shows the matin to be near
And 'gins to pale his uneffectual fire.   90
Adieu, adieu, adieu. Remember me.   *Exit*

---

75 *dispatched* deprived
76–9 *Cut off . . . With all my imperfections on my head.* Hamlet remembers this at III.3.80–81.
76 *in the blossoms of my sin* when my sins were at their height
77 *Unhouseled* without having received the sacrament
    disappointed unprepared (for death, as having had no opportunity for repentance, confession, and absolution)
    unaneled (rhyming with 'healed') without having been given extreme unction
78 *reckoning* assessing and settling of my debts (his sins) to God
    my account (at God's judgement seat)
80 *O . . . Most horrible!* On the stage,

from Garrick's time, this line has often been transferred to Prince Hamlet. The interruption serves to break up the Ghost's long speech.
81 *nature* natural feelings of a son for a father
83 *luxury* lechery
86 *Leave her to heaven* entrust her to God's judgement. According to usual religious teaching, revenge upon Claudius should also be left *to heaven.*
89 *matin* morning
90 *uneffectual* (becoming feeble as day dawns). The glow-worm's *fire* contrasts imaginatively with the purgatorial fires to which the Ghost is about to return (lines 11–13).

HAMLET

O all you host of heaven! O earth! What else?
And shall I couple hell? O, fie! Hold, hold, my heart.
And you, my sinews, grow not instant old,
But bear me stiffly up. Remember thee?
Ay, thou poor ghost, whiles memory holds a seat
In this distracted globe. Remember thee?
Yea, from the table of my memory
I'll wipe away all trivial fond records,
100   All saws of books, all forms, all pressures past
That youth and observation copied there,
And thy commandment all alone shall live
Within the book and volume of my brain,
Unmixed with baser matter. Yes, by heaven!
O most pernicious woman!
O villain, villain, smiling, damnèd villain!
My tables – meet it is I set it down
That one may smile, and smile, and be a villain.
At least I am sure it may be so in Denmark.
          He writes
110   So, uncle, there you are. Now to my word:

92 *host of heaven* (angels)
93 *couple hell* include hell in my invocation
    O, fie! (presumably a rejection of the powers of hell)
    Hold hold together, remain unbroken
94 *instant* immediately
95 *stiffly* strongly. This is F's reading; Q2 has 'swiftly', which, though awkward, perhaps has some support from lines 29–30.
97 *this distracted globe* (probably his head, which he holds, rather than the world itself or 'the little world of man')
98 *the table of my memory* my memory, which is now like a memorandum tablet on which experience writes. The *table* was generally made of thin leaves of ivory or slate, from which one could *wipe away* previous *records* or notes. The customary contents of such notebooks are listed in lines 99–101.
99 *fond* foolish
    records (accented on the second syllable)
100 *saws* (usually somewhat derogatory) wise sayings, platitudes
    forms general ideas
    pressures past impressions previously received
110 *there you are* (I have set down my comment on you, accordingly, in my notebook)
    word watchword, motto (or perhaps 'promise given')

It is 'Adieu, adieu, remember me'.
I have sworn't.

Enter Horatio and Marcellus

HORATIO
My lord, my lord!

MARCELLUS   Lord Hamlet!

HORATIO   Heavens secure him!

HAMLET
So be it!

MARCELLUS
Illo, ho, ho, my lord!

HAMLET
Hillo, ho, ho, boy! Come, bird, come.

MARCELLUS
How is't, my noble lord?

HORATIO   What news, my lord?

HAMLET
O, wonderful!

HORATIO
Good my lord, tell it.

HAMLET   No, you will reveal it.

HORATIO
Not I, my lord, by heaven.

MARCELLUS   Nor I, my lord.   120

HAMLET
How say you then? Would heart of man once think it?
But you'll be secret?

HORATIO *and* MARCELLUS Ay, by heaven, my lord.

---

113 *secure him* keep him safe
114 *So be it* (either a continuation of his own thought, *I have sworn't*, or a response to Horatio's *Heavens secure him!*)
115 *Illo, ho, ho* (originally the falconer's cry in calling a hawk down)

116 *Come, bird, come.* In his excited mood, Hamlet mocks his friends' cries as if they were bird calls.
121 *once think it* ever believe what the Ghost has told me

HAMLET

There's never a villain dwelling in all Denmark –
But he's an arrant knave.

HORATIO

There needs no ghost, my lord, come from the grave
To tell us this.

HAMLET   Why, right, you are in the right,
And so, without more circumstance at all,
I hold it fit that we shake hands and part:
You, as your business and desire shall point you,
130 For every man hath business and desire,
Such as it is; and for my own poor part
I will go pray.

HORATIO

These are but wild and whirling words, my lord.

HAMLET

I am sorry they offend you, heartily.
Yes, faith, heartily.

HORATIO   There's no offence, my lord.

HAMLET

Yes, by Saint Patrick, but there is, Horatio,
And much offence too. Touching this vision here,
It is an honest ghost, that let me tell you.
For your desire to know what is between us,
140 O'ermaster't as you may. And now, good friends,

---

124 *But he's an arrant knave*. Probably
Hamlet intends to say 'who is worse
than King Claudius', or something
similar, but checks himself, deciding
not to tell anyone what the Ghost
has revealed to him.

127 *without more circumstance* cutting the
matter short

136 *Saint Patrick*. Hamlet swears by him
because Saint Patrick was a keeper
of purgatory (whence the Ghost
comes), having found an entrance to

it in Donegal; or perhaps because he
banished serpents from Ireland (see
Richard II, II.1.157–8), and Hamlet's
task is to get rid of a *serpent* (line 39).

137 *much offence*. Hamlet deliberately mistakes Horatio's word *offence* and takes
it as concerning the revelation of the
Ghost, which has told him of the
terrible *offence* of Claudius.

138 *honest ghost*. Hamlet assures them
that the Ghost is a *spirit of health*, not
a *goblin damned* (1.4.40).

As you are friends, scholars, and soldiers,
Give me one poor request.

HORATIO

What is't, my lord? We will.

HAMLET

Never make known what you have seen tonight.

HORATIO *and* **MARCELLUS**

My lord, we will not.

HAMLET   Nay, but swear't.

HORATIO   In faith,
My lord, not I.

MARCELLUS   Nor I, my lord – in faith.

HAMLET

Upon my sword.

MARCELLUS   We have sworn, my lord, already.

HAMLET

Indeed, upon my sword, indeed.

The Ghost cries under the stage

GHOST

Swear.

HAMLET

Ha, ha, boy, sayst thou so? Art thou there, truepenny?   150
Come on. You hear this fellow in the cellarage.

---

141 *scholars, and soldiers* (probably gen-
eric, including Horatio in the one
category and Marcellus in the other)

142 *Give* grant

146 *not I* I will never make known what
I have seen. (Horatio is not refusing
to take the oath.)

147 *Upon my sword.* The handle of a
sword forms a cross upon which an
oath can be administered. Hamlet is
not content with oaths *in faith*.

149 *Swear.* The Ghost's insistence on, or
approval of, the oath upon the hilt
of the sword as a Cross and its re-

sponse to the appeals to God's mercy
in lines 169 and 180 are further evidence that it is not a diabolical
tempter. Presumably Hamlet's mockery of the Ghost is intended to conceal from Horatio and Marcellus
how seriously he takes it and its
revelations.

150 *truepenny* honest fellow

151 *You hear this fellow.* It is not certain
that they do hear the Ghost any more
than the Queen does in III.4.103–40.
cellarage (not a particularly appropriate word for a *platform* (1.2.252). But

Consent to swear.

HORATIO   Propose the oath, my lord.

HAMLET
Never to speak of this that you have seen,
Swear by my sword.

GHOST (*beneath*)
Swear.

HAMLET
Hic et ubique? Then we'll shift our ground.
Come hither, gentlemen,
And lay your hands again upon my sword.
Swear by my sword
160   Never to speak of this that you have heard.

GHOST (*beneath*)
Swear by his sword.

HAMLET
Well said, old mole! Canst work i'th'earth so fast?
A worthy pioneer! Once more remove, good friends.

HORATIO
O day and night, but this is wondrous strange!

HAMLET
And therefore as a stranger give it welcome.

the space under the stage in the Elizabethan theatre was known as the
cellarage.)
153 *Never to speak of this that you have
seen.* The first oath concerns what
they have *seen*, the second, what they
have *heard* (from each other, not the
Ghost), the third, Hamlet's subsequent behaviour (lines 170–79). So it
seems that they swear three times,
though no words are given to them.
But the scene is usually played as if
their words were interrupted by the
Ghost at lines 155 and 161, and only
at line 181 do they silently complete
their oaths (see the note).

156 *Hic et ubique?* (Latin) here and
everywhere?
Then we'll shift our ground. Hamlet
seems to move his companions
around inexplicably. But Horatio and
Marcellus perhaps flee in terror from
the spot whence the Ghost's voice
comes, and Hamlet follows them to
different parts of the stage.
163 *pioneer* miner
165 *stranger* (punningly, alluding to the
proverb that a guest (*stranger*) should
be received hospitably, with no questions asked)

There are more things in heaven and earth, Horatio,
Than are dreamt of in your philosophy.
But come.
Here as before, never, so help you mercy,
How strange or odd some'er I bear myself –   170
As I perchance hereafter shall think meet
To put an antic disposition on –
That you, at such times seeing me, never shall,
With arms encumbered thus, or this head-shake,
Or by pronouncing of some doubtful phrase,
As 'Well, well, we know', or 'We could, an if we
          would',
Or 'If we list to speak', or 'There be, an if they might',
Or such ambiguous giving out, to note
That you know aught of me – this do swear,
So grace and mercy at your most need help you.   180

GHOST (*beneath*)

Swear.

HAMLET

Rest, rest, perturbèd spirit! So, gentlemen,
With all my love I do commend me to you,
And what so poor a man as Hamlet is

167 *your philosophy.* The exact meaning
of *your* is difficult to decide. It may
refer to Horatio's rationalist philosophy (he was established as a sceptic
at 1.1.23–32); or *your philosophy* may
express a general disdain for rationalizing explanations, not Horatio's
modes of thought particularly.

169 *help you mercy* may God's mercy save
you at his judgement seat

170 *How strange or odd some'er I bear
myself.* Hamlet's assumption of madness in order to lull suspicion seems
to have been an essential element in
the Hamlet story, and would be expected by an audience familiar with
the earlier play on the stage.

172 *antic* fantastically disguised
174 *encumbered* folded
176 *an if* if
177 *list* wished
There be, an if they might (there *are*
persons – meaning themselves – who
could explain things if only they were
at liberty to do so)
178 *giving out* intimation
to note to draw attention to the fact
179 *know   aught* have confidential
knowledge
181 *Swear.* But Horatio and Marcellus
are not given any words of an oath
as they place their hands on the
sword.

May do t'express his love and friending to you,
God willing, shall not lack. Let us go in together,
And still your fingers on your lips, I pray.
The time is out of joint. O, cursèd spite,
That ever I was born to set it right!
190   Nay, come, let's go together.   *Exeunt*

II.1   *Enter Polonius, with his man Reynaldo*

POLONIUS
Give him this money and these notes, Reynaldo.

REYNALDO
I will, my lord.

POLONIUS
You shall do marvellous wisely, good Reynaldo,
Before you visit him, to make inquire
Of his behaviour.

REYNALDO   My lord, I did intend it.

---

185 *friending* friendliness
186 *lack* be lacking
187 *still* always
188–9 *cursèd spite,* | *That ever I was born to set it right!* Hamlet seems to be following Job (3.1–3) in cursing the day of his nativity. He laments, not merely his task, but that he was ever born.
188 *spite* (of Fortune)
190 *together* (without an order of precedence. Hamlet's friendliness and avoidance of formality seem to be emphasized.)

II.1 Some time has elapsed: Laertes has

arrived in Paris and is settling down there; Ophelia has repelled Hamlet's letters and *denied* | *His access* (lines 109–10); the King already knows of *Hamlet's transformation* (II.2.5) and has summoned Rosencrantz and Guildenstern. This scene reveals that the King's chief minister is skilful at organizing spying – in this case, upon his own son. So Hamlet's danger, and the justification of his putting on an *antic disposition*, are understandable.

1 *Reynaldo* (a suitable name for a 'foxy' character)

3 *marvellous* very

POLONIUS

    Marry, well said. Very well said. Look you, sir,
    Inquire me first what Danskers are in Paris,
    And how, and who, what means, and where they keep,
    What company, at what expense; and finding
    By this encompassment and drift of question   10
    That they do know my son, come you more nearer
    Than your particular demands will touch it.
    Take you as 'twere some distant knowledge of him,
    As thus, 'I know his father and his friends,
    And in part him' – do you mark this, Reynaldo?

REYNALDO

    Ay, very well, my lord.

POLONIUS

    'And in part him, but', you may say, 'not well;
    But if't be he I mean, he's very wild,
    Addicted so and so'. And there put on him
    What forgeries you please – marry, none so rank   20
    As may dishonour him – take heed of that –
    But, sir, such wanton, wild, and usual slips
    As are companions noted and most known
    To youth and liberty.

REYNALDO   As gaming, my lord.

POLONIUS

    Ay, or drinking, fencing, swearing, quarrelling,

---

7 *me* (the indefinite indirect object (the 'ethic dative'), used so as to give an air of ingratiating ease)
   Danskers Danes (his fellow-countrymen). The unusually correct form of the word seems to imply Shakespeare's interest in giving local colour.

8 *what means* what their financial position is
   keep maintain an establishment

10 *encompassment and drift of question* roundabout and gradual inquiry

11 *more nearer*. The 'double comparative' is common in Shakespeare's grammar.

12 *particular demands will touch it* detailed questions would achieve
   it (the scheme for finding out how Laertes is behaving)

13 *Take you* assume

19 *put on* attribute to

20 *forgeries* fictions (invented accounts of wrong-doing)
   rank gross

Drabbing. You may go so far.

REYNALDO
My lord, that would dishonour him.

POLONIUS
Faith, no, as you may season it in the charge.
You must not put another scandal on him,
30   That he is open to incontinency.
That's not my meaning. But breathe his faults so
        quaintly
That they may seem the taints of liberty,
The flash and outbreak of a fiery mind,
A savageness in unreclaimèd blood,
Of general assault.

REYNALDO   But, my good lord –

POLONIUS
Wherefore should you do this?

REYNALDO   Ay, my lord,
I would know that.

POLONIUS   Marry, sir, here's my drift,
And I believe it is a fetch of warrant.
You laying these slight sullies on my son,
40   As 'twere a thing a little soiled i'th'working,
Mark you,
Your party in converse, him you would sound,
Having ever seen in the prenominate crimes
The youth you breathe of guilty, be assured

---

26 *Drabbing* pursuing loose women
28 *season it in the charge* modify (or soften) the accusation
30 *incontinency* habitual sexual indulgence
31 *breathe . . . quaintly* allude to, hint at . . . subtly
32 *taints of liberty* faults resulting from freedom
34-5 *A savageness . . . | Of general assault* a wildness . . . that attacks all indiscriminately
34 *unreclaimèd* unreformed (like an untamed hawk)
38 *fetch of warrant* justifiable device. For F's 'warrant', Q2 reads 'wit'.
39 *sullies*. See the note to I.2.129.
40 *a little soiled i'th' working* somewhat blemished as a result of contact with the world
42 *converse* conversation
43 *Having* if he has
    prenominate before-mentioned

He closes with you in this consequence:
'Good sir', or so, or 'friend', or 'gentleman' –
According to the phrase or the addition
Of man and country –
REYNALDO   Very good, my lord.
POLONIUS And then, sir, does 'a this – 'a does – What
was I about to say? By the mass, I was about to say   50
something! Where did I leave?
REYNALDO At 'closes in the consequence', at 'friend',
'or so', and 'gentleman'.
POLONIUS At 'closes in the consequence' – Ay, marry!
He closes thus: 'I know the gentleman.
I saw him yesterday, or th'other day,
Or then, or then, with such or such, and, as you say,
There was 'a gaming; there o'ertook in's rouse;
There falling out at tennis'; or perchance
'I saw him enter such a house of sale',   60
Videlicet, a brothel, or so forth.
See you now –
Your bait of falsehood takes this carp of truth,
And thus do we of wisdom and of reach,
With windlasses and with assays of bias,
By indirections find directions out.
So, by my former lecture and advice,
Shall you my son. You have me, have you not?

45 *closes with you in this consequence* will
end by becoming confidential with
you and speak as follows
47 *addition* polite form of address
49 *does 'a* he does
50 *By the mass* (an oath)
58 *o'ertook in's rouse* overcome by drunkenness when carousing
61 *Videlicet* that is to say
64 *we of wisdom and of reach* those of us
characterized by (or 'we who by
means of') wisdom and penetration

65 *windlasses and . . . assays of bias* roundabout methods and indirect attacks.
A *windlass* in this sense was a circuit
made by a portion of a hunting party
to intercept and head back the game.
In the game of bowls, the *bias* is the
curved course of a bowl which
reaches its aim (the jack) by not
going in a straight line.
66 *indirections* indirect approaches
directions ways of proceeding
68 *have* understand

REYNALDO
  My lord, I have.

POLONIUS   God bye ye, fare ye well.

REYNALDO
70 Good my lord.

POLONIUS
  Observe his inclination in yourself.

REYNALDO
  I shall, my lord.

POLONIUS
  And let him ply his music.

REYNALDO   Well, my lord.

POLONIUS
  Farewell.   *Exit Reynaldo*

     Enter Ophelia
         How now, Ophelia, what's the matter?

OPHELIA
  O my lord, my lord, I have been so affrighted!

POLONIUS
  With what, i'th'name of God?

OPHELIA
  My lord, as I was sewing in my closet,
  Lord Hamlet, with his doublet all unbraced,
  No hat upon his head, his stockings fouled,
80 Ungartered, and down-gyvèd to his ankle,

---

69 *God bye ye* God be with you
71 *in yourself* for yourself (as well as by
    report)
73 *let him ply his music* (perhaps with a
    literal meaning, or perhaps 'let him
    go his own way')
77 *closet* small private room
78–80 *his doublet . . . ankle.* Hamlet's dis-
    ordered clothing, presumably deliber-
    ately assumed, and the rest of his
    behaviour here, resemble the usual
    symptoms of love-sickness as de-

scribed in *As You Like It*, III.2.363–
6.
78 *doublet* close-fitting jacket with short
    skirt
    unbraced not laced up or fastened
79 *No hat upon his head.* Elizabethans
    normally wore hats indoors, even in
    church and at meals. Compare
    v.2.93.
80 *down-gyvèd to his ankle* fallen down like
    fetters ('gyves') around the ankles

Pale as his shirt, his knees knocking each other,
And with a look so piteous in purport
As if he had been loosèd out of hell
To speak of horrors – he comes before me.

POLONIUS

Mad for thy love?

OPHELIA   My lord, I do not know,
But truly I do fear it.

POLONIUS   What said he?

OPHELIA

He took me by the wrist and held me hard.
Then goes he to the length of all his arm,
And with his other hand thus o'er his brow
He falls to such perusal of my face   90
As 'a would draw it. Long stayed he so.
At last, a little shaking of mine arm
And thrice his head thus waving up and down,
He raised a sigh so piteous and profound
As it did seem to shatter all his bulk
And end his being. That done, he lets me go;
And, with his head over his shoulder turned,
He seemed to find his way without his eyes;
For out o'doors he went without their helps
And to the last bended their light on me.   100

POLONIUS

Come, go with me. I will go seek the King.
This is the very ecstasy of love,
Whose violent property fordoes itself
And leads the will to desperate undertakings

82 *purport* expression
89 *his other hand thus o'er his brow*. Ophelia
places her open hand palm down-
wards shading her eyes.
91 *As* as if

95 *bulk* body from neck to waist
102 *ecstasy* madness
103 *violent property* quality of being
violent
fordoes damages

As oft as any passion under heaven
That does afflict our natures. I am sorry.
What, have you given him any hard words of late?

OPHELIA

No, my good lord. But, as you did command,
I did repel his letters and denied
110   His access to me.

POLONIUS   That hath made him mad.
I am sorry that with better heed and judgement
I had not quoted him. I feared he did but trifle
And meant to wrack thee. But beshrew my jealousy.
By heaven, it is as proper to our age
To cast beyond ourselves in our opinions
As it is common for the younger sort
To lack discretion. Come, go we to the King.
This must be known, which, being kept close, might
        move
More grief to hide than hate to utter love.
120   Come.   Exeunt

---

105 *passion* violent state of feeling
112 *quoted* made my observation of
113 *wrack* dishonour (by seducing)
     beshrew my jealousy a curse upon my
     suspiciousness
114 *proper to* characteristic of
     our age (that is, old age)
115 *cast beyond ourselves* over-estimate in
     our calculations
117 *go we to the King.* But Q2 and F give
     no indication of Ophelia's being
     present in the next scene, and there
     are strong reasons for not introduc-
     ing her there.
118 *This must be known* we must make
     this known to the King (probably,

rather than 'whatever we may do to
conceal it, the story of this will soon
become common knowledge')
     close secret
118–19 *move | More grief to hide than hate
     to utter love* cause more ill-feeling if I
     conceal this love (by leading to fur-
     ther derangement of Hamlet's mind)
     than will be the indignation pro-
     voked in the King if I reveal (*utter*)
     it. Polonius feels that his daughter
     is no match for Hamlet; but later
     the Queen approves, discreetly at
     III.1.38–42 and (after Ophelia's
     death) plainly at V.1.240–41.

Flourish   II.2
Enter the King and Queen, Rosencrantz and
Guildenstern, with attendants

KING

Welcome, dear Rosencrantz and Guildenstern.
Moreover that we much did long to see you,
The need we have to use you did provoke
Our hasty sending. Something have you heard
Of Hamlet's transformation – so call it,
Sith nor th'exterior nor the inward man
Resembles that it was. What it should be,
More than his father's death, that thus hath put him
So much from th'understanding of himself
I cannot dream of. I entreat you both   10
That, being of so young days brought up with him,
And sith so neighboured to his youth and 'haviour,
That you vouchsafe your rest here in our court
Some little time, so by your companies
To draw him on to pleasures, and to gather
So much as from occasion you may glean,
Whether aught to us unknown afflicts him thus,
That, opened, lies within our remedy.

II.2 (stage direction) *attendants* (an interpretation of F's *'Cum alijs'* ('with
others'); not in Q2. *Go, some of you*
(line 36) implies that attendants are
on stage, or easily summoned.)
1 *Rosencrantz and Guildenstern*. They seem
to be young noblemen, chosen as the
childhood companions of the Prince.
2 *Moreover that* in addition to the fact
that
5 *transformation* metamorphosis, involving both the *exterior* (his appearance)
and *the inward man* (his mental
qualities)

6 *Sith nor* since neither
11 *of so young days* from such an early age
12 *sith* since that time (probably, rather
than 'because' as in line 6)
13 *vouchsafe* be pleased to agree to
rest residence
14 *your companies* the company of each of
you
16 *occasion* opportunity
18 *opened* when it is revealed (perhaps
a medical image: 'lanced')

QUEEN

Good gentlemen, he hath much talked of you,
20   And sure I am two men there is not living
To whom he more adheres. If it will please you
To show us so much gentry and good will
As to expend your time with us awhile
For the supply and profit of our hope,
Your visitation shall receive such thanks
As fits a king's remembrance.

ROSENCRANTZ   Both your majesties
Might, by the sovereign power you have of us,
Put your dread pleasures more into command
Than to entreaty.

GUILDENSTERN   But we both obey,
30   And here give up ourselves in the full bent
To lay our service freely at your feet,
To be commanded.

KING

Thanks, Rosencrantz and gentle Guildenstern.

QUEEN

Thanks, Guildenstern and gentle Rosencrantz.
And I beseech you instantly to visit
My too much changèd son. – Go, some of you,
And bring these gentlemen where Hamlet is.

GUILDENSTERN

Heavens make our presence and our practices

20 *is*. F amends Q2's 'is' to 'are', but
such lack of concord, often in emphatic speech, is not uncommon in
Shakespeare.
21 *adheres* feels united
22 *gentry* courtesy
24 *For the supply and profit of our hope* in
order to feed our hopes and cause
them to progress successfully

26 *fits a king's remembrance* would be fitting to be paid by a king who takes
note of the services rendered him
27 *of us* over us
28 *dread pleasures* revered wishes
30 *in the full bent* completely (like a bow
in archery)
38 *practices* conduct of this affair (but
perhaps implying 'sharp practices')

Pleasant and helpful to him!

QUEEN   Ay, amen!

*Exeunt Rosencrantz and
Guildenstern with attendants*

Enter Polonius

POLONIUS

The ambassadors from Norway, my good lord,   40
Are joyfully returned.

KING

Thou still hast been the father of good news.

POLONIUS

Have I, my lord? Assure you, my good liege,
I hold my duty as I hold my soul,
Both to my God and to my gracious King.
And I do think — or else this brain of mine
Hunts not the trail of policy so sure
As it hath used to do — that I have found
The very cause of Hamlet's lunacy.

KING

O, speak of that! That do I long to hear.   50

POLONIUS

Give first admittance to th'ambassadors.
My news shall be the fruit to that great feast.

KING

Thyself do grace to them and bring them in.

Exit Polonius

He tells me, my dear Gertrude, he hath found
The head and source of all your son's distemper.

40–41 *The ambassadors ... returned.* This
indicates the passage of time since
1.2, where Cornelius and Voltemand
were dispatched on their embassy.

42 *still* always

47 *Hunts ... the trail* (like a dog following the scent)
policy investigation

52 *fruit* (at the end of the *feast*)

53 *do grace to them* conduct them into the
royal presence (as if he were saying
grace before a *feast*). This gives Claudius an opportunity for a private
word with Gertrude.

55 *distemper* malady

QUEEN

I doubt it is no other but the main,
His father's death and our o'erhasty marriage.

KING

Well, we shall sift him.

*Enter Voltemand and Cornelius, the ambassadors, with
Polonius*

Welcome, my good friends.
Say, Voltemand, what from our brother Norway?

VOLTEMAND

60 Most fair return of greetings and desires.
Upon our first, he sent out to suppress
His nephew's levies, which to him appeared
To be a preparation 'gainst the Polack,
But, better looked into, he truly found
It was against your highness; whereat grieved,
That so his sickness, age, and impotence
Was falsely borne in hand, sends out arrests
On Fortinbras; which he in brief obeys,
Receives rebuke from Norway, and in fine
70 Makes vow before his uncle never more
To give th'assay of arms against your majesty.
Whereon old Norway, overcome with joy,
Gives him three thousand crowns in annual fee

57 *His father's death and our o'erhasty marriage.* Gertrude shrewdly enough interprets Hamlet's original state of
mind, but she is ignorant of the
murder, knowledge of which has
transformed Hamlet.
57 *sift him* question Polonius carefully
59 *brother.* Monarchs of different countries were 'brothers'.
60 *desires* good wishes
61 *Upon our first* immediately upon our
making our representations
62 *His nephew's levies* (described at
I.I.95–104)

63 *the Polack* the inhabitants of Poland
66 *impotence* helplessness
67 *falsely borne in hand* deluded
arrests summons to desist
69 *fine* conclusion
71 *give th'assay of arms* make trial of a
military engagement
73 *three thousand.* Q2 reads 'threescore
thousand', but this is unmetrical, and
60,000 crowns is rather a large *annual*
sum for a comparatively small expedition; moreover, F's reading, adopted
here, is supported by Q1.

And his commission to employ those soldiers,
So levied as before, against the Polack,
With an entreaty, herein further shown,
  (*He gives a paper to the King*)
That it might please you to give quiet pass
Through your dominions for this enterprise,
On such regards of safety and allowance
As therein are set down.
KING   It likes us well.   80
And at our more considered time we'll read,
Answer, and think upon this business.
Meantime we thank you for your well-took labour.
Go to your rest. At night we'll feast together.
Most welcome home!   *Exeunt the ambassadors*
POLONIUS   This business is well ended.
My liege and madam, to expostulate
What majesty should be, what duty is,
Why day is day, night night, and time is time,
Were nothing but to waste night, day, and time.
Therefore, since brevity is the soul of wit,   90
And tediousness the limbs and outward flourishes,
I will be brief. Your noble son is mad.
Mad call I it. For, to define true madness,
What is't but to be nothing else but mad?
But let that go.
QUEEN   More matter, with less art.

76-80 *herein . . . therein* (in the document which they have brought. The change from *herein* to *therein* seems to justify the addition of the stage direction.)

77 *quiet pass* peaceful passage

79 *regards of safety* conditions concerning safety (or 'conditions that may be safely granted')
allowance the permission granted

80 *likes* pleases

81 *considered* fit for considering

86 *expostulate* expound

90 *wit* intelligence, wisdom

93-4 *to define . . . mad?* Polonius probably means 'it would be madness to try to define madness, for everyone knows what it is', rather than 'the definition of madness is to be mad'. It may be an intentional bathos: Polonius embarks on a definition and breaks down.

95 *art* rhetorical art

POLONIUS

> Madam, I swear I use no art at all.
> That he's mad, 'tis true. 'Tis true, 'tis pity,
> And pity 'tis 'tis true – a foolish figure.
> But farewell it; for I will use no art.
100 Mad let us grant him then. And now remains
> That we find out the cause of this effect –
> Or rather say, the cause of this defect,
> For this effect defective comes by cause.
> Thus it remains, and the remainder thus.
> Perpend.
> I have a daughter – have while she is mine –
> Who in her duty and obedience, mark,
> Hath given me this. Now gather, and surmise.
>> (*He reads the letter*)
> *To the celestial, and my soul's idol, the most beautified*
110 *Ophelia* – That's an ill phrase, a vile phrase; 'beautified'
> is a vile phrase. But you shall hear. Thus:
>> (*He reads*)
> *In her excellent white bosom, these*, et cetera.

QUEEN

> Came this from Hamlet to her?

97 *'Tis true, 'tis pity* of course it is a pity
98 *figure* (of speech)
102 *defect* (weakness of Hamlet's mind)
103 *this effect defective* the effect we have been aware of, which is a mental deficiency
104 *Thus it remains, and the remainder thus* this is the situation; and now here is the solution (in so far as one can paraphrase Polonius's verbal tangles)
105 *Perpend* consider carefully (probably a comic pomposity)
106 *while she is mine* (until she is married)
109, 110 *beautified*. Probably an affected word for 'beautiful' (Robert Greene in 1592 described Shakespeare as an 'upstart crow, beautified with our feathers'). Presumably Polonius objects to the word as being a past participle of the verb 'to beautify' and therefore an incorrect usage for 'beautiful'.
112 *these* this letter (a common phrase)
et cetera (sometimes interpreted as if Polonius were omitting indecorous allusions suggested by *bosom*; but probably he is merely indicating that he is glancing at, and omitting, some superfluous comments)

POLONIUS

    Good madam, stay awhile. I will be faithful.

        (He reads)

    Doubt thou the stars are fire.

      Doubt that the sun doth move.

    Doubt truth to be a liar.

      But never doubt I love.

    O dear Ophelia, I am ill at these numbers. I have not art

    to reckon my groans. But that I love thee best, O most best,   120

    believe it. Adieu.

        Thine evermore, most dear lady, whilst

        this machine is to him,

                                   Hamlet

    This in obedience hath my daughter shown me,

    And more above hath his solicitings,

    As they fell out by time, by means, and place,

    All given to mine ear.

KING   But how hath she

    Received his love?

POLONIUS   What do you think of me?

KING

    As of a man faithful and honourable.   130

POLONIUS

    I would fain prove so. But what might you think

    When I had seen this hot love on the wing –

    As I perceived it, I must tell you that,

114 *faithful* (to the contents of the letter)

115–18 *Doubt thou . . . I love.* This little poem is a clever epitome of some of the poetical tendencies of the 1590s: cosmological imagery, the Copernican revolution, moral paradoxes, all illustrating amorous responses.

117 *Doubt truth.* In this line *Doubt* means 'suspect' (as at 1.2.256).

119 *ill at* unskilful in making
    numbers verses

123 *this machine* (his body)
    to him his

126–8 *more above hath . . . given* she has in addition given

126 *solicitings* (not necessarily deceitful or immoral importunings)

127 *fell out* took place
    by according to

131 *would fain* should very much wish to

Before my daughter told me – what might you,
Or my dear majesty your Queen here, think
If I had played the desk or table-book,
Or given my heart a winking, mute and dumb,
Or looked upon this love with idle sight?
What might you think? No, I went round to work,
140   And my young mistress thus I did bespeak:
'Lord Hamlet is a prince, out of thy star.
This must not be.' And then I prescripts gave her,
That she should lock herself from his resort,
Admit no messengers, receive no tokens.
Which done, she took the fruits of my advice,
And he, repellèd, a short tale to make,
Fell into a sadness, then into a fast,
Thence to a watch, thence into a weakness,
Thence to a lightness, and, by this declension,
150   Into the madness wherein now he raves
And all we mourn for.

KING   Do you think 'tis this?

QUEEN

It may be, very like.

POLONIUS

Hath there been such a time – I would fain know that –
That I have positively said ''Tis so'

136 *played the desk or table-book* served as
    a mute and useful means of communi-
    cation (between the lovers; or poss-
    ibly 'noted the matter privately for
    myself')
    table-book notebook (like *table*, 1.5.98)
137 *given my heart a winking* shut my eyes
    (to what was going on). For F's
    'winking', Q2 reads 'working', a
    word Shakespeare often uses of the
    heart and of mental activities (com-
    pare line 551 and 1.1.67); but it seems
    to have the contrary meaning to what
    is required here.

138 *idle sight* careless observation
139 *round* roundly, straightforwardly
140 *bespeak* summon to address her
141 *star* sphere
142 *prescripts* orders. F's reading, 'Pre-
    cepts', seems a simplification.
143 *resort* visits
148 *watch* sleeplessness
149 *lightness* lightheadedness
    declension downward course
151 *all* (into) everything that
152 *like* likely

When it proved otherwise?

KING   Not that I know.

POLONIUS

Take this from this, if this be otherwise.
If circumstances lead me, I will find
Where truth is hid, though it were hid indeed
Within the centre.

KING   How may we try it further?

POLONIUS

You know sometimes he walks four hours together   160
Here in the lobby.

QUEEN   So he does indeed.

POLONIUS

At such a time I'll loose my daughter to him.
Be you and I behind an arras then.
Mark the encounter. If he love her not,
And be not from his reason fallen thereon,
Let me be no assistant for a state,
But keep a farm and carters.

KING   We will try it.

       Enter Hamlet

QUEEN

But look where sadly the poor wretch comes reading.

---

156 *Take this from this* (generally interpreted as 'Cut my head off'; but Polonius might more decorously point to his staff or chain of office – 'Remove me from my office as your chief minister'; compare lines 166–7)

159 *centre* (of the earth, which, according to medieval cosmology, was the centre of the universe)
    try judge

162 *loose* release (like an animal in a stud)

163 *arras* (a tapestry hanging, such as covered the full height of the walls of rooms in great Elizabethan houses)

165 *thereon* on account of this (disappointed love)

166 *assistant for a state* government minister

167 (stage direction) *Enter Hamlet*. It has been suggested that Hamlet should enter a little earlier and overhear something of the plot in lines 159–67. This would provide a justification for his bitterness to Polonius in lines 171–219 and his treatment of Ophelia at III.1.89–150.

168 *sadly* seriously (not 'sorrowfully')
    reading. The symbol of his detachment from revenge is striking.

POLONIUS

    Away, I do beseech you both, away.

170   I'll board him presently. O, give me leave.

        Exeunt the King and Queen

    How does my good Lord Hamlet?

HAMLET Well, God-a-mercy.

POLONIUS Do you know me, my lord?

HAMLET Excellent well. You are a fishmonger.

POLONIUS Not I, my lord.

HAMLET Then I would you were so honest a man.

POLONIUS Honest, my lord?

HAMLET Ay, sir. To be honest, as this world goes, is to be
    one man picked out of ten thousand.

180 POLONIUS That's very true, my lord.

HAMLET For if the sun breed maggots in a dead dog,
    being a good kissing carrion – have you a daughter?

POLONIUS I have, my lord.

HAMLET Let her not walk i'th'sun. Conception is a bless-

---

170 *board him presently* accost him immediately (drawing alongside like a sea-
vessel)
  give me leave excuse me (as he
hurries the King and Queen off
stage)
  In Q1 the soliloquy *To be, or not
to be* is placed here; see the note to
III.1.56–88.

172 *God-a-mercy* thank you

174 *fishmonger.* Probably the primary allusion is to the smell of corruption
that seems to emanate from Polonius,
though the word is sometimes
thought to imply 'bawd'. This is the
first occasion on which the audience
sees Hamlet assume his *antic disposition* (1.5.170–72). He deceives Polonius, who has been boasting of his
own shrewdness.

181–2 *For if . . . carrion* (possibly spoken
from the book Hamlet is carrying)

182 *a good kissing carrion.* The phrase is
difficult: the carrion is good for kissing, as the sun shines on a dead dog
and breeds maggots in it. Hamlet is
deliberately indulging in mad-talk;
but there is generally *method in't* (line
206), and it is not easy to see the
point here. Eighteenth-century editors emended *good* to 'god' (the sun-
god Apollo), with great probability.
Perhaps Hamlet is obscurely saying
'Honesty is rare in this world, which
is so corrupt that even the sun produces nothing but maggots in shining upon carrion'.

184 *walk i'th'sun.* Spenser in *The Faerie
Queene* (III.vi) had told how Amoret
and Belphoebe were begotten by the
impregnating rays of the sun.

ing. But as your daughter may conceive, friend, look
to't.

POLONIUS (*aside*) How say you by that? Still harping on
my daughter. Yet he knew me not at first. 'A said I was
a fishmonger. 'A is far gone, far gone. And truly in my
youth I suffered much extremity for love, very near   190
this. I'll speak to him again. – What do you read, my
lord?

HAMLET Words, words, words.

POLONIUS What is the matter, my lord?

HAMLET Between who?

POLONIUS I mean the matter that you read, my lord.

HAMLET Slanders, sir. For the satirical rogue says here
that old men have grey beards, that their faces are
wrinkled, their eyes purging thick amber and plum-tree
gum, and that they have a plentiful lack of wit, together   200
with most weak hams; all which, sir, though I most
powerfully and potently believe, yet I hold it not
honesty to have it thus set down. For yourself, sir, shall
grow old as I am – if, like a crab, you could go backward.

POLONIUS (*aside*) Though this be madness, yet there
is method in't. – Will you walk out of the air, my lord?

HAMLET Into my grave?

POLONIUS Indeed, that's out of the air. (*Aside*) How
pregnant sometimes his replies are! A happiness that

---

187 *harping on* (like a harper playing on
one string)
194 *matter* subject-matter
199 *purging* exuding
199–200 *plum-tree gum* (sap from the bark
of a plum-tree)
201 *hams* thighs and buttocks
203 *honesty* decent
set down (in print)
204 *backward* (actually, of course, crabs
move sideways)
206 *method* logical organization of

thought. Polonius does not mean
that Hamlet is using his apparent
madness as a device for certain ends.
out of the air (probably) out of the
fresh air into a confined room (since
the open air was regarded as dangerous to the sick)
209 *pregnant* full of meaning. The image
is continued in *be delivered of* (line
211).
209–10 *A happiness that often madness
hits on.* This was the doctrine of

210 often madness hits on, which reason and sanity could
not so prosperously be delivered of. I will leave him
and suddenly contrive the means of meeting between
him and my daughter. – My honourable lord, I will
most humbly take my leave of you.

HAMLET You cannot, sir, take from me anything that I
will not more willingly part withal – except my life,
except my life, except my life.

POLONIUS Fare you well, my lord.

HAMLET These tedious old fools!

Enter Guildenstern and Rosencrantz

220 POLONIUS You go to seek the Lord Hamlet. There he is.

ROSENCRANTZ (*to Polonius*) God save you, sir!

Exit Polonius

GUILDENSTERN My honoured lord!

ROSENCRANTZ My most dear lord!

HAMLET

My excellent good friends.

How dost thou, Guildenstern? Ah, Rosencrantz!

Good lads, how do you both?

ROSENCRANTZ

As the indifferent children of the earth.

GUILDENSTERN

Happy in that we are not over-happy.

On Fortune's cap we are not the very button.

HAMLET

230 Nor the soles of her shoe?

ROSENCRANTZ   Neither, my lord.

'poetic fury' (*furor poeticus*), to which
Theseus also refers in linking 'The
lunatic, the lover, and the poet' (*A
Midsummer Night's Dream*, v.1.7).
209 *happiness* felicity of expression
212 *suddenly* immediately
216 *not more.* F makes the sentence more
rational by omitting *not*. But Q2 is
probably correct, as confusing Polonius's wits still further by the double

negatives – which the audience will
take as emphatic.
withal with
227 *indifferent* average
children of the earth ordinary
fellows
229 *button* (summit)
230 *soles of her shoe* (so as to be trodden
underfoot by Fortune)

HAMLET Then you live about her waist, or in the middle of her favours?

GUILDENSTERN Faith, her privates we.

HAMLET In the secret parts of Fortune? O, most true! She is a strumpet. What news?

ROSENCRANTZ None, my lord, but that the world's grown honest.

HAMLET Then is Doomsday near. But your news is not true. Let me question more in particular. What have you, my good friends, deserved at the hands of Fortune that she sends you to prison hither?   240

GUILDENSTERN Prison, my lord?

HAMLET Denmark's a prison.

ROSENCRANTZ Then is the world one.

HAMLET A goodly one; in which there are many confines, wards, and dungeons, Denmark being one o'th'worst.

ROSENCRANTZ We think not so, my lord.

HAMLET Why, then 'tis none to you. For there is nothing either good or bad but thinking makes it so. To me it is a prison.   250

ROSENCRANTZ Why, then your ambition makes it one. 'Tis too narrow for your mind.

HAMLET O God, I could be bounded in a nutshell and count myself a king of infinite space, were it not that I have bad dreams.

GUILDENSTERN Which dreams indeed are ambition. For the very substance of the ambitious is merely the shadow of a dream.

232 *favours*. Hamlet alludes bawdily to her sexual *favours*; Guildenstern follows this by *her privates* ('intimates', and so 'sexual organs'), and Hamlet again by her *secret parts*. The progress then is to the commonplace notion of *Fortune* as a *strumpet* who bestows her favours in a fickle and indiscriminate manner (see line 491).

245 *confines* places of confinement
254 *count* (nevertheless) account
255 *bad*. As nothing develops from *bad* in the subsequent dialogue, emendation to 'had' is attractive.
257–8 *the very substance ... a dream* what an ambitious man actually achieves is only a pale shadow of what he had set out to achieve

HAMLET A dream itself is but a shadow.

260   ROSENCRANTZ Truly; and I hold ambition of so airy and
light a quality that it is but a shadow's shadow.

HAMLET Then are our beggars bodies, and our monarchs
and outstretched heroes the beggars' shadows. Shall
we to th'court? For, by my fay, I cannot reason.

ROSENCRANTZ *and* GUILDENSTERN We'll wait upon
you.

HAMLET No such matter. I will not sort you with the rest
of my servants. For, to speak to you like an honest man,
I am most dreadfully attended. But in the beaten way

270   of friendship, what make you at Elsinore?

ROSENCRANTZ To visit you, my lord. No other occasion.

HAMLET Beggar that I am, I am even poor in thanks.
But I thank you. And sure, dear friends, my thanks are
too dear a halfpenny. Were you not sent for? Is it your
own inclining? Is it a free visitation? Come, come, deal

262–3 *Then are our beggars bodies, and our
monarchs and outstretched heroes the
beggars' shadows* if this is so, the beggars have substance, because they
have no ambition, whereas great
people are unreal (*shadows*) because
they are filled with ambition. Therefore, as it is *bodies* that cast *shadows*,
the great people may be regarded as
the *shadows* of *beggars*. Or perhaps
Hamlet means that *beggars* too have
ambitions and long to be *monarchs*
and *heroes*; since ambitions are *shadows*, *monarchs* and *heroes* are therefore
beggars' shadows. Presumably this cryptic utterance baffles Rosencrantz and
Guildenstern, for Hamlet promptly
breaks off.

263 *outstretched heroes* great men whose
ambitions stretch them. But *outstretched* also suggests their strutting
gait and the length of their shadows.

264 *fay* faith

reason carry on an intellectual conversation at this level

265–6 *wait upon you* accompany you (but
Hamlet takes it to mean 'act as your
servants')

267 *sort you with* put you in the category
of

269 *dreadfully attended* incompetently
waited upon

269–70 *in the beaten way of friendship* as
the course of our friendship has been
well-tried and reliable

274 *too dear a halfpenny* cost a little too
much. Presumably Hamlet is being
cryptically insulting: his friends' visit
is not worth his thanks because it is
not a voluntary kindness on their
part. Or, if *a halfpenny* means 'at a
halfpenny' rather than 'by a halfpenny', he may mean: 'the thanks of
a beggar such as I am are worthless'.

275 *free* voluntary

justly with me. Come, come. Nay, speak.

GUILDENSTERN What should we say, my lord?

HAMLET Why, anything but to th'purpose. You were
sent for. And there is a kind of confession in your looks,
which your modesties have not craft enough to colour.   280
I know the good King and Queen have sent for you.

ROSENCRANTZ To what end, my lord?

HAMLET That you must teach me. But let me conjure
you by the rights of our fellowship, by the consonancy
of our youth, by the obligation of our ever-preserved
love, and by what more dear a better proposer can charge
you withal, be even and direct with me whether you
were sent for or no.

ROSENCRANTZ (*aside to Guildenstern*) What say you?

HAMLET (*aside*) Nay then, I have an eye of you. – If you   290
love me, hold not off.

GUILDENSTERN My lord, we were sent for.

HAMLET I will tell you why. So shall my anticipation
prevent your discovery, and your secrecy to the King
and Queen moult no feather. I have of late – but wherefore I know not – lost all my mirth, forgone all custom
of exercises. And indeed it goes so heavily with my
disposition that this goodly frame the earth seems to

278 *but to th'purpose* except a straightforward answer
280 *modesties* sense of shame
colour disguise
283 *conjure* solemnly ask
284 *consonancy* harmony
286–7 *what more dear a better proposer can
charge you withal* whatever motive a
more skilful speaker than I am might
propose in order to appeal to you
(that you should be frank with me)
287 *even* straightforward

290 *of* on
290 *hold not off* do not remain aloof
293–4 *my anticipation prevent your discovery*
my own statement about the matter
be made before you have any opportunity of revealing the truth to me
294 *discovery* disclosure
295 *moult no feather* be quite unimpaired
296 *forgone* done without
296–7 *custom of exercises* practice of
manly sports
298 *frame* ordered arrangement

me a sterile promontory. This most excellent canopy,
the air, look you, this brave o'erhanging firmament,
this majestical roof fretted with golden fire – why, it
appeareth nothing to me but a foul and pestilent congregation of vapours. What a piece of work is a man,
how noble in reason, how infinite in faculties, in form
and moving how express and admirable, in action how
like an angel, in apprehension how like a god: the
beauty of the world, the paragon of animals! And yet
to me what is this quintessence of dust? Man delights
not me – nor woman neither, though by your smiling
you seem to say so.

ROSENCRANTZ My lord, there was no such stuff in my
thoughts.

HAMLET Why did ye laugh then, when I said 'Man
delights not me'?

ROSENCRANTZ To think, my lord, if you delight not
in man, what lenten entertainment the players shall

299 *sterile promontory.* Presumably this striking image is that of a barren headland jutting out into the sea, contrasted with the fertile cultivated countryside inland.

299, 301 *canopy . . . roof.* The roof overhanging the stage in an Elizabethan public playhouse was known as the 'heavens' and seems to have been painted with stars. This may have given special point to Hamlet's imagery here.

300 *brave* fine

301 *fretted with golden fire* adorned with the heavenly bodies, as a chamber roof is decorated (*fretted*) with bosses

302–3 *pestilent congregation of vapours.* It was widely believed that diseases were borne upon the air and spread by winds.

congregation mass

303 *piece of work* masterpiece

305 *express* (probably) direct. This seems to go with *moving* rather than with *form.*

306 *apprehension* powers of comprehension

307 *paragon* pattern of supreme excellence

308 *quintessence of dust.* The reference is to Genesis 3.19: 'For dust thou art, and into dust shalt thou be turned again'.

309 *woman.* Q2 reads 'women', which may well be right.

316 *lenten entertainment* (the kind of meagre reception one would expect in Lent, not in a season of festivity when theatrical activities would be welcomed)

receive from you. We coted them on the way. And hither are they coming to offer you service.

HAMLET He that plays the king shall be welcome – his majesty shall have tribute of me; the adventurous 320
knight shall use his foil and target; the lover shall not sigh gratis; the humorous man shall end his part in peace; the clown shall make those laugh whose lungs are tickle o'th'sere; and the lady shall say her mind freely, or the blank verse shall halt for't. What players are they?

ROSENCRANTZ Even those you were wont to take such delight in, the tragedians of the city.

HAMLET How chances it they travel? Their residence, both in reputation and profit, was better both ways. 330

ROSENCRANTZ I think their inhibition comes by the means of the late innovation.

317 *coted* caught up with and passed

320 *tribute*. The Prince will pay money to *the king*.

321 *foil and target* sword (blunted for fencing or for stage use) and light shield

322 *gratis* without payment

humorous man (not the comic, but the eccentric, capricious, or carping character, whose state of mind, according to Elizabethan physiology, was due to some excess of one of the humours)

324 *tickle o'th'sere* easily provoked. The image is of a gun whose trigger-catch (*sere*) was sensitive or unstable (*tickle*) and easily went off.

325 *freely* (perhaps 'with a certain amount of ad-libbing' because the boy actor might not know his part very well; or perhaps 'with complete freedom of speech' (without feeling

a need to omit indecent words or allusions). There is not much evidence for either explanation.)

halt limp (scan badly)

328 *tragedians* actors (not necessarily performing only tragedies)

the city. In spite of the dramatic situation, London is in Shakespeare's mind, as the following dialogue makes clear.

329 *travel* are on tour

residence normal place of performance

331 *inhibition*. The word was used of the official indictment of stage plays by the authorities, but here seems to refer metaphorically to the players' inability to continue acting in the city.

332 *late* recent

innovation fashion (the popularity of the boy actors in 1600–1601)

HAMLET Do they hold the same estimation they did when
I was in the city? Are they so followed?

ROSENCRANTZ No, indeed are they not.

HAMLET How comes it? Do they grow rusty?

ROSENCRANTZ Nay, their endeavour keeps in the wonted
pace. But there is, sir, an eyrie of children, little eyases,
that cry out on the top of question and are most tyran-
340 nically clapped for't. These are now the fashion, and so
berattle the common stages – so they call them – that
many wearing rapiers are afraid of goosequills and dare
scarce come thither.

HAMLET What, are they children? Who maintains 'em?
How are they escoted? Will they pursue the quality no
longer than they can sing? Will they not say afterwards,
if they should grow themselves to common players – as
it is most like, if their means are not better – their
writers do them wrong to make them exclaim against
350 their own succession?

336–61 This passage, giving the reason
for the decline in *estimation of the
tragedians of the city*, is not in Q2. The
discussion of the success of the child
actors is somewhat intrusive into the
play and the tone is more personal
and acerbic than we like to associate
with Shakespeare. Its inclusion in F
is surprising, because the episode
must have become more obscure
with the passage of years.

337 *keeps* continues

338 *eyrie* nestful
eyases hawk nestlings

339 *on the top of question*. This probably
means that their voices are heard
above all others in the argument.

339–40 *tyrannically* outrageously

341 *berattle* clamour abusively against
common stages (that is, public theatres,

as distinct from the 'private' play-
houses, occupied by the boys'
companies)

342 *rapiers* (the sign of a gentleman and
man of quality)
are afraid of goosequills fear the satire
and ridicule they would hear in the
plays written for the boys'
companies
goosequills (the usual writing imple-
ment in Shakespeare's time)

345 *escoted* paid for

345–6 *pursue the quality no longer than they
can sing* follow their profession as
actors only until their voices break

348 *their means are not better* they have no
other resources for earning their
livelihood

349–50 *exclaim against their own succession*
speak disdainfully about the profes-

ROSENCRANTZ Faith, there has been much to-do on both sides, and the nation holds it no sin to tarre them to controversy. There was, for a while, no money bid for argument unless the poet and the player went to cuffs in the question.

HAMLET Is't possible?

GUILDENSTERN O, there has been much throwing about of brains.

HAMLET Do the boys carry it away?

ROSENCRANTZ Ay, that they do, my lord – Hercules and his load too.   360

HAMLET It is not very strange. For my uncle is King of Denmark, and those that would make mows at him while my father lived give twenty, forty, fifty, a hundred ducats apiece for his picture in little. 'Sblood, there is something in this more than natural, if philosophy could find it out.

    A flourish

sion to which they will themselves belong (as actors in adult companies)
351 *to-do* (an Elizabethan usage as well as a modern colloquialism) bustle, turmoil
352 *nation* people in general (that is, the audiences)
   tarre (pronounced like 'tar') incite
353–4 *money bid for argument* payment offered (to an author) for the plot of a play (or perhaps 'money paid (by the audience) unless this particular controversy formed part of the entertainment')
354 *went to cuffs* (metaphorically) came to blows
355 *in the question* about the controversy
357–8 *much throwing about of brains* a great battle of wits

359 *carry it away* win the day
360–61 *Hercules and his load too.* The sign of the Globe Theatre was Hercules bearing up the globe (relieving Atlas). This passage implies, perhaps ironically, that the success of the boys' companies had had its effect on Shakespeare's company too.
363 *make mows* put on a mocking expression of face
365 *ducats.* The ducat was a gold coin, worth about nine shillings, so Hamlet is speaking of considerable sums.
   picture in little miniature painting
   'Sblood by God's blood (in the eucharist)
366 *philosophy* 'natural philosophy' or (as we now call it) science

GUILDENSTERN There are the players.

HAMLET Gentlemen, you are welcome to Elsinore. Your
370   hands. Come then. Th'appurtenance of welcome is
fashion and ceremony. Let me comply with you in this
garb, lest my extent to the players, which I tell you must
show fairly outwards, should more appear like entertainment than yours. You are welcome. But my uncle-
father and aunt-mother are deceived.

GUILDENSTERN In what, my dear lord?

HAMLET I am but mad north-north-west. When the wind
is southerly, I know a hawk from a handsaw.

Enter Polonius

POLONIUS Well be with you, gentlemen.

380   HAMLET Hark you, Guildenstern – and you too – at each
ear a hearer. That great baby you see there is not yet
out of his swaddling clouts.

ROSENCRANTZ Happily he is the second time come to
them. For they say an old man is twice a child.

HAMLET I will prophesy he comes to tell me of the
players. Mark it. – You say right, sir. 'A Monday morning, 'twas then, indeed.

370 *appurtenance* proper or usual
accompaniment
371 *fashion and ceremony* conventional ceremonious behaviour
371-2 *comply with you in this garb* show
you polite conduct in this manner
(shaking your hands)
372 *my extent to* the politeness that I
intend to extend towards
373 *show fairly outwards* give every evidence of cordiality
373-4 *entertainment* a good reception
375 *deceived* mistaken (in thinking him to
be mad)
377 *I am but mad north-north-west.* In the
very assertion of his sanity Hamlet
makes such a cryptic remark that

they must regard him as having lost
his senses: 'I am only a very little off
compass – one point ($22\frac{1}{2}°$) out of
sixteen ($360°$)'.
378 *handsaw.* This is usually interpreted
as a variant of 'hernshaw', heron.
Hamlet seems to be warning his companions that, though he may seem a
bit mad, he usually has his wits about
him and can distinguish between true
and false friends.
383 *Happily* perhaps
384 *twice* for the second time
386-7 *You say . . . indeed.* As Polonius
comes on stage, Hamlet pretends to
be engaged in conversation.
386 *'A* on

POLONIUS My lord, I have news to tell you.

HAMLET My lord, I have news to tell you. When Roscius
was an actor in Rome –   390

POLONIUS The actors are come hither, my lord.

HAMLET Buzz, buzz.

POLONIUS Upon my honour –

HAMLET Then came each actor on his ass –

POLONIUS The best actors in the world, either for
tragedy, comedy, history, pastoral, pastoral-comical,
historical-pastoral, tragical-historical, tragical-comical-
historical-pastoral, scene individable, or poem unlimited. Seneca cannot be too heavy, nor Plautus too
light. For the law of writ and the liberty, these are the   400
only men.

HAMLET O Jephthah, judge of Israel, what a treasure
hadst thou!

POLONIUS What a treasure had he, my lord?

389 *Roscius* (the most famous actor in ancient Rome)

392 *Buzz* (a contemptuous exclamation on hearing stale news)

396–9 *tragedy, comedy . . . unlimited.* This is a jest at the expense of the Renaissance theories of the specific 'kinds' of drama, with their special rules or principles.

397–8 *tragical-comical-historical-pastoral.* This mixture may seem absurd until one remembers that Shakespeare later wrote *Cymbeline*.

398 *scene individable* (plays in which the scene is not changed, so that the so-called 'unity of place' is preserved)

398–9 *poem unlimited* (more imaginative plays in which the classicizing unities of place and time are not preserved – like nearly all of Shakespeare's)

399 *Seneca.* The ten tragedies attributed to him were well-known in Shakespeare's time and represented the clas- sical type of tragedy more than did those of Aeschylus, Sophocles, and Euripides. They were performed in academic circles in Latin and in English translation.

Plautus. The two Latin comic playwrights Plautus and Terence had a considerable influence on Elizabethan drama. Shakespeare's *The Comedy of Errors* is based on Plautus's *Menaechmi* and *Amphitruo*.

400 *the law of writ and the liberty* plays (like those of Ben Jonson) in which the classical principles are followed, and plays (like those of Shakespeare) with greater freedom of structure

402 *Jephthah, judge of Israel.* Jephthah made a vow to Jehovah that, if he were successful over the Ammonites, he would sacrifice the first living thing that came to meet him (Judges 11.9–40). This was his daughter.

HAMLET Why,
> 'One fair daughter, and no more,
> The which he lovèd passing well.'

POLONIUS (aside) Still on my daughter.

HAMLET Am I not i'th'right, old Jephthah?

410 POLONIUS If you call me Jephthah, my lord, I have a
daughter that I love passing well.

HAMLET Nay, that follows not.

POLONIUS What follows then, my lord?

HAMLET Why,
> 'As by lot, God wot,'

and then you know,
> 'It came to pass, as most like it was.'

The first row of the pious chanson will show you more.
For look where my abridgement comes.

Enter the Players

420 You are welcome, masters, welcome, all. – I am glad to
see thee well. – Welcome, good friends. – O old friend,
why, thy face is valanced since I saw thee last. Comest
thou to beard me in Denmark? – What, my young lady

406-7 *One fair daughter . . . well.* In 1567–8 the printing of 'A ballad entitled the song of Jephthah's daughter at her death' was authorized. No copy of this is known, but it is probably the same as a ballad authorized in 1624 with the title 'Jephthah Judge of Israel', which begins:

I read that many year ago
When Jephthah, Judge of Israel,
Had one fair daughter and no more,
  Whom he loved passing well,
And as by lot, God wot,
It came to pass most like it was
Great wars there should be,
  And who should be the chief but he.

407 *passing well* very well indeed

412 *that follows not* what you have just said is not the next line of the ballad I was quoting

415 *lot* chance

417 *as most like it was* as was very probable

418 *row* stanza
pious (because it has a biblical subject)
chanson song

419 *abridgement* (1) interruption; (2) entertainment

422 *valanced* fringed (with a beard). A valance is a draped edging of cloth.

423 *beard* defy (punningly)

423-4 *my young lady and mistress.* Hamlet is addressing the boy (probably in his early teens) who takes the female roles in the plays.

and mistress? By'r Lady, your ladyship is nearer to heaven than when I saw you last by the altitude of a chopine. Pray God your voice, like a piece of uncurrent gold, be not cracked within the ring. – Masters, you are all welcome. We'll e'en to't like French falconers: fly at anything we see. We'll have a speech straight. Come, give us a taste of your quality. Come, a passionate speech.   430

FIRST PLAYER What speech, my good lord?

HAMLET I heard thee speak me a speech once, but it was never acted, or if it was, not above once. For the play, I remember, pleased not the million. 'Twas caviary to the general. But it was – as I received it, and others, whose judgements in such matters cried in the top of mine – an excellent play, well digested in the scenes, set down with as much modesty as cunning. I remember one said there were no sallets in the lines to make the matter   440 savoury, nor no matter in the phrase that might indict the author of affectation, but called it an honest method,

---

424–5 *is nearer to heaven* has grown taller

426 *chopine*. The high bases on the fashionable Venetian-styled women's shoes ('chopines') raised them several inches. Hamlet continues to jest with the boy by allusions to women's roles.

426–7 *a piece of uncurrent gold*. A gold coin was regarded as no longer legally current at its full value if it had been 'clipped' or *cracked* within the ring surrounding the monarch's head.

428–9 *like French falconers: fly at anything we see*. This was the British opinion of French sportsmen, who allegedly did not select the prey for their falcons with sufficient care. Hamlet asks for a speech at once, without worrying much what it is to be. (In fact, however, he chooses one carefully.)

429 *straight* straightaway

430 *taste of your quality* specimen of what your profession (acting) can provide

435 *caviary*. Caviare, introduced into England in Shakespeare's time, was an expensive delicacy, unpalatable to those without an acquired taste for it.

436 *general* ordinary people
received considered

437 *cried in the top of* were spoken more loudly and with more authority than

438 *digested* arranged

439 *modesty* moderation in writing
cunning skill

440 *sallets* tasty bits (probably he means 'bawdy')

441 *indict* convict

442 *affectation*. Q2 reads 'affection', perhaps a variant form.

as wholesome as sweet, and by very much more handsome than fine. One speech in't I chiefly loved. 'Twas
Aeneas' tale to Dido; and thereabout of it especially
when he speaks of Priam's slaughter. If it live in your
memory, begin at this line – let me see, let me see.
　　'The rugged Pyrrhus, like th'Hyrcanian beast –'
'Tis not so. It begins with Pyrrhus.

450　　　'The rugged Pyrrhus, he whose sable arms,
Black as his purpose, did the night resemble
When he lay couchèd in th'ominous horse,
Hath now this dread and black complexion smeared
With heraldy more dismal. Head to foot
Now is he total gules, horridly tricked
With blood of fathers, mothers, daughters, sons,
Baked and impasted with the parching streets,
That lend a tyrannous and a damnèd light

443–4 *more handsome than fine* not showy
　　in decoration, but genuinely beauti-
　　ful in proportions
444 *One speech in't I chiefly loved.* It con-
　　cerns a revenge taken by a son and a
　　vigorous homicide. At certain points
　　– *blood of fathers* (line 456), *Did nothing*
　　(line 480) – Hamlet probably re-
　　sponds with personal feeling.
445 *Aeneas' tale to Dido.* This is given in
　　Books 2 and 3 of Virgil's *Aeneid*.
　　The murder of King Priam by Pyr-
　　rhus, son of Achilles, during the
　　night of the fall of Troy is in 2.526–
　　88. In writing the speech, Shake-
　　speare derived many hints from
　　Virgil.
448–516 The old-fashioned style of this
　　speech marks it off from the rest of
　　the play as 'theatrical'. It is a serious
　　performance, and the First Player is
　　a distinguished actor.
448 *Hyrcanian beast.* The tigers of Hyr-
　　cania (a province in Asia Minor near
　　the Caspian Sea) were a common-

place image of ferocity. In the *Aeneid*
(4.367) Dido says of Aeneas that Hyrcanian tigresses must have suckled
him.
450 *rugged* hairy
　　sable black
452 *ominous* fateful
　　horse (the wooden horse used by
　　the Greeks to intrude men secretly
　　inside the walls of Troy)
454 *dismal* (a strong word) disastrous
455 *total* entirely
　　gules (a heraldic term; pronounced
　　with a hard 'g') red
　　tricked (a heraldic term) spotted
457 *Baked and impasted with the parching
　　streets.* The hot air (from the burning
　　city of Troy) has congealed the blood
　　smeared upon Pyrrhus as he went
　　through the streets killing Trojans.
　　impasted made into a paste
458 *tyrannous* cruel
　　damnèd (because resembling the
　　flames of hell)

To their lord's murder; roasted in wrath and fire,
And thus o'er-sizèd with coagulate gore,   460
With eyes like carbuncles, the hellish Pyrrhus
Old grandsire Priam seeks.'
So, proceed you.

POLONIUS 'Fore God, my lord, well spoken, with good
accent and good discretion.

FIRST PLAYER.   'Anon he finds him,
Striking too short at Greeks. His antique sword,
Rebellious to his arm, lies where it falls,
Repugnant to command. Unequal matched,
Pyrrhus at Priam drives, in rage strikes wide,   470
But with the whiff and wind of his fell sword
Th'unnervèd father falls. Then senseless Ilium,
Seeming to feel this blow, with flaming top
Stoops to his base, and with a hideous crash
Takes prisoner Pyrrhus' ear. For lo! his sword,
Which was declining on the milky head
Of reverend Priam, seemed i'th'air to stick.
So as a painted tyrant Pyrrhus stood,
And like a neutral to his will and matter
Did nothing.   480

459 *their lord's murder*. Pyrrhus will soon be the murderer of Priam, the rightful *lord* of Troy and its *streets*.

460 *o'er-sizèd* covered with something like size, painted over

461 *carbuncles* (red and fiery precious stones)

466 *Anon* soon afterwards

467 *too short* with blows which fall short

468 *Rebellious to* not obeying

469 *Repugnant to command* offering resistance to its orders. The old man misses his blow and his arm is so jarred by this that he is unable to raise the sword again.

471 *fell* cruel

472 *unnervèd* without energy
senseless although lacking the senses of a human being
Ilium (pronounced 'eye-li-um') Troy

475 *Takes prisoner* captures (so that he cannot act)

476 *declining* falling
milky white-haired

478 *as a painted tyrant* like a tyrant represented in a painting (in which his sword is shown as held up in the act of descending but never descends)

479 *a neutral to his will and matter* one who is inactive despite both his will and his duty. For a moment Pyrrhus becomes like Hamlet.

But as we often see, against some storm,
A silence in the heavens, the rack stand still,
The bold winds speechless, and the orb below
As hush as death; anon the dreadful thunder
Doth rend the region; so after Pyrrhus' pause,
A rousèd vengeance sets him new a-work,
And never did the Cyclops' hammers fall
On Mars's armour, forged for proof eterne,
With less remorse than Pyrrhus' bleeding sword
490   Now falls on Priam.
Out, out, thou strumpet Fortune! All you gods,
In general synod, take away her power!
Break all the spokes and fellies from her wheel,
And bowl the round nave down the hill of heaven,
As low as to the fiends!'

POLONIUS   This is too long.

HAMLET   It shall to the barber's, with your beard. –
Prithee say on. He's for a jig or a tale of bawdry, or he
sleeps. Say on. Come to Hecuba.

FIRST PLAYER
500   'But who, ah woe!, had seen the mobled Queen –'

481 *against* just before
482 *rack* cloud-formation
485 *region* sky
487 *the Cyclops' hammers.* The Cyclops
assisted Vulcan in forging armour
for the gods.
488 *Mars's armour.* In the *Iliad* it is Achilles' armour, in the *Aeneid* Aeneas's,
that is forged by Vulcan and the
Cyclops. Neither hero is suitable for
mention in this context. So Mars is
reasonably supposed as having a suit
of Cyclopean armour too.
    for proof eterne to remain strong and
impenetrable for ever
489 *remorse* pity
491 *strumpet Fortune.* See the note to line
232.
492 *synod* assembly
493 *fellies* (the curved wooden pieces

which, when joined together, make
the rim of a wheel)
    wheel. Fortune was generally ima-
gined as standing on a wheel which
revolved (compare III.3.17–22).
494 *nave* hub of the wheel
497 *shall to* will have to go to
498 *jig.* In some theatres, but probably
not at Shakespeare's Globe, performances concluded with a farcical
playlet, called a *jig*, including singing
and lively dancing.
499 *Hecuba.* Hamlet is interested in the
effect of her husband's murder upon
the wife.
500 *who . . . had* anyone who had
    mobled (a rare and homely word,
rhyming with 'cobbled') muffled up,
veiled

HAMLET 'The mobled Queen'?

POLONIUS That's good. 'Mobled Queen' is good.

FIRST PLAYER

> 'Run barefoot up and down, threatening the flames
> With bisson rheum; a clout upon that head
> Where late the diadem stood; and for a robe,
> About her lank and all o'er-teemèd loins,
> A blanket in the alarm of fear caught up –
> Who this had seen, with tongue in venom steeped
> 'Gainst Fortune's state would treason have
>   pronounced.
> But if the gods themselves did see her then,   510
> When she saw Pyrrhus make malicious sport
> In mincing with his sword her husband's limbs,
> The instant burst of clamour that she made,
> Unless things mortal move them not at all,
> Would have made milch the burning eyes of heaven
> And passion in the gods.'

POLONIUS Look whe'er he has not turned his colour, and has tears in's eyes. Prithee no more.

HAMLET 'Tis well. I'll have thee speak out the rest of this soon. – Good my lord, will you see the players well   520 bestowed? Do you hear? Let them be well used, for they are the abstract and brief chronicles of the time.

503-4 *threatening the flames | With bisson rheum* (her profuse tears seem likely to put out the fires which are burning Troy)

504 *bisson* blinding
clout piece of cloth

505 *late* recently

506 *all o'er-teemèd loins*. According to Homer and Virgil, Priam's wives and concubines bore him fifty sons. Perhaps this gave an impression that his chief wife, Hecuba, was worn-out with bearing children.

508 *tongue in venom steeped* extremely bitter words

515 *milch* moist (literally 'milky')
burning eyes of heaven heavenly bodies

516 *passion* (would have made) sympathetic sorrow

521 *bestowed* accommodated

522 *abstract* summary. F has 'Abstracts', an easier reading.

After your death you were better have a bad epitaph
than their ill report while you live.

POLONIUS My lord, I will use them according to their
desert.

HAMLET God's bodkin, man, much better! Use every
man after his desert, and who shall 'scape whipping?
Use them after your own honour and dignity. The less
530   they deserve, the more merit is in your bounty. Take
them in.

POLONIUS Come, sirs.

HAMLET Follow him, friends. We'll hear a play tomorrow. (*Aside to First Player*) Dost thou hear me, old
friend? Can you play *The Murder of Gonzago*?

FIRST PLAYER Ay, my lord.

HAMLET We'll ha't tomorrow night. You could for a
need study a speech of some dozen lines or sixteen lines,
which I would set down and insert in't, could you not?

540   FIRST PLAYER Ay, my lord.

HAMLET Very well. – Follow that lord, and look you mock
him not.

                          Exeunt Polonius and Players

My good friends, I'll leave you till night. You are welcome to Elsinore.

ROSENCRANTZ Good my lord.

HAMLET Ay, so, God bye to you.

                      Exeunt Rosencrantz and Guildenstern
                          Now I am alone.

O, what a rogue and peasant slave am I!
Is it not monstrous that this player here,

---

523 *you were better* it would be better for
you to
527 *God's bodkin* (one of the nails of
Christ on the Cross; or *bodkin* may be
a form of 'bodykin', a diminutive of
'body' referring originally to the un-
consecrated wafer in the mass)
528 *after* according to
537–8 *for a need* if necessary

538 *study* learn by heart
541 *mock* make fun by mimicking (not
merely 'deride')
547 *rogue and peasant slave* (on the one
hand a cheat, and on the other a
spiritless coward)
peasant (usually derogatory in Shakespeare) base

But in a fiction, in a dream of passion,
Could force his soul so to his own conceit   550
That from her working all his visage wanned,
Tears in his eyes, distraction in his aspect,
A broken voice, and his whole function suiting
With forms to his conceit? And all for nothing.
For Hecuba!
What's Hecuba to him, or he to her,
That he should weep for her? What would he do
Had he the motive and the cue for passion
That I have? He would drown the stage with tears
And cleave the general ear with horrid speech,   560
Make mad the guilty and appal the free,
Confound the ignorant, and amaze indeed
The very faculties of eyes and ears. Yet I,
A dull and muddy-mettled rascal, peak
Like John-a-dreams, unpregnant of my cause,
And can say nothing, no, not for a king
Upon whose property and most dear life
A damned defeat was made. Am I a coward?
Who calls me villain? Breaks my pate across?
Plucks off my beard and blows it in my face?   570

549 *But* merely
550 *force his soul so to his own conceit* make
his imagination so control the workings of his mind and body
551 *from her working* as a result of this
activity of his soul (commonly
thought of as feminine)
wanned grew pale
553-4 *his whole function suiting | With
forms to his conceit* all his bodily
powers responding with physical
expressiveness appropriate to these
fictitious imaginings
560 *the general ear* the ears of people
generally
horrid horrifying

561 *appal* turn pale (and so 'dismay')
the free the innocent
562 *ignorant* (of the crime that has been
committed)
amaze bewilder, stun
564 *muddy-mettled* sluggish
peak mope
565 *John-a-dreams* (apparently a byword
for 'a dreamer')
unpregnant of my cause not stirred to
action by my just cause
568 *defeat* destruction
570 *beard.* Presumably Hamlet must be
imagined as bearded in the fashion
of a young man of the early seventeenth century.

Tweaks me by the nose? Gives me the lie i'th'throat
As deep as to the lungs? Who does me this?
Ha, 'swounds, I should take it. For it cannot be
But I am pigeon-livered and lack gall
To make oppression bitter, or ere this
I should ha' fatted all the region kites
With this slave's offal. Bloody, bawdy villain!
Remorseless, treacherous, lecherous, kindless villain!
O, vengeance!
580   Why, what an ass am I! This is most brave,
That I, the son of a dear father murdered,
Prompted to my revenge by heaven and hell,
Must like a whore unpack my heart with words
And fall a-cursing like a very drab,
A stallion! Fie upon't, foh!
About, my brains. Hum – I have heard
That guilty creatures sitting at a play
Have by the very cunning of the scene
Been struck so to the soul that presently
590   They have proclaimed their malefactions.
For murder, though it have no tongue, will speak
With most miraculous organ. I'll have these players
Play something like the murder of my father
Before mine uncle. I'll observe his looks.

571 *Gives me the lie i'th'throat* calls me a
    downright liar
572 *to the lungs* (making him swallow the
    insult)
573 *'swounds* by God's wounds
    take it accept the insult
574 *pigeon-livered and lack gall.* Pigeons
    were believed not to secrete gall (the
    reputed cause of anger)
575 *To make oppression bitter* which
    would make me resent the
    oppression
576 *region kites* kites in the sky
578 *kindless* inhuman
580 *brave* fine (ironically)

582 *heaven and hell* (that is, a sense of
    natural justice and the fury of his
    anger)
585 *stallion* a prostitute (like *drab*). F
    reads 'Scullion', an acceptable read-
    ing sometimes preferred by editors.
    But *whore* and *drab* perhaps lead nat-
    urally to *stallion*.
586 *About* to work
588 *by the very cunning of the scene* simply
    by the skill in presentation of the
    play
589 *presently* at once
591–2 *murder . . . organ.* Compare
    1.2.257–8.

I'll tent him to the quick. If 'a do blench,
I know my course. The spirit that I have seen
May be a devil, and the devil hath power
T'assume a pleasing shape, yea, and perhaps
Out of my weakness and my melancholy,
As he is very potent with such spirits,   600
Abuses me to damn me. I'll have grounds
More relative than this. The play's the thing
Wherein I'll catch the conscience of the King.   *Exit*

Enter the King and Queen, Polonius, Ophelia,   III.I
Rosencrantz, Guildenstern, and lords

KING
And can you by no drift of conference
Get from him why he puts on this confusion,
Grating so harshly all his days of quiet

---

595 *tent him to the quick* probe him until
he feels the pain
blench flinch (not 'turn pale')
596–601 *The spirit . . . damn me.* Hamlet
now explains or excuses his inactivity
by distrusting the Ghost's statements. Though he and his friends
had already envisaged the possibility
that the Ghost might be an evil spirit
(*a spirit of health or goblin damned*,
1.4.40–42, and Horatio's warning at
1.4.69–74), Hamlet had concluded *It
is an honest ghost* (1.5.138).
599–600 *my melancholy, | As he is very
potent with such spirits.* According to
Elizabethan physiology, persons suffering from an excess of black bile
(*melancholy*) were prone to exercising
strong imaginations, and were therefore subject to mental instability and

hallucinations. So they were an easy
prey to the devil.
601 *Abuses* deceives
602 *relative* closely related to fact
this (the narrative and promptings of
the Ghost)

III.I (stage direction) Unlike 1.2 and 11.2,
here the royal entry is not marked with a
'Flourish' in Q2 or F. This may indicate
a more private interview than the formal,
though genial, reception of Rosencrantz
and Guildenstern in 11.2.
1 *drift of conference* directing of your conversations with him
2 *puts on.* This indicates suspicion that
Hamlet's *antic disposition* is a pose.
confusion mental distraction
3 *Grating* harassing

    With turbulent and dangerous lunacy?

ROSENCRANTZ

    He does confess he feels himself distracted,
    But from what cause 'a will by no means speak.

GUILDENSTERN

    Nor do we find him forward to be sounded,
    But with a crafty madness keeps aloof
    When we would bring him on to some confession
    Of his true state.

10   QUEEN   Did he receive you well?

ROSENCRANTZ

    Most like a gentleman.

GUILDENSTERN

    But with much forcing of his disposition.

ROSENCRANTZ

    Niggard of question, but of our demands
    Most free in his reply.

QUEEN   Did you assay him
    To any pastime?

ROSENCRANTZ

    Madam, it so fell out that certain players
    We o'er-raught on the way. Of these we told him,
    And there did seem in him a kind of joy
    To hear of it. They are here about the court,
20   And, as I think, they have already order
    This night to play before him.

POLONIUS   'Tis most true,
    And he beseeched me to entreat your majesties
    To hear and see the matter.

KING

    With all my heart, and it doth much content me
    To hear him so inclined.

---

7 *forward* readily disposed   forcing himself to be in an accom-
  sounded questioned   modating mood
8 *crafty* cunning   14 *assay him* try to win him
12 *forcing of his disposition* constraint,   17 *o'er-raught* overtook

Good gentlemen, give him a further edge
And drive his purpose into these delights.

ROSENCRANTZ
We shall, my lord.

Exeunt Rosencrantz, Guildenstern, and lords

KING   Sweet Gertrude, leave us too.
For we have closely sent for Hamlet hither,
That he, as 'twere by accident, may here   30
Affront Ophelia.
Her father and myself, lawful espials,
We'll so bestow ourselves that, seeing unseen,
We may of their encounter frankly judge,
And gather by him, as he is behaved,
If't be th'affliction of his love or no
That thus he suffers for.

QUEEN   I shall obey you. –
And for your part, Ophelia, I do wish
That your good beauties be the happy cause
Of Hamlet's wildness. So shall I hope your virtues   40
Will bring him to his wonted way again,
To both your honours.

OPHELIA   Madam, I wish it may.

Exit the Queen

POLONIUS
Ophelia, walk you here. – Gracious, so please you,

---

26 *give him a further edge* stimulate him to
a keener desire

29 *closely* privately

31 *Affront* come face to face with

32 *lawful espials* spies made excusable by
the circumstances

38–42 *for your part . . . honours.* This probably shows that Ophelia hears the
plotting against Hamlet, so that she
must take responsibility for deceiving him. But it cannot be regarded
as certain, for the Elizabethan stage
was large, and she could have been

so placed that (by convention) she
did not hear lines 32–7. Nothing in
what she says in lines 90–162 implies
that she knows she is being spied
upon.

40 *wildness.* This is a mild word for
Hamlet's *confusion, lunacy, affliction.* To
Ophelia the Queen tactfully avoids
the word 'madness'.

42 *To both your honours* to the credit of
you both

43 *Gracious* (to the King)

We will bestow ourselves. (*To Ophelia*) Read on this
    book,
That show of such an exercise may colour
Your loneliness. We are oft to blame in this,
'Tis too much proved, that with devotion's visage
And pious action we do sugar o'er
The devil himself.

KING   O, 'tis too true.

50   (*Aside*) How smart a lash that speech doth give my
    conscience!
The harlot's cheek, beautied with plastering art,
Is not more ugly to the thing that helps it
Than is my deed to my most painted word.
O, heavy burden!

POLONIUS
I hear him coming. Let's withdraw, my lord.

                    Exeunt the King and Polonius

    Enter Hamlet

HAMLET
To be, or not to be – that is the question;

---

44 *bestow* conceal
    book (clearly a prayer book: lines 45,
    47–8, 89–90)
45 *exercise* religious exercise
    colour provide plausible explanation
    of
46 *loneliness* being alone (without a
    chaperon)
47 *proved* found by experience
    devotion's visage an outward appearance
    of religious devotion
48 *pious action* performance of religious
    acts
49 *O, 'tis too true*. Probably this is spoken
    aloud, for the King is a self-control-
    led character. The '*Aside*' direction
    in line 50 is added by editors.
50–54 *How smart . . . burden!* This is the
    first sign that the King has a bad
    conscience. From now on, the audi-

ence has no reason to doubt the
Ghost's veracity. It is just at this
point that Hamlet has begun to have
doubts (II.2.596–601).

52 *to the thing* in comparison with the
    cosmetic. But the meaning is
    strained. Possibly *the thing that helps
    it* is the harlot's servant who arranges
    her toilet and so knows how ugly
    she really is.

53 *painted* hypocritically disguised

55 (stage direction) *Enter Hamlet*. It is
    possible that Hamlet enters reading a
    book and speaks his soliloquy while
    ruminating upon it. For Q1 has the
    introductory line spoken by the
    King: 'see where hee comes poring
    vpon a booke', which probably indi-
    cates what the actor who reported
    the text had seen upon the stage. If,

Whether 'tis nobler in the mind to suffer
The slings and arrows of outrageous fortune
Or to take arms against a sea of troubles
And by opposing end them. To die, to sleep –   60
No more – and by a sleep to say we end
The heartache and the thousand natural shocks
That flesh is heir to. 'Tis a consummation
Devoutly to be wished. To die, to sleep –
To sleep – perchance to dream. Ay, there's the rub.
For in that sleep of death what dreams may come
When we have shuffled off this mortal coil

as seems probable, the soliloquy was originally spoken at II.2.170 (where Q1 places it), the Queen's *But look where sadly* ... is a vestige of this 'business'.

56–88 *To be, or not to be ... action.* Q1 prints this soliloquy, and the meeting with Ophelia, after II.2.170, which may well indicate stage practice in early productions. Some modern directors have found that placing the soliloquy there, at a low point in Hamlet's despair, is more effective than it is here, just after his vigorous decision to test Claudius. The placing of the soliloquy here may indicate an afterthought – not altogether successful – influenced by the fact that including it in II.2 gives the actor a very long period on stage.

56 *To be, or not to be* whether or not to continue this mortal existence (the choice is between continuing to live and committing suicide). An alternative explanation is: 'is there an after-life, or not?' This, though congruous with the line of thought later in the soliloquy, is more difficult to communicate on the stage.

57–60 *Whether 'tis nobler ... end them* it does not matter (in discussing *the question* of the advantages and disadvantages of suicide) whether we think a stoical attitude to misfortune or an active fighting back against the blows of fate is the more honourable course for a man to take. An alternative explanation is that lines 57–8 expand *To be* and lines 59–60 expand *not to be*: Hamlet can either endure his misfortunes (and so continue to live) or follow an active plan of attacking the King (and so expose himself to an inevitable avenger's death or suicide). At II.2.547 Hamlet had supposed that such an endurance of wrongs was fit only for a *rogue and peasant slave.*

57 *in the mind* (probably goes with *to suffer* rather than with *nobler*)

58 *outrageous.* Hamlet seems to be emphasizing the unbearable irrationality of Fortune.

60 *by opposing* (as distinct from using other methods of ending one's troubles, such as stoical endurance or suicide)

61 *No more* (than to sleep)

63 *consummation* final completion (of life)

65 *rub* obstacle (in the game of bowls)

67 *shuffled off this mortal coil* (like a snake shedding its slough, or perhaps a butterfly – a symbol of the soul – emerging from its chrysalis)
this mortal coil the turmoil of this mortal life

Must give us pause. There's the respect
That makes calamity of so long life.
70   For who would bear the whips and scorns of time,
Th'oppressor's wrong, the proud man's contumely,
The pangs of despised love, the law's delay,
The insolence of office, and the spurns
That patient merit of th'unworthy takes,
When he himself might his quietus make
With a bare bodkin? Who would fardels bear,
To grunt and sweat under a weary life,
But that the dread of something after death,
The undiscovered country, from whose bourn
80   No traveller returns, puzzles the will,
And makes us rather bear those ills we have
Than fly to others that we know not of?
Thus conscience does make cowards of us all;

---

68 *give us pause* cause us to hesitate
respect consideration
69 *makes calamity of so long life* makes
those afflicted by calamity willing to
endure it for so long
70 *time* the world in which one lives,
'the times'
72 *despised* (not necessarily by the lady).
F has 'dispriz'd' ('unvalued'), which
also makes good sense.
the law's delay (a typically Elizabethan
misfortune)
73 *office* those who hold official
positions
74 *patient merit of th'unworthy takes* the
deserving have to endure patiently
from the unworthy
75 *quietus* release from a debt (*quietus est*,
'it is discharged') and so from the
troubles of life
76 *a bare* merely a
bodkin dagger (but *bodkin* had come
also to mean 'a large pin', and possibly that is the vivid image here)

fardels burdens
79-80 *from whose bourn* | *No traveller
returns*. The inconsistency between
this statement and Hamlet's experience of his father's ghost is obvious.
It might be intended to indicate his
waning faith in the authenticity of
the Ghost (see II.2.596–601). But it
is more likely to be an imaginative
intensification of his thoughts on
death, not to be related too literally
to the action in other parts of the
play. Moreover, the image is that of
a *traveller* returning to his home from
a sojourn elsewhere – which is quite
unlike the transitory visitation of a
ghost.
79 *bourn* region, boundary
80 *puzzles* (a strong word) bewilders
83 *conscience* introspection, reflection on
the contents of the consciousness

And thus the native hue of resolution
Is sicklied o'er with the pale cast of thought,
And enterprises of great pitch and moment
With this regard their currents turn awry
And lose the name of action. Soft you now,
The fair Ophelia! – Nymph, in thy orisons
Be all my sins remembered.

OPHELIA   Good my lord,   90
How does your honour for this many a day?

HAMLET
I humbly thank you, well, well, well.

84 *native hue* (complexion characteristic of a state of natural health)
85 *cast* tinge
   thought anxiety
86 *pitch* (the height of a soaring falcon's flight) high aspiration
   moment importance
87 *With this regard* owing to this consideration (because this is thought about)
88 *Soft you now* (an interjection expressing moderate surprise)
89–150 The interview between Hamlet and Ophelia is difficult to interpret. We do not know whether Hamlet is talking with the knowledge that there are eavesdroppers; whether he thinks Ophelia is in the plot and is acting as a decoy; whether he becomes suspicious of her halfway through and thereupon turns nasty. The scene is usually played as if Hamlet were merely suspicious up to line 130, when he asks *Where's your father?* From that point, realizing that the King and Polonius are listening, he puts on a vicious act intended for their ears.

The first part of the interview can be spoken by Hamlet in his typical cryptic ironic manner. At line 130,

it seems, he wonders what Ophelia is doing alone and unchaperoned after having been kept immured from him so long, and learns that her father is not with her. It is an easy step to suppose that she was brought here by the Queen and that, if anyone, it is the Queen who is listening to their conversation. Hamlet therefore begins an attack on womanhood intended for her ears. The irony is that it is not his mother but the King, with Polonius, who overhears his bitter words, and so he unknowingly betrays himself (*all but one – shall live*, line 149) and prepares the King for the trick in the play scene (III.2).

There is no exit for the Queen at line 42 in either Q2 or F. If the audience can be made aware of the Queen's curiosity in observing what goes on between Hamlet and Ophelia, then the revelation at line 162 that Hamlet has been mistaken, and the eavesdropper is, not the Queen, but – more importantly and more dangerously – the King, can be an exciting moment.

89 *orisons* prayers (because Ophelia carries a book of devotions, and is perhaps visibly at prayer)

OPHELIA

My lord, I have remembrances of yours
That I have longèd long to re-deliver.
I pray you now receive them.

HAMLET   No, not I.
I never gave you aught.

OPHELIA

My honoured lord, you know right well you did,
And with them words of so sweet breath composed
As made the things more rich. Their perfume lost,
100   Take these again. For to the noble mind
Rich gifts wax poor when givers prove unkind.
There, my lord.

HAMLET Ha, ha! Are you honest?

OPHELIA My lord?

HAMLET Are you fair?

OPHELIA What means your lordship?

HAMLET That if you be honest and fair, your honesty
should admit no discourse to your beauty.

OPHELIA Could beauty, my lord, have better commerce
110   than with honesty?

HAMLET Ay, truly. For the power of beauty will sooner
transform honesty from what it is to a bawd than the
force of honesty can translate beauty into his likeness.

---

93 *remembrances* gifts as souvenirs of
affection

99 *perfume* (given by the *words of so sweet
breath composed*)

103, 107 *honest* (of a woman) chaste

108 *admit no discourse* to permit no parley-
ing with

109–13 *Could beauty . . . likeness.* Ophelia
supposes Hamlet to have said that
beauty and chastity should not go
together, and he accepts the misinter-
pretation as interesting and develops
it.

109 *commerce* intercourse

111–13 *the power of beauty . . . likeness.*
This is very like the typical paradox
on which academic wits exercised
themselves in Shakespeare's time. In
the second element, Hamlet is presumably referring obscurely to the
failure of his *honest* father to keep his
beautiful mother in the path of
virtue.

113 *translate* transform (probably with
some implication of 'elevate')
his likeness the likeness of *honesty*

This, was sometime a paradox, but now the time gives it
proof. I did love you once.

OPHELIA Indeed, my lord, you made me believe so.

HAMLET You should not have believed me. For virtue
cannot so inoculate our old stock but we shall relish of
it. I loved you not.

OPHELIA I was the more deceived.   120

HAMLET Get thee to a nunnery. Why wouldst thou be a
breeder of sinners? I am myself indifferent honest, but
yet I could accuse me of such things that it were better
my mother had not borne me. I am very proud, revengeful, ambitious, with more offences at my beck than I
have thoughts to put them in, imagination to give them
shape, or time to act them in. What should such fellows
as I do crawling between earth and heaven? We are
arrant knaves all. Believe none of us. Go thy ways to a
nunnery. Where's your father?   130

OPHELIA At home, my lord.

114 *sometime* formerly (before his
mother's disillusioning behaviour)
the time 'the times' (but, in particular,
his experience of his mother's
behaviour)

118 *inoculate our old stock* be grafted (by
the insertion of a bud) into the
human inheritance of original sin
(occasioned by an apple tree; and
no doubt Hamlet is thinking of his
family inheritance from his mother)

118–19 *relish of it* have a flavour of the
original *stock*, with its inheritance of
original sin

121 *Get thee to a nunnery* (so avoiding
sexual temptation, marriage, and the
begetting of children). *Hamlet* is a
play of long ago, set in a foreign
country but in Christian times; and it
is given a vaguely Catholic setting.
The withdrawal of a noble young
lady to a convent to avoid the wickedness of the world is a not unreasonable suggestion. After Shakespeare's
time, 'nunnery' was used facetiously
to mean 'brothel', but in this context (*Why wouldst thou be a breeder
of sinners?*) that meaning seems
impossible.

122 *indifferent honest* of average
honourableness

124–5 *I am very proud, revengeful, ambitious.* This, although it bitterly misrep-
resents Hamlet himself, is not unlike
the character of a hero-villain in a
revenge story, such as that derived
from Belleforest in *The History of
Hamblet.*

131 *At home.* Ophelia's lie (if it is a lie
and she knows Polonius is listening)
is the beginning of the calamity that
falls upon her, though she thinks she
is only humouring a madman.

HAMLET Let the doors be shut upon him, that he may
play the fool nowhere but in's own house. Farewell.

OPHELIA O, help him, you sweet heavens!

HAMLET If thou dost marry, I'll give thee this plague for
thy dowry: be thou as chaste as ice, as pure as snow,
thou shalt not escape calumny. Get thee to a nunnery.
Go, farewell. Or if thou wilt needs marry, marry a fool.
For wise men know well enough what monsters you
140   make of them. To a nunnery, go, and quickly too. Farewell.

OPHELIA O heavenly powers, restore him!

HAMLET I have heard of your paintings too, well enough.
God hath given you one face, and you make yourselves
another. You jig and amble, and you lisp. You nickname God's creatures and make your wantonness your
ignorance. Go to, I'll no more on't. It hath made me
mad. I say we will have no more marriage. Those that
are married already – all but one – shall live. The rest
150   shall keep as they are. To a nunnery, go.   *Exit*

133 *play the fool* ('I have sinned ...
behold, I have played the fool, and
have erred exceedingly', 1 Samuel
26.21)

139 *monsters* (probably) cuckolds (who
traditionally wear horns and so look
like monstrous animals. The actor
can make the gesture of horns with
his fingers on his head.)
   you (women in general, not Ophelia
in particular)

143 *paintings* use of cosmetics

145 *jig* dance, move jerkily
   amble walk affectedly
   lisp talk affectedly

145–6 *nickname God's creatures* use foolish
(or indecent) invented names for creatures which were given their proper
names by Adam at God's direction
(Genesis 2.19)

146–7 *make your wantonness your ignorance*

affect ignorance and use this as an
excuse for your foolishness or
wanton speech

148 *marriage*. So Q2; in F (as often happens) the meaning is simplified by
reading 'Marriages', the concrete for
the abstract word.

149 *all but one*. This clearly refers to the
King. It is an uncharacteristically and
dangerously open warning if Hamlet
suspects that the King is listening.
Perhaps it is his first mistake, putting
the King on his guard (as is expressed in lines 163–76). But if he
supposes that his mother is listening
(see the note to lines 89–150), then it
is a warning to her about what is
going to happen. Or the phrase may
be spoken aside, rather than shouted
as a threat.

OPHELIA

O, what a noble mind is here o'erthrown!
The courtier's, soldier's, scholar's, eye, tongue, sword,
Th'expectancy and rose of the fair state,
The glass of fashion and the mould of form,
Th'observed of all observers, quite, quite down!
And I, of ladies most deject and wretched,
That sucked the honey of his music vows,
Now see that noble and most sovereign reason
Like sweet bells jangled, out of time and harsh,
That unmatched form and feature of blown youth   160
Blasted with ecstasy. O, woe is me
T'have seen what I have seen, see what I see!

    Enter the King and Polonius

KING

Love? His affections do not that way tend;
Nor what he spake, though it lacked form a little,
Was not like madness. There's something in his soul
O'er which his melancholy sits on brood,

---

152 *The courtier's, soldier's, scholar's, eye, tongue, sword.* The *eye*, *tongue*, and *sword* do not seem to apply independently to the three types of a man, though *tongue* and *sword* would go with the *scholar* and *soldier* Rather, Ophelia seems to be insisting on the unity of qualities in Hamlet in his various capacities.

153 *expectancy* hope for the future
rose 'the very flower'
fair (perhaps 'made fair by Hamlet's presence and participation', rather than vaguely approving of the state of Denmark)

154 *glass* mirror
mould of form pattern of behaviour (as distinct from garments and physical appearance)

155 *of* by

157 *music.* This is the F reading. Q2 has 'musickt'.

159 *Out of time.* F has 'tune' for Q2's *time.* The image of the harmony of the human faculties under the government of reason is common in Shakespeare.

160 *feature* general physical appearance (not only the face)
blown youth youth in its bloom

161 *Blasted* withered
ecstasy madness

162 *have seen what I have seen, see what I see* see now such a great change from what I have seen

163 *affections* emotions

164–5 *Nor ... Was not* (the emphatic negative, not uncommon in Shakespeare)

166 *sits on brood* (like a bird on its eggs, leading to *hatch* in line 167)

And I do doubt the hatch and the disclose
Will be some danger; which for to prevent,
I have in quick determination
170   Thus set it down: he shall with speed to England
For the demand of our neglected tribute.
Haply the seas, and countries different,
With variable objects, shall expel
This something-settled matter in his heart,
Whereon his brains still beating puts him thus
From fashion of himself. What think you on't?

POLONIUS
It shall do well. But yet do I believe
The origin and commencement of his grief
Sprung from neglected love. – How now, Ophelia?
180   You need not tell us what Lord Hamlet said.
We heard it all. – My lord, do as you please,
But if you hold it fit, after the play
Let his Queen mother all alone entreat him
To show his grief. Let her be round with him,
And I'll be placed, so please you, in the ear

---

167 *doubt* feel anxious that
disclose. This also means 'hatching',
as at v.1.283.
170 *he shall with speed to England*. Similarly in *The History of Hamblet* the
prince is sent to England. The King
has now changed his mind from
1.2.112–17, where he was intent on
keeping Hamlet at home. At this
point the King still claims to hope
that Hamlet may be cured of his
melancholy. But after he and Hamlet
have confronted each other in the
play scene he resolves to use the
expedition to England as a means
of sending Hamlet to his death
(IV.3.60–70).
171 *tribute*. Shakespeare has a sense of

the historical background of the play;
this is the famous Dangelt.
173 *variable objects* variety of surround-
ings for him to observe
174 *something-settled matter* somewhat
settled matter (*idée fixe*)
175 *still beating* for ever hammering in
his head
176 *From fashion of himself* out of his
ordinary way of conducting himself
178 *grief* grievance
180–81 *You need not ... all.* This could
be taken to mean that Ophelia had
not known that their conversation
was being overheard. See the note to
lines 38–42.
184 *be round with* speak bluntly to
185 *in the ear* within earshot

Of all their conference. If she find him not,
To England send him, or confine him where
Your wisdom best shall think.

KING   It shall be so.
Madness in great ones must not unwatched go. *Exeunt*

Enter Hamlet and the Players   III.2

HAMLET Speak the speech, I pray you, as I pronounced
it to you, trippingly on the tongue. But if you mouth it
as many of our players do, I had as lief the town crier
spoke my lines. Nor do not saw the air too much with
your hand, thus. But use all gently. For in the very tor-
rent, tempest, and, as I may say, whirlwind of your
passion, you must acquire and beget a temperance that
may give it smoothness. O, it offends me to the soul to
hear a robustious periwig-pated fellow tear a passion to
tatters, to very rags, to split the ears of the groundlings,   10
who for the most part are capable of nothing but inexplicable dumb shows and noise. I would have such a
fellow whipped for o'erdoing Termagant. It out-Herods
Herod. Pray you avoid it.

186 *find him not* fails to discover what is the matter with him
187 *confine him* lock him up (as a madman rather than as a political danger)
189 *great ones* highly-placed persons

III.2.1–53 *Speak the speech ... of it.* Hamlet begins by referring only to the elocution of *my lines*, the inserted *speech of some dozen lines or sixteen lines* (II.2.538) which he had himself written. But he soon moves to a consideration of the principles of acting generally.
5 *use all* treat everything
9 *robustious* boisterous

periwig-pated with his head covered with a wig
passion passionate speech
10 *groundlings* (the part of the audience who stood on the ground in the open yard of the theatre, paying only a penny for entrance)
11 *capable of* capable of understanding
13 *o'erdoing* outdoing
Termagant. This imaginary deity believed to be worshipped by Mohammedans appears in the medieval religious plays as violent and overbearing.
13–14 *out-Herods Herod* gives a performance which is even more violent than

FIRST PLAYER I warrant your honour.

HAMLET Be not too tame neither. But let your own discretion be your tutor. Suit the action to the word, the
word to the action, with this special observance, that
you o'erstep not the modesty of nature. For anything so
o'erdone is from the purpose of playing, whose end,
both at the first and now, was and is to hold, as 'twere,
the mirror up to nature, to show virtue her own feature,
scorn her own image, and the very age and body of the
time his form and pressure. Now this overdone, or come
tardy off, though it make the unskilful laugh, cannot
but make the judicious grieve; the censure of the which
one must in your allowance o'erweigh a whole theatre
of others. O, there be players that I have seen play, and
heard others praise, and that highly, not to speak it
profanely, that, neither having th'accent of Christians
nor the gait of Christian, pagan, nor man, have so
strutted and bellowed that I have thought some of
Nature's journeymen had made men, and not made
them well, they imitated humanity so abominably.

that of Herod (represented in medieval religious plays as a wild tyrant)
19 *modesty* moderation
20 *from* contrary to
22 *the mirror up to nature*. This image of
art as a mirror of reality had had a
long history before Shakespeare used
it.
22-3 *show virtue her own feature, scorn her
own image*. The virtues and vices, by
being represented in a lifelike way,
are to be immediately recognizable
for what they are, without confusing
the spectator.
23 *scorn* folly (the object of scorn)
23-4 *very age and body of the time* (that is,
present state of things)
24 *his* its (grammatically, their)
   pressure impression (as in wax)

24-5 *come tardy off* imperfectly achieved
25 *unskilful* uneducated part of the audience (contrasted with *the judicious*)
26-7 *censure of the which one* judgement of
one of *the judicious*
27 *must in your allowance* you should allow
to
29-30 *not to speak it profanely* (by suggesting impiously that they were made
not by God but by *some of Nature's
journeymen*)
33 *journeymen* (that is, indifferent
workmen)
34 *abominably*. This word was generally
(but incorrectly) supposed to derive
from the Latin *ab homine*, interpreted
as 'inhuman'; and both Q2 and F
here spell it 'abhominably'. So
Hamlet is punning on *humanity*.

FIRST PLAYER I hope we have reformed that indifferently with us, sir.

HAMLET O, reform it altogether! And let those that play your clowns speak no more than is set down for them. For there be of them that will themselves laugh to set on some quantity of barren spectators to laugh too, though 40 in the meantime some necessary question of the play be then to be considered. That's villainous, and shows a most pitiful ambition in the fool that uses it. And then you have some again that keeps one suit of jests, as a man is known by one suit of apparel; and gentlemen quote his jests down in their tables before they come to the play; as thus, 'Cannot you stay till I eat my porridge?', and 'You owe me a quarter's wages', and 'My coat wants a cullison', and 'Your beer is sour', and blabbering with his lips, and thus keeping in his cinquepace of 50 jests, when, God knows, the warm clown cannot make a jest unless by chance, as the blind man catcheth a hare. Masters, tell him of it.

FIRST PLAYER We will, my lord.

HAMLET Well, go make you ready.   *Exeunt Players*

35–6 *indifferently* to some extent. The First Player seems to give only a half-hearted assurance of reformation.

39 *there be of them that* there are some of those (clowns) who

43–55 *And then you . . . Well.* This passage is found only in Q1. This is generally unreliable, but there are good reasons for regarding this expansion of Hamlet's speech as a fairly accurate report of a passage later cut. It gives examples of the silly 'character' jests of the comic actors. This part of the scene is quite well remembered by the actor who betrayed the play to a piratical printer – he was obviously interested in this discussion of acting and appreciated the satirical comments on bad actors. Moreover, it is just the kind of passage which would soon become out-of-date and would therefore be cut in later performances. Since, however, we are dependent upon the actor's memory, we cannot trust the exact wording.

45 *quote* note

46 *tables* notebooks

49 *cullison* (a corruption of 'cognizance', a badge)

49–50 *blabbering* babbling

50 *keeping in* (perhaps 'accompanying', that is, the *gentlemen* speak the catch-phrases along with the clown)
cinquepace (a lively dance)

51 *warm* (presumably as the result of his strenuous efforts to amuse)

Enter Polonius, Rosencrantz, and Guildenstern

How now, my lord? Will the King hear this piece of
work?

POLONIUS And the Queen too, and that presently.

HAMLET Bid the players make haste.   *Exit Polonius*

60   Will you two help to hasten them?

ROSENCRANTZ Ay, my lord.

                    Exeunt Rosencrantz and Guildenstern

HAMLET What, ho, Horatio!

        Enter Horatio

HORATIO

Here, sweet lord, at your service.

HAMLET

Horatio, thou art e'en as just a man

As e'er my conversation coped withal.

HORATIO

O my dear lord –

HAMLET   Nay, do not think I flatter.

For what advancement may I hope from thee,

That no revenue hast but thy good spirits

To feed and clothe thee? Why should the poor be
        flattered?

70   No, let the candied tongue lick absurd pomp,

And crook the pregnant hinges of the knee

Where thrift may follow fawning. Dost thou hear?

Since my dear soul was mistress of her choice

56-7 *piece of work* masterpiece (ironic-
    ally). Compare II.2.303.
58 *presently* immediately
64 *e'en* indeed
    just honourable
65 *conversation coped withal* dealings with
    people brought me into contact with
70-71 *let the candied tongue ... hinges of
    the knee.* Hamlet is describing an al-
    legorical scene in which a figure of
    Flattery first licks another figure
    (Pomp), and then kneels down before

him, expecting to be flattered.
Hamlet is thinking of Rosencrantz
and Guildenstern, whom he has just
now dismissed.
70 *absurd* ridiculously unreasonable
71 *crook the pregnant hinges of the knee*
    curtsy or kneel (as a gesture of
    respect)
    pregnant productive of profit
72 *thrift may follow fawning* personal
    profit may derive from sycophantic
    behaviour

And could of men distinguish her election,
Sh'hath sealed thee for herself. For thou hast been
As one, in suffering all, that suffers nothing,
A man that Fortune's buffets and rewards
Hast ta'en with equal thanks. And blest are those
Whose blood and judgement are so well commeddled
That they are not a pipe for Fortune's finger   80
To sound what stop she please. Give me that man
That is not passion's slave, and I will wear him
In my heart's core, ay, in my heart of heart,
As I do thee. Something too much of this.
There is a play tonight before the King.
One scene of it comes near the circumstance,
Which I have told thee, of my father's death.
I prithee, when thou seest that act afoot,
Even with the very comment of thy soul
Observe my uncle. If his occulted guilt   90
Do not itself unkennel in one speech,
It is a damnèd ghost that we have seen,
And my imaginations are as foul
As Vulcan's stithy. Give him heedful note.

74 *of men distinguish her election* make discriminating choice among men
75 *sealed* marked as a possession (like a
legal document)
76 *one, in suffering all, that suffers nothing*
one who, however great his suffer-
ings may be, shows none of the
effects of suffering
79 *blood and judgement* passion and reason
commeddled mixed. F has 'co-mingled',
a more usual word.
81 *stop* finger-hole (and the note produced by 'stopping' it)
83 *core . . . heart* (probably a pun, on the
supposition that 'core' is related to
Latin *cor*, 'heart')
89 *the very comment of thy soul* your closest
observation
90 *occulted* hidden

91 *unkennel* reveal (like a dog emerging
from its lair)
in one speech at one speech. It is natural
to suppose that this is the speech
that Hamlet proposed to insert. This
is not certain. He has chosen the
play, *The Murder of Gonzago*, because
of the resemblance of its plot to the
actual situation in Denmark, and it
may already contain a speech which
will strike Claudius *to the soul* and
make him *blench* (II.2.589, 595).
Hamlet may from the first have intended his speech to be directed at
his mother. See the note to lines
196–225.
94 *Vulcan's stithy* the anvil of Vulcan,
the blacksmith god, whose forge was
supposed to be under Mount Etna,

For I mine eyes will rivet to his face,
And after we will both our judgements join
In censure of his seeming.

HORATIO   Well, my lord.
If 'a steal aught the whilst this play is playing,
And 'scape detecting, I will pay the theft.

100   HAMLET They are coming to the play. I must be idle. Get
you a place.

> *Danish march. Flourish*
> *Trumpets and kettledrums*
> *Enter the King and Queen, Polonius, Ophelia, Rosen-*
> *crantz, Guildenstern, and other lords attendant, with*
> *the guard carrying torches*

KING How fares our cousin Hamlet?

HAMLET Excellent, i'faith; of the chameleon's dish. I eat
the air, promise-crammed. You cannot feed capons so.

---

and so came to be connected with
the idea of hell (therefore *foul*). Compare *the Cyclops' hammers* (II.2.487).

96 *after* afterwards

96–7 *we will both our judgements join | In
censure of his seeming.* It is noteworthy that Hamlet has no plan for action if
Claudius reveals his guilt, and he
ignores the consequences of his revealing to Claudius that he is aware
of the crime.

97 *censure of his seeming* assessment of the
way he behaves outwardly

98 *steal* hide by stealth (any emotion)

100 *be idle* seem to have nothing on my
mind

101 (stage direction) *Danish march. Flourish. Trumpets and kettledrums . . . guard
carrying torches.* The *Trumpets and kettledrums* are in the Q2 direction, the
Flourish, the *guard carrying torches*, and
the *Danish march* in F. They indicate
stage business for a formal entry with
royal and national music. Probably
early productions were content with

trumpets and drums. The F direction
suggests later elaboration. The
phrase *Danish march* is interesting.
The fact that King James I's consort
was Anne of Denmark and that
Christian IV of Denmark visited him
in 1606 and 1614 may have meant
that a *Danish march* had come to be
recognizable to some of Shakespeare's audiences and was appropriately inserted into the play.

Trumpets and kettledrums (probably to
be heard off stage)

torches. Perhaps some of these are
extinguished when the play begins
(line 144), to give point to the King's
and Polonius's demands for *light*
(lines 278–9).

102 *cousin* (used of any close relative)

103 *chameleon's dish.* The chameleon was
alleged to live on air alone. Hamlet
takes up Claudius's *fares* as if it were
an inquiry about his food.

104 *air* (doubtless punning on 'heir')
promise-crammed. This alludes to Clau-

KING I have nothing with this answer, Hamlet. These words are not mine.

HAMLET No, nor mine now. (*To Polonius*) My lord, you played once i'th'university, you say?

POLONIUS That did I, my lord, and was accounted a good actor. 110

HAMLET What did you enact?

POLONIUS I did enact Julius Caesar. I was killed i'th'Capitol. Brutus killed me.

HAMLET It was a brute part of him to kill so capital a calf there. Be the players ready?

ROSENCRANTZ Ay, my lord. They stay upon your patience.

QUEEN Come hither, my dear Hamlet, sit by me.

HAMLET No, good mother. Here's metal more attractive.

POLONIUS (*to the King*) O ho! Do you mark that? 120

HAMLET Lady, shall I lie in your lap?

OPHELIA No, my lord.

---

dius's promise of the succession to the throne (I.2.108–9 and lines 348–52 below).

105 *have nothing with* understand nothing of

105–6 *These words are not mine* what you have said is irrelevant to my remark

107 *nor mine now* (because he has spoken them and they have left him)

113 *Capitol.* In fact Caesar was not killed in the Capitol at Rome, but the error (found also in *Julius Caesar* and *Antony and Cleopatra*) was common. *Brutus killed me.* Hamlet encourages references to the murder of a tyrant.

114 *brute ... capital.* Hamlet's jeering puns have an extra irony in that he will soon kill Polonius (III.4.24–34). *calf* fool

116–17 *stay upon your patience* await your permission to begin

119 *metal more attractive* (of Ophelia)

more magnetic metal. By his behaviour Hamlet encourages Polonius's belief that distracted love is the cause of his trouble. But his other reason for sitting near Ophelia is that it is a position from which he can watch the King closely.

121 *shall I lie in your lap?* Hamlet's sexual innuendos in this scene are quite unlike any other lover's speech to his beloved in Shakespeare, but it must be admitted that several of Shakespeare's pure heroines listen to and tolerate ribald raillery from a man (e.g. Helena from Parolles, *All's Well That Ends Well*, I.1.109–61, and Desdemona from Iago, *Othello*, II.1.100–161).

122 *No, my lord.* Ophelia keeps Hamlet at a distance by addressing him in almost every speech as *my lord*, emphasizing her inferior position.

HAMLET I mean, my head upon your lap?

OPHELIA Ay, my lord.

HAMLET Do you think I meant country matters?

OPHELIA I think nothing, my lord.

HAMLET That's a fair thought – to lie between maids' legs.

OPHELIA What is, my lord?

130 HAMLET Nothing.

OPHELIA You are merry, my lord.

HAMLET Who, I?

OPHELIA Ay, my lord.

HAMLET O God, your only jig-maker! What should a man do but be merry? For look you how cheerfully my mother looks, and my father died within's two hours.

OPHELIA Nay, 'tis twice two months, my lord.

HAMLET So long? Nay then, let the devil wear black, for I'll have a suit of sables. O heavens! Die two months
140 ago, and not forgotten yet? Then there's hope a great man's memory may outlive his life half a year. But, by'r Lady, 'a must build churches then, or else shall 'a suffer

124 *Ay*. Probably she is accepting his interpretation of what he had said, rather than consenting to his suggestion.

125 *meant country matters* was referring to sexual intercourse

130 *Nothing* (the figure nought). Presumably the actor makes the point about *country matters* by some such gesture as putting his thumb and first finger together to make a circle, representing the female organ, the *fair thought . . . between maids' legs*. Ophelia understands the obscenity: *You are merry, my lord*.

134 *your only jig-maker* the very representative of mindless jesting. Compare II.2.498.

136 *within's* within these

137 *twice two months*. As the Ghost appeared when he was *But two months dead, nay, not so much, not two* (1.2.138), the information is thus given us that it is now more than two months since the apparition, during which time Hamlet has done nothing.

138-9 *let the devil wear black, for I'll have a suit of sables* (that is, to hell with mourning! I'll wear a rich garment). 'Sables' could mean both 'black mourning garments' and 'expensive furs'.

139-40 *Die two months ago*. Hamlet seems to ignore the *twice two months* of Ophelia and to revert to *But two months dead*.

142 *build churches* (that is, endow chapels where prayers may be said for his soul)

142-3 *else shall 'a suffer not thinking on*

not thinking on, with the hobby-horse, whose epitaph
is 'For O, for O, the hobby-horse is forgot!'

> *The trumpets sound*
> *Dumb show follows: Enter a King and a Queen very
> lovingly, the Queen embracing him, and he her. She
> kneels, and makes show of protestation unto him. He
> takes her up, and declines his head upon her neck. He
> lies him down upon a bank of flowers. She, seeing him
> asleep, leaves him. Anon come in another man; takes
> off his crown, kisses it, pours poison in the sleeper's
> ears, and leaves him. The Queen returns, finds the King
> dead, makes passionate action. The poisoner, with some
> three or four, come in again, seem to condole with her.
> The dead body is carried away. The poisoner woos the
> Queen with gifts. She seems harsh awhile, but in the
> end accepts love*
>
> *Exeunt dumb show*

OPHELIA What means this, my lord?
HAMLET Marry, this is miching mallecho. It means mischief.

---

otherwise he will have to endure
being forgotten

143 *with* like
the hobby-horse (in morris dancing, a
man with a figure of a horse strapped
around his waist. The word could
also mean 'unchaste woman', and
some association of thought may be
intended here.)

144 *For O ... forgot!* This *epitaph* is
apparently from some ballad not
extant.

(stage direction) *The trumpets sound.*
This is the direction in Q2. F has
'*Hoboyes play*', which may represent
later theatrical practice. Perhaps the
oboe was felt to be more suitable
than the trumpet to accompany the
following love scenes.

Dumb show a mime, common in Eliza-

bethan drama, usually foreshadowing
part or all of a play, or summarizing
part of the action. Claudius can sit
through this dumb show with an
outward appearance of calm because
he is a practised hypocrite. It is only
on the second telling of the story,
where it is made a more intense experience, that he breaks down.

makes show of protestation gives a performance of one affirming strongly
her love. There is no question of
insincerity; the boy player is performing a role.

declines leans

146 *miching mallecho* (an obscure phrase;
mallecho may be related to the Spanish
malhecho, 'mischief'. It is usually pronounced to rhyme with 'calico' or
'pal echo'.)

OPHELIA Belike this show imports the argument of the play.

Enter the Fourth Player as Prologue

150 HAMLET We shall know by this fellow. The players cannot keep counsel. They'll tell all.

OPHELIA Will 'a tell us what this show meant?

HAMLET Ay, or any show that you will show him. Be not you ashamed to show, he'll not shame to tell you what it means.

OPHELIA You are naught, you are naught. I'll mark the play.

FOURTH PLAYER (*as Prologue*)
   For us and for our tragedy,
   Here stooping to your clemency,
160   We beg your hearing patiently.

                                                        Exit

HAMLET Is this a prologue, or the posy of a ring?

OPHELIA 'Tis brief, my lord.

HAMLET As woman's love.

Enter two Players as King and Queen

FIRST PLAYER (*as King*)
   Full thirty times hath Phoebus' cart gone round
   Neptune's salt wash and Tellus' orbèd ground,
   And thirty dozen moons with borrowed sheen

---

148 *Belike* probably
   show dumb show
   imports represents
   argument story
149 (stage direction) *Prologue* (that is, speaker of the Prologue, a chorus-figure)
151 *keep counsel* keep a secret
153–4 *Be not you* provided that you are not
156 *naught* improper
161 *the posy of a ring* a motto inscribed in a ring (therefore short, and often in rhyme)
163 *As woman's love.* The injustice of

this statement to Ophelia would be shocking were it not obvious that Hamlet is observing his mother and thinking of her. It also anticipates the situation in the playlet, where the Queen succumbs to the seductions of the poisoner.
164 *Phoebus' cart* the chariot of Apollo, the sun-god
165 *Neptune's salt wash and Tellus' orbèd ground* the sea and the earth
   Tellus (goddess of the earth)
   orbèd rounded (the earth being a sphere)
166 *borrowed sheen* (because the light of

About the world have times twelve thirties been
Since love our hearts, and Hymen did our hands,
Unite commutual in most sacred bands.

SECOND PLAYER (*as Queen*)

So many journeys may the sun and moon   170
Make us again count o'er ere love be done!
But woe is me, you are so sick of late,
So far from cheer and from your former state
That I distrust you. Yet, though I distrust,
Discomfort you, my lord, it nothing must.
For women fear too much, even as they love,
And women's fear and love hold quantity,
In neither aught, or in extremity.
Now what my love is, proof hath made you know,
And as my love is sized, my fear is so.   180
Where love is great, the littlest doubts are fear.
Where little fears grow great, great love grows there.

FIRST PLAYER (*as King*)

Faith, I must leave thee, love, and shortly too.
My operant powers their functions leave to do.
And thou shalt live in this fair world behind,
Honoured, beloved; and haply one as kind
For husband shalt thou –

the moon is only the reflection of
the sun's)
168 *Hymen* (the pagan god of marriage)
169 *commutual* mutually
173 *cheer* cheerfulness
174 *distrust you* am anxious about you
175 *Discomfort* trouble
176 As there is no rhyme, a line may
have been accidentally omitted.
love (love too much)
177 *hold quantity* are of equivalent
amount
178 *In neither aught, or in extremity* either
there is nothing of either of them

(*fear and love*) or both are present to
the utmost limit
179 *proof* your experience
180 *as my love is sized* according to the
amount of my love for you
182 *Where little fears grow great, great love
grows there* where great anxiety develops from only small causes, that is
evidence of great love. The meaning
is close to that of line 176.
184 *operant powers* vital faculties
leave to do cease to perform
185 *behind* after I have gone

SECOND PLAYER (*as Queen*)
> O, confound the rest!
> Such love must needs be treason in my breast.
> In second husband let me be accurst!
190 > None wed the second but who killed the first.

HAMLET (*aside*)
> That's wormwood.

SECOND PLAYER (*as Queen*)
> The instances that second marriage move
> Are base respects of thrift, but none of love.
> A second time I kill my husband dead
> When second husband kisses me in bed.

FIRST PLAYER (*as King*)
> I do believe you think what now you speak,
> But what we do determine oft we break.
> Purpose is but the slave to memory,
> Of violent birth, but poor validity,

---

190 *None wed the second but who* let no woman marry a second husband except the one who

191 *wormwood* (a plant of bitter taste, and so 'something bitter to a person's feelings')

192 *instances that ... move* motives that lead to

193 *base respects of thrift* a dishonourable concern for personal advantage

194 *A second time I kill my husband dead* I give offence to the memory of my first husband and trouble his spirit

196–225 *I do believe ... dead.* This is sometimes believed to be the speech which Hamlet said (II.2.538–9) he would insert into *The Murder of Gonzago*. It would be an ingenious device of Shakespeare to have Hamlet write a speech about his own vacillations and his mother's miscon-duct when he was expected to be writing one about his uncle's guilt. But probably the promised lines do not appear at all: it is enough for Hamlet to declare that the playlet will contain something that will frighten the King and then to keep us in suspense. Be that as it may, this is an important speech, echoed by Hamlet and the Ghost at III.4.107–12, by Hamlet at IV.4.32–66, by Claudius at IV.7.110–22, and by Hamlet to Horatio at V.2.10–11.

196 *you think* your real opinion is

198 *Purpose is but the slave to memory* our decisions about what we are going to do depend entirely upon our being able to remember them afterwards

199 *Of violent birth, but poor validity* (our initial declarations of our intentions may be emphatic, but they have little stamina)

Which now, like fruit unripe, sticks on the tree,   200
But fall unshaken when they mellow be.
Most necessary 'tis that we forget
To pay ourselves what to ourselves is debt.
What to ourselves in passion we propose,
The passion ending, doth the purpose lose.
The violence of either grief or joy
Their own enactures with themselves destroy.
Where joy most revels, grief doth most lament.
Grief joys, joy grieves, on slender accident.
This world is not for aye, nor 'tis not strange   210
That even our loves should with our fortunes change.
For 'tis a question left us yet to prove,
Whether love lead fortune, or else fortune love.
The great man down, you mark his favourite flies.
The poor advanced makes friends of enemies.
And hitherto doth love on fortune tend,
For who not needs shall never lack a friend,
And who in want a hollow friend doth try
Directly seasons him his enemy.
But, orderly to end where I begun,   220
Our wills and fates do so contrary run

200 *Which* (*Purpose*, line 198)
202 *Most necessary 'tis* it is inevitable
203 *pay ourselves what to ourselves is debt* fulfil the promises we have made about actions which we ourselves have to perform
204 *passion* the heat of the moment
207 *Their own enactures with themselves destroy* destroys them even by putting them into action
209 *joys . . . grieves* turns to joy . . . turns to grief
on slender accident for trivial causes
210 *is not for aye* will not last for ever
nor and so
212 *prove* decide by experience
213 *lead* determine the direction of

214 *down* being displaced
215 *The poor advanced makes friends of enemies* when a humble man is promoted to a position of importance, his enemies become his friends
216 *hitherto* to this extent
217 *who not needs* the rich and important, who do not need friends
218 *try* test (by making an appeal for help)
219 *seasons him* confirms him as, converts him into
221 *Our wills and fates* what we want to happen and what is fated to happen to us
contrary in contrary directions

That our devices still are overthrown.
Our thoughts are ours, their ends none of our own.
So think thou wilt no second husband wed,
But die thy thoughts when thy first lord is dead.

SECOND PLAYER (*as Queen*)
Nor earth to me give food, nor heaven light,
Sport and repose lock from me day and night,
To desperation turn my trust and hope,
An anchor's cheer in prison be my scope,
Each opposite that blanks the face of joy
Meet what I would have well, and it destroy,
Both here and hence pursue me lasting strife,
If, once a widow, ever I be wife!

230

HAMLET (*aside*)
If she should break it now!

FIRST PLAYER (*as King*)
'Tis deeply sworn. Sweet, leave me here awhile.
My spirits grow dull, and fain I would beguile
The tedious day with sleep.

SECOND PLAYER (*as Queen*)
                                        Sleep rock thy brain,
And never come mischance between us twain!

The Player-King sleeps. Exit the Player-Queen

HAMLET
Madam, how like you this play?

---

222 *devices* plans for the future
still always
223 *their ends* what happens as a result of
our *thoughts*
none of our own outside our control
224 *think* you may think now
225 *die thy thoughts* what you think will
come to nothing
226 *Nor* let neither
227 *Sport* recreation
lock from me deprive me of (*Sport and
repose*)
229 *An anchor's cheer* the food of an

anchorite (hermit). The Q2 reading
'cheere' is sometimes interpreted as
'chair'. But both this spelling and
the meaning are difficult.
my scope what I have in prospect
230 *Each opposite* whatever is in opposition
blanks the face of joy changes a happy
face to a miserable one
232 *here and hence* in the present and in
the future (or possibly 'in this world
and the next')

QUEEN

The lady doth protest too much, methinks. 240

HAMLET

O, but she'll keep her word.

KING Have you heard the argument? Is there no offence in't?

HAMLET No, no, they do but jest, poison in jest. No offence i'th' world.

KING What do you call the play?

HAMLET *The Mousetrap*. Marry, how? Tropically. This play is the image of a murder done in Vienna. Gonzago is the duke's name; his wife, Baptista. You shall see anon. 'Tis a knavish piece of work. But what of that? 250 Your majesty, and we that have free souls, it touches us not. Let the galled jade wince. Our withers are unwrung.

Enter the Third Player, as Lucianus

This is one Lucianus, nephew to the King.

OPHELIA You are as good as a chorus, my lord.

240 *protest* promise publicly

242-3 *Have you heard . . . in't?* The King presumably speaks to Polonius, though Hamlet replies to him.

244 *poison in jest.* Poison has not been mentioned so far in the playlet; and Hamlet again anticipates the action by referring to *murder* in line 248. Apparently the King begins to reveal his distress or anger *Upon the talk of the poisoning* (line 298).

245 *offence.* Hamlet's meaning is different from Claudius's in line 242: this is only a play; there is no reality in it, so no actual injury is done by this pretence of poisoning.

247 *The Mousetrap.* The new name for the play seems to derive from Hamlet's belief that he could *catch* the King's *conscience* (II.2.603).
Tropically figuratively (like a 'trope', a rhetorical figure). There may be a

pun on 'trap'.

248 *image* imitation of the reality

250 *knavish* wicked

251 *free* innocent

252 *galled* made sore
jade ill-conditioned horse (also a contemptuous term for a woman, possibly glancing at the Queen)
withers shoulder-bones (of a horse)
unwrung not chafed

253 *nephew.* Although the circumstances of the murder in the playlet correspond to the murder of King Hamlet by his brother Claudius, the agent is the murdered man's *nephew*, not his brother. So the playlet could reasonably be interpreted as a threat against Claudius by his nephew Hamlet. Only Claudius knows that it is also an accusation of murder.
the King (the King in the playlet)

HAMLET I could interpret between you and your love, if
I could see the puppets dallying.

OPHELIA You are keen, my lord, you are keen.

HAMLET It would cost you a groaning to take off mine
edge.

260 OPHELIA Still better, and worse.

HAMLET So you must take your husbands. – Begin, murderer. Pox, leave thy damnable faces and begin. Come;
the croaking raven doth bellow for revenge.

THIRD PLAYER *(as Lucianus)*

Thoughts black, hands apt, drugs fit, and time agreeing,
Confederate season, else no creature seeing,
Thou mixture rank, of midnight weeds collected,

255 *interpret* provide dialogue (that is,
act as a pander). Hamlet imagines
Ophelia and a supposed lover (*love*)
as puppets, and himself as presenter
speaking the words of their play.

256 *dallying* indulging in dalliance (that
is love-play)

257 *keen* bitter, quick-witted. Hamlet
seems to take the word as meaning
'eager for sexual intercourse'.

258–9 *It would cost you a groaning to take
off mine edge* you would have to pay
for it if you were to satisfy my sexual
appetite, because it would cause you
the pangs of childbirth

260 *Still better, and worse* your words are
getting both more witty and more
disgraceful

261 *So you must take your husbands* ('for
better, for worse . . .': the marriage
service)
must take. This reading comes from
Q1. Both Q2 and F read 'mistake',
from which it is difficult to get any
satisfactory meaning (unless it is another sneer at his mother, who had
'mis-taken' her husbands by going
from a good to a bad one).

262 *Pox* a pox on you, may (venereal)
disease afflict you. The oath is inserted in F.

263 *the croaking raven doth bellow for revenge*. These words seem irrelevant to
the situation portrayed. They sound
like a fragment of an 'old play', and
something like them occurs in the
anonymous *True Tragedy of Richard
III* (printed in 1594). They also seem
to be a cue for Lucianus, but they do
not begin his speech. The word *bellow*
applied to the sound of a raven reduces the line to burlesque.

264 *apt* skilful (perhaps in preparing the
poison or in pouring it into his
victim's ear)

265 *Confederate season* a helpful opportunity being provided which acts as
an ally
else no creature seeing no other living
creature observing me

266 *rank* evil-smelling
midnight weeds collected. It was supposed that poisonous or magical
herbs were especially potent when
gathered at midnight.

With Hecat's ban thrice blasted, thrice infected,
Thy natural magic and dire property
On wholesome life usurps immediately.

He pours the poison in the King's ears

HAMLET 'A poisons him i'th'garden for his estate. His   270
name's Gonzago. The story is extant, and written in very
choice Italian. You shall see anon how the murderer
gets the love of Gonzago's wife.

OPHELIA The King rises.

HAMLET What, frighted with false fire?

QUEEN How fares my lord?

POLONIUS Give o'er the play.

KING Give me some light. Away!

POLONIUS Lights, lights, lights!

Exeunt all but Hamlet and Horatio

HAMLET

Why, let the strucken deer go weep,   280
   The hart ungallèd play.
For some must watch, while some must sleep.
   Thus runs the world away.
Would not this, sir, and a forest of feathers – if the rest

---

267 *Hecat* (two syllables: 'hekkett'; goddess of the underworld and hence
supposed to be the ruler of witchcraft)
ban curse
268 *natural magic* inherent magic power
dire property terribly dangerous
power
270 *estate* high rank (as king)
275 *false fire* blank cartridges
280–83 This and lines 290–93 are probably fragments of an old, lost ballad.
Hamlet is contrasting those who are
wounded in some way (*the strucken
deer*) with those who are in a more
fortunate position (*The hart ungallèd*):
that is, the King and himself.
280 *the strucken deer*. It was believed

that a deer would shed tears when
wounded to death (see *As You Like
It*, II.1.33–40).
282 *watch* remain awake (with pain or
sorrow)
283 *Thus runs the world away* it's the way
of the world
284 *this*. Perhaps this refers to Hamlet's
skill in play-revision, or to his mana-
gerial ability in selecting a play and
bringing about its intended effect on
its audience (King Claudius). Characteristically Hamlet, while excitedly tri-
umphing in his theatrical success, has
no thought of any action to deal
with the new situation.
feathers (as worn by actors)

of my fortunes turn Turk with me – with two Provincial
roses on my razed shoes, get me a fellowship in a cry of
players, sir?

HORATIO Half a share.

HAMLET A whole one, I.

290　For thou dost know, O Damon dear
　　　　This realm dismantled was
　　Of Jove himself; and now reigns here
　　　　A very, very – peacock.

HORATIO You might have rhymed.

HAMLET O good Horatio, I'll take the ghost's word for a
thousand pound. Didst perceive?

HORATIO Very well, my lord.

HAMLET Upon the talk of the poisoning?

HORATIO I did very well note him.

300　HAMLET Aha! Come, some music! Come, the recorders!
　　　For if the King like not the comedy,
　　　　Why then, belike he likes it not, perdy.
　　Come, some music!

Enter Rosencrantz and Guildenstern

GUILDENSTERN Good my lord, vouchsafe me a word
with you.

HAMLET Sir, a whole history.

285　*turn Turk* make a complete change
for the worse (like a Christian becoming a renegade to the Turks, the
great non-Christian power in the
seventeenth century)

285-6　*Provincial roses* (double rose patterns, made of ribbons, worn on
shoes, and named from Provins, a
town in northern France famous for
its roses)

286　*razed* (with 'open work', sometimes
showing inside cloth of another
colour)

　fellowship partnership (in a company
of actors)

　cry company. The word is normally
used of a pack of hounds; so Hamlet

is thinking of the way they *mouth*
their lines (line 2).

290　*O Damon dear*. Perhaps Hamlet is
thinking of Horatio and himself as
like Damon and Pythias, the legendary friends.

291-2　*This realm dismantled was | Of Jove
himself*. Presumably he is still thinking of his father (who had *the front of
Jove himself*, III.4.57), whose kingdom
was usurped by a *peacock* (Claudius)
or (as the rhyme suggests) an 'ass'.

292　*dismantled* deprived, stripped

301　*comedy*. The word could be used
generally of a play.

302　*perdy* by God (*par Dieu*)

GUILDENSTERN The King, sir –

HAMLET Ay, sir, what of him?

GUILDENSTERN Is in his retirement marvellous dis-   310
tempered.

HAMLET With drink, sir?

GUILDENSTERN No, my lord, with choler.

HAMLET Your wisdom should show itself more richer to
signify this to the doctor. For for me to put him to his
purgation would perhaps plunge him into more choler.

GUILDENSTERN Good my lord, put your discourse into
some frame, and start not so wildly from my affair.

HAMLET I am tame, sir. Pronounce.

GUILDENSTERN The Queen your mother in most great
affliction of spirit hath sent me to you.   320

HAMLET You are welcome.

GUILDENSTERN Nay, good my lord, this courtesy is not
of the right breed. If it shall please you to make me a
wholesome answer, I will do your mother's commandment. If not, your pardon and my return shall be the
end of my business.

HAMLET Sir, I cannot.

ROSENCRANTZ What, my lord?

HAMLET Make you a wholesome answer. My wit's
diseased. But, sir, such answer as I can make, you shall   330
command; or rather, as you say, my mother. Therefore
no more, but to the matter. My mother, you say –

309 *retirement* withdrawal (from the play
to his private apartments)

309–10 *distempered* sick (in mind or
body)

312 *choler* anger (supposed to be caused
by bile in the stomach)

314 *signify* report

315 *purgation* (of the *choler*; one cure was
by bleeding)

317 *frame* order
start jump away (like a horse that is
startled, or not *tame*)

323 *breed* sort

324 *wholesome* reasonable

325 *pardon* permission to leave your
presence

328 *What, my lord?* Q2 attributes this to
Rosencrantz, but F to Guildenstern
(perhaps rightly), waiting until line
333 for Rosencrantz to take over the
dialogue.

331 *command* have for the asking

332 *to the matter* come to the point

ROSENCRANTZ Then thus she says: your behaviour hath struck her into amazement and admiration.

HAMLET O wonderful son, that can so 'stonish a mother! But is there no sequel at the heels of this mother's admiration? Impart.

ROSENCRANTZ She desires to speak with you in her closet ere you go to bed.

340   HAMLET We shall obey, were she ten times our mother. Have you any further trade with us?

ROSENCRANTZ My lord, you once did love me.

HAMLET And do still, by these pickers and stealers.

ROSENCRANTZ Good my lord, what is your cause of distemper? You do surely bar the door upon your own liberty if you deny your griefs to your friend.

HAMLET Sir, I lack advancement.

ROSENCRANTZ How can that be, when you have the voice of the King himself for your succession in Den-
350   mark?

HAMLET Ay, sir, but 'while the grass grows' – the proverb is something musty.

      Enter a Player with recorders

O, the recorders. Let me see one. – To withdraw with

---

334 *admiration* bewilderment

338-9 *She desires ... bed.* Rosencrantz and Guildenstern are the messengers of the plot devised by Polonius (III.1. 182-6).

339 *closet* small private room. It is not a bedroom, though modern directors sometimes turn it into one in order to communicate Hamlet's Oedipal condition.

341 *trade* (an insulting word) business

343 *these pickers and stealers* (his hands, or perhaps those of Rosencrantz who is holding them out in protestation). The allusion is to the Catechism in the Prayer Book: 'My duty towards my neighbour is to ... keep my hands from picking and stealing'. In-

stead of the usual oath 'by this hand', Hamlet swears one that is not valid, as if the only purpose of hands was theft.

346 *liberty* liberation (from your *distemper*). But perhaps this contains a threat, preparing for the dialogue with the King in III.3.1-26.
   deny refuse to speak about

349 *voice* vote, support

351-2 *the proverb* ('While the grass grows the starving horse dies')

353-4 *To withdraw with you.* Presumably he takes Guildenstern aside, so that the Player does not hear. Perhaps he gets him at a disadvantage by separating him from Rosencrantz.

you – why do you go about to recover the wind of me, as if you would drive me into a toil?

GUILDENSTERN O my lord, if my duty be too bold, my love is too unmannerly.

HAMLET I do not well understand that. Will you play upon this pipe?

GUILDENSTERN My lord, I cannot.   360

HAMLET I pray you.

GUILDENSTERN Believe me, I cannot.

HAMLET I do beseech you.

GUILDENSTERN I know no touch of it, my lord.

HAMLET It is as easy as lying. Govern these ventages with your fingers and thumb; give it breath with your mouth; and it will discourse most eloquent music. Look you, these are the stops.

GUILDENSTERN But these cannot I command to any utterance of harmony. I have not the skill.   370

HAMLET Why, look you now, how unworthy a thing you make of me! You would play upon me. You would seem to know my stops. You would pluck out the heart of my mystery. You would sound me from my lowest note to the top of my compass. And there is much music, excellent voice, in this little organ. Yet cannot you make it speak. 'Sblood, do you think I am easier to be played

354 *recover the wind* get to windward (like a huntsman trying to get the quarry to run with the wind, so that the scent of the nets and of the men who have prepared them is not perceived)

355 *toil* net

356–7 *if my duty be too bold, my love is too unmannerly*. This is an evasive response to Hamlet's accusation. It is difficult to work out any exact meaning: perhaps 'if my manner of behaving to you (in lines 316–26) seemed rather insolent, it was only the strength of my love for you which

made me discourteous.' But the antithesis is merely verbal, and it produces Hamlet's tart rejoinder.

365 *ventages* finger-holes

368 *stops*. Hamlet shows how the finger-holes can be covered with his *fingers and thumb*.

374 *sound* fathom (with a quibble on 'produce sound from a musical instrument')

375 *top of my compass* uppermost range of my notes

376 *organ* (the recorder)

377 *'Sblood* by God's blood (on the Cross)

on than a pipe? Call me what instrument you will, though you can fret me, you cannot play upon me.

Enter Polonius

380 God bless you, sir!

POLONIUS My lord, the Queen would speak with you, and presently.

HAMLET Do you see yonder cloud that's almost in shape of a camel?

POLONIUS By th'mass, and 'tis like a camel indeed.

HAMLET Methinks it is like a weasel.

POLONIUS It is backed like a weasel.

HAMLET Or like a whale.

POLONIUS Very like a whale.

390 HAMLET Then I will come to my mother by and by.
(*Aside*) They fool me to the top of my bent. – I will come by and by.

POLONIUS I will say so.

HAMLET

'By and by' is easily said.   *Exit Polonius*

Leave me, friends.

     Exeunt all but Hamlet

'Tis now the very witching time of night,
When churchyards yawn, and hell itself breathes out
Contagion to this world. Now could I drink hot blood
And do such bitter business as the day
Would quake to look on. Soft, now to my mother.
400 O heart, lose not thy nature. Let not ever
The soul of Nero enter this firm bosom.
Let me be cruel, not unnatural.

---

379 *fret* (punning on the meanings 'a mark on the finger-board of a stringed instrument' and 'irritate')

383 *yonder cloud*. In an Elizabethan theatre open to the sky, Hamlet's pointing to a cloud would not seem incongruous.

390 *by and by* at once

391 *to the top of my bent* till I can put up with it no longer (like a bow *bent* to the full)

396 *yawn* open wide

400 *nature* (natural feelings)

401 *Nero* (the emperor who slew his mother, Agrippina)

I will speak daggers to her, but use none.
My tongue and soul in this be hypocrites.
How in my words somever she be shent,
To give them seals never, my soul, consent!   *Exit*

Enter the King, Rosencrantz, and Guildenstern   III.3

KING

I like him not; nor stands it safe with us
To let his madness range. Therefore prepare you.
I your commission will forthwith dispatch,
And he to England shall along with you.
The terms of our estate may not endure
Hazard so near us as doth hourly grow
Out of his brows.

GUILDENSTERN   We will ourselves provide.
Most holy and religious fear it is

---

404 *be hypocrites* (deceive her by a show
of bitter censure without meaning
actually to harm her)
405 *shent* shamed
406 *give them seals* confirm my words by
actions

III.3.1 *like him not* am nervous about his
actions and intentions
2 *range* roam at liberty
3 *your commission* (the *letters sealed* and
the *mandate* (III.4.203–5). It is nowhere made clear that Rosencrantz
and Guildenstern are aware of the
murderous instructions given in the
letters.)
dispatch quickly prepare (for you to
take)
5 *The terms of our estate* my position as
ruler of the state
7 *brows*. This Q2 reading is difficult.
Perhaps the King is thinking of the

intensely attentive face, with knitted
brows, watching him during the play
scene; and so the meaning is something like 'bold opposition'. The compiler of the F text found the word
unreasonable, and substituted 'Luna-
cies', regardless of metre, perhaps an
echo of *turbulent and dangerous lunacy*
(III.1.4). Emendations proposed include 'blows', 'brains', 'braves',
'brawls', 'frowns', and 'lunes'.
provide act with careful foresight
8–23 This view of kingship, although
put into the mouths of the ingratiating Guildenstern and Rosencrantz,
was the orthodox Elizabethan one.
Its expression here shows the dangerous position into which Hamlet has
got himself: his enemies now have
political morality on their side and
he has offended against it.
8 *religious fear* sacred duty

> To keep those many many bodies safe
10 > That live and feed upon your majesty.

ROSENCRANTZ
> The single and peculiar life is bound
> With all the strength and armour of the mind
> To keep itself from noyance; but much more
> That spirit upon whose weal depends and rests
> The lives of many. The cess of majesty
> Dies not alone, but like a gulf doth draw
> What's near it with it; or 'tis a massy wheel
> Fixed on the summit of the highest mount,
> To whose huge spokes ten thousand lesser things
20 > Are mortised and adjoined; which when it falls,
> Each small annexment, petty consequence,
> Attends the boisterous ruin. Never alone
> Did the king sigh, but with a general groan.

KING
> Arm you, I pray you, to this speedy voyage.
> For we will fetters put about this fear,
> Which now goes too free-footed.

ROSENCRANTZ   We will haste us.

Exeunt Rosencrantz and Guildenstern

Enter Polonius

POLONIUS
> My lord, he's going to his mother's closet.

---

10 *upon* (that is, at the expense of (like parasites))

11 *single and peculiar life* private individual (contrasted with a king)

13 *noyance* harm

14 *That spirit* (the life of a king)
weal welfare

15 *cess of majesty* cessation of royal rule (by the death or deposition of the king). In F the more familiar word 'cease' has replaced the unusual *cess*.

16 *Dies not alone* is not a single death
gulf whirlpool

17–20 *a massy wheel . . . adjoined*. The king

is described as resembling the wheel of Fortune.

20 *mortised and adjoined* fitted together (like joints of wood)

21 *annexment* appendage
petty consequence unimportant follower

22 *Attends* accompanies
boisterous ruin tumultuous downfall

23 *a general groan* (the people share in the misery)

24 *Arm you* prepare

25 *about this fear* upon this cause of our fear

Behind the arras I'll convey myself
To hear the process. I'll warrant she'll tax him home.
And, as you said, and wisely was it said,   30
'Tis meet that some more audience than a mother,
Since nature makes them partial, should o'erhear
The speech, of vantage. Fare you well, my liege.
I'll call upon you ere you go to bed
And tell you what I know.
KING   Thanks, dear my lord.

Exit Polonius

O, my offence is rank. It smells to heaven.
It hath the primal eldest curse upon't,
A brother's murder. Pray can I not,
Though inclination be as sharp as will.
My stronger guilt defeats my strong intent,   40
And like a man to double business bound
I stand in pause where I shall first begin,
And both neglect. What if this cursèd hand
Were thicker than itself with brother's blood,
Is there not rain enough in the sweet heavens

28 *arras.* Again Polonius enjoys spying on Hamlet from a hiding-place.
convey surreptitiously place
29 *the process* what happens
tax him home reproach him unsparingly
30 *as you said.* In fact the suggestion came from Polonius himself (III.1. 185–6).
32 *them* (mothers)
33 *of vantage* (perhaps 'in addition', or 'from the vantage-ground of concealment')
36–72 This is the first time we see the King alone and the only occasion we have a full confession from him (but see III.1.50–54). The conscience-stricken King, unlike Hamlet, knows his theological position exactly, and argues about his situation with clarity

of mind. Ironically, only after Hamlet's departure (with the same erroneous belief as ourselves) do we learn that the King has not achieved a state of grace.
37 *the primal eldest curse* (the oldest curse upon mankind)
39 *Though inclination be as sharp as will* (he sincerely desires to pray; he is not merely forcing himself to do so by an act of will)
41 *like a man to double business bound* (he wishes to repent and wishes to persist in his guilty situation)
43 *both neglect* fail to deal with either
44 *thicker* deeply covered (made more than double its usual thickness)
45 *Is there not rain enough in the sweet heavens* ('How fair a thing is mercy in the time of anguish and trouble? It is

To wash it white as snow? Whereto serves mercy
But to confront the visage of offence?
And what's in prayer but this twofold force,
To be forestallèd ere we come to fall
Or pardoned being down? Then I'll look up.
My fault is past. But, O, what form of prayer
Can serve my turn? 'Forgive me my foul murder'?
That cannot be, since I am still possessed
Of those effects for which I did the murder,
My crown, mine own ambition, and my Queen.
May one be pardoned and retain th'offence?
In the corrupted currents of this world
Offence's gilded hand may shove by justice;
And oft 'tis seen the wicked prize itself
Buys out the law. But 'tis not so above.
There is no shuffling. There the action lies

like a cloud of rain that cometh in
the time of drought', Ecclesiasticus
35.19)

46 *wash it white as snow* ('thou shalt wash
me, and I shall be whiter than snow',
Psalm 51.7)
Whereto serves what is the use of
47 *confront the visage of offence* meet sin
face to face
48 *twofold force* double efficacy, in preventing us from sinning and in helping us to win pardon when we have
sinned ('lead us not into temptation,
but deliver us from evil', Matthew
6.13)
49 *forestallèd* prevented
51 *My fault is past* once I have appealed
to God for mercy, my sin will have
been forgiven. (But he knows that
appealing to God brings with it certain conditions.)
54 *effects* resulting benefits
55 *mine own ambition* (that is, the fulfil-

ment of my ambition)
56 *retain th'offence* continue to enjoy what
has been gained by the wicked deed
57 *corrupted currents* corrupt ways of
behaviour
58 *Offence's gilded hand* the hand of an
offender bearing gold as bribes to
the judges
shove by thrust aside
59–60 *the wicked prize itself | Buys out the
law* what has been gained by wicked
actions – such as power and riches –
is used to obtain exemption from the
laws against those very actions
60 *above* in heaven
61 *There ... There* (emphasized) in
heaven
shuffling trickery
61–2 *the action lies | In* (probably 'legal
action can be brought against us
according to', as well as 'the wicked
deed is revealed in')

In his true nature, and we ourselves compelled,
Even to the teeth and forehead of our faults,
To give in evidence. What then? What rests?
Try what repentance can. What can it not?
Yet what can it when one cannot repent?
O, wretched state! O, bosom black as death!
O limed soul, that struggling to be free
Art more engaged! Help, angels! Make assay.
Bow, stubborn knees, and, heart with strings of steel,   70
Be soft as sinews of the new-born babe.
All may be well.
          The King kneels. Enter Hamlet

HAMLET

Now might I do it pat, now 'a is a-praying.
And now I'll do't. And so 'a goes to heaven.
And so am I revenged. That would be scanned.
A villain kills my father, and for that
I, his sole son, do this same villain send
To heaven.
Why, this is hire and salary, not revenge.

62 *his* its

62–4 *we ourselves ... evidence.* In the law courts a man may not be constrained to give evidence that will incriminate himself; but before God's seat of judgement it is different.

62 *compelled* are compelled

63 *to the teeth and forehead* in the very face

64 *give in* provide
What rests? what remains for me to do?

65 *can* can do

68 *limèd soul.* The soul is like a bird which has been caught by the laying of 'lime', a glue-like substance.

69 *engaged* entangled
Make assay make a vigorous attempt (probably addressed to himself rather than to the angels or to his knees)

70 *strings of steel.* He imagines his heart-strings have hardened to steel as a result of his crime.

73 *pat* neatly, opportunely

74 *'a goes to heaven.* At first Hamlet uses the conventional phrase, meaning 'he dies'. Then he begins to analyse it literally. He supposes that the King is in a state of contrition, and so his death at this moment will, quite literally, enable him to go *to heaven*.

75 *would be scanned* needs to be subjected to scrutiny

77 *sole son* only son (and therefore the only person upon whom the duty of revenge lies)

79 *hire and salary* (like a payment for services, instead of punishment for crimes)

80   'A took my father grossly, full of bread,
With all his crimes broad blown, as flush as May;
And how his audit stands, who knows save heaven?
But in our circumstance and course of thought,
'Tis heavy with him. And am I then revenged,
To take him in the purging of his soul,
When he is fit and seasoned for his passage?
No.
Up, sword, and know thou a more horrid hent.
When he is drunk asleep, or in his rage,
90   Or in th'incestuous pleasure of his bed,
At game, a-swearing, or about some act
That has no relish of salvation in't –
Then trip him, that his heels may kick at heaven,
And that his soul may be as damned and black
As hell, whereto it goes. My mother stays.
This physic but prolongs thy sickly days.   *Exit*

---

80 *took* (took at a disadvantage and killed)
grossly, full of bread (in a condition of gross unpreparedness, without having had an opportunity of a penitential fast)

81 *crimes* sins. See the first note to 1.5.12.
broad blown, as flush as May in full bloom, like the vigorous vegetation in the month of May. Hamlet is recalling that the Ghost said he was *Cut off even in the blossoms of my sin* (1.5.76).

82 *audit* account (with God)

83 *our circumstance and course of thought*. The exact meaning is difficult to decide, but, roughly interpreted, Hamlet is saying 'so far as we, here on earth, can judge' or 'according to our evidence and speculation'.

86 *seasoned* prepared
passage (to the next world)

88 *Up* (that is, come out of your sheath)
a more horrid hent a grasp causing more horror (that is, when he is

about to execute a more terrible deed of vengeance upon Claudius)

89 *drunk asleep* dead drunk

91 *game* gambling

91–2 *some act | That has no relish of salvation in't*. This is what Hamlet ultimately achieves in V.2.316–21, stabbing the King when he is engaged in acts of murderous treachery.

92 *relish* savour

93 *trip him* (still addressing his sword) take him by a quick act of treachery
his heels may kick at heaven. Hamlet imagines his enemy as receiving a deadly blow and sprawling forwards, so that in his death throes his legs bend upwards from his knees.

95 *stays* awaits me

96 *This physic but prolongs thy sickly days* the spiritual medicine you (the King) are now taking (by praying to God, and in *the purging of his soul*, line 85) only gives you a respite; you are like

KING (*rising*)

    My words fly up, my thoughts remain below.

    Words without thoughts never to heaven go.   *Exit*

       Enter the Queen and Polonius   III.4

POLONIUS

    'A will come straight. Look you lay home to him.

    Tell him his pranks have been too broad to bear with, ·

    And that your grace hath screened and stood between

    Much heat and him. I'll silence me even here.

    Pray you be round with him.

HAMLET (*within*) Mother, mother, mother!

QUEEN I'll warrant you. Fear me not. Withdraw. I hear

    him coming.

        Polonius hides behind the arras

        Enter Hamlet

HAMLET

    Now, mother, what's the matter?

QUEEN

    Hamlet, thou hast thy father much offended.   10

HAMLET

    Mother, you have my father much offended.

---

a sick man who takes medicine, but thereby only postpones the inevitable approach of death

97 *My words fly up, my thoughts remain below.* The King has been uttering the *words* of prayers, but has not been thinking about them. His mind has been busy with *thoughts* of his worldly affairs. So he has not been in a state of contrition.

III.4 This scene takes place in Gertrude's *closet* (III.2.339).

1 *lay home* talk severely

2 *broad* unrestrained

4 *heat* anger (of the court, and of the King in particular)

silence. This is the reading of both Q2 and F. Editors often accept the emendation 'sconce' (hide). But *silence* may be right, as a stroke of irony against the *foolish prating knave* who can only be *still* when dead (lines 215–16).

5 *round with* plain-spoken to

7 *Fear me not* do not doubt that I will do what you have suggested

9 *Now, mother* . . . Q1 makes Hamlet say 'but first weele make all safe'. This may be a genuine memory of a piece of stage business by which Hamlet bolts the door.

10 *thy father* your stepfather

QUEEN

Come, come, you answer with an idle tongue.

HAMLET

Go, go, you question with a wicked tongue.

QUEEN

Why, how now, Hamlet?

HAMLET   What's the matter now?

QUEEN

Have you forgot me?

HAMLET   No, by the Rood, not so!

You are the Queen, your husband's brother's wife,

And, would it were not so, you are my mother.

QUEEN

Nay, then I'll set those to you that can speak.

HAMLET

Come, come, and sit you down. You shall not budge.

20   You go not till I set you up a glass

Where you may see the inmost part of you.

QUEEN

What wilt thou do? Thou wilt not murder me?

Help, ho!

POLONIUS (behind)

What, ho! Help!

HAMLET (drawing his sword)

How now? A rat? Dead for a ducat, dead!

He makes a thrust through the arras and kills Polonius

---

12 *idle* foolish

15 *forgot me* forgotten that I am your
mother
the Rood Christ's Gross*a*

18 *I'll set those to you that can speak.* Presumably she rises, resentful of
Hamlet's insult.

21 *see the inmost part of you.* The Queen
interprets this as a threat of personal
violence. But Hamlet means merely
'see the bottom of your soul'.

23 *Help, ho!* That Hamlet behaves in a
way that genuinely frightens his
mother is suggested by the absurd
lines which the reporter of Q1 based
on his memory of the action: 'I first
bespake him faire, | But then he
throwes and tosses me about, | As
one forgetting that I was his mother'
(to the King at IV.1.8).

25 *Dead for a ducat* I would wager a
ducat that I have killed it

POLONIUS

O, I am slain!

QUEEN   O me, what hast thou done?

HAMLET

Nay, I know not. Is it the King?

QUEEN

O, what a rash and bloody deed is this!

HAMLET

A bloody deed – almost as bad, good mother,

As kill a king and marry with his brother.   30

QUEEN

As kill a king!

HAMLET   Ay, lady, it was my word.

He sees Polonius

Thou wretched, rash, intruding fool, farewell!

I took thee for thy better. Take thy fortune.

Thou findest to be too busy is some danger. –

Leave wringing of your hands. Peace, sit you down,

And let me wring your heart. For so I shall,

If it be made of penetrable stuff,

If damned custom have not brassed it so

That it be proof and bulwark against sense.

QUEEN

What have I done that thou darest wag thy tongue   40

In noise so rude against me?

HAMLET   Such an act

That blurs the grace and blush of modesty;

31 *As kill a king!* The Queen's amazement and horror both remind the
audience of the terrible nature of the
King's crime and confirm our impression of her innocence of any knowledge of it.

34 *busy* interfering (like a busy-body)

38 *damnèd custom* vice that has become
habitual. See Hamlet's lines on *that
monster custom* (162–71).
brassed. Q2 reads 'brasd', which prob-

ably indicates *brassed* 'hardened like
brass'. But F reads 'braz'd', which
makes it possible that 'brazed' ('made
brazen') is correct.

39 *proof* impenetrable
sense feeling

40 *wag* (not a ludicrous word) move

41 *act* (presumably incest; the accusation
of adultery is scarcely evidenced: see
the note to 1.5.42)

Calls virtue hypocrite; takes off the rose
From the fair forehead of an innocent love
And sets a blister there; makes marriage vows
As false as dicers' oaths; O, such a deed
As from the body of contraction plucks
The very soul, and sweet religion makes
A rhapsody of words! Heaven's face does glow,
50 Yea, this solidity and compound mass,
With heated visage, as against the Doom,
Is thought-sick at the act.

QUEEN   Ay me, what act,
That roars so loud and thunders in the index?

HAMLET
Look here upon this picture, and on this,

43 *Calls virtue hypocrite* makes all virtue
seem a mere pretence
43-4 *takes off the rose ... innocent love.*
Presumably he is thinking of his love
for Ophelia, and is summarizing his
interview with her at III.1.89-150.
Compare Laertes's language at
IV.5.120-22: *brands the harlot | ...
between the chaste unsmirchèd brows | Of
my true mother.*
45 *blister* mark made by the branding
iron. Criminals, including harlots,
were branded on the forehead.
47 *contraction* witnessed ceremony and
contract of marriage
48-9 *sweet religion makes | A rhapsody of
words* (probably referring to the marriage service; but Hamlet's attitude is
scarcely justified, for the vows undertaken are to last 'so long as ye both
shall live')
49 *rhapsody* medley of items strung together without meaningful order
words (merely, and nothing more)
glow blush
50 *this solidity and compound mass* (the
earth)
compound composed of the various
elements

51 *heated.* F has 'tristfull' ('sad'), which
many editors adopt.
as against the Doom as if the Day of
Judgement were at hand
52 *thought-sick* sick with horror
53 *index* table of contents (as in a book
– the index was formerly at the beginning, not at the end – and so 'prelude
to what you are going to say')
54 *upon this picture, and on this.* It is uncertain whether these are miniatures or
large pictures hanging on the wall.
Miniatures have generally been preferred; Hamlet wears one and his
mother another, and he can force her
to gaze upon them as he puts them
together. Moreover, two large pictures would be inconvenient stage
properties, quite apart from the
indecorum of the Queen's having
portraits of both her husbands in
her closet. Nevertheless, the pose
described in lines 55–63 would best
suit a full-length portrait; and in the
first illustration of this scene (in
Rowe's edition, 1709) wall portraits
(but half-lengths) are shown. Some
actors have preferred to suppose the
pictures to be in the mind's eye only,

The counterfeit presentment of two brothers.
See what a grace was seated on this brow:
Hyperion's curls, the front of Jove himself,
An eye like Mars, to threaten and command,
A station like the herald Mercury
New lighted on a heaven-kissing hill –   60
A combination and a form indeed
Where every god did seem to set his seal
To give the world assurance of a man.
This was your husband. Look you now what follows.
Here is your husband; like a mildewed ear,
Blasting his wholesome brother. Have you eyes?
Could you on this fair mountain leave to feed,
And batten on this moor? Ha! Have you eyes?
You cannot call it love. For at your age
The heyday in the blood is tame; it's humble,   70
And waits upon the judgement; and what judgement
Would step from this to this? Sense sure you have,
Else could you not have motion. But sure that sense
Is apoplexed. For madness would not err,

but *counterfeit presentment* (line 55) is
strongly against this.

55 *counterfeit presentment* presentation by
artistic portraiture

57 *Hyperion*. See the second note to
1.2.140.
front forehead

59 *station* stance
Mercury (the winged messenger of the
gods, and so an image of graceful
movement and poise)

60 *New lighted* newly alighted

61 *combination* (of the elements)

62 *every god did seem to set his seal*. This
seems to be a reminiscence of the
classical story of the creation of man,
in which each of the gods gave
something.

63 *assurance* confirmation

65 *ear* (of wheat)

66 *Blasting* blighting

67–8 *this fair mountain leave to feed,* | *And
batten on this moor*. The contrast is
difficult to explain. Presumably it is
suggested by *hill* (line 60) and *mildewed ear* (line 65). Neither mountains
nor moors (uncultivated highlands)
are especially attractive for sheep-
fattening. We should expect the
contrast to be between the healthful
pasturage on the hillsides and the
unhealthful pasturage in the rank
lower ground.

68 *batten* fatten (like sheep)

70 *heyday* time of wildness in youth
blood passion, sexual urge

71 *waits upon* obeys

72 *Sense*. The exact meaning is uncertain;
perhaps 'control of the senses', or
'ability to apprehend and distinguish', or 'sexual desire'.

74 *apoplexed* paralysed (as by a stroke)

Nor sense to ecstasy was ne'er so thralled
But it reserved some quantity of choice
To serve in such a difference. What devil was't
That thus hath cozened you at hoodman-blind?
Eyes without feeling, feeling without sight,
80   Ears without hands or eyes, smelling sans all,
Or but a sickly part of one true sense
Could not so mope.
     O shame, where is thy blush? Rebellious hell,
If thou canst mutine in a matron's bones,
To flaming youth let virtue be as wax
And melt in her own fire. Proclaim no shame
When the compulsive ardour gives the charge,
Since frost itself as actively doth burn,
And reason panders will.

QUEEN   O Hamlet, speak no more.
90   Thou turnest mine eyes into my very soul,
And there I see such black and grainèd spots
As will not leave their tint.

HAMLET   Nay, but to live
In the rank sweat of an enseamèd bed,
Stewed in corruption, honeying and making love
Over the nasty sty —

QUEEN   O, speak to me no more.

75 *ecstasy* madness
     thralled enslaved
76 *reserved some quantity* preserved some
     small element
78 *cozened you at hoodman-blind* tricked
     you in playing blind-man's buff (into
     choosing the very worst)
80 *sans all* without using any of the other
     senses
82 *so mope* behave so aimlessly
84 *mutine* make a mutiny
85–6 *be as wax | And melt in her own fire.*
     The image is probably of a stick of
     sealing-wax, which is ignited and

then nearly inverted so that drops of
the melting wax fall from it.
87 *charge* command (to go forward)
88 *frost* (of middle age)
89 *reason panders will* reason (the powers
     of judgement appropriate to middle
     age) acts as a pander to lust
91 *grainèd* deeply ingrained
92 *will not leave their tint* cannot have
     the stain washed out of them
93 *enseamèd* greasy
94 *Stewed* soaked. ('Stews' were
     brothels.)
95 *sty* (place like a pig-sty)

These words like daggers enter in mine ears.
No more, sweet Hamlet.

HAMLET   A murderer and a villain,
A slave that is not twentieth part the tithe
Of your precedent lord, a vice of kings,
A cutpurse of the empire and the rule,   100
That from a shelf the precious diadem stole
And put it in his pocket –

QUEEN   No more.

HAMLET
A king of shreds and patches –
        (*Enter the Ghost*)
Save me and hover o'er me with your wings,
You heavenly guards! – What would your gracious
        figure?

QUEEN
Alas, he's mad.

HAMLET
Do you not come your tardy son to chide,
That, lapsed in time and passion, lets go by
Th'important acting of your dread command?
O, say!   110

GHOST
Do not forget. This visitation

---

98 *tithe* tenth part
99 *precedent lord* previous husband
    vice of kings king who behaves like a
    buffoon (like the Vice in the Morality
    plays of the sixteenth century)
103 *of shreds and patches* (as if he were
    wearing the clown's motley)
    (stage direction) Q1 has '*Enter the
    ghost in his night gowne*' (i.e. dressing-
    gown), probably reflecting stage
    practice. It appears at the climax of
    Hamlet's tirade, presumably as he is

about to tell his mother the circumstances of the murder.
106 *he's mad.* It is clear from this and
    lines 125 and 133 that the Queen
    cannot see the Ghost.
108 *lapsed in time and passion* having
    allowed time to slip by and his
    passionate commitment to his task of
    revenge to cool (also sometimes inter-
    preted as 'deteriorated into mere
    emotion')
109 *important* urgent

Is but to whet thy almost blunted purpose.
But look, amazement on thy mother sits.
O, step between her and her fighting soul!
Conceit in weakest bodies strongest works.
Speak to her, Hamlet.

HAMLET   How is it with you, lady?

QUEEN

Alas, how is't with you,
That you do bend your eye on vacancy,
And with th'incorporal air do hold discourse?
120   Forth at your eyes your spirits wildly peep,
And, as the sleeping soldiers in th'alarm,
Your bedded hair like life in excrements
Start up and stand an end. O gentle son,
Upon the heat and flame of thy distemper
Sprinkle cool patience. Whereon do you look?

HAMLET

On him, on him! Look you, how pale he glares!
His form and cause conjoined, preaching to stones,
Would make them capable. – Do not look upon me,
Lest with this piteous action you convert
130   My stern effects. Then what I have to do

---

113 *amazement* distraction (at Hamlet's
  behaviour, not at the Ghost)
114 *fighting soul* mind in agony
115 *Conceit* imagination
118 *bend* aim
  vacancy space, thin air
119 *incorporal* incorporeal
120 *Forth ... peep* (that is, you look
  astonished)
121 *in th'alarm* when an alarm is
  sounded
122 *bedded* normally lying flat (like *soldiers* on their beds)
  hair. This is sometimes emended to
  'hairs', but the plural forms *Start*
  and *stand* may be influenced by *excrements*.

excrements outgrowths (hair grows
  out of the body, but has no independent *life*)
123 *an* on
127 *form and cause* physical appearance
  (which inspires pity) and the reason
  he has for appealing to us
  conjoined united
128 *capable* (of responding to what he
  said)
129 *this piteous action* these gestures (like
  an actor's) stirring pity
129–30 *convert | My stern effects* transform
  the results of my stern intentions

Will want true colour – tears perchance for blood.

QUEEN

To whom do you speak this?

HAMLET   Do you see nothing there?

QUEEN

Nothing at all. Yet all that is I see.

HAMLET

Nor did you nothing hear?

QUEEN   No, nothing but ourselves.

HAMLET

Why, look you there! Look how it steals away!

My father, in his habit as he lived!

Look where he goes, even now, out at the portal!

Exit the Ghost

QUEEN

This is the very coinage of your brain.

This bodiless creation ecstasy

Is very cunning in.

HAMLET   Ecstasy?   140

My pulse as yours doth temperately keep time

And makes as healthful music. It is not madness

That I have uttered. Bring me to the test,

And I the matter will re-word, which madness

Would gambol from. Mother, for love of grace,

Lay not that flattering unction to your soul,

That not your trespass but my madness speaks.

It will but skin and film the ulcerous place

Whiles rank corruption, mining all within,

---

131 *want true colour* lack its proper appearance (look pale and bloodless; with a
quibble on *colour* meaning 'motive')
tears . . . for blood shedding tears
instead of blood

136 *his habit as he lived* his familiar everyday clothing

138 *very coinage* complete invention

139 *This bodiless creation* this kind of

hallucination

139–40 *ecstasy | Is very cunning in* madness
is very skilful in creating

141 *temperately keep time* beat steadily

144 *re-word* repeat word for word

145 *gambol* capriciously lead me astray

146 *that flattering unction* the soothing
balm of that flattery

149 *mining* undermining

150   Infects unseen. Confess yourself to heaven.
         Repent what's past. Avoid what is to come;
         And do not spread the compost on the weeds
         To make them ranker. Forgive me this my virtue.
         For in the fatness of these pursy times
         Virtue itself of vice must pardon beg,
         Yea, curb and woo for leave to do him good.

    QUEEN
         O Hamlet, thou hast cleft my heart in twain.

    HAMLET
         O, throw away the worser part of it,
         And live the purer with the other half.
160   Good night. But go not to my uncle's bed.
         Assume a virtue, if you have it not.
         That monster custom, who all sense doth eat,
         Of habits devil, is angel yet in this,
         That to the use of actions fair and good
         He likewise gives a frock or livery
         That aptly is put on. Refrain tonight,
         And that shall lend a kind of easiness
         To the next abstinence; the next more easy;
         For use almost can change the stamp of nature,
170   And either master the devil or throw him out

151 *what is to come* further opportunities
    of sinful behaviour
154 *fatness* grossness
    pursy short-winded (and so in bad
    condition morally)
156 *curb* bow
    him (vice)
161 *Assume* acquire
162 *who all sense doth eat* which destroys
    all sensibility
163 *Of habits devil* being the evil genius
    of our habits. For *devil* many editors
    prefer the emendation 'evil'; the
    meaning is then 'custom, which de-
    prives one of all feeling for the evil
    nature of habits'.
    angel yet nevertheless our good

    genius
164 *use* habitual practice
165 *frock or livery* (new) dress or
    uniform
166 *aptly* easily
169 *stamp of nature* inborn characteristics
    of personality
170 *And either master the devil.* Q2 omits
    the verb, doubtless accidentally. (The
    passage is not in F.) The fourth
    quarto edition (1611) has 'And
    maister the devil'; and, although this
    quarto's changes have no known
    authority, the choice of this word to
    fill the gap could be due to stage
    practice. Other plausible suggestions
    are 'curb', 'lay', 'oust', 'quell',

With wondrous potency. Once more, good night.
And when you are desirous to be blest,
I'll blessing beg of you. For this same lord,
I do repent. But heaven hath pleased it so,
To punish me with this, and this with me,
That I must be their scourge and minister.
I will bestow him and will answer well
The death I gave him. So again good night.
I must be cruel only to be kind.
This bad begins, and worse remains behind.   180
One word more, good lady.

QUEEN   What shall I do?

HAMLET

Not this, by no means, that I bid you do:
Let the bloat King tempt you again to bed,
Pinch wanton on your cheek, call you his mouse,
And let him, for a pair of reechy kisses,
Or paddling in your neck with his damned fingers,
Make you to ravel all this matter out,
That I essentially am not in madness,
But mad in craft. 'Twere good you let him know.
For who that's but a queen, fair, sober, wise,   190

'shame', or 'tame', or to replace *either* by 'exorcize'. Perhaps, however, the use of *either . . . or* demands a word contrasting with *throw . . . out*, such as 'aid', 'house', or 'speed'.

172–3 *when you are desirous to be blest, | I'll blessing beg of you* that is, I shall not ask for your blessing (as a son would normally do on departure) until you are repentant and seek God's blessing

174 *heaven hath pleased it so* such has been the will of heaven. Hamlet seems to transfer the responsibility for Polonius's death to Providence.

175 *this* (Polonius's corpse)

176 *scourge and minister* both the lash which inflicts punishment and the officer who administers it

177 *bestow* put away somewhere
answer account for

179 *only to be kind* (purely to fulfil my filial love for my father and to effect a reformation of character in you)

180 *This bad begins* this calamity (the killing of Polonius) is a beginning of trouble

183 *bloat* bloated

184 *wanton* wantonly
mouse (a common term of endearment)

185 *reechy* dirty (literally, 'smoky')

186 *paddling* playing wantonly

187 *ravel . . . out* disentangle, make clear

188 *essentially* in my essential nature

189 *in craft* by cunning
'Twere good (sarcastic)

Would from a paddock, from a bat, a gib,
Such dear concernings hide? Who would do so?
No, in despite of sense and secrecy,
Unpeg the basket on the house's top.
Let the birds fly, and like the famous ape,
To try conclusions, in the basket creep
And break your own neck down.

QUEEN

Be thou assured, if words be made of breath,
And breath of life, I have no life to breathe
200   What thou hast said to me.

HAMLET

I must to England. You know that?

QUEEN   Alack,
I had forgot. 'Tis so concluded on.

HAMLET

There's letters sealed, and my two schoolfellows,
Whom I will trust as I will adders fanged,
They bear the mandate. They must sweep my way
And marshal me to knavery. Let it work.
For 'tis the sport to have the enginer

191 *paddock* toad
    gib tom-cat
192 *Such dear concernings* matters that con-
    cern his so closely
193 *sense and secrecy* instinct and your
    impulse towards secrecy
194-7 *Unpeg the basket ... down.* This
    story is not known from any other
    source. It can be reconstructed as fol-
    lows: an ape steals a wickerwork cage
    (*basket*) of birds and carries it to the
    top of a house. Out of curiosity, or
    by accident, he releases the pegs of
    the cage, and the birds fly out. The
    ape is prompted to imitate them; he
    creeps into the basket and then leaps
    out, supposing that he will be able
    to fly like the birds. But, of course,
    he falls to the ground and breaks his
    neck.

Hamlet's application of the fable
is as follows: if you reveal my secrets
to the King, you will be like this
ape. You will gain nothing by it; and
if you imagine you can act with the
King as cleverly as I can, independently of me, you will be like the ape
trying to fly, and so will come to grief.
196 *try conclusions* see what will happen
197 *down* in the fall
205 *mandate* command
    sweep my way prepare the way for
    me (literally, sweep a path before
    me)
206 *marshal me to knavery* conduct me
    into some trap. Hamlet guesses that
    the King is plotting some treachery.
    work go forward
207 *enginer* maker of military 'engines'

Hoist with his own petar; and't shall go hard
But I will delve one yard below their mines
And blow them at the moon. O, 'tis most sweet   210
When in one line two crafts directly meet.
This man shall set me packing.
I'll lug the guts into the neighbour room.
Mother, good night. Indeed, this counsellor
Is now most still, most secret, and most grave,
Who was in life a foolish prating knave.
Come, sir, to draw toward an end with you.
Good night, mother.

> *Exeunt Hamlet, tugging in Polonius, and the Queen*

Enter the King and Queen, with Rosencrantz and   IV.I
Guildenstern

KING
There's matter in these sighs. These profound heaves
You must translate. 'Tis fit we understand them.
Where is your son?

QUEEN
Bestow this place on us a little while.

208 *Hoist* hoisted (here, 'blown up')
     petar bomb
208-9 *'t shall go hard | But I will delve* it
     will be unlucky if I don't succeed in
     delving
209-10 *delve one yard . . . moon.* Hamlet
     imagines that, like the garrison of a
     besieged town whose walls have been
     mined, he will dig a counter-mine
     below the attackers' mine and so
     blow them up.
211 *in one line two crafts directly meet* (like
     mining and counter-mining). Per-
     haps Hamlet is quibbling on *crafts*
     meaning 'ships'.

212 *set me packing* make me start plotting
     (with a quibble on the other meaning,
     'cause me to be sent away quickly')
217 *draw toward an end with you* conclude
     my conversation with you (who were
     such a *prating* fellow)

IV.I As there is clearly no real lapse of
     time between this and the previous
     scene, the traditional act division is un-
     reasonable; but it is preserved here for
     readers' convenience.
1 *matter* significance
     heaves heavy sighs
2 *translate* explain

Exeunt Rosencrantz and Guildenstern

Ah, mine own lord, what have I seen tonight!

KING

What, Gertrude? How does Hamlet?

QUEEN

Mad as the sea and wind when both contend
Which is the mightier. In his lawless fit,
Behind the arras hearing something stir,
10 Whips out his rapier, cries 'A rat, a rat!'
And in this brainish apprehension kills
The unseen good old man.

KING   O, heavy deed!

It had been so with us, had we been there.
His liberty is full of threats to all,
To you yourself, to us, to everyone.
Alas, how shall this bloody deed be answered?
It will be laid to us, whose providence
Should have kept short, restrained, and out of haunt
This mad young man. But so much was our love,
20 We would not understand what was most fit,
But, like the owner of a foul disease,
To keep it from divulging let it feed
Even on the pith of life. Where is he gone?

QUEEN

To draw apart the body he hath killed;
O'er whom his very madness, like some ore
Among a mineral of metals base,
Shows itself pure. 'A weeps for what is done.

---

10 *Whips* he whips
11 *brainish apprehension* headstrong illusion
12 *heavy* grievous
13 *us ... we* (the royal plural. Claudius knows that the blow was intended for him.)
16 *answered* explained
17 *laid to* blamed upon
    providence foresight
18 *short* under control

out of haunt away from public places
22 *divulging* becoming known in public
25 *O'er whom his very madness* over which his madness itself
    ore vein of gold
26 *mineral of metals base* mine of nonprecious metals
27 *'A weeps* (probably an invention of Gertrude's to palliate Hamlet's conduct)

KING

O Gertrude, come away!
The sun no sooner shall the mountains touch
But we will ship him hence; and this vile deed   30
We must with all our majesty and skill
Both countenance and excuse. Ho, Guildenstern!

Enter Rosencrantz and Guildenstern

Friends both, go join you with some further aid.
Hamlet in madness hath Polonius slain,
And from his mother's closet hath he dragged him.
Go seek him out. Speak fair. And bring the body
Into the chapel. I pray you haste in this.

Exeunt Rosencrantz and Guildenstern

Come, Gertrude, we'll call up our wisest friends
And let them know both what we mean to do
And what's untimely done. So haply slander,   40
Whose whisper o'er the world's diameter
As level as the cannon to his blank
Transports his poisoned shot, may miss our name
And hit the woundless air. O, come away!
My soul is full of discord and dismay.   *Exeunt*

Enter Hamlet   IV.2

HAMLET Safely stowed.
GENTLEMEN (*within*) Hamlet! Lord Hamlet!

29 *The sun . . . touch* (a reminder that it is still the middle of the night)
32 *countenance* assume responsibility for
40 *So haply slander.* There is a gap in the Q2 text here (F omits the whole sentence). Some extra words are needed for both metre and sense. Those printed here, proposed by eighteenth-century editors, seem more satisfactory than other suggestions.
41 *the world's diameter* the extent of the world from side to side
42 *level* straight
     his blank its point of aim (the 'white' in the middle of the target)
44 *woundless* invulnerable

IV.2 Again, no time elapses between this and the previous scene.
1 *Safely stowed.* By hiding the body, Hamlet makes his murder of Polonius seem to be an act of madness.

HAMLET
But soft, what noise? Who calls on Hamlet?
O, here they come.

Enter Rosencrantz, Guildenstern, and attendants

ROSENCRANTZ
What have you done, my lord, with the dead body?

HAMLET
Compounded it with dust, whereto 'tis kin.

ROSENCRANTZ
Tell us where 'tis, that we may take it thence
And bear it to the chapel.

HAMLET Do not believe it.

10 ROSENCRANTZ Believe what?

HAMLET That I can keep your counsel and not mine own.
Besides, to be demanded of a sponge, what replication
should be made by the son of a king?

ROSENCRANTZ Take you me for a sponge, my lord?

HAMLET Ay, sir, that soaks up the King's countenance,
his rewards, his authorities. But such officers do the
King best service in the end. He keeps them, like an ape
an apple, in the corner of his jaw, first mouthed, to be

---

6 *Compounded it with dust* (hardly true; Hamlet has only *stowed* it in a cupboard on the stairs: IV.3.35–6)
Compounded. Shakespeare normally accents this word on the first syllable, so Q2's 'Compound' may be correct.

11 *I can keep your counsel and not mine own.* Hamlet's riddling speech is as baffling to us as to Rosencrantz. Perhaps *counsel* means 'secret', and Hamlet is referring to his not betraying their confession at II.2.292 that they had been *sent for*. His own *counsel* (or 'secret') is the whereabouts of the body.

12 *to be demanded of* on being questioned by
replication (a legal term) reply

15 *countenance* favour

16 *his authorities* the exercise of his powers. Doubtless Hamlet is speaking scornfully of their position of new authority over him.

17–18 *like an ape an apple.* F's reading is 'like an Ape'; Q2 has 'like an apple'. Each gives only a very strained meaning. Q1 transfers this conversation to follow III.2.379 and reads 'hee doth keep you as an Ape doth nuttes, | In the corner of his Iaw, first mouthes you, | Then swallowes you.' It is tempting to adopt the clear reading of Q1 ('as an ape doth nuts'). But it seems most likely that the Q2 and F readings are each a confusion of *like an ape an apple.*

18 *first* at first
mouthed taken into the mouth

last swallowed. When he needs what you have gleaned,
it is but squeezing you and, sponge, you shall be dry   20
again.

ROSENCRANTZ I understand you not, my lord.

HAMLET I am glad of it. A knavish speech sleeps in a
foolish ear.

ROSENCRANTZ My lord, you must tell us where the body
is, and go with us to the King.

HAMLET The body is with the King, but the King is not
with the body. The King is a thing –

GUILDENSTERN A thing, my lord?

HAMLET Of nothing. Bring me to him. Hide fox, and all   30
after.   *Exeunt*

Enter the King and two or three attendants   IV.3

KING

I have sent to seek him and to find the body.
How dangerous is it that this man goes loose!
Yet must not we put the strong law on him.
He's loved of the distracted multitude,

19 *last* at last

23–4 *A knavish speech sleeps in a foolish ear*
a sarcastic remark is wasted upon an
unintelligent hearer

27–8 *The body is ... body.* Hamlet may
mean 'the body is now in the next
world with the King (my father
Hamlet), but King Claudius has not
yet been killed.' Or he may be talking
deliberate, sinister nonsense.

28–30 *The King is a thing ... Of nothing.*
Again Hamlet is using suggestive
threatening language, echoing the
passage in the Psalms about the trans-
itoriness of mortal life: 'Man is like
a thing of nought. His time passeth
away like a shadow' (144.4; Prayer
Book version). Claudius is doomed

to death.

30–31 *Hide fox, and all after.* These
words in F are not in Q2, and may
be an interpolation to introduce a bit
of exit business, such as Hamlet's
eluding his captors and running off
stage. This has become common
theatrical practice, but is not justified
by Hamlet's entry at IV.3.15. The
words probably refer to some children's game of hide-and-seek.

IV.3 (stage direction) *attendants* (presumably a group of counsellors or supporters, perhaps the *wisest friends* of IV.1.38)

4 *of* by

distracted unreasonable, unstable

Who like not in their judgement but their eyes;
And where 'tis so, th'offender's scourge is weighed,
But never the offence. To bear all smooth and even,
This sudden sending him away must seem
Deliberate pause. Diseases desperate grown
10   By desperate appliance are relieved,
Or not at all.

       Enter Rosencrantz, Guildenstern, and all the rest
       How now? What hath befallen?

ROSENCRANTZ

Where the dead body is bestowed, my lord,
We cannot get from him.

KING   But where is he?

ROSENCRANTZ

Without, my lord; guarded, to know your pleasure.

KING

Bring him before us.

ROSENCRANTZ   Ho! Bring in the lord.

       Enter attendants with Hamlet

KING Now, Hamlet, where's Polonius?

HAMLET At supper.

KING At supper? Where?

HAMLET Not where he eats, but where 'a is eaten. A cer-
20   tain convocation of politic worms are e'en at him. Your

---

5 *like not in* choose not by

6 *scourge* punishment. Claudius supposes
that the people will not allow Hamlet
to be punished for murdering
Polonius.

7 *bear all smooth and even* conduct the
affair so as not to give offence or
seem high-handed

9 *Deliberate pause* the result of deliberately and unhurriedly considering the
matter

9–11 *Diseases desperate grown ... at all* (a
proverbial idiom, which occurs in
the form 'A desperate disease must
have a desperate cure')

10 *appliance* remedies

11 (stage direction) *all the rest* (probably,
in Shakespeare's theatre, any extras
who could be spared to stand in as
courtiers)

20 *convocation of politic worms*. There is
doubtless a punning allusion to the
Diet of Worms (a city on the Rhine),
opened by the Emperor (see line 21)
Charles V in 1521, which brought
together the dignitaries of the Roman
Empire.
convocation parliament
politic crafty
e'en even now

worm is your only emperor for diet. We fat all creatures else to fat us, and we fat ourselves for maggots. Your fat king and your lean beggar is but variable service – two dishes, but to one table. That's the end.

KING Alas, alas!

HAMLET A man may fish with the worm that hath eat of a king, and eat of the fish that hath fed of that worm.

KING What dost thou mean by this?

HAMLET Nothing but to show you how a king may go a progress through the guts of a beggar.   30

KING Where is Polonius?

HAMLET In heaven. Send thither to see. If your messenger find him not there, seek him i'th'other place yourself. But if indeed you find him not within this month, you shall nose him as you go up the stairs into the lobby.

KING (*to attendants*) Go seek him there.

HAMLET 'A will stay till you come.   *Exeunt attendants*

KING
  Hamlet, this deed, for thine especial safety,
  Which we do tender as we dearly grieve   40
  For that which thou hast done, must send thee hence
  With fiery quickness. Therefore prepare thyself.
  The bark is ready and the wind at help,
  Th'associates tend, and everything is bent
  For England.

21 *fat* fatten
23 *but variable service* just different courses of a meal
30 *progress* (the usual word for a monarch's official journeys through his kingdom)
35 *nose* smell
39 *thine especial safety.* Claudius is presumably referring to possible retribution upon Hamlet by Polonius's son or friends rather than to Hamlet's judicial prosecution for murder.

49 *tender* feel concern for
   dearly keenly
42 *With fiery quickness* as quickly as spreading flames
43 *at help* ready to help
44 *associates* companions (Rosencrantz and Guildenstern)
   tend await you
   bent prepared (like a drawn bow)

HAMLET For England?

KING Ay, Hamlet.

HAMLET Good.

KING

So is it, if thou knewest our purposes.

50   HAMLET I see a cherub that sees them. But come, for
England! Farewell, dear mother.

KING Thy loving father, Hamlet.

HAMLET My mother. Father and mother is man and wife;
man and wife is one flesh; and so, my mother. Come,
for England!   *Exit*

KING

Follow him at foot. Tempt him with speed aboard.
Delay it not. I'll have him hence tonight.
Away! For everything is sealed and done
That else leans on the affair. Pray you make haste.
                                    Exeunt all but the King

60   And, England, if my love thou holdest at aught –
As my great power thereof may give thee sense,
Since yet thy cicatrice looks raw and red
After the Danish sword, and thy free awe
Pays homage to us – thou mayst not coldly set
Our sovereign process, which imports at full,

---

50 *cherub* (a heavenly spirit with exceptional powers of vision: Ezekiel 1.18
and 10.12)

54 *man and wife is one flesh.* Hamlet ironically uses the language of the marriage service.

56 *at foot* close behind him

58 *everything is sealed and done.* Claudius is
here referring ostensibly to *the demand
of our neglected tribute* (III.1.171) but,
in his thoughts, to the letters ordering *The present death of Hamlet* (lines
66–7). There is an emphasis on the
secrecy of these instructions.
Hamlet has to *unseal | Their grand*

commission at v.2.17–18 and seal
the new one with his *father's signet*
(v.2.49).

59 *leans* depends

60 *England* (probably) King of England

61 *As* for so
   thereof may give thee sense may well
   give you a just appreciation of the
   importance of that love

62 *cicatrice* scar

63 *free awe* awe of us which is still felt
   though without military occupation

64 *coldly set* set a low value upon

65 *sovereign process* royal instructions
   imports at full calls in detail for

By letters congruing to that effect,
The present death of Hamlet. Do it, England.
For like the hectic in my blood he rages,
And thou must cure me. Till I know 'tis done,
Howe'er my haps, my joys were ne'er begun.   *Exit*   70

FORTINBRAS
Go, captain, from me greet the Danish King.
Tell him that by his licence Fortinbras
Craves the conveyance of a promised march
Over his kingdom. You know the rendezvous.
If that his majesty would aught with us,
We shall express our duty in his eye.
And let him know so.

CAPTAIN   I will do't, my lord.

FORTINBRAS Go softly on.   *Exeunt all but the Captain*

66 *congruing* agreeing. Claudius seems to
be referring to a second letter with
more explicit instructions. Nothing
further is made of this. F reads 'con-
iuring' ('earnestly requesting'), which
would correspond to *earnest conjuration* (v.2.38).

67 *present* immediate

68 *hectic* persistent fever

70 *Howe'er my haps* whatever my fortunes
may be
were ne'er begun. This is the F reading.
Q2 reads 'will nere begin', which is
perhaps better grammar, but fails to
rhyme.

IV.4 (stage direction) *Fortinbras*. We
have not heard about old Norway and
Fortinbras since II.2.60–80. The vigour
of Fortinbras, like that of Laertes, is an
adverse reflection upon Hamlet's inactivity, as he himself recognizes (lines 46–

53).

3 *the conveyance of* escort during
promised previously agreed
(II.2.80–82, where a favourable
answer to the Norwegian request is
implied)

5–6 *If that his majesty . . . eye.* Fortinbras
expresses his respect for the King of
Denmark and accepts his authority,
in accordance with the vow (shown
now to be sincere) he had given to
his uncle (II.2.70–71).

5 *would aught* wishes to have any
communication

6 *in his eye* by presenting myself (*us*, the
royal plural) personally before him

8 *Go softly on.* This is probably addressed
to his troops, not to the Captain.
softly slowly, leisurely (perhaps;
but the word seems to imply the
respectful march of the army through
the Danish territory)

*Enter Hamlet, Rosencrantz, Guildenstern and
attendants*

HAMLET Good sir, whose powers are these?

10 CAPTAIN They are of Norway, sir.

HAMLET How purposed, sir, I pray you?

CAPTAIN Against some part of Poland.

HAMLET Who commands them, sir?

CAPTAIN

The nephew to old Norway, Fortinbras.

HAMLET

Goes it against the main of Poland, sir,
Or for some frontier?

CAPTAIN

Truly to speak, and with no addition,
We go to gain a little patch of ground
That hath in it no profit but the name.

20 To pay five ducats, five, I would not farm it;
Nor will it yield to Norway or the Pole
A ranker rate, should it be sold in fee.

HAMLET

Why, then the Polack never will defend it.

CAPTAIN

Yes, it is already garrisoned.

HAMLET

Two thousand souls and twenty thousand ducats

---

9 *powers* troops

15 *main* central part

16 *frontier* frontier-fortress

17 *addition* fine words to exaggerate the matter

19 *name* (reputation for having conquered it)

20 *five ducats, five.* The repeated numeral emphasizes its smallness: it would not be worth paying an annual rent of a mere five ducats (a coin worth about nine shillings) for the lease of the land as a farm.

22 *ranker rate* higher rate of interest (on the purchase money)

in fee as a freehold property

25-6 *Two thousand souls ... straw.* It has been plausibly suggested that these two lines belong to the Captain, who is in a better position to speak of *Two thousand* and *twenty thousand* than is Hamlet. Perhaps the repetition of *straw* in line 55 supports this.

25 *Two thousand souls* (his estimate of the size of the armies involved)

twenty thousand ducats (his estimate of the expenditure on the war)

Will not debate the question of this straw.
This is th'imposthume of much wealth and peace,
That inward breaks, and shows no cause without
Why the man dies. I humbly thank you, sir.

CAPTAIN

God bye you, sir.   *Exit*

ROSENCRANTZ   Will't please you go, my lord?   30

HAMLET

I'll be with you straight. Go a little before.

Exeunt all but Hamlet

How all occasions do inform against me
And spur my dull revenge! What is a man,
If his chief good and market of his time
Be but to sleep and feed? A beast, no more.
Sure He that made us with such large discourse,
Looking before and after, gave us not
That capability and godlike reason
To fust in us unused. Now, whether it be
Bestial oblivion, or some craven scruple   40

---

26 *Will not debate the question* are not
enough to settle the dispute
straw trivial matter

27 *imposthume* abscess. The consequences
of the luxury of society and its vices
accumulate unperceived during
peace, like the pus in a swollen
abscess.

28 *inward . . . without* internally . . . externally (of the body)

32–66 *How all occasions . . . worth.* The
importance of this soliloquy is that it
enables Hamlet to make a strong
impression on the audience before
his long absence, and gives a reassurance that he is still true to his oath of
vengeance. It is the most 'reasonable'
of his soliloquies, and is probably
intended to reveal his developing
maturity.

32 *occasions* (such dissimilar chance meet-
ings as with the players and with this
Norwegian army)
inform against me denounce me,
provide evidence to my discredit (as
in a law-suit)

34 *market* profitable employment

36 *large discourse* wide-ranging faculty of
understanding

37 *Looking before and after* able to review
the past and to use experience as a
guide in facing the future

38 *capability* capacity of mind
godlike (because shared with the
Creator Himself)

39 *fust* go mouldy

40 *Bestial oblivion* animal-like inability to
retain past impressions
craven scruple cowardly scrupulous-
ness

Of thinking too precisely on th'event –
A thought which, quartered, hath but one part wisdom
And ever three parts coward – I do not know
Why yet I live to say 'This thing's to do',
Sith I have cause, and will, and strength, and means
To do't. Examples gross as earth exhort me.
Witness this army of such mass and charge,
Led by a delicate and tender prince,
Whose spirit, with divine ambition puffed,
Makes mouths at the invisible event,
Exposing what is mortal and unsure
To all that fortune, death, and danger dare,
Even for an eggshell. Rightly to be great
Is not to stir without great argument,
But greatly to find quarrel in a straw
When honour's at the stake. How stand I then,
That have a father killed, a mother stained,
Excitements of my reason and my blood,
And let all sleep, while to my shame I see
The imminent death of twenty thousand men
That for a fantasy and trick of fame

41-3 *thinking . . . coward.* Anxiety about
the precise consequences of one's actions is due to cowardice much more
than to prudence (a remarkably unil-
lusioned analysis by Hamlet of his
own feelings and motives).
41 *event* outcome
44 *to do* still to be done
45 *Sith* since
46 *gross* weighty
47 *mass and charge* size and expense
49 *puffed* (not necessarily derogatory)
swollen
50 *Makes mouths at* scorns
52 *dare* could inflict upon him
53-6 *Rightly to be . . . stake* true greatness
does not consist in rushing into
action on account of any trivial
cause; but when the cause is one
involving honour, it is noble to act,
however trivial the subject of dispute
may be
54 *argument* cause
55 *greatly* nobly
58 *Excitements* incentives
blood passions
60 *twenty thousand men.* Hamlet has con-
fusedly transferred the number of
ducats in line 25 to the men (who
were then only *Two thousand*).
61 *trick of fame* whim of seeking fame.
Probably *of fame* goes with both *fantasy* and *trick.*

Go to their graves like beds, fight for a plot
Whereon the numbers cannot try the cause,
Which is not tomb enough and continent
To hide the slain? O, from this time forth,
My thoughts be bloody, or be nothing worth!   *Exit*

Enter the Queen, Horatio, and a Gentleman   IV.5

QUEEN
I will not speak with her.

GENTLEMAN
She is importunate, indeed distract.
Her mood will needs be pitied.

QUEEN   What would she have?

GENTLEMAN
She speaks much of her father; says she hears
There's tricks i'th'world, and hems, and beats her heart,
Spurns enviously at straws, speaks things in doubt
That carry but half sense. Her speech is nothing.
Yet the unshapèd use of it doth move
The hearers to collection. They aim at it,

---

62 *plot* (of ground)
63 *Whereon the numbers cannot try the cause* where there is not enough space for the two armies to fight out the dispute
64 *continent* receptacle (that is, earth to cover the bodies of those who are killed in battle)
66 *thoughts.* He speaks only of *thoughts*, not of deeds.

IV.5 There is clearly a considerable lapse of time between the previous scene and the opening of this.
1 *I will not speak with her.* The Queen is reluctant to see her son's beloved, the daughter of the man he has murdered.
2 *distract* distracted
3 *mood will needs be* mental condition

cannot fail to be
5 *hems.* She makes a noise like 'hmm', confirming her knowledge that *There's tricks i'th'world.*
6 *Spurns* (with her foot)
   enviously spitefully
   straws trifles
   in doubt ambiguous
7 *Her speech is nothing* she talks nonsense
8 *unshapèd* uncontrolled
9 *to collection* to gather something of a meaning
   aim at it make a guess at its meaning. This is the F reading ('ayme'). Q2 has 'yawne', which can hardly be right, though in an appropriate context 'yawn' can mean 'let the mouth gape open with surprise'.

10 And botch the words up fit to their own thoughts,
Which, as her winks and nods and gestures yield them,
Indeed would make one think there might be thought,
Though nothing sure, yet much unhappily.

HORATIO
'Twere good she were spoken with, for she may strew
Dangerous conjectures in ill-breeding minds.

QUEEN
Let her come in.   *Exit the Gentleman*
(*Aside*) To my sick soul, as sin's true nature is,
Each toy seems prologue to some great amiss.
So full of artless jealousy is guilt
20 It spills itself in fearing to be spilt.

                 Enter Ophelia

OPHELIA
Where is the beauteous majesty of Denmark?
QUEEN How now, Ophelia?
OPHELIA (*sings*)
         How should I your true-love know
         From another one?

---

10 *botch* patch clumsily
fit to their own thoughts to suit their own inferences (about her state of mind and the meaning she is trying to convey)
11 *Which* (her words)
yield them deliver (interpret) her words
13 *nothing* not at all
much unhappily very unskilfully
15 *Dangerous conjectures* (about the murder of Polonius and ill-treatment of herself)
16 *Let her come in.* Q2 attributes these words to Horatio. If this were retained, the Queen must give some silent assent to Horatio's request.
17 *as sin's true nature is* (that is, as is characteristic of someone in a state of sin)

18 *toy* trifling event. Apparently she does not yet take Ophelia's madness as a serious thing.
amiss misfortune
19 *artless jealousy* uncontrolled suspicion
20 *spills* reveals and destroys
(stage direction) Q1 has '*Enter Ofelia playing on a Lute, and her haire downe singing*'. This doubtless is a memory of a performance.
21 *Where is the beauteous majesty of Denmark?* This may mean merely 'Where is the Queen?', or possibly 'Where has your queenly beauty gone?' (addressed to the Queen, who, now conscience-ridden, may be looking very different from the happy woman of the scenes up to III.4)
23–40 *How should I . . . showers.* In these snatches of ballads Ophelia seems to

By his cockle hat and staff
And his sandal shoon.

QUEEN
Alas, sweet lady, what imports this song?

OPHELIA Say you? Nay, pray you, mark.
(*sings*) He is dead and gone, lady.
He is dead and gone.   30
At his head a grass-green turf,
At his heels a stone.

O, ho!

QUEEN Nay, but, Ophelia —

OPHELIA Pray you, mark.
(*sings*) White his shroud as the mountain snow —
Enter the King

QUEEN Alas, look here, my lord.

OPHELIA (*sings*)
Larded all with sweet flowers,
Which bewept to the ground did not go
With true-love showers.   40

KING How do you, pretty lady?

---

be confusing recollections of her lost lover with her dead father. They hint that the cause of her madness is not only her father's death but her estrangement from Hamlet and his banishment. Shakespeare does not reveal whether she knows that Hamlet killed her father. Her song to the Queen about *your true-love* and *another one* may seem to hint at the difference between her first and second husbands. The next two stanzas remind the Queen of the death of King Hamlet as well as of Polonius. For the music of Ophelia's songs see F. W. Sternfeld's *Music in Shakespearean Tragedy* (London, 1963).

25 *cockle hat*. A hat with a cockle-shell on it signified that the wearer had made a pilgrimage to the shrine of St James at Compostela (in north-west Spain), famous medieval place of pilgrimage.

staff pilgrim's walking-staff

26 *shoon* (archaic plural) shoes

28 *Say you?* what do you say?

38 *Larded* garnished

39 *ground*. F and Q1 read '*graue*' ('grave'), which many editors prefer.
did not go. It has been suggested that the original song had 'did go' (which would give an easier rhythm) and that Ophelia inserts *not* because of her father's not having received an adequate funeral ceremony (*In hugger-mugger to inter him*, line 85 below).

40 *showers* (of tears)

OPHELIA Well, God dild you! They say the owl was a baker's daughter. Lord, we know what we are, but know not what we may be. God be at your table!

KING Conceit upon her father –

OPHELIA Pray let's have no words of this, but when they ask you what it means, say you this:

(*sings*) Tomorrow is Saint Valentine's day,
All in the morning betime,
50   And I a maid at your window
To be your Valentine.

Then up he rose and donned his clothes,
And dupped the chamber door;
Let in the maid, that out a maid
Never departed more.

KING Pretty Ophelia!

OPHELIA Indeed, la, without an oath, I'll make an end on't.

42 *God dild* may God reward ('yield')

42–3 *They say the owl was a baker's daughter.* This may refer to a folk-tale in which Christ begged for a loaf of bread and punished the baker's daughter, who insisted on his being given only a small one, by transforming her into an owl. Perhaps Ophelia is trying to say that she knows she is changed from what she was but is not so badly done by as that other wicked daughter.

43–4 *we know ... may be.* Presumably this is a comment on the transformation of the baker's daughter.

44 *God be at your table!* Perhaps the emphasis is on *your*: 'The benediction before eating may save you from such a fate as that of the inhospitable baker's daughter.'

45 *Conceit upon her father* – these imaginings of hers about her father – (Clau-

dius is interrupted by Ophelia). Or perhaps this is an aside, spoken in anxiety about what Ophelia may reveal. Or it may be addressed to the Queen, a kind of warning about her son's dangerous violence.

48–67 *Tomorrow is ... bed.* The song seems to be prompted by her imagining herself to have been disobedient to her father about associating with Hamlet.

48 *Saint Valentine's day.* 14 February, when the birds choose their mates, according to popular tradition. There were also folk-customs: the first girl seen by a man was his 'Valentine'.

49 *betime* early

53 *dupped* opened (by lifting *up* the latch)

57 *la* (a very mild substitute for an oath)

57–8 *make an end on't* finish the song (in spite of its immodesty)

(sings) By Gis and by Saint Charity,
    Alack, and fie for shame!   60
  Young men will do't if they come to't.
    By Cock, they are to blame.

  Quoth she, 'Before you tumbled me,
    You promised me to wed.'
He answers:
    'So would I ha' done, by yonder sun,
    An thou hadst not come to my bed.'

KING How long hath she been thus?

OPHELIA I hope all will be well. We must be patient. But
I cannot choose but weep to think they would lay him   70
i'th'cold ground. My brother shall know of it. And so I
thank you for your good counsel. Come, my coach!
Good night, ladies, good night. Sweet ladies, good
night, good night.   *Exit*

KING

Follow her close. Give her good watch, I pray you.

                                 Exit Horatio

O, this is the poison of deep grief. It springs
All from her father's death – and now behold!
O Gertrude, Gertrude,
When sorrows come, they come not single spies,

59 *Gis* Jesus
  Saint Charity (the personification of the virtue)
62 *Cock* God (probably with a quibble on the popular name for the penis)
63 *tumbled me* took my virginity
72 *Come, my coach!* Perhaps she imagines herself to be a stately princess or Hamlet's queen.
73 *ladies . . . Sweet ladies.* The only female present is the Queen (unless she has attendants).
75 *Follow her . . . you.* There is no indica-

tion whom the King is addressing; but except for Gertrude (and, possibly, unspecified attendants) Horatio is the only other character on stage, and editors usually leave the King and Queen alone for their obviously private conversation.
76–7 *It springs | All from her father's death.* Claudius does not consider – or wish Gertrude to consider – that Ophelia's love for Hamlet has anything to do with her madness.

80   But in battalions: first, her father slain;
        Next, your son gone, and he most violent author
        Of his own just remove; the people muddied,
        Thick and unwholesome in their thoughts and whispers
        For good Polonius' death, and we have done but greenly
        In hugger-mugger to inter him; poor Ophelia
        Divided from herself and her fair judgement,
        Without the which we are pictures or mere beasts;
        Last, and as much containing as all these,
        Her brother is in secret come from France,
90   Feeds on his wonder, keeps himself in clouds,
        And wants not buzzers to infect his ear
        With pestilent speeches of his father's death,
        Wherein necessity, of matter beggared,
        Will nothing stick our person to arraign
        In ear and ear. O my dear Gertrude, this,
        Like to a murdering-piece, in many places

81 *author* originator
82 *remove* removal
    muddied turbulent with suspicion
    (stirred up, as a pool of water be-
    comes muddy)
83 *Thick and unwholesome* (like bad
    blood)
    whispers malicious gossip
84 *greenly* in an inexperienced way
85 *In hugger-mugger* with haste and in se-
    crecy. The King could not allow an
    inquiry into the circumstances of
    Polonius's death, exposing Hamlet's
    guilt; for he knows that Hamlet has
    the secret of the fratricide. To the
    Queen he must pretend that his ac-
    tions are prompted by a desire to
    protect Hamlet from the conse-
    quences of his crime.
87 *pictures or mere beasts* (that is, lacking
    a soul)
88 *as much containing* quite as important
89 *come from France*. This indicates the
    passage of some time since the night

of Polonius's death and the morning
of Hamlet's departure (IV.4).
90 *Feeds on his wonder* nurses his shocked
    grievance (perhaps). For *his* Q2 reads
    'this', which is even more difficult; it
    can hardly refer to Ophelia's distrac-
    tion (and in any case it is implied
    that Laertes does not know of it
    until he sees her at line 155); and the
    hugger-mugger funeral of Polonius is
    grammatically too far away to be re-
    ferred to by 'this'.
    keeps himself in clouds holds himself
    sullenly aloof
91 *wants* lacks
    buzzers rumour-mongers
93-4 *Wherein necessity ... arraign* in this
    gossip, as the speakers have nothing
    definite to go on, they are obliged to
    invent things and so do not scruple
    to spread accusations against me
95 *In ear and ear* in many ears one after
    the other
96 *murdering-piece* (mortar or cannon

Gives me superfluous death.

    A noise within

QUEEN

Alack, what noise is this?

KING

Attend. Where is my Switzers? Let them guard the
    door.

    Enter a Messenger

What is the matter?

MESSENGER   Save yourself, my lord.   100

The ocean, overpeering of his list,

Eats not the flats with more impiteous haste

Than your Laertes, in a riotous head,

O'erbears your officers. The rabble call him lord,

And, as the world were now but to begin,

Antiquity forgot, custom not known,

The ratifiers and props of every word,

They cry 'Choose we! Laertes shall be king!'

which scattered a variety of lethal small shot and pieces of metal instead of a single shot)

99 *Attend* (a call to his guards, imagined as just off stage)

  Switzers. Swiss mercenary soldiers were employed in many European courts to form a royal bodyguard (they survive in the Vatican). Their mention here implies that Claudius is usually well guarded; so Hamlet's task is not easy.

101 *overpeering of* rising above

  list boundary, barrier (perhaps the shore)

102 *Eats not the flats.* Shakespeare is doubtless thinking of the advancing tide of such places as the Essex coast and the Thames estuary, where it moves a considerable distance in a short time.

  impiteous. Probably this is another form of 'impetuous', influenced by the meaning of the word 'piteous'.

But perhaps Shakespeare uses it to mean 'pitiless'.

103 *head* onset

104 *officers* household servants and guards

105 *as the world were now but to begin* as if civilized life were only now to be created (instead of having been in existence from time immemorial)

107 *The ratifiers and props of every word.* Traditional practices, inherited from earlier times, are the things which give authority and stability to society. This leisurely comment hardly suits the excited tone of the speech. Editors have often emended *word*. It may mean 'pledge, honourable undertakings according to promise', or 'oath of allegiance', or 'title of rank'. But all these interpretations are strained.

108 *Choose we! Laertes shall be king!* Claudius had intimated that Hamlet was the people's favourite (IV.3.4–5). The

Caps, hands, and tongues applaud it to the clouds:
110   'Laertes shall be king! Laertes king!'

A noise within

QUEEN

How cheerfully on the false trail they cry!
O, this is counter, you false Danish dogs!

KING

The doors are broke.

Enter Laertes with his followers

LAERTES

Where is this King? – Sirs, stand you all without.

HIS FOLLOWERS

No, let's come in.

LAERTES   I pray you give me leave.

HIS FOLLOWERS

We will, we will.

LAERTES

I thank you. Keep the door.   *Exeunt his followers*
                                   O thou vile King,

Give me my father.

QUEEN   Calmly, good Laertes.

fickleness of the *multitude* is illustrated by their support for Laertes when the opportunity is offered. The demand *Choose we!* is remarkable. It implies that the election of Claudius was an oligarchic move, not a popular one. But Laertes soon comes to terms with Claudius, and this hint of a democratic revolt is immediately forgotten.

109 *Caps* (which they wave or throw into the air)

111 *How cheerfully on the false trail they cry!* Gertrude, with unusual bitterness of language, imagines the intruders as a pack of baying hounds pursuing a false scent (*false* because the King is not guilty of Polonius's murder).

112 *counter* hunting the trail backwards (like hounds going in the direction contrary to the game). The Danes elected Claudius as their king, and now are going back on their oaths of allegiance.

you false Danish dogs! Presumably Shakespeare took it for granted that the queen-consort of the monarch was a foreigner.

false perfidious

117 *Keep* guard

118 *Give me my father.* Apparently Laertes does not yet know that it was Hamlet who killed Polonius.

LAERTES

That drop of blood that's calm proclaims me bastard,
Cries cuckold to my father, brands the harlot   120
Even here between the chaste unsmirchèd brows
Of my true mother.

KING   What is the cause, Laertes,
That thy rebellion looks so giant-like?
Let him go, Gertrude. Do not fear our person.
There's such divinity doth hedge a king
That treason can but peep to what it would,
Acts little of his will. Tell me, Laertes,
Why thou art thus incensed. Let him go, Gertrude.
Speak, man.

LAERTES

Where is my father?

KING   Dead.

QUEEN   But not by him.   130

KING

Let him demand his fill.

LAERTES

How came he dead? I'll not be juggled with.
To hell allegiance! Vows to the blackest devil!
Conscience and grace to the profoundest pit!
I dare damnation. To this point I stand,
That both the worlds I give to negligence,

121 *the chaste unsmirchèd brows.* See the note to III.4.43–4.
122 *true* faithful in marriage
124 *fear our* fear for my royal
125 *divinity* (alluding to the doctrine of kings as divine representatives on earth, the Lord's anointed). Claudius's brave assertion of this doctrine in order to intimidate Laertes comes ironically from one who is himself a regicide.
hedge protect as with a rampart
126 *peep to.* Claudius's language belittles

the power of treason by supposing it to peer furtively out of, or over, its hiding place or *hedge*.
127 *Acts little of his will* (and) performs little of what it intends
132 *juggled with* deceived
134 *grace* the grace of God
135 *To this point I stand* I have gone so far as this
136 *both the worlds I give to negligence* I care nothing of what happens to me in this world or the next

Let come what comes, only I'll be revenged
Most throughly for my father.

KING   Who shall stay you?

LAERTES

My will, not all the world's.

140   And for my means, I'll husband them so well
They shall go far with little.

KING   Good Laertes,
If you desire to know the certainty
Of your dear father, is't writ in your revenge
That, swoopstake, you will draw both friend and foe,
Winner and loser?

LAERTES

None but his enemies.

KING   Will you know them then?

LAERTES

To his good friends thus wide I'll ope my arms
And like the kind life-rendering pelican
Repast them with my blood.

KING   Why, now you speak

150   Like a good child and a true gentleman.

---

138 *throughly* thoroughly
139 *My will, not all the world's* nothing in
the world shall stop me, except my
own decision (when my desire for
revenge is satisfied)
140–41 *for my means ... little* I will
employ my resources so econom-
ically that I shall be able to make
them go a long way
142–3 *certainty | Of* truth about
143 *writ* specified
144 *swoopstake* (a gambling term used
when a winner took the stakes of all
his opponents)
draw take from
148 *life-rendering* giving life to its young.

The pelican was supposed to feed its
young with the blood that flowed
from self-inflicted wounds upon its
breast. No one, as far as I can discover, has yet suggested that
Laertes, with his arms stretched out
in the form of a cross and with the
blood flowing from his wounded
breast, is a Christ figure. Yet the
religious metaphor seems clear:
Laertes's image of himself feeding
his father's friends with his own
blood is offensive bombast, typical
of the man.
149 *Repast* feed

That I am guiltless of your father's death,
And am most sensibly in grief for it,
It shall as level to your judgement 'pear
As day does to your eye.
          A noise within

VOICES (*within*)   Let her come in.

LAERTES

How now? What noise is that?
          Enter Ophelia
O heat, dry up my brains! Tears seven times salt
Burn out the sense and virtue of mine eye!
By heaven, thy madness shall be paid with weight
Till our scale turn the beam. O rose of May,
Dear maid, kind sister, sweet Ophelia!   160
O heavens, is't possible a young maid's wits
Should be as mortal as an old man's life?
Nature is fine in love, and where 'tis fine,
It sends some precious instance of itself
After the thing it loves.

---

152 *most sensibly* with very intense feeling

153 *level* plain (like a path on the level)
'pear appear. Q2 reads 'peare', which some editors have interpreted as 'peer'. F reads 'pierce'.

155 (stage direction) *Enter Ophelia*. Presumably Ophelia behaves in such a way as reveals immediately to Laertes that she is mad. It is not clear whether she still carries her lute or whether she now has a bunch of flowers instead. Perhaps it is intended that she has gone to collect the flowers for her father's grave (lines 178–85). Q1 has '*Enter Ofelia as before*', but this may refer only to her madness. In her first speech in Q1 she says 'I a bin gathering of floures'.

156 *heat, dry up my brains*. Laertes is prob-

ably referring to his own fiery anger.

157 *Burn out the sense and virtue* (let scalding tears) destroy the sense and power

158 *paid with weight* paid for in full measure

159 *our scale turn the beam*. (His revenge will weigh heavier than Ophelia's madness.)
beam horizontal bar of a balance
rose of May. The English wild rose first flowers in May; Ophelia is in her early bloom.

163–5 *Nature is fine ... loves* filial love is, by nature, very sensitive; and such is its sensitivity that it sends some most precious token of itself to the object of its love – in this case, Ophelia's sanity departs with her father Polonius. Laertes's language is typically strained. These three lines are not in Q2.

OPHELIA *(sings)*

> They bore him barefaced on the bier,
>   Hey non nony, nony, hey nony,
>   And in his grave rained many a tear –
> Fare you well, my dove!

LAERTES

170   Hadst thou thy wits, and didst persuade revenge,
    It could not move thus.

OPHELIA You must sing 'A-down a-down, and you call
    him a-down-a.' O, how the wheel becomes it! It is the
    false steward, that stole his master's daughter.

LAERTES This nothing's more than matter.

OPHELIA There's rosemary, that's for remembrance.
    Pray you, love, remember. And there is pansies, that's
    for thoughts.

169 *my dove* (perhaps Laertes)

171 *move thus* persuade me as strongly as
your madness does

172–3 *A-down a-down, and you call him a-
down-a.* Perhaps Ophelia is thinking
of Polonius as having been called
down to his grave, and therefore says
that this is a preferable refrain to *Hey
non nony* ... It is possible that the
correct reading is 'You must sing
"A-down a-down", and you call him
a-down-a' (if you refer to Polonius
as being dead).

173 *wheel.* Perhaps the spinning-wheel,
to which she imagines she is singing
the song; or perhaps *wheel* means
'refrain' ('how appropriate is that
refrain "A-down a-down" to my
song of woe!'); or perhaps it is a
movement in her dance.

173–4 *the false steward, that stole his
master's daughter.* This story (perhaps

a ballad) is unknown. It may be that
the three lines sung by Ophelia at 166–
8 above are from the ballad, of which
she is here giving the title or subject.

175 *This nothing's more than matter* this
nonsense has more significance than
any coherent sense could have

176–85 Presumably these flowers are dis-
tributed by Ophelia to be taken to
her father's undecked grave. We can
only guess who are the recipients,
nor do we know whether the flowers
are intended to be real or fantasies of
Ophelia's disordered brain.

176–8 *rosemary ... for remembrance ...
pansies ... for thoughts.* These are probably gifts to a lover. Perhaps she
imagines Laertes to be her lover, and
gives these flowers to him.

177–8 *pansies ... thoughts.* The name
comes from French *pensées.*

LAERTES A document in madness: thoughts and re-
membrance fitted.   180

OPHELIA There's fennel for you, and columbines. There's
rue for you, and here's some for me. We may call it
herb of grace o'Sundays. O, you must wear your rue
with a difference. There's a daisy. I would give you some
violets, but they withered all when my father died. They
say 'a made a good end.

     (sings) For bonny sweet Robin is all my joy.

LAERTES

Thought and afflictions, passion, hell itself,
She turns to favour and to prettiness.

OPHELIA *(sings)*

     And will 'a not come again?   190
     And will 'a not come again?
     No, no, he is dead.

179 *document in madness* something from which one can gain instruction in the study of madness

179–80 *thoughts and remembrance fitted.* By *thoughts* Laertes probably means 'melancholy thoughts': 'she appropriately brings together melancholy and memories (of happier things)'.

181 *fennel* suggests flattery and *columbines* ingratitude or marital infidelity. Perhaps these are given to the King.

182 *rue.* Perhaps she gives this to the Queen, as suggesting contrition, and then to herself, as suggesting sorrow.

183 *herb of grace o'Sundays.* As 'herb (of) grace' is an ordinary name for *rue*, the idea that such a pious-sounding name is appropriate for use on Sunday seems to be a mere fancy.

184 *with a difference.* The heraldic phrase refers to an alteration or addition to a coat of arms to distinguish one branch of a family from another. But it is only remotely, if at all, applied here: the rue has a different signifi-

cance for each of the wearers.
daisy (the flower of dissembling; perhaps given to the Queen)

185 *violets.* These represent faithfulness in love, and Ophelia now has none to give. Perhaps in her fantasy she gives them to Hamlet – all faith in love has disappeared after the murder of Polonius.

185–6 *They say 'a made a good end.* If she is thinking of Polonius, the statement is strikingly untrue; he was killed suddenly, with no opportunity for contrition and for receiving the sacraments.

187 *For bonny sweet Robin ... joy.* The words of this song, probably relating to Robin Hood, are lost; but the tune, which was exceptionally popular, survives.

188 *Thought* gloomy thought
passion suffering
hell itself (presumably 'torment of soul')

189 *favour* beauty

Go to thy deathbed.
He never will come again.

His beard was as white as snow,
All flaxen was his poll.
He is gone, he is gone,
And we cast away moan.
God 'a' mercy on his soul!
200   And of all Christian souls, I pray God. God bye you.

Exit

LAERTES
Do you see this? O God!

KING
Laertes, I must commune with your grief,
Or you deny me right. Go but apart,
Make choice of whom your wisest friends you will,
And they shall hear and judge 'twixt you and me.
If by direct or by collateral hand
They find us touched, we will our kingdom give,
Our crown, our life, and all that we call ours,
To you in satisfaction. But if not,
210   Be you content to lend your patience to us,
And we shall jointly labour with your soul

196 *flaxen was his poll* his head was pale
  like flax
198 *cast away moan* are wasting our time
  in grieving
201 *Do you see this? O God!* Q2 reads
  'Doe you this ô God'. F reads 'Do
  you see this, you Gods?' F's 'Gods'
  is unsuitable in a Christian play, especially immediately after Ophelia's
  exit-line; but its *see* is probably right.
  There is no punctuation in Q2 to
  help us decide whether Laertes, in an
  expostulatory tone, is asking God to
  observe what is going on here on
  earth ('Do you see this, O God?') or
  whether he is making two broken-
hearted utterances, first a general
appeal and then an anguished interjection. On the whole the second seems
more likely. Perhaps *you* refers to the
King, who responds.

202 *commune with your grief* have your
  grief in common with you
  commune (accented on the first
  syllable)
204 *whom* whichever among
206 *collateral hand* indirect agency
207 *touched* infected with guilt (of the
  murder of Polonius)
209 *in satisfaction* as recompense
210 *lend your patience to us* be patient for
  a while at my request

To give it due content.

LAERTES   Let this be so.
His means of death, his obscure funeral –
No trophy, sword, nor hatchment o'er his bones,
No noble rite nor formal ostentation –
Cry to be heard, as 'twere from heaven to earth,
That I must call't in question.

KING   So you shall.
And where th'offence is, let the great axe fall.
I pray you go with me.   *Exeunt*

Enter Horatio and a Gentleman   IV.6

HORATIO
What are they that would speak with me?

GENTLEMAN Seafaring men, sir. They say they have
letters for you.

HORATIO
Let them come in.   *Exit the Gentleman*
I do not know from what part of the world
I should be greeted if not from Lord Hamlet.
    Enter Sailors

---

213 *His means of death* the manner of
Polonius's death
obscure (accented on the first
syllable)
214 *trophy, sword . . . hatchment.* Memorial
emblems, such as the knightly sword
and the coat of arms, accompanied
the coffin in the funeral procession.
The *hatchment* (or 'achievement') was
an escutcheon blazoning the arms of
the dead person. Many of these old
painted escutcheons still hang in
churches in England
215 *ostentation* ceremony
217 *That* so that
call't in question demand an explanation of it

218 *where th'offence is, let the great axe fall.*
The Queen can hardly fail to hear
this threat to Hamlet. But Claudius
is doubtless thinking of his secret
instructions to the King of England
not to stay the grinding of the axe but
Hamlet's *head should be struck off*
(v.2.24–5). He comes to terms with
Laertes for his own safety. Not until
IV.7.43 does the news come that
Hamlet, contrary to expectations, is
returning to Elsinore; and then Claudius sees the advantages of allying
himself with Laertes against Hamlet.

IV.6.6 *greeted* addressed in a letter

SAILOR God bless you, sir.

HORATIO Let him bless thee, too.

SAILOR 'A shall, sir, an't please him. There's a letter for
you, sir – it came from th'ambassador that was bound
for England – if your name be Horatio, as I am let to
know it is.

HORATIO (*reads the letter*) *Horatio, when thou shalt have
overlooked this, give these fellows some means to the King.
They have letters for him. Ere we were two days old at sea,
a pirate of very warlike appointment gave us chase. Finding ourselves too slow of sail, we put on a compelled valour,
and in the grapple I boarded them. On the instant they got
clear of our ship. So I alone became their prisoner. They
have dealt with me like thieves of mercy. But they knew
what they did. I am to do a good turn for them. Let the
King have the letters I have sent, and repair thou to me
with as much speed as thou wouldst fly death. I have words
to speak in thine ear will make thee dumb. Yet are they
much too light for the bore of the matter. These good fellows will bring thee where I am. Rosencrantz and Guildenstern hold their course for England. Of them I have much
to tell thee. Farewell.*

      He that thou knowest thine,

                                         Hamlet

Come, I will give you way for these your letters,

10 *th'ambassador.* The sailor does not name Hamlet, presumably as a disguise. He can hardly be unaware of his identity.

14 *overlooked* looked over
   means (of access)

16 *appointment* equipment

17 *put on a compelled valour* decided to assume an appearance of courage, because we had no alternative

20 *of mercy* merciful. There seems to be a slight allusion to the thieves crucified with Christ, as is supported by the phraseology of *they knew what they did.*

20–21 *knew what they did* (were aware that Hamlet was a prince, who would have influence to get them pardoned if they treated him well)

22 *repair* come

25 *much too light for the bore of the matter* weak in comparison with the importance of the matter, like a small projectile in a gun with a *large bore*

26 *will bring thee where I am.* This may suggest that Hamlet is in hiding, but the idea is not developed.

31 *I will give you way for these your letters.* Compare IV.7.39–41.

And do't the speedier that you may direct me
To him from whom you brought them.   *Exeunt*

Enter the King and Laertes   IV.7

KING
Now must your conscience my acquittance seal,
And you must put me in your heart for friend,
Sith you have heard, and with a knowing ear,
That he which hath your noble father slain
Pursued my life.
LAERTES   It well appears. But tell me
Why you proceeded not against these feats
So criminal and so capital in nature,
As by your safety, greatness, wisdom, all things else,
You mainly were stirred up.
KING   O, for two special reasons,
Which may to you perhaps seem much unsinewed,   10
But yet to me they're strong. The Queen his mother
Lives almost by his looks, and for myself —
My virtue or my plague, be it either which —

IV.7 This scene continues the talk between the King and Laertes which was
broken off at the end of IV.5. In the
interval, the King has been able to give
Laertes an account (which the audience
does not need) of Hamlet's misdeeds.
1 *my acquittance seal* confirm my acquittal
(as guiltless of the misdeeds you had
attributed to me)
3 *with a knowing ear.* (Laertes is an intelligent listener, says the ingratiating
King.)
6 *feats* deeds
7 *capital* punishable by death
8 *your safety* your care for your own
safety
greatness. This word is omitted in F,
probably in order to reduce the line

to ten syllables.
wisdom political prudence
9 *mainly* strongly
two special reasons. The King omits
the really powerful reason: if he
were to take public proceedings
against Hamlet for the murder of
Polonius, Hamlet would be likely to
reveal the fratricide. The King is
confident in dealing with Laertes because he expects shortly to receive
from England the news of Hamlet's
death.
10 *unsinewed* without strength
13 *My virtue or my plague, be it either which*
whether it is a good side of my
character or a serious misfortune
(that I have these feelings contrary
to my self-interest)

She is so conjunctive to my life and soul
That, as the star moves not but in his sphere,
I could not but by her. The other motive
Why to a public count I might not go
Is the great love the general gender bear him,
Who, dipping all his faults in their affection,
20 Work like the spring that turneth wood to stone,
Convert his gyves to graces; so that my arrows,
Too slightly timbered for so loud a wind,
Would have reverted to my bow again,
And not where I had aimed them.

LAERTES

And so have I a noble father lost,
A sister driven into desperate terms,
Whose worth, if praises may go back again,
Stood challenger, on mount, of all the age
For her perfections. But my revenge will come.

14 *conjunctive* closely united (also an astronomical term, and so leading to the image in the next line)
15 *the star moves not but in his sphere.* In astronomy before Copernicus, the earth, at the centre of the universe, was believed to be surrounded by a series of hollow transparent concentric spheres. On the surface of each a planet was fixed. The sphere revolved around the earth and carried the planet with it.
16 *I could not but by her* (because she is, as it were, my sphere, and with her motion I move) I could not live without her
17 *count* trial
18 *general gender* common people
20 *Work* act
    the spring that turneth wood to stone. Several of these lime-laden springs, able to 'petrify' (with a limestone

deposit) objects placed in them, were known in Shakespeare's time.
21 *Convert his gyves to graces* would make the fetters he wore as a prisoner seem to be emblems of his personal honour
22 *Too slightly timbered for* too light in weight to be effective in
    loud (suggesting popular clamour on Hamlet's behalf)
23 *reverted* returned
26 *desperate terms* a condition of despair
27 *if praises may go back again* if one may praise what has been and is now no more
28 *Stood challenger . . . of all the age* was able to challenge all competitors in the world nowadays
on mount conspicuously, for all to see. An alternative reading is 'challenger-on-mount' ('a challenger mounted and ready in the lists'), but this usage is difficult to parallel.

KING

    Break not your sleeps for that. You must not think   30
    That we are made of stuff so flat and dull
    That we can let our beard be shook with danger,
    And think it pastime. You shortly shall hear more.
    I loved your father, and we love ourself,
    And that, I hope, will teach you to imagine –
        Enter a Messenger with letters
    How now? What news?

MESSENGER   Letters, my lord, from Hamlet.
    These to your majesty. This to the Queen

KING

    From Hamlet? Who brought them?

MESSENGER

    Sailors, my lord, they say. I saw them not.
    They were given me by Claudio. He received them   40
    Of him that brought them.

KING   Laertes, you shall hear them. –
    Leave us.   *Exit the Messenger*
        (He reads)
    High and mighty, you shall know I am set naked on your
    kingdom. Tomorrow shall I beg leave to see your kingly

---

30 *Break not your sleeps for that.* Laertes need not worry about taking vengeance for his father's murder, for the King has already arranged for Hamlet's death. He is, up to this point, only concerned with pacifying Laertes, not with arousing him to revenge.

32 *let our beard be shook with danger* allow such insulting behaviour to come close to me

33 *You shortly shall hear more.* Claudius has in mind the news he expects of Hamlet's execution in England. But soon quite different news arrives.

37 *This to the Queen.* No more is heard of this letter.

40 *Claudio* (an odd name for Shakespeare to use, as the King's name is Claudius)

41 *you shall hear them.* The King is showing off his confidence in Laertes, and his openness: he will read the letter without previously examining its contents.

43 *naked* (without resources, or unarmed, rather than without clothes)

44 *Tomorrow.* The time-scheme of the play scarcely allows this. Some interval of time is assumed between the end of this scene and v.1, allowing for the inquest on Ophelia. See the headnote to v.1.

eyes; when I shall, first asking your pardon thereunto,
recount the occasion of my sudden and more strange return.

Hamlet

What should this mean? Are all the rest come back?
Or is it some abuse, and no such thing?

LAERTES

Know you the hand?

50 KING   'Tis Hamlet's character. 'Naked'!
And in a postscript here, he says 'alone'.
Can you devise me?

LAERTES

I am lost in it, my lord. But let him come.
It warms the very sickness in my heart
That I shall live and tell him to his teeth
'Thus didest thou'.

KING   If it be so, Laertes –
As how should it be so? How otherwise? –
Will you be ruled by me?

LAERTES   Ay, my lord,
So you will not o'errule me to a peace.

KING

60 To thine own peace. If he be now returned,

---

46 *more strange* (than *sudden*)
48 *What should this mean?* The King receives the news with consternation,
as it shows that his English plot has
failed. But Laertes is delighted.
all the rest (Rosencrantz, Guildenstern, and others in the party for
England)
49 *abuse* deception
50 *character* handwriting
51 *alone.* Perhaps Hamlet is avoiding suspicion of having raised support for
himself.
52 *devise me* explain it for me. The King
is surprised, but is thinking rapidly,
and by line 58 has made up his mind
about his next move.
53 *lost in* perplexed at

56 *didest.* Q2 has 'didst', possibly a misreading of 'diest'.
it (Hamlet's return, rather than
Laertes's impulse to revenge)
57 *how should it be so? How otherwise?*
The King is almost incredulous of
Hamlet's return, yet the evidence of
the letter is strong.
58 *Will you be ruled by me?* The King has
recovered his equilibrium. Now he
must stir Laertes to revenge against
Hamlet.
59 *So you will not* provided that you do
not
60 *thine own peace* (peace of mind
achieved by taking full vengeance,
not the 'reconciliation' rejected by
Laertes in the previous line)

As checking at his voyage, and that he means
No more to undertake it, I will work him
To an exploit now ripe in my device,
Under the which he shall not choose but fall;
And for his death no wind of blame shall breathe,
But even his mother shall uncharge the practice
And call it accident.

LAERTES   My lord, I will be ruled;
The rather if you could devise it so
That I might be the organ.

KING   It falls right.
You have been talked of since your travel much,   70
And that in Hamlet's hearing, for a quality
Wherein they say you shine. Your sum of parts
Did not together pluck such envy from him
As did that one, and that, in my regard,
Of the unworthiest siege.

LAERTES   What part is that, my lord?

KING
A very riband in the cap of youth,
Yet needful too, for youth no less becomes
The light and careless livery that it wears
Than settled age his sables and his weeds,
Importing health and graveness. Two months since,   80

---

61 *As checking at* because he has turned
aside from (like a hawk swerving
aside from its prey and pursuing
some inferior object)
that if
63 *ripe in my device* matured in my
invention
66 *uncharge the practice* be unable to make
any accusation as a consequence of
our plot (or 'not suspect a plot')
69 *organ* agent
72 *Your sum of parts* all your talents put
together
75 *siege* rank
76 *A very riband in the cap of youth* a

typical accomplishment of a young
man, like a ribbon worn as an ornament in his hat
77 *needful* (it being a necessary accomplishment for a man to defend himself with his sword)
no less becomes is no less suited by
78 *livery* garments
79 *his sables and his weeds* its (dark) fur-
lined garments
80 *Importing health* indicating a care for
health (or perhaps health means 'prosperity' in general: 'giving an impression of being well-to-do')

Here was a gentleman of Normandy.
I have seen myself, and served against, the French,
And they can well on horseback. But this gallant
Had witchcraft in't. He grew unto his seat,
And to such wondrous doing brought his horse
As had he been incorpsed and demi-natured
With the brave beast. So far he topped my thought
That I, in forgery of shapes and tricks,
Come short of what he did.

LAERTES   A Norman was't?

KING

90   A Norman.

LAERTES

Upon my life, Lamord.

KING   The very same.

LAERTES

I know him well. He is the brooch indeed
And gem of all the nation.

KING

He made confession of you,
And gave you such a masterly report
For art and exercise in your defence,

81 *Normandy*. As the play is vaguely set
    in late Anglo-Saxon times, the intro-
    duction of a Norman is appropriate
    enough.
83 *can well* are very skilful
84 *in't* (in his horsemanship)
86 *As had he* as if he had
86–7 *incorpsed and demi-natured | With the
    . . . beast* grown to have one body
    with the horse, and so half-man and
    half-beast. Shakespeare is doubtless
    thinking of the centaurs.
87 *topped my thought* surpassed my
    estimate
88–9 *I, in forgery of shapes and tricks, |
    Come short of what he did* whatever I
    am able to describe as figures and

tricks (in managing a horse), he ex-
    ceeded in actual execution
91 *Lamord*. F reads '*Lamound*', which
    editors often spell as '*Lamond*'. If
    Lamord is accurate, it is curiously
    ominous (*mort*, 'death'), especially
    when accompanied by the oath *Upon
    my life*.
92–3 *brooch . . . gem* ornament . . . jewel
94 *made confession of you* felt compelled,
    although he was a Frenchman, to
    acknowledge the truth about you
95 *masterly report* report of your masterly
    skill
96 *For art and exercise in your defence* in
    respect of your knowledge and skil-
    ful practice in the use of your sword

And for your rapier most especial,
That he cried out 'twould be a sight indeed
If one could match you; the scrimers of their nation
He swore had neither motion, guard, nor eye,   100
If you opposed them. Sir, this report of his
Did Hamlet so envenom with his envy
That he could nothing do but wish and beg
Your sudden coming o'er to play with you.
Now, out of this —

LAERTES   What out of this, my lord?

KING

Laertes, was your father dear to you?
Or are you like the painting of a sorrow,
A face without a heart?

LAERTES   Why ask you this?

KING

Not that I think you did not love your father,
But that I know love is begun by time,   110
And that I see, in passages of proof,
Time qualifies the spark and fire of it.

---

99 *one could match you* an equal opponent
could be found for you
scrimers (pronounced to rhyme
with 'rhymers') fencers
100 *motion* attack (as distinct from *guard*,
'parrying')
101–4 *this report ... with you.* There is
no other mention in the play of
Hamlet's envy of Laertes. It sounds
like a ruse of Hamlet, giving himself
an excuse for improving his swordsmanship. Or perhaps the actor can
convey that the whole thing is an
invention of the King's. Compare
*Since he went into France I have been in
continual practice* (V.2.204–5).
104 *sudden* immediate
play fence
you. Grammatically we might have
expected 'him' (which is, in fact, the
F reading).

109–22 This discourse of the King on
the effects of time upon will-power
is an interesting and ironical comment on Hamlet's situation. Hamlet
had given his view of the matter at
IV.4.32–66, and had acknowledged
to the Ghost that he, *lapsed in time
and passion, lets go by | The important
acting of your dread command*
(III.4.108–9). Claudius seems, moreover, to be repeating the assertion
of the Player-King in III.2.198–225,
that *Purpose is but the slave to
memory.*
110 *love is begun by time* circumstances
give rise to love (and they change)
111 *in passages of proof* by definite incidents that prove the truth of what I
am saying
112 *qualifies* moderates

There lives within the very flame of love
A kind of wick or snuff that will abate it,
And nothing is at a like goodness still;
For goodness, growing to a pleurisy,
Dies in his own too-much. That we would do
We should do when we would. For this 'would' changes,
And hath abatements and delays as many
120   As there are tongues, are hands, are accidents.
And then this 'should' is like a spendthrift sigh,
That hurts by easing. But to the quick o'th'ulcer –
Hamlet comes back. What would you undertake
To show yourself in deed your father's son
More than in words?

LAERTES   To cut his throat i'th'church!

KING

No place, indeed, should murder sanctuarize.

---

114 *snuff*. The image is that of a candle; the *snuff* is the charred part of the candle wick, which, if neglected, spoils and eventually puts out the flame.

115 *is at a like goodness still* remains at the same constant level of goodness

116 *pleurisy* excess. The word is spelt 'plurisy' in the early texts, by association with Latin *plus*, 'more', and not with Greek *pleura*, 'rib', from which is derived modern 'pleurisy', inflammation of the pleura (coverings of the lungs).

117 *his* its

117–18 *That we would do | We should do when we would* when we want to do something, we should do it immediately we know we want to do it

119 *abatements* diminutions of energy

120 *As there are tongues, are hands, are accidents* as the ways in which we are influenced by what people say, and by what they help us to do or restrain us from doing, and by the mere chances of life

121–2 *this 'should' is like a spendthrift sigh, | That hurts by easing* a sigh is a relief to our feelings, though it also harms us (alluding to the belief that with every sigh a drop of blood was lost); likewise, when we say 'I know what I ought to do', it may ease the conscience but the self-reproach also weakens our will-power. (This is the probable explanation of a difficult passage.)

122 *the quick o'th'ulcer* (that is, the main point)

124–5 *in deed . . . More than in words* (contrasting with Hamlet)

125 *cut his throat i'th'church.* Laertes's words contrast strongly with Hamlet's unwillingness to kill the King while he was at his prayers (III.3.73–96).

126 *No place . . . should murder sanctuarize* for a murderer (such as Hamlet) there should be no rights of sanctuary; so there would be no objection to your killing him anywhere, even in church

Revenge should have no bounds. But, good Laertes,
Will you do this: keep close within your chamber?
Hamlet returned shall know you are come home.
We'll put on those shall praise your excellence   130
And set a double varnish on the fame
The Frenchman gave you; bring you in fine together,
And wager on your heads. He, being remiss,
Most generous, and free from all contriving,
Will not peruse the foils, so that with ease,
Or with a little shuffling, you may choose
A sword unbated, and, in a pass of practice,
Requite him for your father.
LAERTES   I will do't,
And for that purpose I'll anoint my sword.
I bought an unction of a mountebank,   140
So mortal that, but dip a knife in it,
Where it draws blood no cataplasm so rare,

127 *Revenge should have no bounds*. This is
   Hamlet's doctrine, expounded by
   him at III.3.73–96.
128 *keep close within your chamber*. Presumably the King is guarding against the
   possibility that Hamlet might win
   Laertes over to his side.
130 *We'll put on those shall praise* I will
   arrange that some persons shall
   praise
132 *fine* conclusion
133 *remiss* careless (as not expecting any
   treachery)
134 *Most generous, and free from all contriving*. Claudius is not speaking the
   truth, for he knows that Hamlet has
   already engaged in a complicated con-
   trivance, *The Mousetrap*.
135 *foils* (blunt-edged swords with buttons on the point for use in fencing)
136 *a little shuffling* some little trick of
   substitution
137 *unbated* without a button on the
   point

in a pass of practice. This probably
   means 'in making a treacherous thrust
   at him', rather than 'while playing a
   practice-bout' or than 'while making
   a pass in which you are well practised'. But perhaps the King is deliberately ambiguous.
139–47 Part of the treacherous plan
   comes from Laertes; in Q1 the proposal to poison the sword comes
   from the King himself. This may
   represent what happened in a performance earlier than the Q2 text,
   the change being intended to indicate
   the deterioration of Laertes under
   the King's influence. At V.2.307–14
   Laertes does not confess that the en-
   venoming of the sword was his own
   idea.
140 *unction* ointment
   of a mountebank from a quack doctor
   (or itinerant drug-seller)
142 *cataplasm* poultice

Collected from all simples that have virtue
Under the moon, can save the thing from death
That is but scratched withal. I'll touch my point
With this contagion, that, if I gall him slightly,
It may be death.

KING   Let's further think of this,
Weigh what convenience both of time and means
May fit us to our shape. If this should fail,
And that our drift look through our bad performance,
'Twere better not assayed. Therefore this project
Should have a back or second, that might hold
If this did blast in proof. Soft, let me see.
We'll make a solemn wager on your cunnings –
I ha't!
When in your motion you are hot and dry –
As make your bouts more violent to that end –
And that he calls for drink, I'll have preferred him
A chalice for the nonce, whereon but sipping,
If he by chance escape your venomed stuck,
Our purpose may hold there. – But stay, what noise?

143-4 *Collected . . . Under the moon.* It was
believed that herbs were especially
efficacious when gathered by moon-
light (see III.2.266). But perhaps
Under the moon goes with *have virtue*
and merely means 'anywhere on
earth'.
143 *simples* medicinal herbs
146 *gall* graze
148-9 *Weigh what convenience both of time
and means | May fit us to our shape* con-
sider carefully what arrangements of
time and of opportunity may suit us
in assuming the roles we have decided to act
149 *shape* role
150 *drift* intention, plan
     look through become visible
151 *assayed* attempted
152 *back* support

hold stand firm
153 *blast in proof* (like a gun exploding
     when it is tested by being fired)
154 *cunnings* respective skills in fencing
157 *As* and therefore
158 *preferred* proffered. This seems to
     be the meaning of Q2's reading,
     'prefard'. But F reads 'prepar'd',
     which may well be right.
159 *chalice* (a special ceremonial cup)
     nonce occasion
160 *stuck* thrust
161 *may hold there* will be achieved by
     that
161-2 *But stay, what noise? | How, sweet
     Queen!* Q2 has only the first sentence,
     F only the second. One or other may
     be an accidental omission. It seems
     best to include both in the text; a
     director can choose either or both.

Enter the Queen

How, sweet Queen!

QUEEN

One woe doth tread upon another's heel,
So fast they follow. Your sister's drowned, Laertes.

LAERTES

Drowned! O, where?

QUEEN

There is a willow grows askant the brook,
That shows his hoar leaves in the glassy stream.
Therewith fantastic garlands did she make
Of crowflowers, nettles, daisies, and long purples,
That liberal shepherds give a grosser name,   170
But our cold maids do dead-men's-fingers call them.
There on the pendent boughs her crownet weeds
Clambering to hang, an envious sliver broke,
When down her weedy trophies and herself

165 *O, where?* Presumably these words represent a numbed reaction to the deeply felt calamity. Or Laertes may speak as if about to run to her.

166 *willow* (the emblem of forsaken love, appropriately)
askant sideways, leaning over. F has 'aslant', a more usual word.

167 *shows his hoar leaves in the glassy stream.* The underside of the willow leaf is greyish, and this, not the green upper side, would be reflected in the *glassy stream* underneath.

168 *Therewith* (of the willow). F reads 'There with', and alters *make* to 'come'.
fantastic extravagant

169 *crowflowers* buttercups
long purples purple orchises

170 *liberal* free-spoken
grosser more obscene

171 *cold maids* (distinguished from *liberal*

shepherds; the maidens are chaste and therefore ignore obscene names for flowers)
dead-men's-fingers (so named from the pale tuber-like roots of some kinds of orchids)

172–3 *There . . . | Clambering to hang.* As one forsaken in love, Ophelia tries to hang her garland on a willow tree. Or perhaps she imagines herself to be decorating her father's monument.

172 *crownet weeds* garlands made of weeds

173 *an envious sliver broke.* There is no word here of Ophelia's death's being suicide, though the strong suspicion of this is voiced in the next scene (v.1.1–25 and 223–34).
envious malicious
sliver branch

Fell in the weeping brook. Her clothes spread wide,
And mermaid-like awhile they bore her up;
Which time she chanted snatches of old tunes,
As one incapable of her own distress,
Or like a creature native and indued
180   Unto that element. But long it could not be
Till that her garments, heavy with their drink,
Pulled the poor wretch from her melodious lay
To muddy death.

LAERTES   Alas, then she is drowned?

QUEEN
Drowned, drowned.

LAERTES
Too much of water hast thou, poor Ophelia,
And therefore I forbid my tears. But yet
It is our trick. Nature her custom holds,
Let shame say what it will. When these are gone,
The woman will be out. Adieu, my lord.
190   I have a speech o'fire that fain would blaze,
But that this folly drowns it.   *Exit*

KING   Let's follow, Gertrude.
How much I had to do to calm his rage!
Now fear I this will give it start again.
Therefore let's follow.   *Exeunt*

---

175 *clothes*. Ophelia is imagined as wearing the elaborate farthingale of an
Elizabethan court lady.

177 *tunes*. Q2 has 'laudes', a strange
word in this context, but just possible, referring to parts of the Psalms
sung at the service of Lauds. The F
reading 'tunes' is supported by Q1,
'Chaunting olde sundry tunes'.

178 *incapable of* unable to comprehend

179–80 *indued | Unto that element* having
the qualities appropriate for living in
the water

182 *lay* song

187 *our trick* the way of us men

187–8 *Nature her custom holds, | Let shame
say what it will* Nature follows her
usual course, even though our shame
(at being unmanly) rebukes us

188–9 *When these are gone, | The woman
will be out* after my tears are over, the
woman-like side of my human nature
will cease to appear

191 *this folly* these foolish tears
drowns. So Q2; F reads 'doubts',
which could be interpreted as 'douts'
(puts out).

192 *calm his rage* (not a true statement of
what has happened)

Enter two Clowns   V.I

FIRST CLOWN Is she to be buried in Christian burial
when she wilfully seeks her own salvation?

SECOND CLOWN I tell thee she is. Therefore make her
grave straight. The crowner hath sat on her, and finds
it Christian burial.

FIRST CLOWN How can that be, unless she drowned
herself in her own defence?

SECOND CLOWN Why, 'tis found so.

FIRST CLOWN It must be *se offendendo*. It cannot be else.
For here lies the point: if I drown myself wittingly, it   10
argues an act, and an act hath three branches — it is to

---

v.1 It seems that this remarkable scene
was an afterthought. v.2 would follow
naturally upon IV.7, where we are told
(line 44) that Hamlet will arrive at the
court *Tomorrow*. v.2 opens with
Hamlet's narration to Horatio of what
had happened to bring him back to
Elsinore.

(stage direction) *Enter two Clowns*.
This is the direction in Q2 and F.
But Q1 has '*enter Clowne and an other*'.
This probably indicates the principal
comic actor and his 'feed', who
appear as rustics ('clowns'). The First
Clown plays the part of a gravedigger: he is addressed as *Goodman Delver*
(line 14) and called a *sexton* (lines 88
and 160) and *grave-maker* (line 140).
It would be wrong to regard the
Second Clown as another; for two men
cannot easily dig the same grave.

1 *in Christian burial* with the authorized
funeral services of the Church and in
consecrated ground (as was not permitted to suicides)

2 *salvation*. He presumably should say
'damnation', but he has muddled no-
tions of her presumptuousness in

dying and going to heaven before
her due time.

4 *straight* straightaway

4–22 *The crowner . . . law*. The Clowns give
a burlesque of the arguments in the
coroner's court over Ophelia's death.

4 *crowner* coroner. This colloquial form
occurs in common Elizabethan
usage, and not only in uneducated
speech.

sat on her conducted an inquest into the
cause of her death

4–5 *finds it* has given his verdict that the
cause of her death does not prohibit

8 *'tis found so* this verdict has been given
by the coroner

9 *se offendendo*. He means '*se defendendo*'
('in self-defence'), the phrase used in
a plea of justifiable homicide. But it
is, of course, comically misapplied in
a case of suicide. Q2's reading, 'so
offended', may be a further comic
corruption of the phrase, rather than
a misprint.

11 *branches* divisions of an argument.
Shakespeare is doubtless making fun
of the over-systematic distinctions
and quibbles of lawyers.

act, to do, and to perform. Argal, she drowned herself
wittingly.

SECOND CLOWN Nay, but hear you, Goodman Delver.

FIRST CLOWN Give me leave. Here lies the water – good.
Here stands the man – good. If the man go to this water
and drown himself, it is, will he nill he, he goes, mark
you that. But if the water come to him and drown him,
he drowns not himself. Argal, he that is not guilty of
20   his own death shortens not his own life.

SECOND CLOWN But is this law?

FIRST CLOWN Ay, marry, is't – crowner's quest law.

SECOND CLOWN Will you ha' the truth on't? If this had
not been a gentlewoman, she should have been buried
out o'Christian burial.

FIRST CLOWN Why, there thou sayst. And the more pity
that great folk should have countenance in this world
to drown or hang themselves more than their even-
Christian. Come, my spade. There is no ancient gentle-
30   men but gardeners, ditchers, and grave-makers. They
hold up Adam's profession.

SECOND CLOWN Was he a gentleman?

FIRST CLOWN 'A was the first that ever bore arms.

SECOND CLOWN Why, he had none.

FIRST CLOWN What, art a heathen? How dost thou
understand the Scripture? The Scripture says Adam

---

12 *Argal.* The Clown is attempting the
Latin *ergo*, 'therefore'.
14 *Goodman* (a polite form of address to
a working-man)
Delver gravedigger
17 *will he nill he* willy-nilly
22 *crowner's quest law* (that is, according
to the formalities governing a coroner's inquest (*quest*))
26 *there thou sayst* what you say is true
27-9 *great folk ... even-Christian.* This
looks forward to the Priest's remarks
at lines 223-34, including the reveal-

ing information that *great command
o'ersways the order.*
27 *countenance* social and legal privilege
28-9 *even-Christian* ordinary fellow-
Christians (who are all equal, whatever their social rank, in the sight of
God)
31 *hold up* continue
33 *arms* (both 'a coat of arms' and 'arms
to hold a spade with')
34 *none* (no coat of arms)
36 *the Scripture* (Genesis 2.15 and 3.19)

digged. Could he dig without arms? I'll put another question to thee. If thou answerest me not to the purpose, confess thyself —

SECOND CLOWN Go to!   40

FIRST CLOWN What is he that builds stronger than either the mason, the shipwright, or the carpenter?

SECOND CLOWN The gallows-maker, for that frame outlives a thousand tenants.

FIRST CLOWN I like thy wit well, in good faith. The gallows does well. But how does it well? It does well to those that do ill. Now thou dost ill to say the gallows is built stronger than the church. Argal, the gallows may do well to thee. To't again, come.

SECOND CLOWN Who builds stronger than a mason, a   50
shipwright, or a carpenter?

FIRST CLOWN Ay, tell me that, and unyoke.

SECOND CLOWN Marry, now I can tell.

FIRST CLOWN To't.

SECOND CLOWN Mass, I cannot tell.

FIRST CLOWN Cudgel thy brains no more about it, for your dull ass will not mend his pace with beating. And when you are asked this question next, say 'a gravemaker'. The houses he makes lasts till Doomsday. Go, get thee in, and fetch me a stoup of liquor.   60

Exit Second Clown

(*sings*) In youth when I did love, did love,
          Methought it was very sweet

---

37 *Could he dig without arms?* This mocks the absurd claims of writers on heraldry about the antiquity of their branch of knowledge

39 *confess thyself* – (to be a fool. Or perhaps this is the first half of the proverb 'Confess yourself and be hanged', which may prompt the Second Clown to guess *gallows-maker* (line 43) as the answer to the riddle.)

40 *Go to!* (an interjection of impatience: 'come on!')

43 *frame* (the 'framework' of the gallows)

52 *unyoke* (after this great effort, you can have your yoke taken off, like a beast of burden whose day's task is done, and can give your brain a rest)

55 *Mass* by the mass

60 *stoup* (pronounced like 'stoop'; a flagon containing two quarts)

61-119 *In youth … meet.* The Clown sings three garbled stanzas of a well-known poem attributed to Thomas

To contract – O – the time for – a – my behove,
O, methought there – a – was nothing – a – meet.

Enter Hamlet and Horatio

HAMLET Has this fellow no feeling of his business? 'A sings in grave-making.

HORATIO Custom hath made it in him a property of easiness.

HAMLET 'Tis e'en so. The hand of little employment hath the daintier sense.

70

FIRST CLOWN (*sings*)

But age with his stealing steps
Hath clawed me in his clutch,
And hath shipped me into the land,
As if I had never been such.

He throws up a skull

HAMLET That skull had a tongue in it, and could sing once. How the knave jowls it to the ground, as if 'twere Cain's jawbone, that did the first murder! This might be the pate of a politician, which this ass now o'erreaches; one that would circumvent God, might it not?

Lord Vaux (1510–56), first printed in the book of *Songs and Sonnets* (by the Earl of Surrey and others) published by Tottel in 1557, with the title 'The Aged Lover Renounceth Love', and printed separately as a ballad in 1563.

63 *O ... a* (presumably grunts made by the digger at his labours rather than interpolated vowels in the song)
   behove (that is, 'behoof') benefit, advantage

65 *feeling of his business* response to the sombre nature of his job

67–8 *in him a property of easiness* natural for him to carry out his distressing task without any painful sensations

70 *hath the daintier sense* is more fastidious

(than the hard hand of a working man)

74 *such* (as I was in my youth)

76 *jowls* thrusts or knocks forcibly (presumably with a play upon *jawbone*)

77 *Cain's jawbone, that did* the jawbone used by Cain, who committed. According to legend, he used an ass's jawbone to murder his brother Abel. Hamlet's mind reverts to fratricide, as does the King's (III.3.37–8).

78 *politician.* This word generally had a derogatory meaning: 'schemer'.
   this ass (the gravedigger)
   o'erreaches gets the better of (perhaps with a pun on the sense 'reach over')

79 *circumvent* outwit

HORATIO It might, my lord.   80

HAMLET Or of a courtier, which could say 'Good morrow, sweet lord! How dost thou, sweet lord?' This
might be my Lord Such-a-one, that praised my Lord
Such-a-one's horse when 'a meant to beg it, might it
not?

HORATIO Ay, my lord.

HAMLET Why, e'en so, and now my Lady Worm's, chopless, and knocked about the mazzard with a sexton's
spade. Here's fine revolution, an we had the trick to
see't. Did these bones cost no more the breeding but   90
to play at loggats with them? Mine ache to think on't.

FIRST CLOWN (sings)

> A pickaxe and a spade, a spade,
>   For and a shrouding sheet.
> O, a pit of clay for to be made
>   For such a guest is meet.

He throws up another skull

HAMLET There's another. Why may not that be the skull
of a lawyer? Where be his quiddities now, his quillets,
his cases, his tenures, and his tricks? Why does he
suffer this mad knave now to knock him about the
sconce with a dirty shovel, and will not tell him of his   100
action of battery? Hum! This fellow might be in's

83–4 *praised my Lord Such-a-one's horse when 'a meant to beg it.* Shakespeare gives an instance of this kind of deviousness in *Timon of Athens*, 1.2.210–16.

87 *my Lady Worm's* it belongs to my Lady Worm

87–8 *chopless* without the lower jaw

88 *mazzard* skull (the upper part)

89 *revolution* reversal of fortune brought about by time

89–90 *trick to see* knack of seeing

90 *cost no more the breeding but* cost so little to raise that men are willing

91 *loggats* (a game played by throwing pear-shaped pieces of wood – *loggats* – at wooden pins stuck in the ground)
Mine (my own *bones*)

93 *For and* (an emphatic form) and

97 *quiddities* subtleties
quillets small distinctions

98 *tenures* (modes of holding property from a superior owner, or periods of time during which it may be so held)

100 *sconce* head

101 *action of battery* suing for physical violence upon himself

time a great buyer of land, with his statutes, his recognizances, his fines, his double vouchers, his recoveries. Is this the fine of his fines, and the recovery of his recoveries, to have his fine pate full of fine dirt? Will his vouchers vouch him no more of his purchases, and double ones too, than the length and breadth of a pair of indentures? The very conveyances of his lands will scarcely lie in this box, and must th'inheritor himself have no more, ha?

HORATIO Not a jot more, my lord.

HAMLET Is not parchment made of sheep-skins?

HORATIO Ay, my lord, and of calves' skins too.

HAMLET They are sheep and calves which seek out assurance in that. I will speak to this fellow. – Whose grave's this, sirrah?

FIRST CLOWN Mine, sir.

102 *statutes* (legal documents acknowledging debts, by which creditors acquired rights over the debtors' lands and goods)

102–3 *recognizances* (certain kinds of statutes)

103 *fines* (legal documents by which entailed property was changed into freehold possession)
double vouchers (persons (generally two) who played their part in the legal devices of *recoveries*)
recoveries (the process including *fines*)

104 *fine of his fines* end of his fines (as in line 103). In this sentence Hamlet achieves four puns on the word *fine*.
recovery successful attainment

106 *vouch him . . . of* guarantee his legal title to

107–8 *the length and breadth of a pair of indentures*. (Two of his legal documents would together be of the same size as his grave.)

108 *indentures* joint agreements. The document was cut or torn into two parts so that the exact fitting together

of the irregularly indented edges was a proof of genuineness. Perhaps Hamlet is punning, referring to the two teeth-bearing jaws.

108–10 *The very conveyances . . . more* the documents themselves, symbols of ownership, are too bulky to go into this grave (or coffin), and must the owner of all these lands occupy no more space?

108 *conveyances* (documents legalizing the transfer of ownership of property)

109 *box* (grave, or coffin, compared to the box in which a lawyer keeps his documents)
inheritor owner

114 *sheep and calves* foolish fellows

114–15 *assurance* security (with a pun on the legal sense, 'documentary conveyance of property')

115 *in that* (by trusting to legal documents, which are only made of parchment)

115–16 *Whose grave's this*. Horatio, as well as Hamlet, is ignorant of Ophelia's death, having left the court at the end of IV.6.

(*sings*) O, a pit of clay for to be made
            For such a guest is meet.

HAMLET I think it be thine indeed, for thou liest in't.   120

FIRST CLOWN You lie out on't, sir, and therefore 'tis
    not yours. For my part, I do not lie in't, yet it is mine.

HAMLET Thou dost lie in't, to be in't and say it is thine.
    'Tis for the dead, not for the quick. Therefore thou
    liest.

FIRST CLOWN 'Tis a quick lie, sir. 'Twill away again
    from me to you.

HAMLET What man dost thou dig it for?

FIRST CLOWN For no man, sir.

HAMLET What woman then?   130

FIRST CLOWN For none neither.

HAMLET Who is to be buried in't?

FIRST CLOWN One that was a woman, sir. But, rest her
    soul, she's dead.

HAMLET How absolute the knave is! We must speak by
    the card, or equivocation will undo us. By the Lord,
    Horatio, this three years I have took note of it, the age
    is grown so picked that the toe of the peasant comes so
    near the heel of the courtier he galls his kibe. – How
    long hast thou been grave-maker?   140

FIRST CLOWN Of all the days i'th'year, I came to't that
    day that our last King Hamlet overcame Fortinbras.

120 *thou liest.* Hamlet jestingly uses the
formula of insult among gentlemen.
126 *a quick lie* a lie that will return from
me to you quickly
126–7 *'Twill away again from me to you*
(the Clown 'gives him the lie' back
again)
135 *absolute* positively precise (in
language)
135–6 *by the card* precisely, as if according to the directions given on a
seaman's chart or on his compass
(divided into thirty-two points)
136 *equivocation* deliberate use of ambigu-

ity in words. It was notorious in
Shakespeare's time as a device, attributed to the Roman Catholics, for
taking oaths with mental reservations
and double meanings.
137 *the age* our contemporaries of all
classes (both *peasant* and *courtier*)
138 *picked* over-refined
138–9 *the toe of the peasant comes so near
the heel of the courtier* (a curious echo
of the Queen's image at IV.7.163:
One woe doth tread upon another's heel)
139 *kibe* chilbain

HAMLET How long is that since?

FIRST CLOWN Cannot you tell that? Every fool can tell
that. It was that very day that young Hamlet was born –
he that is mad, and sent into England.

HAMLET Ay, marry, why was he sent into England?

FIRST CLOWN Why, because 'a was mad. 'A shall recover his wits there. Or, if 'a do not, 'tis no great matter
150 there.

HAMLET Why?

FIRST CLOWN 'Twill not be seen in him there. There
the men are as mad as he.

HAMLET How came he mad?

FIRST CLOWN Very strangely, they say.

HAMLET How strangely?

FIRST CLOWN Faith, e'en with losing his wits.

HAMLET Upon what ground?

FIRST CLOWN Why, here in Denmark. I have been
160 sexton here, man and boy, thirty years.

HAMLET How long will a man lie i'th'earth ere he rot?

FIRST CLOWN Faith, if 'a be not rotten before 'a die, as
we have many pocky corses nowadays that will scarce
hold the laying in, 'a will last you some eight year or
nine year. A tanner will last you nine year.

HAMLET Why he more than another?

FIRST CLOWN Why, sir, his hide is so tanned with his
trade that 'a will keep out water a great while, and your
water is a sore decayer of your whoreson dead body.

---

145 *that very day that young Hamlet was
born.* There seems to be a curious
symbolism in the gravedigger's
having entered upon his occupation
at the same time as Hamlet entered
into being, as if preparation for death
began from the day of birth.

158 *Upon what ground?* from what cause?
(But the Clown chooses to take
ground literally.)

160 *thirty years.* This seems conclusive

that at this point Shakespeare intended Hamlet to be aged thirty. See
the notes to 1.1.171 and lines 170–71
below.

163 *pocky corses nowadays.* The ravages of
the 'great pox' (venereal diseases)
were serious in Elizabethan
England.

164 *hold* last out

169 *sore* (an intensifying epithet:
'terrible')

Here's a skull now hath lien you i'th'earth three-and-   170
twenty years.

HAMLET Whose was it?

FIRST CLOWN A whoreson mad fellow's it was. Whose
do you think it was?

HAMLET Nay, I know not.

FIRST CLOWN A pestilence on him for a mad rogue!
'A poured a flagon of Rhenish on my head once. This
same skull, sir, was, sir, Yorick's skull, the King's jester.

HAMLET This?

FIRST CLOWN E'en that.   180

HAMLET Let me see. Alas, poor Yorick! I knew him,
Horatio. A fellow of infinite jest, of most excellent fancy.
He hath bore me on his back a thousand times. And
now how abhorred in my imagination it is! My gorge
rises at it. Here hung those lips that I have kissed I
know not how oft. Where be your gibes now? Your
gambols, your songs, your flashes of merriment that
were wont to set the table on a roar? Not one now to
mock your own grinning? Quite chop-fallen? Now get
you to my lady's table and tell her, let her paint an inch   190
thick, to this favour she must come. Make her laugh at
that. Prithee, Horatio, tell me one thing.

HORATIO What's that, my lord?

---

170 *lien* (an old form) lain

170–71 *three-and-twenty years.* Q1 has a
passage which combines lines 139–46
and 170–71 and gives about twelve
years since Yorick's death, so that in
Q1 Hamlet could be in his late teens.

177 *Rhenish.* See the note to 1.4.10.

178 *Yorick.* This (like 'Osrick' in v.2) is
a Scandinavian-sounding name, suggesting Jörg (George) and Eric.

182 *fancy* imagination

183–9 *He hath . . . grinning.* This passage
is a wonderful glimpse of the privileged position of the jester in a great
Elizabethan household.

189 *grinning* (as a skull appears to be)
chop-fallen with the lower jaw hanging down (as if miserable)

189–90 *get you to my lady's table.* There
were engravings of Death (represented by a skeleton) coming into a
young lady's bedchamber while she
sits at her toilet-table. For *table* F
reads 'Chamber', which may be right;
table could be due to a repetition
from line 188.

190–91 *paint an inch thick* (the frequent
hostility to face-painting; compare
III.1.51 and 143–5)

191 *favour* facial appearance

HAMLET Dost thou think Alexander looked o'this fashion
i'th'earth?

HORATIO E'en so.

HAMLET And smelt so? Pah!

HORATIO E'en so, my lord.

HAMLET To what base uses we may return, Horatio! Why
200   may not imagination trace the noble dust of Alexander
till 'a find it stopping a bunghole?

HORATIO. 'Twere to consider too curiously to consider so.

HAMLET No, faith, not a jot. But to follow him thither
with modesty enough, and likelihood to lead it; as thus:
Alexander died, Alexander was buried, Alexander
returneth to dust; the dust is earth; of earth we make
loam; and why of that loam whereto he was converted
might they not stop a beer barrel?

    Imperious Caesar, dead and turned to clay,
210   Might stop a hole to keep the wind away.
    O, that that earth which kept the world in awe
    Should patch a wall t'expel the winter's flaw!
But soft, but soft awhile!

> *Enter the King and Queen, Laertes, and the corpse of*
> *Ophelia, with lords attendant and a Priest*

                      Here comes the King,
The Queen, the courtiers. Who is this they follow?
And with such maimèd rites? This doth betoken
The corse they follow did with desperate hand
Fordo it own life. 'Twas of some estate.

---

194 *Alexander* (the Great)

202 *too curiously* with unreasonably
minute attention

203 *follow him* (in imagination)

204 *with modesty* moderately and reasonably (that is, not *too curiously*, which
would make the idea improbable)

207 *loam* (mortar or plaster made of clay
and straw)

209–12 *Imperious Caesar . . . winter's flaw.*
Perhaps this impromptu verse-
epigram (a characteristic specimen

of its kind) serves, like the love poem
to Ophelia (II.2.115–18), to identify
Hamlet as a 'university wit'.

209 *Imperious* imperial

211 *earth* (piece of earth, that is, Caesar's
remains)

212 *expel the winter's flaw* keep out a
sudden gust of winter wind

215 *maimèd* incomplete

217 *Fordo* undo, destroy
    it its
    some estate rather high social station

Couch we awhile, and mark.

He withdraws with Horatio

LAERTES

What ceremony else?

HAMLET

That is Laertes, a very noble youth. Mark.   220

LAERTES

What ceremony else?

PRIEST

Her obsequies have been as far enlarged

As we have warranty. Her death was doubtful,

And, but that great command o'ersways the order,

She should in ground unsanctified have lodged

Till the last trumpet. For charitable prayers,

Shards, flints, and pebbles should be thrown on her.

Yet here she is allowed her virgin crants,

Her maiden strewments, and the bringing home

Of bell and burial.   230

LAERTES

Must there no more be done?

PRIEST   No more be done.

218 *Couch we* let us lie down and so be concealed

219 *What ceremony else?* Laertes irritably repeats his question, following an embarrassed or indignant silence by the Priest.

222 PRIEST. For his two speeches Q2 has the heading '*Doct.*'. This presumably means 'Doctor of Divinity' and would point to a Protestant rather than a Catholic cleric. But Laertes calls him a *priest* at line 236.
enlarged extended

223 *warranty* authorization
doubtful (owing to the suspicion of suicide. There was nothing, however, in the Queen's description of Ophelia's death (IV.7.166–83) to suggest that it was suicide; and we are told at V.1.4–5 that the coroner gave

his judgement that it was to be *Christian burial*.)

224 *great* (that is, of the King)
order regulations prescribed by the ecclesiastical authorities

226 *For* instead of

227 *Shards* broken pieces of pots

228 *crants* (an unusual and foreign word, apparently Germanic, whose use may be a bit of local colour) garlands

229 *strewments* flowers strewn on the grave or coffin
bringing home. Ophelia's funeral has followed the usual custom of being made to resemble a wedding festival. Instead of being taken to her husband's house, she is brought to her 'last home'.

230 *Of* with
burial burial service

We should profane the service of the dead
To sing a requiem and such rest to her
As to peace-parted souls.

LAERTES   Lay her i'th'earth,
And from her fair and unpolluted flesh
May violets spring! I tell thee, churlish priest,
A ministering angel shall my sister be
When thou liest howling.

HAMLET   What, the fair Ophelia?

QUEEN
Sweets to the sweet! Farewell.
                    She scatters flowers
240 I hoped thou shouldst have been my Hamlet's wife.
I thought thy bride-bed to have decked, sweet maid,
And not have strewed thy grave.

LAERTES   O, treble woe
Fall ten times double on that cursèd head
Whose wicked deed thy most ingenious sense
Deprived thee of! Hold off the earth awhile,
Till I have caught her once more in mine arms.
                    He leaps in the grave
Now pile your dust upon the quick and dead
Till of this flat a mountain you have made
T'o'ertop old Pelion or the skyish head
Of blue Olympus.

HAMLET (*coming forward*)
250   What is he whose grief
Bears such an emphasis, whose phrase of sorrow

---

234 *peace-parted souls* those who die pi-
ously in peace ('Lord, now lettest
thou thy servant depart in peace',
Luke 2.29)
238 *howling* (as a damned soul in hell)
244 *Whose wicked deed* (the killing of
Polonius, to which alone Laertes
seems to attribute Ophelia's loss of
reason)

ingenious sense naturally quick (or perhaps 'noble') powers of mind
246 *caught her . . . in mine arms*. This implies an open coffin.
249 *Pelion* (a mountain in Thessaly;
presumably it is old because of its
reputation in ancient literature)
250 *blue* (presumably like a distant
mountain)

Conjures the wandering stars, and makes them stand
Like wonder-wounded hearers? This is I,
Hamlet the Dane.

LAERTES   The devil take thy soul!

HAMLET

Thou prayest not well.
I prithee take thy fingers from my throat.
For, though I am not splenitive and rash,
Yet have I in me something dangerous,
Which let thy wisdom fear. Hold off thy hand.

KING

Pluck them asunder.

QUEEN   Hamlet, Hamlet!   260

ALL

Gentlemen!

HORATIO   Good my lord, be quiet.

HAMLET

Why, I will fight with him upon this theme
Until my eyelids will no longer wag.

QUEEN

O my son, what theme?

HAMLET

I loved Ophelia. Forty thousand brothers

252 *Conjures* puts a magic spell upon
   wandering stars planets (contrasted with
   the 'fixed stars')
   stand stand still
253 *wonder-wounded* awe-struck
   This is I. Presumably he throws off
   his cloak or *sea-gown* (V.2.13).
254 *Hamlet the Dane* (a defiant way of
   describing himself, asserting his
   princely rank or his claim to the
   throne)
   The devil take thy soul! Perhaps with
   this Laertes leaps out of the grave and
   flies at Hamlet. Before it, Q1 has the
   direction '*Hamlet leapes in after Leartes*',
   but this turns Hamlet into the physical

aggressor, though the text (lines 256
and 259) indicates otherwise.
257 *splenitive* of an angry temperament.
   In sixteenth-century physiology the
   spleen was regarded as one of the seats
   of emotion, particularly of choler.
259 *Which let thy wisdom fear* which your
   good sense should cause you to fear
263 *wag* (not a ludicrous word) move.
   The movement of the eyelids is
   among the last visible ones to cease
   in a human being.
265 *I loved Ophelia.* Hamlet is shown
   briefly as having lost most of his
   self-consciousness and as being moved
   by serious feelings. Or perhaps it is

Could not with all their quantity of love
Make up my sum. What wilt thou do for her?

KING

O, he is mad, Laertes.

QUEEN

For love of God, forbear him.

HAMLET

270 'Swounds, show me what thou't do.
Woo't weep? Woo't fight? Woo't fast? Woo't tear
   thyself?
Woo't drink up eisel? Eat a crocodile?
I'll do't. Dost thou come here to whine?
To outface me with leaping in her grave?
Be buried quick with her, and so will I.
And if thou prate of mountains, let them throw
Millions of acres on us, till our ground,
Singeing his pate against the burning zone,
Make Ossa like a wart! Nay, an thou'lt mouth,
I'll rant as well as thou.

280 QUEEN   This is mere madness.

another self-dramatization? *Forty* (its use as an indefinitely large number seems to derive from its frequent biblical use)

266 *quantity* (comparatively small quantity)

269 *forbear him* refrain from conflicting with him (Hamlet)

271 *Woo't* wouldst thou

272 *eisel* vinegar. This is the common emendation of the word 'Esill' in Q2 and '*Esile*' (italicized, as if the printer thought it might be a proper name or a foreign word) in F. The difficulty is that something more violently absurd may be expected than the notion of eagerly drinking vinegar. This has prompted such conjectures as 'Nilus' (the river Nile — which might have suggested *Eat a*

crocodile), 'Yssel' in Flanders, 'Weissel' (Vistula), which flows into the Baltic, and others.

crocodile (regarded as a venomous beast; perhaps alluding also to its hypocritical trick of counterfeiting tears)

275 *quick* alive

278 *burning zone* (part of the sky representing the path of the sun between the tropics of Cancer and Capricorn)

279 *Make Ossa like a wart.* Hamlet derides Laertes's mention of *Pelion* (line 249) by naming the other mountain of Thessaly, always associated with Pelion: when the giants made war upon the gods of Olympus they tried to scale heaven by piling Pelion upon Ossa.

280 *mere* pure

And thus a while the fit will work on him.
Anon, as patient as the female dove
When that her golden couplets are disclosed,
His silence will sit drooping.

HAMLET   Hear you, sir.
What is the reason that you use me thus?
I loved you ever. But it is no matter.
Let Hercules himself do what he may,
The cat will mew, and dog will have his day.

KING
I pray thee, good Horatio, wait upon him.

Exeunt Hamlet and Horatio

(*To Laertes*)
Strengthen your patience in our last night's speech.   290
We'll put the matter to the present push.
Good Gertrude, set some watch over your son.
This grave shall have a living monument.
An hour of quiet shortly shall we see.
Till then in patience our proceeding be.   *Exeunt*

---

282 *Anon* soon afterwards
  dove (symbol of peace and quiet)
283 *golden couplets.* The newly hatched
  two chicks of a dove are covered
  with a yellow down.
  disclosed hatched
285 *use* treat
288 *cat . . . dog.* Presumably Hamlet is
  comparing Laertes to a cat for his
  whining lamentation and to a dog
  for his snarling. But perhaps *dog will
  have his day* refers to Hamlet: 'My
  turn will come soon'.
290 *Strengthen your patience in our last
  night's speech* let thoughts of our conversation last night enable you to
  preserve your patience (under such
  provocation by Hamlet)

291 *the present push* an immediate test
293-5 *This grave shall . . . be.* The King
  speaks these lines publicly, but they
  have an additional meaning for
  Laertes, as continuing lines 290-91:
  Hamlet will soon be in his grave,
  too, and then we can rest safe; but
  meanwhile, looking forward to the
  duel, we can remain patient.
293 *living monument* enduring memorial
  (but the King knows that Laertes
  will take his remark ironically)
294 *An hour of quiet shortly shall we see.*
  The King expects that Hamlet's
  death, which he has plotted, will
  solve his anxieties. But he himself
  will soon find *quiet* in death.

V.2   *Enter Hamlet and Horatio*

HAMLET

So much for this, sir. Now shall you see the other.
You do remember all the circumstance?

HORATIO

Remember it, my lord!

HAMLET

Sir, in my heart there was a kind of fighting
That would not let me sleep. Methought I lay
Worse than the mutines in the bilboes. Rashly,
And praised be rashness for it – let us know
Our indiscretion sometime serves us well
When our deep plots do pall, and that should learn us

10   There's a divinity that shapes our ends,
Rough-hew them how we will –

HORATIO   That is most certain.

HAMLET

Up from my cabin,
My sea-gown scarfed about me, in the dark

v.2.1 *this*. Possibly the letter to England given to Hamlet, *the other* being the *commission* given to Rosencrantz and Guildenstern (line 26); the contrast shows the King's treachery.

4 *fighting* agitation

5–6 *Methought I lay | Worse than the mutines in the bilboes* it seemed to me that I felt more uncomfortable in my bed than do mutineers in their iron fetters

6 *Rashly* . . . After five lines of interpolation, the sentence is resumed, not quite logically, at line 12: *Up from my cabin*.

7 *praised be rashness*. The praise of impetuous conduct and the confidence in divine providence are ill connected logically. Hamlet speaks eloquently, but without philosophical compet-

ence, of the old dilemma of human action and reliance on the will of God. At v.1.257 he boasted *I am not splenitive and rash*.

8 *indiscretion* lack of judgement

9 *pall* fail
  learn teach

10–11 *There's a divinity . . . will*. This is the first evidence of Hamlet's new piety or Christian patience, preparing us for lines 213–18. Perhaps Shakespeare is interesting the audience by showing, after the excited reasoning of iv.4.32–66, the meditative force of v.1.65–212 and the anxieties of v.1.250–88, a new kind of irresponsibility in Hamlet.

11 *Rough-hew* (like a piece of timber)

13 *sea-gown* (described in the 1611 dictionary of Cotgrave as 'a coarse,

Groped I to find out them, had my desire,
Fingered their packet, and in fine withdrew
To mine own room again, making so bold,
My fears forgetting manners, to unseal
Their grand commission; where I found, Horatio –
Ah, royal knavery! – an exact command,
Larded with many several sorts of reasons,   20
Importing Denmark's health, and England's too,
With, ho! such bugs and goblins in my life,
That on the supervise, no leisure bated,
No, not to stay the grinding of the axe,
My head should be struck off.

HORATIO   Is't possible?

HAMLET
Here's the commission. Read it at more leisure.
But wilt thou hear now how I did proceed?

HORATIO
I beseech you.

HAMLET
Being thus be-netted round with villainies,
Or I could make a prologue to my brains   30

---

high-collared, and short-sleeved gown, reaching down to the mid-leg')
scarfed about me wrapped around me like a sash. He had not dressed properly, but merely put his gown around him without using the sleeves.
14 *them* (Rosencrantz and Guildenstern)
15 *Fingered* stole
in fine finally
18 *grand* (sarcastic)
commission (the *commission* of III.3.3 and the *letters sealed* of III.4.203. See the note to IV.3.58.)
20 *Larded* garnished
many several a variety of different
21 *Importing* deeply concerned with
22 *bugs and goblins* terrors and dangers

(spoken contemptuously, for Hamlet believes them to be imaginary)
bugs (literally) bogies, bugbears
in my life if I am allowed to live (or perhaps 'in my daily behaviour')
23 *supervise* viewing
no leisure bated without any delay being permitted
24 *stay* wait for
26 *Here's the commission.* Presumably he hands it to Horatio.
29 *be-netted* ensnared
30 *Or* before
make a prologue to my brains go through the initial steps of submitting the problem to my intelligence (as often with Hamlet, a theatrical metaphor)

They had begun the play. I sat me down,
Devised a new commission, wrote it fair.
I once did hold it, as our statists do,
A baseness to write fair, and laboured much
How to forget that learning. But, sir, now
It did me yeoman's service. Wilt thou know
Th'effect of what I wrote?

HORATIO   Ay, good my lord.

HAMLET

An earnest conjuration from the King,
As England was his faithful tributary,
40   As love between them like the palm might flourish,
As peace should still her wheaten garland wear
And stand a comma 'tween their amities,
And many such-like as's of great charge,
That on the view and knowing of these contents,

---

31 *They* (his brains, without his conscious will)

32 *fair* (in a clear hand, like a professional scrivener)

33 *statists* men involved in business of state

34 *A baseness to write fair* evidence of ungentlemanly birth to have a clear handwriting, like a professional

36 *yeoman's service* (the kind of admirably loyal and reliable military service which an English yeoman rendered to his feudal lord)

37 *effect* import

38 *conjuration* appeal or injunction (as from a person able to rely upon some special authority)

40 *As* so that (whereas the *As* in line 39 means 'because')
    like the palm might flourish. Hamlet is mocking the high-flown style of diplomatic correspondence, which borrowed biblical phrases: 'The right-

eous shall flourish like the palm tree', Psalm 92.12.

41 *wheaten garland* (emblematic of *peace*)

42 *comma.* This, the reading of both Q2 and F, is difficult. Perhaps it is used in the sense 'a short part of a sentence'. But the word may be wrong. The suggested emendations ('commere', 'cement', 'column', 'concord', 'calm', 'compact', etc.) are unsatisfactory.
    amities. Perhaps Hamlet is ironical; for England's *cicatrice looks raw and red | After the Danish sword* (IV.3.62–3), and Shakespeare could hardly have been ignorant of the terrible conflicts between the Anglo-Saxons and the Danes.

43 *as's of great charge.* Hamlet characteristically puns on 'asses bearing heavy burdens'.

44 *That* (follows *conjuration*, line 38)

Without debatement further, more or less,
He should those bearers put to sudden death,
Not shriving time allowed.

HORATIO   How was this sealed?

HAMLET
Why, even in that was heaven ordinant.
I had my father's signet in my purse,
Which was the model of that Danish seal,   50
Folded the writ up in the form of th'other,
Subscribed it, gave't th'impression, placed it safely,
The changeling never known. Now, the next day
Was our sea-fight, and what to this was sequent
Thou knowest already.

HORATIO
So Guildenstern and Rosencrantz go to't.

HAMLET
Why, man, they did make love to this employment.

46 *those bearers* (Rosencrantz and Guildenstern)
47 *shriving time* (a period of time for confession and absolution before execution)
48 *ordinant* in control (compare lines 10–11)
49 *signet* seal
50 *model* replica
   that Danish seal (probably pointing to the seal on the commission now in Horatio's hand). Hamlet seems to be saying that, by good luck, he had his father's seal, and, equally luckily, the Danish seal of state of the new monarch was not (as one would expect) different from that of his predecessor.
52 *Subscribed it* (by forging King Claudius's signature)
   impression (of the seal)
53 *changeling* (like a human child taken by the fairies and replaced by one of their own)
53–4 *the next day | Was our sea-fight* . . . Shakespeare makes it clear that Hamlet's substitution of the *commission* to be carried to England had nothing to do with his accidental return to Denmark.
54 *our sea-fight*. This is described in IV.6.15 as *Ere we were two days old at sea*. So the substitution of the commission took place during the first night aboard ship.
56 *to't* to their death
57 *did make love to this employment* were willing and active collaborators in Claudius's schemes against me

They are not near my conscience. Their defeat
Does by their own insinuation grow.
60   'Tis dangerous when the baser nature comes
Between the pass and fell incensèd points
Of mighty opposites.

HORATIO   Why, what a king is this!

HAMLET
Does it not, think thee, stand me now upon –
He that hath killed my King and whored my mother,
Popped in between th'election and my hopes,
Thrown out his angle for my proper life,
And with such cozenage – is't not perfect conscience
To quit him with this arm? And is't not to be damned
To let this canker of our nature come
70   In further evil?

HORATIO
It must be shortly known to him from England
What is the issue of the business there.

HAMLET
It will be short. The interim is mine;
And a man's life's no more than to say 'one'.
But I am very sorry, good Horatio,

58 *defeat* destruction
59 *insinuation* intrusive intervention
61 *pass* thrust (of the rapier)
    fell incensèd points fiercely angered
    sword-points
62 *mighty opposites* (Hamlet and
    Claudius)
63 *Does it not . . . stand me now upon* is it
    not now my duty
66 *angle* fishing-hook
    my proper life my very life
67 *cozenage* cheating by inspiring confid-
    ence in one's victim
    is't not perfect conscience may I not with
    a clear conscience
68 *quit* pay back
    be damned act sinfully

69 *canker* cancer, ulcer
    nature (human nature)
69–70 *come | In* grow into
74 *a man's life's no more than to say 'one'*.
    The probable meaning is that the
    short time will be enough: he needs
    only a single successful thrust of his
    rapier into Claudius to end his life
    (*one* is the swordsman's claim to
    have hit his opponent's body). But
    perhaps it is another of Hamlet's
    newly acquired fatalistic generaliza-
    tions, like *There's a divinity* . . . (line
    10) and *The readiness is all* . . . (line
    216), and so refers to his own life,
    not the King's.

That to Laertes I forgot myself.
For by the image of my cause I see
The portraiture of his. I'll court his favours.
But sure the bravery of his grief did put me
Into a towering passion.

HORATIO   Peace, who comes here?   80

    Enter Osrick

OSRICK Your lordship is right welcome back to Denmark.

HAMLET I humbly thank you, sir. (*Aside to Horatio*) Dost
know this waterfly?

HORATIO (*aside to Hamlet*) No, my good lord.

HAMLET (*aside to Horatio*) Thy state is the more gracious,
for 'tis a vice to know him. He hath much land, and
fertile. Let a beast be lord of beasts, and his crib shall
stand at the king's mess. 'Tis a chough, but, as I say,
spacious in the possession of dirt.

OSRICK Sweet lord, if your lordship were at leisure, I   90
should impart a thing to you from his majesty.

---

78 *favours* friendship
79 *bravery* bravado
80 (stage direction) *Osrick*. The first
form of the name in Q2 is '*Os-
tricke*', and this is used for his
speech headings in the duel scene.
In view of the many references to
birds in this episode, it is tempting
to suppose that 'Ostrick' was Shakespeare's original intention. But at
lines 343–4 Q2 has '*Osrick*', and F
has '*Osricke*' ('*Osr.*') throughout. Q1
has '*Enter a Bragart Gentleman*',
which indicates how he appeared on
the stage. Hamlet's easy wit in rag-
ging poor Osrick, showing a mind
free from vacillation and anxiety,
confirms the change of mood revealed in the earlier part of the
scene.

83 *waterfly* (vain and meddlesome
creature)
85 *state* (of soul)
more gracious happier (as being in a
state of grace)
87 *Let a beast be lord of beasts, and* if a
man, however contemptible he may
be, owns large flocks and herds and
is therefore rich (he will be received
at the royal court). Wealth brings its
position at court, regardless of merit.
crib manger
88 *mess* (a division of the company at a
banquet)
chough jackdaw (which is able to
make a chatter resembling human
speech)
89 *spacious in the possession of dirt* the
owner of many acres of land

HAMLET I will receive it, sir, with all diligence of spirit. Put your bonnet to his right use. 'Tis for the head.

OSRICK I thank your lordship, it is very hot.

HAMLET No, believe me, 'tis very cold. The wind is northerly.

OSRICK It is indifferent cold, my lord, indeed.

HAMLET But yet methinks it is very sultry and hot for my complexion.

100 OSRICK Exceedingly, my lord. It is very sultry, as 'twere – I cannot tell how. But, my lord, his majesty bade me signify to you that 'a has laid a great wager on your head. Sir, this is the matter –

HAMLET I beseech you remember.

He invites Osrick to put on his hat

OSRICK Nay, good my lord. For my ease, in good faith. Sir, here is newly come to court Laertes; believe me, an absolute gentleman, full of most excellent differences, of very soft society and great showing. Indeed, to speak feelingly of him, he is the card or calendar of gentry.

---

92 *diligence of spirit* attention. Hamlet begins to mock Osrick's style of speech.

93 *Put your bonnet to his right use.* It was customary to wear hats indoors. Probably Osrick's excessive cap-doffing was an affectation of respect. But he politely pretends he has taken his hat off for his comfort in the hot weather.
bonnet (any kind of headwear)
his its

97 *indifferent* fairly

98-9 *for my complexion.* This is F's reading. Q2 has 'or' instead of *for*; this could be right if one puts a dash after *complexion* and supposes that Hamlet is interrupted by Osrick before he can finish his sentence with

'judges it wrongly' (or something of the sort).

99 *complexion* bodily state

105 *Nay* . . . Osrick apparently wins, and does not put on his hat until he departs at line 179.

107-11 *an absolute gentleman . . . see.* Osrick's panegyric has been arranged by the King (IV.7.130).

107 *absolute* perfect
differences distinguishing qualities

108 *soft society* sociable disposition
great showing impressive appearance

109 *card* accurate guide, to be used as a seaman uses his chart or compass (see V.1.135-6 and note)
calendar directory which one may consult for information
gentry gentlemanliness

For you shall find in him the continent of what part a   110
gentleman would see.

HAMLET Sir, his definement suffers no perdition in you,
though, I know, to divide him inventorially would dizzy
th'arithmetic of memory, and yet but yaw neither in
respect of his quick sail. But, in the verity of extolment,
I take him to be a soul of great article, and his infusion
of such dearth and rareness as, to make true diction of
him, his semblable is his mirror, and who else would
trace him, his umbrage, nothing more.

OSRICK Your lordship speaks most infallibly of him.   120

HAMLET The concernancy, sir? Why do we wrap the
gentleman in our more rawer breath?

OSRICK Sir?

HORATIO Is't not possible to understand in another
tongue? You will to't, sir, really.

HAMLET What imports the nomination of this gentleman?

110 *continent* embodiment
110–11 *what part a gentleman would see*
every quality a gentleman would like
to see
112 *his definement suffers no perdition in you*
he loses nothing by being described
by you
113 *divide him inventorially* list his qualities
one by one
113–14 *dizzy th'arithmetic of memory* (the
number of his qualities would be so
large that one's memory would
become confused in trying to remember them)
114 *yaw* move unsteadily (of a boat)
neither for all that
115 *the verity of extolment* praising him
truly
116 *article* importance
infusion mixture of good qualities
117 *dearth and rareness* 'dearness' (pre-

ciousness) and rarity
make true diction of speak truthfully
about
118 *his semblable is his mirror* the only
thing that resembles him is his own
image in a mirror
who whoever
119 *trace* follow in his footsteps (that is,
imitate)
his umbrage (is) a shadow of him
120 *infallibly* accurately
121 *concernancy* (apparently a word invented for the occasion) purpose of
all this
122 *more rawer breath* too little refined
way of speech
125 *You will to't* you can succeed, if you
try
126 *imports the nomination of* is your purpose in naming

OSRICK Of Laertes?

HORATIO (*aside to Hamlet*) His purse is empty already.
130   All's golden words are spent.

HAMLET Of him, sir.

OSRICK I know you are not ignorant –

HAMLET I would you did, sir. Yet, in faith, if you did, it
would not much approve me. Well, sir?

OSRICK You are not ignorant of what excellence Laertes
is –

HAMLET I dare not confess that, lest I should compare
with him in excellence. But to know a man well were to
know himself.

140   OSRICK I mean, sir, for his weapon. But in the imputation laid on him by them, in his meed he's unfellowed.

HAMLET What's his weapon?

OSRICK Rapier and dagger.

HAMLET That's two of his weapons. But well!

OSRICK The King, sir, hath wagered with him six Barbary
horses, against the which he has impawned, as I take it,
six French rapiers and poniards, with their assigns, as

134 *approve me* demonstrate the truth
about me (or perhaps 'be to my
credit')
137 *compare* vie
138–9 *to know a man well were to know
himself.* This exercise in logical nonsense seems to be based on an extension of 'Judge not, that you be not
judged' (Matthew 7.1). It would be
wrong for Hamlet to judge Laertes's
excellence, unless he were to consider
himself worthy to be judged to be of
equal excellence, and that would be a
presumptuous self-opinion, for he
cannot really *know himself*; therefore
he cannot really know (or estimate)
Laertes's excellence.
139 *himself* oneself

140 *for* with
140–41 *imputation* reputation
141 *by them* by people in general. Some
editors, following Q2's punctuation,
read 'by them in his meed' ('by those
who are in his pay, his retainers'),
but this seems to indicate an irony
that is beyond Osrick.
meed merit (probably, but the word is
difficult)
unfellowed without a rival
145–6 *Barbary horses.* North African
horses were much esteemed.
146 *he has impawned* Laertes has wagered
147 *poniards* daggers
' *assigns* appurtenances
as such as

girdle, hangers, and so. Three of the carriages, in faith, are very dear to fancy, very responsive to the hilts, most delicate carriages, and of very liberal conceit. 150

HAMLET What call you the carriages?

HORATIO (*aside to Hamlet*) I knew you must be edified by the margent ere you had done.

OSRICK The carriages, sir, are the hangers.

HAMLET The phrase would be more germane to the matter if we could carry a cannon by our sides. I would it might be 'hangers' till then. But on! Six Barbary horses against six French swords, their assigns, and three liberal-conceited carriages. That's the French bet against the Danish. Why is this all impawned, as you 160 call it?

OSRICK The King, sir, hath laid, sir, that in a dozen

148 *hangers* straps by which the sword (or its scabbard) was attached to the man's belt (*girdle*)
carriages (an affected word for *hangers*)
149 *very dear to fancy* (probably 'delightful to think about')
responsive to (perhaps 'matching' or 'in keeping with'; the two items 'go well together')
150 *delicate* finely wrought
of very liberal conceit (perhaps) tasteful in design and decoration
152–3 *I knew you must be edified by the margent* I expected that you would fail to understand something he said and have some word or phrase explained. (Explanations of difficult words or phrases were usually printed in the *margent* (margin) rather than at the foot of the page.)
152 *edified* enlightened
155–6 *germane to the matter* appropriate to the thing itself (*the matter* contrasts with *The phrase*)
156–7 *I would it might be 'hangers' till then* I had rather we kept the word 'hangers' until that time comes (when we can carry cannons at our sides and not merely rapiers)
162 *laid* wagered
162–4 *in a dozen passes ... he shall not exceed you three hits. He hath laid on twelve for nine.* These odds are difficult to interpret, but must have been immediately intelligible to Shakespeare's audience, familiar with the art of fencing and with the conventions of fencing matches. It seems that the King wagers that, in twelve bouts or rounds, Laertes's score will not exceed Hamlet's by three. That means that if the score were Laertes 8 and Hamlet 4, Laertes would win; and that if the score were Laertes 7 and Hamlet 5, Hamlet would win. This explanation seems to be supported by Q1, where the reporter is doubtless remembering what he saw

passes between yourself and him he shall not exceed you three hits. He hath laid on twelve for nine; and it would come to immediate trial if your lordship would vouchsafe the answer.

HAMLET How if I answer no?

OSRICK I mean, my lord, the opposition of your person in trial.

170 HAMLET Sir, I will walk here in the hall. If it please his majesty, it is the breathing time of day with me. Let the foils be brought, the gentleman willing, and the King hold his purpose, I will win for him an I can. If not, I will gain nothing but my shame and the odd hits.

OSRICK Shall I re-deliver you e'en so?

HAMLET To this effect, sir, after what flourish your nature will.

on the stage. Hamlet asks 'And howe's the wager?' and receives the reply 'Mary sir, that yong Leartes in twelue venies | At Rapier and Dagger do not get three oddes of you.' In the event, Hamlet wins the first two bouts (lines 275 and 280 below). The score of two-nil against him is serious for Laertes, for it means he must win at least eight of the remaining ten bouts in order to win the match. The King thereupon says *Our son shall win* (line 281). But what is the meaning of *He hath laid on twelve for nine*? By the natural run of the sentences *He* would be the King. The actor might convey that *He* was Laertes. It would be natural to take *twelve for nine* as being related to Hamlet's 'advantage' of *three hits*. Perhaps *for nine* means 'instead of nine': Laertes wants a larger number of bouts than usual, in order to achieve a lead of at least four hits over Hamlet. Unfortunately there is no evidence that nine was the usual number of bouts. Perhaps the wager is that Laertes will not achieve twelve

hits before Hamlet has achieved nine. If so, they might have to fight as many as twenty bouts; for the score, after the nineteenth, could be 11 to 8.

163 *passes* (probably means 'bouts' or 'rounds', which ended when one of the contestants scored a hit)

165–6 *vouchsafe the answer* accept the challenge. But Hamlet deliberately misunderstands the words as merely 'give a reply'.

167 *How if I answer no?* (a moment of suspense, when Hamlet comes near to spoiling the treacherous plot)

168–9 *I mean . . . in trial.* Osrick assumes that it is unthinkable that a gentleman should refuse to respond to a challenge of this kind, and so he pretends that Hamlet may have misunderstood him.

171 *breathing time* time for taking exercise

174 *the odd hits* my small score of successful hits

175 *re-deliver you* report what you have said

176 *flourish* verbal decoration

OSRICK I commend my duty to your lordship.

HAMLET Yours, yours.   *Exit Osrick*

He does well to commend it himself. There are no   180
tongues else for's turn.

HORATIO This lapwing runs away with the shell on his
head.

HAMLET 'A did comply, sir, with his dug before 'a sucked
it. Thus has he, and many more of the same bevy that I
know the drossy age dotes on, only got the tune of the
time and, out of an habit of encounter, a kind of yeasty
collection, which carries them through and through the
most fanned and winnowed opinions; and do but blow
them to their trial, the bubbles are out.   190

    Enter a Lord

LORD My lord, his majesty commended him to you by
young Osrick, who brings back to him that you attend

---

178 *I commend my duty*. This is a merely
complimentary phrase, and Hamlet's
immediate response is conventional
too. But after Osrick has left he plays
with the words, taking them separately and literally as 'I praise my
performance of duty'.

182–3 *This lapwing runs away with the shell
on his head* Presumably Osrick puts
his hat on at his departure. The
image is of a precocious young bird
which, just hatched, starts running
away with a piece of its shell still
clinging to its head.

184 *comply . . . with his dug* behave with
ingratiating good manners towards
his nurse's breast ('he was born a
courtier')

185 *bevy* covey of birds. Q2 has 'breede',
which is acceptable; but the appropriateness of F's 'Beauy' ('bevy') is
strongly in its favour.

186 *drossy age* present times, which are
worthless
dotes on makes a cult of

186–7 *got the tune of the time* acquired the

fashionable mannerisms of speech

187 *out of an habit of encounter* by practice
in having constant conversational
contact with other gallants. F reads
'outward habite of encounter' ('exterior manner of address'), which is
parallel to *the tune of the time*.

187–8 *yeasty collection* frothy accumulation (of modes of expression)

188 *carries* sustains
through and through right through

189 *fanned and winnowed* carefully considered. Q2 reads 'prophane and tren-
nowed', which does not make sense.
F reads 'fond and winnowed'; but
'fond' is difficult, for the meaning
the context requires is the opposite
of 'foolish'. The emendation to
'fand', that is, 'fanned' ('sifted'), is
commonly accepted, though it is
rather close to *winnowed* in meaning.
An equally probable emendation is
'profound'.

190 *are out* (soon burst)

192 *attend* await

him in the hall. He sends to know if your pleasure hold
to play with Laertes, or that you will take longer time.

HAMLET I am constant to my purposes. They follow the
King's pleasure. If his fitness speaks, mine is ready,
now or whensoever, provided I be so able as now.

LORD The King and Queen and all are coming down.

HAMLET In happy time.

200   LORD The Queen desires you to use some gentle entertainment to Laertes before you fall to play.

HAMLET She well instructs me.   *Exit the Lord*

HORATIO You will lose this wager, my lord.

HAMLET I do not think so. Since he went into France I
have been in continual practice. I shall win at the odds.
But thou wouldst not think how ill all's here about my
heart. But it is no matter.

HORATIO Nay, good my lord –

HAMLET It is but foolery. But it is such a kind of gain-
210   giving as would perhaps trouble a woman.

HORATIO If your mind dislike anything, obey it. I will
forestall their repair hither and say you are not fit.

HAMLET Not a whit. We defy augury. There is special

194 *that* if

196 *his fitness speaks* his (the King's)
readiness is declared

199 *In happy time* (a polite phrase) it is
an opportune moment

200–201 *gentle entertainment* friendliness
of attitude

204–5 *Since he went . . . continual practice.*
This is more or less consistent with
the King's words at IV.7.101–4; nevertheless at II.2.296–7 Hamlet told
Rosencrantz and Guildenstern that
he had *forgone all custom of exercises.*

205 *at the odds* with the advantage given
me (at lines 162–4)

209–10 *gaingiving* misgiving

212 *repair* coming

213 *We defy augury* I shall disdain fore-
bodings. For a moment Hamlet be-

comes almost like his admired Horatio (III.2.75–81 – though Horatio's
stoicism has no religious foundation). But it is perhaps felt to be a
moment of carelessness, rather than
heroism, before the catastrophe of
the duel.

213–14 *There is special providence in the
fall of a sparrow.* 'And fear ye not
them which kill the body, but are
not able to kill the soul; but rather
fear him which is able to destroy
both body and soul in hell. Are not
two little sparrows sold for a farth-
ing? And one of them shall not light
on the ground without your
father. Yea, even all the hairs of
your head are numbered. Fear ye
not, therefore; ye are of more value

providence in the fall of a sparrow. If it be now, 'tis not
to come. If it be not to come, it will be now. If it be not
now, yet it will come. The readiness is all. Since no man
knows of aught he leaves, what is't to leave betimes?
Let be.

> *Trumpets and drums*
> *A table prepared, with flagons of wine on it*
> *Enter officers with cushions, and other attendants with*
> *foils, daggers, and gauntlets*
> *Enter the King and Queen, Osrick, Laertes, and all*
> *the state*

KING

Come, Hamlet, come, and take this hand from me.
> *He puts Laertes's hand into Hamlet's*

HAMLET

Give me your pardon, sir. I have done you wrong.   220
But pardon't, as you are a gentleman.
This presence knows, and you must needs have heard,
How I am punished with a sore distraction.

than many sparrows', Matthew
10.28–31. The phrase is also influenced by *augury*, which originally
meant the foretelling of the future
by observing the behaviour of birds.
214 *it* my death
216–17 *The readiness is all. Since no man
knows of aught he leaves, what is't to
leave betimes?* Q2 places *knows* after
leaves. F reads: 'the readinesse is all,
since no man ha's ought of what he
leaues. What is't to leaue betimes?'
Many amendments have been suggested. On the whole, the simplest is
to suppose that *knows* in Q2 has got
out of place. The meaning is then:
'To be ready (for death) is all that
matters. As no one has knowledge
of what happens after his death, what
does an early death matter?'
218 *Let be* do not try to postpone the
fencing match. Alternatively *Let be*

may be part of the previous sentence,
giving the meaning 'since a man
cannot find out from anything on
earth (*of aught he leaves*) what is the
appropriate moment for his dying,
don't bother about it'. The words
are in Q2, not in F.
(stage direction) Q2 and F differ
slightly; see collations list 4.
state (that is, courtly attendants)
220–38 Hamlet is loyally carrying out
his mother's request (lines 200–201)
and adopts her explanation of his
behaviour (v.1.280–84).
222 *presence* royal assembly (or perhaps
only the King and Queen)
223 *punished* afflicted
a sore distraction. The excuse of madness must be regarded as disingenu-
ous. In the episode of the killing of
Polonius, Hamlet is conspicuously
sane in his discourse and expressly

What I have done
That might your nature, honour, and exception
Roughly awake, I here proclaim was madness.
Was't Hamlet wronged Laertes? Never Hamlet.
If Hamlet from himself be ta'en away,
And when he's not himself does wrong Laertes,
230   Then Hamlet does it not. Hamlet denies it.
Who does it then? His madness. If 't be so,
Hamlet is of the faction that is wronged.
His madness is poor Hamlet's enemy.
Sir, in this audience,
Let my disclaiming from a purposed evil
Free me so far in your most generous thoughts
That I have shot my arrow o'er the house
And hurt my brother.

LAERTES   I am satisfied in nature,
Whose motive in this case should stir me most
240   To my revenge. But in my terms of honour
I stand aloof, and will no reconcilement
Till by some elder masters of known honour
I have a voice and precedent of peace
To keep my name ungored. But till that time
I do receive your offered love like love,
And will not wrong it.

HAMLET   I embrace it freely,

denies to his mother that he is really
mad (III.4.140–45).
225 *exception* right to take exception
232 *faction* contending party
237 *That I have* as if I had
238 *my brother*. As Ophelia's brother,
Laertes might have been Hamlet's
brother-in-law. But the allusion
would be awkward, and perhaps,
rather, the echoes of the fratricide
are heard even here.
in nature so far as my personal feelings
are concerned (but not as regards
my position in society)

239 *Whose motive* the impulse from
which
240 *terms of honour* condition as a man of
honour
241 *will* desire
243 *voice* opinion
precedent of peace knowledge of a
precedent for my making peace with
you
245 *receive* accept
246 *will not wrong it*. Laertes's plain speaking is the extreme of treachery.
embrace welcome

And will this brothers' wager frankly play.
Give us the foils. Come on.

LAERTES   Come, one for me.

HAMLET
I'll be your foil, Laertes. In mine ignorance
Your skill shall, like a star i'th'darkest night,   250
Stick fiery off indeed.

LAERTES   You mock me, sir.

HAMLET
No, by this hand.

KING
Give them the foils, young Osrick. Cousin Hamlet,
You know the wager?

HAMLET   Very well, my lord.
Your grace has laid the odds o'th'weaker side.

KING
I do not fear it. I have seen you both.
But since he is bettered, we have therefore odds.

LAERTES
This is too heavy. Let me see another.

HAMLET
This likes me well. These foils have all a length?

---

247 *frankly* without ill-feeling
249 *foil* (a characteristic pun: 'the gold-
    leaf used to set off the brightness of
    a gem' and 'a blunted sword')
251 *Stick fiery off* shine out brightly in
    contrast
257 *But since he is bettered, we have therefore
    odds.* Perhaps *since* means 'since then',
    giving the meaning 'Since I saw you
    both fence, Laertes has improved
    himself. Therefore we are giving
    three points to Hamlet.' Another sug-
    gestion is that the King's stake is so
    much more valuable than Laertes's
    that he has asked for favourable odds.
    But it is difficult to see how this could
    be communicated to an audience.
    bettered more skilful than you (or

perhaps 'improved by his training' in
France). Q2 has 'better' for F's
'better'd'.
258 *Let me see another.* This begins the
    process (also covered by the King's
    elaborate speech at lines 261-72)
    through which Laertes secures the
    Unbated and envenomed rapier.
259 *likes* pleases
    a length one and the same length.
    From surviving rapiers it seems that
    the length of the blades varied consid-
    erably. Hamlet's question increases
    the suspense by suggesting that he
    may, contrary to the King's expecta-
    tion (IV.7.135), inspect the weapons
    and so discover the plot.

OSRICK

260 Ay, my good lord.

They prepare to play

KING

Set me the stoups of wine upon that table.
If Hamlet give the first or second hit,
Or quit in answer of the third exchange,
Let all the battlements their ordnance fire.
The King shall drink to Hamlet's better breath,
And in the cup an union shall he throw
Richer than that which four successive kings
In Denmark's crown have worn. Give me the cups,
And let the kettle to the trumpet speak,

270 The trumpet to the cannoneer without,
The cannons to the heavens, the heaven to earth,
'Now the King drinks to Hamlet.' Come, begin.

(Trumpets the while)

And you, the judges, bear a wary eye

HAMLET

Come on, sir.

LAERTES   Come, my lord.

They play

HAMLET   One.

LAERTES   No.

HAMLET   Judgement?

OSRICK

A hit, a very palpable hit.

---

263 *quit in answer of the third exchange*
  (probably) win the third bout, which
  will pay Laertes back for his having
  won the first and second. The King
  is thinking of the need to bring into
  effect his *back or second* (IV.7.152) and
  to get Hamlet to drink from the
  poisoned cup as soon as possible.
266 *cup* (the *chalice* of IV.7.159)

union large pearl
268 *Denmark's crown* (presumably that
  which he is now wearing)
269 *kettle* kettledrum
273 *judges* (of whom Osrick is the only
  active one)
274 *Judgement* (appealing to the *judges* for
  a decision)

Drum, trumpets, and shot. Flourish. A piece goes off

LAERTES   Well, again.

KING

Stay, give me drink. Hamlet, this pearl is thine.
Here's to thy health. Give him the cup.

HAMLET

I'll play this bout first; set it by awhile.
Come.

  They play
    Another hit. What say you?

LAERTES

A touch, a touch. I do confess't.   280

KING

Our son shall win.

QUEEN   He's fat and scant of breath.
Here, Hamlet, take my napkin. Rub thy brows.
The Queen carouses to thy fortune, Hamlet.

---

275 (stage direction) *Drum, trumpets, and shot.* Presumably the King or an official gives the order.
piece piece of ordnance, cannon
276 *this pearl is thine.* Presumably this is the moment when the King throws the poison into the cup, as Hamlet later believes (line 320). We would assume that the King has drunk from the cup first, but the placing of *Here's to thy health* suggests that he throws in the poison and takes a sip before it has time to dissolve; the cup will have been shaken and enough time will have elapsed before it reaches Hamlet.
278 *I'll play this bout first* (presumably a grave discourtesy, a refusal of the King's amity)
281 *He's fat and scant of breath.* The word *fat* (in both Q2 and F) is incongruous. There is slight evidence that it

could mean 'sweaty', but the usual meaning was the same as today. Possibly the Queen's tone is bantering, giving expression to her motherly happiness at her now well-behaved son. But the word may be wrong. What the sense needs is something like 'he sweats and scants his breath.' None of the emendations suggested so far (e.g. 'faint', 'hot') is satisfactory.
282 *take my napkin.* This move of the Queen can appear significant: she openly goes over to Hamlet's 'side', leaving the throne and the King. It may be a relic of the old motivation which appears in Q1: having secretly allied herself with Hamlet against the King, she suspects some treachery and is warning her son.
napkin handkerchief
283 *The Queen* (as well as the King)

HAMLET
  Good madam!

KING   Gertrude, do not drink.

QUEEN
  I will, my lord. I pray you, pardon me.
        She drinks

KING (*aside*)
  It is the poisoned cup. It is too late.

HAMLET
  I dare not drink yet, madam. By and by.

QUEEN
  Come, let me wipe thy face.

LAERTES (*aside to the King*)
  My lord, I'll hit him now.

KING (*aside to Laertes*)   I do not think't.

LAERTES (*aside*)
290 And yet it is almost against my conscience.

HAMLET
  Come for the third, Laertes. You do but dally.
  I pray you, pass with your best violence.
  I am afeard you make a wanton of me.

LAERTES
  Say you so? Come on.
        They play

OSRICK
  Nothing neither way.

284, 286 *do not drink . . . It is the poisoned cup. It is too late.* At this sudden turn of events the King, for all his usual skill and promptitude, cannot summon the energy to face the peril of abandoning the plot by saving his Queen.

289 *I do not think't.* Perhaps this is almost a moment of despair in the King, though he retains his self-control as he waits for the Queen to show the effects of the poison.

292 *pass* make your thrusts

293 *make a wanton of me* are playing with me as if I were a child (unworthy of your serious swordsmanship). Perhaps the implication is that Laertes's bad *conscience* is affecting his skill.

LAERTES

Have at you now!

In scuffling they change rapiers, and both are wounded
with the poisoned weapon

KING   Part them. They are incensed.

HAMLET

Nay, come. Again!

The Queen falls

OSRICK   Look to the Queen there. Ho!

HORATIO

They bleed on both sides. How is it, my lord?

OSRICK

How is't, Laertes?

LAERTES

Why, as a woodcock to mine own springe, Osrick.   300
I am justly killed with mine own treachery.

HAMLET

How does the Queen?

KING   She swounds to see them bleed.

---

296 *Have at you now!* This is usually interpreted as indicating that Laertes suddenly thrusts at Hamlet, without warning, and wounds him, thus apprising him of the treachery.

(stage direction) Q2 has no stage direction for the exchange of rapiers. F has '*In scuffling they change Rapiers*'. The compiler of Q1 remembered the situation as '*They catch one anothers Rapiers, and both are wounded, Leartes falles downe, the Queene falles downe and dies*'. Probably Burbage displayed a virtuoso piece of swordsmanship as Hamlet. When in a tight corner a swordsman would throw down his own weapon and seize the blade of his opponent's, securing enough leverage to wrench it away. The opponent then had no alternative but to pick up the other

weapon, by which time his opponent would have recovered himself.

Part them. The King wishes to save Laertes.

297 *Ho!* Perhaps this is Osrick's cry to stop the duel in accordance with the King's instructions. Q2 reads 'howe' here and 'how' at line 305; this was a common spelling of 'ho', though 'how' could be an exclamatory interrogative.

300 *as a woodcock to mine own springe* (a curious echo of Polonius's *springes to catch woodcocks*, 1.3.115)

302 *She swounds to see them bleed.* He tries to keep up appearances and to cover the cause of the Queen's collapse. Knowing that the Queen, Hamlet, and Laertes will soon be dead, he can still hope to escape exposure.

swounds swoons

QUEEN

No, no, the drink, the drink! O my dear Hamlet!
The drink, the drink! I am poisoned.

  She dies

HAMLET

O, villainy! Ho! Let the door be locked.
Treachery! Seek it out.

LAERTES

It is here, Hamlet. Hamlet, thou art slain.
No medicine in the world can do thee good.
In thee there is not half an hour's life.
310 The treacherous instrument is in thy hand,
Unbated and envenomed. The foul practice
Hath turned itself on me. Lo, here I lie,
Never to rise again. Thy mother's poisoned.
I can no more. The King, the King's to blame.

HAMLET

The point envenomed too?
Then, venom, to thy work.

  He wounds the King

ALL

Treason! Treason!

KING

O, yet defend me, friends. I am but hurt.

---

304 *poisoned.* The terrible word arouses
Hamlet's fury.

(stage direction) *She dies.* There is no
indication in Q2 or F; perhaps the
Queen, speechless, hears and sees
some of the later words and actions
before dying. Hamlet's *Follow my
mother* (line 321) implies that he
knows she is dying, if not dead; his
Wretched Queen, adieu! (line 327) may
be an immediate response, accompanied by some gesture, to her death.

311 *Unbated ... practice* (an echo of the
King's words at IV.7.137)

practice plot

314 *can no more* can say no more. But in
fact Laertes is able to give the first
public evidence of the King's guilt.

316 *Then, venom, to thy work.* Hamlet
never really becomes a contriving
revenger. He kills the King, as he
had killed Polonius, on the spur of
the moment.

318 *but hurt* only wounded. Perhaps he
is intended to suppose that the
poison on the sword-point has been
used up on Hamlet and Laertes.

HAMLET
   Here, thou incestuous, murderous, damnèd Dane,
   Drink off this potion.
      He forces the King to drink
                 Is thy union here?   320
   Follow my mother.
      The King dies
LAERTES   He is justly served.
   It is a poison tempered by himself.
   Exchange forgiveness with me, noble Hamlet.
   Mine and my father's death come not upon thee,
   Nor thine on me!
      He dies

HAMLET
   Heaven make thee free of it! I follow thee.
   I am dead, Horatio. Wretched Queen, adieu!
   You that look pale and tremble at this chance,
   That are but mutes or audience to this act,
   Had I but time – as this fell sergeant, Death,   330
   Is strict in his arrest – O, I could tell you –
   But let it be. Horatio, I am dead.
   Thou livest. Report me and my cause aright
   To the unsatisfied.
HORATIO   Never believe it.
   I am more an antique Roman than a Dane.

---

320 *Is thy union here?* Hamlet is probably
   still making a pun, referring to his
   uncle's *union* in marriage with his
   mother.
321 (stage direction) *The King dies*. Claudius dies without contrition or forgiveness, unlike Laertes.
322 *tempered* compounded
326 *make thee free* acquit you of the guilt
328 *You that look pale* ... (the courtiers
   and attendants)
329 *mutes* actors with wordless parts in a
   play

330 *as* which I have not, because
   sergeant (an officer of the sheriff, responsible for arrests)
331 *arrest* (doubtless a final pun: death
   stops him from proceeding with his
   story)
334 *the unsatisfied* those who are in doubt
   about my conduct
335 *more an antique Roman than a Dane*.
   The common notion that, among the
   Romans, suicide was an acceptable
   way of escaping from an intolerable
   situation derived from the many

Here's yet some liquor left.

HAMLET   As th' art a man,
Give me the cup. Let go. By heaven, I'll ha't!
O God, Horatio, what a wounded name,
Things standing thus unknown, shall I leave behind me!
340   If thou didst ever hold me in thy heart,
Absent thee from felicity awhile,
And in this harsh world draw thy breath in pain,
To tell my story.
          A march afar off, and shout within
                    What warlike noise is this?

OSRICK
Young Fortinbras, with conquest come from Poland,
To the ambassadors of England gives
This warlike volley.

HAMLET   O, I die, Horatio!
The potent poison quite o'er-crows my spirit.

---

stories in which stoical Roman nobles foiled the dishonour they suffered from wicked emperors. A Christian Dane would know that *the Everlasting had ... fixed | His canon 'gainst self-slaughter* (1.2.131–2). But Horatio's Roman allusion is congruous with the classical education he showed at 1.1.113–25. Here he temporarily loses the imperturbability of one who *Fortune's buffets and rewards* has *ta'en with equal thanks* (III.2.77–8).

338 *wounded name* damaged reputation

339 *shall I leave behind me.* This is the Q2 reading. F has 'shall liue behind me', and Q1 'wouldst thou leaue behinde'. The excellent suggestion has been made that the Q2 reading is a mistake for an original 'shall't leave behind me', which improves the scansion and the meaning.

341 *felicity.* Hamlet refers to the happiness of release from life's miseries (compare III.1.63–4) rather than to

the joys of heaven.

343 (stage direction) *and shout within.* This is only in F. Many editors have emended *shout* to *shot* or *shoot*, to connect with the *warlike volley* in line 346. Both Q2 and F have an entry for Osrick at the end of the line, though there has been no reasonable point of exit for him. Probably no more is implied than that he comes forward to give his explanation of the *warlike noise.*

344 *with conquest come from Poland.* This is the first news of the outcome of Fortinbras's expedition (II.2.72–80, IV.4).

345 *the ambassadors of England* the Englishmen coming as ambassadors to the King of Denmark (see lines 71–2). The dramatic time has been drastically shortened.

347 *o'er-crows* triumphs over (like the victor in cock-fighting)

I cannot live to hear the news from England.
But I do prophesy th'election lights
On Fortinbras. He has my dying voice.   350
So tell him, with th'occurrents, more and less,
Which have solicited – the rest is silence.
        He dies

HORATIO

Now cracks a noble heart. Good night, sweet Prince,
And flights of angels sing thee to thy rest!
        (*March within*)
Why does the drum come hither?
        *Enter Fortinbras, with the Ambassadors and with his
        train of drum, colours, and attendants*

FORTINBRAS

Where is this sight?

HORATIO   What is it you would see?

349–50 *But I do prophesy ... Fortinbras.*
This does not mean that there is any
connexion between *the news from England* and *the election* (to the Danish
throne). Rather, Hamlet turns aside
from the triviality of the fate of
Rosencrantz and Guildenstern to his
serious concern for the future of the
Danish crown. Perhaps some stage
business is required: he is handed
the crown of Denmark (taken from
the dead Claudius), and his dying
thoughts, self-forgetful and calm, are
upon its inheritance by a worthy
successor.
    Shakespeare does not intend us to
regard Fortinbras as a tyrant, or his
assumption of power as arbitrary.
The praise bestowed on him by
Hamlet (*a delicate and tender prince*,
IV.4.48) is important, confirming the
good impression of Fortinbras given
throughout the play (II.2.68–80 and
IV.4.1–8). In many respects Fortinbras seems to embody Hamlet's ideal

of kingship.
    lights | On alights upon
350 *voice* vote
351 *occurrents, more and less* incidents,
    great and small
352 *solicited* – incited me to –. Probably
    Hamlet breaks off in mid-sentence,
    intending to continue with some-
    thing like 'my various actions over
    the last few months'.
    silence. F somewhat incongruously
    adds 'O, o, o, o' (presumably indicat-
    ing the actor's dying groans).
354 *flights of angels sing* may companies
    of angels sing
355 (stage direction) *his train.* As there
    are now four dead bodies on the
    stage, requiring at least eight men
    for their simultaneous removal,
    Shakespeare has good reason to
    bring on a stage-army. It provides a
    splendid military finale.
    drum drummer
    colours military ensigns

If aught of woe or wonder, cease your search.

FORTINBRAS

This quarry cries on havoc. O proud Death,
What feast is toward in thine eternal cell

360 That thou so many princes at a shot
So bloodily hast struck?

AMBASSADOR   The sight is dismal,
And our affairs from England come too late.
The ears are senseless that should give us hearing,
To tell him his commandment is fulfilled,
That Rosencrantz and Guildenstern are dead.
Where should we have our thanks?

HORATIO   Not from his mouth,
Had it th'ability of life to thank you.
He never gave commandment for their death.
But since, so jump upon this bloody question,

370 You from the Polack wars, and you from England,
Are here arrived, give order that these bodies
High on a stage be placèd to the view.
And let me speak to th'yet unknowing world
How these things came about. So shall you hear
Of carnal, bloody, and unnatural acts,

---

358 *quarry cries on havoc* heap of dead
   proclaims that the hunters have carried out their slaughter (rather than
   '. . . cries out for revenge')
359 *toward* in preparation
   thine eternal cell (the grave)
361 *dismal* (a strong word) calamitous
363 *The ears* (Claudius's)
366 *Where should we have our thanks?* The
   Ambassador seems to be politely inquiring about the succession to the
   throne of Denmark.
   his (Claudius's)
367 *Had it th'ability of life* even if it
   could utter words

369 *jump* exactly
   question conflict
371 *give order* (presumably addressed to
   Fortinbras, who has his military
   power with him)
372 *stage* platform
373 *let me speak*. Horatio is proposing to
   speak to the people, rather like Mark
   Antony in *Julius Caesar*, III.2.
375 *carnal, bloody, and unnatural acts* (the
   murder of King Hamlet by his
   brother Claudius and the Queen's
   remarriage; the plot against Prince
   Hamlet which was to lead to his
   execution in England)

Of accidental judgements, casual slaughters,
Of deaths put on by cunning and forced cause,
And, in this upshot, purposes mistook
Fallen on th'inventors' heads. All this can I
Truly deliver.

FORTINBRAS Let us haste to hear it,   380
And call the noblest to the audience.
For me, with sorrow I embrace my fortune.
I have some rights of memory in this kingdom,
Which now to claim my vantage doth invite me.

HORATIO

Of that I shall have also cause to speak,
And from his mouth whose voice will draw on more.

---

376 *accidental judgements, casual slaughters*
(the unpremeditated killing of Polonius behind the arras; Ophelia's drowning; the Queen's unintended death by poison; the killing of Laertes by his own *Unbated and envenomed* sword)

377 *deaths put on by cunning and forced cause*
(the intended death of Hamlet by execution in England; the consequent deaths of Rosencrantz and Guildenstern)
  put on instigated
  forced not genuine

378 *in this upshot* as a final result of this

378–9 *purposes mistook | Fallen on th'inventors' heads* (the death of Laertes by the unbated sword intended for use on Hamlet; the Queen's death by the poison intended for Hamlet; the King's death by the poisoned sword and drink)

383 *I have some rights of memory.* Fortinbras's claims to the Danish throne have not hitherto been mentioned, nor are we told what they are. But we remember that old Fortinbras forfeited his personal lands to old Hamlet (1.1.80–104 and 1.2.17–25) and so his son might regard himself

as the residual heir to the throne after the expiring of the Hamlet lineage. It is notable that Fortinbras speaks only of *rights of memory* in Denmark. He is not like Malcolm in *Macbeth* or Richmond in *Richard III*, the rightful heir to the throne who ousts a regicide and usurper and so can cleanse the kingdom of corruption. A peaceful transfer of the throne to a strong, worthy, and rightful claimant, and so an avoidance of political disorder, is what the ending of this tragedy requires (and perhaps supplies).
  of memory ('not forgotten' (by you) or 'ancient' (claims). Perhaps both meanings are implied.)

384 *Which* (this kingdom)
  my vantage good fortune

386 *from his mouth.* See lines 350–51.
  whose voice will draw on more. Denmark being an elective monarchy, Fortinbras's claims will be dependent upon his winning support. The approval of him by the popular Prince Hamlet as he died will win him many votes in the election.

But let this same be presently performed,
Even while men's minds are wild, lest more mischance
On plots and errors happen.

FORTINBRAS   Let four captains

390   Bear Hamlet like a soldier to the stage.
For he was likely, had he been put on,
To have proved most royal. And for his passage
The soldiers' music and the rites of war
Speak loudly for him.
Take up the bodies. Such a sight as this
Becomes the field, but here shows much amiss.
Go, bid the soldiers shoot.

Exeunt marching; after the which a peal of
ordnance is shot off

387 *this same* (Horatio's proposal that he give *to the yet unknowing world* a full account, which will include Hamlet's recommendation of Fortinbras) *presently* immediately

389 *On plots and errors* on top of the plots and misjudgements. Horatio fears disorder as a result of the disasters to the ruling house.

391–2 *he was likely, had he been put on,* | *To have proved most royal.* The tribute over the dead body of the tragic hero is conventional. It does not necessarily cast a light over the whole of the preceding play. A similar problem faces us in *Julius Caesar*, where Mark Antony praises Brutus as 'the noblest Roman of them all' (v.5.68–75), and in *Coriolanus*, where Aufidius praises Coriolanus: 'he shall have a noble memory' (v.6.155). But Fortinbras's strong words are consistent with Ophelia's *Th'expectancy and rose of the fair state* (III.1.153).

391 *put on* put to the test (by his accession to the throne, rather than by following a career as a soldier)

392 *passage* (from this life to the other world)

393 *The soldiers' music and the rites of war.* A military funeral is described by Aufidius at the end of *Coriolanus,* v.5.149–52:

> Take him up.
> Help three o'th'chiefest soldiers; I'll be one.
> Beat thou the drum, that it speak mournfully.
> Trail your steel pikes.

394 *Speak* ('let them speak')

396 *field* battlefield

397 *shoot . . . a peal of ordnance is shot off.* This again reminds us, unhappily or ironically, of Claudius's partiality for gunshot (1.2.124–8, 1.4.8–12, and v.2.269–72).

OTHELLO

Introduction

Othello was written between 1602 and 1604, soon after *Hamlet* and not long before *King Lear*. It was performed at Court, not necessarily for the first time, in the autumn of 1604. Shakespeare found the plot in Giraldi Cinthio's collection of tales, *Hecatommithi* (1565); and his departures from his source throw light on his dramatic purpose.

Cinthio's is a sordid, melodramatic tale of sexual jealousy, and at first sight it may seem strange that Shakespeare should have been attracted by it. The heroine, called Disdemona, does not elope with the Moor (whose name is not given); her family agree to the marriage, though with some reluctance; and the couple live together in great happiness in Venice. The Moor is appointed to the command in Cyprus (Cinthio makes no mention of the Turkish danger). The Moor and his wife travel on the same boat. The villain's sole motive for his actions is his unsuccessful love for Disdemona, for which he blames the Captain (Shakespeare's Cassio). His plot is directed not against the Moor, but against Disdemona; and he is sexually, but not professionally, jealous of the Captain. The latter draws his sword upon one of the guard. He is not made drunk by the Ensign and there is no Roderigo. The Ensign steals the handkerchief while Disdemona is caressing his child. The Captain finds it in his house and, knowing it to be Disdemona's, he tries to return it; but he leaves hurriedly on hearing the Moor's voice. The murder of Disdemona is carried out by the villain and the Moor together: they knock her senseless with a sandbag and make the roof fall, so as to make the deed look like an accident. Finally, the Moor is killed by Disdemona's kinsmen. The

Ensign is tortured to death for another crime; and his wife was privy to the whole story. We have some pity for his victim, but no sympathy for the Moor.

There are several points in Cinthio's tale which may have fired Shakespeare's imagination. Jealousy was a theme to which he returned again and again, farcically in *The Merry Wives of Windsor*, tragi-comically in *Much Ado about Nothing* (where Claudio is deluded by a villain into believing Hero is unchaste), and he was later to deal with the subject again in the plays of his last period: in *Cymbeline* Posthumus is tricked by a villain into believing his wife has committed adultery; and in *The Winter's Tale*, where Leontes's jealousy of Hermione is self-begotten. In all these plays, as in Cinthio's story, the suspected woman is innocent. Then it was obvious that the misalliance of a white woman with a Moor offered dramatic opportunities; and the repentance of the Moor after the murder:

It came about that the Moor, who had loved the lady more than his very eyes, felt his loss and began to suffer so much longing for her that he went about like one out of his mind, looking for her in all sorts of places in the house

would suggest the tragedy of the man who kills the thing he loves. Above all, perhaps, Cinthio's description of the Ensign:

although he was a most detestable character, nevertheless with high-sounding words he concealed the malice he bore in his heart, in such a way that he showed himself outwardly like another Hector or Achilles

would chime with one of Shakespeare's obsessive themes – the contrast between appearance and reality, and the difficulty of distinguishing between the two. Claudio, confronted with the evidence of Hero's unchastity, exclaims:

> *Out on thee! Seeming! . . .*
> *You seemed to me as Dian in her orb.*

Isabella, in *Measure for Measure*, determines to unmask the 'seeming' of Angelo. Troilus finds it difficult to believe that the Cressida who capitulates to Diomed is the same person as the one he had loved. Hamlet discovers that one may smile and be a villain. Henry V's chief complaint of the conspirators against him was their hypocrisy. The villain in Cinthio's tale, whose persona was accepted by all his associates as his real character, posed the question of 'seeming' in its extreme form. It has been suggested that the question had a professional interest to Shakespeare. If an actor could play the role of a saint or even a woman so as to convince an audience, how was it possible to tell in real life whether a man was what he seemed? Iago, in a sense, is the apotheosis of the actor.

To transform the melodramatic story into tragedy necessit-ated a number of important changes. First, the character of the Moor, if it was to arouse tragic sympathy, had to be invested with nobility and greatness. This Shakespeare achieved prim-arily by the poetry he gave him to speak, which characterizes him as noble, magnanimous, royal, exotic, and (some critics believe) egotistical. Then Shakespeare added the threat to Cyprus by the Turks to show Othello's indispensability to the Venetian state: as even Iago admits,

> *Another of his fathom they have none*
> *To lead their business.*

The background of Othello's life is filled in, partly by his autobiographical account of his 'travels' history' and partly by references throughout the play to incidents in his past life, from the death of his brother at his side, recounted by Iago, to the slaying of the malignant Turk in Aleppo. Most important of all is the way Shakespeare convinces us that Othello never ceases to love the bride he murders: he does not merely allow the love to be revived after the murder. Othello commits the murder himself and he executes justice on himself as soon as he knows that Desdemona was innocent.

Secondly, Shakespeare rejected the simple motivation of Cinthio's villain and made Iago direct his hatred, not against Desdemona, but against the Moor.

Thirdly, he invented the character of Roderigo, 'a gull'd Gentleman' as he is called in the Folio Dramatis Personae. He seems to have taken a hint from his own *Twelfth Night*, where Sir Toby Belch extracts money from Sir Andrew Aguecheek by promising to arrange for his marriage to Olivia, just as Iago promises Desdemona to Roderigo. Desdemona's marriage threatens to cut off Iago's supply of money from his dupe, and he therefore holds out the promise that she will take a lover – and this suggests to Iago the accusation of Cassio.

Fourthly, Shakespeare altered the character of Cassio. In Cinthio's tale he is wounded after supping with a prostitute. Shakespeare softens this by making the relationship between Cassio and Bianca less mercenary. He gives the handkerchief not to the *donna* in his lodgings – usually translated 'wife', though this is not necessarily Cinthio's meaning – but to Bianca. This tightens the structure, eliminates an inessential character, and gives Iago a useful instrument for arousing Othello's fury. The brawl which leads to the Captain's dismissal is not engineered by Cinthio's villain. Shakespeare reduces the element of chance by making Iago incite Roderigo to brave Cassio, by making Cassio have a poor head for drinking, by making Iago suggest to Cassio that he should ask Desdemona to intercede for him, and by making Cassio privy to Othello's courtship of Desdemona.

Fifthly, Shakespeare alters the way in which Iago gets possession of the handkerchief. In the source, as we have seen, the villain steals the handkerchief from Disdemona's girdle while she is fondling his child. Shakespeare may have altered this incident so that he could dispense with the child, or because the Iago he had created would not have had a child. The incident he substituted for it is at first sight less plausible: Desdemona drops the handkerchief and Emilia picks it up and gives it to Iago. It has been argued that this change turns accident into design. She forgets about the handkerchief, which she prizes as Othello's first gift to her, only at the moment when she is worried about his headache. Her forgetfulness is in the circumstances a sign of her love, not of carelessness.

Sixthly, Shakespeare alters the character of Emilia. Cinthio makes the villain's wife privy to his plot, but afraid to reveal it. Emilia, though she steals the handkerchief, is deceived, like everyone else, by her husband; and she turns against him as soon as she learns the truth.

It has been suggested that Shakespeare's treatment of the plot was influenced by a tale in Geoffrey Fenton's *Certaine Tragicall Discourses* (1567), in which a foreign soldier, an Albanian captain, kills his innocent wife out of jealousy. The wife bewails her 'wretched fortune' but continues to love her husband; the Captain, when about to stab his wife, 'embraced and kissed her, in such sort as Judas kissed our Lord the same night he betrayed him', as Othello kisses Desdemona; the wife's confession to God is cut short by her want of breath; and the Captain, like Othello, commits suicide, commending his soul 'to the reprobate society of Judas and Cain'. If Shakespeare was influenced by Fenton's tale, it would lend some support to those who believe that there is an allusion to Judas's kiss of betrayal in Othello's last speech.

We are on more certain ground in supposing that Shakespeare went to Lewkenor's translation of Cardinal Contarini's *Commonwealth and Government of Venice* for some of his information about the Venetian state and that he made copious use of Philemon Holland's translation of Pliny's *Natural History* for filling in the exotic background of Othello's career. The Anthropophagi and other details of his defence before the senate, the simile of the Pontic Sea, and the reference to chrysolite are the most striking examples.

Richard Burbage, the leading actor in Shakespeare's company, played the part of the 'grieved Moor' and it was one of his greatest successes. We are told by Shakespeare's neighbour, Leonard Digges, that audiences were bored with Jonson's tragedies:

> *They prized more*
> *Honest Iago, or the jealous Moor.*

After the Restoration the play was attacked by Thomas Rymer for its improbabilities and for its failure to satisfy the demands of poetic justice. He concluded that the play was 'a bloody farce without salt or savour'; that the character of Iago was incredible because soldiers are genuinely honest; that the morals to be drawn from it are to warn 'all maidens of quality, without their parents' consent', not to run away with blackamoors, to warn 'all good wives, that they look well to their linen', and a warning to husbands 'that before their jealousy be tragical, the proof may be mathematical'. But Rymer's most serious complaint is that the innocent Desdemona is murdered:

What instruction can we make out of this catastrophe? Or whither must our reflection lead us? Is not this to envenom and sour our spirits, to make us repine and grumble at Providence, and the government of the world? If this be our end, what boots it to be virtuous?

Few later critics have taken Rymer's complaints seriously. But there have been several who have felt uneasy about the conclusion. Johnson found the last scene unendurable; Bradley thought the play evoked feelings of depression; and Granville-Barker declared that it was a tragedy without meaning. It is not merely that an innocent woman is murdered – for Lady Macduff and Cordelia are as innocent and Ophelia's fate is equally undeserved – but that the hero himself is degraded and destroyed by the villainy of his subordinate. It will be necessary to examine in some detail the characters of Iago and Othello to see how far these feelings of disquiet are justifiable.

Some actors playing the part of Iago make him into such an obvious villain that he deceives no one; but the essential thing about him, as of Cinthio's villain, is that he appears to be honest. That is the point of the iteration of *honest* and *honesty* right down to the moment of his unmasking. He deceives not merely Othello and Cassio, but Montano, Lodovico, and even

Emilia. Even Roderigo, indeed, who knows Iago is not honest, does not at first suspect that he himself is being duped.

One actor who realized how the part should be played was Bensley, whom Charles Lamb described as

the only endurable one which I remember to have seen. No spectator, from his action, could divine more of his artifice than Othello was supposed to do. His confessions in soliloquy alone put you in possession of the mystery. There were no by-intimations to make the audience fancy their own discernment so much greater than that of the Moor. The Iago of Bensley did not go to work so grossly. There was a triumphant tone about the character, natural to a general consciousness of power; but none of that petty vanity which chuckles and cannot contain itself upon any little successful stroke of its knavery — as is common with your small villains, and green probationers in mischief. It did not clap or crow before its time. It was not a man setting his wits at a child, and winking all the while at other children, who are mightily pleased at being let into the secret; but a consummate villain entrapping a noble nature into toils against which no discernment was available, where the manner was as fathomless as the purpose seemed dark, and without motive.

Apart from the last two words of this description, to which we shall have occasion to return, Lamb's account of Bensley's performance shows that the actor had precisely the right conception of the part. It was followed by Edwin Booth, the American actor, of whose Iago we are told that 'if Othello had suddenly turned upon him, at any moment in their interview, he would have seen only the grave, sympathetic, respectful, troubled face that was composed for him to see'. He advised any actor playing the part to 'try to impress even the audience with your sincerity . . . Iago should appear to be what all but the audience believe he is.' A great actor of our own day, Sir Ralph Richardson, played the part in the same way. If Iago is played as an obvious villain, Othello and the other characters are reduced to credulous fools, whereas Shakespeare, as we have suggested, was concerned with the difficulty of distinguishing between appearance and reality, with the impossibility of detecting an absolute hypocrite.

Lamb, as we have seen, accepts Coleridge's view that Iago's malignity was motiveless. It was accepted, too, by Hazlitt, Swinburne, Bradley and Granville-Barker and by many other critics, who assume that he loves evil for its own sake, that he has said, with Satan, 'Evil be thou my good', and that the various motives he acknowledges are mere rationalizations. The Ensign of Shakespeare's source, as we have seen, is motivated simply by his hatred of Disdemona, arising from his thwarted lust. This motive is mentioned by Iago only once. In addition to this motive taken from Cinthio, Shakespeare provides several more, presented with equal casualness, and seldom referred to more than once. In the first scene Iago tells Roderigo that he hates Othello for choosing Cassio, rather than himself, as his Lieutenant; but this motive is not directly mentioned after the first scene of the play, except once, casually, in the soliloquy at the end of the Act:

> To get his place and to plume up my will
> In double knavery.

Even his desire to get Cassio's place fades into the background, though we are later reminded of it by Emilia in the lines:

> I will be hanged if some eternal villain,
> Some busy and insinuating rogue,
> Some cogging, cozening slave, to get some office,
> Have not devised this slander . . .

In his first soliloquy (I.3.377–82) Iago mentions another motive, that Othello is 'thought abroad' to have seduced Emilia. This is mentioned again in his second soliloquy (II.1.286–7) with the addition that he also suspects Cassio of cuckolding him. Neither of these motives is mentioned again. Iago's ultimate motives for getting Roderigo to murder Cassio are not mentioned until the last Act (v.1.11–22) – that Othello may reveal Iago's accusations to him, and that

> *He hath a daily beauty in his life*
> *That makes me ugly.*

It is not, therefore, surprising that Coleridge should describe one of the soliloquies as 'the motive-hunting of a motiveless malignity'.

Yet, from the nature of Iago's role, he cannot reveal himself except in soliloquy; and there are no soliloquies in Shakespeare's plays – or, indeed, in any Elizabethan plays – which do not express the genuine feelings or beliefs of the characters speaking them. We ought, therefore, to be suspicious of everything that Iago says to another person, unless it is afterwards corroborated, and to accept what he says in soliloquy, not of course as true, but as the expression of his actual feelings.

The soliloquy at the end of Act I is, in fact, a displaced aside in which Iago removes the mask for the first time: it throws a retrospective light on his dialogues with Roderigo. The marriage of Othello and Desdemona has come as a shock to Iago, because it threatens to cut off his main source of income. Since he can no longer get paid by Roderigo for assisting his suit with Desdemona, he has to convince his dupe that he hates Othello and that he will assist Roderigo to seduce Desdemona. As a proof of his hatred, he mentions the way Cassio has obtained the lieutenantship he thought that he himself deserved; and he shows this hatred in action by the foul images he uses about Othello's marriage in awakening Brabantio. It is significant that only Iago and Brabantio seem to have any colour prejudice against Othello. In the third scene Iago, anxious to persuade Roderigo that Desdemona is still attainable, assures him that when her lust for the Moor is sated she will find it 'as acerbe as the coloquintida' and she will turn to a younger man. Up to this point in the play the audience may assume that Iago hates Othello for his appointment of Cassio, that he hates Cassio for the same reason, that he is pretending loyalty to Othello for his own ends, and that he purports to have the lowest opinion of Desdemona's motives in marrying a coloured man. Then he is left alone; and before he begins to frame his plot against Othello he reveals his suspicion that he has been cuckolded (lines 380-84):

> *I hate the Moor,*
> *And it is thought abroad that 'twixt my sheets*
> *He's done my office. I know not if't be true*
> *But I, for mere suspicion in that kind,*
> *Will do as if for surety.*

It is noteworthy that Iago does not say he hates the Moor *because* the latter has cuckolded him, or even because people think it, but that he hates the Moor, '*and* it is thought abroad . . .' Bernard Spivack stresses the significance of the conjunction as 'The seam between the drama of allegory and the drama of nature, as well as between the kind of motivation proper to each'. In other words, Iago is both a stage devil, deriving ultimately from the Vice of the Morality plays, and a character in a more sophisticated Elizabethan tragedy. He hates goodness, at the same time as he has psychological motives for hating Othello.

We have some confirmation, not of the truth of Iago's suspicion, as some critics have absurdly supposed, but of the fact that he had indeed suspected his wife in Emilia's words in Act IV (2.144-6):

> *Some such squire he was*
> *That turned your wit the seamy side without*
> *And made you to suspect me with the Moor.*

Shakespeare, we may suppose, would not have inserted these lines in a later scene if he had wanted us to think that Iago's suspicions were invented on the spur of the moment to justify his villainy. Iago, however, is not so much concerned with Emilia's unfaithfulness, as with the fact that he is despised or pitied, or an object of ridicule as a cuckold; and this is intolerable to his self-esteem. The fact that this motive is not mentioned until this point does not in itself prove that it is merely a rationalization, for, of course, he would not mention it to Roderigo or to anyone else. It is considered respectable to act from feelings of injured merit: he could never admit that he feared he was an object of ridicule.

Booth was quite right to make Iago wince when Cassio kisses Emilia, for it leads on to the revelation in the second soliloquy that he fears Cassio with his night-cap too. His aside, spoken while Cassio is conversing with Desdemona, suggests that he is not merely pretending for his own ends that Cassio and Desdemona are in love with each other, but that he is, perhaps unconsciously, identifying himself with the supposedly amorous Cassio – 'Would they were clyster-pipes for your sake!' – and in the next soliloquy we learn why (II.1.282–98):

> *Now, I do love her too;*
> *Not out of absolute lust – though peradventure*
> *I stand accountant for as great a sin –*
> *But partly led to diet my revenge*
> *For that I do suspect the lusty Moor*
> *Hath leaped into my seat, the thought whereof*
> *Doth, like a poisonous mineral, gnaw my inwards,*
> *And nothing can, or shall, content my soul*
> *Till I am evened with him, wife for wife;*
> *Or failing so, yet that I put the Moor*
> *At least into a jealousy so strong*
> *That judgement cannot cure . . .*
> *I'll have our Michael Cassio on the hip,*
> *Abuse him to the Moor in the rank garb –*
> *For I fear Cassio with my night-cap too . . .*

Here, if anywhere, is the motive-hunting of which Coleridge speaks. But, as Kittredge and others have argued, Iago's jealousy is not a pretence but 'a raging torment'. The image of the poisonous mineral convinces one by its force and vividness. We may suspect that the professional jealousy at Cassio's appointment only rankled so much because Iago thought he had reason to hate Othello and Cassio on other grounds.

We learn one other thing from these lines: that Iago loves Desdemona, not, he tells us, 'out of absolute lust' but partly to feed his revenge, either by cuckolding Othello or getting someone else to do it for him. In Shakespeare's source, as we have seen, the Ancient's love for Disdemona is the primary motive for his actions. Shakespeare makes it subordinate to others; but there are several hints earlier in the play, and others on the first night in Cyprus, that Iago is jealous of Othello's success with Desdemona, as well as of his supposed seduction of Emilia. It is therefore not surprising that in Act III, scene 3, Iago should be able to describe the pangs of jealousy so vividly: he is drawing on his own experience. He knows only too well

> *the green-eyed monster, which doth mock*
> *The meat it feeds on*

and he knows that

> *Dangerous conceits are in their natures poisons,*
> *Which at the first are scarce found to distaste,*
> *But, with a little act upon the blood,*
> *Burn like the mines of sulphur.*

The secret of Iago is not a motiveless malignity – though, being evil, he has a natural hatred of good – but a pathological jealousy of his wife, a suspicion of every man with whom she is acquainted, and a jealous love of Desdemona, which makes him take a vicarious pleasure in other men's actual or prospective enjoyment of her at the same time as it arouses his hatred of the successful Moor.

As Lily B. Campbell has shown, the Elizabethans recognized several different kinds of jealousy. Tofte in *The Blazon of Jealousie* (1613) described one sort, very like Iago's, as 'when we would not have that any one should obtain . . . that which we wish and desire to obtain'. Iago's jealousy is a kind of envy, which, Bacon tells us, is

the vilest affection, and the most depraved; for which cause, it is the
proper attribute of the Devil, who is called The Envious Man, that
soweth tares amongst the wheat by night. *As it always cometh to*
pass, that Envy worketh subtilly, and in the dark; and to the prejudice
of good things, such as is the wheat.

Jealousy and envy are thus the springs of Iago's conduct, and
his plot against Othello has the advantage of hurting the three
people against whom he bears a grudge. Nor need we regard
this multiplication of motives as incredible, for they all spring
from the same basic attitude to life, the self-love of which he
boasts to Roderigo, what Bacon called 'wisdom for a man's
self'.

Iago has one more important soliloquy at the end of Act II,
after he has suggested that Cassio should beg Desdemona to
plead for him. Its main function is to explain to the audience
why he has made this suggestion. But in the course of the
speech he pays an indirect tribute to the depth of Othello's love
for Desdemona; he admits that Desdemona is virtuous, despite
his previous remarks about her, and that he is going to use her
goodness to enmesh Othello and Cassio as well as her, and he
speaks of the 'Divinity of hell' by which he is governed. His
dedication to evil, revealed both here and in his first soliloquy,
is as important to an understanding of his character as the
psychological motives we have attempted to analyse. Othello is
right to speak of him in the last scene as a demi-devil.

At the end of the play Iago is perfectly willing to confess
what he has done, but he refuses to answer Othello's question
(v.2.299):

Why he hath thus ensnared my soul and body?

Some critics believe that he could not have answered the
question, even if he had wanted to; but if the above analysis of
his character has been sound, the reason for his obstinate
silence is that he will reveal neither his own jealousy, nor his
dedication to evil.

It is important to believe in the reality for him of Iago's motives. As with all Shakespeare's mature plays the dramatic relationship of one character to another is of great importance. It has often been pointed out that in *Hamlet* there are four young men who have the task of avenging their fathers – Laertes, Fortinbras and Pyrrhus, as well as Hamlet himself. So in *Othello* we observe the operations of jealousy in several different characters – in the comic dupe, Roderigo, in Bianca, in Iago and in Othello himself. The main theme is the way in which a jealous villain – whose villainy cannot be penetrated by anyone because of the impossibility of distinguishing between genuine and apparent honesty – succeeds in infecting an essentially noble man, one who is 'not easily jealous', with his own jealousy; and, in so doing, drags him down to his own level.

Those who have written on the imagery of the play have shown how the hold Iago has over Othello is illustrated by the language Shakespeare puts into their mouths. Both characters use a great deal of animal imagery, and it is interesting to note its distribution. Iago's occurs mostly in the first three Acts of the play: he mentions, for example, ass, daws, flies, ram, jennet, guinea-hen, baboon, wild-cat, snipe, goats, monkeys, monster and wolves. Othello, on the other hand, who makes no use of animal imagery in the first two Acts of the play, catches the trick from Iago in Acts III and IV. The fondness of both characters for mentioning repulsive animals and insects is one way by which Shakespeare shows the corruption of the Moor's mind by his subordinate. Seven of Othello's animals had been previously mentioned by Iago. Iago, for example, had said (III.3.400) it would be impossible to catch Desdemona and Cassio in the act of adultery,

> *Were they as prime as goats, as hot as monkeys.*

Later in the play, Othello, exasperated by Desdemona's pleasure at Cassio's appointment as Governor of Cyprus, exclaims 'Goats and monkeys!'

The same transference from Iago to Othello may be observed in what S. L. Bethell called diabolic imagery. He estimated that of the 64 images relating to hell and damnation – many of them are allusions rather than strict images – Iago has 18 and Othello 26. But 14 of Iago's are used in the first two Acts, and 25 of Othello's in the last three. The theme of hell originates with Iago and is transferred to Othello only when Iago has succeeded in infecting the Moor with his jealousy.

If, then, this is the thematic structure of the play, it is impossible to accept the view, which dates from Coleridge, that jealousy was not the point of Othello's passion, or Pushkin's remark, quoted by Dostoevsky in *The Brothers Karamazov*, that 'Othello was not jealous, he was trustful'. We are told that in all the 78 productions of *Othello* in the Soviet Union between 1945 and 1957 only one actor interpreted the Moor as a man obsessed by jealousy. It is partly a matter of definition. Jealousy covers a wide variety of feelings from a crude sexual possessiveness to spiritual disillusionment, from groundless suspicion to a certain knowledge of marital unfaithfulness. Othello is not jealous in the same pathological way as Leontes, who needs no proof or prompter to make him certain that Hermione has played him false with his best friend. But, all the same, as Stoll pointed out, Othello does display the very characteristics of jealousy mentioned by Coleridge in his attempt to show that the Moor was not jealous: eagerness to snatch at proofs (for example, Cassio's dream, the handkerchief), a disposition to degrade the object of his passion by sensual fancies and images (for example, IV.1.35–43), catching occasions to ease the mind by ambiguities, a dread of vulgar ridicule, and a spirit of selfish vindictiveness (for example, 'I will chop her into messes'). This aspect of Othello cannot be ignored; but, at the same time, he is unable to stop loving the wife who, as he believes, has betrayed him. The love is partly sexual infatuation, but not merely that. In the scene in which he sees Bianca return the handkerchief to Cassio, Othello oscillates between ungovernable rage and pity for Desdemona's fall (IV.1.177–99):

A fine woman, a fair woman, a sweet woman! ... *Ay, let her rot and perish, and be damned tonight* ... *She might lie by an emperor's side and command him tasks* ... *so delicate with her needle, an admirable musician!* ... *but yet the pity of it, Iago! O, Iago, the pity of it, Iago!* ... *I will chop her into messes!*

The same ambivalence is to be seen in iv.2, where Othello treats Desdemona,

> *Who art so lovely fair, and smell'st so sweet*
> *That the sense aches at thee,*

as a whore; and in the last scene, where her snow-white skin and balmy breath

> *almost persuade*
> *Justice to break her sword.*

Mingled with his furious jealousy, and his fear of being despised as a cuckold, is the feeling that chaos is come again because he has garnered up his heart in Desdemona. His feelings are similar to those of Troilus when he witnesses Cressida's unfaithfulness:

> *The bonds of heaven are slipped, dissolved and loosed . . .*

But Othello is an older man than Troilus, and his dedication to love is more absolute because Desdemona was a worthier object than Cressida; and the corresponding disillusionment is more devastating. In Othello's case there is an additional complication. Like the jealous husbands in many French and Spanish plays of the seventeenth century and in plays by some Jacobean dramatists, Othello believes that his own honour is tarnished by his wife's unfaithfulness, and that he can only restore his honour by killing her and her paramour. It has been pointed out that this drama of marital honour is preceded in Act i by a drama of parental honour – Brabantio feels himself disgraced by his daughter's elopement – and in Act ii by a drama of professional honour centred on Cassio, who feels he has lost the immortal part of himself in losing his reputation as a soldier.

Othello claims in his final apologia that he was 'not easily jealous'; and some critics have regarded this statement as a delusion. Iago begins his temptation at line 35 of III.3, and some two hundred lines later Othello has become a prey to jealousy, when he says 'Set on thy wife to observe'. Until that point Othello has been worried by Iago's accusations, but he has not fallen. His comment on Iago's warning against jealousy 'O misery!' is not an admission that he has already fallen a victim. Even as late as line 223, when he says

> I do not think but Desdemona's honest

he is still not quite vanquished, though he has obviously been shaken by Iago's echo (line 204) of Brabantio's final warning (I.3.290):

> She has deceived her father, and may thee . . .

> She did deceive her father, marrying you.

The most poisonous shafts in Iago's armoury are the suggestion that Othello knows nothing about the real nature of sophisticated Venetian ladies and that Desdemona's choice of a Moor showed a perverted taste (III.3.230–31) –

> a will most rank,
> Foul disproportion, thoughts unnatural.

But even after he has asked Iago to get Emilia to spy on Desdemona, as soon as he sees her he is reconverted to a belief in her fidelity (III.3.275–6):

> If she be false, O, then heaven mocks itself!
> I'll not believe't.

Those who suppose that Othello was easily jealous point to the fact that the scene we have been considering takes only ten or twelve minutes to perform. But, of course, the playing-time is not intended to correspond exactly to the time supposed to elapse in real life: inevitably there is some telescoping. Shakespeare, indeed, plays some strange tricks with time. Iago begins his temptation on the morning after the arrival in Cyprus. At the end of the scene he promises to murder Cassio within three days, and the impression we get from the remainder of the play is that the attempt on Cassio's life was made within the stipulated period. Certainly the action of the last two Acts of the play is more or less continuous and so is the section from the beginning of Act II to the end of Act III, scene 3. The only possible break occurs between the third and fourth scenes of Act III, and, although an interval of a week or more at this point would help to explain Bianca's complaint that Cassio had stayed away for a week, such an interval would conflict with the impression we get that events are moving very swiftly. From Iago's point of view, every hour increases the danger of his exposure. Shakespeare was faced with an acute problem. The action has to be exceedingly swift or it becomes incredible; and yet considerable time has to elapse or the action becomes incredible in another way. News of the dispersal of the Turkish fleet has to be conveyed to Venice and Lodovico has to travel to Cyprus with the appointment of Cassio as Governor. Shakespeare uses a double clock, as many critics have recognized; but no one will notice the discrepancies during an actual performance of the play.

There is one, more serious, difficulty. Iago accuses Desdemona of adultery on the day following the consummation of her marriage. As she travels to Cyprus on one boat and Cassio on another, there was no possible occasion between her elopement and her reunion with Othello when she could have committed adultery with Cassio. Shakespeare could have arranged for Desdemona and Cassio to travel to Cyprus on the same boat, or have allowed some time to elapse after the arrival in Cyprus before the brawl which leads to Cassio's dismissal. Presumably he avoided these solutions to his problem either because he did not wish to slow down the action, or because

Iago's plot depends on Othello's comparative ignorance of his wife, or because he wished to deprive the Moor of all rational grounds for his jealousy.

In the crucial scene (III.3), Iago makes no attempt to provide even the flimsiest circumstantial evidence of Desdemona's guilt, until Othello is no longer in a fit state to think logically about it. He first exclaims 'I like not that' when Cassio hurries off to avoid meeting Othello. Then he picks up Desdemona's mention of the fact that Cassio had come a-wooing with Othello – either before his avowal of love or between the proposal and the elopement – warns Othello against jealousy, and then suggests that Desdemona is too friendly with Cassio. Up to this point, Iago can withdraw his imputations, protest that he has been misunderstood; and Othello can assume that Desdemona has been carrying on a more or less innocent flirtation with Cassio during his own wooing, and that their cordial friendship may lead to something less innocent. The seed of suspicion is planted, and Othello is left to himself.

Before Iago resumes the temptation he comes into possession of the handkerchief; but it is to be noticed that he does not use it at once. He waits to see how far Othello's mind has been poisoned. When by his talk of Desdemona's stolen hours of lust and by his demand for ocular proof of her adultery, Othello shows that he has gone much further in his imagination than Iago had done in his accusations, Iago produces his story of Cassio's dream. (If Othello were capable of rational thought at this point, he would know that Iago and Cassio had had no recent opportunity of sharing a bed.) Even after his account of the dream, Iago might still retreat. As he himself is careful to point out, it might be a true dream and yet prove only that Cassio was in love with Desdemona, not that he had seduced her, or that she was in love with him. But from Othello's reaction to the dream, Iago knows that he can safely mention the handkerchief. If he had mentioned it at first, Othello might have guessed that Desdemona had mislaid it, but now he is so blinded with passion that he can believe impossibilities. Cassio and Desdemona could not, during the action of the play, have committed 'the act of shame | A thousand times' as Othello asserts after the murder. Othello, as Iago had planned, has been put

> *At least into a jealousy so strong*
> *That judgement cannot cure.*

If one were to consider the play as an exact replica of real life, one would be worried not merely by Shakespeare's treatment of time, but also by some improbabilities in the action. The success of Iago's plot depends on the assumption that Othello would avoid a specific accusation of Desdemona until too late, that Emilia, in spite of her love for Desdemona, would not realize earlier the way in which Iago was using the handkerchief, and that Othello would not confront Cassio with Iago's accusations. From the point of view of naturalism, Iago has astonishing luck. But, of course, the conventions of poetic drama do not require this kind of verisimilitude; and we must never forget that Shakespeare wrote his plays to be performed, not to be read.

When Othello claims that he is 'not easily jealous' he means that it would never have entered his head to suspect Desdemona of infidelity but for Iago's plot. In spite of the reputation of Moors in this respect, there is no doubt that Shakespeare intended this claim to be true. Othello's final speech, just before his suicide, is not a last example of his lack of self-knowledge, but an objective statement, for the audience as well as for the people on stage, of the tragedy. Those critics who think that Othello was self-deluded and self-dramatizing to the death are as mistaken as those who suppose that his character is flawless. It is true, of course, that if it had been flawless, Iago could not have succeeded; but it is quite wrong to regard his nobility as hollow. The testimony of all the main characters in the play is decisive. Brabantio loved him; Lodovico speaks of him as 'the noble Moor' 'once so good'; Cassio, who has good cause to hate him, addresses him as 'Dear General' and speaks his epitaph: 'he was great of heart'. The Duke declares that he is more fair than black. Montano is delighted to hear of Othello's appointment as Governor. But the most significant testimony to Othello's character comes from the one man who hates him. Iago confesses that the state 'Cannot with safety cast him' because 'Another of his fathom they have none'. When he first outlines his plot he declares (1.3.393–4):

> *The Moor is of a free and open nature,*
> *That thinks men honest that but seem to be so . . .*

In a later soliloquy he is even more emphatic (II.1.279–80):

> *The Moor – howbeit that I endure him not –*
> *Is of a constant, loving, noble nature . . .*

This testimony cannot be brushed aside as a corporate delusion.

Nor, indeed, should Othello's sense of drama be regarded as a tendency to self-dramatization. His quiet authority when he encounters Brabantio's servants (1.2.59) –

> *Keep up your bright swords, for the dew will rust them*

– his defence of his marriage before the senate, and the last speech which leads to his account of stabbing the 'malignant and . . . turbaned Turk' as a preparation for his own suicide, are examples of his sense of occasion, which is perfectly fitting in a great soldier of royal birth. Even his frequent expressions of self-esteem would be regarded by Shakespeare's audience, not as vanity, but as legitimate and proper pride. It was not then considered that a great man should pretend to be unconscious of his merits. Othello, after all, was perfectly justified in believing that his services to the state would out-tongue the complaints of Brabantio; he was right in believing that his royal birth and his merits made him worthy of Desdemona; and, as he put it in his final apologia (v.2.335):

> *I have done the state some service and they know't.*

Far from being a braggart soldier, Othello is modest in his claims.

It has nevertheless been argued by some critics that to the end of the play the Moor fails to realize the whole truth: that he blames the arts of the demi-devil, Iago, and fate, but does not recognize the extent of his own guilt. Such an interpretation is incompatible with the text of the last scene. Immediately after the murder, while he still believes in Desdemona's guilt, Othello regrets what he has done (lines 98–102):

> *I have no wife.*
> *O, insupportable! O heavy hour!*
> *Methinks it should be now a huge eclipse*
> *Of sun and moon, and that th'affrighted globe*
> *Should yawn at alteration.*

A few lines later, he tells Emilia:

> *It is the very error of the moon;*
> *She comes more nearer earth than she was wont,*
> *And makes men mad.*

The implication is that he has been driven mad. But when Desdemona tries to shield him by pretending she has committed suicide, Othello shows how horribly his reason has been darkened – or possibly, that the truth is beginning to dawn on it – by exclaiming (line 130):

> *She's like a liar gone to burning hell.*

A little later he admits:

> *O, I were damned beneath all depth in hell*
> *But that I did proceed upon just grounds . . .*

When he learns that he has not proceeded on just grounds, he first attempts to avenge himself on Iago; but it is clear that he intends to kill himself. He asks 'why should honour outlive honesty?' Why should reputation outlive inner integrity? He admits that he has reached his journey's end.

It is true that he asks 'Who can control his fate?' and speaks of Desdemona as ill-starred, referring possibly to the derivation of her name, which means 'unfortunate'. But it is only Shakespeare's evil characters, such as Edmund in *King Lear*, who completely discount the influence of the stars; and Othello does not disclaim his responsibility for his actions. He recognizes that he is damned and he looks forward to an eternity of torture for his crime (lines 271–8):

> *When we shall meet at compt*
> *This look of thine will hurl my soul from heaven*
> *And fiends will snatch at it . . .*
> > *Whip me, ye devils,*
> *From the possession of this heavenly sight!*
> *Blow me about in winds! Roast me in sulphur!*
> *Wash me in steep-down gulfs of liquid fire!*

It is odd, in the light of these lines, that anyone should think that Othello is 'cheering himself up', or that he refuses to recognize his own guilt. In his final speech, after urging his hearers to extenuate nothing, nor to set down aught in malice, he stabs himself as he had once in Aleppo stabbed a traducer of the state.

We have seen how Cinthio's Moor lives happily in Venice with his bride for some unspecified time. Shakespeare eliminated this period of happiness because if Othello were to have had this experience of peaceful marriage he would not have believed Iago's insinuations against Desdemona. The consummation of his marriage has to be postponed by the exigencies of war; and the first night in Cyprus is disturbed by the brawl which leads to the dismissal of Cassio. Iago begins his temptation on the following morning, and he is able to exploit Othello's comparative ignorance of his wife.

This ignorance is only partly due to the fact that they have had no opportunity of living together. It is due to a number of other factors. Othello comes of royal birth but he has won for himself a place of distinction in the service of the Venetian state by his military prowess. He confesses the one-sidedness of his experience (1.3.86–7):

> *little of this great world can I speak*
> *More than pertains to feats of broil and battle . . .*

From the age of seven he has lived in the camp. He is very conscious of his lack of sophistication; and, although he is a natural orator, he thinks of himself as rude in his speech, and as being ignorant of the arts of polite conversation. He is a Christian, but we are conscious that he has not entirely out-grown some pagan superstitions. Brabantio 'loves' him, but it does not enter his head that the Moor is a possible son-in-law, because of the difference of race. Desdemona falls in love with his autobiography rather than with him. She loves him for the dangers he has undergone, partly because she pities past sufferings, partly because she wishes she could have had such exciting adventures herself – she is not called 'fair warrior' for nothing – and partly because she responded to the nobility, the integrity, and the simplicity of the great soldier. She 'saw Othello's visage in his mind' and this made the difference of colour seem irrelevant. But though her instinct about Othello was sound, she was acting on faith rather than know-ledge.

But the difference of race and colour remains: the very feeling of 'otherness', which can be a recurrent miracle in marriage, can also be the seed from which distrust will spring. In a marriage of two different races this 'otherness' can be distorted and warped into alienation. The strangeness can come to seem a mask, hiding the real self. The act of faith and commitment can be interpreted as a perversion, as it was by Iago; but Shakespeare actually proves the essential innocence of the marriage by raising and quashing the suspicions an audience was bound to have.

Apart from the major difference of race between the couple, there is a great difference of age. Othello has reached middle age, apparently without any previous experience of love. At

least he knows nothing about the manners and morals of
Venetian ladies which, to judge not merely from Iago's satire
but from Emilia's conversation and Roderigo's ambitions, leave
something to be desired. In one respect Othello is lacking in
self-knowledge. He believes that he has reached an age in
which the violent passions of youth have died down, so that
his affections are guided by reason. He speaks scornfully of
'light-winged toys | Of feathered Cupid'; he is confident that
love will never interfere with his duties as a soldier; and he
claims (1.3.258–62) that he wishes Desdemona to accompany
him to Cyprus not primarily 'To please the palate of [his]
appetite',

> But to be free and bounteous to her mind.

What he does not fully realize at first is the absoluteness of his
commitment to his love, and his dependence on her love for
him. If he ceased to love her, chaos would come again; if he
ceased to love her, his whole life would be drained of meaning
and, full as it had been before he met her, his occupation would
be gone. Equally important is his failure to know his own
capacity for jealousy – that, though 'not easily jealous', he
could be wrought by spurious evidence and become perplexed
in the extreme.

Because of his lack of experience of women and because he
has no reason to suspect Iago's integrity or to know of his
hidden hatred for himself, he trusts his comrade-in-arms instead
of the bride, who is still a comparative stranger. As Chapman
remarked of a hero who has something in common with
Othello:

> He would believe, since he would be believed:
> Your noblest natures are most credulous.

Edgar in *King Lear* is another character to whom these words
could be applied; and it must be remembered that Othello's
credulity with regard to Iago is shared by nearly all the
characters in the play, even if Shakespeare was relying partly

on the convention, common in Elizabethan drama, of 'the calumniator believed'.

Johnson gave as one of the proofs of Shakespeare's knowledge of human nature 'the fiery openness of Othello, magnanimous, artless, and credulous, boundless in his confidence, ardent in his affection, inflexible in his resolution and obdurate in his revenge'. This is a fair summary of the character of the Moor. It properly avoids the two extremes of interpretation – the assumption that he is faultless and the assumption that his nobility is hollow, which, as we have seen, is disproved even by Iago who is desperately anxious to believe the worst about human nature, and to drag everyone down to his own level. Love is merely lust, a proper pride is bragging, nobility is ostentation, and honesty a cloak for hypocrisy. To look at the play through the eyes of the villain is bound to give one a false impression. What Iago does is to exploit the virtues as well as the weaknesses of the Moor and of Desdemona, weaknesses both of character and situation. The noble simplicity of Othello,

> *Whose nature is so far from doing harm*
> *That he suspects none,*

and the warmth of Desdemona in championing Cassio's cause are the two qualities which provide Iago with his opportunity; but he would not have succeeded without the defects in the two characters. Desdemona's advocacy of Cassio is an interference in professional matters, and she is prepared to carry it almost to the extent of nagging. Equally serious, perhaps, is the fib she tells about the handkerchief, though we can excuse this by the fact that she is shocked and frightened by Othello's first outburst of fury. Othello's weaknesses are also vulnerable. His freedom from suspicion which is based on his own transparent sincerity leads to an absurd credulity and it reveals an ignorance of human nature. His pride in his own achievements and his sense of honour are linked with the common delusion that a man's honour can be smirched by his wife's misbehaviour and redeemed only by her death. Above all, he is too confident of his own rationality and of the way his passions are under his control.

Iago makes use of these weaknesses of character, but he seizes too on the peculiarities of the marriage – the fact that it involved deception of Brabantio; the difference of race which could be represented as being an unnatural basis for marriage between 'an erring barbarian and a super-subtle Venetian', which would collapse as soon as she was sated with his body; the difference of age, which could be used to plant doubts in Othello's mind about his competence as a lover compared with a younger man; and the separation of the couple on the day of their secret marriage. Add to this the fact that Iago is not merely cunning but lucky: he obtains possession of the handkerchief at the very moment when he needs some circumstantial evidence, and Bianca accosts Cassio with the handkerchief in Othello's sight so that Iago can turn the incident to his advantage.

Iago ruins himself in the end because of his degraded view of human nature. He was afraid that Roderigo would demand the return of his presents, because he knew that men were animated by self-interest; he was afraid that Othello would have it out with Cassio; but he was too obtuse to realize that his wife, because of her love for Desdemona, would court death rather than let her memory be smirched. But, before his exposure, Iago has succeeded in his aim of driving Othello 'into a jealousy so strong | That judgement cannot cure' and of destroying both the Moor and his wife, although this was not his original intention.

In the course of the play we watch the gradual destruction of Othello's integrity, and the nobler we take him to be in the first Act the more painful is the spectacle. Little by little we see the devout Christian revert to barbarism, the great soldier reduced to being a powerless puppet, the man of noble self-control driven into unreasoning frenzy, the chivalric lover striking his wife in public, the devoted husband murdering the woman he still loves. In *Twelfth Night*, Orsino, when he believes that Olivia has married Cesario, asks her why he should not

> Kill what I love – a savage jealousy
> That sometime savours nobly?

Othello kills what he loves, because he believes in his state of darkened reason that this is the only way to restore his lost honour (v.2.1–2):

> It is the cause, it is the cause, my soul:
> Let me not name it to you, you chaste stars!

In this last scene Othello has recovered something of his dignity and self-control. But he is still deluded. He thinks that the murder he is committing is a sacrifice to his ideal of love; that what he is doing is an act of justice, not of revenge for his wounded self-esteem; that he is doing it lest she 'betray more men'. Some memory of the Christian ethic he is violating makes him offer Desdemona a chance of making her peace with God; but the actual murder is committed in a rage, when Desdemona weeps for Cassio. His savage jealousy does not savour nobly; but when, after the murder, he learns how he has been deluded and what he has lost, he recovers his former nobility, his greatness of heart.

In speaking his own epitaph, Othello claims that he had 'loved not wisely, but too well'. This is true. If he had loved less intensely, if he had not garnered up his heart in Desdemona, if she had not been the fountain from which his current ran, his reaction to her supposed unfaithfulness would not have been so violent, or so disastrous. He retains some sympathy, even in his most horrible behaviour, because we remember his earlier nobility, reflected in the poetry, because we are conscious all the time that he has become Iago's puppet, because we are aware of the struggle in his mind between love and perverted views of 'honour', and because he is not merely sexually jealous and 'Perplexed in the extreme', but also suffering from a profound spiritual disillusionment. Coleridge, as we have seen, was wrong in supposing that jealousy was not the point in Othello's passion, but he was right in seeing that it was also

an agony that the creature, whom he had believed angelic . . . whom he could not help still loving, should be proved impure and worthless . . . It was a moral indignation that virtue should so fall.

Critics, on the whole, have looked on *Othello* as inferior to *King Lear* and *Macbeth*, the tragedies which immediately followed it; but it was 'preeminently dear' to Wordsworth; and Landor, in answering the criticism that Shakespeare was less grand in his designs than other poets, replied:

To the eye. But Othello was loftier than the citadel of Troy; and what a Paradise fell before him! Let us descend; for from Othello we must descend, whatever road we take.

Landor implies that the play is the equal of the *Iliad* and *Paradise Lost* in the magnitude of its theme. But most critics today would regard such praise as excessive; partly because they feel that the play depends too much on theatrical convention – a gullible hero deceived by a melodramatic villain – and also on codes of behaviour which can no longer be regarded as valid. *Hamlet* is not damaged for us by the fact that we no longer believe in the revenge code, which its hero in fact transcends, and the mythological impression given by *King Lear* prevents us from expecting verisimilitude. *Othello* is Shakespeare's only domestic tragedy, and the only one which is set in his own age; and we are likely to be more disturbed by the operations of poetic licence. We may also be inclined to feel that it lacks the universality and cosmic overtones of the other great tragedies. If, however, the interpretation offered above is sound, *Othello* is clearly not without universal significance, for, apart from its dramatization of the difficulty of discovering reality behind appearance, its two main characters exemplify opposing principles which together constitute the human psyche. Othello believes in love, in complete commitment, in nobility, in vocation, and in absolutes. Iago believes in nothing, and least of all in other human beings. Love to him is merely sex, 'a lust of the blood and a permission of the will'. He is unable to love, as can be seen from the fact that his professed love for Desdemona is merely a means to an end – of revenging himself on Othello: love is an instrument of hate. Virtue to him is an illusion or an absurdity, Desdemona's admitted goodness being an opportunity for exploitation. The sensible man is governed entirely by self-interest. The good are simpletons who can be led by the nose; other people, good or bad, are objects to be manipulated. Iago is the Italianate villain raised to the highest pitch of intensity; he is what the Elizabethans called a malcontent; he is the intellect divorced from the imagination; he is the corrosive which eats away love and trust; 'he publishes doubt and calls it knowledge' (in Blake's phrase); he is the spirit that denies; he is Shakespeare's most penetrating vision of evil, beside which Edmund in *King Lear* seems almost amiable.

Keats remarked that Shakespeare took as much delight in conceiving an Iago as an Imogen. We may go further and suggest that he knew the psychology of Iago from the inside. It has often been observed that Iago, like Shakespeare himself, was an actor; and Bradley pointed out that, in formulating his plots, Iago resembles a dramatist in the early stages of composition. It may be added that a dramatist manipulates his characters, as Iago manipulated other people. This does not mean, of course, that Shakespeare had a similar dedication to evil; but, the greater the dramatist, the greater his capacity to imagine himself in all kinds of characters. Thersites is as convincing as Troilus; and though, as we can see from the *Sonnets*, Shakespeare affirmed his faith in love, there must have been occasions when the vision of Iago seemed more rational. However much we are appalled by Iago's actions, most of us are occasionally tempted to see things from his point of view. In a sense, therefore, the conflict between Othello and Iago is one which has a much wider application than the particular circumstances of the play.

*

We have concentrated attention on the two principal characters, on whom any interpretation of the play mainly depends and about whom there is most critical debate, and commented only incidentally on the remaining characters. A few words may be added on these.

Some modern critics have spoken harshly of Desdemona. They have stressed her deceit of her father, her unwise intervention on behalf of Cassio, and her lie to Othello about the loss of the handkerchief: they have even blamed her last words in which she mendaciously exonerates her murderer. But those who speak of the 'guilt' of Desdemona are surely as far from the truth as those who regard her as a female Christ-figure. For her essential goodness, in which she 'Does tire the ingener', is vouched for both by her actions and by the testimony of the other characters. Brabantio, in accusing Othello, stresses his daughter's innocence; Iago finds it difficult to persuade Roderigo that she is not full of 'most blessed condition'; Cassio's chaste admiration is apparent throughout the play; he describes her hyperbolically as 'a maid | That paragons description' and politely but firmly repudiates Iago's lascivious imputations; the worldly-wise and cynical Emilia is inspired by her love for her mistress to die in defence of her memory; and even Iago, in framing his plot against the Moor, admits that he is going to use Desdemona's 'goodness' as a net to enmesh both Othello and Cassio. Othello refers to her, and she refers to herself, as a warrior; she falls in love with Othello because of his adventures, which she envies; the extraordinary abnegation and selflessness of her character are revealed in her reactions to Othello's jealousy and in her last sublime falsehood. What faults of judgement she displays are all due to her youth and inexperience.

Cassio is defined partly by the exigencies of the plot, which require him to have a poor head for drinking and to have a mistress; but his chivalric worship of Desdemona, his affectionate admiration for Othello, which enables him even at the end to call him 'Dear General' and to speak of his greatness of heart, and his professional reputation, which only Iago impugns, build up a complex portrait of an attractive, if flawed, character. In spite of his weaknesses, we can understand why Iago should be envious of the 'daily beauty in his life' and why Desdemona should speak so warmly for his reinstatement.

Emilia's character, too, is determined by the plot. In the source, the villain's wife is privy to his nefarious designs. Shakespeare wisely makes her, like the other characters, ignorant of Iago's character. She knows that she has lost his love, and her unhappy marriage drives her to cynicism about sex; but she tries to win back her husband's affections by carrying out his wishes, even when this involves betrayal of the mistress she loves. If we examine her role too curiously, we may be inclined to think her dull-witted not to realize the truth before the last scene; and her superb defiance of Othello and Iago may appear to be inconsistent with the worldly standards she has previously enunciated. But, during a performance, her failure to penetrate Iago's hypocrisy appears to be an additional proof of its impenetrability, rather than of her stupidity; and her cynical talk is not ultimately incompatible with heroic action.

Roderigo, 'God Almighty's fool', begins as a gulled gentleman, honestly, if sentimentally, in love with Desdemona; and he ends as a would-be adulterer and a potential murderer, his feeble jealousy a parody of Othello's. We see him only in relation to his evil genius, Iago, whose powers of corruption he afterwards exercises on a nobler victim. The scenes in which he appears provide the only substantial comic relief; the Clown himself hardly raises a smile, and Cassio's intoxication, amusing in itself, is overshadowed by our consciousness of Iago's design against him.

The other characters – Brabantio, Montano, Gratiano, Lodovico – are merely sketched; but, within the limits of their presentation, they are perfectly adequate for Shakespeare's purpose.

Lastly, a word should be said about the poetry of the play. We have touched on the question of imagery in relation to the corruption of Othello by Iago. It has often been pointed out that the characters are differentiated by the imagery they use. Both Othello and Iago, for example, use sea imagery, but in a totally different way; the one romantic, as in the famous description of the Black Sea flowing through the Sea of Marmora into the Dardanelles, and the other prosaic. There is a similar difference in the characters' references to their own profession: to Othello it is a vocation, to Iago it is a trade. Both characters, again, use images of wealth. Iago, characteristically, speaks of actual money; Othello talks rather of the chrysolite and the pearl. It has been pointed out, too, that while Othello's characteristic image is the metaphor, Iago's is the simile; and this fits in with the villain's conscious manipulation of all the people with whom he comes in contact.

Several other groups of images (which have been examined in some detail by R. B. Heilman) may be mentioned. The theme of witchcraft, first introduced by Brabantio to account for the unnaturalness of his daughter's marriage, is taken up by Iago in the temptation scene, and finds its most memorable expression in Othello's account of the handkerchief. The fact that the handkerchief was not merely a love-token and the Moor's first gift to Desdemona, but that it was thought also to have magical properties, goes far to explain why he should be 'Perplexed in the extreme' by its loss. It also shows, perhaps, that pagan superstitions have not been entirely eradicated by the Moor's baptism; and Desdemona's half-belief in the magic deters her from admitting that the handkerchief is lost.

The theme of light and darkness is more complex. It begins with the simple contrast between the complexions of Desdemona and Othello; it quickly takes on a moral connotation with the devilish blackness of the Moor covering a noble soul; and, later in the play, to his diseased imagination, the whiteness of Desdemona seems to hide the blackness of sin. In the last scene, Othello is described as a 'blacker devil' for murdering the angelic Desdemona.

A minor example of image-patterns is connected with drugs and poisons. It ranges from the drug which Brabantio accuses Othello of using in order to subdue Desdemona's affections, to the coloquintida to which Iago hopes to reduce the sweetness of Othello's love, the poison of jealousy he administers to his victim, the mandragora which will fail to bring him rest, and the poisonous mineral to which Iago compares his own jealousy.

The imagery is only one form of figurative expression; and the total effect of what Wilson Knight has called 'the Othello music' in creating our imaginative impression of the hero depends on a wide range of poetic devices, including exotic colouring and the actual sound of the verse. As some recent critics have professed to find something hollow in Othello's nobility and have argued that this is revealed by the poetic rhetoric, it may be necessary to affirm that the diction, the imagery and the music of Othello's speech cannot properly be used to undermine his nobility. To most sensitive critics his lines ring true.

Further Reading

Recent editions, with fuller commentary than the present one allows, are the New Cambridge (edited by Alice Walker) and the new Arden (edited by M. R. Ridley). The standard interpretation of the play given in A. C. Bradley's *Shakespearean Tragedy* (1904) was attacked in *Othello* (1915) and *Art and Artifice in Shakespeare* (1933) by E. E. Stoll, who argued that the character of the hero was psychologically inconsistent, and in 'Diabolic Intellect and the Noble Hero' (reprinted in *The Common Pursuit*, 1952; Peregrine Books, 1962) by F. R. Leavis, who stressed the defects of Othello. Stoll has been effectively answered by J. I. M. Stewart in *Character and Motive in Shakespeare* (1949); and there have been replies to Leavis in Helen Gardner's *The Noble Moor* (1956), in John Bayley's *The Characters of Love* (1960) and in John Holloway's *The Story of the Night* (1962). There is a good essay on the play in G. Wilson Knight's *The Wheel of Fire* (1930).

The fullest account of the imagery is to be found in *Magic in the Web* by R. B. Heilman (1956) and there are essays by M. M. Morozov, and S. L. Bethell (*Shakespeare Survey 2, 5*), a chapter in *The Development of Shakespeare's Imagery* by W. H. Clemen (1951), and an essay on the iteration of 'honest' in William Empson's *The Structure of Complex Words* (1951).

The best detailed account of the action of the play is H. Granville-Barker's *Preface* (1930). G. R. Elliott's *Flaming Minister* (1953) is a scene-by-scene interpretation. M. Rosenberg in *The Masks of Othello* (1961) deals with the interaction of stage performance and literary interpretation. C. Stanislavski's *Stanislavski Produces 'Othello'* (1948) and Arthur Colby Sprague's

Shakespearian Players and Performances (1954) may also be recommended.

There is a useful chapter on the play by Robert Hapgood in *Shakespeare: Select Bibliographical Guides*, edited by Stanley Wells (1973). *Shakespeare Survey 21* (1968) includes eight essays on the play and a survey by Helen Gardner of recent criticism. *Aspects of Othello*, edited by Kenneth Muir and Philip Edwards (1977), is a collection of essays reprinted from *Shakespeare Survey*. A book on *Iago* (1971) by Stanley Edgar Hyman, and chapters in *Hero and Saint* by Reuben Brower (1970), *Shakespeare's Living Art* by Rosalie L. Colie (1974), and *Shakespeare's Tragic Sequence* by Kenneth Muir (1972) may also be mentioned. There is an admirable discussion of 'Othello and Colour Prejudice' by G. K. Hunter (reprinted in *Dramatic Identities and Cultural Tradition*, 1978).

The main source of the play is included in *Elizabethan Love Stories*, edited by T. J. B. Spencer (Penguin Shakespeare Library, 1968). Shakespeare's treatment of his various sources is discussed by Kenneth Muir in *The Sources of Shakespeare* (1977). Geoffrey Bullough has a more extensive discussion in *Narrative and Dramatic Sources of Shakespeare*, VII (1973), and he prints the main source, together with a story from *Certaine Tragicall Discourses* of Bandello, translated by Geoffrey Fenton (1567), and an extract from Richard Knolles's *The Generall Historie of the Turkes* (1603).

An Account of the Text

Othello was first published in 1622, after Shakespeare's death, in an edition known as the Quarto (Q). In the following year the play was included in the collected edition of Shakespeare's plays known as the Folio (F): this text was based on a copy of Q which had been corrected by comparison with the prompt-book. A modern edition has to be based on both Q and F. Both texts omit passages. Omissions in Q may be due to inaccurate calculations on the amount of copy required to fill eight pages which led the compositor of the Quarto to omit passages; or these supposed omissions may result from later expansions after the first performance of the play. Omissions in F include many oaths which were cut to comply with the new regulations about profanity; some spurious readings had crept into the prompt-book and the text clearly contains some 'improvements' for which Shakespeare was not responsible.

The nature of the Q text is still debated. Some believe it to be based, directly or indirectly, on Shakespeare's manuscript; others think that it is thoroughly corrupt. Some mistakes – it is impossible to say how many – are common to Q and F, presumably because the man who corrected Q for the printer of F overlooked some errors, and these cannot all be detected. It is, moreover, possible that sometimes where Q and F differ Shakespeare may have been responsible for both readings.

Some editors have assumed that they must follow F, except where its readings are manifestly impossible. But, as A. E. Housman remarked in discussing a similar problem, for all wrong readings to be impossible could only be the result of divine intervention. An editor ought to be prepared to accept readings from Q if he is convinced that they are both Shake-spearian and superior to those of F; and where Q and F both appear to be wrong, he must accept an emendation of others or propose one of his own.

The present edition, therefore, is based mainly on F. It adds passages omitted from F; it deviates from F in about 250 readings, and in nearly 200 of these Q has been followed. In other words, it accepts more Q readings than the New Cambridge or old Penguin editions, but fewer than the new Arden. The 'long s' [ʃ] has been replaced by 's' throughout. A few insignificant variations have been omitted in lists 2 and 3 below.

COLLATIONS

I

Passages Omitted in Quarto

1.1.	122–38	If 't . . . yourself
1.2.	20	Which, when I know
	65	If . . . bound
	72–7	Judge . . . attach thee
1.3.	16	By Signor Angelo
	24–30	For . . . profitless
	63	Being . . . sense
	118	The . . . you
	123	I . . . blood
	192	Which . . . heart
	273	her
	274	it
	280	So
	308	O villainous
	345–6	She must change for youth
	357–8	if . . . issue
	376	I'll sell all my land
11.1.	39–40	Even . . . regard

	63	quirks of
	112	DESDEMONA
	154	See . . . behind
	234	Why, none; why, none
	237	a devilish knave
	246	Blessed pudding
	248	that I did
	249	obscure
	252	Villainous thoughts, Roderigo
	254	master and
	255	Pish
II.2.	9	of feasting
II.3.	67	O
	96	to be
	98–9	and . . . saved
	112	Why
	184	to
	245	dear
	297	O, strange
III.1.	54	CASSIO I am much bound to you
III.3.	163	OTHELLO Ha
	380–87	By . . . satisfied
	450–57	Iago . . . heaven
	465	in me
III.4.	8–10	CLOWN To . . . this
	98	of it
	179	Well, well
	191–2	BIANCA . . . not
IV.1.	37–43	To . . . devil
	120	What! A customer
	123	they
	174–6	IAGO Yours . . . whore
	179	that
IV.2.	50	utmost
	72–5	Committed . . . committed
	185	With naught but truth

	217	what is it
IV.3.	30–50	I have . . . next
	57–60	I . . . question
	85–102	But . . . so
V.1.	21	much
V.2.	83	OTHELLO Being . . . pause
	150–53	EMILIA . . . Iago
	184–92	My . . . villainy
	244–6	EMILIA What . . . willow
	264–70	Be . . . wench
	334	before you go

2

Passages Omitted in Folio

I.I.	1	Tush
	4	'Sblood (*later examples of oaths are not listed*)
	15	And in conclusion
	117	now
I.3.	106	DUKE
	199	Into your favour
	274	You must hence tonight
	372–5	RODERIGO . . . purse
II.I.	82	And . . . comfort
	88	me
	116	thou (*after* wouldst)
	264	with his truncheon
II.3.	322	here
III.I.	29	CASSIO Do . . . friend
	48	To . . . front
III.3.	178	once
	183	well
	221	at
	421	then
	449	perhaps

III.4.   22   of
            37   yet
            84   sir
            90   OTHELLO . . . Cassio
IV.1.   52   No, forbear
           103   now
           110   a
           120   her
           124   shall
         135–6   by this hand
           248   an
IV.2.   32   But not the words
            80   Impudent strumpet
           166   And . . . you
           187   to
           227   of
IV.3.   20   in them
            23   thee
            71   it
V.2.   52   Yes
            85   DESDEMONA O Lord, Lord, Lord
           143   Nay
           239   here
           334   him

3

Readings Accepted from Quarto, with Rejected Folio Reading

I.1.   25   togèd] Tongued
            30   Christian] Christen'd
            67   full] fall
                 thick-lips] Thicks-lips
           101   bravery] knauerie
           104   them] their
           147   produced] producted

	183	night] might
I.2.	10	pray] pray you
	15	and] or
	16	That] The
	21	provulgate] promulgate
	68	darlings] Deareling
	84	Where] Whether
I.3.	1	these] this
	4	and forty] forty
	35	injointed] inioynted them
	45	wish] to
	93	proceedings] proceeding
	99	maimed] main'd
	107	overt] over
	122	till] tell
	129	fortunes] Fortune
	138	travels'] Trauellours
	140	and hills] Hills
		heads] head
	141	the] my
	142	other] others
	144	Do grow] Grew
		This] These things
	146	thence] hence
	154	intentively] instinctively
	158	sighs] kisses
	182	lord of all my] the Lord of
	217	ear] eares
	237–8	If . . . father's.] Why at her Fathers?
	239	Nor I: I would not] Nor would I
	244	you? Speak.] you Desdemona?
	245	did love] loue
	254	which] why
	265	For] When
	267	instruments] Instrument
	274–5	You . . . night] *Sen.* You must away to night

	279	With] And
	296	matters] matter
	306	we have] haue we
	310	a man] man
	327	our (*after* stings)] or
	338–9	be . . . continue] be long that Desdemona should continue
	345	acerbe as the] bitter as
	347	error] errors
	389	ear] eares
II.1.	11	banning] foaming
	19	they] to
	33	prays] praye
	34	heaven] Heauens
	42	arrivance] Arriuancie
	43	this] the
	70	clog] enclogge
	92	the sea] sea
	94	their] this
	104	list] leaue
	155	wight] wightes
	171	an] and
	208	hither] thither
	217–18	And will she] To
	221	again] a game
	230	eminently] eminent
	235	finder out of occasions] finder of occasion
	236	has] he's
	253	mutualities] mutabilities
	290	for wife] for wift
	297	rank] right
II.3.	37	unfortunate] infortunate
	75	expert] exquisite
	124	the prologue] his prologue
	152	God's will] Alas
	156	God's . . . hold] Fie, fie Lieutenant

157 You will be shamed] You'le be asham'd
159 death] death. He dies
227 the] then
234 can I not] cannot I
259 thought] had thought
265 ways] more wayes
292 not so] not
305 I'll] I
344 fortunes] Fortune
352 enmesh] en-mash
367 By th'mass] Introth
374 the while] a while

III.1. 21 hear] heare me
III.3.   4 case] cause
        16 circumstance] Circumstances
        39 sneak] steale
        60 or] on
        66 their] her
        74 By'r Lady] Trust me
       105 By . . . me] Alas, thou ecchos't me
       106 his] thy
       111 In] Of
       134 free to] free
       137 a breast] that breast
       138 But some] Wherein
       139 session] Sessions
       148 conjects] conceits
       180 blown] blow'd
       196 eye] eyes
       200 God] Heauen
       213 In faith] Trust me
       215 my] your
       231 disproportion] disproportions
       246 to hold him] to him
       256 qualities] Quantities
       270 of] to

	274	Desdemona] Look where she
	275	O . . . mocks] Heauen mock'd
	299	A] You haue a
	308	faith] but
	335	of] in
	337	well] well, fed well
	370	defend] forgiue
	383	Her] My
	390	I] and I
	392	supervisor] super-vision
	422	Over . . . sighed . . . kissed] ore . . . sigh . . . kisse
	423	Cried] cry
	426	'Tis . . . dream] *Given to Othello*
	429	but] yet
	444	thy hollow cell] the hollow hell
III.4.	5	one] me
		is] 'tis
	23	that] the
	54	faith . . . That is] indeed . . . That's
	64	wive] Wiu'd
	67	lose] loose't
	94	I'faith] Insooth
	95	Zounds] Away
	133	can he be] is he
	143	that] a
	159	that] the
	167	I'faith] Indeed
	183	by my faith] in good troth
	184	sweet] neither
IV.1.	9	So] If
	21	infected] infectious
	37	confession] Confessions
	45	, work] workes
	60	No] not
	77	unsuiting] resulting F; vnfitting Q (*uncorrected state*)

	79	scuse] scuses
	98	refrain] restraine
	107	power] dowre
	111	i'faith] indeed
	124	Faith] Why
	131	beckons] becomes
	139	hales] shakes
	152	not know] know not
	162	street] streets
	191	a thousand, thousand times] a thousand, a thousand times
	214	Come . . . him] this, comes from the Duke. See, your wife's with him
	216	Senators] the Senators
	238	By my troth] Trust me
	278	this] his
	281	denote] deonte
IV.2.	23	Pray] Pray you
	29	Nay] May
	30	knees] knee
	54	unmoving] and mouing
	91	keep] keepes
	116	As . . . bear] That . . . beare it
	125	all] and
	140	heaven] Heauens
	147	O good] Alas
	154	in] or
	169	stay] staies
	223	takes] taketh
IV.3.	12	He] And
	17	I would] I, would
	22	faith] Father
	24	those] these
	74	Ud's pity] why
V.1.	1	bulk] Barke
	25	think'st] know'st

	35	Forth] For
	38	cry] voyce
	42	It is a] 'Tis
	49	Did] Do
	50	heaven's] heauen
	60	here] there
	90	O heaven] Yes, 'tis
	93	you] your
	104	out o'th'] o'th'
	111	'Las . . . What's] Alas, what is . . . what is
	116	fruit] fruits
	123	Foh! Fie] Fie
v.2.	15	it] thee
	19	this] that's
	32	heaven] Heauens
	35	say so] say
	57	Then Lord] O Heauen
	102	Should] Did
	118	O Lord] Alas
	151	that she] she
	227	steal it] steal't
	249	I die, I die] alas, I dye
	289	damnèd] cursed
	292	did I] I did
	312	to have] t'haue
	313	nick] interim
	314	the] thou
	317	but] it but
	343	Indian] Iudean

4

Some Rejected Quarto Variants

1.1.	33	Moorship's] Worships
	39	affined] assign'd

	66	daws] Doues
	73	chances . . . on't] changes . . . out
	141	thus deluding you] this delusion
	146	place] pate
	166	she deceives] thou deceiuest
	173	maidhood] manhood
I.2.	22	siege] height
	41	sequent] frequent
	46	hath sent about] sent aboue
I.3.	6	the aim] they aym'd
	122	truly] faithfull
	138	portance in] with it all
	165	hint] heate
	175	on my head] lite on me
	246	storm] scorne
	248	very quality] vtmost pleasure
	257	Let . . . voice] Your voyces Lords: beseech you let
		her will	Have a free way
	266	Of . . . seel] And . . . foyles
	267	officed] actiue
	271	estimation] reputation
	280	import] concerne
	289	if thou hast eyes] haue a quicke eye
	347	Therefore] shee must haue change, she must. Therefore
	362	conjunctive] communicatiue
	387	plume] make
II.1.	8	mountains melt on them] the huge mountaine meslt
	12	chidden] chiding
	15	ever-fixèd] euer fired
	20	lads] Lords
	68	high] by
	72	mortal] common
	80	Make . . . in] And swiftly come to
	95	See for the news] So speakes this voyce
	167	gyve] catch

	179	calms] calmenesse
	235	slipper and subtle] subtle slippery
	286	lusty] lustfull
II.3.	51	else] lads
	129	Prizes the virtue] Praises the vertues
	143	twiggen-bottle] wicker bottle
	187	mouths] men
	200	collied] coold
	313	broken joint] braule
	357–8	and so ... Venice] as that comes to, and no money at all, and with that wit returne to Venice
III.1.	41	sure] soone
III.2.	2	senate] State
III.3.	70	mammering] muttering
	114	conceit] counsell
	122	dilations] denotements
	124	be sworn] presume
	153	What dost thou mean] Zouns
	352	rude] wide
	353	dread clamours] great clamor
	358	mine] mans
	373	lov'st] livest
	463	execution] excellency
III.4.	51	sorry] sullen
	62	loathèd] lothely
	145	observancy] obseruances
	174	continuate] conuenient
IV.1.	80	return] retire
	82	fleers] Ieeres
	213	I ... Lodovico] Something from Venice sure, 'tis Lodovico
IV.2.	17	their wives] her sex
	46	I have lost] Why I have left
	47	they rained] he ram'd
	169	The ... meat] And the great Messengers of Venice stay

	190	acquaintance] acquittance
	207	exception] conception
	232	harlotry] harlot
IV.3.	103	uses] vsage
V.1.	7	stand] sword
	8	deed] dead
	11	quat] gnat
	14	gain] game
	34	unblest fate hies] fate hies apace
	76	my sweet Cassio, | O Cassio, Cassio, Cassio] O my sweete Cassio! | Cassio, Cassio
	86	be . . . injury] beare a part in this
	105	gentlemen] Gentlewoman
	106	gastness] ieastures
V.2.	10	thy light] thine
	13	relume] returne
	15	needs must] must needes
	55	conception] conceit
	70	hath used thee] hath – vds death
	111	nearer] neere the
	149	iterance] iteration
	208	reprobance] reprobation
	217	'Twill . . . peace?] 'Twill out, 'twill, I hold my peace sir, no.
	218	I will speak as . . . north] Ile be in speaking . . . ayre
	285	Wrench] wring
	347	med'cinable] medicinal
	359	loading] lodging

5

Emendations

I.1.	30	leed] be-leed F; led Q
	152	stand] stands Q, F

	155	hell pains] hell apines F; hells paines Q
I.2.	11	For be assured] Be assur'd F; For be sure Q
	50	carack] Carract F; Carrick Q
I.3.	58	yet] it Q, F
	87	feats of broil] Feats of Broiles F; feate of broyle Q
	177	company] noble company Q, F
	217	piecèd] pierced Q, F
	228	couch] Cooch Q; Coach F
	232	war] Warres Q, F
	261	In me] In my Q, F
	323	beam] ballance Q; braine F
	336	thou these] thou the F; these Q
II.1.	13	mane] Maine Q, F
	65	tire the ingener] tyre the Ingeniuer F; beare all excellency Q
	67	He's] He has Q; Ha's F
	70	enscarped] ensteep'd F; enscerped Q
	108	of doors] of doore F; adores Q
	195	let's] let vs Q, F
	294	I leash] I trace F; I crush Q
II.2.	5	addiction] addition F; minde Q
II.3.	112	well] well then Q, F
	121	in him] him in Q, F
	161	sense of place] place of sense Q, F
	212	leagued] league Q, F
	221	following] following him Q, F
	260	of sense] sence F; offence Q
	308	denotement] deuotement Q, F
III.1.	25	General's wife] Ceneral's wife Q; General F
III.2.	6	We'll] Well F; We Q
III.3.	119	affright me more] fright me the more F; affright me the more Q
	147	that . . . then] that your wisedome F; I intreate you then Q
	168	fondly] soundly F; strongly Q
	180	exsufflicate] exufflicate Q, F

	182	fair, loves] faire, feeds well, loues Q, F
	202	keep't] kept F; keepe Q
	209	to] too Q, F
	347	make] makes Q, F
	403	circumstance] circumstances Q, F
	437	any that] any it Q, F
	452	feels] keepes F
III.4.	42	there's] heere's Q, F
	82	an] and Q, F
	112	sorrow] sorrowes Q, F
	143	Our] our other Q, F
IV.1.	73	shall] she shall Q, F
	87	gestures] ieasture Q, F
	101	construe] cònster Q; conserue F
	123	win] winnes Q, F
IV.2.	63	Ay, there] I heere Q, F
	79	hear it] hear't Q, F
	167	It is so] It is but so F; Tis but so Q
	175	daff'st] dafts F; doffs Q
IV.3.	38	sighing] singing F
V.1.	22	But ... hear] But so ... heard F; be't so ... hear Q
	114	quite] quite dead F; dead Q
V.2.	107	murder] Murthers Q, F
	216	O God! O heavenly Powers] Oh Heauen! Oh heauenly Powres F; O God, O heauenly God Q
	233	serve] serues Q, F
	288	wast] wert Q; was F
	346	Drop] Drops Q, F

6

Stage Directions

I.1.	82	above F; at a window Q
	145	Exit above] Exit F; *not in* Q

	160	in his night-gown] *not in* F
I.2.	33	Enter . . . torches] Enter Cassio, with Torches F; Enter Cassio with lights, Officers and Torches Q (both at line 27)
	49	*not in* Q, F
	53	*not in* Q, F
I.3.	0	Enter Duke, Senators, and Officers F; Enter Duke, and Senators set at a Table, with lights and Attendants Q
	121	Exit . . . attendants] Exit two or three Q; *not in* F
	291	Exeunt . . . attendants] Exit F; Exeunt Q
	297	Exeunt . . . Desdemona] Exit Moore and Desdemona Q; Exit F
II.1.	55	Salvo] *not in* F; A shot Q
	82	and attendants] *not in* Q, F
	99	He kisses Emilia] *not in* Q, F
	121	(aside)] *not in* Q, F
	164	(aside)] *not in* Q, F
	173	Trumpet] Trumpets within Q; *not in* F
	174	(aloud)], *not in* Q, F
	191	They kiss] *not in* F
	206	Exeunt . . . Roderigo] Exit Q; Exit Othello and Desdemona F
II.3.	11	and attendants] *not in* Q, F
	59	and servants with wine] *not in* Q, F
	132	Exit Roderigo] *not in* F
	139	Cry within] *not in* F
	145	He strikes Roderigo] *not in* Q, F
	154	Bell rings] *not in* Q, F
	247	Montano is led off] Lead him off Q, F
	251	Exeunt . . . Cassio] Exit Moore, Desdemona, and attendants Q; Exit F
III.3.	239	going] *not in* Q, F
	284	He . . . it] *not in* Q, F
	312	snatching it] *not in* Q, F

III.4.	34	(Aside)] *not in* Q, F
IV.1.	43	He falls] Falls in a Traunce F; he fals downe Q
	58	Exit Cassio] *not in* Q, F
	92	Othello retires] *not in* Q, F
	109, 112, 114 etc.	(aside)] *not in* Q, F
	168	Exit Cassio] *not in* F
	169	(coming forward)] *not in* Q, F
	212	Trumpet sounds] *not in* Q, F
	216	He . . . letter] *not in* Q, F
	217	He . . . letter] *not in* Q, F
	240	He strikes her] *not in* Q, F
	262	Exit Desdemona] *not in* Q, F
IV.2.	89	(Calling)] *not in* Q, F
IV.3.	9	Othello . . . attendants] *not in* Q, F
	38	etc. (sings)] *not in* Q, F
	44	etc. (She speaks)] *not in* Q, F
V.1.	7	He retires] *not in* Q, F
	26	He wounds Roderigo] *not in* Q, F
		Iago . . . exit] *not in* Q, F
	27	above] *not in* Q, F
	46	with a light] *not in* F
	61	He stabs Roderigo] *not in* Q, F
	62	He faints] *not in* Q, F
	64	Lodovico . . . forward] *not in* Q, F
	98	Enter . . . chair] *not in* Q, F
	104	Cassio . . . removed] *not in* Q, F
	110	Enter Emilia] *not in* F
	128	(Aside)] *not in* Q, F
V.2.	0	with a light] *not in* F
		Desdemona in her bed] *not in* Q
	15	He kisses her] *not in* F
	85	smothers] Q; stifles F
	106	(He unlocks door)] *not in* Q, F
	120	She . . . curtains] *not in* Q, F
	197	(falling on bed)] Oth. fals on the bed Q; *not in* F
	233	He . . . exit] *not in* F; The Moore runnes at Iago.

Iago kils his wife Q

249　She dies] *not in* F

269　He goes to the bed] *not in* Q, F

279　in a chair] *not in* F

352　He stabs himself] *not in* F

355　falls on the bed and] *not in* Q, F

361　The . . . drawn] *not in* Q, F

The Songs

For a full discussion see *Music in Shakespearean Tragedy* by F. W. Sternfeld (1963), from whose work the following notes are, with his permission, derived.

1. 'And let me the canakin clink' (II.3.64).

The tune for this song is not certainly known, but the following tune called 'A Soldier's Life' fits the words. It appears to be traditional, though not printed until 1651 (in John Playford's *The English Dancing Master*). A version of it is familiar as the tune to which, according to stage tradition, Ophelia sings 'Tomorrow is St Valentine's Day' in *Hamlet* (IV.5.46).

2. 'King Stephen was and-a worthy peer' (II.3.84).

A song with the refrain 'Then take thy auld cloak about thee' is found in the eighteenth century and the music may be a version of that used for this well-known ballad in Shakespeare's time. The tune was first printed in James Oswald's *Caledonian*

Pocket Companion (mid eighteenth century); and the following vocal version appeared in Robert Bremner's *Thirty Scot Songs for a Voice and Harpsichord* (1757, as revised in 1770).

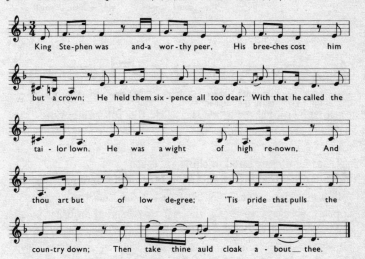

King Ste-phen was and-a wor-thy peer, His bree-ches cost him but a crown; He held them six - pence all too dear; With that he called the tai - lor lown. He was a wight of high re-nown, And thou art but of low de-gree; 'Tis pride that pulls the coun-try down; Then take thine auld cloak a - bout __ thee.

3. 'The poor soul sat sighing by a sycamore tree' (IV.3.38).

This song was well known. Different settings appear in manuscripts of the sixteenth century and later. The following, which is the only one for voice and lute, seems to be the version most easily adjusted to the words in Shakespeare's text. It is found in a manuscript in the British Museum (Add MSS. 15117, folio 18) dated 1616 or earlier.

1. The poor soul set sigh - ing by a
2. The fresh streams ran by her and
3. Let no - bo - dy blame him; his
4. I called my love false love, but

sy - ca - more tree, Sing all a green wil - low;
mur-mured her moans;
scorn I ap - prove;
what said he then?

Her hand on her bo - som, her
Her salt tears fell from her and
If I court moe wo - men, you'll

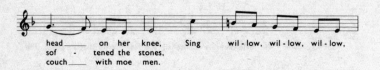

head on her knee, Sing wil - low, wil - low, wil - low,
sof - tened the stones,
couch with moe men.

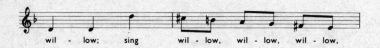

wil - low; sing wil - low, wil - low, wil - low,

wil - low must be my gar - land. Sing all a green

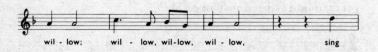

wil - low; wil - low, wil - low, wil - low, sing

all a green wil - low must be my gar - land.

OTHELLO

The Characters in the Play

OTHELLO, a Moor, General in the Venetian army
DESDEMONA, his wife
CASSIO, his Lieutenant
IAGO, his Ancient
EMILIA, wife of Iago
BIANCA, mistress of Cassio
RODERIGO, in love with Desdemona

THE DUKE OF VENICE
BRABANTIO, a Venetian Senator, Desdemona's father
GRATIANO, his brother
LODOVICO, his kinsman
MONTANO, Governor of Cyprus

Senators of Venice
Gentlemen of Cyprus
Musicians
Officers
A Clown in Othello's household
A Herald
A Sailor
A Messenger
Soldiers, attendants, and servants

RODERIGO

    Tush, never tell me! I take it much unkindly

    That thou, Iago, who hast had my purse

    As if the strings were thine, shouldst know of this.

IAGO

    'Sblood, but you will not hear me!

    If ever I did dream of such a matter,

    Abhor me.

RODERIGO

    Thou told'st me thou didst hold him in thy hate.

IAGO

    Despise me, if I do not. Three great ones of the city,

    In personal suit to make me his Lieutenant,

    Off-capped to him: and by the faith of man,   10

    I know my price, I am worth no worse a place.

    But he, as loving his own pride and purposes,

    Evades them with a bombast circumstance

1.1 The play opens at night, in the street outside Brabantio's house in the middle of a conversation between Iago and Roderigo, described in the Folio (F) list of characters as 'a Villaine' and 'a gull'd Gentleman'. Although the opening scenes of Shakespeare's plays are expository, the facts are here distorted by Iago's envy and by his anxiety not to be deprived of Roderigo's money. Iago has been as surprised as his dupe by Desdemona's marriage.

4 *'Sblood* God's blood. This and other oaths were omitted in F because of the new regulations against profanity. Iago's oaths contrast with Roderigo's feeble 'Tush'.

8–33 *Despise me, if I do not . . . his Moorship's Ancient.* We cannot assume that Iago's account is accurate or that the main cause of his hatred of Othello is Cassio's promotion. See Introduction, p. 311.

13 *bombast circumstance* bombastic beating about the bush

Horribly stuffed with epithets of war,
And in conclusion
Non-suits my mediators. For 'Certes,' says he,
'I have already chose my officer.'
And what was he?
Forsooth, a great arithmetician,
20   One Michael Cassio, a Florentine –
A fellow almost damned in a fair wife –
That never set a squadron in the field,
Nor the division of a battle knows
More than a spinster – unless the bookish theoric,
Wherein the togèd consuls can propose
As masterly as he. Mere prattle without practice
Is all his soldiership. But he, sir, had th'election:
And I, of whom his eyes had seen the proof
At Rhodes, at Cyprus, and on other grounds
30   Christian and heathen, must be leed and calmed
By debitor and creditor; this counter-caster,
He in good time must his Lieutenant be,
And I – God bless the mark! – his Moorship's Ancient.

14 *stuffed*. Bombast was originally cotton used for stuffing quilts and clothes.

16 *Non-suits* rejects the suit of
Certes certainly

19 *arithmetician*. Iago means that Cassio's knowledge of war was theoretical.

21 *A fellow almost damned in a fair wife*. Possibly at this point in the play Shakespeare intended to give Cassio a wife and afterwards decided to fuse the harlot and the lady (*donna*) of the source. There were Italian and English proverbs on the damnation involved in having a fair wife – because she was certain to be seduced.

24 *theoric* theory

25 *togèd*. Shakespeare is thinking of the Venetian government in terms of ancient Roman senators, wearing togas. The F reading, 'tongued', accepted by few editors, would mean that the senators could prattle about military matters without having any practical experience of them.

30 *leed* cut off from the wind. This is clearly the intention of the Quarto (Q) 'led'; the F reading 'be be-leed' is awkward to speak. Iago's matter-of-fact nautical imagery contrasts with the imaginative sea-imagery of Othello.

31 *counter-caster* one who reckons with counters

33 *Ancient* ensign

RODERIGO

By heaven, I rather would have been his hangman.

IAGO

Why, there's no remedy. 'Tis the curse of service:
Preferment goes by letter and affection,
And not by old gradation, where each second
Stood heir to th'first. Now sir, be judge yourself
Whether I in any just term am affined
To love the Moor.   40

RODERIGO

I would not follow him then.

IAGO   O, sir, content you:
I follow him to serve my turn upon him.
We cannot all be masters, nor all masters
Cannot be truly followed. You shall mark
Many a duteous and knee-crooking knave
That, doting on his own obsequious bondage,
Wears out his time, much like his master's ass,
For naught but provender, and when he's old –
    cashiered!
Whip me such honest knaves. Others there are
Who, trimmed in forms and visages of duty,   50
Keep yet their hearts attending on themselves,
And, throwing but shows of service on their lords,
Do well thrive by them; and when they have lined
    their coats,
Do themselves homage: these fellows have some soul,
And such a one do I profess myself.

---

36 *letter and affection* influence and nep-
   otism. But Iago had himself pulled
   strings (see line 8).
37 *gradation* process of advancing step
   by step
39 *affined* constrained
44 *truly* faithfully
   shall mark cannot help noticing
45 *knave* servant

47 *ass*. Both Iago and Othello make frequent use of animal imagery. See
   Introduction, p. 316.
48 *cashiered!* he is cashiered. The elliptical expression is characteristic of
   Iago.
49 *Whip me* (ethical dative)
52 *shows* appearances
53 *lined their coats* feathered their nests

For, sir,
It is as sure as you are Roderigo,
Were I the Moor, I would not be Iago:
In following him, I follow but myself.
Heaven is my judge, not I for love and duty,
But seeming so for my peculiar end:
For when my outward action doth demonstrate
The native act and figure of my heart
In compliment extern, 'tis not long after,
But I will wear my heart upon my sleeve
For daws to peck at — I am not what I am.

RODERIGO

What a full fortune does the thick-lips owe
If he can carry't thus!

IAGO   Call up her father,
Rouse him, make after him, poison his delight,
Proclaim him in the streets; incense her kinsmen,
And, though he in a fertile climate dwell,
Plague him with flies: though that his joy be joy,
Yet throw such chances of vexation on't,
As it may lose some colour.

RODERIGO

Here is her father's house; I'll call aloud.

IAGO

Do, with like timorous accent and dire yell,

---

58 *Were I the Moor, I would not be Iago* If I were the General, I would not wish to be a subordinate

61 *peculiar* personal

63 *figure* shape, intention

64 *compliment extern* outward show

66 *I am not what I am*. This is thought by some to be a parody of Exodus 3.14, 'I am that I am', and by others to mean 'I am not what I seem to be'. Iago means merely that, if he were to wear his heart

on his sleeve, he would cease to be himself.

67 *full* perfect
thick-lips. This is the first indication that Othello is negroid.
owe own

68 *If he can carry't thus* if he can get away with it
her father (Desdemona's father, Brabantio)

73 *chances* possibilities

76 *timorous* causing fear

As when, by night and negligence, the fire
Is spied in populous cities.

RODERIGO
What, ho, Brabantio! Signor Brabantio, ho!

IAGO
Awake! What, ho, Brabantio! Thieves, thieves!   80
Look to your house, your daughter, and your bags!
Thieves, thieves!

Enter Brabantio above, at a window

BRABANTIO
What is the reason of this terrible summons?
What is the matter there?

RODERIGO
Signor, is all your family within?

IAGO
Are your doors locked?

BRABANTIO   Why, wherefore ask you this?

IAGO
Zounds, sir, you're robbed; for shame, put on your gown;
Your heart is burst, you have lost half your soul.
Even now, now, very now, an old black ram
Is tupping your white ewe. Arise, arise,   90
Awake the snorting citizens with the bell,
Or else the devil will make a grandsire of you.
Arise, I say!

BRABANTIO   What, have you lost your wits?

RODERIGO
Most reverend signor, do you know my voice?

BRABANTIO
Not I: what are you?

---

82 (stage direction) *at a window*. On the
Elizabethan stage the window would
be at the side on the balcony level.
87 *Zounds* God's wounds
robbed . . . gown. A quibble may be
intended on 'robbed' and 'robed'.

88 *burst* broken
90 *tupping* covering
91 *snorting* snoring
92 *devil*. The devil was depicted as
black.

RODERIGO   My name is Roderigo.

BRABANTIO

The worser welcome!
I have charged thee not to haunt about my doors.
In honest plainness thou hast heard me say
My daughter is not for thee. And now in madness,
Being full of supper and distempering draughts,
Upon malicious bravery dost thou come
To start my quiet.

RODERIGO

Sir, sir, sir —

BRABANTIO   But thou must needs be sure
My spirit and my place have in them power
To make this bitter to thee.

RODERIGO   Patience, good sir.

BRABANTIO

What tell'st thou me of robbing? This is Venice:
My house is not a grange.

RODERIGO   Most grave Brabantio,
In simple and pure soul I come to you . . .

IAGO Zounds, sir, you are one of those that will not serve
God if the devil bid you. Because we come to do you
service, and you think we are ruffians, you'll have your
daughter covered with a Barbary horse; you'll have your
nephews neigh to you, you'll have coursers for cousins,
and jennets for germans.

BRABANTIO What profane wretch art thou?

IAGO I am one, sir, that comes to tell you, your daughter

---

100 *distempering* intoxicating
101 *bravery* show of courage
102 *start* startle
103 *Sir, sir, sir*. Roderigo's words are extra-metrical, and Brabantio continues without a pause.
107 *grange* country house

108 *simple* sincere
112 *Barbary*. The Barbary coast, North Africa, was famous for horse-breeding. Iago is, of course, referring to the Moor.
114 *jennet* a small Spanish horse
   germans near relations

and the Moor are now making the beast with two
backs.

BRABANTIO
Thou art a villain.

IAGO   You are a Senator.

BRABANTIO
This thou shalt answer. I know thee, Roderigo.   120

RODERIGO
Sir, I will answer anything. But I beseech you
If 't be your pleasure and most wise consent,
As partly I find it is, that your fair daughter,
At this odd-even and dull watch o'th'night,
Transported with no worse nor better guard
But with a knave of common hire, a gondolier,
To the gross clasps of a lascivious Moor –
If this be known to you, and your allowance,
We then have done you bold and saucy wrongs;
But if you know not this, my manners tell me   130
We have your wrong rebuke. Do not believe
That from the sense of all civility
I thus would play and trifle with your reverence.
Your daughter, if you have not given her leave,
I say again hath made a gross revolt,
Tying her duty, beauty, wit, and fortunes

117–18 *making the beast with two backs*
engaging in sexual intercourse. In
fact, as we learn later, Othello's marriage is consummated in Act II.

119 *You are a Senator.* Many editors
assume that Iago suppresses an
uncomplimentary word, but he may
either be ironically polite or
pretending that 'Senator' is
uncomplimentary.

123 *partly* in some degree (from your
apparent lack of concern)

124 *odd-even* between midnight and 1
a.m.

126 *knave* servant

127 *Moor –.* Roderigo does not complete
his sentence.

128 *allowance* permission

132 *from the sense of all civility* contrary to
good manners

In an extravagant and wheeling stranger
Of here and everywhere. Straight satisfy yourself:
If she be in her chamber or your house,

140 Let loose on me the justice of the state
For thus deluding you.

BRABANTIO   Strike on the tinder, ho!
Give me a taper; call up all my people!
This accident is not unlike my dream:
Belief of it oppresses me already.
Light, I say, light!   *Exit above*

IAGO   Farewell, for I must leave you.
It seems not meet, nor wholesome to my place,
To be produced — as if I stay, I shall —
Against the Moor. For I do know the state,
However this may gall him with some check,

150 Cannot with safety cast him; for he's embarked
With such loud reason to the Cyprus wars,
Which even now stand in act, that for their souls
Another of his fathom they have none
To lead their business. In which regard,
Though I do hate him as I do hell pains,
Yet for necessity of present life
I must show out a flag and sign of love,
Which is indeed but sign. That you shall surely find him,
Lead to the Sagittary the raisèd search;

160 And there will I be with him. So farewell.   *Exit*
  Enter Brabantio in his night-gown with servants and
  torches

---

137 *extravagant and wheeling* vagrant
143 *accident* event
149 *check* reprimand
150 *cast* dismiss
  embarked engaged
152 *stand in act* are in progress
153 *fathom* ability. This is one of

Iago's admissions about the man he hates.
159 *Sagittary* (the name of the inn or the house where Othello and Desdemona are lodging)
160 (stage direction) *night-gown* dressing-gown

BRABANTIO

It is too true an evil. Gone she is,
And what's to come of my despisèd time
Is naught but bitterness. Now, Roderigo,
Where didst thou see her? – O unhappy girl! –
With the Moor, say'st thou? – Who would be a father? –
How didst thou know 'twas she? – O, she deceives me
Past thought! – What said she to you? – Get more tapers.
Raise all my kindred. – Are they married, think you?

RODERIGO

Truly I think they are.

BRABANTIO

O heaven! How got she out? O treason of the blood!   170
Fathers, from hence trust not your daughters' minds
By what you see them act. Is there not charms
By which the property of youth and maidhood
May be abused? Have you not read, Roderigo,
Of some such thing?

RODERIGO   Yes, sir, I have indeed.

BRABANTIO

Call up my brother – O would you had had her!
Some one way, some another. Do you know
Where we may apprehend her and the Moor?

RODERIGO

I think I can discover him, if you please
To get good guard and go along with me.   180

BRABANTIO

Pray you, lead on. At every house I'll call –
I may command at most. Get weapons, ho!
And raise some special officers of night.
On, good Roderigo, I'll deserve your pains.   *Exeunt*

---

162 *despisèd time*. A father whose daughter married without his permission
would be regarded as dishonoured.
172 *charms* enchantments (the first of
many references to witchcraft)

173 *property* nature
183 *officers of night*. These are mentioned
in *The Commonwealth and Government
of Venice*. See Introduction, p. 12.

I.2   *Enter Othello, Iago, attendants with torches*

IAGO

Though in the trade of war I have slain men,
Yet do I hold it very stuff o'th'conscience
To do no contrived murder: I lack iniquity
Sometimes to do me service. Nine or ten times
I had thought t'have yerked him here under the ribs.

OTHELLO

'Tis better as it is.

IAGO   Nay, but he prated
And spoke such scurvy and provoking terms
Against your honour,
That with the little godliness I have,
10   I did full hard forbear him. But I pray, sir,
Are you fast married? For be assured of this,
That the Magnifico is much beloved,
And hath in his effect a voice potential
As double as the Duke's. He will divorce you,

I.2 The calm dignity of Othello on his first appearance contrasts with what Iago and Brabantio have said about him in the previous scene.

1–10 *Though in the trade of war ... I did full hard forbear him.* Iago is posing as a loyal follower of Othello, in accordance with the hypocritical course of conduct outlined in the first scene, and ascribing to Roderigo his own descriptions of the Moor. He has apparently told Othello that Roderigo was responsible for informing Brabantio of Desdemona's elopement.

2 *very stuff* essence (but carrying on the metaphor of 'trade')

3 *contrived* (accent on first syllable)

5 *yerked* thrust

10 *full hard* with great difficulty

12 *Magnifico* (Brabantio's title)

13–14 *voice potential | As double as the Duke's.* Shakespeare would have found several passages in Lewkenor's translation of Contarini's *Commonwealth and Government of Venice* about the powers of the Duke, and though 'voice' often means 'vote' in Shakespeare's plays, the Duke did not have two votes. Either Shakespeare was careless in his perusal of the book, or he meant simply that Brabantio's voice was as influential as the Duke's and twice as influential as those of the other Senators.

13 *potential* powerful

Or put upon you what restraint and grievance
That law, with all his might to enforce it on,
Will give him cable.

OTHELLO   Let him do his spite:
My services, which I have done the signory,
Shall out-tongue his complaints. 'Tis yet to know –
Which, when I know that boasting is an honour,   20
I shall provulgate – I fetch my life and being
From men of royal siege, and my demerits
May speak, unbonneted, to as proud a fortune
As this that I have reached. For know, Iago,
But that I love the gentle Desdemona,
I would not my unhousèd free condition
Put into circumscription and confine
For the seas' worth. But look, what lights come yond!

IAGO
Those are the raised father and his friends:
You were best go in.

OTHELLO   Not I: I must be found.   30
My parts, my title, and my perfect soul
Shall manifest me rightly. Is it they?

IAGO
By Janus, I think no.

            Enter Cassio, with men bearing torches

OTHELLO
The servants of the Duke and my Lieutenant!
The goodness of the night upon you, friends.

18 *signory* Venetian government
19 *yet to know* not yet known
21 *provulgate* publish abroad. As this is a
    rarer word than 'promulgate' (F), it
    is unlikely to have been a misprint.
22 *siege* rank
    demerits deserts
23 *unbonneted* without my hat on, with
    all due modesty

26 *unhousèd* without a house
27 *circumscription and confine* restriction
    and restraint
28 *yond* yonder
31 *parts* natural gifts
    perfect soul clear conscience
33 *Janus* (a two-faced Roman god – the
    oath is appropriate to the two-faced
    Iago)

What is the news?

CASSIO   The Duke does greet you, General,
And he requires your haste-post-haste appearance
Even on the instant.

OTHELLO   What is the matter, think you?

CASSIO
Something from Cyprus, as I may divine:
It is a business of some heat. The galleys
Have sent a dozen sequent messengers
This very night at one another's heels;
And many of the consuls, raised and met,
Are at the Duke's already. You have been hotly called for,
When being not at your lodging to be found.
The senate hath sent about three several quests
To search you out.

OTHELLO   'Tis well I am found by you:
I will but spend a word here in the house
And go with you.

CASSIO ·   Ancient, what makes he here?   *Exit*

IAGO
Faith, he tonight hath boarded a land carack:
If it prove lawful prize, he's made for ever.

CASSIO
I do not understand.

IAGO   He's married.

CASSIO   To who?

IAGO
Marry, to – Come, Captain, will you go?
          Enter Othello

OTHELLO   Have with you.

40

50

---

39 *divine* guess
40 *heat* urgency
44 *hotly* urgently
50 *carack* large ship

52 *who* whom
53 *Marry* the Virgin Mary (with a quib-
    ble on the word)
    Have with you I'll go with you

CASSIO

Here comes another troop to seek for you.

Enter Brabantio, Roderigo, with officers and torches

IAGO

It is Brabantio: General, be advised,

He comes to bad intent.

OTHELLO   Holla, stand there.

RODERIGO

Signor, it is the Moor.

BRABANTIO   Down with him, thief!

IAGO

You, Roderigo? Come, sir, I am for you.

OTHELLO

Keep up your bright swords, for the dew will rust them.

Good signor, you shall more command with years   60

Than with your weapons.

BRABANTIO

O thou foul thief! Where hast thou stowed my daughter?

Damned as thou art, thou hast enchanted her:

For I'll refer me to all things of sense,

If she in chains of magic were not bound,

Whether a maid, so tender, fair, and happy,

So opposite to marriage that she shunned

The wealthy curlèd darlings of our nation,

Would ever have – t'incur a general mock –

Run from her guardage to the sooty bosom   70

Of such a thing as thou: to fear, not to delight.

Judge me the world, if 'tis not gross in sense

That thou hast practised on her with foul charms,

---

58 *Come, sir, I am for you.* Iago pretends
to fight Roderigo.

59 *Keep up your bright swords, for the dew
will rust them.* This exhibits Othello's
calm authority rather than his sup-

posed tendency to self-dramatization.

63 *enchanted.* See note to 1.1.172.

67 *opposite* opposed

70 *guardage* guardianship

72 *gross in sense* quite obvious

Abused her delicate youth with drugs or minerals
That weakens motion. I'll have't disputed on;
'Tis probable, and palpable to thinking:
I therefore apprehend, and do attach thee
For an abuser of the world, a practiser
Of arts inhibited, and out of warrant.

80 Lay hold upon him: if he do resist,
Subdue him, at his peril.

OTHELLO   Hold your hands,
Both you of my inclining and the rest.
Were it my cue to fight, I should have known it
Without a prompter. Where will you that I go
To answer this your charge?

BRABANTIO   To prison, till fit time
Of law and course of direct session
Call thee to answer.

OTHELLO   What if I do obey?
How may the Duke be therewith satisfied,
Whose messengers are here about my side,

90 Upon some present business of the state
To bring me to him?

OFFICER   'Tis true, most worthy signor:
The Duke's in council, and your noble self
I am sure is sent for.

BRABANTIO   How? The Duke in council?
In this time of the night? Bring him away.
Mine's not an idle cause; the Duke himself,
Or any of my brothers of the state,
Cannot but feel this wrong as 'twere their own:

---

74 *minerals*. This is one of many references to poison.
75 *motion* impulses, faculties
77 *attach* arrest
79 *arts inhibited* the black art

out of warrant unwarrantable
86 *direct session* immediate sitting of
court
95 *idle* trifling

For if such actions may have passage free,
Bondslaves and pagans shall our statesmen be.   *Exeunt*

The Duke and Senators sitting at a table; with lights   I.3
and attendants

DUKE
There is no composition in these news
That gives them credit.

FIRST SENATOR   Indeed they are disproportioned.
My letters say a hundred and seven galleys.

DUKE
And mine, a hundred and forty.

SECOND SENATOR   And mine two hundred;
But though they jump not on a just accompt —
As in these cases where the aim reports
'Tis oft with difference — yet do they all confirm
A Turkish fleet, and bearing up to Cyprus.

DUKE
Nay, it is possible enough to judgement:

99 *Bondslaves and pagans shall our statesmen be.* This reference to slavery was perhaps suggested by the Venetian constitution. Brabantio implies that if blackamoors are allowed to intermarry with Venetian citizens, either the Senators would be reduced to the level of slaves or else the government would be taken over by former slaves.

I.3 The early part of this scene, concerned with the Turkish danger, is a means of building up Othello's reputation as a soldier; the second part, containing Othello's defence of his wooing, is an effective rebuttal of Iago's slanders and Brabantio's accusations of witchcraft, and it shows that Desdemona was half the wooer; the third part, after the departure of the Senators, reveals Iago's plot to retain his hold over Roderigo and the birth of his scheme to make Othello jealous of Cassio. This is prepared for by the accounts of Cassio in the first scene and his brief and colourless appearance in the second.

1 *composition* consistency
2 *disproportioned* inconsistent
5 *jump* tally
6-7 *where the aim reports | 'Tis oft with difference* where there are discrepancies between one report and another

10   I do not so secure me in the error,
But the main article I do approve
In fearful sense.

SAILOR (*without*)   What, ho! What, ho! What, ho!

FIRST OFFICER
A messenger from the galleys.

      Enter Sailor

DUKE   Now, what's the business?

SAILOR
The Turkish preparation makes for Rhodes;
So was I bid report here to the state
By Signor Angelo.

DUKE
How say you by this change?

FIRST SENATOR   This cannot be,
By no assay of reason. 'Tis a pageant
To keep us in false gaze. When we consider
20   Th'importancy of Cyprus to the Turk,
And let ourselves again but understand
That as it more concerns the Turk than Rhodes,
So may he with more facile question bear it,
For that it stands not in such warlike brace,
But altogether lacks th'abilities
That Rhodes is dressed in. If we make thought of this,
We must not think the Turk is so unskilful
To leave that latest which concerns him first,
Neglecting an attempt of ease and gain

---

10 *I do not so secure me in the error* I do
not feel myself so secure from the
discrepancy between the various reports as not to believe the thing
common to all
11 *approve* endorse
18 *assay* test
   pageant show

19 *in false gaze* looking in the wrong
direction
20 *importancy* importance
23 *with more facile question bear it* capture
it more easily
24 *brace* readiness
26 *dressed in* equipped with

To wake and wage a danger profitless.   30

DUKE

Nay, in all confidence he's not for Rhodes.

FIRST OFFICER

Here is more news.

Enter a Messenger

MESSENGER

The Ottomites, reverend and gracious,
Steering with due course toward the isle of Rhodes,
Have there injointed with an after fleet.

FIRST SENATOR

Ay, so I thought. How many, as you guess?

MESSENGER

Of thirty sail; and now they do re-stem
Their backward course, bearing with frank appearance
Their purposes toward Cyprus. Signor Montano,
Your trusty and most valiant servitor,   40
With his free duty recommends you thus,
And prays you to believe him.

DUKE

'Tis certain then for Cyprus.
Marcus Luccicos, is not he in town?

FIRST SENATOR

He's now in Florence.

DUKE   Write from us: wish him
Post-post-haste dispatch.

FIRST SENATOR

Here comes Brabantio and the valiant Moor.

Enter Brabantio, Othello, Iago, Roderigo, and officers

DUKE

Valiant Othello, we must straight employ you
Against the general enemy Ottoman.

30 *wage* risk   37 *re-stem* re-trace
35 *injointed* united

50   (*To Brabantio*) I did not see you: welcome, gentle signor;
      We lacked your counsel and your help tonight.

BRABANTIO
      So did I yours. Good your grace, pardon me:
      Neither my place, nor aught I heard of business,
      Hath raised me from my bed; nor doth the general care
      Take hold on me; for my particular grief
      Is of so flood-gate and o'erbearing nature
      That it engluts and swallows other sorrows
      And yet is still itself.

DUKE   Why? What's the matter?

BRABANTIO
      My daughter! O, my daughter!

SENATORS   Dead?

BRABANTIO   Ay, to me.
60   She is abused, stolen from me, and corrupted
      By spells and medicines bought of mountebanks;
      For nature so preposterously to err,
      Being not deficient, blind, or lame of sense,
      Sans witchcraft could not.

DUKE
      Whoe'er he be that in this foul proceeding
      Hath thus beguiled your daughter of herself
      And you of her, the bloody book of law
      You shall yourself read in the bitter letter
      After your own sense, yea, though our proper son
      Stood in your action.

70   BRABANTIO   Humbly I thank your grace.
      Here is the man: this Moor, whom now it seems
      Your special mandate for the state affairs

50 *I did not see you.* The Duke has been
   absorbed in his papers.
57 *engluts* swallows up
64 *Sans* without
67–9 *the bloody book of law | You shall
   yourself read in the bitter letter | After*

your own sense you shall be judge in
   your own cause and sentence the
   guilty one to death
69 *proper* own
70 *Stood* were accused

Hath hither brought.

ALL   We are very sorry for't.

DUKE

What in your own part can you say to this?

BRABANTIO

Nothing, but this is so.

OTHELLO

Most potent, grave and reverend signors,
My very noble and approved good masters,
That I have ta'en away this old man's daughter,
It is most true; true I have married her;
The very head and front of my offending   80
Hath this extent, no more. Rude am I in my speech
And little blessed with the soft phrase of peace;
For since these arms of mine had seven years' pith
Till now some nine moons wasted, they have used
Their dearest action in the tented field;
And little of this great world can I speak
More than pertains to feats of broil and battle;
And therefore little shall I grace my cause
In speaking for myself. Yet, by your gracious patience,
I will a round unvarnished tale deliver   90
Of my whole course of love: what drugs, what charms,
What conjuration and what mighty magic –
For such proceedings I am charged withal –
I won his daughter.

BRABANTIO   A maiden never bold;
Of spirit so still and quiet that her motion
Blushed at herself: and she, in spite of nature,

---

80 *head and front* height and breadth
81 *Rude am I in my speech.* There is nothing in the splendid poetry put into
Othello's mouth to support this
modest admission; but he is given an
exotic vocabulary and a style which
distinguishes his speech from that of
the other characters.
90 *round* plain
92 *conjuration* incantation
95 *motion* movement of the soul,
impulse
96 *herself* itself

Of years, of country, credit, everything,
To fall in love with what she feared to look on!
It is a judgement maimed and most imperfect
That will confess perfection so could err
Against all rules of nature, and must be driven
To find out practices of cunning hell
Why this should be. I therefore vouch again
That with some mixtures powerful o'er the blood,
Or with some dram conjured to this effect,
He wrought upon her.

DUKE   To vouch this is no proof,
Without more wider and more overt test
Than these thin habits and poor likelihoods
Of modern seeming do prefer against him.

FIRST SENATOR
But, Othello, speak:
Did you by indirect and forcèd courses
Subdue and poison this young maid's affections?
Or came it by request and such fair question
As soul to soul affordeth?

OTHELLO   I do beseech you,
Send for the lady to the Sagittary,
And let her speak of me before her father.
If you do find me foul in her report,
The trust, the office I do hold of you
Not only take away, but let your sentence
Even fall upon my life.

DUKE   Fetch Desdemona hither.

OTHELLO
Ancient, conduct them: you best know the place.

---

105 *conjured* induced by magic spells (the
    accent is on the second syllable)
107 *more wider* fuller
108 *thin habits* tenuous arguments

likelihood hypotheses
109 *modern* ordinary
113 *question* talk

Exit Iago with attendants

And till she come, as truly as to heaven
I do confess the vices of my blood,
So justly to your grave ears I'll present
How I did thrive in this fair lady's love,
And she in mine.

DUKE   Say it, Othello.

OTHELLO

Her father loved me, oft invited me,
Still questioned me the story of my life
From year to year – the battles, sieges, fortunes
That I have passed.   130
I ran it through, even from my boyish days
To th'very moment that he bade me tell it:
Wherein I spake of most disastrous chances,
Of moving accidents by flood and field,
Of hair-breadth scrapes i'th'imminent deadly breach,
Of being taken by the insolent foe,
And sold to slavery; of my redemption thence,
And portance in my travels' history:
Wherein of antres vast and deserts idle,
Rough quarries, rocks, and hills whose heads touch   140
      heaven,
It was my hint to speak – such was the process:
And of the Cannibals that each other eat,
The Anthropophagi, and men whose heads

122–3 *as truly as to heaven* | *I do confess the vices of my blood.* Othello, as we are reminded often, is a Christian.

128 *Still* continually

138 *portance* behaviour

travels'. This reading is superior to that of F, since 'Trauellers' would imply that Othello's story had been embroidered.

139–44 *Wherein of antres vast and deserts idle . . . Do grow beneath their shoulders.* These details were derived from Pliny's *Natural History* and from Elizabethan narratives of travel.

139 *antres* caves
    idle uninhabited, sterile

141 *hint* occasion

143 *Anthropophagi* man-eaters

Do grow beneath their shoulders. This to hear
Would Desdemona seriously incline:
But still the house affairs would draw her thence,
Which ever as she could with haste dispatch
She'd come again, and with a greedy ear
Devour up my discourse; which I observing
Took once a pliant hour, and found good means
To draw from her a prayer of earnest heart
That I would all my pilgrimage dilate
Whereof by parcels she had something heard,
But not intentively. I did consent,
And often did beguile her of her tears
When I did speak of some distressful stroke
That my youth suffered. My story being done,
She gave me for my pains a world of sighs:
She swore, in faith 'twas strange, 'twas passing strange,
'Twas pitiful, 'twas wondrous pitiful;
She wished she had not heard it, yet she wished
That heaven had made her such a man. She thanked me,
And bade me, if I had a friend that loved her,
I should but teach him how to tell my story,
And that would woo her. Upon this hint I spake:
She loved me for the dangers I had passed,
And I loved her, that she did pity them.
This only is the witchcraft I have used.
Here comes the lady: let her witness it.

Enter Desdemona, Iago, and attendants

DUKE

I think this tale would win my daughter too.

---

150 *pliant* favourable
152 *dilate* relate in full
153 *by parcels* piecemeal
154 *intentively* attentively, continuously
158 *sighs*. The F reading, 'kisses', is obviously impossible.
162 *her*. Desdemona wished she could have been a man to have had such

adventures; she was not suggesting that she would like to have such a husband.
165 *hint* opportunity. Othello is not suggesting that Desdemona was fishing for a proposal, although the previous words seem to be a fairly direct hint.

Good Brabantio, take up this mangled matter at the best:
Men do their broken weapons rather use
Than their bare hands.

BRABANTIO   I pray you hear her speak.
If she confess that she was half the wooer,
Destruction on my head, if my bad blame
Light on the man! Come hither, gentle mistress;
Do you perceive in all this company
Where most you owe obedience?

DESDEMONA   My noble father
I do perceive here a divided duty:
To you I am bound for life and education;   180
My life and education both do learn me
How to respect you. You are lord of all my duty,
I am hitherto your daughter. But here's my husband;
And so much duty as my mother showed
To you, preferring you before her father,
So much I challenge, that I may profess
Due to the Moor, my lord.

BRABANTIO   God bu'y! I have done.
Please it your grace, on to the state affairs.
I had rather to adopt a child than get it.
Come hither, Moor: 190
I here do give thee that with all my heart
Which, but thou hast already, with all my heart
I would keep from thee. For your sake, jewel,
I am glad at soul I have no other child,
For thy escape would teach me tyranny
To hang clogs on them. I have done, my lord.

171 *take up this mangled matter at the best*
      make the best of a bad job
180 *education* upbringing
181 *learn* teach
186 *challenge* claim
187 *bu'y* be with you
189 *get* beget
193 *For your sake* on your own account
195 *escape* elopement
196 *clogs* (blocks of wood fastened to
      legs)

DUKE
    Let me speak like yourself and lay a sentence
    Which as a grise or step may help these lovers
    Into your favour.
200   When remedies are past the griefs are ended
    By seeing the worst which late on hopes depended.
    To mourn a mischief that is past and gone
    Is the next way to draw new mischief on.
    What cannot be preserved when fortune takes,
    Patience her injury a mockery makes.
    The robbed that smiles steals something from the thief;
    He robs himself that spends a bootless grief.

BRABANTIO
    So let the Turk of Cyprus us beguile,
    We lose it not so long as we can smile;
210   He bears the sentence well that nothing bears
    But the free comfort which from thence he hears;
    But he bears both the sentence and the sorrow
    That to pay grief must of poor patience borrow.
    These sentences, to sugar or to gall
    Being strong on both sides, are equivocal.
    But words are words; I never yet did hear
    That the bruised heart was piecèd through the ear.
    I humbly beseech you proceed to th'affairs of state.

DUKE The Turk with a most mighty preparation makes for
220   Cyprus. Othello, the fortitude of the place is best known
    to you: and though we have there a substitute of most
    allowed sufficiency, yet opinion, a more sovereign mistress

---

198 *grise* step
200–217 *When remedies are past ... piecèd through the ear.* The rhymed verse suggests that both the Duke and Brabantio are indulging in proverbial wisdom, and the speeches have a choric effect.
207 *bootless* vain
217 *piecèd* mended

through the ear by listening to consolation
218 *I humbly beseech you proceed to th'affairs of state.* The drop into prose indicates the change of subject.
220 *fortitude* strength
222 *allowed* acknowledged
    opinion public opinion

of effects, throws a more safer voice on you. You
must therefore be content to slubber the gloss of your
near fortunes with this more stubborn and boisterous
expedition.

OTHELLO
The tyrant, custom, most grave Senators,
Hath made the flinty and steel couch of war
My thrice-driven bed of down. I do agnize
A natural and prompt alacrity   230
I find in hardness; and do undertake
This present war against the Ottomites.
Most humbly, therefore, bending to your state,
I crave fit disposition for my wife,
Due reference of place and exhibition,
With such accommodation and besort
As levels with her breeding.

DUKE   If you please,
Be't at her father's.

BRABANTIO   I'll not have it so.

OTHELLO
Nor I.

DESDEMONA Nor I: I would not there reside
To put my father in impatient thoughts   240
By being in his eye. Most gracious Duke,
To my unfolding lend your prosperous ear,
And let me find a charter in your voice

---

223 *more safer* safer
224 *slubber* spoil
225 *stubborn* inflexible
227 *tyrant, custom* (proverbial)
229 *agnize* acknowledge
230–31 *A natural and prompt alacrity | I
        find in hardness* that I am eager to
        embrace hardship
233 *bending to your state* bowing to your
        office

234 *disposition* arrangements
235 *Due reference of place* treatment as
        becomes her rank
        exhibition financial provision
236 *besort* retinue
237 *levels* fits
242 *unfolding* proposal
        prosperous favourable
243 *charter* pledge

T'assist my simpleness.

DUKE   What would you? Speak.

DESDEMONA

That I did love the Moor to live with him,
My downright violence and storm of fortunes
May trumpet to the world. My heart's subdued
Even to the very quality of my lord.
I saw Othello's visage in his mind
250 And to his honours and his valiant parts
Did I my soul and fortunes consecrate.
So that, dear lords, if I be left behind
A moth of peace, and he go to the war,
The rites for which I love him are bereft me,
And I a heavy interim shall support
By his dear absence. Let me go with him.

OTHELLO

Let her have your voice.
Vouch with me, heaven, I therefore beg it not
To please the palate of my appetite,
260 Nor to comply with heat – the young affects
In me defunct – and proper satisfaction;

246 *storm.* The Q reading 'scorne' is attractive, but 'storm' is supported by Lewkenor, from whom the phrase is echoed.

247–8 *My heart's subdued | Even to the very quality of my lord* I am in love with Othello's virtues

253 *moth* (condemned to useless idleness)

254 *rites* (of marriage). Desdemona's frankness about sex contrasts with her husband's later protestations that he is anxious merely for companionship; but several editors prefer 'rights' – her right to share Othello's life.

257 *Let her have your voice.* Some critics suppose that the Senators here show

astonishment that Othello should ask to take his wife on active service; but if this had been Shakespeare's intention he would have made the Duke express surprise.

260 *comply with* satisfy
   affects desires

261 *In me defunct – and proper satisfaction.* The line is probably corrupt in both texts, but the general meaning is clear. Othello is explaining that he is no longer a young man swayed by passion, and that he wants Desdemona's companionship more than the gratification of his own 'proper' desires. Those who think that Othello is deceived about himself fasten on this line.

But to be free and bounteous to her mind.
And heaven defend your good souls that you think
I will your serious and great business scant
For she is with me. No, when light-winged toys
Of feathered Cupid seel with wanton dullness
My speculative and officed instruments,
That my disports corrupt and taint my business,
Let housewives make a skillet of my helm,
And all indign and base adversities   270
Make head against my estimation!

DUKE

Be it as you shall privately determine,
Either for her stay, or going. Th'affair cries haste,
And speed must answer it. You must hence tonight.

DESDEMONA

Tonight, my lord?

DUKE   This night.

OTHELLO   With all my heart.

DUKE

At nine i'th'morning, here we'll meet again.
Othello, leave some officer behind,
And he shall our commission bring to you,
With such things else of quality and respect
As doth import you.

OTHELLO   So please your grace, my Ancient.   280
A man he is of honesty and trust:
To his conveyance I assign my wife,

---

263 *defend* forbid
266 *seel* blind (from the practice of sewing up the eyelids of a hawk)
267 *speculative and officed instruments* eyes and other faculties
268 *disports* sexual pleasures
269 *skillet* (small metal pot, used in cooking)
270 *indign* unworthy

271 *estimation* reputation
279 *quality and respect* importance and relevance
280 *import* concern
281 *A man he is of honesty and trust.* The audience is aware that Othello is completely deceived about Iago and has no idea that he bears resentment at being passed over.

With what else needful your good grace shall think
To be sent after me.

DUKE   Let it be so.
Good night to everyone. And, noble signor,
If virtue no delighted beauty lack,
Your son-in-law is far more fair than black.

FIRST SENATOR
Adieu, brave Moor: use Desdemona well.

BRABANTIO
Look to her, Moor, if thou hast eyes to see.
290   She has deceived her father, and may thee.

OTHELLO
My life upon her faith!

                              Exeunt Duke, Senators, and attendants
                              Honest Iago,
My Desdemona must I leave to thee.
I prithee let thy wife attend on her,
And bring them after in the best advantage.
Come, Desdemona, I have but an hour
Of love, of worldly matters and direction
To spend with thee. We must obey the time.

                              Exeunt Othello and Desdemona

RODERIGO Iago.

IAGO What say'st thou, noble heart

300   RODERIGO What will I do, think'st thou?

IAGO Why, go to bed and sleep.

RODERIGO I will incontinently drown myself.

---

286 *delighted* delightful
287 *far more fair than black.* This contrast
between black and white recurs frequently throughout the play.
289-90 *Look to her, Moor, if thou hast eyes
to see. | She has deceived her father, and
may thee.* Iago remembers this couplet
(see III.3.204).

294 *in the best advantage* at the best
opportunity
296 *direction* instructions
298-398 *Iago . . . the world's light.* On
Shakespeare's unlocalized stage, the
scene ceases to be the council-
chamber when Roderigo and Iago
are left alone.
302 *incontinently* forthwith

IAGO If thou dost, I shall never love thee after. Why, thou silly gentleman!

RODERIGO It is silliness to live, when to live is torment: and then we have a prescription to die, when death is our physician.

IAGO O villainous! I have looked upon the world for four times seven years, and since I could distinguish betwixt a benefit and an injury, I never found a man that knew   310
how to love himself. Ere I would say I would drown myself for the love of a guinea-hen, I would change my humanity with a baboon.

RODERIGO What should I do? I confess it is my shame to be so fond, but it is not in my virtue to amend it.

IAGO Virtue? A fig! 'Tis in ourselves that we are thus, or thus. Our bodies are our gardens, to the which our wills are gardeners. So that if we will plant nettles or sow lettuce, set hyssop and weed up thyme, supply it with one gender of herbs or distract it with many, either to   320
have it sterile with idleness or manured with industry, why the power and corrigible authority of this lies in our wills. If the beam of our lives had not one scale of reason to poise another of sensuality, the blood and baseness of our natures would conduct us to most preposterous conclusions. But we have reason to cool our raging motions, our carnal stings, our unbitted lusts: whereof I take this, that you call love, to be a sect or scion.

RODERIGO It cannot be.   330

IAGO It is merely a lust of the blood and a permission of

306 *prescription*. This is a quibble on medical prescription and 'immemorial right' (A. Walker).
312 *guinea-hen* prostitute
320 *gender* kind
322 *corrigible authority* corrective power
323 *beam* balance
327 *unbitted* unbridled

328 *sect* cutting
331–2 *It is merely a lust of the blood and a permission of the will*. This is Iago's real opinion, though he is using it to corrupt Roderigo. He has been paid by Roderigo to arrange a marriage with Desdemona: he now holds out the hope that she can be seduced.

the will. Come, be a man. Drown thyself? Drown cats
and blind puppies. I have professed me thy friend, and
I confess me knit to thy deserving with cables of perdurable toughness. I could never better stead thee than
now. Put money in thy purse. Follow thou these wars;
defeat thy favour with an usurped beard. I say, put
money in thy purse. It cannot be that Desdemona should
long continue her love to the Moor – put money in thy
purse – nor he his to her. It was a violent commencement, and thou shalt see an answerable sequestration –
put but money in thy purse. These Moors are changeable in their wills – fill thy purse with money. The food
that to him now is as luscious as locusts shall be to him
shortly as acerbe as the coloquintida. She must change
for youth: when she is sated with his body she will find
the error of her choice. Therefore put money in thy
purse. If thou wilt needs damn thyself, do it a more
delicate way than drowning. Make all the money thou
canst. If sanctimony and a frail vow betwixt an erring
barbarian and a super-subtle Venetian be not too hard
for my wits and all the tribe of hell, thou shalt enjoy
her – therefore make money. A pox of drowning thyself!
It is clean out of the way. Seek thou rather to be hanged
in compassing thy joy than to be drowned and go without her.

RODERIGO Wilt thou be fast to my hopes, if I depend on
the issue?

IAGO Thou art sure of me. Go make money. I have told
thee often, and I re-tell thee again and again, I hate

334–5 *perdurable* long-lasting
335 *stead* benefit
337 *defeat thy favour* disguise your face
usurped wrongly appropriated (because Roderigo is unmanly) or false
341 *sequestration* separation

344 *locusts* (cobs of the carob tree)
345 *acerbe* bitter (the reading of F)
coloquintida colocynth (bitter apple
used as purgative drug)
349 *Make* raise
350 *erring* wandering, sinful

the Moor. My cause is hearted: thine hath no less reason. Let us be conjunctive in our revenge against him. If thou canst cuckold him, thou dost thyself a pleasure, me a sport. There are many events in the womb of time, which will be delivered. Traverse! Go, provide thy money. We will have more of this tomorrow. Adieu.

RODERIGO Where shall we meet i'th'morning?

IAGO At my lodging.

RODERIGO I'll be with thee betimes.   370

IAGO Go to; farewell. Do you hear, Roderigo?

RODERIGO What say you?

IAGO No more of drowning, do you hear?

RODERIGO I am changed.

IAGO Go to; farewell. Put money enough in your purse.

RODERIGO I'll sell all my land.   *Exit*

IAGO

Thus do I ever make my fool my purse:
For I mine own gained knowledge should profane
If I would time expend with such a snipe
But for my sport and profit. I hate the Moor,   380
And it is thought abroad that 'twixt my sheets
He's done my office. I know not if't be true
But I, for mere suspicion in that kind,
Will do as if for surety. He holds me well:
The better shall my purpose work on him.
Cassio's a proper man: let me see now;
To get his place and to plume up my will

---

361 *hearted* heart-felt
362 *conjunctive* allied
365 *Traverse!* about turn!
370 *betimes* early
377–98 *Thus do I ever make my fool my purse ... the world's light.* In Iago's

soliloquy we see him for the first time without a mask.
384 *holds me well* esteems me
386 *proper* handsome
387 *plume up* set a feather in the cap of

In double knavery. How? How? Let's see.
After some time, to abuse Othello's ear
390   That he is too familiar with his wife;
He hath a person and a smooth dispose
To be suspected, framed to make women false.
The Moor is of a free and open nature,
That thinks men honest that but seem to be so,
And will as tenderly be led by th'nose
As asses are.
I have't. It is engendered. Hell and night
Must bring this monstrous birth to the world's light.

Exit

II.1   *Enter Montano and two Gentlemen*

MONTANO
What from the cape can you discern at sea?

FIRST GENTLEMAN
Nothing at all; it is a high-wrought flood.
I cannot 'twixt the heaven and the main
Descry a sail.

MONTANO
Methinks the wind does speak aloud at land;

391 *dispose* disposition
393–4 *The Moor is of a free and open nature,
| That thinks men honest that but seem to
be so.* This is another tribute from
the villain about the hero, though it
is said with a sneer.
397–8 *Hell and night | Must bring this
monstrous birth to the world's light.* Iago
deliberately chooses evil.

II.1 The rest of the play is set in Cyprus.

Enough time has elapsed to enable the
chief characters to sail to the island from
Venice. The scene is near the harbour.
The function of the storm is to show, by
the anxiety for Othello's safety, the
esteem in which he is held, to exhibit the
mutual love of Othello and Desdemona,
to dispose of the Turkish danger, which
is now dramatically unnecessary, and to
symbolize the tempest of passion which
is soon to overwhelm Othello.

A fuller blast ne'er shook our battlements.
If it hath ruffianed so upon the sea,
What ribs of oak, when mountains melt on them,
Can hold the mortise? What shall we hear of this?

SECOND GENTLEMAN
A segregation of the Turkish fleet: 10
For do but stand upon the banning shore,
The chidden billow seems to pelt the clouds;
The wind-shaked surge, with high and monstrous mane,
Seems to cast water on the burning Bear
And quench the guards of th'ever-fixèd Pole.
I never did like molestation view
On the enchafèd flood.

MONTANO   If that the Turkish fleet
Be not ensheltered and embayed, they are drowned:
It is impossible they bear it out.

Enter a Gentleman

THIRD GENTLEMAN
News, lads! Our wars are done: 20
The desperate tempest hath so banged the Turks
That their designment halts. A noble ship of Venice
Hath seen a grievous wrack and sufferance
On most part of their fleet.

MONTANO
How! Is this true?

THIRD GENTLEMAN The ship is here put in,

7 *ruffianed* raged
8 *mountains* mountainous seas
10 *segregation* dispersal
11 *banning* cursing. This reading is superior to the colourless 'foaming'.
13 *monstrous mane*. The seas are compared to a wild beast.
15 *guards of th'ever-fixèd Pole* (two stars
in the Little Bear known as the
Guardians)

16 *molestation* disturbance
17 *enchafèd* angry
22 *designment* design. The Turkish
danger, necessary for displaying Othello's reputation, is ended before his
arrival in Cyprus.
23 *sufferance* damage

A Veronesa; Michael Cassio,
Lieutenant to the warlike Moor, Othello,
Is come on shore; the Moor himself at sea,
And is in full commission here for Cyprus.

MONTANO

30   I am glad on't; 'tis a worthy governor.

THIRD GENTLEMAN

But this same Cassio, though he speak of comfort
Touching the Turkish loss, yet he looks sadly
And prays the Moor be safe; for they were parted
With foul and violent tempest.

MONTANO   Pray heaven he be:
For I have served him, and the man commands
Like a full soldier. Let's to the sea-side, ho!
As well to see the vessel that's come in,
As to throw out our eyes for brave Othello,
Even till we make the main and th'aerial blue
An indistinct regard.

40   THIRD GENTLEMAN Come, let's do so;
For every minute is expectancy
Of more arrivance.

          Enter Cassio

CASSIO

Thanks, you the valiant of this warlike isle
That so approve the Moor! O, let the heavens
Give him defence against the elements,
For I have lost him on a dangerous sea.

MONTANO

Is he well shipped?

---

26 *Veronesa.* Presumably this was a vessel fitted out by Verona, which belonged to Venice; but it has been suggested that the word should be *verrinessa*, or cutter. (Shakespeare, to judge from *The Two Gentlemen of Verona*, thought that town was a port.)

30 *'tis a worthy governor* (another tribute to Othello)

32 *sadly* gravely

39 *th'aerial blue* the sky

40 *An indistinct regard* indistinguishable

41 *expectancy* expectation

42 *more arrivance* the arrival of more ships

CASSIO

His bark is stoutly timbered, and his pilot
Of very expert and approved allowance;
Therefore my hopes, not surfeited to death,   50
Stand in bold cure.
        (*Cry within* 'A sail, a sail, a sail!')

CASSIO

What noise?

FOURTH GENTLEMAN

The town is empty; on the brow o'th'sea
Stand ranks of people, and they cry 'A sail!'

CASSIO

My hopes do shape him for the Governor.
        Salvo

SECOND GENTLEMAN

They do discharge their shot of courtesy:
Our friends at least.

CASSIO   I pray you, sir, go forth,
And give us truth who 'tis that is arrived.

SECOND GENTLEMAN

I shall.   *Exit*

MONTANO

But, good Lieutenant, is your General wived?   60

CASSIO

Most fortunately: he hath achieved a maid
That paragons description and wild fame;
One that excels the quirks of blazoning pens,
And in th'essential vesture of creation

---

49 *allowance* reputation
50–51 *not surfeited to death,* | *Stand in bold
    cure* are not excessive, but healthy
55 *My hopes do shape him for* I hope it is
60 *is your General wived?* There has been
    no previous mention of Othello's
    marriage. Possibly some lines have
    dropped out, for Montano has had
    no private conversation with Cassio.
62 *paragons* equals or excels

64–5 *And in th'essential vesture of creation* |
    Does tire the ingener 'in real beauty or
    outward form goes beyond the
    power of the artist's inventive or
    expressive pencil' (Hudson). But
    'ingener' is an emendation of 'In-
    geniuer' and 'tyre' can mean 'attire',
    as well as 'weary'. Possibly 'tire' was
    suggested by 'vesture' through an
    unconscious quibble.

Does tire the ingener.

    Enter Second Gentleman

                    How now? Who has put in?

SECOND GENTLEMAN

'Tis one Iago, Ancient to the General.

CASSIO

He's had most favourable and happy speed:
Tempests themselves, high seas, and howling winds,
The guttered rocks and congregated sands,
70   Traitors enscarped to clog the guiltless keel,
As having sense of beauty, do omit
Their mortal natures, letting go safely by
The divine Desdemona.

MONTANO   What is she?

CASSIO

She that I spake of, our great Captain's Captain,
Left in the conduct of the bold Iago,
Whose footing here anticipates our thoughts
A se'nnight's speed. Great Jove, Othello guard,
And swell his sail with thine own powerful breath,
That he may bless this bay with his tall ship,
80   Make love's quick pants in Desdemona's arms,
Give renewed fire to our extinct spirits,
And bring all Cyprus comfort.

    Enter Desdemona, Emilia, Iago, Roderigo, and
      attendants

                    O, behold,
The riches of the ship is come on shore!

---

69 *guttered* with gullies, jagged

70 *enscarped to clog.* Nearly all editors accept 'ensteeped' from F but reject 'enclogge'. It seems probable that 'enscerped' was a misprint for 'enscarped' (that is, shelved abruptly). This fits the rocks, if not the sands; and Shakespeare may have been responsible for both readings.

72 *mortal* deadly. Here again the alternative reading 'common' makes good sense.

76 *footing* landing

77 *se'nnight* week

80 *Make love's quick pants.* This weak phrase was substituted for an even feebler phrase in Q.

You men of Cyprus, let her have your knees.
Hail to thee, lady! And the grace of heaven,
Before, behind thee, and on every hand,
Enwheel thee round.

DESDEMONA   I thank you, valiant Cassio.
What tidings can you tell me of my lord?

CASSIO
He is not yet arrived; nor know I aught
But that he's well, and will be shortly here.   90

DESDEMONA
O, but I fear! How lost you company?

CASSIO
The great contention of the sea and skies
Parted our fellowship.
          (*Cry within*) 'A sail, a sail!'

GENTLEMAN   But hark, a sail!
They give their greeting to the citadel:
This likewise is a friend.

CASSIO   See for the news.
Good Ancient, you are welcome. Welcome, mistress.
Let it not gall your patience, good Iago,
That I extend my manners. 'Tis my breeding
That gives me this bold show of courtesy.
          He kisses Emilia

IAGO
Sir, would she give you so much of her lips   100
As of her tongue she oft bestows on me,
You'd have enough.

DESDEMONA
Alas, she has no speech.

IAGO   In faith, too much.

---

87 *Enwheel* encircle
94 *greeting* (by firing a salvo)
99 *courtesy*. Kissing was a normal

method of greeting, and does not
imply that Cassio was flirting with
Emilia.

I find it still when I have list to sleep.
Marry, before your ladyship, I grant
She puts her tongue a little in her heart
And chides with thinking.

EMILIA   You have little cause to say so.

IAGO Come on, come on: you are pictures out of doors,
bells in your parlours, wild-cats in your kitchens, saints
in your injuries, devils being offended, players in your
housewifery, and housewives in your beds.

DESDEMONA
O, fie upon thee, slanderer!

IAGO
Nay, it is true, or else I am a Turk:
You rise to play and go to bed to work.

EMILIA
You shall not write my praise.

IAGO   No, let me not.

DESDEMONA
What wouldst thou write of me, if thou shouldst praise
me?

IAGO
O, gentle lady, do not put me to't,
For I am nothing if not critical.

DESDEMONA
Come on, assay. There's one gone to the harbour?

IAGO
Ay, madam.

DESDEMONA
(aside) I am not merry, but I do beguile

---

107 *chides with thinking* does not utter her
shrewish thoughts
108 *pictures* (that is, silent)
109 *bells* (that is, noisy)
111 *housewives* hussies
119 *assay* try

121–2 *I am not merry, but I do beguile |
The thing I am by seeming otherwise.*
This is merely an explanation to the
audience, so that Desdemona should
not appear too little concerned for
Othello's safety.

The thing I am by seeming otherwise.
Come, how wouldst thou praise me?

IAGO

I am about it, but indeed my invention
Comes from my pate as birdlime does from frieze –
It plucks out brains and all. But my muse labours,
And thus she is delivered.
If she be fair and wise, fairness and wit,
The one's for use, the other useth it.

DESDEMONA

Well praised! How if she be black and witty?   130

IAGO

If she be black, and thereto have a wit,
She'll find a white that shall her blackness fit.

DESDEMONA

Worse and worse.

EMILIA   How if fair and foolish?

IAGO

She never yet was foolish that was fair,
For even her folly helped her to an heir.

DESDEMONA These are old fond paradoxes to make fools
laugh i'th'alehouse. What miserable praise hast thou for
her that's foul and foolish?

IAGO

There's none so foul and foolish thereunto,
But does foul pranks which fair and wise ones do.   140

DESDEMONA O heavy ignorance! Thou praisest the worst
best. But what praise couldst thou bestow on a deserving

125 *as birdlime does from frieze.* Frieze or
frize is a coarse cloth, and when one
tries to remove birdlime from it, one
pulls out the threads at the same
time. So Iago's powers of invention
are 'sticky'.

130 *black* brunette
witty clever
132 *white* (with a quibble on 'wight')
135 *folly* wantonness
136 *fond* foolish
138 *foul* ugly or sluttish

woman indeed? One that in the authority of her merit
did justly put on the vouch of very malice itself?

IAGO

She that was ever fair and never proud,
Had tongue at will, and yet was never loud;
Never lacked gold, and yet went never gay;
Fled from her wish, and yet said 'Now I may';
She that being angered, her revenge being nigh,
150   Bade her wrong stay, and her displeasure fly;
She that in wisdom never was so frail
To change the cod's head for the salmon's tail;
She that could think and ne'er disclose her mind:
See suitors following and not look behind:
She was a wight, if ever such wight were –

DESDEMONA

To do what?

IAGO

To suckle fools and chronicle small beer.

DESDEMONA

O, most lame and impotent conclusion!
Do not learn of him, Emilia, though he be thy husband.
160   How say you, Cassio, is he not a most profane and
liberal counsellor?

CASSIO He speaks home, madam; you may relish him more
in the soldier than in the scholar.

IAGO (aside) He takes her by the palm. Ay, well said,
whisper. With as little a web as this will I ensnare as
great a fly as Cassio. Ay, smile upon her, do. I will

---

144 *put on the vouch* compel the approval
152 *change the cod's head for the salmon's
tail.* This passage is obscure, probably obscene, in view of the connotations of cod's 'head' and 'tail'; but it
may merely mean exchange a foolish
husband for a handsome lover.

157 *small beer* trivial events
160 *profane* worldly
161 *liberal* licentious
162 *home* bluntly
162-3 *relish him more in* appreciate more
in the role of

gyve thee in thine own courtship. You say true, 'tis so
indeed. If such tricks as these strip you out of your
lieutenantry, it had been better you had not kissed your
three fingers so oft, which now again you are most apt   170
to play the sir in. Very good: well kissed, an excellent
courtesy! 'Tis so indeed. Yet again your fingers to your
lips? Would they were clyster-pipes for your sake!

>   *Trumpet*

(*aloud*) The Moor! I know his trumpet.

CASSIO   'Tis truly so.

DESDEMONA

Let's meet him and receive him.

CASSIO   Lo, where he comes!

>   *Enter Othello and attendants*

OTHELLO

O, my fair warrior!

DESDEMONA   My dear Othello!

OTHELLO

It gives me wonder great as my content
To see you here before me. O, my soul's joy!
If after every tempest come such calms,
May the winds blow till they have wakened death,   180
And let the labouring bark climb hills of seas,
Olympus-high, and duck again as low
As hell's from heaven. If it were now to die,
'Twere now to be most happy; for I fear

---

167 *gyve* fetter, ensnare

167–8 *You say true, 'tis so indeed.* This is
either a comment on the animated
conversation between Cassio and
Desdemona or a reply (not spoken
aloud) to Cassio's last remark (lines
162–3).

171 *sir* gentleman

173 *clyster-pipes* tubes used for injection
(here used obscenely)

176 *fair warrior.* Othello is referring to
her courage in accompanying him to
the wars, and unconsciously echoing
the language of sonneteers. He may
also be thinking of her wish she had
been a man.

183–9 *If it were now to die . . . Amen to
that, sweet Powers!* (dramatic irony)

My soul hath her content so absolute
That not another comfort like to this
Succeeds in unknown fate.

DESDEMONA   The heavens forbid
But that our loves and comforts should increase,
Even as our days do grow.

OTHELLO   Amen to that, sweet Powers!
190   I cannot speak enough of this content;
It stops me here; it is too much of joy.

> *They kiss*

And this, and this the greatest discords be
That e'er our hearts shall make.

IAGO (*aside*)   O, you are well tuned now!

But I'll set down the pegs that make this music,
As honest as I am.

OTHELLO   Come, let's to the castle.
News, friends; our wars are done; the Turks are drowned.
How does my old acquaintance of this isle?
Honey, you shall be well desired in Cyprus:
I have found great love amongst them. O my sweet,
200   I prattle out of fashion and I dote
In mine own comforts. I prithee, good Iago,
Go to the bay and disembark my coffers;
Bring thou the Master to the citadel;
He is a good one, and his worthiness
Does challenge much respect. Come, Desdemona,
Once more well met at Cyprus!

> *Exeunt all except Iago and Roderigo*

IAGO (*to soldiers, who go off*) Do thou meet me presently at
the harbour. (*To Roderigo*) Come hither. If thou be'st

---

194 *set down the pegs* slacken the
        strings
198 *desired* liked
200 *out of fashion* unbecomingly
205 *challenge* claim

207–8 *Do thou meet me presently at the
harbour.* These lines are spoken not
to Roderigo, but to one of the soldiers who are to fetch Othello's
luggage.

valiant – as they say base men being in love have then a
nobility in their natures more than is native to them –   210
list me. The Lieutenant tonight watches on the court of
guard. First, I must tell thee this: Desdemona is directly
in love with him.

RODERIGO With him? Why, 'tis not possible!

IAGO Lay thy finger thus, and let thy soul be instructed.
Mark me with what violence she first loved the Moor,
but for bragging and telling her fantastical lies. And
will she love him still for prating? Let not thy discreet
heart think it. Her eye must be fed. And what delight
shall she have to look on the devil? When the blood is   220
made dull with the act of sport, there should be, again
to inflame it and give satiety a fresh appetite, loveliness
in favour, sympathy in years, manners and beauties: all
which the Moor is defective in. Now for want of these
required conveniences, her delicate tenderness will find
itself abused, begin to heave the gorge, disrelish and
abhor the Moor. Very nature will instruct her in it and
compel her to some second choice. Now, sir, this granted
– as it is a most pregnant and unforced position – who
stands so eminently in the degree of this fortune as   230
Cassio does? – a knave very voluble; no further conscionable than in putting on the mere form of civil and
humane seeming for the better compassing of his salt
and most hidden loose affection. Why, none; why, none
– a slipper and subtle knave, a finder out of occasions;
that has an eye can stamp and counterfeit advantages,
though true advantage never present itself; a devilish

207 *presently* at once
215 *thus* (on the lips)
223 *favour* appearance
225 *conveniences* points of fitness
229 *pregnant* cogent
231–2 *conscionable* conscientious

233 *humane* polite
    salt lustful
235 *slipper* slippery
    occasions opportunities
236 *stamp* coin

knave! Besides, the knave is handsome, young, and hath all those requisites in him that folly and green minds look after. A pestilent complete knave; and the woman hath found him already.

RODERIGO I cannot believe that in her: she's full of most blessed condition.

IAGO Blessed fig's end! The wine she drinks is made of grapes. If she had been blessed, she would never have loved the Moor. Blessed pudding! Didst thou not see her paddle with the palm of his hand? Didst not mark that?

RODERIGO Yes, that I did: but that was but courtesy.

IAGO Lechery, by this hand: an index and obscure prologue to the history of lust and foul thoughts. They met so near with their lips that their breaths embraced together. Villainous thoughts, Roderigo! When these mutualities so marshal the way, hard at hand comes the master and main exercise, th'incorporate conclusion. Pish! But, sir, be you ruled by me. I have brought you from Venice. Watch you tonight: for the command, I'll lay't upon you. Cassio knows you not; I'll not be far from you. Do you find some occasion to anger Cassio, either by speaking too loud, or tainting his discipline, or from what other course you please, which the time shall more favourably minister.

RODERIGO Well.

IAGO Sir, he's rash and very sudden in choler, and haply with his truncheon may strike at you: provoke him that he may, for even out of that will I cause these of Cyprus to mutiny, whose qualification shall come into no true taste again but by the displanting of Cassio. So shall you have a shorter journey to your desires by the means I shall then have to prefer them, and the impediment most

243 *condition* characteristics
244 *fig's end* a worthless thing
247 *paddle with* stroke
254 *incorporate* bodily

259 *tainting* sneering at
261 *minister* provide
263 *choler* anger
266 *qualification* dilution, appeasement

profitably removed, without the which there were no   270
expectation of our prosperity.

RODERIGO I will do this, if you can bring it to any opportunity.

IAGO I warrant thee. Meet me by and by at the citadel. I
must fetch his necessaries ashore. Farewell.

RODERIGO Adieu.   *Exit*

IAGO
That Cassio loves her, I do well believe't:
That she loves him, 'tis apt and of great credit.
The Moor – howbeit that I endure him not –
Is of a constant, loving, noble nature,   280
And, I dare think, he'll prove to Desdemona
A most dear husband. Now, I do love her too;
Not out of absolute lust – though peradventure
I stand accountant for as great a sin –
But partly led to diet my revenge
For that I do suspect the lusty Moor
Hath leaped into my seat, the thought whereof
Doth, like a poisonous mineral, gnaw my inwards,
And nothing can, or shall, content my soul
Till I am evened with him, wife for wife;   290
Or failing so, yet that I put the Moor
At least into a jealousy so strong
That judgement cannot cure. Which thing to do
If this poor trash of Venice, whom I leash
For his quick hunting, stand the putting on,
I'll have our Michael Cassio on the hip,

271 *prosperity* success
277–303 *That Cassio loves her . . . never
seen till used.* See Introduction, p. 313.
280 *constant, loving, noble* (a notable testi-
monial from an enemy)
284 *accountant* accountable
285 *diet* feed
294 *leash.* Neither 'crush' (Q) nor 'trace'
(F) makes good sense. The usual

emendation 'trash' (check) is inappropriate to Roderigo, though it, like
'quick hunting', may be ironical. J.
Dover Wilson adopts 'leash' from an
earlier conjecture.
295 *stand the putting on* do what I incite
him to
296 *on the hip* at my mercy

Abuse him to the Moor in the rank garb –
For I fear Cassio with my night-cap too –
Make the Moor thank me, love me, and reward me
300   For making him egregiously an ass,
And practising upon his peace and quiet,
Even to madness. 'Tis here, but yet confused:
Knavery's plain face is never seen till used.   *Exit*

II.2   *Enter Herald, with a proclamation*
HERALD It is Othello's pleasure, our noble and valiant
General, that upon certain tidings now arrived importing
the mere perdition of the Turkish feet, every man put
himself into triumph: some to dance, some to make
bonfires, each man to what sport and revels his addiction
leads him. For, besides these beneficial news, it is the
celebration of his nuptial. So much was his pleasure
should be proclaimed. All offices are open, and there is
full liberty of feasting from this present hour of five
10   till the bell have told eleven. Heaven bless the isle of
Cyprus and our noble General Othello!   *Exit*

II.3   *Enter Othello, Desdemona, Cassio, and attendants*
OTHELLO
Good Michael, look you to the guard tonight.
Let's teach ourselves that honourable stop,

297 *rank garb* gross manner, as a
    cuckold

II.2 This proclamation is a preparation
for the drinking-scene which follows. It
was addressed to the audience rather
than to a crowd on the stage.
3 *mere* absolute
8 *offices* (for the supply of food and
    drink)

II.3 This scene is in the guardroom of
the castle. The remaining scenes of the
play are in or near the castle. Iago engineers the brawl between Roderigo and
Cassio – Shakespeare deviates from his
source in this respect – and persuades
Cassio to appeal to Desdemona for
reinstatement.
1, 7 *Michael*. Note the affectionate use of
    Cassio's Christian name.

Not to outsport discretion.

CASSIO
Iago hath direction what to do;
But, notwithstanding, with my personal eye
Will I look to't.

OTHELLO   Iago is most honest.
Michael, good night. Tomorrow with your earliest
Let me have speech with you. (*To Desdemona*) Come,
      my dear love,
The purchase made, the fruits are to ensue:
That profit's yet to come 'tween me and you.   10
Good night.   *Exeunt Othello, Desdemona, and attendants*
      Enter Iago

CASSIO Welcome, Iago; we must to the watch.

IAGO Not this hour, Lieutenant; 'tis not yet ten o'th'clock.
Our General cast us thus early for the love of his
Desdemona; who let us not therefore blame. He hath
not yet made wanton the night with her; and she is
sport for Jove.

CASSIO She is a most exquisite lady.

IAGO And, I'll warrant her, full of game.

CASSIO Indeed, she is a most fresh and delicate creature.   20

IAGO What an eye she has! Methinks it sounds a parley to
provocation.

CASSIO An inviting eye, and yet methinks right modest.

IAGO And when she speaks, is it not an alarum to love?

CASSIO She is indeed perfection.

IAGO Well, happiness to their sheets! Come, Lieutenant,
I have a stoup of wine; and here without are a brace of
Cyprus gallants that would fain have a measure to the
health of black Othello.

---

7 *with your earliest* at your earliest
convenience
9 *the fruits are to ensue* (the marriage has
not been consummated)
13–25 *Not this hour . . . She is indeed perfection.* Iago's pruriency about Desde-

mona is contrasted with Cassio's
chaste admiration.
14 *cast* dismissed
21–2 *sounds a parley to provocation* arouses
lustful thoughts
27 *stoup* jug

30 CASSIO Not tonight, good Iago. I have very poor and
unhappy brains for drinking. I could well wish courtesy
would invent some other custom of entertainment.

IAGO O, they are our friends! But one cup; I'll drink for
you.

CASSIO I have drunk but one cup tonight, and that was
craftily qualified too; and behold what innovation it
makes here. I am unfortunate in the infirmity and dare
not task my weakness with any more.

IAGO What, man! 'Tis a night of revels; the gallants desire
40 it.

CASSIO Where are they?

IAGO Here, at the door: I pray you call them in.

CASSIO I'll do't, but it dislikes me.   _Exit_

IAGO
  If I can fasten but one cup upon him,
  With that which he hath drunk tonight already,
  He'll be as full of quarrel and offence
  As my young mistress' dog. Now my sick fool Roderigo,
  Whom love hath turned almost the wrong side out,
  To Desdemona hath tonight caroused
50 Potations pottle-deep; and he's to watch.
  Three else of Cyprus, noble swelling spirits –
  That hold their honours in a wary distance,
  The very elements of this warlike isle –
  Have I tonight flustered with flowing cups,
  And they watch too. Now 'mongst this flock of
        drunkards,
  Am I to put our Cassio in some action
  That may offend the isle. But here they come;

33–4 _I'll drink for you_ I'll drink in your place (that is, drink more than my share, to cover your abstemiousness)
36 _qualified_ mixed with water
43 _dislikes_ displeases
50 _pottle-deep_ to the bottom of a two-quart tankard
51 _swelling_ lively
52 _hold their honours in a wary distance_ are quick to take offence at any suspected insult
53 _elements_ quintessence

If consequence do but approve my dream,
My boat sails freely both with wind and stream.
> *Enter Cassio with Montano and Gentlemen, and
> servants with wine*

CASSIO 'Fore God, they have given me a rouse already.   60

MONTANO Good faith, a little one; not past a pint, as I am
a soldier.

IAGO Some wine, ho!
(*sings*)   And let me the canakin clink, clink;
And let me the canakin clink;
A soldier's a man
O, man's life's but a span;
Why, then, let a soldier drink.
Some wine, boys.

CASSIO 'Fore God, an excellent song.   70

IAGO I learned it in England, where indeed they are most
potent in potting. Your Dane, your German, and your
swag-bellied Hollander – drink, ho! – are nothing to
your English.

CASSIO Is your Englishman so expert in his drinking?

IAGO Why, he drinks you with facility your Dane dead
drunk; he sweats not to overthrow your Almaine; he
gives your Hollander a vomit, ere the next pottle can be
filled.

CASSIO To the health of our General!   80

MONTANO I am for it, Lieutenant; and I'll do you justice.

IAGO O, sweet England!
(*sings*) King Stephen was and-a worthy peer,

---

58 *consequence* what happens
   approve substantiate
60 *rouse* large glass
64–8 *And let me the canakin clink*. See
   The Songs, p. 358.
64 *canakin* small can
67 *life's but a span*. Compare Psalm 39.5:
   'Behold thou hast made my days as

it were a span long.'
72 *potting* drinking
77 *Almaine* German
84–91 *King Stephen . . . cloak about thee.*
   This song was earlier than 1600. See
   The Songs, p. 358.
84 *and-a*. The syllable was inserted for
   the sake of the tune.

His breeches cost him but a crown;
He held them sixpence all too dear;
With that he called the tailor lown.
He was a wight of high renown,
And thou art but of low degree;
90 'Tis pride that pulls the country down;
Then take thine auld cloak about thee.

Some wine, ho!

CASSIO 'Fore God, this is a more exquisite song than the
other.

IAGO Will you hear't again?

CASSIO No, for I hold him to be unworthy of his place
that does those things. Well, God's above all; and there
be souls must be saved, and there be souls must not be
saved.

100 IAGO It's true, good Lieutenant.

CASSIO For mine own part – no offence to the General,
nor any man of quality – I hope to be saved.

IAGO And so do I too, Lieutenant.

CASSIO Ay, but, by your leave, not before me. The
Lieutenant is to be saved before the Ancient. Let's have
no more of this; let's to our affairs. God forgive us our
sins. Gentlemen, let's look to our business. Do not
think, gentlemen, I am drunk: this is my Ancient, this
is my right hand, and this is my left. I am not drunk
110 now: I can stand well enough and I speak well enough.

GENTLEMEN Excellent well.

CASSIO Why, very well; you must not think then that I
am drunk.   *Exit*

MONTANO To th'platform, masters; come, let's set the
watch.

---

87 *lown* loon, rogue
96–9 *No, for I hold him to be unworthy . . .*
souls must not be saved. Cassio is already
drunk, as Shakespeare indicates by
his moralizing and theology.

104–5 *The Lieutenant is to be saved before
the Ancient.* This is likely to rub salt
in Iago's wounds.

108 *my Ancient* (another reference to
Cassio's superior rank)

IAGO
    You see this fellow that is gone before:
    He is a soldier, fit to stand by Caesar
    And give direction; and do but see his vice:
    'Tis to his virtue a just equinox,
    The one as long as th'other. 'Tis pity of him.   120
    I fear the trust Othello puts in him,
    On some odd time of his infirmity,
    Will shake this island.
MONTANO   But is he often thus?
IAGO
    'Tis evermore the prologue to his sleep:
    He'll watch the horologe a double set,
    If drink rock not his cradle.
MONTANO   It were well
    The General were put in mind of it:
    Perhaps he sees it not, or his good nature
    Prizes the virtue that appears in Cassio
    And looks not on his evils. Is not this true?   130
        Enter Roderigo
IAGO
    (*aside*) How now, Roderigo!
    I pray you after the Lieutenant go!   *Exit Roderigo*
MONTANO
    And 'tis great pity that the noble Moor
    Should hazard such a place as his own second
    With one of an ingraft infirmity.
    It were an honest action to say
    So to the Moor.
IAGO   Not I, for this fair island!
    I do love Cassio well and would do much
    To cure him of this evil.
        (*Cry within*) 'Help! Help!'
                But hark, what noise?

125 *horologe* clock   135 *ingraft* ingrafted
    a double set twice round

Enter Cassio, pursuing Roderigo

140 CASSIO Zounds, you rogue, you rascal!

MONTANO What's the matter, Lieutenant?

CASSIO A knave teach me my duty? I'll beat the knave into a twiggen-bottle.

RODERIGO Beat me?

CASSIO Dost thou prate, rogue?

He strikes Roderigo

MONTANO Nay, good Lieutenant; I pray you, sir, hold your hand.

CASSIO Let me go, sir, or I'll knock you o'er the mazzard.

MONTANO Come, come, you're drunk.

150 CASSIO Drunk!

IAGO (*to Roderigo*) Away, I say; go out and cry a mutiny.

Exit Roderigo

Nay, good Lieutenant. God's will, gentleman!

Help, ho! Lieutenant. Sir! Montano! Sir!

Help, masters. Here's a goodly watch indeed.

Bell rings

Who's that which rings the bell? Diablo, ho!

The town will rise. God's will, Lieutenant, hold!

You will be shamed for ever!

Enter Othello and attendants

OTHELLO

What is the matter here?

MONTANO   Zounds, I bleed still.

I am hurt to th'death.

OTHELLO   Hold for your lives!

IAGO

160 Hold, ho, Lieutenant, sir, Montano, gentlemen!

Have you forgot all sense of place and duty?

Hold! The General speaks to you: hold, for shame!

---

143 *twiggen-bottle* bottle cased in wicker-work. This may mean (1) beat Roderigo till he resembles wicker-work, or (2) chase him through the holes in a wicker-work case. The second explanation is more probable.

148 *mazzard* head

155 *Diablo* the Devil

OTHELLO

    Why, how now, ho! From whence ariseth this?
    Are we turned Turks and to ourselves do that
    Which heaven hath forbid the Ottomites?
    For Christian shame, put by this barbarous brawl.
    He that stirs next to carve for his own rage
    Holds his soul light: he dies upon his motion.
    Silence that dreadful bell: it frights the isle
    From her propriety. What is the matter, masters?   170
    Honest Iago, that looks dead with grieving,
    Speak, who began this? On thy love I charge thee.

IAGO

    I do not know. Friends all but now, even now,
    In quarter and in terms like bride and groom
    Devesting them for bed: and then but now –
    As if some planet had unwitted men –
    Swords out, and tilting one at others' breasts
    In opposition bloody. I cannot speak
    Any beginning to this peevish odds;
    And would in action glorious I had lost   180
    Those legs that brought me to a part of it.

OTHELLO

    How comes it, Michael, you are thus forgot?

CASSIO

    I pray you pardon me: I cannot speak.

OTHELLO

    Worthy Montano, you were wont to be civil:
    The gravity and stillness of your youth
    The world hath noted; and your name is great
    In mouths of wisest censure. What's the matter
    That you unlace your reputation thus
    And spend your rich opinion for the name

---

174 *quarter* friendship
176 *unwitted* bereft of their wits. Believ-
    ers in astrology thought that planets
    could drive men mad (compare
    V.2.111–12).

179 *odds* quarrel
185 *stillness* quietness, sobriety
187 *censure* judgement
189 *rich opinion* high reputation

190   Of a night-brawler? Give me answer to it.

MONTANO

    Worthy Othello, I am hurt to danger.
    Your officer, Iago, can inform you,
    While I spare speech, which something now offends me,
    Of all that I do know; nor know I aught
    By me that's said or done amiss this night,
    Unless self-charity be sometimes a vice,
    And to defend ourselves it be a sin
    When violence assails us.

OTHELLO   Now, by heaven,

    My blood begins my safer guides to rule,
200   And passion, having my best judgement collied,
    Assays to lead the way. Zounds, if I stir,
    Or do but lift this arm, the best of you
    Shall sink in my rebuke. Give me to know
    How this foul rout began, who set it on;
    And he that is approved in this offence,
    Though he had twinned with me, both at a birth,
    Shall lose me. What! In a town of war
    Yet wild, the people's hearts brimful of fear,
    To manage private and domestic quarrel
210   In night, and on the court and guard of safety,
    'Tis monstrous. Iago, who began't?

MONTANO

    If partially affined or leagued in office,
    Thou dost deliver more or less than truth,
    Thou art no soldier.

IAGO   Touch me not so near.

---

193 *offends* hurts
200 *collied* blackened
204 *rout* brawl
205 *approved* proved guilty
210 *on the court and guard of safety* in the guard-room, while actually members of the watch (who should protect the safety of the town)

212 *partially*   *affined* bounded by partiality
leagued in office unwilling to testify against a superior
214–40 *Touch me not so near ... Which patience could not pass.* Iago has the difficult task of persuading both Othello and Cassio that he is minimizing

I had rather have this tongue cut from my mouth
Than it should do offence to Michael Cassio.
Yet, I persuade myself, to speak the truth
Shall nothing wrong him. This it is, General.
Montano and myself being in speech,
There comes a fellow, crying out for help,   220
And Cassio following with determined sword
To execute upon him. Sir, this gentleman
Steps in to Cassio and entreats his pause:
Myself the crying fellow did pursue
Lest by his clamour — as it so fell out —
The town might fall in fright. He, swift of foot,
Outran my purpose and I returned the rather
For that I heard the clink and fall of swords
And Cassio high in oath, which till tonight
I ne'er might say before. When I came back —   230
For this was brief — I found them close together
At blow and thrust, even as again they were
When you yourself did part them.
More of this matter can I not report:
But men are men; the best sometimes forget.
Though Cassio did some little wrong to him,
As men in rage strike those that wish them best,
Yet surely Cassio, I believe, received
From him that fled some strange indignity
Which patience could not pass.
OTHELLO   I know, Iago,   240
Thy honesty and love doth mince this matter,
Making it light to Cassio. Cassio, I love thee,
But nevermore be officer of mine.
          Enter Desdemona, attended
Look, if my gentle love be not raised up.
I'll make thee an example.

the latter's fault, and of persuading
Montano that he is not doing this.
245 *I'll make thee an example.* This seems
to suggest that Othello is being
severe because his wife has been
disturbed.

DESDEMONA   What is the matter, dear?

OTHELLO

All's well now, sweeting: come away to bed.

Sir, for your hurts myself will be your surgeon.

Montano is led off

Iago, look with care about the town

And silence those whom this vile brawl distracted.

250   Come, Desdemona, 'tis the soldiers' life

To have their balmy slumbers waked with strife.

Exeunt all but Iago and Cassio

IAGO What, are you hurt, Lieutenant?

CASSIO Ay, past all surgery.

IAGO Marry, God forbid!

CASSIO Reputation, reputation, reputation! O, I have lost
my reputation! I have lost the immortal part of myself,
and what remains is bestial. My reputation, Iago, my
reputation!

IAGO As I am an honest man I thought you had received

260   some bodily wound: there is more of sense in that
than in reputation. Reputation is an idle and most false
imposition; oft got without merit and lost without
deserving. You have lost no reputation at all, unless you
repute yourself such a loser. What, man! There are
ways to recover the General again. You are but now cast
in his mood – a punishment more in policy than in
malice – even so as one would beat his offenceless dog to
affright an imperious lion. Sue to him again, and he's
yours.

270   CASSIO I will rather sue to be despised than to deceive so
good a commander with so slight, so drunken, and so
indiscreet an officer. Drunk! And speak parrot! And

---

247 (stage direction) *Montano is led off.*
Both Q and F ascribe 'Lead him off'
to Othello, but it is probably a stage
direction.

261–4 *Reputation is an idle and most false
imposition . . . repute yourself such a loser.*
Compare III.3.154–60, where Iago

says the opposite.

265 *cast* dismissed

267–8 *beat his offenceless dog to affright an
imperious lion* punish the innocent to
deter the great criminal

271 *slight* worthless

272 *parrot* nonsense

squabble! Swagger! Swear! And discourse fustian with one's own shadow! O, thou invisible spirit of wine, if thou hast no name to be known by, let us call thee devil.

IAGO What was he that you followed with your sword? What had he done to you?

CASSIO I know not.

IAGO Is't possible?

CASSIO I remember a mass of things, but nothing distinctly: a quarrel, but nothing wherefore. O God, that men should put an enemy in their mouths to steal away their brains! That we should with joy, pleasance, revel and applause transform ourselves into beasts!   280

IAGO Why, but you are now well enough! How came you thus recovered?

CASSIO It hath pleased the devil drunkenness to give place to the devil wrath: one unperfectness shows me another, to make me frankly despise myself.

IAGO Come, you are too severe a moraller. As the time, the place and the condition of this country stands, I could heartily wish this had not so befallen: but since it is as it is, mend it for your own good.   290

CASSIO I will ask him for my place again; he shall tell me I am a drunkard. Had I as many mouths as Hydra, such an answer would stop them all. To be now a sensible man, by and by a fool, and presently a beast! O, strange! Every inordinate cup is unblessed and the ingredience is a devil.

IAGO Come, come; good wine is a good familiar creature if it be well used: exclaim no more against it. And, good Lieutenant, I think you think I love you.   300

CASSIO I have well approved it, sir. I drunk!

IAGO You or any man living may be drunk at a time, man. I'll tell you what you shall do. Our General's wife is

---

273 *fustian* bombast

284 *applause* desire for applause

295 *Hydra* (snake with many heads slain

by Hercules)

298 *ingredience* ingredients

300 *familiar creature* friendly spirit

now the General. I may say so in this respect, for that
he hath devoted and given up himself to the contemplation, mark, and denotement of her parts and graces.
Confess yourself freely to her; importune her help to
310 put you in your place again. She is of so free, so kind, so
apt, so blessed a disposition, that she holds it a vice in her
goodness not to do more than she is requested. This
broken joint between you and her husband, entreat her
to splinter; and my fortunes against any lay worth
naming, this crack of your love shall grow stronger than
it was before.

CASSIO You advise me well.

IAGO I protest in the sincerity of love and honest kindness.

320 CASSIO I think it freely; and betimes in the morning I will
beseech the virtuous Desdemona to undertake for me.
I am desperate of my fortunes if they check me here.

IAGO You are in the right. Good night, Lieutenant, I must
to the watch.

CASSIO Good night, honest Iago.   *Exit*

IAGO
And what's he then that says I play the villain,
When this advice is free I give, and honest,
Probal to thinking, and indeed the course
To win the Moor again? For 'tis most easy
330 Th'inclining Desdemona to subdue
In any honest suit. She's framed as fruitful
As the free elements; and then for her
To win the Moor, were't to renounce his baptism,
All seals and symbols of redeemèd sin,

---

310 *free* open
314 *splinter* put a splint on
326–52 *And what's he then that says I play
the villain . . . That shall enmesh them
all.* See Introduction, p. 315.
328 *Probal* reasonable

330 *subdue* persuade
331 *fruitful* generous
333 *renounce his baptism.* The statement is
one of several references to Othello's
faith.

His soul is so enfettered to her love,
That she may make, unmake, do what she list,
Even as her appetite shall play the god
With his weak function. How am I then a villain
To counsel Cassio to this parallel course
Directly to his good? Divinity of hell!   340
When devils will the blackest sins put on,
They do suggest at first with heavenly shows
As I do now. For whiles this honest fool
Plies Desdemona to repair his fortunes
And she for him pleads strongly to the Moor,
I'll pour this pestilence into his ear:
That she repeals him for her body's lust,
And by how much she strives to do him good,
She shall undo her credit with the Moor.
So will I turn her virtue into pitch,   350
And out of her own goodness make the net
That shall enmesh them all.
    Enter Roderigo
                      How now, Roderigo?
RODERIGO I do follow here in the chase, not like a hound
that hunts, but one that fills up the cry. My money is
almost spent; I have been tonight exceedingly well
cudgelled; and I think the issue will be, I shall have so
much experience for my pains; and so, with no money
at all, and a little more wit, return again to Venice.
IAGO
How poor are they that have not patience!
What wound did ever heal but by degrees?   360
Thou know'st we work by wit, and not by witchcraft,
And wit depends on dilatory time.
Does't not go well? Cassio hath beaten thee,

337 *appetite* desire
338 *function* exercise of faculties
339 *parallel* (to Iago's plot)
340 *Divinity* theology
341 *put on* incite
354 *cry* pack

And thou by that small hurt hath cashiered Cassio.
Though other things grow fair against the sun,
Yet fruits that blossom first will first be ripe.
Content thyself awhile. By th'mass, 'tis morning:
Pleasure and action make the hours seem short.
Retire thee; go where thou art billeted.

370   Away, I say, thou shalt know more hereafter:
Nay, get thee gone.   *Exit Roderigo*
                Two things are to be done.
My wife must move for Cassio to her mistress:
I'll set her on.
Myself the while to draw the Moor apart,
And bring him jump when he may Cassio find
Soliciting his wife. Ay, that's the way.
Dull not device by coldness and delay.   *Exit*

III.1   *Enter Cassio and Musicians*

CASSIO

Masters, play here – I will content your pains –
Something that's brief; and bid 'Good morrow, General'.
     They play
     Enter Clown

CLOWN Why, masters, have your instruments been in

365–6 *Though other things grow fair against the sun,* | *Yet fruits that blossom first will first be ripe* the fact that you have already got Cassio dismissed means that you will soon enjoy Desdemona, despite the apparent happiness of her marriage

375 *jump* exactly

III.1 This scene follows soon after the conclusion of Act II, when day was

already breaking. It was an Elizabethan custom to awaken a newly married couple with music. The Clown has little individuality and his jests are feeble. It has been argued that Shakespeare did not wish to lower the tension by arousing hearty laughter, but he need not have introduced a clown at all to act as a messenger.

1 *I will content your pains* I will reward you for your trouble

Naples, that they speak i'th'nose thus?

FIRST MUSICIAN How, sir, how?

CLOWN Are these, I pray you, wind instruments?

FIRST MUSICIAN Ay, marry are they, sir.

CLOWN O, thereby hangs a tail.

FIRST MUSICIAN Whereby hangs a tale, sir?

CLOWN Marry, sir, by many a wind instrument that I   10
know. But, masters, here's money for you: and the
General so likes your music that he desires you, for
love's sake, to make no more noise with it.

FIRST MUSICIAN Well, sir, we will not.

CLOWN If you have any music that may not be heard,
to't again. But, as they say, to hear music the General
does not greatly care.

FIRST MUSICIAN We have none such, sir.

CLOWN Then put up your pipes in your bag, for I'll
away. Go, vanish into air, away.   *Exeunt Musicians*   20

CASSIO Dost thou hear, mine honest friend?

CLOWN No, I hear not your honest friend: I hear you.

CASSIO Prithee keep up thy quillets – there's a poor piece
of gold for thee. If the gentlewoman that attends the
General's wife be stirring, tell her there's one Cassio
entreats her a little favour of speech. Wilt thou do this?

CLOWN She is stirring, sir. If she will stir hither, I shall
seem to notify unto her.

CASSIO Do, good my friend.   *Exit Clown*
        Enter Iago

In happy time, Iago.

IAGO   You have not been abed then?   30

CASSIO

Why, no: the day had broke before we parted.

3–4 *have your instruments been in Naples.*
    This is an allusion to the results of
    the pox.
8–9 *tail . . . tale* (indecent quibble)
19–20 *for I'll away* (either a snatch of

song or a misprint)
23 *quillets* quibbles
30 *In happy time* you come at the right
    moment

I have made bold, Iago,
To send in to your wife. My suit to her
Is that she will to virtuous Desdemona
Procure me some access.

IAGO   I'll send her to you presently;
And I'll devise a mean to draw the Moor
Out of the way, that your converse and business
May be more free.

CASSIO   I humbly thank you for't.   *Exit Iago*
I never knew a Florentine more kind and honest.
        Enter Emilia

EMILIA

40   Good morrow, good Lieutenant; I am sorry
For your displeasure: but all will sure be well.
The General and his wife are talking of it,
And she speaks for you stoutly. The Moor replies
That he you hurt is of great fame in Cyprus,
And great affinity; and that in wholesome wisdom
He might not but refuse you; but he protests he loves
            you
And needs no other suitor but his likings
To take the safest occasion by the front
To bring you in again.

CASSIO   Yet I beseech you,
50   If you think fit, or that it may be done,
Give me advantage of some brief discourse
With Desdemona alone.

EMILIA   Pray you, come in:
I will bestow you where you shall have time
To speak your bosom freely.

CASSIO   I am much bound to you.
                                    Exeunt

---

39 *Florentine.* Cassio is surprised that
Iago, a Venetian, should be as kind as
one of his own fellow-countrymen.

48 *take the safest occasion by the front* seize
on the first safe occasion

54 *bosom* heart

Enter Othello, Iago, and Gentlemen III.2

OTHELLO
These letters give, Iago, to the pilot,
And by him do my duties to the senate.
That done, I will be walking on the works:
Repair there to me.

IAGO   Well, my good lord, I'll do't. *Exit*

OTHELLO
This fortification, gentlemen, shall we see't?

GENTLEMEN
We'll wait upon your lordship.   *Exeunt*

Enter Desdemona, Cassio, and Emilia III.3

DESDEMONA
Be thou assured, good Cassio, I will do
All my abilities in thy behalf.

EMILIA
Good madam, do: I warrant it grieves my husband
As if the case were his.

DESDEMONA
O, that's an honest fellow! Do not doubt, Cassio,
But I will have my lord and you again
As friendly as you were.

III.2 This little scene has two functions – to remind us of Othello's military responsibilities, and to prepare the way for his entrance with Iago in the next scene.
2 *do* convey
3 *works* fortifications

III.3 This is the longest scene in the play. At the beginning, Othello is perfectly happy in his marriage; at the end, he has decided to murder Desdemona and Cassio. Unless we realize the extent to which Shakespeare has telescoped the action, we shall be bound to think that Othello was absurdly prone to jealousy, instead of 'not easily jealous' as he claims at the end of the play. Desdemona's promise to Cassio to get him reinstated is a sign of her innocence and inexperience; not because she has any reason to fear Othello's jealousy, but because in her natural warmth and generosity she does not realize that she is interfering in professional matters.

CASSIO   Bounteous madam,
Whatever shall become of Michael Cassio,
He's never anything but your true servant.

DESDEMONA

10   I know't: I thank you. You do love my lord;
You have known him long, and be you well assured
He shall in strangeness stand no farther off
Than in a politic distance.

CASSIO   Ay, but, lady,
That policy may either last so long,
Or feed upon such nice and waterish diet,
Or breed itself so out of circumstance,
That I being absent and my place supplied,
My General will forget my love and service.

DESDEMONA

Do not doubt that. Before Emilia here,
20   I give thee warrant of thy place. Assure thee,
If I do vow a friendship, I'll perform it
To the last article. My lord shall never rest.
I'll watch him tame and talk him out of patience;
His bed shall seem a school, his board a shrift;
I'll intermingle everything he does
With Cassio's suit. Therefore be merry, Cassio,
For thy solicitor shall rather die
Than give thy cause away.
                    Enter Othello and Iago

EMILIA

Madam, here comes my lord.

12 *strangeness* estrangement
15 *nice* thin
16 *breed itself so out of circumstance* be so
   long delayed
17 *supplied* filled up
19 *doubt* fear
20 *give thee warrant of* guarantee

22 *My lord shall never rest.* Desdemona,
   however charmingly, is proposing to
   nag Othello until she gets her way.
23 *watch him tame* prevent him from
   sleeping (as hawks were tamed)
24 *shrift* confessional
27 *solicitor* advocate

CASSIO

    Madam, I'll take my leave.   30

DESDEMONA

    Why, stay and hear me speak

CASSIO

    Madam, not now: I am very ill at ease,

    Unfit for mine own purposes.

DESDEMONA

    Well, do your discretion.   *Exit Cassio*

IAGO

    Ha! I like not that.

OTHELLO   What dost thou say?

IAGO

    Nothing, my lord; or if – I know not what.

OTHELLO

    Was not that Cassio parted from my wife?

IAGO

    Cassio, my lord? No, sure, I cannot think it

    That he would sneak away so guilty-like,

    Seeing you coming.

OTHELLO   I do believe 'twas he.   40

DESDEMONA

    How now, my lord?

    I have been talking with a suitor here,

    A man that languishes in your displeasure.

OTHELLO

    Who is't you mean?

DESDEMONA

    Why, your Lieutenant, Cassio. Good my lord,

    If I have any grace or power to move you,

    His present reconciliation take.

    For if he be not one that truly loves you,

35 *I like not that.* Iago begins his tempta-   47 *present* immediate
tion.

That errs in ignorance, and not in cunning,
50   I have no judgement in an honest face.
I prithee call him back.

OTHELLO   Went he hence now?

DESDEMONA
Yes, faith; so humbled
That he hath left part of his grief with me
To suffer with him. Good love, call him back.

OTHELLO
Not now, sweet Desdemon; some other time.

DESDEMONA
But shall't be shortly?

OTHELLO   The sooner, sweet, for you.

DESDEMONA
Shall't be tonight, at supper?

OTHELLO   No, not tonight.

DESDEMONA
Tomorrow dinner then?

OTHELLO   I shall not dine at home.
I meet the captains at the citadel.

DESDEMONA
60   Why, then, tomorrow night, or Tuesday morn,
On Tuesday noon, or night; on Wednesday morn.
I prithee name the time, but let it not
Exceed three days. In faith, he's penitent:
And yet his trespass in our common reason –
Save that, they say, the wars must make example
Out of their best – is not almost a fault
T'incur a private check. When shall he come?
Tell me, Othello. I wonder in my soul
What you would ask me that I should deny,
70   Or stand so mammering on? What! Michael Cassio,

67 *check* reprimand   70 *mammering* stammering, hesitating

That came a-wooing with you? And so many a time –
When I have spoke of you dispraisingly –
Hath ta'en your part, to have so much to do
To bring him in? By'r Lady, I could do much.

OTHELLO

Prithee, no more: let him come when he will;
I will deny thee nothing.

DESDEMONA   Why, this is not a boon:
'Tis as I should entreat you wear your gloves
Or feed on nourishing dishes, or keep you warm,
Or sue to you to do a peculiar profit
To your own person. Nay, when I have a suit   80
Wherein I mean to touch your love indeed
It shall be full of poise and difficult weight,
And fearful to be granted.

OTHELLO   I will deny thee nothing.
Whereon, I do beseech thee, grant me this:
To leave me but a little to my self.

DESDEMONA

Shall I deny you? No; farewell, my lord.

OTHELLO

Farewell, my Desdemona, I'll come to thee straight.

DESDEMONA

Emilia, come. Be as your fancies teach you.

---

71 *came a-wooing with you?* This is the
first we hear of Cassio's part in
Othello's wooing and it is difficult
to reconcile with the Moor's own
account in 1.3. There are four possible explanations: (1) Desdemona supposed that Othello was wooing her
before he realized it himself; (2) Othello gave a slightly distorted account
of the events leading up to his declaration; (3) Desdemona is referring

to the period between the declaration
and the elopement, though she
would hardly dispraise him then; (4)
Shakespeare wanted to give a lead to
Iago's words later in the scene (lines
93–4) and did not bother about the
discrepancy.
74 *bring him in* get him reinstated
79 *peculiar* personal
82 *poise* weight

Whate'er you be, I am obedient.

                           Exeunt Desdemona and Emilia

OTHELLO

90   Excellent wretch! Perdition catch my soul
But I do love thee! And when I love thee not,
Chaos is come again.

IAGO   My noble lord –

OTHELLO

What dost thou say, Iago?

IAGO   Did Michael Cassio,
When you wooed my lady, know of your love?

OTHELLO

He did, from first to last. Why dost thou ask?

IAGO

But for a satisfaction of my thought –
No further harm.

OTHELLO   Why of thy thought, Iago?

IAGO

I did not think he had been acquainted with her.

OTHELLO

O yes, and went between us very oft.

IAGO

100   Indeed!

OTHELLO

Indeed? Ay, indeed. Discern'st thou aught in that?
Is he not honest?

IAGO   Honest, my lord?

OTHELLO   Honest? Ay, honest.

IAGO

My lord, for aught I know.

OTHELLO   What dost thou think?

---

90 *wretch* (term of endearment)
91 *But I do* if I do not
91–2 *And when I love thee not,* | *Chaos is*

come again. This proves to be prophetic.

IAGO
  Think, my lord?
OTHELLO
  Think, my lord! By heaven, he echoes me,
  As if there were some monster in his thought
  Too hideous to be shown. Thou dost mean something.
  I heard thee say even now, thou lik'st not that,
  When Cassio left my wife. What didst not like?
  And when I told thee he was of my counsel   110
  In my whole course of wooing, thou cried'st 'Indeed!'
  And didst contract and purse thy brow together,
  As if thou then hadst shut up in thy brain
  Some horrible conceit. If thou dost love me,
  Show me thy thought.
IAGO
  My lord, you know I love you.
OTHELLO   I think thou dost:
  And for I know thou'rt full of love and honesty,
  And weigh'st thy words before thou giv'st them breath,
  Therefore these stops of thine affright me more:
  For such things in a false disloyal knave   120
  Are tricks of custom; but in a man that's just,
  They're close dilations, working from the heart,
  That passion cannot rule.
IAGO   For Michael Cassio,
  I dare be sworn I think that he is honest.
OTHELLO
  I think so too.
IAGO   Men should be what they seem;

106 *monster*. Compare line 164.   121 *of custom* customary
114 *conceit* idea   122 *close dilations* involuntary delays
119 *stops* pauses

Or those that be not, would they might seem none!

OTHELLO

Certain, men should be what they seem.

IAGO

Why, then, I think Cassio's an honest man.

OTHELLO

Nay, yet there's more in this.
130   I prithee speak to me as to thy thinkings,
As thou dost ruminate, and give thy worst of thoughts
The worst of words.

IAGO   Good my lord, pardon me;
Though I am bound to every act of duty,
I am not bound to that all slaves are free to:
Utter my thoughts. Why, say they are vile and false?
As where's that palace whereinto foul things
Sometimes intrude not? Who has a breast so pure,
But some uncleanly apprehensions
Keep leets and law-days, and in session sit
140   With meditations lawful?

OTHELLO

Thou dost conspire against thy friend, Iago,
If thou but think'st him wronged, and mak'st his ear
A stranger to thy thoughts.

IAGO   I do beseech you,
Though I perchance am vicious in my guess –
As I confess it is my nature's plague
To spy into abuses, and of my jealousy
Shapes faults that are not – that your wisdom then,
From one that so imperfectly conjects,
Would take no notice, nor build yourself a trouble

---

126 *none* (not to be men)   really necessary.
139 *leets* (days on which courts are held)   *jealousy* suspicious nature
146 *of*. The emendation 'oft' for 'of'   148 *conjects* conjectures
    would improve the syntax but is not

Out of his scattering and unsure observance.   150
It were not for your quiet nor your good,
Nor for my manhood, honesty, and wisdom,
To let you know my thoughts.

OTHELLO   What dost thou mean?

IAGO
Good name in man and woman, dear my lord,
Is the immediate jewel of their souls.
Who steals my purse, steals trash; 'tis something,
          nothing;
'Twas mine, 'tis his, and has been slave to thousands:
But he that filches from me my good name
Robs me of that which not enriches him
And makes me poor indeed.

OTHELLO   By heaven, I'll know thy thoughts.   160

IAGO
You cannot, if my heart were in your hand,
Nor shall not, whilst 'tis in my custody.

OTHELLO
Ha!

IAGO O, beware, my lord, of jealousy!
It is the green-eyed monster, which doth mock
The meat it feeds on. That cuckold lives in bliss
Who certain of his fate loves not his wronger,
But O, what damnèd minutes tells he o'er,
Who dotes yet doubts, suspects yet fondly loves!

OTHELLO
O misery!

---

150 *scattering* random
154–5 *Good name in man and woman, dear my lord, | Is the immediate jewel of their souls* (proverbial)
155 *immediate* nearest the heart
167–8 *But O, what damnèd minutes tells he*
o'er, | *Who dotes yet doubts, suspects yet fondly loves!* This proves to be Othello's fate.
169 *O misery!* Othello is not referring to himself.

IAGO

170   Poor and content is rich, and rich enough;
      But riches fineless is as poor as winter,
      To him that ever fears he shall be poor.
      Good God, the souls of all my tribe defend
      From jealousy!

OTHELLO   Why, why is this?
      Think'st thou I'd make a life of jealousy,
      To follow still the changes of the moon
      With fresh suspicions? No, to be once in doubt
      Is once to be resolved. Exchange me for a goat,
      When I shall turn the business of my soul
180   To such exsufflicate and blown surmises,
      Matching thy inference. 'Tis not to make me jealous
      To say my wife is fair, loves company,
      Is free of speech, sings, plays, and dances well:
      Where virtue is, these are more virtuous.
      Nor from mine own weak merits will I draw
      The smallest fear or doubt of her revolt,
      For she had eyes and chose me. No, Iago,
      I'll see before I doubt; when I doubt, prove;
      And on the proof, there is no more but this:
190   Away at once with love or jealousy!

IAGO

      I am glad of this: for now I shall have reason
      To show the love and duty that I bear you
      With franker spirit. Therefore, as I am bound,
      Receive it from me. I speak not yet of proof.

---

170 *Poor and content is rich, and rich enough*
    (proverbial)
171 *fineless* boundless
176-7 *To follow still the changes of the moon
    | With fresh suspicions* indulge in new
    suspicions several times a month
177-8 *No, to be once in doubt | Is once to be
    resolved* if I once doubt, I will settle

the question one way or the other
(compare lines 188-90)
178 *goat* (supposed to be lustful)
180 *exsufflicate and blown* inflated and
    blown up (but some think the words
    mean 'spat out and fly-blown')
186 *doubt* suspicion

Look to your wife; observe her well with Cassio.
Wear your eye thus: not jealous, nor secure.
I would not have your free and noble nature,
Out of self-bounty, be abused. Look to't.
I know our country disposition well:
In Venice they do let God see the pranks   200
They dare not show their husbands; their best
          conscience
Is not to leave't undone, but keep't unknown.

OTHELLO
Dost thou say so?

IAGO
She did deceive her father, marrying you,
And when she seemed to shake, and fear your looks,
She loved them most.

OTHELLO   And so she did.

IAGO   Why, go to, then!
She that so young could give out such a seeming,
To seel her father's eyes up close as oak –
He thought 'twas witchcraft. – But I am much to blame,
I humbly do beseech you of your pardon   210
For too much loving you.

OTHELLO   I am bound to thee for ever.

IAGO
I see this hath a little dashed your spirits.

OTHELLO
Not a jot, not a jot.

IAGO   In faith, I fear it has.

---

198 *self-bounty* inherent generosity
200–202 *In Venice they do let God see the pranks . . . but keep't unknown.* Othello begins to be worried at this point because of his comparative ignorance of Venetian society.
204 *She did deceive her father, marrying you*

(echoing Brabantio's last words in I.3)
208 *seel* blind
     oak the grain of oak
211 *I am bound to thee for ever* (with a possible quibble on 'bound')

I hope you will consider what is spoke
Comes from my love. But I do see you're moved.
I am to pray you, not to strain my speech
To grosser issues, nor to larger reach
Than to suspicion.

OTHELLO

I will not.

IAGO   Should you do so, my lord,

220   My speech should fall into such vile success
Which my thoughts aimed not at. Cassio's my worthy
        friend.
My lord, I see you're moved.

OTHELLO   No, not much moved.
I do not think but Desdemona's honest.

IAGO

Long live she so! And long live you to think so!

OTHELLO

And yet, how nature erring from itself —

IAGO

Ay, there's the point: as, to be bold with you,
Not to affect many proposèd matches
Of her own clime, complexion, and degree,
Whereto we see in all things nature tends,

230   Foh! One may smell in such a will most rank,
Foul disproportion, thoughts unnatural.
But, pardon me, I do not in position
Distinctly speak of her, though I may fear
Her will, recoiling to her better judgement,

217 *issues* conclusions
220 *success* result
223 *honest* chaste
227 *affect* like
230–31 *Foh! One may smell in such a will most rank,* | *Foul disproportion, thoughts unnatural*. This mention of difference

of colour is Iago's strongest card. His earlier exclamation 'Pish!' (II.1.255) and 'Foh!' here suggest there is a streak of puritanism in him.
232 *in position* positively

May fall to match you with her country forms,
And happily repent.

OTHELLO   Farewell, farewell.
If more thou dost perceive, let me know more.
Set on thy wife to observe. Leave me, Iago.

IAGO
(*going*) My lord, I take my leave.

OTHELLO
Why did I marry? This honest creature doubtless   240
Sees and knows more, much more than he unfolds.

IAGO
(*returning*) My lord, I would I might entreat your
          honour
To scan this thing no farther. Leave it to time.
Although 'tis fit that Cassio have his place,
For sure he fills it up with great ability,
Yet, if you please to hold him off awhile,
You shall by that perceive him and his means;
Note if your lady strain his entertainment
With any strong or vehement importunity –
Much will be seen in that. In the meantime,   250
Let me be thought too busy in my fears,
As worthy cause I have to fear I am,
And hold her free, I do beseech your honour.

OTHELLO
Fear not my government.

IAGO   I once more take my leave.
                                         Exit

OTHELLO
This fellow's of exceeding honesty,
And knows all qualities with a learnèd spirit

---

235 *fall to match* happen to compare   248 *entertainment* reinstatement
    country country's   251 *busy* interfering
236 *happily* maybe   253 *free* innocent
247 *means* (to recover his post)   254 *government* self-control

Of human dealings. If I do prove her haggard,
Though that her jesses were my dear heart-strings,
I'd whistle her off, and let her down the wind
To prey at fortune. Haply, for I am black
And have not those soft parts of conversation
That chamberers have; or for I am declined
Into the vale of years – yet that's not much –
She's gone: I am abused, and my relief
Must be to loathe her. O, curse of marriage!
That we can call these delicate creatures ours
And not their appetites! I had rather be a toad
And live upon the vapour of a dungeon
Than keep a corner in the thing I love
For others' uses. Yet 'tis the plague of great ones;
Prerogatived are they less than the base.
'Tis destiny unshunnable, like death:
Even then this forkèd plague is fated to us
When we do quicken. Desdemona comes:
            Enter Desdemona and Emilia
If she be false, O, then heaven mocks itself!
I'll not believe't.

DESDEMONA   How now, my dear Othello!
Your dinner, and the generous islanders
By you invited, do attend your presence.

OTHELLO
I am to blame.

257 *haggard* wild (a term in falconry)
258 *jesses* straps tied to legs of hawks
260 *prey at fortune* fend for herself. At
this point Othello is not thinking of
killing Desdemona but only of casting her off.
Haply perhaps
261 *soft parts* pleasant arts
262 *chamberers* gallants
267 *toad.* Othello begins to use the

characteristic animal imagery of
Iago.
271 *Prerogatived* privileged
273 *forkèd plague* cuckold's horns
274 *do quicken* are conceived
276 *I'll not believe't.* As soon as he sees
Desdemona, Othello repudiates
Iago's temptation; but the recovery
of faith is only temporary.
277 *generous* noble

DESDEMONA   Why do you speak so faintly?
Are you not well?

OTHELLO   280
I have a pain upon my forehead here.

DESDEMONA
Faith, that's with watching: 'twill away again.
Let me but bind it hard, within this hour
It will be well.

OTHELLO   Your napkin is too little.
    He puts the handkerchief from him, and she drops it
Let it alone. Come, I'll go in with you.

DESDEMONA
I am very sorry that you are not well.
                              Exeunt Othello and Desdemona

EMILIA
I am glad I have found this napkin:
This was her first remembrance from the Moor.
My wayward husband hath a hundred times
Wooed me to steal it; but she so loves the token –   290
For he conjured her she should ever keep it –
That she reserves it evermore about her
To kiss and talk to. I'll have the work ta'en out,
And give't Iago.
What he will do with it, heaven knows, not I:
I nothing, but to please his fantasy.
        Enter Iago

IAGO
How now? What do you here alone?

EMILIA
Do not you chide: I have a thing for you.

282 *watching* not getting enough sleep
284 *napkin* handkerchief. The loss of the handkerchief is Shakespeare's invention. In Cinthio's tale it is stolen. (See Introduction, p. 306.) Desdemona forgets the precious love-token because, in her love for Othello, she is concerned about his 'headache'.
293 *ta'en out* copied
296 *fantasy* whim

IAGO

A thing for me? It is a common thing.

EMILIA

300   Ha!

IAGO

To have a foolish wife.

EMILIA

O, is that all? What will you give me now
For that same handkerchief?

IAGO   What handkerchief?

EMILIA

What handkerchief!
Why that the Moor first gave to Desdemona;
That which so often you did bid me steal.

IAGO

Hast stol'n it from her?

EMILIA

No, faith, she let it drop by negligence,
And to th'advantage, I, being here, took't up.
Look, here it is.

310   IAGO   A good wench! Give it me.

EMILIA

What will you do with't, that you have been so earnest
To have me filch it?

IAGO (snatching it)   Why, what is that to you?

EMILIA

If it be not for some purpose of import,
Give't me again. Poor lady, she'll run mad
When she shall lack it.

IAGO

Be not acknown on't: I have use for it.
Go, leave me.   Exit Emilia

---

299 *A thing* (the female pudenda)   316 *Be not acknown on't* don't acknow-
313 *import* importance   ledge anything about it

I will in Cassio's lodging lose this napkin,
And let him find it. Trifles light as air
Are to the jealous confirmations strong   320
As proofs of holy writ. This may do something.
The Moor already changes with my poison.
Dangerous conceits are in their natures poisons,
Which at the first are scarce found to distaste,
But, with a little act upon the blood,
Burn like the mines of sulphur.

     Enter Othello

                                     I did say so.
Look where he comes! Not poppy, nor mandragora,
Nor all the drowsy syrups of the world,
Shall ever medicine thee to that sweet sleep
Which thou owed'st yesterday.

OTHELLO   Ha, ha, false to me!   330

IAGO

Why, how now, General! No more of that.

OTHELLO

Avaunt! Be gone! Thou hast set me on the rack.
I swear 'tis better to be much abused,
Than but to know't a little.

IAGO   How now, my lord!

OTHELLO

What sense had I of her stolen hours of lust?
I saw't not, thought it not, it harmed not me.
I slept the next night well, was free and merry;
I found not Cassio's kisses on her lips.

---

323 *conceits* ideas
324 *distaste* be distasteful
325 *act* action
327 *poppy* opium (derived from the poppy)

mandragora narcotic plant
328 *drowsy* causing sleep
330 *owed'st* didst own
337 *free* untroubled

He that is robbed, not wanting what is stolen,
340   Let him not know't, and he's not robbed at all.

IAGO
I am sorry to hear this.

OTHELLO
I had been happy if the general camp,
Pioners and all, had tasted her sweet body,
So I had nothing known. O, now, for ever
Farewell the tranquil mind! Farewell content!
Farewell the plumèd troops and the big wars
That make ambition virtue – O, farewell!
Farewell the neighing steed, and the shrill trump,
The spirit-stirring drum, th'ear-piercing fife,
350   The royal banner and all quality,
Pride, pomp and circumstance of glorious war!
And, O you mortal engines, whose rude throats
Th'immortal Jove's dread clamours counterfeit,
Farewell! Othello's occupation's gone.

IAGO
Is't possible, my lord?

OTHELLO
Villain, be sure thou prove my love a whore;
Be sure of it: give me the ocular proof,
Or by the worth of mine eternal soul,
Thou hadst been better have been born a dog
Than answer my waked wrath!

360   IAGO   Is't come to this?

OTHELLO
Make me to see't: or, at the least, so prove it
That the probation bear no hinge nor loop

339–40 *He that is robbed, not wanting what*   344 *So* if
  is stolen, | *Let him not know't, and he's*   351 *circumstance* pageantry
  not robbed at all (proverbial)   352 *mortal* deadly
339 *wanting* missing   353 *Jove's dread clamours* (thunder)
343 *Pioners* sappers   362 *probation* proof

To hang a doubt on – or woe upon thy life!

IAGO

My noble lord –

OTHELLO

If thou dost slander her and torture me,
Never pray more; abandon all remorse;
On horror's head horrors accumulate;
Do deeds to make heaven weep, all earth amazed:
For nothing canst thou to damnation add
Greater than that.

IAGO   O grace! O heaven defend me!   370
Are you a man? Have you a soul? Or sense?
God bu'y you: take mine office. O wretched fool,
That lov'st to make thine honesty a vice!
O monstrous world! Take note, take note, O world!
To be direct and honest is not safe.
I thank you for this profit, and from hence
I'll love no friend, sith love breeds such offence.

OTHELLO

Nay, stay: thou shouldst be honest.

IAGO

I should be wise; for honesty's a fool
And loses that it works for.

OTHELLO   By the world,   380
I think my wife be honest, and think she is not;
I think that thou art just, and think thou art not.
I'll have some proof. Her name that was as fresh
As Dian's visage is now begrimed and black
As mine own face. If there be cords or knives,

372 *bu'y* be with
373 *make thine honesty a vice* (by carrying
    it to excess)
376–7 *I thank you ... such offence.* The
    couplet underlines the fact that he is
    about to exit.
377 *sith* since
379 *should* ought to be (quibbling on
    'shouldst' in the previous line)
381 *honest* chaste
384 *Dian* Diana (goddess of chastity)
385–7 *If there be cords or knives, | Poison or
    fire or suffocating streams, | I'll not endure
    it.* Othello is thinking of suicide.

Poison or fire or suffocating streams,
I'll not endure it. Would I were satisfied!

IAGO

I see, sir, you are eaten up with passion.
I do repent me that I put it to you.
You would be satisfied?

390 OTHELLO　　　　　　　　Would! Nay, I will.

IAGO

And may. But how? How satisfied, my lord?
Would you, the supervisor, grossly gape on?
Behold her topped?

OTHELLO　　　　　　Death and damnation! O!

IAGO

It were a tedious difficulty, I think,
To bring them to that prospect. Damn them then
If ever mortal eyes do see them bolster
More than their own! What then? How then?
What shall I say? Where's satisfaction?
It is impossible you should see this,
400 Were they as prime as goats, as hot as monkeys,
As salt as wolves in pride, and fools as gross
As ignorance made drunk. But yet, I say,
If imputation and strong circumstance,
Which lead directly to the door of truth,
Will give you satisfaction, you might have't.

OTHELLO

Give me a living reason she's disloyal.

IAGO

I do not like the office.
But sith I am entered in this cause so far –

392 *supervisor* looker-on
396 *bolster* share a bolster
400 *prime* lecherous
401 *salt* lustful

pride heat
403 *imputation and strong circumstance*
strong circumstantial evidence

Pricked to't by foolish honesty and love –
I will go on. I lay with Cassio lately,   410
And being troubled with a raging tooth
I could not sleep.
There are a kind of men so loose of soul
That in their sleeps will mutter their affairs:
One of this kind is Cassio.
In sleep I heard him say: 'Sweet Desdemona,
Let us be wary, let us hide our loves';
And then, sir, would he gripe and wring my hand,
Cry 'O sweet creature!' and then kiss me hard,
As if he plucked up kisses by the roots,   420
That grew upon my lips; then laid his leg
Over my thigh, and sighed and kissed, and then
Cried 'Cursèd fate that gave thee to the Moor!'

OTHELLO

O monstrous! Monstrous!

IAGO   Nay, this was but his dream.

OTHELLO

But this denoted a foregone conclusion.

IAGO

'Tis a shrewd doubt, though it be but a dream:
And this may help to thicken other proofs
That do demonstrate thinly.

OTHELLO   I'll tear her all to pieces!

IAGO

Nay, but be wise: yet we see nothing done,
She may be honest yet. Tell me but this: 430
Have you not sometimes seen a handkerchief,

425 *foregone conclusion* previous consummation

426 *shrewd doubt* cursed suspicion. This line is given to Othello in F, perhaps rightly.

429 *yet we see nothing done* (referring to Othello's demand for ocular proof)

431 *Have you not sometimes seen a handkerchief.* Iago reserves this 'proof' till Othello is too upset to think clearly.

Spotted with strawberries, in your wife's hand?

OTHELLO

I gave her such a one: 'twas my first gift.

IAGO

I know not that: but such a handkerchief –
I am sure it was your wife's – did I today
See Cassio wipe his beard with.

OTHELLO   If it be that –

IAGO

If it be that, or any that was hers,
It speaks against her with the other proofs.

OTHELLO

O, that the slave had forty thousand lives!
440   One is too poor, too weak for my revenge.
Now do I see 'tis true. Look here, Iago –
All my fond love thus do I blow to heaven:
'Tis gone.
Arise, black vengeance, from thy hollow cell!
Yield up, O love, thy crown and hearted throne
To tyrannous hate! Swell, bosom, with thy fraught,
For 'tis of aspics' tongues!

IAGO   Yet be content.

OTHELLO

O, blood, blood, blood!

IAGO

Patience, I say: your mind perhaps may change.

OTHELLO

450   Never, Iago. Like to the Pontic sea,
Whose icy current and compulsive course

---

445 *hearted* seated in the heart
446 *fraught* burden
447 *aspics'* venomous snakes'
450–53 *Like to the Pontic sea ... and the*
Hellespont. The simile, like several
others in the play, was derived from

Holland's translation of Pliny's *Nat-*
ural History. Either it was a late addition to the text, or omitted from Q.
Actors would be unlikely to omit
the lines.

450 *Pontic sea* Black Sea

Ne'er feels retiring ebb, but keeps due on
To the Propontic and the Hellespont,
Even so my bloody thoughts with violent pace
Shall ne'er look back, ne'er ebb to humble love,
Till that a capable and wide revenge
Swallow them up. Now, by yond marble heaven,
In the due reverence of a sacred vow
I here engage my words.
          He kneels

IAGO   Do not rise yet.
          He kneels
Witness you ever-burning lights above,   460
You elements, that clip us round about,
Witness that here Iago doth give up
The execution of his wit, hands, heart,
To wronged Othello's service. Let him command,
And to obey shall be in me remorse,
What bloody business ever.
          They rise

OTHELLO   I greet thy love,
Not with vain thanks, but with acceptance bounteous;
And will upon the instant put thee to't.
Within these three days let me hear thee say
That Cassio's not alive.

IAGO   My friend is dead;   470
'Tis done at your request. But let her live.

OTHELLO
Damn her, lewd minx! O, damn her, damn her!
Come go with me apart. I will withdraw
To furnish me with some swift means of death
For the fair devil. Now art thou my Lieutenant.

---

453 *Propontic* Sea of Marmora
    Hellespont Dardanelles
456 *capable* ample
461 *clip* encompass
463 *execution* activities
    wit intelligence

465 *remorse* compassion. Iago means that
    the utmost cruelty will be reckoned
    as kindness because he is doing it for
    Othello.
466 *ever* soever

IAGO
    I am your own for ever.   *Exeunt*

III.4   *Enter Desdemona, Emilia, and Clown*

    DESDEMONA Do you know, sirrah, where Lieutenant
        Cassio lies?
    CLOWN I dare not say he lies anywhere.
    DESDEMONA Why, man?
    CLOWN He's a soldier, and for one to say a soldier lies is
        stabbing.
    DESDEMONA Go to! Where lodges he?
    CLOWN To tell you where he lodges is to tell you where I
        lie.
10 DESDEMONA Can anything be made of this?
    CLOWN I know not where he lodges, and for me to devise a
        lodging, and say he lies here, or he lies there, were to lie
        in mine own throat.
    DESDEMONA Can you inquire him out? And be edified by
        report?
    CLOWN I will catechize the world for him, that is, make
        questions, and by them answer.
    DESDEMONA Seek him; bid him come hither; tell him I
        have moved my lord on his behalf, and hope all will be
20   well.
    CLOWN To do this is within the compass of man's wit, and
        therefore I will attempt the doing of it.   *Exit*
    DESDEMONA
        Where should I lose that handkerchief, Emilia?

---

476 *I am your own* (1) I am your faithful
    servant; (2) you have become pos-
    sessed with my spirit

III.4.1–22 *Do you know, sirrah . . . attempt*
    the doing of it. The feeble quibbling
    provides some slight relief between
    the intensity of the previous scene
    and that which follows.

EMILIA

I know not, madam.

DESDEMONA

Believe me, I had rather have lost my purse
Full of crusadoes; and, but my noble Moor
Is true of mind, and made of no such baseness
As jealous creatures are, it were enough
To put him to ill-thinking.

EMILIA   Is he not jealous?

DESDEMONA

Who? He? I think the sun where he was born   30
Drew all such humours from him.

EMILIA   Look where he comes.

                Enter Othello

DESDEMONA

I will not leave him now till Cassio
Be called to him. How is't with you, my lord?

OTHELLO

Well, my good lady. (*Aside*) O, hardness to dissemble!
How do you, Desdemona?

DESDEMONA   Well, my good lord.

OTHELLO

Give me your hand. This hand is moist, my lady.

DESDEMONA

It yet has felt no age, nor known no sorrow.

OTHELLO

This argues fruitfulness and liberal heart.
Hot, hot and moist. This hand of yours requires
A sequester from liberty, fasting and prayer,   40

24 *I know not*. Emilia's lie makes it difficult for her to explain matters after
Othello has shown his jealousy.
26 *crusadoes* gold coins
31 *humours* bodily fluids determining
temperament

38 *fruitfulness* generosity or amorousness
liberal generous or licentious
40 *sequester* sequestration, removal

Much castigation, exercise devout;
For there's a young and sweating devil here
That commonly rebels. 'Tis a good hand,
A frank one.

DESDEMONA   You may, indeed, say so:
For 'twas that hand that gave away my heart.

OTHELLO
A liberal hand! The hearts of old gave hands;
But our new heraldry is hands, not hearts.

DESDEMONA
I cannot speak of this. Come now, your promise.

OTHELLO
What promise, chuck?

DESDEMONA

50   I have sent to bid Cassio come speak with you.

OTHELLO
I have a salt and sorry rheum offends me:
Lend me thy handkerchief.

DESDEMONA   Here, my lord.

OTHELLO
That which I gave you.

DESDEMONA   I have it not about me.

OTHELLO
Not?

DESDEMONA   No, faith, my lord.

OTHELLO   That is a fault.
That handkerchief
Did an Egyptian to my mother give:

---

47 *our new heraldry*. Possibly this is a
topical reference. The meaning is that
people used 'to give their hands and
their hearts together, but we think it
a finer grace to look asquint, our
hand looking one way, and our heart

another' (Sir William Cornwallis,
1601).

49 *chuck* (term of endearment)
51 *salt and sorry rheum* wretched running
cold

She was a charmer and could almost read
The thoughts of people. She told her, while she kept it,
'Twould make her amiable and subdue my father
Entirely to her love; but, if she lost it   60
Or made a gift of it, my father's eye
Should hold her loathèd, and his spirits should hunt
After new fancies. She, dying, gave it me,
And bid me, when my fate would have me wive,
To give it her. I did so; and take heed on't:
Make it a darling, like your precious eye.
To lose or give't away were such perdition
As nothing else could match.

DESDEMONA   Is't possible?

OTHELLO
'Tis true: there's magic in the web of it.
A sibyl, that had numbered in the world   70
The sun to course two hundred compasses,
In her prophetic fury sewed the work:
The worms were hallowed that did breed the silk,
And it was dyed in mummy, which the skilful
Conserved of maidens' hearts.

DESDEMONA   Indeed! Is't true?

OTHELLO
Most veritable; therefore look to't well.

DESDEMONA
Then would to God that I had never seen it!

OTHELLO
Ha! Wherefore?

57 *charmer* enchantress
59 *amiable* beloved
63 *fancies* loves
69–72 *there's magic in the web of it* ...
       prophetic fury sewed the work. The lines
       derive from Ariosto, *Orlando Furioso*,
       XLVI.80.

72 *prophetic fury* 'il furor profetico'
       (Ariosto)
74 *mummy* preparation made from
       mummies

DESDEMONA
Why do you speak so startlingly and rash?

OTHELLO
80   Is't lost? Is't gone? Speak: is't out o'th'way?

DESDEMONA
Heaven bless us!

OTHELLO   Say you?

DESDEMONA   It is not lost.
But what an if it were?

OTHELLO   How!

DESDEMONA
I say it is not lost.

OTHELLO   Fetch't: let me see't.

DESDEMONA
Why, so I can, sir; but I will not now.
This is a trick to put me from my suit.
Pray you let Cassio be received again.

OTHELLO
Fetch me the handkerchief: my mind misgives.

DESDEMONA
Come, come:
You'll never meet a more sufficient man.

OTHELLO
The handkerchief!

90   DESDEMONA   I pray, talk me of Cassio.

OTHELLO
The handkerchief!

DESDEMONA   A man that all his time
Hath founded his good fortunes on your love;
Shared dangers with you –

OTHELLO
The handkerchief!

DESDEMONA   I'faith you are to blame.

79 *rash* rashly   90 *talk* talk to

OTHELLO
Zounds!   *Exit*

EMILIA
Is not this man jealous?

DESDEMONA   I ne'er saw this before.
Sure, there's some wonder in this handkerchief:
I am most unhappy in the loss of it.

EMILIA
'Tis not a year or two shows us a man.
They are all but stomachs, and we all but food;   100
They eat us hungerly, and when they are full,
They belch us. Look you, Cassio and my husband.
            Enter Iago and Cassio

IAGO
There is no other way: 'tis she must do't.
And lo, the happiness! Go, and importune her.

DESDEMONA
How now, good Cassio! What's the news with you?

CASSIO
Madam, my former suit. I do beseech you
That by your virtuous means I may again
Exist and be a member of his love,
Whom I, with all the office of my heart,
Entirely honour. I would not be delayed.   110
If my offence be of such mortal kind
That nor my service past, nor present sorrow,
Nor purposed merit in futurity,
Can ransom me into his love again,
But to know so must be my benefit:
So shall I clothe me in a forced content,
And shut myself up in some other course

101 *hungerly* hungrily   109 *office* loyal service
104 *happiness* good luck   117 *shut myself up* confine myself

To Fortune's alms.

DESDEMONA   Alas, thrice-gentle Cassio!
My advocation is not now in tune:
My lord is not my lord; nor should I know him,
Were he in favour as in humour altered.
So help me every spirit sanctified
As I have spoken for you all my best,
And stood within the blank of his displeasure
For my free speech! You must awhile be patient.
What I can do, I will; and more I will,
Than for myself I dare. Let that suffice you.

IAGO
Is my lord angry?

EMILIA   He went hence but now
And certainly in strange unquietness.

IAGO
Can he be angry? I have seen the cannon
When it hath blown his ranks into the air,
And like the devil from his very arm
Puffed his own brother — and can he be angry?
Something of moment then. I will go meet him.
There's matter in't indeed if he be angry.

DESDEMONA
I prithee do so.   *Exit Iago*
              Something, sure, of state,
Either from Venice, or some unhatched practice
Made demonstrable here in Cyprus to him,
Hath puddled his clear spirit; and in such cases
Men's natures wrangle with inferior things,
Though great ones are their object. 'Tis even so.
For let our finger ache, and it endues

121 *favour* appearance
124 *blank* centre of target, range
137 *unhatched practice* undisclosed plot
139 *puddled* made muddy

141–4 *'Tis even so . . . that sense* | *Of pain.*
See An Account of the Text, p. 354.
Neither Q nor F gives a satisfactory
text, but the sense is clear.

Our healthful members even to that sense
Of pain. Nay, we must think men are not gods,
Nor of them look for such observancy
As fits the bridal. Beshrew me much, Emilia,
I was – unhandsome warrior as I am –
Arraigning his unkindness with my soul;
But now I find I had suborned the witness
And he's indicted falsely.   150

EMILIA

Pray heaven it be state matters, as you think,
And no conception nor no jealous toy
Concerning you.

DESDEMONA

Alas the day, I never gave him cause.

EMILIA

But jealous souls will not be answered so;
They are not ever jealous for the cause,
But jealous for they're jealous. It is a monster
Begot upon itself, born on itself.

DESDEMONA

Heaven keep that monster from Othello's mind.

EMILIA

Lady, amen!   160

DESDEMONA

I will go seek him. Cassio, walk here about.
If I do find him fit, I'll move your suit,
And seek to effect it to my uttermost.

CASSIO

I humbly thank your ladyship.

Exeunt Desdemona and Emilia

---

146 *bridal* wedding
147 *unhandsome* inadequate
  warrior. Desdemona is thinking of
  Othello's greeting on his arrival in
  Cyprus (II.1.176).

151–3 *Pray heaven it be state matters . . .*
  Concerning you. Emilia is feeling guilty
  about the handkerchief.
152 *toy* fancy
157 *monster.* Compare III.3.164.

Enter Bianca

BIANCA

'Save you, friend Cassio.

CASSIO   What make you from home?

How is it with you, my most fair Bianca?

I'faith, sweet love, I was coming to your house.

BIANCA

And I was going to your lodging, Cassio.

What! Keep a week away? Seven days and nights?

170   Eight score eight hours? And lovers' absent hours

More tedious than the dial eight score times!

O weary reckoning!

CASSIO   Pardon me, Bianca.

I have this while with leaden thoughts been pressed:

But I shall in a more continuate time

Strike off this score of absence. Sweet Bianca,

Take me this work out.

BIANCA   O Cassio, whence came this?

This is some token from a newer friend.

To the felt absence now I feel a cause.

Is't come to this? Well, well.

CASSIO   Go to, woman!

180   Throw your vile guesses in the devil's teeth

From whence you have them. You are jealous now

That this is from some mistress, some remembrance:

No, by my faith, Bianca.

BIANCA   Why, whose is it?

CASSIO

I know not, sweet. I found it in my chamber.

169 *week.* Cassio, according to one time-scheme, arrived in Cyprus only on the previous day; but a week could elapse between III.3 and III.4. This, however, would conflict with Othello's demand at the end of III.3 that Cassio should be killed within three

days and with the natural assumption that Othello would demand the handkerchief at the first opportunity.

174 *continuate* uninterrupted

176 *Take me this work out* copy this embroidery for me

I like the work well. Ere it be demanded –
As like enough it will – I'd have it copied.
Take it and do't, and leave me for this time.

BIANCA
Leave you? Wherefore?

CASSIO
I do attend here on the General,
And think it no addition, nor my wish,   190
To have him see me womaned.

BIANCA   Why, I pray you?

CASSIO
Not that I love you not.

BIANCA   But that you do not love me.
I pray you, bring me on the way a little,
And say if I shall see you soon at night.

CASSIO
'Tis but a little way that I can bring you,
For I attend here: but I'll see you soon.

BIANCA
'Tis very good: I must be circumstanced.   *Exeunt*

                Enter Othello and Iago   IV.1

IAGO
Will you think so?

OTHELLO   Think so, Iago?

IAGO   What!

---

197 *circumstanced*   give   way   to
   circumstance

IV.1 The opening of this scene indicates
that despite Othello's determination to
kill Desdemona he still loves her;

and Iago, knowing that every hour she
lives increases his own exposure, is
driven to arouse Othello's rage by harping on the sexual relations of Cassio and
Desdemona.

To kiss in private?

OTHELLO   An unauthorized kiss.

IAGO

Or to be naked with her friend in bed
An hour or more, not meaning any harm?

OTHELLO

Naked in bed, Iago, and not mean harm?
It is hypocrisy against the devil.
They that mean virtuously and yet do so,
The devil their virtue tempts, and they tempt heaven.

IAGO

So they do nothing, 'tis a venial slip.

10   But if I give my wife a handkerchief –

OTHELLO

What then?

IAGO

Why, then, 'tis hers, my lord, and being hers,
She may, I think, bestow't on any man.

OTHELLO

She is protectress of her honour too.
May she give that?

IAGO

Her honour is an essence that's not seen:
They have it very oft that have it not.
But for the handkerchief –

OTHELLO

By heaven, I would most gladly have forgot it!

20   Thou said'st – O, it comes o'er my memory
As doth the raven o'er the infected house,
Boding to all! – he had my handkerchief.

IAGO

Ay, what of that?

9 *So if*
21 *As doth the raven o'er the infected house.*
   A croaking raven was thought to portend death to the plague-stricken inmates of a house.

OTHELLO   That's not so good now.

IAGO   What

If I had said, I had seen him do you wrong,
Or heard him say – as knaves be such abroad,
Who having by their own importunate suit
Or voluntary dotage of some mistress
Convincèd or supplied them, cannot choose
But they must blab –

OTHELLO   Hath he said anything?

IAGO

He hath, my lord; but be you well assured,   30
No more than he'll unswear.

OTHELLO   What hath he said?

IAGO

Faith, that he did – I know not what he did.

OTHELLO

What? What?

IAGO

Lie –

OTHELLO With her?

IAGO   With her, on her, what you will.

OTHELLO Lie with her? Lie on her? We say lie on her
when they belie her. Lie with her! Zounds, that's ful-
some! Handkerchief – confession – handkerchief! To
confess and be hanged for his labour. First to be hanged
and then to confess! I tremble at it. Nature would not
invest herself in such shadowing passion without some   40
instruction. It is not words that shakes me thus! Pish!

25 *abroad* in the world
27 *voluntary dotage* willing infatuation
28 *Convincèd or supplied* overcome or grati-
fied sexually
38–9 *First to be hanged and then to confess!*
This impossibility indicates Othello's
hopeless confusion of mind.
40 *shadowing* foreshadowing, darkening
40–41 *without some instruction* if there
were no basis of fact
41 *shakes* shake

Noses, ears, and lips! Is't possible? – Confess? Handkerchief! O devil!

> *He falls*

IAGO

Work on,
My medicine, work! Thus credulous fools are caught,
And many worthy and chaste dames even thus,
All guiltless, meet reproach. What ho, my lord!
My lord, I say! Othello!

> *Enter Cassio*

How now, Cassio!

CASSIO

What's the matter?

IAGO

50   My lord is fallen into an epilepsy.
This is his second fit: he had one yesterday.

CASSIO

Rub him about the temples.

IAGO   No, forbear.
The lethargy must have his quiet course.
If not, he foams at mouth; and by and by
Breaks out to savage madness. Look, he stirs.
Do you withdraw yourself a little while:
He will recover straight. When he is gone,
I would on great occasion speak with you.

> *Exit Cassio*

How is it, General? Have you not hurt your head?

OTHELLO

Dost thou mock me?

60   IAGO   I mock you? No, by heaven!

---

42 *Noses, ears, and lips.* Othello is thinking of the supposed love-making between Cassio and Desdemona.

50–51 *epilepsy.* | *This is his second fit* (poss-
ibly an invention)

53 *lethargy* unconsciousness

58 *on great occasion* on an important
matter

60 *mock.* Othello thinks Iago is referring
to the cuckold's horns.

Would you would bear your fortune like a man!

OTHELLO

A hornèd man's a monster and a beast.

IAGO

There's many a beast then in a populous city,
And many a civil monster.

OTHELLO

Did he confess it?

IAGO   Good sir, be a man.
Think every bearded fellow that's but yoked
May draw with you. There's millions now alive
That nightly lie in those unproper beds
Which they dare swear peculiar. Your case is better.
O, 'tis the spite of hell, the fiend's arch-mock,   70
To lip a wanton in a secure couch,
And to suppose her chaste! No, let me know;
And knowing what I am, I know what shall be.

OTHELLO

O, thou art wise, 'tis certain.

IAGO   Stand you awhile apart;
Confine yourself but in a patient list.
Whilst you were here, o'erwhelmèd with your grief –
A passion most unsuiting such a man –
Cassio came hither. I shifted him away
And laid good scuse upon your ecstasy;
Bade him anon return and here speak with me,   80
The which he promised. Do but encave yourself,
And mark the fleers, the gibes, and notable scorns
That dwell in every region of his face.

64 *civil* civilized
67 *May draw with you* (as though they were horned cattle)
68 *unproper* shared with a lover
69 *peculiar* their own alone
71 *lip* kiss
   secure free from suspicion
73 *what I am* (that is, a cuckold)

what shall be what will be my action (see An Account of the Text, p. 354)
75 *a patient list* bounds of patience
79 *ecstasy* fit
81 *encave* hide
82 *fleers* sneers

For I will make him tell the tale anew,
Where, how, how oft, how long ago, and when
He hath, and is again, to cope your wife.
I say, but mark his gestures. Marry, patience!
Or I shall say you're all in all in spleen
And nothing of a man.

OTHELLO   Dost thou hear, Iago?
90   I will be found most cunning in my patience,
But – dost thou hear? – most bloody.

IAGO   That's not amiss,
But yet keep time in all. Will you withdraw?

                              Othello retires

Now will I question Cassio of Bianca,
A housewife, that by selling her desires
Buys herself bread and clothes. It is a creature
That dotes on Cassio – as 'tis the strumpet's plague
To beguile many and be beguiled by one.
He, when he hears of her, cannot refrain
From the excess of laughter. Here he comes.

              Enter Cassio

100   As he shall smile, Othello shall go mad;
And his unbookish jealousy must construe
Poor Cassio's smiles, gestures, and light behaviour
Quite in the wrong. How do you now, Lieutenant?

CASSIO
The worser that you give me the addition
Whose want even kills me.

IAGO
Ply Desdemona well and you are sure on't.
Now if this suit lay in Bianca's power,

---

86 *cope* meet (with a sexual undertone)
88 *all in all in spleen* quite transformed
    by passion
92 *keep time* be restrained

94 *housewife* (pronounced 'huzif') hussy
101 *unbookish* ignorant
104 *addition* title

How quickly should you speed!

CASSIO   Alas, poor caitiff!

OTHELLO

(*aside*) Look, how he laughs already!

IAGO

I never knew a woman love man so.   110

CASSIO

Alas, poor rogue! I think i'faith she loves me.

OTHELLO

(*aside*) Now he denies it faintly, and laughs it out.

IAGO

Do you hear, Cassio?

OTHELLO

(*aside*) Now he importunes him to tell it o'er.

Go to, well said, well said!

IAGO

She gives it out that you shall marry her.

Do you intend it?

CASSIO

Ha, ha, ha!

OTHELLO

(*aside*) Do you triumph, Roman? Do you triumph?

CASSIO I marry her! What! A customer! Prithee bear some   120
charity to my wit: do not think it so unwholesome. Ha,
ha, ha!

OTHELLO (*aside*) So, so, so, so: they laugh that win.

IAGO Faith, the cry goes that you shall marry her.

CASSIO Prithee, say true.

IAGO I am a very villain else.

OTHELLO (*aside*) Have you scored me? Well.

CASSIO This is the monkey's own giving out. She is

---

108 *caitiff* wretch   120 *customer* harlot
119 *Roman* (referring to Roman tri-   127 *scored* branded
umphs)

persuaded I will marry her out of her own love and
130 flattery, not out of my promise.

OTHELLO (*aside*) Iago beckons me. Now he begins the
story.

CASSIO She was here even now. She haunts me in every
place. I was the other day talking on the sea-bank with
certain Venetians, and thither comes the bauble and, by
this hand, falls me thus about my neck.

OTHELLO (*aside*) Crying 'O dear Cassio!' as it were. His
gesture imports it.

CASSIO So hangs and lolls and weeps upon me, so hales
140 and pulls me. Ha, ha, ha!

OTHELLO (*aside*) Now he tells how she plucked him to
my chamber. O, I see that nose of yours, but not that
dog I shall throw it to!

CASSIO Well, I must leave her company.

IAGO Before me! Look where she comes.

CASSIO 'Tis such another fitchew! Marry, a perfumed one!
   Enter Bianca

What do you mean by this haunting of me?

BIANCA Let the devil and his dam haunt you! What did
you mean by that same handkerchief you gave me even
150 now? I was a fine fool to take it. I must take out the
work! A likely piece of work, that you should find it in
your chamber, and not know who left it there! This is
some minx's token, and I must take out the work?
There, give it your hobby-horse, wheresoever you had
it. I'll take out no work on't.

---

134 *sea-bank* sea-shore
135 *bauble* plaything
142–3 *but not that dog I shall throw it to!*
   (when he has cut it off)
146 *such another.* This does not imply
   that Cassio fails to recognize Bianca;
   it is merely an idiomatic way of referring to a person one knows only too
   well. Pandarus, commenting on

Cressida's bawdy talk in *Troilus and
Cressida*, says 'You are such another!'
fitchew polecat, strumpet
(stage direction) The arrival of Bianca
   with the handkerchief is a stroke of
   luck which Iago turns to good
   account.
154 *hobby-horse* harlot

CASSIO How now, my sweet Bianca! How now, how now!

OTHELLO (*aside*) By heaven, that should be my handkerchief!

BIANCA If you'll come to supper tonight, you may. If you will not, come when you are next prepared for.   *Exit*   160

IAGO After her, after her!

CASSIO Faith I must: she'll rail in the street else.

IAGO Will you sup there?

CASSIO Faith, I intend to.

IAGO Well, I may chance to see you: for I would very fain speak with you.

CASSIO Prithee come, will you?

IAGO Go to! Say no more.   *Exit Cassio*

OTHELLO (*coming forward*) How shall I murder him, Iago?

IAGO Did you perceive how he laughed at his vice?   170

OTHELLO O, Iago!

IAGO And did you see the handkerchief?

OTHELLO Was that mine?

IAGO Yours, by this hand! And to see how he prizes the foolish woman your wife: she gave it him, and he hath giv'n it his whore.

OTHELLO I would have him nine years a-killing! – A fine woman, a fair woman, a sweet woman!

IAGO Nay, you must forget that.

OTHELLO Ay, let her rot and perish, and be damned   180 tonight, for she shall not live! No, my heart is turned to stone: I strike it, and it hurts my hand. – O, the world hath not a sweeter creature! She might lie by an emperor's side and command him tasks.

IAGO Nay, that's not your way.

OTHELLO Hang her! I do but say what she is: so delicate

169–211 *How shall I murder him, Iago? ... You shall hear more by midnight.* This dialogue brings out the conflict between love and jealousy in Othello's mind, 'the struggle not to love her' (Coleridge).

with her needle, an admirable musician! O, she will sing
the savageness out of a bear! Of so high and plenteous
wit and invention!

190 IAGO She's the worse for all this.

OTHELLO O, a thousand, thousand times! – And then of
so gentle a condition.

IAGO Ay, too gentle.

OTHELLO Nay, that's certain – but yet the pity of it, Iago!
O, Iago, the pity of it, Iago!

IAGO If you are so fond over her iniquity, give her patent
to offend, for if it touch not you, it comes near nobody.

OTHELLO I will chop her into messes! Cuckold me!

200 IAGO O, 'tis foul in her!

OTHELLO With mine officer!

IAGO That's fouler.

OTHELLO Get me some poison, Iago, this night. I'll not
expostulate with her, lest her body and beauty unprovide
my mind again – this night, Iago.

IAGO Do it not with poison; strangle her in her bed, even
the bed she hath contaminated.

OTHELLO Good, good! The justice of it pleases; very
good!

210 IAGO And for Cassio, let me be his undertaker. You shall
hear more by midnight.

OTHELLO
Excellent good!

Trumpet sounds
                    What trumpet is that same?

IAGO
I warrant, something from Venice.

Enter Lodovico, Desdemona, and attendants
                              'Tis Lodovico,

---

199 *messes* pieces of meat   210 *be his undertaker* deal with him
204 *unprovide* make reluctant

Come from the Duke; and see your wife is with him.

LODOVICO

God save you, worthy General!

OTHELLO   With all my heart, sir.

LODOVICO

The Duke and Senators of Venice greet you.
          He gives him a letter

OTHELLO

I kiss the instrument of their pleasures.
          He reads the letter

DESDEMONA

And what's the news, good cousin Lodovico?

IAGO

I am very glad to see you, signor:
Welcome to Cyprus.   220

LODOVICO

I thank you. How does Lieutenant Cassio?

IAGO

Lives, sir.

DESDEMONA

Cousin, there's fallen between him and my lord
An unkind breach; but you shall make all well.

OTHELLO

Are you sure of that?

DESDEMONA

My lord?

OTHELLO

'This fail you not to do, as you will' –

LODOVICO

He did not call: he's busy in the paper.
Is there division 'twixt my lord and Cassio?

DESDEMONA

A most unhappy one; I would do much   230
T'atone them, for the love I bear to Cassio.

OTHELLO

Fire and brimstone!

DESDEMONA
  My lord?

OTHELLO
  Are you wise?

DESDEMONA
  What, is he angry?

LODOVICO   Maybe the letter moved him.
  For, as I think, they do command him home,
  Deputing Cassio in his government.

DESDEMONA
  By my troth, I am glad on't.

OTHELLO   Indeed!

DESDEMONA   My lord?

OTHELLO
  I am glad to see you mad.

DESDEMONA   Why, sweet Othello!

OTHELLO
240 Devil!

     He strikes her

DESDEMONA
  I have not deserved this.

LODOVICO
  My lord, this would not be believed in Venice,
  Though I should swear I saw't. 'Tis very much.
  Make her amends; she weeps.

OTHELLO   O devil, devil!
  If that the earth could teem with woman's tears,
  Each drop she falls would prove a crocodile.
  Out of my sight!

DESDEMONA   I will not stay to offend you.

---

238 *on't* of it
239 *I am glad to see you mad* (to rejoice at
  your lover's promotion. But possibly
  'mad' is an abbreviation of 'madam'

and Desdemona is astonished at
Othello's cold politeness.)
245 *teem* be impregnated
246 *falls* let fall

LODOVICO

Truly an obedient lady.

I do beseech your lordship call her back.

OTHELLO

Mistress!   250

DESDEMONA

My lord?

OTHELLO

What would you with her, sir?

LODOVICO

Who? I, my lord?

OTHELLO

Ay, you did wish that I would make her turn.

Sir, she can turn, and turn, and yet go on,

And turn again. And she can weep, sir, weep.

And she's obedient; as you say, obedient,

Very obedient – proceed you in your tears –

Concerning this, sir – O, well-painted passion! –

I am commanded home – get you away!   260

I'll send for you anon. – Sir, I obey the mandate,

And will return to Venice. – Hence, avaunt!

                                        Exit Desdemona

Cassio shall have my place. And sir, tonight

I do entreat that we may sup together.

You are welcome, sir, to Cyprus. Goats and monkeys!

                                                        Exit

LODOVICO

Is this the noble Moor, whom our full senate

Call all-in-all sufficient? Is this the nature

Whom passion could not shake? Whose solid virtue

252–6 *What would you with her . . . And*   259 *passion* grief
turn again. Othello is pretending that   265 *Goats and monkeys!* Compare
Desdemona is a harlot and Lodovico   III.3.400.
a potential client.

The shot of accident nor dart of chance
Could neither graze nor pierce?

270 IAGO   He is much changed.

LODOVICO
Are his wits safe? Is he not light of brain?

IAGO
He's that he is: I may not breathe my censure
What he might be. If what he might he is not,
I would to heaven he were.

LODOVICO   What! Strike his wife!

IAGO
Faith, that was not so well: yet would I knew
That stroke would prove the worst!

LODOVICO   Is it his use?
Or did the letters work upon his blood
And new-create this fault?

IAGO   Alas, alas!
It is not honesty in me to speak
280   What I have seen and known. You shall observe him,
And his own courses will denote him so,
That I may save my speech. Do but go after,
And mark how he continues.

LODOVICO
I am sorry that I am deceived in him.

Enter Othello and Emilia

IV.2 OTHELLO
You have seen nothing then?

269 *accident* fate
272 *censure* judgement
276 *use* custom

IV.2 In this scene Othello treats his wife
as though she were a prostitute and
Emilia as a bawd; but though he accuses
Desdemona of adultery, he does not give
her a chance of defending herself by
naming her supposed lover, her accuser,
or the evidence against her.

EMILIA

Nor ever heard, nor ever did suspect.

OTHELLO

Yes, you have seen Cassio and she together.

EMILIA

But then I saw no harm; and then I heard
Each syllable that breath made up between them.

OTHELLO

What! Did they never whisper?

EMILIA   Never, my lord.

OTHELLO

Nor send you out o'th'way?

EMILIA   Never.

OTHELLO

To fetch her fan, her gloves, her mask, nor nothing?

EMILIA

Never, my lord.

OTHELLO

That's strange.   10

EMILIA

I durst, my lord, to wager she is honest,
Lay down my soul at stake. If you think other,
Remove your thought: it doth abuse your bosom.
If any wretch have put this in your head,
Let heaven requite it with the serpent's curse!
For if she be not honest, chaste, and true,
There's no man happy. The purest of their wives
Is foul as slander.

OTHELLO   Bid her come hither: go!

Exit Emilia

She says enough; yet she's a simple bawd
That cannot say as much. This is a subtle whore,   20
A closet lock and key of villainous secrets;

20 *whore* (Desdemona)   21 *closet lock and key* concealer

And yet she'll kneel and pray – I have seen her do't.

Enter Desdemona and Emilia

DESDEMONA

My lord, what is your will?

OTHELLO   Pray, chuck, come hither.

DESDEMONA

What is your pleasure?

OTHELLO   Let me see your eyes.

Look in my face.

DESDEMONA   What horrible fancy's this?

OTHELLO *(to Emilia)*

Some of your function, mistress.

Leave procreants alone and shut the door.

Cough or cry 'hem' if anybody come.

Your mystery, your mystery! Nay, dispatch!

Exit Emilia

DESDEMONA

30   Upon my knees, what doth your speech import?

I understand a fury in your words,

But not the words.

OTHELLO   Why, what art thou?

DESDEMONA

Your wife, my lord; your true and loyal wife.

OTHELLO

Come, swear it; damn thyself;

Lest being like one of heaven, the devils themselves

Should fear to seize thee. Therefore be double-damned:

Swear thou art honest.

DESDEMONA   Heaven doth truly know it.

OTHELLO

Heaven truly knows that thou art false as hell.

---

26 *Some of your function* do your office   29 *mystery* trade (of procuress)
27 *procreants* those engaged in pro-
creation

DESDEMONA

    To whom, my lord? With whom? How am I false?

OTHELLO

    Ah, Desdemon! Away, away, away! 40

DESDEMONA

    Alas, the heavy day! Why do you weep?
    Am I the motive of these tears my lord?
    If haply you my father do suspect
    An instrument of this your calling back,
    Lay not your blame on me. If you have lost him,
    I have lost him too.

OTHELLO   Had it pleased heaven
    To try me with affliction, had they rained
    All kind of sores and shames on my bare head,
    Steeped me in poverty to the very lips,
    Given to captivity me and my utmost hopes, 50
    I should have found in some place of my soul
    A drop of patience. But alas, to make me
    A fixèd figure for the time of scorn
    To point his slow unmoving finger at!
    Yet could I bear that too, well, very well:
    But there where I have garnered up my heart,
    Where either I must live, or bear no life,
    The fountain from the which my current runs,
    Or else dries up – to be discarded thence
    Or keep it as a cistern for foul toads 60
    To knot and gender in! Turn thy complexion there,

42 *motive* cause
46–7 *heaven . . . they.* Shakespeare possibly wrote 'God . . . he'. See An Account of the Text, p. 351.
53–4 *A fixèd figure for the time of scorn | To point his slow unmoving finger at!* Othello thinks of himself as an object of mockery, pointed at by the scornful time, as the figure on a clock or dial is pointed at by the hand, which moves so slowly that it seems not to move at all.
56 *garnered* stored
61 *gender* engender
    Turn thy complexion change colour

Patience, thou young and rose-lipped cherubin,
Ay, there look grim as hell!

DESDEMONA

I hope my noble lord esteems me honest.

OTHELLO

O, ay! As summer flies are in the shambles,
That quicken even with blowing, O, thou weed,
Who art so lovely fair, and smell'st so sweet
That the sense aches at thee, would thou hadst ne'er
   been born!

DESDEMONA

Alas, what ignorant sin have I committed?

OTHELLO

70 Was this fair paper, this most goodly book,
Made to write 'whore' upon? What committed!
Committed? O, thou public commoner!
I should make very forges of my cheeks,
That would to cinders burn up modesty,
Did I but speak thy deeds. What committed?
Heaven stops the nose at it, and the moon winks;
The bawdy wind, that kisses all it meets,
Is hushed within the hollow mine of earth
And will not hear it. What committed?
Impudent strumpet!

80 DESDEMONA   By heaven, you do me wrong.

OTHELLO

Are you not a strumpet?

DESDEMONA   No, as I am a Christian.
If to preserve this vessel for my lord

---

64 *honest* chaste
65 *shambles* butchers' slaughter-house
66 *quicken* receive life
72 *commoner* whore
76 *moon* (symbolizing chastity)
 winks shuts her eyes

82 *vessel* body. Compare 1 Thessalonians 4.3–4: 'that ye should abstain from fornication: That every one of you should know how to possess his vessel in holiness and honour.'

From any other foul unlawful touch,
Be not to be a strumpet, I am none.

OTHELLO
What! Not a whore?

DESDEMONA   No, as I shall be saved.

OTHELLO
Is't possible?

DESDEMONA
O, heaven forgive us!

OTHELLO   I cry you mercy then:
I took you for that cunning whore of Venice
That married with Othello. (*Calling*) You, mistress,
That have the office opposite to Saint Peter   90
And keep the gate of hell!
        Enter Emilia
                        You, you, ay, you!
We have done our course: there's money for your pains.
I pray you turn the key, and keep our counsel.   *Exit*

EMILIA
Alas, what does this gentleman conceive?
How do you, madam? How do you, my good lady?

DESDEMONA
Faith, half asleep.

EMILIA
Good madam, what's the matter with my lord?

DESDEMONA
With who?

EMILIA
Why, with my lord, madam.

DESDEMONA
Who is thy lord?

EMILIA   He that is yours, sweet lady.   100

83 *other* of another man   87 *I cry you mercy* I beg your pardon

DESDEMONA
> I have none. Do not talk to me, Emilia:
> I cannot weep; nor answers have I none,
> But what should go by water. Prithee tonight
> Lay on my bed my wedding sheets, remember,
> And call thy husband hither.

EMILIA   Here's a change indeed!
>   *Exit*

DESDEMONA
> 'Tis meet I should be used so, very meet.
> How have I been behaved, that he might stick
> The smallest opinion on my least misuse?
>> *Enter Emilia and Iago*

IAGO
> What is your pleasure, madam? How is't with you?

DESDEMONA
110 > I cannot tell: those that do teach young babes
> Do it with gentle means and easy tasks:
> He might have chid me so, for, in good faith,
> I am a child to chiding.

IAGO   What is the matter, lady?

EMILIA
> Alas, Iago, my lord hath so bewhored her,
> Thrown such despite and heavy terms upon her
> As true heart cannot bear.

DESDEMONA
> Am I that name, Iago?

IAGO   What name, fair lady?

DESDEMONA
> Such as she said my lord did say I was.

---

103 *water* (tears)
107–8 *stick* | *The smallest opinion on my
least misuse* have the least suspicion
of my least misbehaviour (Q reads

'greatest abuse': perhaps Shakespeare
wrote 'worst misuse')
113 *I am a child to chiding* I have had
little experience of chiding

EMILIA

He called her whore: a beggar in his drink
Could not have laid such terms upon his callet.   120

IAGO

Why did he so?

DESDEMONA

I do not know: I am sure I am none such.

IAGO

Do not weep, do not weep. Alas the day!

EMILIA

Hath she forsook so many noble matches,
Her father, and her country, all her friends,
To be called whore? Would it not make one weep?

DESDEMONA

It is my wretched fortune.

IAGO   Beshrew him for't!
How comes this trick upon him?

DESDEMONA   Nay, heaven doth know.

EMILIA

I will be hanged if some eternal villain,
Some busy and insinuating rogue,   130
Some cogging, cozening slave, to get some office,
Have not devised this slander; I'll be hanged else.

IAGO

Fie, there is no such man! It is impossible.

DESDEMONA

If any such there be, heaven pardon him.

EMILIA

A halter pardon him and hell gnaw his bones!
Why should he call her whore? Who keeps her company?
What place, what time, what form, what likelihood?
The Moor's abused by some most villainous knave,

120 *callet* drab
128 *trick* whim, delusion
131 *cogging* deceiving

to get some office. But Emilia does not
suspect Iago.
137 *form* appearance

Some base notorious knave, some scurvy fellow.
140   O heaven, that such companions thou'dst unfold,
And put in every honest hand a whip
To lash the rascals naked through the world,
Even from the east to th'west!

IAGO   Speak within door.

EMILIA
O fie upon them! Some such squire he was
That turned your wit the seamy side without
And made you to suspect me with the Moor.

IAGO
You are a fool, go to.

DESDEMONA   O good Iago,
What shall I do to win my lord again?
Good friend, go to him; for, by this light of heaven,
150   I know not how I lost him. Here I kneel:
If e'er my will did trespass 'gainst his love,
Either in discourse of thought or actual deed;
Or that mine eyes, mine ears, or any sense
Delighted them in any other form;
Or that I do not yet, and ever did,
And ever will – though he do shake me off
To beggarly divorcement – love him dearly,
Comfort forswear me! Unkindness may do much,
And his unkindness may defeat my life,
160   But never taint my love. I cannot say 'whore':
It does abhor me now I speak the word;
To do the act that might the addition earn
Not the world's mass of vanity could make me.

---

140 *companions* fellows
143 *within door* less loudly
144 *squire* fellow
146 *suspect me with the Moor.* Compare
    II.1.286.
147 *go to.* This is an expression with a

variety of meanings, here 'be quiet'.
152 *discourse* course
154 *Delighted them* took delight
155 *yet* still
159 *defeat* destroy
162 *addition* title

IAGO

I pray you, be content: 'tis but his humour;
The business of the state does him offence,
And he does chide with you.

DESDEMONA

If 'twere no other —

IAGO   It is so, I warrant.

Hark how these instruments summon to supper!
The messengers of Venice stay the meat.
Go in, and weep not; all things shall be well.   170

Exeunt Desdemona and Emilia

Enter Roderigo

How now, Roderigo?

RODERIGO I do not find that thou deal'st justly with
me.

IAGO What in the contrary?

RODERIGO Every day thou daff'st me with some device,
Iago, and rather, as it seems to me now, keep'st from me
all conveniency, than suppliest me with the least advantage of hope. I will indeed no longer endure it. Nor
am I yet persuaded to put up in peace what already I
have foolishly suffered.   180

IAGO Will you hear me, Roderigo?

RODERIGO Faith, I have heard too much; for your words
and performances are no kin together.

IAGO You charge me most unjustly.

RODERIGO With naught but truth. I have wasted myself
out of my means. The jewels you have had from me to
deliver to Desdemona would half have corrupted a
votarist. You have told me she hath received them, and
returned me expectations and comforts of sudden respect

---

170 (stage direction) *Enter Roderigo*. On   175 *daff'st* dost put me off
Shakespeare's unlocalized stage, it   177 *conveniency* opportunity
would not seem that Roderigo had   188 *votarist* a nun, vowed to chastity
sought out Iago in a private room of   189 *sudden respect* immediate notice
the castle.

190   and acquaintance, but I find none.

IAGO Well, go to; very well.

RODERIGO Very well, go to! I cannot go to, man, nor 'tis
not very well. Nay, I think it is scurvy and begin to
find myself fopped in it.

IAGO Very well.

RODERIGO I tell you, 'tis not very well. I will make myself
known to Desdemona. If she will return me my jewels,
I will give over my suit and repent my unlawful solicita-
tion. If not, assure yourself I will seek satisfaction of
200   you.

IAGO You have said now.

RODERIGO Ay, and said nothing but what I protest
intendment of doing.

IAGO Why, now I see there's mettle in thee; and even from
this instant do build on thee a better opinion than ever
before. Give me thy hand, Roderigo. Thou hast taken
against me a most just exception; but yet I protest I have
dealt most directly in thy affair.

RODERIGO It hath not appeared.

210   IAGO I grant indeed it hath not appeared; and your suspicion is not without wit and judgement. But, Roderigo,
if thou hast that in thee indeed, which I have greater
reason to believe now than ever – I mean purpose, courage, and valour – this night show it. If thou the next
night following enjoy not Desdemona, take me from
this world with treachery, and devise engines for my life.

RODERIGO Well, what is it? Is it within reason and
compass?

IAGO Sir, there is especial commission come from Venice
220   to depute Cassio in Othello's place.

191–2 *go to*. See note to IV.2.147. Iago's
use of the expression is probably
accompanied by an obscene gesture.
Roderigo means he cannot have

sexual intercourse with Desdemona.
194 *fopped* duped
203 *intendment* intention
216 *engines for* plots against

RODERIGO Is that true? Why, then Othello and Desdemona return again to Venice.

IAGO O, no: he goes into Mauritania and takes away with him the fair Desdemona, unless his abode be lingered here by some accident: wherein none can be so determinate as the removing of Cassio.

RODERIGO How do you mean 'removing' of him?

IAGO Why, by making him uncapable of Othello's place – knocking out his brains.

RODERIGO And that you would have me to do?   230

IAGO Ay, if you dare do yourself a profit and a right. He sups tonight with a harlotry; and thither will I go to him. He knows not yet of his honourable fortune. If you will watch his going thence – which I will fashion to fall out between twelve and one – you may take him at your pleasure. I will be near to second your attempt, and he shall fall between us. Come, stand not amazed at it, but go along with me. I will show you such a necessity in his death that you shall think yourself bound to put it on him. It is now high supper-time and   240 the night grows to waste. About it!

RODERIGO I will hear further reason for this.

IAGO And you shall be satisfied.   *Exeunt*

Enter Othello, Lodovico, Desdemona, Emilia, and   IV.3
attendants

LODOVICO
I do beseech you, sir, trouble yourself no further.

225–6 *determinate* conclusive
232 *harlotry* harlot
240 *high* fully

IV.3 Now the time of Desdemona's murder approaches Othello has recov-

ered his self-control. The song is omitted from the Q text probably because the boy who played Desdemona could no longer sing. But some critics think the song was added later.

OTHELLO

O, pardon me: 'twill do me good to walk.

LODOVICO

Madam, good night. I humbly thank your ladyship.

DESDEMONA

Your honour is most welcome.

OTHELLO   Will you walk, sir?

O, Desdemona!

DESDEMONA

My lord?

OTHELLO   Get you to bed on th'instant. I will be returned
forthwith. Dismiss your attendant there. Look't be done.

DESDEMONA   I will, my lord.

                   Exeunt Othello, Lodovico, and attendants

EMILIA

10   How goes it now? He looks gentler than he did.

DESDEMONA

He says he will return incontinent.

He hath commanded me to go to bed,

And bade me to dismiss you.

EMILIA   Dismiss me?

DESDEMONA

It was his bidding: therefore, good Emilia,

Give me my nightly wearing, and adieu.

We must not now displease him.

EMILIA

I would you had never seen him.

DESDEMONA

So would not I: my love doth so approve him

That even his stubbornness, his checks, his frowns –

20   Prithee, unpin me – have grace and favour in them.

EMILIA

I have laid those sheets, you bade me, on the bed.

---

11 *incontinent* forthwith   19 *checks* rebukes

DESDEMONA
　All's one. Good faith, how foolish are our minds!
　If I do die before thee, prithee shroud me
　In one of those same sheets.

EMILIA　　　　　　　　　　　Come, come, you talk.

DESDEMONA
　My mother had a maid called Barbary:
　She was in love: and he she loved proved mad
　And did forsake her. She had a song of willow;
　An old thing 'twas; but it expressed her fortune,
　And she died singing it. That song tonight
　Will not go from my mind: I have much to do　　　　30
　But to go hang my head all at one side,
　And sing it like poor Barbary – prithee, dispatch.

EMILIA
　Shall I go fetch your night-gown?

DESDEMONA　　　　　　　　　　No, unpin me here.
　This Lodovico is a proper man.

EMILIA
　A very handsome man.

DESDEMONA　　　　　He speaks well.

EMILIA　I know a lady in Venice would have walked bare-
　foot to Palestine for a touch of his nether lip.

DESDEMONA (*sings*)
　　The poor soul sat sighing by a sycamore tree,
　　　Sing all a green willow;
　　Her hand on her bosom, her head on her knee,　　　40
　　　Sing willow, willow, willow;
　　The fresh streams ran by her and murmured her moans;

22 *All's one* all right
26 *mad* faithless
30–31 *I have much to do* | *But* I find it
　difficult not
33 *night-gown* dressing-gown
34 *proper* handsome
38–54 *The poor soul sat sighing . . . you'll*

couch with moe men. This is adapted
from an old song in which the forsaken lover is a man. See The Songs,
p. 359.
38 *sycamore* fig mulberry (not the modern sycamore)
39 *willow* (an emblem of forsaken love)

       Sing willow, willow, willow;
      Her salt tears fell from her and softened the stones –
         (*She speaks*)
Lay by these.
         (*She sings*)
      Sing willow, willow, willow
         (*She speaks*)
Prithee hie thee; he'll come anon.
         (*She sings*)
      Sing all a green willow must be my garland.
      Let nobody blame him; his scorn I approve –
         (*She speaks*)

50   Nay, that's not next. Hark, who is't that knocks?

EMILIA It's the wind.

DESDEMONA (*Sings*)
      I called my love false love, but what said he then?
        Sing willow, willow, willow:
      If I court moe women, you'll couch with moe men.
         (*She speaks*)
      So get thee gone; good night. Mine eyes do itch:
      Does that bode weeping?

EMILIA   'Tis neither here nor there.

DESDEMONA
      I have heard it said so. O, these men, these men!
      Dost thou in conscience think – tell me, Emilia –
      That there be women do abuse their husbands
      In such gross kind?

60 EMILIA   There be some such, no question.

DESDEMONA
      Wouldst thou do such a deed for all the world?

---

45 *these* (necklace, jewels or other ornaments)
54 *moe* more
58–104 *Dost thou in conscience think ... but by bad mend!* This dialogue brings out the difference between Desdemona's innocence and idealism and Emilia's worldly-wise cynicism and realism.

EMILIA
Why, would not you?

DESDEMONA   No, by this heavenly light.

EMILIA Nor I neither by this heavenly light: I might do't
as well i'th'dark.

DESDEMONA Wouldst thou do such a deed for all the
world?

EMILIA The world's a huge thing: it is a great price for a
small vice.

DESDEMONA In troth, I think thou wouldst not.

EMILIA In troth I think I should, and undo't when I had   70
done it. Marry, I would not do such a thing for a joint
ring, nor for measures of lawn, nor for gowns, petticoats,
nor caps, nor any petty exhibition. But for all the whole
world! Ud's pity, who would not make her husband a
cuckold, to make him a monarch? I should venture
purgatory for't.

DESDEMONA Beshrew me, if I would do such a wrong for
the whole world!

EMILIA Why, the wrong is but a wrong i'th'world; and
having the world for your labour, 'tis a wrong in your   80
own world, and you might quickly make it right.

DESDEMONA I do not think there is any such woman.

EMILIA Yes, a dozen: and as many to th'vantage as would
store the world they played for.
But I do think it is their husbands' faults
If wives do fall. Say that they slack their duties,

---

62 *heavenly light* the moon
67–8 *it is a great price for a small vice.* The
  rhyme suggests that it is meant to be
  a quotation.
71–2 *joint ring* ring made in two separate
  parts
73 *exhibition* gift, allowance
74 *Ud's* God's

83 *to th'vantage* in addition
84 *store* populate
85 *But I do think it is their husbands' faults.*
  Emilia, who has been speaking in
  prose, now drops into verse, to give
  her words a kind of choric tone.
86 *duties.* Emilia is probably referring to
  sexual duties and to Iago.

And pour our treasures into foreign laps;
Or else break out in peevish jealousies,
Throwing restraint upon us; or say they strike us,
90   Or scant our former having in despite –
Why, we have galls, and though we have some grace,
Yet have we some revenge. Let husbands know
Their wives have sense like them: they see and smell,
And have their palates both for sweet and sour
As husbands have. What is it that they do,
When they change us for others? Is it sport?
I think it is. And doth affection breed it?
I think it doth. Is't frailty that thus errs?
It is so too. And have not we affections,
100   Desires for sport, and frailty, as men have?
Then let them use us well: else let them know
The ills we do, their ills instruct us so.

DESDEMONA
Good night, good night. God me such uses send,
Not to pick bad from bad, but by bad mend!   *Exeunt*

V.I   *Enter Iago and Roderigo*
   IAGO
Here, stand behind this bulk: straight will he come.
Wear thy good rapier bare, and put it home.

---

87 *foreign* other than their wives'
88 *peevish jealousies.* This could refer to
    Iago or Othello.
90 *having* allowance
    in despite out of spite
91 *galls* spirits to resent
103 *uses* habits
104 *Not to pick bad from bad, but by bad
    mend* not to get worse through evil
    chance or suffering but to learn from
    it

v.i. Iago, characteristically, gets Roderigo to attack Cassio, though he has
to intervene himself; but he fails to kill
either Cassio or Roderigo. Even without
Emilia's evidence he would be ruined.
1 *bulk* projecting part of building. On
    the Elizabethan stage Roderigo
    would hide behind the pillar support-
    ing the canopy.
2 *bare* unsheathed

Quick, quick; fear nothing: I'll be at thy elbow.
It makes us, or it mars us; think on that,
And fix most firm thy resolution.

RODERIGO

Be near at hand; I may miscarry in't.

IAGO

Here, at thy hand: be bold, and take thy stand.

He retires

RODERIGO

I have no great devotion to the deed,
And yet he hath given me satisfying reasons.
'Tis but a man gone. Forth my sword! He dies!   10

IAGO

I have rubbed this young quat almost to the sense,
And he grows angry. Now, whether he kill Cassio,
Or Cassio him, or each do kill the other,
Every way makes my gain. Live Roderigo,
He calls me to a restitution large
Of gold and jewels, that I bobbed from him
As gifts to Desdemona.
It must not be. If Cassio do remain
He hath a daily beauty in his life
That makes me ugly: and besides, the Moor   20
May unfold me to him – there stand I in much peril.
No, he must die. But soft, I hear him coming.

Enter Cassio

RODERIGO

I know his gait; 'tis he. Villain, thou diest!

---

5 *resolution* (pronounced with five syllables)

10 *'Tis but a man gone.* Roderigo is quoting Iago.
Forth my sword! He dies! He is rehearsing the murder in his mind.

11 *I have rubbed this young quat almost to the sense* I have rubbed this pimple almost to the quick

16 *bobbed* swindled

19–20 *He hath a daily beauty in his life | That makes me ugly.* Cassio is handsome and popular. It is significant that Iago should confess that his envy is a more important motive than the danger that Othello would have it out with Cassio.

CASSIO

That thrust had been mine enemy indeed,
But that my coat is better than thou think'st.
I will make proof of thine.

He wounds Roderigo

RODERIGO   O, I am slain!

Iago wounds Cassio in the leg, and exit

CASSIO

I am maimed for ever. Help, ho! Murder, murder!

Enter Othello, above

OTHELLO

The voice of Cassio: Iago keeps his word.

RODERIGO

O, villain that I am!

OTHELLO   It is even so.

CASSIO

30   O, help, ho! Light! A surgeon!

OTHELLO

'Tis he! O brave Iago, honest and just,
That hast such noble sense of thy friend's wrong,
Thou teachest me! Minion, your dear lies dead,
And your unblest fate hies. Strumpet, I come!
Forth of my heart those charms, thine eyes, are blotted;
Thy bed, lust-stained, shall with lust's blood be spotted.

Exit Othello

Enter Lodovico and Gratiano

25 *coat* (coat of mail, or leather jerkin)
27 (stage direction) *above* on the balcony
29 *It is even so.* Othello either mistakes
    Roderigo's voice for Cassio's and
    agrees that he is a villian, or else he
    continues his previous speech.
34-6 *And your unblest fate hies ... with
    lust's blood be spotted.* Neither F nor

Q is satisfactory and some critics
think the lines were interpolated. It
is odd that Othello should speak of
'lust's blood' when he has decided to
strangle or smother Desdemona.
36 (stage direction) *Enter Lodovico and
    Gratiano.* Gratiano has just arrived
    with news of Brabantio's death.

CASSIO

What, ho! No watch? No passage? Murder, murder!

GRATIANO

'Tis some mischance: the cry is very direful.

CASSIO

O, help!

LODOVICO

Hark!   40

RODERIGO

O wretched villain!

LODOVICO

Two or three groan. It is a heavy night.

These may be counterfeits. Let's think't unsafe

To come in to the cry without more help.

RODERIGO

Nobody come? Then shall I bleed to death.

LODOVICO

Hark!

     Enter Iago, with a light

GRATIANO

Here's one comes in his shirt, with light and weapons.

IAGO

Who's there? Whose noise is this that cries on murder?

LODOVICO

We do not know.

IAGO   Did you not hear a cry?

CASSIO

Here, here: for heaven's sake help me!

IAGO   What's the matter?   50

GRATIANO

This is Othello's Ancient, as I take it.

LODOVICO

The same indeed, a very valiant fellow.

---

37 *passage* passers-by   44 *come in to* approach
42 *heavy* gloomy, dark

IAGO

What are you here, that cry so grievously?

CASSIO

Iago? O, I am spoiled, undone by villains!
Give me some help.

IAGO

O me, Lieutenant! What villains have done this?

CASSIO

I think that one of them is hereabout
And cannot make away.

IAGO   O treacherous villains!
What are you there? Come in, and give some help.

RODERIGO

60   O, help me here!

CASSIO

That's one of them.

IAGO   O murd'rous slave! O villain!
He stabs Roderigo

RODERIGO

O damned Iago! O inhuman dog!
He faints

IAGO

Kill men i'th'dark? Where be these bloody thieves?
How silent is this town! Ho, murder, murder!
Lodovico and Gratiano come forward
What may you be? Are you of good or evil?

LODOVICO

As you shall prove us, praise us.

IAGO

Signor Lodovico?

LODOVICO

He, sir.

IAGO

I cry you mercy. Here's Cassio hurt by villains.

69 *I cry you mercy* pardon me

GRATIANO
　Cassio?　　　　　　　　　　　　　　　　　　　　　　　70

IAGO
　How is't, brother?

CASSIO
　My leg is cut in two.

IAGO　　　　　　　　　Marry, heaven forbid!
　Light, gentlemen. I'll bind it with my shirt.
　　　　Enter Bianca

BIANCA
　What is the matter, ho? Who is't that cried?

IAGO
　Who is't that cried?

BIANCA
　O, my dear Cassio, my sweet Cassio,
　O Cassio, Cassio, Cassio!

IAGO
　O notable strumpet! Cassio, may you suspect
　Who they should be that have thus mangled you?

CASSIO
　No.　　　　　　　　　　　　　　　　　　　　　　　80

GRATIANO
　I am sorry to find you thus: I have been to seek you.

IAGO
　Lend me a garter: so. O, for a chair
　To bear him easily hence!

BIANCA　　　　　　　　　Alas, he faints!
　O Cassio, Cassio, Cassio!

IAGO
　Gentlemen all, I do suspect this trash
　To be a party in this injury.
　Patience awhile, good Cassio. Come, come,
　Lend me a light. Know we this face or no?
　Alas, my friend, and my dear countryman
　Roderigo? No – yes, sure – O heaven, Roderigo!　　90

GRATIANO
　What! Of Venice?

IAGO

Even he, sir. Did you know him?

GRATIANO   Know him? Ay.

IAGO

Signor Gratiano? I cry you gentle pardon.
These bloody accidents must excuse my manners
That so neglected you.

GRATIANO   I am glad to see you.

IAGO

How do you, Cassio? O, a chair, a chair!

GRATIANO

Roderigo!

IAGO

He, he, 'tis he.

Enter attendants with chair

O, that's well said, the chair!
Some good man bear him carefully from hence.
I'll fetch the General's surgeon. For you, mistress,
Save you your labour. He that lies slain here, Cassio,
Was my dear friend. What malice was between you?

CASSIO

None in the world, nor do I know the man.

IAGO

(*to Bianca*) What, look you pale? O, bear him out
o'th'air.

Cassio is borne in. Roderigo's body is removed

Stay you, good gentlemen. Look you pale, mistress?
Do you perceive the gastness of her eye?
Nay, if you stare, we shall hear more anon.
Behold her well; I pray you look upon her.
Do you see, gentlemen? Nay, guiltiness will speak
Though tongues were out of use.

---

98 *that's well said* well done!   Cassio.
101 *Save you your labour*. Bianca is tending   106 *gastness* frightened look

Enter Emilia

EMILIA

'Las, what's the matter? What's the matter, husband?

IAGO

Cassio hath here been set on in the dark

By Roderigo and fellows that are scaped:

He's almost slain and Roderigo quite.

EMILIA

Alas, good gentleman! Alas, good Cassio!

IAGO

This is the fruit of whoring. Prithee, Emilia,

Go know of Cassio where he supped tonight.

What, do you shake at that?

BIANCA

He supped at my house, but I therefore shake not.

IAGO

O, did he so? I charge you go with me.   120

EMILIA

O, fie upon thee, strumpet!

BIANCA

I am no strumpet, but of life as honest

As you that thus abuse me.

EMILIA   As I? Foh! Fie upon thee!

IAGO

Kind gentlemen, let's see poor Cassio dressed.

Come, mistress, you must tell's another tale.

Emilia, run you to the citadel,

And tell my lord and lady what hath happed.

Will you go on afore? (*Aside*) This is the night

That either makes me, or fordoes me quite.   *Exeunt*

122–3 *of life as honest* | *As you that thus*
abuse me. Bianca is perhaps more
honest, in one sense of the word,
than Emilia.   129 *fordoes* undoes

V.2   *Enter Othello, with a light, Desdemona in her bed*

OTHELLO
It is the cause, it is the cause, my soul:
Let me not name it to you, you chaste stars!
It is the cause. Yet I'll not shed her blood,
Nor scar that whiter skin of hers than snow,
And smooth as monumental alabaster:
Yet she must die, else she'll betray more men.
Put out the light, and then put out the light:
If I quench thee, thou flaming minister,
I can again thy former light restore,
10   Should I repent me; but once put out thy light,
Thou cunning'st pattern of excelling nature,
I know not where is that Promethean heat
That can thy light relume. When I have plucked thy
              rose,
I cannot give it vital growth again,
It needs must wither. I'll smell it on the tree.
              He kisses her
O balmy breath, that dost almost persuade
Justice to break her sword! One more, one more.
Be thus when thou art dead and I will kill thee,
And love thee after. One more, and this the last.
20   So sweet was ne'er so fatal. I must weep.

---

v.2 The bed was probably pushed forward from the curtained space under the balcony, as otherwise much of the action would be invisible to part of the audience. It has often been observed that Othello has recovered something of his nobility at the beginning of this scene, but in his 'darkened reason' he believes he is sacrificing his wife to an ideal rather than committing a brutal murder. The actual deed, however, is committed not calmly but in a blind fury when Desdemona weeps for Cassio.

1 *cause* (adultery)

4 *whiter skin of hers than snow* her skin whiter than snow

7 *light . . . light* (1) the torch; (2) Desdemona's life

8 *flaming minister* serviceable torch. Compare Psalm 104.4: 'He maketh his angels spirits and his ministers a flame of fire.'

12 *Promethean*. Prometheus brought fire to men.

13 *relume* relight

But they are cruel tears: this sorrow's heavenly –
It strikes where it doth love. She wakes.

DESDEMONA

Who's there? Othello?

OTHELLO

Ay, Desdemona.

DESDEMONA   Will you come to bed, my lord?

OTHELLO

Have you prayed tonight, Desdemon?

DESDEMONA   Ay, my lord.

OTHELLO

If you bethink yourself of any crime
Unreconciled as yet to heaven and grace,
Solicit for it straight.

DESDEMONA

Alack, my lord, what may you mean by that?

OTHELLO

Well, do it, and be brief; I will walk by: 30
I would not kill thy unprepared spirit;
No – heaven forfend! – I would not kill thy soul.

DESDEMONA

Talk you of killing?

OTHELLO   Ay, I do.

DESDEMONA   Then heaven
Have mercy on me!

OTHELLO   Amen, with all my heart!

DESDEMONA

If you say so, I hope you will not kill me.

OTHELLO

Hum!

DESDEMONA

And yet I fear you: for you're fatal then

22 *It strikes where it doth love.* Compare
Hebrews 12.6: 'For whom the Lord
loveth, he chasteneth.'

When your eyes roll so. Why I should fear I know not,
Since guiltiness I know not; but yet I feel I fear.

OTHELLO

Think on thy sins.

40   DESDEMONA   They are loves I bear to you.

OTHELLO

Ay, and for that thou diest.

DESDEMONA

That death's unnatural that kills for loving.
Alas, why gnaw you so your nether lip?
Some bloody passion shakes your very frame:
These are portènts; but yet I hope, I hope
They do not point on me.

OTHELLO   Peace, and be still!

DESDEMONA

I will – so. What's the matter?

OTHELLO

That handkerchief which I so loved and gave thee,
Thou gav'st to Cassio.

DESDEMONA   No, by my life and soul!
Send for the man and ask him.

50   OTHELLO   Sweet soul, take heed,
Take heed of perjury: thou art on thy death-bed.

DESDEMONA

Ay, but not yet to die.

OTHELLO   Yes, presently.
Therefore confess thee freely of thy sin;
For to deny each article with oath
Cannot remove nor choke the strong conception
That I do groan withal. Thou art to die.

---

38 *When your eyes roll so.* This description
   was probably necessary on the Jacobean stage, where there was no artificial lighting. Compare line 43 below.
40 *They are loves I bear to you* (in deceiving
   her father)

47 *will – so.* There is a pause between
   these two words while Desdemona
   controls herself.
52 *presently* at once
55 *conception* belief

DESDEMONA
Then Lord have mercy on me!

OTHELLO   I say, amen.

DESDEMONA
And have you mercy too! I never did
Offend you in my life; never loved Cassio
But with such general warranty of heaven   60
As I might love. I never gave him token.

OTHELLO
By heaven, I saw my handkerchief in's hand!
O perjured woman! Thou dost stone my heart,
And mak'st me call what I intend to do
A murder, which I thought a sacrifice.
I saw the handkerchief.

DESDEMONA   He found it then.
I never gave it him. Send for him hither.
Let him confess a truth.

OTHELLO   He hath confessed.

DESDEMONA
What, my lord?

OTHELLO
That he hath used thee.

DESDEMONA   How? Unlawfully?   70

OTHELLO
Ay.

DESDEMONA
He will not say so.

OTHELLO   No, his mouth is stopped:
Honest Iago hath ta'en order for't.

DESDEMONA
O, my fear interprets! What, is he dead?

OTHELLO
Had all his hairs been lives, my great revenge

59 *Offend* wrong   73 *ta'en order* taken steps
63 *stone* turn to stone

Had stomach for them all.

DESDEMONA

Alas, he is betrayed, and I undone.

OTHELLO

Out, strumpet! Weep'st thou for him to my face?

DESDEMONA

O banish me, my lord, but kill me not!

OTHELLO

80   Down, strumpet!

DESDEMONA

Kill me tomorrow: let me live tonight!

OTHELLO

Nay, if you strive –

DESDEMONA

But half an hour!

OTHELLO   Being done, there is no pause.

DESDEMONA

But while I say one prayer!

OTHELLO   It is too late.

DESDEMONA

O Lord, Lord, Lord!
     He smothers her

EMILIA

(*without*) My lord, my lord! What, ho! My lord, my
     lord!

OTHELLO

What noise is this? Not dead? Not yet quite dead?
I, that am cruel, am yet merciful:
I would not have thee linger in thy pain.
So, so.

83 *Being done, there is no pause* now the
   deed is begun, I cannot stop
85 *O Lord, Lord, Lord!* Desdemona tries
   to pray; and Emilia's words in the
   next line seem like a macabre echo.
90 *So, so.* As suffocated persons do not

recover consciousness, some actors
and critics make Othello stab Desdemona. But Shakespeare may have
been ignorant or, as some medical
authorities suggest, Desdemona may
die of shock.

EMILIA (*without*) What, ho! My lord, my lord!

OTHELLO   Who's there?   90

EMILIA

(*without*) O, good my lord, I'd speak a word with you.

OTHELLO

Yes, 'tis Emilia. – By and by. – She's dead.
'Tis like she comes to speak of Cassio's death:
The noise was high. Ha! No more moving?
Still as the grave. Shall she come in? Were't good?
I think she stirs again. No. What's best to do?
If she come in, she'll sure speak to my wife –
My wife! My wife! What wife? I have no wife.
O, insupportable! O heavy hour!
Methinks it should be now a huge eclipse   100
Of sun and moon, and that th'affrighted globe
Should yawn at alteration.

EMILIA   I do beseech you
That I may speak with you. O, good my lord!

OTHELLO

I had forgot thee. O, come in, Emilia.
Soft; by and by. Let me the curtains draw.
Where art thou? (*He unlocks door.*) What's the matter
     with thee now?
          Enter Emilia

EMILIA

O, my good lord, yonder's foul murder done.

OTHELLO

What! Now?

EMILIA

But now, my lord.

---

94 *high* loud
99 *O, insupportable! O heavy hour!* Othello
     already repents.
102 *yawn* (with an earthquake)

alteration (the change brought about
     by Desdemona's death)
105 *curtains* (of the bed, to hide the
     body)

OTHELLO

110   It is the very error of the moon;
She comes more nearer earth than she was wont,
And makes men mad.

EMILIA

Cassio, my lord, hath killed a young Venetian
Called Roderigo.

OTHELLO   Roderigo killed?
And Cassio killed?

EMILIA   No, Cassio is not killed.

OTHELLO

Not Cassio killed! Then murder's out of tune,
And sweet revenge grows harsh.

DESDEMONA

O, falsely, falsely murdered!

EMILIA   O, Lord! What cry is that?

OTHELLO

That? What?

EMILIA

120   Out and alas, that was my lady's voice!
        She draws back the curtains
Help, help, ho, help! O, lady, speak again!
Sweet Desdemona, O sweet mistress, speak!

DESDEMONA

A guiltless death I die.

EMILIA

O, who hath done this deed?

DESDEMONA

Nobody – I myself – farewell.
Commend me to my kind lord – O, farewell!   *She dies*

OTHELLO

Why, how should she be murdered?

EMILIA   Alas, who knows?

110 *error* straying off course
125 *I myself.* Desdemona's lie, oddly condemned by some critics, is a final
proof of her loving heart.

OTHELLO

You heard her say herself it was not I.

EMILIA

She said so: I must needs report the truth.

OTHELLO

She's like a liar gone to burning hell: 130
'Twas I that killed her.

EMILIA   O, the more angel she,
And you the blacker devil!

OTHELLO

She turned to folly; and she was a whore.

EMILIA

Thou dost belie her, and thou art a devil.

OTHELLO

She was false as water.

EMILIA   Thou art rash as fire to say
That she was false. O, she was heavenly true!

OTHELLO

Cassio did top her: ask thy husband else.
O, I were damned beneath all depth in hell
But that I did proceed upon just grounds
To this extremity. Thy husband knew it all. 140

EMILIA

My husband!

OTHELLO   Thy husband.

EMILIA   That she was false to wedlock?

OTHELLO

Ay, with Cassio. Nay, had she been true,
If heaven would make me such another world
Of one entire and perfect chrysolite,

130 *She's like a liar gone to burning hell.* It
has been suggested that Othello's violent repudiation of the lie indicates
that he subconsciously realizes that if
she had been unfaithful she would
not have lied to save him.

131 *O, the more angel she.* Emilia's love

for Desdemona leads her to risk her
life, and finally to lose it. She is
credibly transformed from the cynical spokesman of worldly wisdom at
the end of the previous scene.

144 *chrysolite* (a semi-precious stone)

I'd not have sold her for it.

EMILIA   My husband!

OTHELLO

Ay, 'twas he that told me on her first.
An honest man he is, and hates the slime
That sticks on filthy deeds.

EMILIA   My husband!

OTHELLO

What needs this iterance, woman? I say thy husband.

EMILIA

150   O mistress, villainy hath made mocks with love!
My husband say that she was false?

OTHELLO   He, woman;
I say thy husband; dost understand the word?
My friend, thy husband, honest, honest Iago.

EMILIA

If he say so, may his pernicious soul
Rot half a grain a day! He lies to th'heart.
She was too fond of her most filthy bargain.

OTHELLO

Ha!

EMILIA

Do thy worst:
This deed of thine is no more worthy heaven
Than thou wast worthy her.

160   OTHELLO   Peace, you were best.

EMILIA

Thou hast not half that power to do me harm
As I have to be hurt. O gull! O dolt!
As ignorant as dirt! Thou hast done a deed –
I care not for thy sword – I'll make thee known,
Though I lost twenty lives. Help! Help, ho! Help!

---

149 *iterance* repetition
150 *made mocks with love* used love as a
plaything (referring either to Desdemona's love for Othello, or to her
friendly intervention on behalf of
Cassio)

The Moor hath killed my mistress! Murder! Murder!
Enter Montano, Gratiano, and Iago

MONTANO

What is the matter? How now, General?

EMILIA

O, are you come, Iago? You have done well,
That men must lay their murders on your neck.

GRATIANO

What is the matter?   170

EMILIA

Disprove this villain, if thou be'st a man:
He says thou told'st him that his wife was false.
I know thou didst not: thou'rt not such a villain.
Speak, for my heart is full.

IAGO

I told him what I thought, and told no more
Than what he found himself was apt and true.

EMILIA

But did you ever tell him she was false?

IAGO

I did.

EMILIA

You told a lie, an odious damnèd lie:
Upon my soul, a lie, a wicked lie!   180
She false with Cassio! Did you say with Cassio?

IAGO

With Cassio, mistress! Go to, charm your tongue.

EMILIA

I will not charm my tongue; I am bound to speak:
My mistress here lies murdered in her bed.

ALL

O heavens forfend!

EMILIA

And your reports have set the murder on.

182 *charm your tongue* be silent

OTHELLO
Nay, stare not masters: it is true indeed.

GRATIANO
'Tis a strange truth.

MONTANO
O monstrous act!

EMILIA   Villainy, villainy, villainy!
190   I think upon't, I think – I smell't – O villainy!
I thought so then; I'll kill myself for grief.
O villainy, villainy!

IAGO
What, are you mad? I charge you get you home.

EMILIA
Good gentlemen, let me have leave to speak.
'Tis proper I obey him, but not now.
Perchance, Iago, I will ne'er go home.

OTHELLO
(*falling on bed*) O! O! O!

EMILIA   Nay, lay thee down and roar,
For thou hast killed the sweetest innocent
That e'er did lift up eye.

OTHELLO (*rising*)   O, she was foul!
200   I scarce did know you, uncle; there lies your niece,
Whose breath indeed these hands have newly stopped.
I know this act shows horrible and grim.

GRATIANO
Poor Desdemon, I am glad thy father's dead:
Thy match was mortal to him, and pure grief
Shore his old thread in twain. Did he live now,
This sight would make him do a desperate turn,
Yea, curse his better angel from his side,
And fall to reprobance.

191 *I thought so then.* This is a reference   206 *turn* deed
either to IV.2.129 or to her misgiving   208 *reprobance* (the state of damnation)
when Iago takes the handkerchief.

OTHELLO

'Tis pitiful: but yet Iago knows
That she with Cassio hath the act of shame   210
A thousand times committed. Cassio confessed it,
And she did gratify his amorous works
With that recognizance and pledge of love
Which I first gave her. I saw it in his hand:
It was a handkerchief, an antique token
My father gave my mother.

EMILIA   O God! O heavenly Powers!

IAGO

Zounds, hold your peace!

EMILIA   'Twill out, 'twill out. I peace?
No, I will speak as liberal as the north;
Let heaven, and men, and devils, let them all,
All, all cry shame against me, yet I'll speak.   220

IAGO

Be wise, and get you home.

EMILIA   I will not.

    Iago draws his sword

GRATIANO   Fie!
Your sword upon a woman!

EMILIA

O thou dull Moor, that handkerchief thou speak'st of
I found by fortune and did give my husband,

---

211 *A thousand times*. This, obviously, could not have happened during the course of the play, even when every allowance has been made for 'double time'; but Othello may be vaguely referring to the period before and after his marriage.

212 *gratify* reward

213 *recognizance* token

216 *My father gave my mother*. But earlier (III.4.55–6) Othello has told Desdemona that the handkerchief was given to his mother by an Egyptian. The discrepancy is probably an oversight, and could be resolved by the assumption that Othello's father purchased the handkerchief from the Egyptian. But some critics implausibly suggest that the earlier account was invented by Othello to frighten Desdemona.

218 *liberal* unrestrainedly
north (north wind)

For often, with a solemn earnestness –
More than indeed belonged to such a trifle –
He begged of me to steal it.

IAGO   Villainous whore!

EMILIA
She give it Cassio? No, alas, I found it
And I did give't my husband.

IAGO   Filth, thou liest!

EMILIA
230   By heaven I do not, I do not, gentlemen.
O murderous coxcomb, what should such a fool
Do with so good a wife?

OTHELLO   Are there no stones in heaven
But what serve for the thunder? Precious villain!

> *He runs at Iago; Montano disarms him;*
> *Iago stabs Emilia from behind and exit*

GRATIANO
The woman falls: sure he hath killed his wife.

EMILIA
Ay, ay: O, lay me by my mistress' side.

GRATIANO
He's gone, but his wife's killed.

MONTANO
'Tis a notorious villain. Take you this weapon,
Which I have here recovered from the Moor.
Come guard the door without: let him not pass,
240   But kill him rather. I'll after that same villain,
For 'tis a damnèd slave.

> *Exeunt Montano and Gratiano*

OTHELLO   I am not valiant neither,
But every puny whipster gets my sword.

---

231 *coxcomb* fool
232–3 *Are there no stones in heaven | But
what serve for the thunder?* (to punish
such wickedness)
237 *notorious* notable

242 *whipster* one who whips out his
sword (though Montano, an experienced soldier, hardly deserves the
description)

But why should honour outlive honesty?
Let it go all.

EMILIA   What did thy song bode, lady?
Hark, canst thou hear me? I will play the swan
And die in music. (*Singing*) Willow, willow, willow.
Moor, she was chaste; she loved thee, cruel Moor,
So come my soul to bliss, as I speak true;
So speaking as I think, I die, I die.   *She dies*

OTHELLO
I have another weapon in this chamber: 250
It was a sword of Spain, the ice-brook's temper.
O, here it is. Uncle, I must come forth.

GRATIANO
(*within*) If thou attempt it, it will cost thee dear;
Thou hast no weapon, and perforce must suffer.

OTHELLO
Look in upon me then, and speak with me,
Or naked as I am I will assault thee.
          Enter Gratiano

GRATIANO
What is the matter?

OTHELLO   Behold, I have a weapon:
A better never did itself sustain
Upon a soldier's thigh. I have seen the day
That with this little arm and this good sword,   260
I have made my way through more impediments
Than twenty times your stop. But, O vain boast! –
Who can control his fate? – 'Tis not so now.
Be not afraid, though you do see me weaponed:
Here is my journey's end, here is my butt

---

243 *why should honour outlive honesty?* why
should reputation outlive desert?
251 *ice-brook's*. The sword was tempered
by plunging it into icy water. (It has
been argued that 'Isebrookes' – the
reading of Q – is a spelling of Inns-
bruck's; but the definite article makes
this impossible.)
256 *naked* unarmed
262 *stop* power to stop me
265 *butt* goal

And very sea-mark of my utmost sail.
Do you go back dismayed? 'Tis a lost fear:
Man but a rush against Othello's breast,
And he retires. Where should Othello go?

He goes to the bed

270   Now, how dost thou look now? O ill-starred wench,
Pale as thy smock! When we shall meet at compt
This look of thine will hurl my soul from heaven
And fiends will snatch at it. Cold, cold, my girl,
Even like thy chastity.
O cursèd, cursèd slave! Whip me, ye devils,
From the possession of this heavenly sight!
Blow me about in winds! Roast me in sulphur!
Wash me in steep-down gulfs of liquid fire!
O Desdemon! Dead Desdemon! Dead! O! O!

Enter Lodovico, Cassio in a chair, Montano and Iago
with officers

LODOVICO

280   Where is this rash and most unfortunate man?

OTHELLO

That's he that was Othello: here I am.

LODOVICO

Where is that viper? Bring the villain forth.

OTHELLO

I look down towards his feet; but that's a fable.
If that thou be'st a devil, I cannot kill thee.

He wounds Iago

LODOVICO

Wrench his sword from him.

IAGO   I bleed, sir, but not killed.

---

266 *sea-mark* beacon
268 *Man* wield
271 *compt* Judgement day
272–3 *This look of thine will hurl my soul*
from heaven | *And fiends will snatch at*

it. Othello recognizes that he is
damned.
275 *slave.* Othello is speaking of himself,
not of Iago.
283 *fable* (that a devil has cloven feet)

OTHELLO

    I am not sorry neither; I'd have thee live,

    For in my sense 'tis happiness to die.

LODOVICO

    O, thou Othello, that wast once so good,

    Fallen in the practice of a damnèd slave,

    What shall be said to thee?

OTHELLO   Why, anything: 290

    An honourable murderer, if you will:

    For naught did I in hate, but all in honour.

LODOVICO

    This wretch hath part confessed his villainy.

    Did you and he consent in Cassio's death?

OTHELLO

    Ay.

CASSIO

    Dear General, I never gave you cause.

OTHELLO

    I do believe it, and I ask your pardon.

    Will you, I pray, demand that demi-devil

    Why he hath thus ensnared my soul and body?

IAGO

    Demand me nothing; what you know, you know: 300

    From this time forth I never will speak word.

LODOVICO

    What! Not to pray?

GRATIANO

    Torments will ope your lips.

OTHELLO   Well, thou dost best.

LODOVICO

    Sir, you shall understand what hath befallen,

---

289 *practice* plot
    slave villain
291 *An honourable murderer, if you will*
    (spoken, presumably, with bitter
    irony)

294 *consent* agree
296 *Dear.* The epithet shows Cassio's
    noble forgiveness as well as his love
    for Othello.

Which, as I think, you know not. Here is a letter
Found in the pocket of the slain Roderigo,
And here another: the one of them imports
The death of Cassio, to be undertook
By Roderigo.

OTHELLO   O villain!

CASSIO   Most heathenish and most gross!

LODOVICO

310   Now here's another discontented paper
Found in his pocket too; and this, it seems
Roderigo meant to have sent this damnèd villain,
But that, belike, Iago, in the nick,
Came in and satisfied him.

OTHELLO   O the pernicious caitiff!
How came you, Cassio, by that handkerchief
That was my wife's?

CASSIO   I found it in my chamber;
And he himself confessed but even now
That there he dropped it for a special purpose
Which wrought to his desire.

OTHELLO   O fool, fool, fool!

CASSIO

320   There is besides, in Roderigo's letter,
How he upbraids Iago, that he made him
Brave me upon the watch, whereon it came
That I was cast; and even but now he spake
After long seeming dead – Iago hurt him,
Iago set him on.

LODOVICO

You must forsake this room and go with us.
Your power and your command is taken off
And Cassio rules in Cyprus. For this slave,
If there be any cunning cruelty

---

310 *discontented* full of discontent   his deeds, but not his motives.
313 *in the nick* (of time)   323 *cast* dismissed
317 *confessed.* Iago is willing to confess

That can torment him much, and hold him long,   330
It shall be his. You shall close prisoner rest,
Till that the nature of your fault be known   .
To the Venetian state. Come, bring him away.

OTHELLO

Soft you; a word or two before you go.
I have done the state some service and they know't:
No more of that. I pray you in your letters
When you shall these unlucky deeds relate
Speak of me as I am: nothing extenuate,
Nor set down aught in malice. Then must you speak
Of one that loved not wisely, but too well;   340
Of one, not easily jealous but, being wrought,
Perplexed in the extreme; of one whose hand
Like the base Indian threw a pearl away
Richer than all his tribe; of one whose sùbdued eyes,
Albeit unusèd to the melting mood,
Drop tears as fast as the Arabian trees
Their med'cinable gum. Set you down this:
And say, besides, that in Aleppo once
Where a malignant and a turbaned Turk
Beat a Venetian and traduced the state,   350
I took by th'throat the circumcisèd dog
And smote him thus.

     He stabs himself

LODOVICO

O bloody period!

GRATIANO   All that's spoke is marred!

---

330 *hold him long* keep him long alive
334 *Soft you* one moment
337 *unlucky* unfortunate
342 *Perplexed* bewildered
343 *Indian.* There are many stories of Indians throwing away precious stones; but the F reading, 'Iudean', also makes good sense if it is taken to refer to Judas. Compare line 355.
344 *sùbdued eyes* overcome by grief, weeping
347 *med'cinable gum* (myrrh, 'associated with incense, and therefore atonement and sacrifice' – A. Walker)
353 *period* ending

OTHELLO

I kissed thee, ere I killed thee: no way but this,
Killing myself, to die upon a kiss.

He falls on the bed and dies

CASSIO

This did I fear, but thought he had no weapon,
For he was great of heart.

LODOVICO   O, Spartan dog,
More fell than anguish, hunger, or the sea,
Look on the tragic loading of this bed:

360   This is thy work. The object poisons sight:
Let it be hid.

The curtains are drawn

Gratiano, keep the house
And seize upon the fortunes of the Moor,
For they succeed on you. To you, Lord Governor,
Remains the censure of this hellish villain:
The time, the place, the torture, O, enforce it!
Myself will straight aboard, and to the state
This heavy act with heavy heart relate.   *Exeunt*

---

357 *Spartan dog* (notorious for their   362 *seize upon* take legal possession of
fierceness)   363 *Lord Governor* (Cassio)
358 *fell* deadly   364 *censure* trial

KING LEAR

Introduction

King Lear is generally agreed today to be Shakespeare's 'greatest play', not only by the learned (who have long approved it) but also by the general public; and this latter approval is more recent. It seems to have been some time during the Second World War that the more grim and overwhelming work replaced *Hamlet* in popular esteem. But before we endorse this general approval too heartily we should consider a little what 'greatness' means in such a context. *King Lear* is certainly a play in which everything is at full stretch: extremes of cruelty and suffering face extremes of loyalty and self-sacrifice. The play as a whole gives an impression of a monolithic and rough-hewn grandeur, as if it were some Stonehenge of the mind. But not every work that claims these qualities justifies possession of them. André Gide, watching Laurence Olivier play King Lear in 1946, did not think of Beethoven and Michelangelo, but only of Victor Hugo. He found in the play nothing which was not 'forced, arbitrary, wished upon us . . . Hugo himself could not have imagined anything more gigantically factitious, more false.'

Acquaintance with the play teaches us that these charges cannot be sustained. Lear's giant features do not lack humanity; they are impressive not simply because of the scope and sweep of the conception, but also because of the detail and accurate grain of experience. The imperious monarch is also the tedious father; the demonic energy he manifests – those who think of him as an enfeebled old man should read again – shows itself in 'pranks', in 'unsightly tricks', as his literal-minded daughters call them, in transformations of domestic trivia into the symbols of the Apocalypse. The world that his energy works upon is littered with the jumbled reality of common experience; it is the constantly asserted relationship between this and the gigantic vision that gives the play its integrity inside its power.

Alas, this is not what people usually talk about when they discuss the 'greatness' of *King Lear*. The modern popularity of the play is closely associated with a movement which uses as its touchstone the 'meaning' attributed to Shakespeare's plays, the spiritual messages they convey to us. Of course the idea that the work of art is a 'message' from the author is not new. Hazlitt tells us that '*King Lear* is the best of Shakespeare's plays, for it is the one in which he was most in earnest'. But modern critics are usually unable to stop at this point; they want to ask the next question: 'What is Shakespeare in earnest about?' One trouble with asking this question is that it produces answers of unbearable obviousness; it is a long way round about to learn only that Shakespeare felt love to be superior to hate or was strongly against sin. One aspect of the enormous energy of the play, of which I spoke above, is its perpetually renewed capacity for discovering life. Characters are all the time learning new and surprising truths, and we in the audience are learning with them. But this is quite different from supposing that the play is about learning a general lesson (for example, that love matters more than power) which can be stated in words other than the author's.

Those who attack the vague uplifting piety of such 'meanings' are not always, however, in a stronger position. Attacking mere moralizing they tend to substitute mere plot. The play, they tell us, cannot be about 'the salvation of Lear through the redeeming love of Cordelia' since the moments when redemption might seem to be asserted – in the reunion scene (IV.7) and the 'Come, let's away to prison' speech (V.3.8–25) – are discarded by a process which leads on to deprivation 'All dark and comfortless', indeed all the more dark and comfortless because of the hint of redemption that has preceded it. I cannot pretend that these points about the plot are untrue; but I note that it does the play a disservice to make them a limiting truth. What seems to be needed is a description of the play which relates plot to meaning in such a way that the two dimensions support each other. In this Introduction I seek to describe such a relationship, assuming that the play is not only a great work of art but also a successful one and that form and content are therefore totally compatible.

The first thing that we must notice about the plot of *King Lear* is its defectiveness by ordinary standards. To measure its weaknesses we need refer to no tradition outside that of the King Lear story itself. In all versions other than Shakespeare's there is a happy ending. Holinshed's *Chronicles*, Spenser's version in *The Faerie Queene*, that in *A Mirror for Magistrates*, the old play of *King Leir* (Shakespeare's main source), all restore Lear and Cordelia to power and happiness. Even though Cordelia may have killed herself later in history (as is reported by the first three), they all fulfil in terms of this particular story what Dr Johnson was to call 'the natural ideas of justice and the hope of the readers'. Not only Shakespeare's predecessors but also Nahum Tate, who refashioned the play in the form which was to hold the English stage from 1681 to 1834, give it a happy ending. The sense of moral logic and the sense of narrative logic seem to point naturally in only one direction.

But Shakespeare chose to divert both tradition and logic. If we ask why, and believe that the play is unified, we must seek our answer especially among those elements that are absent from the other versions of the story. Tate's version is like one of those modern miracles of steel rods and concrete piles with which engineers hold up tottering cathedrals; most of the fabric is preserved, but the weight is now carried by quite different systems, by believable or conventional characterization, by conflicts of personal loyalties, by unbroken lines of motivation. Shakespeare's Gothic structure distributes its weight in quite different places; and it is to these that we must pay particular attention.

The preceding versions of the King Lear story (and in many cases Tate's version) lack features that modern readers think of as central: there is no Fool, Lear does not go mad, there is no Poor Tom – indeed the addition of the parallel Gloucester plot is Shakespeare's largest single change – there is no powerfully generalizing and interrelating integument of verse. All these in various ways alter the nature of the story that is being told.

We may begin by thinking about the function of the madness (and the poetry which focuses it on our attention). Why does Shakespeare take us, in cardinal middle scenes of the play, into a world not only of social deprivation (as the story requires) but of mental deprivation as well, and not only in the case of the King but in the parallel and complementary cases of Edgar and the Fool? It is not that madness augments the pathos that the King's position already presents. Indeed the effect is opposite. The pathos of the old *King Leir* play is almost wholly swallowed up in the terrifying maelstrom of words and images that express man's need to see himself as meaningful. And this is a depersonalizing process. In the scenes on the heath Lear joins Tom and the Fool in a world of fragmentary reactions to the present, a world without a connected past and therefore without personal purpose. They have become 'voices' rather than people, bound together by the orchestration of the scene rather than by anything that might be called social contact or individual expression.

The orchestration is skilfully and spaciously laid out: the three kinds of madness are carefully differentiated from one another. The Fool has a quality of savage innocence that the other two lack. The role is clearly designed for Robert Armin, the member of Shakespeare's company who also played Feste and Lavatch. Like these he is a professional Fool. His stock consists in the main of songs and riddles, nonsense-rhymes and a mock prophecy. These he deploys as oblique and self-protective comments on the real world. It is easy to sentimentalize him; too much is often made of a supposed relationship with Cordelia, based on the slender evidence of 1.4.72–3: 'Since my young lady's going into France, sir, the Fool hath much pined away'. This certainly indicates an intention to make fragility one of his characteristics; but literally it says no more than that the Fool feels keenly the pressures of the new world of Gonerill and Regan. Unlike Cordelia he has the destructive energy of innocence. We should remember also what Gonerill says of him, that he is 'more knave than fool' (1.4.311). He is a living manifestation of that world of irony and metaphor in which every experience can throw light on every other one, in which Lear too would 'make a good fool', and which the daughters seek to reduce to the literalism of appetite. In such a world, where bitterness and innocence, correction and irresponsibility effortlessly co-exist, it is pointless to ask if he is mad or sane. He knows as much as the next man; but he is exempted from the need to put his knowledge in logical order.

Edgar's Poor Tom is the possessed or demented man. Shakespeare had been reading about 'possession' (or pretended possession) in an anti-papist pamphlet of 1603, Samuel Harsnet's *Declaration of Egregious Popish Impostures*, and was obviously exercised by the idea of man in the grip of an identity he believes he can control but which assumes a reality in the world outside which he never anticipated. Poor Tom is in thrall to his obsessions, cold, hunger, lice and other incommodities, which he expresses as the local effects of 'the foul fiend', but which we (like Lear) may see as the basic features of unprotected humanity. In these terms we are all in danger of 'possession'. The Fool sees folly everywhere; Tom sees torment. His vision is of Hell; his song-snatches are free-wheeling phantasmagorias, not pointed social comments like the Fool's.

Lear's madness shares characteristics with both of these, but is different from each. He uses no songs or rhymes. His forms are the sermon, the prayer, the trial. His role is always a commanding one; though he may become a voice rather than a person, his is always the leading voice. It is he who directs our attention to circle round and round the obsessive centres of *need, nature, kind,* and the idea of identity. These, of course, are key ideas in sanity as well.

We may see how the two mental states relate by looking at *need* both in sanity and in terms of the madness which takes it up and develops it. 'But for true need', says Lear before rushing out into the storm, 'You heavens, give me that patience, patience I need'. Almost straight away his speech modulates from patience to anger and revenge (traditionally the opposite of patience). But the problem of *need* remains central in the mad scenes which follow and grow out of anger. Patience would be a way of expressing man's need, if it could in fact hold together the various passions – rage at injustice and hypocrisy; pity for the oppressed, disgust at human depravity, incomprehension at offences against that social solidarity of human beings that Shakespeare calls 'kind'. If patience could hold all these together then the need to understand oneself in relation to them could begin to be defined. But at the very end of this same speech an alternative to patience is declared:

> *this heart*
> *Shall break into a hundred thousand flaws . . .*
> *O Fool, I shall go mad!*
>
> II.4.279–81

The madness is a bursting apart of the coherence which holds the hundred thousand flaws in a connected sequence. It does not involve any change in the nature of the obsessions. The need to find a respectable answer to the question

> *Who is it that can tell me who I am?*   I.4.22

moves into more radical questioning about the bonds of 'kind' which seem to guarantee identity. Lear asserts, in his sanity, that he cannot tell who he is, for the defining family relationship is denied by his daughters. In the mad scenes it is not only the relationship between a man and his family that he finds denied; it is the whole sequence of loyalties, duties, and respects that everywhere in Shakespeare describes the final good:

> *Piety and fear,*
> *Religion to the gods, peace, justice, truth,*
> *Domestic awe, night-rest, and neighbourhood,*
> *Instruction, manners, mysteries, and trades,*
> *Degrees, observances, customs, and laws.*
>
> *Timon of Athens*, IV.1.15–19

It is not only the individual Lear's identity that comes to be in question; it is the whole status of man. If humankind cannot satisfy the individual's need for a sense of himself, how then is man different from a beast? The relationship between man and beast, the potential for bestiality in man, is constantly referred to by the imagery. Man wears clothes, it is true. But he *need* not. Even the beggar's rags are *superfluous* (II.4.260). This is why it is the idea of Edgar's nakedness (however it was represented in the theatre of Shakespeare's day) that gives the final impulse to Lear's madness:

Thou art the thing itself! Unaccommodated man is no more but such a poor, bare, forked animal as thou art. Off, off, you lendings!

III.4.103–5

Here, when he tears off his own clothes, we have the point at which Lear's fear of madness becomes, unambiguously, the thing itself. The boundary separating his inner world from the outer 'reality' of things seems to dissolve. If Poor Tom 'out there' can fulfil so exactly the inner vision of man's deprivation, why should not a joint-stool be Regan (III.6.51) or Gloucester be 'Gonerill with a white beard' (IV.6.96)?

The external storm plays a preparatory part in this loosening of the baffle between inner and outer:

> *this tempest in my mind*
> *Doth from my senses take all feeling else*
> *Save what beats there.*   III.4.12–14

As the two worlds begin to dissolve into each other, it is the external world of duties and continuities, of business and homes and clothing that loses its shape. Its elements are re-formed as part of an infernal Bosch-like landscape centred on

Poor Tom ... whom the foul fiend hath led through fire and through flame, through ford and whirlpool, o'er bog and quagmire, that hath laid knives under his pillow and halters in his pew, set ratsbane by his porridge, made him proud of heart, to ride on a bay trotting horse over four-inched bridges to course his own shadow for a traitor.

III.4.49-55

In this unstructured and disparate world Lear comes to know things he (and we) could not know in sanity. The whirlpools of his obsession dredge up truths that are normally concealed. That there is any progression in these mad scenes (III.2, III.4, III.6, IV.6) is very doubtful. At the end of Act IV, scene 6, Lear's obsessions shift from the particular crimes of his own life-time to a more general vision of depravity in which the 'rascal beadle' whips the whore he lusts after, in which 'The usurer hangs the cozener' and the 'scurvy politician' seems to 'see the things' he does not. But the only real progression is towards the establishment of a vision which may stand in the play as one of the buttresses of its value-system. Lear's madness is a means of diverting our attention out of the natural world of effects (where the other versions of the story have their being) and into the metaphorical world of causes. In the mad scenes nothing 'happens', in the ordinary meaning of the word. But these scenes convey that sense of an irreversible change of state which an earlier dramaturgy (*The Spanish Tragedy, Titus Andronicus*) derived from Ovid's horrific stories of metamorphosis – the sense of a world now frozen in the grotesque forms of despair, and using the grotesque actions that derive from this. In *King Lear* this world is focused, not (as in the earlier plays) on public revenge, but on spiritual change, and the actions reflect this. But as in *Titus Andronicus* and *The Spanish Tragedy*, so here we are given a new vision of reality which the play must carry forward to whatever resolutions its end can achieve. In this sense Lear's recovery from madness cannot be regarded as more than a personal emergence from a vision we can still see everywhere around him. His own sense of coherence is restored; but the paradisal calm of his reunion with Cordelia is achieved, we must feel, by avoiding the irreducibles. For the first time it is possible here to think of Lear's age as enfeebling. The family pieties are restored, but so muted and ironic are the restorations that they carry with them almost the flavour of a loss.

The madness, I have suggested, translates the story into a mode of vision that is absent from the other versions, and it burdens the denouement with meanings which they do not have. Other Shakespearian inventions operate in the same direction. The history of King Lear belongs to the sequence that Geoffrey of Monmouth invented to bridge the gap between Aeneas and the coming of the Romans to Britain. It is presented as history, but it is fabulous history, closer to folk legend than to politics, and acceptable as part of the English royal story only because of the extreme remoteness of the time in which it is set – 'in the year of the world 3105, at what time Joas reigned in Judah', says Holinshed's *Chronicles*. The old play of *King Leir* conveys very well the sense of an antique (though Christian) life; but it gives no sense of the tension between the dreamy piety of that ancient time and the bustling modern world. Shakespeare on the other hand gives us a very clear sense of antique pieties dissolving under the impact of a modernism which is always around (raising the rational arguments for euthanasia, free love, etc.), but which in his day must have carried the particular stamp of Montaigne's scepticism and Machiavelli's cynical infidelity.

It seems clear that Shakespeare went to some pains to create the image of a society which had not yet received the Christian revelation. His art is usually quite happy to be anachronistic, and we must assume that his pains were designed to secure more than the establishment of Lear's antiquity. He seems to have wished to explore, with almost scientific thoroughness, the problem of Providence in a context which does not exact the Christian answer. In his picture of Gloucester's superstition, of Edmund's atheist determinism, of Lear's pagan piety and loss and recovery of faith, he raises the largest questions of man's relationship to destiny and leaves them unanswered, hanging like a cloud over the play. And this he could hardly do if he were writing about a Christian society.

The same effort to avoid dogmatic answers and to push the open hypothetical questions to the limit can be seen in more secular terms. One of the key ideas in the play is *nature*; set around this word are opposed and historically differentiated views of its meaning. For Gloucester as for Lear the 'bias of nature' (1.2.111) requires children and parents to love and protect one another; the 'offices of nature' (11.4.173) cause the young to respect the old, the subordinate to yield to the superior, the passionate to bow to the rational, as female to male or human to divine. All this follows inevitably from an assumption that *nature* is a reflection of the *status quo*, of an order without which things could not hold together and meaning would not exist. And the *status quo* is thought of not simply as 'the way things happen to be' but rather as 'the way things must be', since God made them so, placing the king (as God's vicegerent) at the top of the hierarchy (like the father in a household) and giving every other creature a justified place in an explained and explaining total system. In Shakespeare's own day the noise of challenge to this view of *nature* was not hard to hear; perhaps it is never stifled. The 'generation gap', the sense of the child's need to outrage and replace the father (and his values) are not entirely strange to us today. The anarchic individual points to his own *nature* as wilful and wayward, owing no natural allegiance to 'the system'. And he points also at the system itself, noting that the *status quo* is held together by force and fraud, not by love and loyalty. What is *natural* may be quite other than what the system thinks is desirable; the individual may be able to defend his own nature only by 'illegal acts' against a system in bland possession of legality, by fighting it with the standards of another kind of nature – animal nature:

> Thou, Nature, art my goddess; to thy law
> My services are bound. Wherefore should I
> Stand in the plague of custom . . .
> When my dimensions are as well-compact,
> My mind as generous, and my shape as true
> As honest madam's issue? Why brand they us
> With 'base'? with 'baseness'? 'bastardy'? 'base, base'?
> Who in the lusty stealth of nature take
> More composition and fierce quality . . .
>
> 1.2.1–3, 7–12

What Shakespeare is doing here is rather interesting. He is taking a paradox on bastardy which first appeared in Ortensio Landi's *Paradossi* (1543), translated into French in 1553 and perhaps into English in the lost second part of Anthony Munday's *The Defence of Contraries* (1602). In Thomas Milles's *A Treasury of Ancient and Modern Times* (1613) it is headed 'A paradox in the defence of bastardy, approving that the bastard is more worthy to be esteemed than he that is lawfully born', and runs:

bastards generally are begot in more heat and vigour of love . . . than the most part of our legitimate children. Consider withal that their conception is performed by stolen opportunities . . . Besides it seemeth as a certainty that Nature hath some peculiar respect of bastards . . .

Such a 'paradox' was one of the smart 'new' literary forms of the turn of the seventeenth century, a favourite in advanced circles (such as those of John Donne), exploring the witty possibilities of infidelity without actually endorsing it. What Shakespeare does is to take it out of the merely theoretical context in which he found it. He dramatizes it as part of a world in which the structure of set beliefs (which kept the thought as a mere paradox) is weakened. 'What if the smart toy came alive; what if these entertaining propositions had to be accepted as part of our daily life?' he seems to be asking. 'What if the true Law of Nature were not the Christian Humanist one, centred on reason, but another, more red in tooth and claw, based on animal rapacity?' It may be that this is the 'kind' to which man belongs, and will always return:

> *It will come —*
> *Humanity must perforce prey on itself*
> *Like monsters of the deep.*   IV.2.48–50

In these terms Edmund stands for a whole class of anti-Establishment individualists, who, in every age, are thought to be finding it too easy to pull down the decencies of society.

The play dramatizes a crisis in the history of society. Shakespeare has chosen to widen the gap between opposites to its maximum, giving to the old a patriarchal Old Testament flavour (of 'what time Joas reigned in Judah') and to the young the newest cut of brash impiety:

I have heard him oft maintain it to be fit that, sons at perfect age and fathers declined, the father should be as ward to the son, and the son manage his revenue.   I.2.72–5

The Revolution fails, not for an absence of power in the revolutionaries but because its aims are (as in Kant's definition of evil) incapable of being universalized. The three revolutionary children are justifiably proud of their individual vigour, cunning, and determination. But one individual vigour only cancels another. Edmund comments when the deaths of Gonerill and Regan are announced:

> *I was contracted to them both. All three*
> *Now marry in an instant.*   V.3.226–7

This strange moment of concert is the most concerted the three have been able to achieve. It was easy for them to exploit and destroy the system they belonged to; but they have proved quite incapable of building another. The survivors, Edgar and Albany, in whom we have to repose such final confidence as remains in us, are characterized as men in whom the individual will has been completely subordinated to social duty.

The story that Shakespeare inherited showed the swing back to virtue at the end as an inevitable function of an unbreached moral system. In Shakespeare, the system with which the play began is, in effect, destroyed. The scything swing of assumptions throughout the play leaves the end desolated, hesitant, minimal, more certain of what has been lost than of what can survive:

> *we that are young*
> *Shall never see so much nor live so long.*

As I have said above, the most obvious modification of the source is the addition of the story of the Paphlagonian unkind king, found in Sidney's *Arcadia* (Book II, chapter 10) and turned into the Gloucester plot. The things that are usually said about this addition are undoubtedly true: the doubling of the fable of ingratitude, the paralleling of betrayals by a favoured child and rescue by one outcast and persecuted, direct our attention away from the particularities of either story and fasten it on a general image of a world where betrayal and monstrous ingratitude are customary laws. Of course it is important to notice that the overall effect is made by differences as well as similarities in the two plots. The active will to self-destruction in Lear is answered by daughters who take every advantage but only in response to a situation he creates. The more shallow and passive nature of Gloucester, happy to lay blame beyond his own reach – on the King or the stars – and pushed from compromise to compromise, is answered by the positive exploitations of Edmund. The two old men are joined to one another as if to exclude any further possibility of escape from the fate that catches both, for all their radical divergence of temper.

A. C. Bradley censured the sub-plot as one of the principal agents in what he takes to be the play's 'undramatic' quality:

The number of essential characters is so large, their actions and movements are so complicated, and events towards the end crowd on one another so thickly that the reader's attention . . . is overstrained.

I believe this to be a misjudgement of the meaning of 'dramatic', deriving from too uncritical an acceptance of the realistic theatre of the nineteenth century as *the* theatre. It is difficult in *King Lear* to focus on single characters, single places, or single lines of development in action, and the double plot (the only one in Shakespeare's tragedies) undoubtedly contributes to these difficulties. But Shakespeare's vision in this play seems to have required a vagueness about place, a broadening and flattening of action and character. 'The reader's attention' is *meant* to be prised loose from individual motives and actions, I suspect, and attached to a different but equally dramatic sense of man's general status, rather than his individual destiny. Our attention is also, I suspect, meant to be detached from any sense of implausibility in the speed of plot development. The rapidity of the sub-plot (where the speed of Edmund's success is a function of his character) diverts our notice from the inexplicable speed of the Lear plot.

The madness and the questions it raises, the religious and social problems that rear up, the duplications of the double plot, all help to divert our attention from too narrow a focus in terms of cause and effect, motive and consequence. The effects of action are expressed in a variety of parallel symbolic and realistic channels. This does not imply that now we attend to the meaning and now follow the plot. The enlargements I have been speaking about are not departures from the story. It may be appropriate in this context to draw on the anthropologist Claude Lévi-Strauss's approach to myth – for 'the King Lear choice' is a recurrent folk-tale motif. Lévi-Strauss interprets myth in terms not only of its narrative (or 'diachronous') linear dimension but also of its recurrent (or 'synchronous') thematic elements, and finds meaning only by the relationship of these two (which co-exist like harmony and melody). It is interesting to observe that the addition of the Gloucester story to the Lear story produces precisely the same kind of dense synchronous dimension as Lévi-Strauss discovers in the repetitions and parallelisms of the Oedipus story. The vocabulary in which we focus the relationship between these two dimensions is unimportant; but it is important to notice the elaboration of attention which takes the emphases of the play away from the linear processes of motive and sequence. When Nahum Tate described the play as 'a heap of jewels, unstrung' he was of course referring to this weakness of linear connexion. The progress of the action is, in fact, extraordinarily elliptical. Albany's change of heart in Act IV, scene 2, the double love of the sisters for Edmund, the King of France's love for Cordelia, the death of Cornwall – all these come quite unprepared, as if being shown in pools of light surrounded by darkness. The battle is the most perfunctory of military actions, even in Shakespeare. On the other hand, the conflict between Albany and Cornwall, always being prepared for, never comes to anything.

There is another way of thinking about this lack of concern with motive and sequence. We may start from the point that the language of the play is not so much an imitation of the way people speak as an evocation of the realities *behind* what people say. The metaphors that characters use are not commonly chosen to represent their personal vocabulary or delineate their natures. They are more like trains of gunpowder laid across the play, capable of exploding into action when the poet requires it. Take the blinding of Gloucester. Why blinding? The most cogent answer to this question derives not from motive (Cornwall and Regan do have to be cruel, but not this way) nor from narrative convenience, but from the poetic vision of what man is doing to man. The blinding of Gloucester is a climax to the great series of comments on eyes and seeing that the play contains. When Gloucester says

> *I have no way and therefore want no eyes;*
> *I stumbled when I saw . . .*
>
> > *O dear son Edgar . . .*
> *Might I but live to see thee in my touch*
> *I'd say I had eyes again*   IV.1.18–19, 21, 23–4

the relationship between Gloucester's physical eyeballs and his metaphorical insight does not clearly subordinate the latter to the former, even though we can see his physical eyelessness in front of us. On the other hand it would be wrong to think of Gloucester's blindness as simply a metaphor for his impercipience. He is a man, and not a walking allegory. The 'reality' of the blind Gloucester as a thinking and acting individual is great, but no greater than the 'reality' of the language in which the potential meanings of 'sight' have been explored. The effect of what Gloucester does and the meaning of what Gloucester is are not divisible, for these are two dimensions of one and the same object.

Take as another example the many expressions of clothing and stripping that the play contains. In the light of these it can be seen that Lear's tearing off his own clothes is like the blinding of Gloucester – the climactic moment when the narrative and the language coalesce, giving the narrative event a force and density it could not have in another telling.

The use of ideas of number and of *nothing* reflects the same tendencies in the play. When the force of Lear's will is suddenly dammed up at Cordelia's 'Nothing' (1.1.87) it is clear that we are at a key moment. But it is not as yet clear what the moment means. That is the business of the play's language as a whole. We have to hear a repetition of Lear's 'Nothing will come of nothing' in the parallel history of Gloucester: 'The quality of nothing hath not such need to hide itself. Let's see! Come! If it be nothing I shall not need spectacles' (1.2.34–6). We have to learn that both Lear and Gloucester begin with an assurance that *nothing* is always at the empty end of the scale, far away from them. And we have to see the process of the play bringing them to *nothing* – by a plain system of arithmetic in Lear's case, reducing his train through a hundred, fifty, five-and-twenty, ten, five to the nothing that lies behind the final line of the sequence:

What need one?   II.4.258

It is at this moment when Lear returns to the *nothing* he had scorned in Cordelia that the arc of movement begun in the first scene comes to rest; and from the same moment springs the second span of the play, which is to carry Lear through the heath and the madness. In the great speech which marks the junction of the two spans ('O, reason not the need . . .') he rejects all numbers as superfluous and begins that exploration of *nothing* which is the substance of the central portion of the play. As often, it is the sub-plot that makes the more explicit statement: Edgar sinks through his own nothingness to take up another identity. On the other side of nothing he can survive as the 'horrible object' Poor Tom:

That's something yet; Edgar I nothing am.   II.3.21

More obliquely the Fool makes the same point to Lear:

Thou hast pared thy wit o' both sides and left nothing i' the middle . . . Now thou art an O without a figure. I am better than thou art now; I am a fool; thou art nothing.

1.4.183–4, 188–90

Not until the end of the play, with its impassioned negatives, however, do we reach the end proposed for this pursuit of *nothing*. With Cordelia dead, Lear's passion turns to a rejection of a world full of unimportant somethings: 'No, no, no life', 'Thou'lt come no more', and then the climactic fivefold

Never, never, never, never, never.   V.3.306

The action of the play has reached the final *nothing*, not only of death, but of a world emptied of meaningful content. It has often been remarked that Lear's refusal to listen to Cordelia in

Act I, scene I, finds its mirror-image in Act V, scene 3, where her voice 'soft, | Gentle and low' is the only thing in the world he is listening for, and where her silence is his executioner. The choice of words, the metaphors in which the business of the play is expressed are here, as elsewhere, an indivisible part of the dramatic event, determining emphases and the focus of meaning in the action. We cannot separate the plot from the poetic pattern, the symbol from 'the picture of life'. A proper description of the play must not only encompass both of these; it must also reconcile them, or at least base itself on their inter-relation.

The ways in which developing action and poetic pattern grow out of one another can be described only in terms of detail. Here, the description of a single scene must suffice. Fortunately, Act I, scene I, of *King Lear* is one of the great examples of Shakespeare's power of poetic foreshortening, contraction of human motive into poetic motif, and incorporation of symbol into person. The old *King Leir* play gives an adequate motive for the love-contest, an unsubtle motive, but one that fits perfectly well into the nature of the play. Leir wishes to trick Cordella (Cordelia) into a profession of love so binding that he will be able to demand that she marry the Irish king – which he desires for political as well as personal reasons. Shakespeare removes this (understandably enough), but substitutes nothing else; in his play there is no motive at all, simply

> *Meantime we shall express our darker purpose.*

Indeed, of all Shakespeare's plays this is the least concerned to explain the present by reference to the past. There is no 'exposition', though the traditional expository scene of two court gentlemen stands in front of the play (compare *Cymbeline*, Act I, scene I) almost as if to say 'So you expect an explanation! Well, you're not going to get one.' Shakespeare seems to have wished to make Lear not so much the inheritor as the creator of the world of the play, acting at the start with total responsibility and total freedom. Our response must be a mixture of admiration for the creative energy of this godlike exercise and of dismay or terror at its exercise in terms of a merely human will. We are shown the conundrum of a complete confidence in will coupled to a complete indifference as to means or executive process. We wait for the indifference to catch up with and destroy the will.

I have spoken of the first span or arch of the play, which carries our attention from Act I, scene 1, to Act II, scene 4. The attention we give to this is not, of course, concerned only with forward movement. Our knowledge of the play comes to us also as a series of tableau-like discoveries of separate situations. We see the King divide his kingdom and disinherit his youngest daughter. We see this youngest daughter 'claimed' by the King of France. We see a true-speaking nobleman exiled for speaking true. We also learn how the wicked bastard Edmund tricks his brother out of his inheritance and his father's love; and how Lear comes to regret his abandonment of power to his two daughters, and how, driven frantic by their cruelties, he rushes out into the storm.

These are the bare facts of the case – the facts without their power. For it is not the facts, but the range of value-systems they incorporate that gives *King Lear* the power to be read again and again; and it is in these terms that we should look at the beginning of the first movement, at Act I, scene 1.

The opening dialogue of Kent and Gloucester is concerned with both national politics and domestic affairs. It is not chance, however, that brings these two men together. The father has two sons as the King has (we learn) two Dukes. The father's sons are, respectively, legitimate and bastard; these external distinctions make one 'no dearer in my account' than the other; yet one is to hear himself called a 'whoreson', and learns that 'there was good sport at his making'. He has 'been out nine years, and away he shall again'; I take this to mean that (like the by-blows of the Edwardian aristocracy) Edmund has been sent to distant parts where he can grow up without embarrassing his father – though in the clubman's morality of this dialogue there is not much evidence of embarrassment. In any case we can note that a sense of moral unease is generated in these opening lines, and already this attaches to Lear. The Dukes, like the sons, are weighed against one another in simple computation and found equal. Is the assertion of numerical equality in them as dubious as the similar assertion in respect of the sons? With this question, this unease, already in our minds, we move into the main part of the scene.

The King enters in full panoply of power. This is an abdication ritual. Lear is the medieval sovereign with his 'two bodies', one merely personal, and one belonging to the role. He proposes to divide them, and in his own natural body 'Unburdened crawl toward death'. Unlike the other abdication ritual in Shakespeare – that in *Richard II* – this one is supported by a widely diffused sense of the King's religious and even anthropological meaning. But another point of view is also present; and from that angle the whole ritual is a fake. The first words of the play tell us that the land is already divided. Marshall McLuhan has pointed out that the map denotes a degree of abstraction from the real land, and marks the separation of business (which has been completed) from ritual. Two divergent and incompatible views of what is going on are established. Lear represents both the terrifying and *mana*-laden god-king, whose verse has the sweep and majesty of one whose thoughts are laws:

> *We have this hour a constant will to publish*
> *Our daughters' several dowers, that future strife*
> *May be prevented now.*   1.1.43–5

And at the same time, behind the divine mask, he is the chief executive of a modern state, measuring worth and marking the map.

The land itself shares something of this duality. It can be abstracted into a map; but the terms in which Lear's words describe it are more physical:

> *Of all these bounds, even from this line to this,*
> *With shadowy forests and with champains riched,*
> *With plenteous rivers and wide-skirted meads,*
> *We make thee lady. To thine and Albany's issues*
> *Be this perpetual.*   1.1.63–7

The 'wide-skirted meads' here make explicit what is implied by the whole transaction, that the land is seen as a kind of extension from the physical life of the royal family. Its fertility (the point that is stressed, rather than the extent) is closely associated with Gonerill's own fertility. Fertility, as the form of the good that this part of the play is particularly anxious to stress, appears no less obviously in the first mention of Cordelia:

> to whose young love
> *The vines of France and milk of Burgundy*
> *Strive to be interested.*   1.1.83–5

The fertility of the land and the fertility of the daughters are held, it would seem, inside ritual as part of the blessing conferred by the existence and beneficence of a god-king closely associated with

> *the sacred radiance of the sun,*
> *The mysteries of Hecat and the night,*
> *... all the operation of the orbs*
> *From whom we do exist, and cease to be.*
>
>   1.1.109–12

The full force of Lear's anthropological displeasure is not felt in this scene. The punishment for Cordelia and Kent is that they should be cut off from his life-giving beams. The full inversion of the anthropological gifts conferred in Act 1, scene 1, is postponed till Act 1, scene 4:

> *Hear, Nature, hear! Dear goddess, hear!*
> *Suspend thy purpose if thou didst intend*
> *To make this creature fruitful.*

> *Into her womb convey sterility,*
> *Dry up in her the organs of increase,*
> *And from her derogate body never spring*
> *A babe to honour her.*   1.4.272–8

In rational terms it is a curious curse; but the continuity with which Lear calls on the gods to underwrite his role not as the arbiter of life and death but as the guarantor of fertility marks its central importance. In Lear's view it seems to be the power to promote or deny issue that holds his world together.

But his view of the king's role is not shared by his daughters. Gonerill and Regan reject it at the political level. They are willing to appear in the same ritual as Lear, but their language reveals that to them it is only a charade; the reality is the numerically assessed purchase they achieve by playing him along. As Regan says:

> *I am made of that self mettle as my sister*
> *And price me at her worth. In my true heart*
> *I find she names my very deed of love.*   1.1.69–71

As the chosen language exposes, the two sisters are alike in their concern for the metallic and legalistic aspects of the exchange, statement traded for land, or rather (more abstractly) power. Language for them is not the magical expression of continuity with and control over objects; it is a political expedient by which the individual secures temporary advantages which physical power will make actual.

Cordelia's rejection of Lear's strange conjunction of politics and magic is both similar to her sisters' and different. It is not so much towards a rejection of the political meaning that she moves; it is, rather, a refusal to allow personal relationships to be expressed in these terms. Her care is to insert some emotional realism into her personal situation:

> *Haply when I shall wed,*
> *That lord whose hand must take my plight shall carry*
> *Half my love with him, half my care and duty.*

> *Sure I shall never marry like my sisters,*
> *To love my father all.* I.I.100—104

Computation is once again an enemy to Lear's demand that number be used to express relationship derived from love and affection. If it is number he demands then he must know that he can't have *all*, but only what is appropriate and 'According to my bond'.

What is this 'bond' that prescribes Cordelia's duty? It is basically, I suppose, the bond of nature which ties child to parent. The three other occasions when the word appears in *King Lear* (I.2.108; II.1.46; II.4.173) deal with this relationship. But I believe that 'bond' in the first scene carries a further meaning than this. *Bond* is also 'a uniting or cementing force' (*O.E.D.*7). It is that *bond* of natural sympathy which makes man-kind 'kind' in the modern sense of the word. This is why the family is (in this play and elsewhere) the model of the nation, and the nation the model of the 'kind' or species: at each level survival depends on 'kindness'. Cordelia acknowledges (as Gonerill and Regan do not) that she belongs to that blood-tied community her father describes:

> *You have begot me, bred me, loved me.*
> *I return those duties back as are right fit,*
> *Obey you, love you, and most honour you.* I.I.96–8

But she rejects the connexion between these feelings and the third of the kingdom which is to be their 'reward'. For her, as for Gonerill and Regan, the daughter's role is not the same as the inheritor's. They reject the daughter in order to enjoy power as inheritors. She reject the inheritor in order to retain in its own idiom the role of daughter. All three are united in rejecting the combination of roles that Lear prepares for them, the equation of power and love, of rule with natural fertility. But again the choices differ. Gonerill and Regan choose the metallic barrenness of power; Cordelia remains close to the processes of nature:

All blest secrets,
…published virtues of the earth,
…with my tears.   IV.4.15–17

…y from madness, which these words lead up to, is
…n terms of man's humble acceptance of the healing
… of nature. The full madness is identified with high
su…mer's choking riot of weeds:

> *Crowned with rank fumiter and furrow-weeds,*
> *With hardokes, hemlock, nettles, cuckoo-flowers,*
> *Darnel, and all the idle weeds that grow*
> *In our sustaining corn.*   IV.4.3–6

It is a context which prepares us for the re-entry of Cordelia into the action, part of nature but, like another Eve, intent to 'Lop overgrown, or prune or prop or bind', well adapted to recover the human garden from its 'natural' rankness and promote its proper order.

In the first scene the Britain which is centred on Lear flies apart into its constituent elements, as (in individual terms) Lear's mind flies apart into its 'hundred thousand flaws'. The opening establishes not only individual characters but also a pattern of relationship between them, and between a set of ideas and images which the play is to change and rearrange and draw on throughout its length. A world of competing values is established, and the values are, on the whole, larger, more complex, and more interesting than the people who profess them.

Any temptation to think Lear's character responsible for what happens is in fact much limited by the absence of any dimension of doubt or self-scrutiny in his nature; it would be like assuming an interest in God's character. The question he asks, 'Who is it that can tell me who I am?', is to be answered in terms not of personal idiosyncrasy but of function and role. The division of the kingdom defines him; he does not explain it. In

the sub-plot we find that Edmund begins the action w
very similar definition rather than explanation. 'I am a bastard'
is enough to justify everything that follows. It is a kind of opening which is recurrent in *King Lear*. Edmund, Cordelia, Kent,
all begin with powerful acts of self-definition, strong denials of
their contexts. Gonerill and Regan begin by agreeing only in
order to repudiate. But the strong context of settled beliefs
and assumptions which allows and perhaps even encourages
these acts of denial does not survive beyond the first few
scenes. And as that collapses the power of the individual to
define himself seems also to collapse. Exile and separation
isolate one from another; disguise and madness lock away the
individuals in their private worlds. The play seems to be intent
on hunting down the man who thinks he knows what he
believes or even who he is. This is a general drift of the
plot, as I say; but it is probably easiest to see in the history of
Edgar.

Edgar is the only character in the play who may he said to
choose his own deprivation:

> *I will preserve myself . . .*
> *And with presented nakedness outface*
> *The winds and persecutions of the sky.*

> II.3.6, 11–12

He outfaces persecution by becoming naked, by becoming as it
were transparent, wholly unprotected. He abandons identity in
favour of mere existence, mere survival:

> *That's something yet; Edgar I nothing am.*

But Edgar is not allowed to rest secure even as Poor Tom,

> *the basest and most poorest shape*
> *That ever penury, in contempt of man,*
> *Brought near to beast.*
> II.3.7–9

He constantly complains of the difficulty of keeping up the role
of Poor Tom, and in Act IV he abandons it – the Tom role

With his father he becomes 'A poor ... after the episode at the supposed Dover ... someone else, never defined, and then 'A ... made tame to fortune's blows' (IV.6.221). But ... announcing himself thus he turns into a Mummer- ... it, obviously in antithesis to Oswald's Osric-like court ..., then when Oswald is dead he moves back to a neutral accent. In the final scene he appears as a knight in shining armour, unknown and treading the same isolated path as always, talking chivalric jargon and achieving poetic justice. Finally his wheel of identities can come full circle:

> My name is Edgar, and thy father's son.   V.3.167

The context in which this anagnorisis or recognition occurs defines and limits its meaning. The trumpets, the armour, the stylized rhetoric, the too-neat morality, all serve to place it in the world of art rather than in that bitterer world which at the end of this play undercuts the traditional art-form. It is only in the dream of art that one really recovers that which was lost. What Edgar can find at the end of the play is only the debris of the world which exploded in Act I. The only wisdom that is available to him at the end is the knowledge of insufficiency:

> we that are young
> Shall never see so much nor live so long.

But it is not only in terms of identity that Edgar is hunted throughout the play. His moral sense is equally subject to challenge. He is much given to maxims and has an evident capacity not only to endure but to moralize on his own endurance:

> Welcome, then,
> Thou unsubstantial air that I embrace!
>
> IV.1.6–7

But he has no sooner said this than he sees his blinded father being led towards him:

> *O gods! Who is't can say 'I am at the worst'?*
> *I am worse than e'er I was . . .*
> *The worst is not,*
> *So long as we can say 'This is the worst'.*
>
> IV.1.25–6, 27–8

Every security he reaches for turns out to be illusory. He has to learn that endurance is endless and without satisfaction.

This pattern of insecurity appears in lives other than Edgar's. Albany, late arriving at virtue, is always that minute too late to make it effective. The most reverberant irony in the play is given to him: 'The gods defend her' he says, hearing of Edmund's order on the life of Cordelia. He is immediately answered by '*Enter Lear with Cordelia in his arms*'. The gods seem to have defended her by killing her. But at least Albany has seen the wicked punished, and he proposes a distribution of rewards to the good who have survived:

> *we will resign*
> *During the life of this old majesty*
> *To him our absolute power . . .*
> *All friends shall taste*
> *The wages of their virtue . . .*
>
> V.3.296–8, 300–301

But Lear's only answer is 'No, no, no life'. The offer is hardly made before the recipient dies. The wages of virtue sound suspiciously like the wages of sin.

I began this Introduction by discussing the relationship between the plot and a meaning which is often spoken about in the form of 'what Lear learned'. I believe that it must now be obvious that the process of the play is one to which the idea of 'What have I learned?' is particularly inappropriate, since we see so many men setting up ideas of what they have learned and then see the play knocking them down.

Looked at from this angle the play can be seen to be a series

...ions between disappointment and relief.
... deceive, but Cordelia speaks out; Lear
...ent answers back; Cordelia is banished, but
...up what is cast away; Kent is banished, but
...ius; Lear is forced out of civilization, but the only
...ized people in the play follow him; he goes mad, but
...ers hidden truths; Cornwall triumphs over Gloucester,
b... is killed for his cruelty; Gloucester loses his eyes, but gains
insight; Gonerill bullies, but Albany wins. But the oscillations
do not only work this way; they also move to disappointment.
Edgar's rescue of his father is completed by his inability to tell
him who he is; Kent can present himself to his master, but not
make his message intelligible; Albany wins the battle but loses
the purpose for which it is fought; Lear regains daughter,
crown, and sanity, only to lose almost straight away daughter,
crown, sanity, and life.

The process of the play see-saws between hope and disappointment; and any sense of values that the play is supposed to
affirm must be held against this background of recurrent
betrayal. Certainly no values held by the characters themselves
produce final positive affirmation. We may, if we wish, follow
A. C. Bradley and suppose that Lear dies of joy, thinking that
Cordelia is alive:

> *Do you see this? Look on her! Look, her lips!*
> *Look there! Look there!*

But in its context this can hardly be regarded as an affirmation
of the conquering value of love. Both immediately before –
'No, no, no life' – and immediately after –

> *Vex not his ghost. O, let him pass. He hates him*
> *That would upon the rack of this tough world*
> *Stretch him out longer*

– the negative is strongly asserted. The see-saw motion, which
has throughout the play been betraying, undercutting, and
isolating the sense of achievement we share with those who are

steadfast in suffering, has not ceased to operate. The only value left would seem to be the bare fact of having survived.

One passage in the play points to some of the meaning Shakespeare may initially have seen in such a process. When Gloucester speaks to Edmund of 'These late eclipses' he tells him that the effects fit with 'the prediction':

love cools, friendship falls off, brothers divide. In cities, mutinies; in countries, discord; in palaces, treason; and the bond cracked 'twixt son and father . . . son against father . . . father against child.   1.2.106–11

Two passages are cited as very plausible sources of this; and certainly they show the current context of such words and of the events in the play to which they refer. One is from the Elizabethan 'Homily against Wilful Rebellion', appointed to be read in all churches. This tells of

the mischief and wickedness when the subjects unnaturally do rebel against their prince . . . the brother to seek and often to work the death of his brother; the son of the father; the father to seek or procure the death of his sons, being at man's age, and by their faults to disinherit their innocent children and kinsmen.

Certain Sermons or Homilies, 1817 edition, page 541

Probably behind both this and Gloucester's prediction lies a passage in Mark:

Now the brother shall betray the brother to death and the father the son; and children shall rise up against their parents and shall cause them to be put to death . . . but he that shall endure unto the end, the same shall be saved.   13.12–13

Had Shakespeare been given to epigraphs he might have used either of these passages, for each gives in some sense the substance of *King Lear*. But each gives it in a context that Shakespeare did not use in the play, though I believe he was aware of the pressure of these contexts. To see what Shakespeare chose not to embody is to glimpse something of the nature of his dramatic art.

The *Homilies* passage is set into a discussion of the sin of rebellion against proper authority. Lear's abdication and division of the kingdom – the opening premise of the play – obviously had for the Elizabethans a resonance it does not have for us. The old play of *Gorboduc* (1561) depends almost exclusively on the political meaning of such action, and of the chaos, the worst of worlds, that would ensue (so the Tudors said) if central authority were to be dissipated. The passage from the Gospels is larger in its view, but it does not necessarily contradict the assumptions of the *Homilies*. It comes from a series of verses dealing with the portents which will precede the Last Judgement, including the final chaos of the reign of Antichrist. The last Act of *King Lear* is studded with references to the Last Judgement. People in the play are conscious of the analogy, conscious that this is the direction in which their world seems to be heading. But the play does not end in the same mode of resolution as the Gospel passage ('but he that shall endure unto the end, the same shall be saved') and *could not do so.*

The *Homilies* passage and the Gospel one both see chaos as a horror that the individual is already guarded against. In the political terms of the *Homilies* we can say that the individual need not choose to rebel; good order and obedience are always there waiting to be gripped fast. In the eschatological world of Mark, salvation is an end and an answer available to all men. *King Lear* takes us through a version of the political and spiritual chaos of which these sources speak; but it cannot, as a play, mimic their answers. Endurance is certainly something the play is concerned with, but the endurance of Lear ('The wonder is he hath endured so long') is very different from that endurance in faith of which Christ speaks in the Gospels. The 'endurance' of *King Lear* is rather an endlessly adaptive acceptance of one's self and of the world in which one happens to exist, a process of struggle rather than achievement, a direction of the will rather than a knowledge of the Good, and is certainly far from the fixity of salvation.

Frank Kermode has expressed this quality of the play's ending very well:

In *King Lear* everything tends towards a conclusion that does not occur ... The world may, as Gloucester supposes, exhibit all the symptoms of decay and change, all the terrors of an approaching end, but when the end comes it is not an end, and both suffering and the need for patience are perpetual.

> *The Sense of an Ending* (New York,
> 1967), page 82

In such a world the idea of 'the same shall be saved' can only exist as a potential, in the harmony but not the melody of the piece, as a perpetual hope in the perpetual disappointment.

What the play never allows is that any character should continue to hold a position of security. The role of plot in relation to character is to flatten self-assertion. I have already noted the tendency of people in this play to begin with strong self-definition. But the final scenes are full of statements that these individual lives do not matter. Edmund begins a career devoted to radical revaluation with

> *Thou, Nature, art my goddess.*   I.2.1

But he ends it with the flat

> *The wheel is come full circle; I am here.*   V.3.172

The only trajectory has been the self-defeating circle of his own individuality; the world has not moved for him. Gloucester dies, if not in a mist at least in a mystery – where contact with the mysterious truth of his fate bursts his heart with wonder. Kent's near-death, reported by Edgar immediately after Gloucester's, shows the same pattern. While he is telling 'the most piteous tale of Lear and him | That ever ear received', 'the strings of life | Began to crack ... And there I left him tranced' (V.3.212–16). For all we know at this point, Kent has died (like Gloucester) at the moment of recognition. And even when Kent appears, still alive, a few minutes later, he is still unable to secure recognition from his master. 'I'll see that straight' says Lear, and 'You are welcome hither'. But these vague courtesies have to be heard with Albany's comment attached:

> He knows not what he sees, and vain is it
> That we present us to him.   V.3.291–2

The Fool disappears in the middle of the play without any explanation. Edmund's death is 'but a trifle'; the deaths of Gonerill and Regan are matter for moralization, but not for personal response:

> This judgement of the heavens that makes us tremble
> Touches us not with pity . . .
>   Cover their faces.   V.3.229–30, 240

The 'gigantic' quality of *King Lear* might seem to be tied in with its lack of interest in the details of character which separate one person from another. Shakespeare certainly seems to be more interested in lining up the good against the bad than in discriminating the fine grain of one goodness from another. This is perhaps what Gide and others mean when they complain of the play's inhumanity. The play is true to the detail of our human experience, in fact, not in its characterization but only in the tracing of experiences by which we come to know the irrelevance of characterization. In a play where loss of identity is almost a prerequisite of survival (certainly so in the cases of Kent and Edgar) it is the way in which attitudes and assumptions distort, modify, disappear, under pressure that holds our continuous attention. The text is full of detailed perceptions, but they are all in motion or transformation; to stop the film and make any one perception 'the meaning' is to falsify. Those who wish to think of the whole work as a 'visionary statement' tend to suppose that the perceptions of Lear's madness are Shakespeare's central 'truth', and the process which diminishes these, as it diminishes all human effort, is somehow irrelevant. In fact the perception and the diminution are two sides to one coin.

In Act IV, scene 6, the climactic scene where plot and sub-plot merge, the mad Lear describes to the blind Gloucester a world of horror and anarchy; but it is also a world in which the individual is finally liberated from the pretences of social obligation:

> *Thorough tattered clothes great vices do appear;*
> *Robes and furred gowns hide all. Plate sins with gold,*
> *And the strong lance of justice hurtless breaks;*
> *Arm it in rags, a pygmy's straw does pierce it.*
> *None does offend, none, I say none.*   IV.6.165–9

The anarchic ultimate of the last line marks the furthest point in Lear's 'understanding'. But it is a perception so final that further movement can only back away from it. If 'None does offend' then there is no meaning in the discrimination between innocent and guilty, with which tragedy no less than law is centrally concerned. The play, to be a play (and it is a play), must disown such ideas. The action ends not with the perception of Lear but with the duty of Edgar:

> *The weight of this sad time we must obey.*

Those who carry the burden of time's imperfections are as necessary to the tragic vision as those who destroy the world in the flash of their understanding. Edgar's and Albany's patience with things as they are, with compromise and half-measures, does not rule out Lear's (and our) perception that ultimately 'None does offend'. Neither does Lear's perception obliterate the need for action at a level where some must seem to offend and be punished for it. The life that goes on beyond the end of the tragic process must depend on such good men, whose limitation is their virtue.

'KING LEAR' IN PERFORMANCE

The title-page of the Quarto (see below, page 559) tells us that *King Lear* was performed at court on 26 December; and we learn from another source that the year was 1606. Since the writing of the play is most likely to have taken place in 1605, one must suppose that the court performance was not the first. It was no doubt performed at the Globe, both earlier and later, as part of the normal repertory. We know that Richard Burbage was the original Lear, and may presume that Robert Armin played the Fool. Boys would have performed the parts of Gonerill, Regan, and Cordelia.

The text of the Quarto is unlikely, of course, to be the text of the play as performed in 1606. I argue below (page 561) that a great part of the Quarto text is based on Shakespeare's 'foul papers' or working draft. It follows that the actual court performance would not be recorded in this manuscript which the author handed over to the company for theatrical cutting and smoothing. The Folio text is our first unequivocal witness to what was involved in putting King Lear on to Shakespeare's stage. The cuts in the Folio show obvious ways in which the text can be shortened and simplified, comment, moralization, and indecisive action (the much-discussed wars between the Dukes) being reduced, but explicit action preserved. These cuts have an extraordinary persistence in the stage tradition; and one must presume that they preserve the theatrical fabric to the satisfaction of the stage, however abhorrent they are to literary connoisseurs.

I have argued above against the separation of poetry from action in King Lear. But I think it reasonable to assume that the play has always given peculiar difficulties to producers. Action in King Lear must be of a rather special kind if it is to convey the quality of its poetry. The title-role is demanding but not glamorous. The total effect depends on ensemble playing of chamber-music fidelity but of orchestral magnitude. There has to be a detailed control over the 'reality' projected, but without the usual naturalistic aids of defined place and time. The stage history gives an instructive account of the theatre's capacity to deal with these problems. Certainly it is more usefully seen from this point of view than, as usual, as a document of human perversity.

There is no evidence to suggest that *King Lear* made much impact during the seventeenth century. In the list of allusions to Shakespeare from 1591 to 1700 collected in *The Shakspere Allusion Book*, *King Lear* occupies a very lowly position, less mentioned than even *Pericles* or *The Merry Wives of Windsor*, and far outshone by *Julius Caesar*, *Hamlet*, and *Othello*. In the period after the Restoration, when theatrical records become significant in England, it is hardly mentioned. Downes, the prompter at the Theatre Royal, speaks of two performances by Davenant's company 'between 1662 and 1665'. We know from a surviving 'prompt-copy' that it was performed in Dublin, probably in the early 1680s. But in the main we may say that in this period *King Lear* was waiting for the great event in its theatrical history, Nahum Tate's rewriting in 1681.

Tate's *King Lear* is only one of the many Restoration 'improvements' of Shakespeare; but it is probably the most notorious, perhaps because of the stature of the play and the drastic turning of the ending from tragedy to reconciliation; or perhaps because of the hold Tate's version had in the theatre, and the difficulty experienced in re-establishing Shakespeare's text on the stage, even when the literary critics were united in denouncing Tate. *King Lear* demands a mode of action that is very different from the conventional intrigue-procedures of most drama. But intrigue is the stuff of the modern theatre, and is precisely what Tate supplied. Finding the play, as he says, 'a heap of jewels, unstrung and unpolished, yet dazzling in their disorder', he proceeded to restring them on the motive of Cordelia's love for Edgar – what he calls the 'one expedient to rectify what was wanting in the regularity and probability of the tale'. Cordelia's refusal to please her father in Act I, scene 1, is thus restrung on a motive (which Shakespeare had denied it), and, what is more, on a theatrically conventional motive. Sexual love becomes throughout a dominant motivation. Edmund's intrigue with Gonerill and Regan is amplified: Act IV, scene 1, discovers 'Edmund and Regan amorously seated, listening to music' in 'A Grotto':

EDMUND

> *Why were these beauties made another's right*
> *Which none can prize like me? Charming Queen,*
> *Take all my blooming youth; for ever fold me*
> *In these soft arms . . .*

Moreover, seeing Cordelia (who does not go to France) venturing on to the heath with only her confidante Arante, he sends two 'Ruffians' to detain her for the rape he intends. From this fate worse than death she is (of course) rescued by Edgar. The battle in Act v is no longer a foreign invasion, but a species of peasants' revolt, set afoot by the taxations imposed by Gonerill and Regan, and led by Kent and Edgar. The final scene takes us into the prison with 'Lear asleep, with his head on Cordelia's lap'. An exciting *coup de théâtre* is created by the struggle to hang Cordelia, frustrated by Lear and stopped by Edgar's entrance:

> *Death! Hell! Ye vultures, hold your impious hands*
> *Or take a speedier death than you would give.*

In a general reconciliation, Gloucester, Kent, Albany (shrunk from his Shakespearian importance), and above all Edgar and Cordelia restore order and justice. The last words of the play leave 'this celestial pair' in possession of the kingdom and of one another. Edgar says

> *Divine Cordelia, all the gods can witness*
> *How much thy love to empire I prefer!*
> *Thy bright example shall convince the world*
> *(Whatever storms of fortune are decreed)*
> *That truth and virtue shall at last succeed*

– a moral Shakespeare had been at some pains to deny.

Tate's version took immediate hold of the stage; and the next 150 years of *King Lear* are a history of the tension between Shakespeare's poetry and Tate's patent theatricality. The scholarly and critical interest in Shakespeare as a reading text produced (inevitably) an outcry against Tate. As early as 1711 Addison was writing: '*King Lear* is an admirable tragedy . . . as Shakespeare wrote it; but as it is reformed according to the chimerical notion of poetical justice, in my humble opinion it has lost half its beauties.' On the other hand, Dr Johnson saw that 'in the present case the public has decided, and Cordelia, from the time of Tate, has always retired with victory and felicity'. Dr Johnson's pupil, David Garrick, the leading actor of the eighteenth century, had in King Lear perhaps his most celebrated role, but it was Tate's *Lear* that he played. Inevitably, given the cultural pressure, he had a guilty conscience about this. He tampered with the text, introducing Shakespearian lines and phrases where he could without damaging the Tate framework.

One of the curiosities of the movement against Tate is that it often implies attitudes to *King Lear* which are more remote from Shakespeare than is the 1681 version. George Colman the elder produced in 1768 a text of (for its date) startlingly anti-Tate character. He removed the love story and even thought of restoring the Fool (but decided that in performance this part could only 'sink into burlesque'). On the other hand, we should note, he removes the fall over 'Dover Cliff' which Tate retained. He also initiates the nineteenth-century habit of ending Acts with big climactic 'curtain' speeches. Thus Act I ends with 'Hear, Nature, hear . . .' (1.4.272–86), which had already been moved to a more prominent (though not final) position by Tate. Likewise, Act II now ends with 'O, reason not the need . . .' (II.4.259–81). This marks a notable distortion of Shakespearian dramaturgy. Shakespeare characteristically ends his scenes (and his plays) on diminuendos – movements in which ordinary people try to digest or accept what has happened, or to reduce great events to individual or domestic terms. The stage is cleared and re-entered in the trough of the dramatic wave.

The nineteenth century inherits and develops this complex set of contradictory attitudes to *King Lear*. There is a crescendo of literary protest against Tate, but this is often coupled to a sense that Shakespeare's play is, in any case, unactable, and is his greatest play precisely because it is unactable. Charles Lamb has the most famous expression of this:

To see Lear acted, to see an old man tottering about the stage with a walking stick, turned out of doors by his daughters in a rainy night, has nothing in it but what is painful and disgusting . . . But the Lear of Shakespeare cannot be acted . . . they might more easily propose to personate the Satan of Milton upon a stage, or one of Michelangelo's terrible figures . . . But the play is beyond all art, as the tamperings with it show: it is too hard and stony; it must have love scenes and a happy ending. It is not enough that Cordelia is a daughter; she must shine as a lover too. Tate has put his hook in the nostrils of this Leviathan for Garrick and his followers, the showmen of the scene, to draw the mighty beast about more easily . . . Lear is essentially impossible to be represented on a stage.

At the same time there are theatrical and social developments – gigantic theatres, dominant and isolated actor-managers, a sentimental middle-class audience, a deference to female taste – all of which militated against both Tate, on the one hand, and the real Shakespeare on the other. Given all this, it is not surprising that the Fool was the last Shakespeare character to return to the play (1838). As constructed by Shakespeare the play sets Lear in counterpoint against a series of other important roles, Gloucester, Kent, and above all the Fool, who reflect what he himself does not know; and meaning emerges from the pattern of these quite unnaturalistic relationships. It was only when Macready hit on the expedient of a young lady (Miss Horton) playing the (heavily cut) Fool's role as one of innocent pathos rather than bitter bawdry that the character could be brought back.

With the return of the Fool in 1838 it is often thought that the history of *King Lear* has reached a happy ending: all the elements in Shakespeare are restored and all the Tate additions removed. What this version of the history does not notice is that Macready's *King Lear* – and, even more, Charles Kean's (first performed in 1858) – omit large portions of the play: twelve hundred lines are missing in Charles Kean's. The Tate–Garrick–Kemble–Edmund Kean conflation of III.4 and III.6 is preserved; III.5, III.7, IV.3, and V.2 have disappeared; and restructuring to end every scene with a big 'curtain' effect is carried through with great resolution.

The bowdlerizing of passages is (as one might expect at this date) a fertile source of omission. The blinding of Gloucester was handed over to servants by Tate (such is the progress of civilization); Garrick pushed it into the wings; now it is omitted altogether. The 'Dover Cliff' leap is prevented by the entry of Lear (as in the Kemble and Edmund Kean versions).

The cuts are, inevitably (given the number), widespread. But they tend to curtail parts other than Lear's own, and leave the King's role in greater isolation. The effect of a star part set against a fairly undifferentiated background had earlier been promoted by the omission of the Fool. Now, by judicious cutting, it is confirmed and even developed though the Fool is present.

The effects that Shakespeare had been at some pains to secure by the structure of the double plot and the flattening of character are patiently undone; indeed it is likely that 'Shakespeare' could not have replaced Tate if they had not been undone. Irving's version of the play, the last of the great nineteenth-century impersonations, was also heavily cut. Bernard Shaw's remark that Irving 'does not merely cut plays: he disembowels them' seems to have been amply demonstrated in his 'fearfully mutilated acting version of *King Lear*'. It is likely that Bradley (for example) could not have seen on the stage anything approximating to the play that Shakespeare wrote.

The twentieth-century *King Lear* has been more faithful to the text than the nineteenth-century one. One should note, of course, that the modern director's control of lighting and production allows him to impose 'interpretation' without changing the text. The modern popularity of the play among readers has its obvious counterpart in the theatrical movement which stresses the theatre's social role to shock and distress. If the later nineteenth century stressed the pathetic side of the play and highlighted the healing role of Cordelia, the twentieth century's special contribution has been to stress the inhumanity and impersonality of the processes which crush Lear. The 1962 production by Peter Brook is the most famous expression of this view, by which the play became parallel to the *Waiting for Godot* or *Endgame* of Samuel Beckett. For this purpose Lear had to be made an overbearing belching boor, and his knights shown as in fact a 'deboshed' company of bullies who break up the furniture when their dinner is late. The servants who bind up Gloucester's eyes and prophesy the downfall of wickedness (III.7.98–106) were omitted as providing too sugary an image. The fall over 'Dover Cliff', aimed at a grotesque and nihilistic comedy, was thought to be the central image of the whole structure. The production was enormously successful, for it answered many modern feelings about the play; but it made these powerful contemporary effects largely by turning the play into a contemporary document – which is what the theatre has always done.

Further Reading

Editions and Editorial Problems

The challenge and the greatness of *King Lear* tend to make it an early volume in new Shakespeare series, sometimes to its disadvantage. H. H. Furness's New Variorum edition came out in 1880 before Furness had fully defined the nature of his task and before the modern world of criticism existed. Both W. J. Craig's old Arden edition (1901) and Kenneth Muir's new Arden (1952) are interesting and useful; the latter is the standard annotated text today. Its notes are built on the excellent basis of G. L. Kittredge's edition (1940). The New Cambridge *King Lear*, edited by J. Dover Wilson and G. I. Duthie, is the latest major edition (1960) and is, textually, the most sophisticated. It is based on the elaborately argued text of Duthie (Oxford, 1949).

The basic modern works for the textual study of *King Lear* are W. W. Greg, *The Variants in the First Quarto of 'King Lear'* (1940), Duthie's *Elizabethan Shorthand and the First Quarto of 'King Lear'* (Oxford, 1949) and his edition (Oxford, 1949), and Alice Walker's *Textual Problems of the First Folio* (1953). See also E. A. J. Honigmann, *The Stability of Shakespeare's Text* (1965), and Charlton Hinman, *The Printing and Proof-Reading of the First Folio of Shakespeare* (Oxford, 1963). The Quarto is well reproduced in the Shakespeare Quarto Facsimile series (Oxford, 1939 and 1964), and the Folio text in the various Folio facsimiles (of which Charlton Hinman's Norton facsimile (1968) is the best), and, separately, with an apparatus by J. Dover Wilson (1931).

Sources

The sources of *King Lear* are discussed in Volume vii (1973) of *Narrative and Dramatic Sources of Shakespeare*, edited by Geoffrey Bullough, which includes a reprint of the old *King Leir* play and other relevant extracts from writings available to Shakespeare, including parts of Samuel Harsnet's *Declaration of Egregious Popish Impostures* (1603). Nahum Tate's version of *King Lear* is discussed in Hazelton Spencer, *Shakespeare Improved: The Restoration Versions in Quarto and on the Stage* (1927), and is printed in *Five Restoration Adaptations of Shakespeare*, edited by Christopher Spencer (Urbana, Illinois, 1965), and also edited by James Black for the Regents' Restoration Drama series (Lincoln, Nebraska, 1975; London, 1976). It is reproduced in facsimile (as well as Colman's, Garrick's, Elliston's, and Charles Kean's later versions) in the Cornmarket Press series 'Acting Versions of Shakespeare' (1969). The most complete description of the fortunes of the traditional story is Wilfrid Perrett's *The Story of King Lear from Geoffrey of Monmouth to Shakespeare* (Berlin, 1904).

Criticism

A. C. Bradley's essays on *King Lear* (*Shakespearean Tragedy*, 1904) are full of fine perceptions, but less fully encompass the play, I suspect, than those on *Hamlet* or *Macbeth*. His distinction between the 'poetic' and the 'dramatic' in *King Lear* provides an interesting bridge between Charles Lamb's complaint about the play's unactability in his 'On the Tragedies of Shakespeare, Considered with Reference to their Fitness for Stage Representation' (1811) and the main movement in the *Lear* criticism of this century. This may be thought to have begun with G. Wilson Knight's essay '*King Lear* and the Comedy of the Grotesque' (*The Wheel of Fire*, 1930) and to have reached its fullest expression in Robert B. Heilman's *This Great Stage: Image and Structure in 'King Lear'* (Baton Rouge,

Louisiana, 1948), which devotes itself exclusively to 'themes' rather than narrative or dramatic continuity. J. F. Danby's *Shakespeare's Doctrine of Nature: A Study of 'King Lear'* (1949) is more openly allegorical, and involves another increasingly emphasized element – an explicit Christianizing. This whole 'interpretative' position is the object of a frontal onslaught by Barbara Everett in *Critical Quarterly*, II (1960), 325–39. There is a lucid and undogmatic Preface to *King Lear* by Harley Granville-Barker (*Prefaces to Shakespeare*, First Series, 1927). An interesting and unusual essay on the play appears in Stanley Cavell's *Must We Mean What We Say?* (New York, 1969). Several interesting essays are printed in *Some Facets of 'King Lear'* (Toronto, 1974), edited by R. L. Colie and E. T. Flahiff. Scholarship and criticism on the play are surveyed by Kenneth Muir in a chapter of *Shakespeare: Select Bibliographical Guides* (Oxford, 1973), edited by Stanley Wells.

On more technical issues, Theodore Spencer's *Shakespeare and the Nature of Man* (Cambridge, Mass., 1942) contains an excellent account of *King Lear* in relation to the cross-currents of Renaissance thought. William R. Elton's *King Lear and the Gods* (San Marino, California, 1966) is a wonderfully documented treatment of the religious attitudes in the play. Maynard Mack's *King Lear in Our Time* (1966) is an eloquent account of the play's literary mode and of its modern productions. Jan Kott (*Shakespeare Our Contemporary*, 1964) has tried to present the play as an analogue to Samuel Beckett. The songs are interestingly discussed by F. W. Sternfeld in *Music in Shakespearean Tragedy* (1963). On the Jacobean 'paradox' see R. L. Colie, *Paradoxia Epidemica: the Renaissance Tradition of Paradox* (Princeton, 1966) and (in more detailed relation to *King Lear*) R. C. Bald's essay in *Quincy Adams Memorial Studies*, edited by J. G. McManaway (Washington, D.C., 1948). Marshall McLuhan's comments on *King Lear* appear in *The Gutenberg Galaxy* (1962). The king's 'two bodies' are described (*without reference to Lear*) in Ernst Kantorowicz, *The King's Two Bodies: A Study in Medieval Political Theology* (Princeton, 1957). Sigmund

Freud has a short treatment of the first scene of the play in 'The Theme of the Three Caskets' (1913), reprinted in *Complete Psychological Works*, Volume 12.

An Account of the Text

The great difficulty in establishing a true text for *King Lear* arises from the duplication of evidence, an embarrassment of witnesses, whose credentials can be investigated but not finally tested. The text appears in two separate definitive editions, in the 'first Folio' (1623) of Shakespeare's plays ('F'), and as a 'quarto' (small format) text ('Q') of 1608: *M. William Shakespeare his True Chronicle History of the life and death of King Lear and his three daughters. With the unfortunate life of Edgar, son and heir to the Earl of Gloucester, and his sullen and assumed humour of Tom of Bedlam.* The title-page goes on to tell us that it is printed 'as it was played before the King's Majesty at Whitehall upon S. Stephen's night in Christmas holidays' – that is, on 26 December. The year of this performance must have been 1606, for the text was entered, officially enough, in the Register book of the Stationers' Company on 26 November 1607, with the same title as above, and giving the same indication of performance.

In spite of this official entry, there is good reason to think that the 1608 text is in some sense 'stolen' – one of those 'divers stolen and surreptitious copies' against which the editors of the first Folio warned their readers: '. . . where before you were abused with divers stolen and surreptitious copies, maimed and deformed by the frauds and stealths of injurious impostors that exposed them, even those are now offered to your view cured and perfect of their limbs, and all the rest absolute in their numbers, as he conceived them'. This is, of course, advertisers' copy rather than truth, but (as in the best advertising copy) there is a grain of truth in it. Shakespeare's theatrical company was always anxious to avoid premature publication of the works whose novelty gave them their living. After about 1600 they seem to have been very effective in preventing good copies of Shakespeare's plays from reaching the printers. The printers, however, retained a certain appetite for Shakespeare's plays, and a small number of texts (five in all) filtered through. But in all these cases it is possible to argue that the route to the printing house was an illicit one.

For the company's 'official' first Folio we must suppose that the theatrical playbooks, copied from Shakespeare's working manuscripts, were available (at least for consultation). This certainly seems to be the case for the Folio *King Lear*. For the Quarto of *King Lear* the line back to Shakespeare's manuscript is more tortuous. It is clear that the process of transmission is one which has allowed the product to deteriorate: verse has collapsed into prose, sharp and memorable phrases are rendered as commonplace ones, lines are omitted or cobbled together clumsily, nonsense reaches an epidemic level. An example of what the Quarto can do to the text of *King Lear* can be seen in the last two lines that Lear speaks in the play. These are rendered by the Folio as

> Do you see this? Looke on her? Looke her lips,
> Looke there, looke there.

The same moment is rendered by the Quarto more simply, but rather crudely:

> O, o, o, o.

But this is an extreme example of distortion. It would be easy to exaggerate the badness of the Quarto text. In the main it gives the impression of being quite closely derived from an authoritative original. The differences between Quarto and Folio are many, but most of them are minor, a matter of a word or a line rather than the whole speeches which disfigure the 1603 Quarto of *Hamlet* or the 1602 text of *The Merry Wives of Windsor*. To explain the Quarto of *King Lear* we must seek a hypothesis which will account both for the general faithfulness of the 1608 text and for the film of corruption which keeps it from being satisfactory.

Those who first addressed themselves to this problem thought that the text might have been produced by a shorthand writer sitting in the theatre, taking down what the actors said. Investigation of the systems of shorthand then available has proved, however, that the degree of faithfulness we find in the 1608 *King Lear* could not have been achieved by these methods. Shorthand having failed, scholars turned to the more endlessly debatable mysteries of human memory. The Quarto might have been written down by those who knew the text by heart, and who, at some points, were obliged to use their memory to reconstruct a text they did not have at hand. Various errors in the Quarto suggest mishearing rather than misreading: 'in sight' for 'incite', 'have' for 'of', 'dogge so bade' for 'dog's obeyed'. The idea of 'memorial reconstruction', which is much invoked by those who have to explain the badness of some Elizabethan theatrical texts, is, however, rather unsatisfactory. The obvious persons who could engage in it are the actors; but the major actors were also the shareholders in the company, and so the very people with the greatest interest in preventing publication. Minor actors who were not shareholders would know their own parts, but could hardly produce a text as good as the 1608 *King Lear* on this basis. Moreover, as has been pointed out, the corruptions which stem from memory in the Quarto are concentrated on a small number of scenes; other scenes (for example, III.4, 5, and 6) are too accurate to be the fruit of unaided memory. The latest complete theory of the process by which the Quarto was written comes from Dr Alice Walker. She suggests that the two boy actors who played Gonerill and Regan were (appropriately enough) the agents who betrayed *King Lear* to the mutilations of the printer. They did this by remembering the scenes in which they appeared, and by copying the rest from Shakespeare's rough draft or 'foul papers' at such times as they could catch a glimpse of these – they were probably kept in the theatre as a 'second copy' in case the prompt-book should disappear.

The version of the play produced by this or another such process seems certainly to have posed grave problems for the printer who set it up in type. It is clear that the manuscript was difficult to read. The printing seems to have involved a continuous struggle to get the readings right (or at least plausible), and eventually demanded systematic resetting.

The available evidence suggests that the idea of systematic correction was not at first in the mind of the printer. The first eight pages are without corrections in any of the surviving copies (though not without errors). The first realization of error seems to have come during the printing of the second sheet of eight pages when, at 1.2.37, the omission of the speech prefix 'Ba.' (for 'Bastard' – that is, Edmund) made nonsense of the context. Another error some fifty-four lines later was also corrected. But both of these are *ad hoc* corrections for which, wastefully, the press was stopped while the type actually in the press was changed. The point, however, was taken. From the next sheet onward correction seems to have been systematized. Thereafter the surviving copies of the Quarto (twelve in all) offer a scatter of about 144 substantive variant readings; and some explanation is necessary to indicate why these copies of a single edition differ one from another to the extent they do, not only in this but in many Elizabethan books.

In modern printing practice the printer supplies 'proofs' or trial printings which a responsible person reads and marks for errors. The corrected proof then goes back to the printer, who has kept his type idle waiting for this. He changes the type in accordance with the corrections, and only then proceeds to print his pages. The Elizabethan printer seems to have used a similar but much less time-consuming method. The compositor first set in type the pages which would comprise a single 'sheet' – eight pages in a quarto, four (the first, fourth, fifth, eighth of each sheet) on one (or 'outer') side of the sheet and four (the second, third, sixth, seventh) on the other (or 'inner') side. The printer then took his first proof-sheet printings from these and gave them to the corrector. Meantime the press was standing idle; so, without waiting for corrections, he placed one 'forme' or set of four pages in the press and started printing one side of a succession of sheets. Meantime the corrector was at work. He corrected the pages not in the press and had the type of that 'forme' changed in accordance with the corrections. He could then order the press-man to stop printing – the uncorrected forme in the press could be removed (so that corrections could be carried out in that) and the other, already corrected forme could be placed in the press in substitution. In this way the machine could be kept working almost continuously. At this point, when the corrected forme was placed in the press, the printer had already been printing a great many sheets, on one side only. It seems that he proceeded to complete them by printing these, and the remaining pages, on the other side, from the 'corrected' forme. If half the total run of (say) a thousand sheets had been printed before the press was stopped to take out the uncorrected forme and substitute the other forme, now corrected, then 500 sheets would end up with uncorrected readings on one side, though with corrected readings on the other. When the printing of the second side had got to the end of the (say) 500 sheets already half-done he would work on to the end of the run, ending up with 500 completed sheets and 500 sheets still to be completed by the return to the press of the first-used forme, now corrected. Thus when the printing of the sheet was finally completed he would have produced 500 copies (say) uncorrected on one side (though corrected on the other) and 500 corrected on both sides. There seems to have been no discrimination in the printing house between corrected and uncorrected sheets; they were bound up indifferently. It has taken the resources of modern scholarship to discriminate those words which reflect the original reading of manuscript by the compositor and those which reflect the 'correction' of the press-reader. In some books this was the author himself, but in the case of a surreptitious printing like the 1608 *King Lear* the press-reader could not have been a more authoritative figure than the master-printer. His concern was to make a neat and intelligible piece of work, so that his corrections often reflect only this aim to reduce the text to the nearest intelligible form. But he did have the manuscript and he may have used this from time to time in his search for sense.

Of the 146 substantive 'corrections' which Sir Walter Greg estimates to have been inserted in the Quarto while it was being printed, some certainly show the corrector returning to the manuscript and scrutinizing it afresh in hope to decipher the words actually written.

> *I would deuose me from thy mothers fruit*

says the uncorrected version of II.4.126. The corrector turns this into

> *I would diuorse me from thy mothers tombe,*

which is not only obviously right, but obviously beyond the range of clever guesses. Only the original could have supplied the new reading. On the other hand, the corrector often indulged in mere guesswork, as when he corrected 'deptoued' (II.4.132) to 'depriued' instead of the true reading (found in the Folio), 'deprau'd', or when he curtailed the meaningless 'battero' (IV.6.241) — as the uncorrected Quarto has it — to 'bat' instead of rereading the manuscript and discovering 'ballow', as printed in the Folio.

However 'stolen' or 'surreptitious' the 1608 Quarto might be, from an official point of view, the company editors for the first Folio still saw the advantage of using it as a basis for the new version, 'perfect of [its] limbs', that they were offering to the public. I am not accusing them of bad faith in this; they were doing their best for their author; they had the Quarto compared with the official playbook in the theatre, so that the errors it contained could be corrected. In this way they avoided the danger of letting the official version, with the licence to act written on it, out of their possession; they also avoided the expense of having a completely new transcript made. Compos-

itors traditionally prefer printed copy to manuscript, and this –
no doubt perfectly readable on the whole – they supplied. It
cannot be denied that the comparison with the playhouse copy
vastly improved the text of the play: prose was reassembled as
verse and nonsense as sense. One's pleasure in the restoration
is, however, limited by a number of factors. The text against
which the Quarto was compared was presumably that in current
theatrical use in 1622; but it may have been the text used in the
theatre from the beginning. It is about three hundred lines
shorter than the Quarto, which, on the theory outlined above,
was derived in the main from the manuscript of the text that
Shakespeare originally wrote. One whole scene (IV.3) is missing.
There is recurrent evidence of a desire to simplify the staging.
In IV.7 both the music and the Doctor are gone, the latter
replaced (as in IV.4) by an easier-to-use Gentleman. The invasion of Britain by France is largely concealed, though this may
reflect censorship rather than theatrical cutting. Censorship
should probably be invoked on two other occasions: the cutting
of I.2.143–9 – the account of prophecies to be fulfilled (including 'maledictions against king and nobles' and 'nuptial
breaches') – and I.4.138–53, in which the King is called a fool,
and reference is made to the greed of 'great men' for mono-
polies. Many cuts seem designed, however, simply to reduce the
length of the play. The passages removed, like III.6.100–113
and V.3.202–19, often seem indispensable to the modern reader,
but in theatrical terms the play will hang together all right
without them.

Another reason for reserve about the Folio text derives from
the fact that it was set up by two of the more incompetent
compositors in the printing house, one an apprentice and the
other a careless journeyman. There is evidence of their eyes and
their minds wandering from the line in hand. Thus 'pregnant
and potential spurs' (II.1.75) is misprinted in the Folio 'pregnant
and potentiall spirits', probably because the compositor's eye
caught the '–its' ending of 'profits' in the line before. It is also
evident that the Quarto from which the Folio text was set up

showed the uncorrected readings at some points, and that the Folio corrector did not tamper with these (that is, he misread the manuscript in the same way as the Quarto compositor had misread his manuscript). There is a particularly obvious rash of readings in IV.2 (inner forme of Sheet H in the Quarto) where the corrected Quarto is superior to the Folio, since the latter only reproduces the uncorrected Quarto. The same is true of the outer forme of Sheet K, where the variant readings of v.3.48 give the clearest evidence of the Folio's slavish acceptance of the uncorrected Quarto.

Lastly, in *King Lear* as throughout its length, the Folio is concerned to express its material in up-to-date and 'correct' English, or even in that kind of English that the individual compositor preferred. A number of the new readings in the Folio may be attributed to this rather than to the recovery of truly Shakespearian readings. The substitution of 'squints' (III.4.112) for 'squenies' (printed as 'squemes' in the Quarto) may well be of this kind, like 'sticke' for 'rash' at III.7.57 or 'sterne' for 'dern' at III.7.62. In smaller things modernization is probably commoner and more difficult to detect, but examples I assume are 'yond' for 'yon' (IV.6.18, 118, and 152) and 'if' for 'and' (II.2.42).

The Folio also differs from the Quarto presentation of *King Lear* in modes of clarification and rationalization that are more acceptable. The Quarto is quite without indications of Act and scene divisions. In this it follows the common form of early play publication. The Folio, on the other hand, sets out the enumeration of Acts and scenes with great clarity and exactitude. It need not be supposed that the enumeration reflects Shakespeare's precise intention; it is rather part of the later literary and even classical polish applied to the plays. But it is a rational convenience, and like all modern editors I follow the Folio except in three instances. In Act II of the play *Actus Secundus. Scena Prima* is marked, and then *Scena Secunda*, but the third and fourth scenes of Act II in the modern division are not marked. It could be argued that Kent is present on the stage (in the stocks) continuously from II.2 to II.4 and that the Folio recognizes this in its scene division – it does not give Kent an exit at II.2.171. This is possible, but it does not correspond with normal Elizabethan dramaturgy. Act II, scene 3 is delocalized and separate, whether Kent is on the stage or not. The other place where the Folio misleads is in Act IV, where the F text omits IV.3. It follows that scenes 4, 5, and 6 of this Act are misnumbered as 3, 4, and 5. Act IV, scene 7 is, however, correctly described ('*Scæna Septima*'); this suggests that someone discovered the error during the printing of the Folio, avoided a continuation of it, but did not correct the instances already perpetrated.

The present text is based on the Folio; but all the variants to be discovered in the Quarto (corrected and uncorrected) have been considered, and have been admitted if a good enough argument for their superiority could be discovered. Where the Folio has been printed from the uncorrected state of the Quarto, I have treated the corrected readings (where these are not duplicated by the Folio corrector) as primary authority. A list of the places where the Quarto has been preferred to the Folio is given below (list 1). I also give a list of places where neither Q nor F is accepted (stage directions excluded). The third list is of stage directions. It should be noted that I have assumed a higher degree of authority for the Quarto in stage directions than in text. If Q represents memories of a theatrical performance, then it is likely to be more accurate in describing what happened on the stage than in giving the detail of what was spoken. The two texts often differ in the kind of directions they give. F, as a theatrical text, is not interested in stage directions except where props (the stocks, the thunder machine, trumpets) are concerned, or where persons are to be got on and off the stage. Q on the other hand is more concerned with description and less with business, but only at two points – the fall at 'Dover Cliff', and the fight between Edgar and Oswald – is substantive stage action described which is wholly omitted by the Folio. Both texts leave many important and significant stage actions undescribed, and so I have been fairly free with additional directions, as collation list 3 will show. I assume that this is a play in which the physical relationship of person to person and the range of significant gesture are very important, and often (especially in the scenes of folly and madness) far from obvious. In the elaborately scored scenes in the middle of the play it is sometimes difficult to discover which person is being addressed, and I have sought to clarify this in the stage directions.

The last collation lists 'rejected readings' and will enable the reader to see some ways in which the present text differs from others. It will be seen that it follows the Folio in more places than its contemporaries. The history of modern texts of *King Lear* is (with some exceptions) a history of drift from Quarto to Folio. The old 'Cambridge' text of Clark and Wright (1891), the foundation of modern textual scholarship, differs from the present text in over 260 substantive readings (not including lineation and stage directions). Most of these variants derive from the substitution of Folio for Quarto readings; the greater obviousness of the latter's vocabulary often makes it seem 'safer' or 'more probable', especially in the absence of a general theory of the relationship of the texts. Readings that appear to be unusual if not unique among modern texts appear at 1.1.5 and 70, 1.5.46, II.1.8 and 119, III.6.22, IV.1.10, IV.3.20, IV.7.21, 23, and 53, V.1.16, V.3.158 and 275.

In the text I have normalized the speech prefixes, preferring 'Edmund' to 'Bastard' (the commoner form in Q and F) and 'Oswald' to 'Steward' (the standard form in Q and F). I have kept the F form 'Gonerill' (Q has 'Gonorill') since I know of no relevant authority by which to correct it. I have also preferred F's 'Albany' and 'Corn[e]wall' to Q's 'Duke', and F's 'Gloucester' to Q's 'Gloster', though I accept that 'Gloucester' may reflect only Folio modernization.

COLLATIONS

Quotations from Q and F are given in the original spelling, except that 'long s' (ʃ) has been replaced by 's'.

I

Readings accepted from Q, with substantive alternatives from F which have been rejected (given as the final element in each entry).

I.I.	35	liege] Lord
	74	possesses] professes
	104	To love my father all] *omitted*
	149	stoops] falls
	155	a pawn] pawne
	156	nor fear] nere feare
	168	vow] vowes
	188	GLOUCESTER] (*Glost.*); *Cor.*
	214	best object] obiect
	225	well] will
	241	Lear] King
	289	not been] beene
	302	hit] sit
I.2.	41–2	*prose*] *verse* (. . . it: | . . . them, | . . . blame. |)
	55	waked] wake
	95–7	EDMUND Nor is . . . earth] *omitted*
	127	disposition to] disposition on
	130	Fut] *omitted*
	132	Edgar] *omitted*
	143–9	as of . . . astronomical] *omitted*
I.3.	17–21	Not to . . . abused] (*prose in* Q); *omitted*
	25–6	I would . . . speak] (*prose in* Q); *omitted*
	27	very] *omitted*

1.4.	98	KENT Why, Fool] *Lear.* Why my Boy
	138–53	That lord . . . snatching] *omitted*
	158	thy crown] thy Crownes
	174	fools] Foole
	193	crust nor] crust, not
	228–31	LEAR I would . . . father] *omitted*
	254	O . . . come] *omitted*
	301	Yea . . . this] *omitted*
II.1.	2–4	*prose*] *verse* (. . . bin | . . . notice | . . . Duchesse | . . . night. |)
	2	you] your
	10–11	*prose*] *verse* (. . . toward, | . . . *Albany?* |)
	52	But] And
	69	I should] should I
	70	ay, though] though
	75	spurs] spirits
	77	I never got him] *omitted*
	78	why] wher
	86	strange news] strangenesse
	119	price] (*uncorrected*: prise; *corrected*: poyse); prize
II.2	42	and] if
	76	Renege] Reuenge
	128	respect] respects
	139–43	His fault . . . with] *omitted*
	143	The King] The King his Master, needs
	148	For . . . legs] *omitted*
	149	Come] *Corn.* Come
II.3.	15	mortified bare arms] mortified Armes
II.4.	18–19	LEAR No, no . . . have] *omitted*
	30	panting] painting
	33	whose] those
	181	fickle] fickly
	295	bleak] high
III.1.	7–15	tears . . . take all] *omitted*
	30–42	But true . . . to you] *omitted*
III.2.	3	drowned] drown

III.4.   12   this] *(corrected; uncorrected*: the); the
          51   ford] Sword
          87   I deeply] I deerely
         110   foul fiend] foule
         111   till the first] at first
         128   stock-punished] stockt, punish'd
         129   hath had] hath
III.5.   9   letter he] Letter which hee
          24   dearer] deere
III.6. 17–55 EDGAR The foul . . . 'scape] *omitted*
          69   tike] tight
          76   makes] make
         95–9 KENT Oppressèd . . . behind, GLOUCESTER]
               omitted
       100–113 EDGAR When we . . . lurk] *omitted*
III.7.   rash] sticke
          62   dern] sterne
        98–106 SECOND SERVANT I'll never . . . help him]
               omitted
IV.1.   10   parti-eyed] *(corrected; uncorrected*: poorlie, leed);
               poorely led
          41   Then prithee] *omitted*
        57–62 Five friends . . . master] *omitted*
IV.2.   17   arms] names
          28   A fool] *(corrected; uncorrected*: My foote); My
               Foole
               bed] *(corrected; uncorrected*: body); body
          29   whistling]   *(corrected;   uncorrected*:   whistle);
               whistle
        31–50 I fear . . . deep] *omitted*
        53–9   that not . . . he so] *omitted*
          60   shows] *(corrected; uncorrected*: seemes); seemes
        62–9   ALBANY Thou . . . news] *omitted*
          75   thereat] threat
          79   justicers] *(corrected; uncorrected*: Iustices); Iustices
IV.3.   1–55   KENT Why . . . me] *omitted*

IV.4.   11   DOCTOR] *Gent.*
18   distress] desires
IV.5.   39   meet him] meet
IV.6.   18, 118, 152   yon] yond
71   enridgèd] enraged
83   coining] crying
134   *prose*] *two lines* (. . . first, | . . . Mortality. |)
198   Ay . . . dust] *omitted*
205   one] a
IV.7.   13, 17, 21, 43, 51, 78   DOCTOR] *Gent.* (or *Gen.*)
23   GENTLEMAN] *omitted*
24   doubt not] doubt
24–5   Very . . . there] *omitted*
33–6   To stand . . . helm] *omitted*
59   No, sir,] *omitted*
79–80   and yet . . . lost] (*prose in* Q); *omitted*
85–97   GENTLEMAN Holds . . . fought] *omitted*
V.1.   11–13   EDMUND That . . . hers] *omitted*
18–19   GONERILL I had . . . me] (*prose in* Q); *omitted*
23–8   Where . . . nobly] *omitted*
33   EDMUND I shall . . . tent] *omitted*
46   love] loues
V.3.   39–40   CAPTAIN I cannot . . . do't] *omitted*
48   and appointed guard] (*corrected; uncorrected omits*); *omitted*
55–60   At this time . . . place] *omitted*
84   attaint] arrest
127   it is the privilege] it is my priuiledge, | The priuiledge
194   my] our
202–19   EDGAR This would . . . slave] *omitted*
291   sees] saies

2

Emendations incorporated in the present text (not including stage directions, or variants judged to derive from spelling rather than meaning, or from the obvious correction of obvious error).

THE CHARACTERS IN THE PLAY] *not in* Q, F

I.I.	110	mysteries] mistresse Q; miseries F
	283–5	*verse in* Q, F (. . . say, | . . . both, | . . . to night. |)
I.2.	21	top the] tooth' Q; to'th' F
I.3.	23–7	*prose in* Q, F
I.4. 211–13		*prose in* Q, F
	252–3	*prose in* Q, F
	302	Let] Ha? Let F; (*not in* Q)
	340	a-taxed for] alapt Q *uncorrected*; attaskt for Q *corrected*; at task for F
I.5.	44–5	*prose in* Q, F
	46	KNIGHT] *Gent.* F; *Seruant.* Q
II.2.	45–6	*prose in* Q, F
	141	contemned'st] contaned Q *uncorrected*; temnest Q *corrected*; (*not in* F)
II.4.	55	Hysterica] *Historica* Q, F
	73	ha' . . . use] haue . . . follow Q; hause . . . follow F
III.I.	10	out-storm] outscorne Q; (*not in* F)
III.2.	85–6	Then shall . . . confusion] *placed after* 'build' (*line* 92) *in* F; (*not in* Q)
III.4.	45	*prose in* Q, F
		blow the cold winds] blowes the cold wind Q; blow the windes F
	60	What, has his] What, his Q; Ha's his F
	73	*prose in* Q, F
	95–6	*prose in* Q, F

	112	squenies] queues Q *uncorrected*; squemes Q *corrected*; squints F
	138–9	*prose in* Q, F
III.6.	21	justicer] Iustice Q; (*not in* F)
	24–5	madam? | Come . . . me] madam come . . . mee Q; (*not in* F)
	25	burn] broome Q; (*not in* F)
	33–4	*prose in* Q; (*not in* F)
	47	she kicked] kickt Q; (*not in* F)
	68	lym] him Q; Hym F
	99–101	*prose in* Q; (*not in* F)
III.7.	44–5	*prose in* Q, F
	99–101	*prose in* Q; (*not in* F)
	105–6	*prose in* Q; (*not in* F)
IV.1.	60	Flibberdigibbet] *Stiberdigebit* Q; (*not in* F)
IV.2.	32	its origin] it origin Q *uncorrected*; ith origin Q *corrected*; (*not in* F)
	47	these] the Q *uncorrected*; this Q *corrected*; (not in F)
	57	begins to threat] begin threats Q *uncorrected*; begins thereat Q *corrected*; (*not in* F)
IV.3.	11	Ay, sir] I say Q; (*not in* F)
	16	strove] streme Q; (*not in* F)
	31	moistened] moystened her Q; (*not in* F)
IV.6.118–27		*prose in* Q, F
161–74		*prose in* Q, F
	166	Plate] Place F; (*not in* Q)
	184	This's a] This a Q, F
V.1.	12–13	*prose in* Q; (*not in* F)
V.3.	211	him] me Q; (*not in* F)
	221–2	*prose in* Q, F
	273	SECOND OFFICER] *Cap.* Q; *Gent.* F

3

The following list of stage directions concerns itself only with those added to, or considerably adapted from, the substantive texts, Q and F, where the editor's interpretation of requirements has been involved. Provision of exits, where these are clearly demanded by the context, is not recorded; nor is the common slight adjustment of the point at which entries and exits are mentioned; these are often a line or two early in F. Asides and other indicators of the mode of utterance ('*aloud*', '*sings*', etc.) are always editorial, as are indicators of the person addressed, and these are not collated.

I.I.	35	*Exeunt Gloucester and Edmund*] *Exit*. F
	161	*not in* Q, F
	266	*Flourish. Exeunt Lear, Burgundy, Cornwall, Albany, Gloucester, and attendants*] *Flourish. Exeunt*. F; *Exit Lear and Burgundie*. Q
I.4.	0	*Enter Kent in disguise*] *Enter Kent*. Q, F
	7	*Enter Lear and Knights*] *Enter Lear and Attendants*. F
	8	*not in* Q, F
	43	*Exit Second Knight*] *not in* Q, F
	46	*not in* Q, F
	47	*not in* Q, F
	75	*not in* Q, F
	76	*not in* Q, F
	83	*not in* Q, F
	85	*not in* Q, F
	91	*not in* Q, F
	94	*He gives him money*] *not in* Q, F
	194	*not in* Q, F
	268	*not in* Q, F
	269	*not in* Q, F
	271	*not in* Q, F

I.5.	o	*Enter Lear, Kent, Knight, and the Fool*] Enter Lear, Kent, Gentleman, and Foole. F
II.1.	o	*... by opposite doors*] Enter ... seuerally. F
	35	*not in* Q, F
	42	*not in* Q, F
II.2.	o	*Enter Kent and Oswald by opposite doors*] Enter Kent, and Steward seuerally. F
	30	*not in* Q, F
	38	*not in* Q, F
	39	*not in* Q, F
	148	*not in* Q, F
II.4.	o	*Kent still in the stocks*] not in Q, F
	130	*not in* Q, F
	148	*not in* Q, F
	153	*not in* Q, F
	212	*not in* Q, F
	281	*Exeunt Lear, Gloucester, Kent, the Fool, and Gentleman*] Exeunt Lear, Leister, Kent, and Foole Q; Exeunt. F
III.1.	o	*... by opposite doors*] ..., seuerally. F
	55	*Exeunt by opposite doors*] Exeunt. Q, F
III.4.	37, 43	*Enter the Fool from the hovel ... Enter Edgar disguised as Poor Tom*] Enter Edgar, and Foole. F (*after line 36*)
	105	*not in* Q, F
	153	*not in* Q, F
III.6.	99	*Exeunt Kent, Gloucester, and the Fool, bearing off the King*] Exeunt F
III.7.	20	*not in* Q, F
	23	*not in* Q, F
	32	*not in* Q, F
	34	*not in* Q, F
	76, 77,	*Cornwall draws his sword ... He lunges at him ...*
	78	*drawing his sword ... He wounds Cornwall*] draw and fight. Q (*after line 77*)
	81	*not in* Q, F

	97	*Exit Cornwall, supported by Regan*] *Exeunt,* F
	106	*Exeunt by opposite doors*] *Exit.* Q
IV.2.	21	*not in* Q, F
IV.4.	0	*Enter, with drum and colours, Cordelia, Doctor, and soldiers*] *Enter with Drum and Colours, Cordelia, Gentlemen, and Souldiours.* F; *Enter Cordelia, Docter and others.* Q
IV.6.	0	*Enter Gloucester and Edgar in peasant's clothes*] *Enter Gloucester, and Edgar.* F
	41	*Gloucester throws himself forward*] *He fals.* Q
	80	*Enter Lear fantastically dressed with wild flowers*] *Enter Lear mad.* Q
	95	*not in* Q, F
	132	*not in* Q, F
	170	*not in* Q, F
	181	*not in* Q, F
	188	*He throws down his flowers and stamps on them*] *not in* Q, F
		Enter a Gentleman and two attendants. Gloucester and Edgar draw back] *Enter three Gentlemen.* Q
	203	*Exit running, followed by attendants*] *Exit King running.* Q
	208	*not in* Q, F
	217	*not in* Q, F
	231	*not in* Q, F
IV.7.	22	*Enter Gentleman ushering Lear in a chair carried by servants. All fall to their knees*] *Enter Lear in a chaire carried by Seruants* F
	24	*not in* Q, F
	26	*not in* Q, F
	58	*not in* Q, F
	70	*not in* Q, F
	95	*not in* Q, F
V.1.	37	*As Albany is going out, enter Edgar*] *Enter Edgar* Q, F
V.3.	21	*not in* Q, F

26 *Exeunt Lear and Cordelia, guarded*] *Exit*. F

84 *not in* Q, F

94 *not in* Q, F

98 *not in* Q, F

106 *not in* Q, F

115 *Trumpet answers within. Enter Edgar armed, a trumpet before him*] *Trumpet answers within. Enter Edgar armed*. F; *Enter Edgar at the third sound, a trumpet before him*. Q

126 *not in* Q, F

148 *Alarums. Fights. Edmund falls*] *Alarums. Fights*. F (*after* 'save him!')

149 *to Edgar, about to kill Edmund*] *not in* Q, F

159 *not in* Q, F

219 *Enter a Gentleman with a bloody knife*] *Enter a Gentleman*. F; *Enter one with a bloudie knife*. Q

228 *not in* Q, F

249 *not in* Q, F

254 *Edmund is borne off*] *not in* Q, F
followed by Second Officer and others] *not in* Q, F

4

This list sets against the readings of the present text (printed to the left of the square bracket) substantive readings of other modern editions – in particular those of Peter Alexander (1951), Kenneth Muir (1952), Dover Wilson and Duthie (1960) – which have been considered and rejected. Similar readings can, of course, be found in many other editions. The reading cited from the present text can be understood to derive from F except where an asterisk directs attention to collation-list 1 above (in which case the reading derives from Q) or where it is an emendation recorded above in list 2. In most cases the rejected readings derive from editors' preference for Q, and in such cases '(Q)' indicates the source. In the same way '(F)' is used to indicate derivation from the Folio. Sometimes the rejected reading is an emendation – often to be traced back to the eighteenth-century editors – and in such cases the Q reading (if variant) is supplied before the rejected reading.

I.I.	5	qualities] equalities (Q)
	74	square] spirit (Q)
	128	the third] this third (Q)
	163	Kill] Do. | Kill (Q)
		thy fee] the fee (Q)
	*168	vow] vows (F)
	206	up in] up on (Q)
	237	intends to do] intends (Q)
	239	stands] stand (Q)
	248	and fortunes] of fortune (Q)
	281	covers] (F, Q); covert
I.2.	133	pat] and pat (Q)
I.4.	21	he's] he is (Q)
	40–41	me if . . . dinner. I] me. If . . . dinner I
	111	the Lady Brach] (Ladie oth'e brach Q); Lady the Brach; the Lady's brach
	199	Sir] (F, Q); omitted
	212	it's] it (Q)
	*254	sir] omitted
	*301	Yea] Ha (F)
	302	Let] Ha! Let (F). See note
I. 5.	1	Gloucester] (F, Q); Cornwall
	44	most editors add the direction Enter a Gentleman
	46	KNIGHT] (Seruant. Q); GENTLEMAN (F)
II.I.	8	kissing] bussing (Q)
	39	stand] stand's (Q)
	45	the thunder] their thunder (Q)
	51	latched] lanch'd (Q)
	*52	But] And (F)
	76	O strange] strong (Q)
	77	letter, said he] letter (Q)

	119	price] poise (Q); prize. *See note*
II.2.	55	A tailor] Ay, a tailor (Q)
	75	Being] Bring (Q)
		the] their (Q)
	80	Smile] Smoile (F, Q)
	149	my lord] my good lord (Q)
II.3.	19	Sometimes . . . sometime] Sometimes . . . sometimes (Q)
II.4.	2	messengers] messenger (Q)
	*19	Yes] Yes, yes
	52	for thy] (*not in* Q); from thy
	73	ha' . . . use] have . . . follow (Q). *See note*
	97	commands, tends, service] commands her service (Q); commands their service
	143	his] her (Q)
	163	blister] blast her pride (Q); blister her
	164	rash mood is on] rash mood (Q)
	*181	fickle] sickly (F)
	261	needs –] (needs: F); needs, (Q)
	266	that patience] (F, Q); patience
III.1.	10	out-storm] out-scorn (Q)
	20	is] be (Q)
	48	that] your (Q)
III.2.	9	makes] make (Q)
	54	simular] simular man (Q)
	57	Has] Hast (Q)
	71	And] That (Q)
	78	boy] my good boy (Q)
	85–6	Then shall . . . confusion] *placed after line* 92 (F)
III.4.	45	cold winds] cold wind (Q); winds (F)
	46	thy bed] thy cold bed (Q)
	78	word's justice] words justly (Q); word justly
	96	mun, nonny] (hay no on ny Q); mun, hey no nonny; mun, hey, nonny, nonny
III.6.	*22	No] Now
	*53	store] stone

III.7.	52	answer] first answer (Q)
	58	bare] loved (Q)
	76	What] (F, Q); REGAN What
IV.1.	*10	parti-eyed] poorly led (F); poorly eyed
	38	fool] the fool (Q)
	*60	mopping] mocking
IV.2.	*28	A fool usurps my bed] My Fool usurps my body (F)
	*29	whistling] whistle (F)
	*32	its] (ith Q *corrected*); it (Q *uncorrected*)
IV.3.	*20	seem] seemed
	*29	be believed] believe it
	*31	And clamour] That clamour
IV.6.	15	sampire] (F, Q); samphire
*18, 118, 152		yon] yond (F)
	97	the white] white (Q)
128–32		(*prose*)] (F, Q); *verse*
130–31		civet; good apothecary, sweeten] civet, good apothecary, to sweeten (Q)
158–60		(*prose*)] (F, Q); *verse*
	165	great] small (Q)
	184	This's] This (F, Q); This'
	202	Come] Nay (Q)
	250	English] British (Q)
	260	we] we'ld (Q)
IV.7.	*21	DOCTOR] GENTLEMAN (F)
	*23	GENTLEMAN] DOCTOR
	32	jarring] warring (Q)
	49	Where] when (Q)
	53	even] (eu'n F); e'en (Q)
	58	hand] hands (Q)
V.1.	16	Fear not] Fear me not (Q)
	21	heard] hear (Q)
	36	Pray] pray you (Q)
V.3.	5	I am] am I (Q)
	77	is] (*not in* Q); are

100   the] thy (Q)

102   ho!] ho! | EDMUND A herald, ho, a herald (Q)
Enter a Herald] (F (*after* 'firmly.')); *most editors
place after line* 106

108   this.] this. | OFFICER Sound, trumpet! (Q)

113   *defence.*] defence. | EDMUND Sound (Q); defence.
| EDMUND Sound trumpet

129   place, youth] youth, place (Q)

153   stop] stople (Q)

158   EDMUND] GONERIL (Q)

273   SECOND OFFICER] CAPTAIN (Q); OFFICER

275   him] them (Q)

*291   sees] says (F)

Words for Music in *King Lear*

The traditional expressions of socially accepted madness in the snatches of court Fool and Bedlam beggar in *King Lear* involve the idea of music, and probably were given, in Elizabethan performance, the reality of music. We may take it that the roles of Edgar and the Fool were played by two of the singing actors in the company. Neither the Quarto nor the Folio, however, has any stage directions indicating singing. It has been left to editors to imagine what music was used. Dr F. W. Sternfeld, to whose work I am indebted, has listed eighteen places in the play where one might expect singing (*Music in Shakespearean Tragedy* (1963), pages 174-5). His list is valuable; but it cannot be accepted just as it stands. It includes one item which does not seem to be a lyric – the Fool's 'prophecy' at the end of Act III, scene 2: fourteen lines which can be rearranged as two stanzas, but still lack the regularity of strophic composition. There are also four passages (items 7, 13, 14, and 15 below) which might have been sung but are not included by Dr Sternfeld. My list therefore contains twenty-one items.

It will be seen that these passages all occur in five scenes in the first three Acts of the play; and that the singing role of the Fool is abandoned in III.4 when Poor Tom joins the group on stage – except that 'Come o'er the burn, Bessy' is shared between the two singing actors.

Three of the passages (items 4, 12, and 19) seem to be from ballads with a wide currency; for two of these (4 and 19) music of the early seventeenth century survives, and is transcribed on pages 589-90. Item 12 ('He that has and a little tiny wit') is related, of course, to the last song of *Twelfth Night*, but no music earlier than the eighteenth century has survived. A transcription is printed in the New Penguin edition of *Twelfth Night*.

For the rest, no tunes with any likelihood of authenticity survive. One can only guess from the subject-matter and the metrical form whether these are traditional words using traditional music; brief comments on these probabilities are given in the list. At least ten of the passages seem unlikely to have been associated with traditional tunes.

Below I indicate the metrical form of each passage, listing the number of stresses in each line aligned above the rhyme scheme (represented by letters); the line division and possible stanzaic structure are indicated by commas and semi-colons.

1. 1.4.117–26 (FOOL Have more than thou showest)

```
2 2 2 2 2 2 2 2 2 2
a, a, a, a, a, a, b, b, b, b
```

The repetition of the (anapaestic) rhythmic structure and of the same rhyme suggests an attempt to create an effect of incantation through words alone, making music superfluous.

2. 1.4.138–45 (FOOL That lord that counselled thee)

```
3 3 3 3     3 3 3 3
a, b, a, b;   c, d, d, d,
```

The form is strophically accurate. But the subject-matter is so germane to *King Lear* that if the passage does have a ballad origin the words must have been much modified. There is an obvious parallel with traditional 'counting-out' songs.

3. 1.4.163–6 (FOOL Fools had ne'er less grace in a year)

```
4 3 4 3
a, b, a, b
```

The form is apt for music, but these words cannot be traditional.

4. 1.4.171–4 (FOOL Then they for sudden joy did weep)

4 3 4 3
a, b, a, b

Lines three and four are obviously Shakespeare's invention, but the first two lines appear (with variations) in several ballad scraps and adaptations of the period. One of these supplies the music cited on page 589; it was written in manuscript in a printed book of 1609 (Thomas Ravencroft's *Pammelia*) now in the British Museum, with the following words:

Late as I waked out of sleep
I heard a pretty thing:
Some men for sudden joy do weep,
And some for sorrow sing.

In the transcription below, Shakespeare's words are fitted to the same tune. The words may be sung as a round, the second and third voices entering at the eighth and fifteenth bars; but of course no such effect was sought in *King Lear*.

5. 1.4.192–4 (FOOL Mum, mum! | He that keeps nor crust nor crumb)

2 4 4
a, a, a

On the repeated rhyme see under item 1. The tone is more that of a proverb than a song.

6. 1.4.211–12 (FOOL The hedge-sparrow fed the cuckoo so long)

4 4
a, a

Again, more a proverb than a song.

7. I.4.221 (FOOL Whoop, Jug, I love thee!)

3
a

Sounds like a ballad-refrain, but not otherwise known.

8. I.4.314–18 (FOOL A fox, when one has caught her)

3 2 2 3 2
a, a, a, a, a

Sounds like a comic exercise in rhyming words notoriously difficult to pronounce.

9. II.4.46–51 (FOOL Fathers that wear rags)

3 3 3 3 3 3
a, b, a, b, c, c

Does not sound like traditional ballad material.

10. II.4.74–81 (FOOL That sir which serves and seeks for gain)

4 3 4 3   4 3 4 3
a, b, a, b;   c, d, c, d

There is no reason why this should not be a ballad; but there is no evidence to connect it with one.

11. III.2.27–34 (FOOL The cod-piece that will house)

3 3 3 3   3 3 3 3
a, b, a, b;   c, d, c, d

The compression and obliquity of language makes this unsuitable for music.

12. III.2.74–7 (FOOL He that has and a little tiny wit)

4 4 4 4
a, b, a, c

The stage direction in the Folio printing of *Twelfth Night* ('*Clowne sings*') tells us that this was a song in Shakespeare's day; but no music of that period has survived.

13. III.4.45 (POOR TOM Through the sharp hawthorn blow the cold winds)

4

a

The phrase is obviously related to Edgar's nakedness; but it would have most effect if derived from traditional material.

14. III.4.73 (POOR TOM Pillicock sat on Pillicock Hill)

4

a

Sounds like a ballad-refrain, but not otherwise known. I have assumed that 'Alow, alow, loo, loo!' – the line following – is an imitation of the huntsman's cry and is not part of a traditional song.

15. III.4.95–6 (POOR TOM Still through the hawthorn blows the cold wind)

4 3

a, b

See under item 13. Line 96 *may* be connected with line 95, and I have so printed it; but it may be a quite disparate remark.

16. III.4.115–18 (POOR TOM S'Withold footed thrice the 'old)

4 4 4

a, a, bb, c

Form and content suggest incantation rather than song.

17. III.4.131–3 (POOR TOM Horse to ride and weapon to wear)

4 4 4
a, a, a

The source in *Bevis of Hampton* makes music unlikely.

18. III.4.176–8 (POOR TOM Child Roland to the dark tower came)

4 4 4
a, a, a

The material is, in part at least, traditional. But these do not sound like words for music.

19. III.6.25–8 (POOR TOM *and* FOOL Come o'er the burn, Bessy, to me)

3 2 2 3
a, b, b, a

Various pieces of music with this title have survived. They raise the question whether Tom should sing the full three lines of the original –

> Come o'er the burn, Bessy,
> Thou little pretty Bessy,
> Come o'er the burn, Bessy, to me –

or merely the shortened version. For the transcription on page 589 I have assumed the latter. The first line is, I take it, merely a cue, used to suggest the song to the audience, to provide a basis on which the Fool can embroider his parody.

The transcription gives the refrain sections of the tune with this heading found in a Cambridge lute manuscript (MS. Dd. 2. 11, fol. 80ᵛ). This seems more appropriate than any tune extracted from the elaborate contrapuntal setting in a British Museum manuscript (Additional MS. 5665, fols. 143–4). I have placed inside square brackets the part of the refrain which is not printed in Shakespeare's text.

20. III.6.41–4 (POOR TOM Sleepest or wakest thou, jolly shepherd?)

4 3 4 3
a, b, c, b

Form and content would make a ballad source quite plausible.

21. III.6.65–72 (POOR TOM Be thy mouth or black or white)

4 4 4 4 4 4 4 4
a, a, b, b, c, c, d, d

These trochaic octosyllabics suggest incantation rather than song. They are strongly reminiscent of the witches' incantations in *Macbeth*.

4. 14.171–4 (Then they for sudden joy did weep)

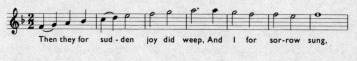

Then they for sud-den joy did weep, And I for sor-row sung,

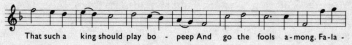

That such a king should play bo - peep And go the fools a-mong. Fa-la-

- la *etc.*

19. III.6.25–8 (Come o'er the burn, Bessy, to me)

KING LEAR
The Characters in the Play

LEAR, King of Britain
GONERILL, Lear's eldest daughter
REGAN, Lear's second daughter
CORDELIA, Lear's youngest daughter
DUKE OF ALBANY, husband of Gonerill
DUKE OF CORNWALL, husband of Regan
KING OF FRANCE
DUKE OF BURGUNDY

EARL OF KENT, later disguised as Caius
EARL OF GLOUCESTER
EDGAR, son of Gloucester, later disguised as Poor Tom
EDMUND, bastard son of Gloucester

OSWALD, Gonerill's steward

Throughout the notes, the abbreviations 'Q' and 'F' refer to the Quarto text of *King Lear* (1608) and the text in the first Folio of Shakespeare's plays (1623). The terms 'Q corrected' and 'Q uncorrected' are explained at length in the Account of the Text (pages 562–4). Other Shakespeare works, where these are not yet published in the New Penguin Shakespeare, are referred to by the lineation in Peter Alexander's edition of the *Complete Works* (1951). Biblical quotations are taken from the Bishops' Bible (1568 etc.), the official English translation of Elizabeth's reign.

The Characters in the Play GENTLEMEN.

'Gentleman' appears in several scenes of the play – II.4, III.1, IV.3, IV.6 (after line 188), IV.7, and V.3. There is no clear carry-over from one scene to another, and all these may be different characters. It is clear that the Folio text has a strong tendency to call all supporting actors 'Gentlemen'. Sometimes the Quarto is more discriminating, sometimes not. If he is a single person the 'Gentleman' (like the 'Knight' in I.5) attends Lear; he leaves Gloucester's castle with him (II.4), is sent by Kent to meet Cordelia (III.1), reports her reactions and is taken to meet Lear (IV.3), comes to find him (IV.6), and attends him in IV.7.

Lear's FOOL
Three KNIGHTS
CURAN, gentleman of Gloucester's household
GENTLEMEN
Three SERVANTS
OLD MAN, a tenant of Gloucester
Two MESSENGERS
DOCTOR, attendant on Cordelia
A CAPTAIN, follower of Edmund
HERALD
Two OFFICERS

Knights of Lear's train, servants, soldiers, attendants,
gentlemen

Enter Kent, Gloucester, and Edmund

KENT I thought the King had more affected the Duke of
Albany than Cornwall.

GLOUCESTER It did always seem so to us. But now in the
division of the kingdom it appears not which of the
Dukes he values most, for qualities are so weighed that
curiosity in neither can make choice of either's moiety.

KENT Is not this your son, my lord?

GLOUCESTER His breeding, sir, hath been at my charge.
I have so often blushed to acknowledge him that now I
am brazed to it.   10

KENT I cannot conceive you.

GLOUCESTER Sir, this young fellow's mother could;
whereupon she grew round-wombed, and had indeed,

1.1 The scene which generates all the subsequent action. A short prelude introducing the names and natures of Gloucester and Edmund leads into a headlong ritual of abdication and 'auction' of the country. Loyalty and sense are exiled from Britain in the persons of Cordelia and Kent, but taken up by the King of France. Hypocrisy and opportunism are left in charge of self-ignorant greatness. (stage direction) *Edmund*. Normally the name used for this character in speech prefixes and stage directions throughout the play, in both Q and F, is '*Bastard*'.

1 *had . . . affected* was fond of

3 *to us* to our people (perhaps an attempt to include Edmund in the conversation)

6 *curiosity in neither can make choice of either's moiety* not even the most scrupulous weighing of advantages can make either prefer the share given to the other
moiety share

8 *His breeding . . . hath been at my charge* I have been financially responsible for his upbringing (or 'I might be held responsible for his birth')

10 *brazed to it* brazen about it

11 *conceive* understand (with secondary reference to 'become pregnant')

sir, a son for her cradle ere she had a husband for her bed. Do you smell a fault?

KENT I cannot wish the fault undone, the issue of it being so proper.

GLOUCESTER But I have a son, sir, by order of law, some year elder than this, who yet is no dearer in my account. Though this knave came something saucily to the world, before he was sent for, yet was his mother fair; there was good sport at his making, and the whoreson must be acknowledged. Do you know this noble gentleman, Edmund?

EDMUND No, my lord.

GLOUCESTER My lord of Kent. Remember him hereafter as my honourable friend.

EDMUND My services to your lordship.

KENT I must love you and sue to know you better.

EDMUND Sir, I shall study deserving.

GLOUCESTER He hath been out nine years, and away he shall again. The King is coming.

> *Sound a sennet. Enter one bearing a coronet*
> *Enter King Lear, Cornwall, Albany, Gonerill, Regan,*
> *Cordelia, and attendants*

LEAR Attend the lords of France and Burgundy, Gloucester.

GLOUCESTER I shall, my liege.

---

15 *smell a fault. A fault* is both (1) a sin; (2) a loss of scent by the hounds.

17 *proper* handsome (but with, perhaps, an ironic undertone of *proper* meaning 'appropriate' (to the *fault*))

18 *by order of law* legitimate

19 *dearer in my account* (the first of the many financial puns in this scene, unless *charge* above, line 8, be so considered)

20 *knave* boy. The sense of 'villain' was available to Shakespeare and may be present by irony.
something somewhat

29 *sue* beg

30 *I shall study deserving* I shall make every effort to deserve your esteem

31 *out* out of the country. This helps to explain the ignorance of Edmund's nature shown both by his brother and by his father.

32 (stage direction) *a sennet* a trumpet call (announcing a movement of important characters)
a coronet. This seems to be designed to be part of a ritual of 'parting' the kingdom, expressed in a no doubt abbreviated form in line 139.

33 *Attend* usher into our presence

Exeunt Gloucester and Edmund

LEAR

Meantime we shall express our darker purpose.
Give me the map there. Know that we have divided
In three our kingdom; and 'tis our fast intent
To shake all cares and business from our age,
Conferring them on younger strengths, while we   40
Unburdened crawl toward death. Our son of Cornwall –
And you, our no less loving son of Albany –
We have this hour a constant will to publish
Our daughters' several dowers, that future strife
May be prevented now. The princes, France and
        Burgundy,
Great rivals in our youngest daughter's love,
Long in our court have made their amorous sojourn,
And here are to be answered. Tell me, my daughters,
Since now we will divest us both of rule,
Interest of territory, cares of state,   50
Which of you shall we say doth love us most,
That we our largest bounty may extend
Where nature doth with merit challenge, Gonerill.

36 *darker* hitherto undivulged
37 *the map.* Marshall McLuhan says 'the map was also a novelty . . . and was key to the new vision of peripheries of power and wealth . . . the map brings forward at once a principal theme of *King Lear*, namely the isolation of the visual sense as a kind of blindness' (*The Gutenberg Galaxy* (1962), page 11).
37–8 *we have divided* | . . . *our kingdom.* The text 'Every kingdom divided against itself is brought to desolation' (Matthew 12.25) would occur to many Elizabethan minds. See Introduction, page 543.
38 *'tis our fast intent. Fast* means 'firm', and sorts oddly with *shake* in the following line. Notice the similar contradiction in line 41, where 'un-

burdening' leads to 'crawling'. The impression is given of the abdication as a charade rather than a necessity.
43 *constant will to publish* settled intention to promulgate
44 *several* separate
45 *prevented* forestalled
46 *Great* noble, powerful
49 *both.* Shakespeare sets 'both' before three (instead of the usual two) cognate nouns in several other places.
50 *Interest of territory* right or title to the territory
52 *largest* most generous
53 *Where nature doth with merit challenge* to the person in whom natural filial affection can be rewarded as if it were objective *merit* (since the merit and the filial love challenge one another as equals)

Our eldest born, speak first.

GONERILL

Sir, I love you more than word can wield the matter,
Dearer than eyesight, space, and liberty,
Beyond what can be valued rich or rare,
No less than life, with grace, health, beauty, honour,
As much as child e'er loved or father found;
60   A love that makes breath poor and speech unable;
Beyond all manner of 'so much' I love you.

CORDELIA (*aside*)

What shall Cordelia speak? Love, and be silent.

LEAR

Of all these bounds, even from this line to this,
With shadowy forests and with champains riched,
With plenteous rivers and wide-skirted meads,
We make thee lady. To thine and Albany's issues
Be this perpetual. – What says our second daughter,
Our dearest Regan, wife of Cornwall?

REGAN

I am made of that self mettle as my sister
70   And price me at her worth. In my true heart

55 *I love you more than word can wield the matter* the *matter* of my love is too weighty to be lifted or expressed by language
56 *space, and liberty* freedom from confinement, and the enjoyment of that freedom
59 *As much as . . . father found* as much as any father ever found himself to be loved
60 *breath* ('speech' rather than 'life' – repeating the idea of line 55)
unable incompetent
61 *Beyond all manner of 'so much'* beyond all manner of ways of saying 'so much'
62 *Love, and be silent.* Gonerill has *spoken* of love. Cordelia therefore finds speech devalued; she cannot speak, but only love in fact, and so be silent.

63 *bounds* boundaries
64 *champains* flat open country
65 *wide-skirted meads* widely spread-out meadows
67 *Be this perpetual.* This is no temporary division of the kingdom. From now on, Britain will cease to exist as an entity.
69 *self* same
mettle spirit. But the pun on 'metal' is given strength by *price* and *worth* in the following line (and by their opposition to *true heart*) – with the implication: 'My price can be measured in metal'.
70 *price me* evaluate myself. F reads 'prize', but the two words were not clearly differentiated, and *price* seems the more appropriate modern form.

I find she names my very deed of love;
Only she comes too short, that I profess
Myself an enemy to all other joys
Which the most precious square of sense possesses,
And find I am alone felicitate
In your dear highness' love.

CORDELIA (*aside*)   Then poor Cordelia!
And yet not so, since I am sure my love's
More ponderous than my tongue.

LEAR

To thee and thine hereditary ever
Remain this ample third of our fair kingdom,   80
No less in space, validity, and pleasure
Than that conferred on Gonerill. – Now, our joy,
Although our last and least, to whose young love
The vines of France and milk of Burgundy
Strive to be interested: what can you say to draw
A third more opulent than your sisters'? Speak!

---

71 *names my very deed* gives the very particulars of my deed
deed (1) action; (2) legal instrument. Regan finds in her heart a document containing the very words that Gonerill has been using.

72 *that* in that

74 *Which the most precious square of sense possesses* which the senses, not 'out of square' (unbalanced) but in their proper constitution – the constitution that is so precious to us – possess

75 *felicitate* joyful

76 *poor* (because (1) she feels the lack of gifts within her; (2) she cannot join in the exchange of these high-flown 'golden' sentiments, and must be *poor* as a result)

77–8 *my love's | More ponderous than my tongue*. Compare line 55 and lines 91–2, where we find the same

sense of the glib tongue as the lever of the heart's weighty affections. This supports F's 'ponderous' against Q's 'richer'.

79 *hereditary ever*. See the note on line 67.

81 *validity*. Shakespeare frequently uses the word in the sense of 'value'.

83 *least* littlest (or perhaps, as youngest, 'last in precedence'). Cordelia's low stature may be implied elsewhere (for example, line 198 of this scene). The Q reading, 'last, not least', is easier, but the text may have been remembered in this form because of the very triteness of the phrase.

84 *milk of Burgundy*. Burgundy was notable for the fertility of its land, though not particularly devoted to milk production.

85 *interested* admitted (as to a privilege)

CORDELIA Nothing, my lord.

LEAR Nothing?

CORDELIA Nothing.

LEAR

90   Nothing will come of nothing. Speak again.

CORDELIA

Unhappy that I am, I cannot heave
My heart into my mouth. I love your majesty
According to my bond, no more nor less.

LEAR

How, how, Cordelia! Mend your speech a little
Lest you may mar your fortunes.

CORDELIA   Good my lord,
You have begot me, bred me, loved me.
I return those duties back as are right fit,
Obey you, love you, and most honour you.
Why have my sisters husbands, if they say

100   They love you all? Haply when I shall wed,
That lord whose hand must take my plight shall carry
Half my love with him, half my care and duty.
Sure I shall never marry like my sisters,
To love my father all.

LEAR

But goes thy heart with this?

CORDELIA   Ay, my good lord.

LEAR So young, and so untender?

---

87 *Nothing* (I can say nothing designed
to draw | *A third more opulent*. I
refuse to enter this charade.)

93 *According to my bond* according to my
bounden duty, the bond of natural
affection and respect between child
and parent

97 *those duties back as are right fit* the
duties that are fitting to be returned,
in answer to your kindnesses, and
According to my bond

98 *Obey you, love you, and most honour you.*

Shakespeare seems to be remembering the marriage service in the Prayer
Book ('Wilt thou obey him, love,
honour, and keep him . . .'), in preparation for the comparison with
these duties owed to a husband.

100 *all* with the whole of themselves
Haply perhaps

101 *take my plight* accept my troth-plight
(vow of marriage)

106 *untender* inflexible, stiff in opinions

CORDELIA So young, my lord, and true.

LEAR

Let it be so! Thy truth then be thy dower!
For by the sacred radiance of the sun,
The mysteries of Hecat and the night,   110
By all the operation of the orbs
From whom we do exist, and cease to be,
Here I disclaim all my paternal care,
Propinquity and property of blood,
And as a stranger to my heart and me
Hold thee from this for ever. The barbarous Scythian,
Or he that makes his generation messes
To gorge his appetite, shall to my bosom
Be as well neighboured, pitied, and relieved
As thou my sometime daughter.

KENT   Good my liege –   120

LEAR Peace, Kent!
Come not between the dragon and his wrath.

---

107 *true* growing straight; stiff, perhaps, but accurate and unerring

110 *mysteries.* F reads 'miseries', Q, 'mistresse'. This provides a good example of the way in which both texts can contribute to the true reading.
Hecat and the night. Following the *radiance of the sun*, and preceding *the orbs*, this may refer to Hecat – more properly 'Hecatè' – as the moon; but *mysteries* suggests the Hecat who presides over witchcraft.

111–12 *the operation of the orbs | From whom we do exist, and cease to be* the influence of the stars on the lives of men, controlling life and death

116 *Scythian* (an inhabitant of the region now occupied by Russia, remarked by the Roman poets as savage and barbarous)

117–18 *he that makes his generation messes |*

To gorge his appetite a barbarian, who chops up his parents (or his children) for food, just out of gluttony. The sense of *generation* as 'parents' gives a slightly better parallel with the actual parent–child situation that Lear sees.

118–19 *shall to my bosom | Be as well neighboured, pitied, and relieved* shall be as close to my bosom, and as within the kindnesses of intimate kinship. The forecast of his own situation in the heath scenes should be noticed.

120 *sometime* former

122 *dragon* (appropriate to the British (as against English) monarchy, imagined as carrying the Welsh red dragon emblem on their coats-of-arms)

I loved her most, and thought to set my rest
On her kind nursery. (*To Cordelia*) Hence and avoid
    my sight! –
So be my grave my peace as here I give
Her father's heart from her. Call France! Who stirs?
Call Burgundy! Cornwall and Albany,
With my two daughters' dowers digest the third.
Let pride, which she calls plainness, marry her.
130   I do invest you jointly with my power,
Pre-eminence, and all the large effects
That troop with majesty. Ourself by monthly course,
With reservation of an hundred knights,
By you to be sustained, shall our abode
Make with you by due turn. Only we shall retain
The name and all th'addition to a king; the sway,
Revenue, execution of the rest,
Beloved sons, be yours; which to confirm,
This coronet part between you.

KENT   Royal Lear,

123 *set my rest* (1) stake all I have on the bet (a term in the card game of primero); (2) repose in retirement

124 *nursery* nursing, loving care
Hence and avoid my sight! (addressed, presumably, to Cordelia; but it appears that she does not obey, and that Lear accepts this, since he calls for France and Burgundy)

126 *Who stirs?* get moving, somebody! Don't stand staring!

128 *digest* assimilate, incorporate

129 *Let pride, which she calls plainness, marry her* instead of a dowry to win a husband, she will have to buy one with the pride which she thinks of as plain-speaking

131-2 *all the large effects | That troop with majesty* all the splendid panoply that accompanies the condition of being a king; and also all that *results*

from being a king. Lear is to be a king outside the world of cause and effect.

132 *by monthly course* moving round, one month with Regan, one month with Gonerill, and so on

133 *With reservation* the privilege (of having the knights) being reserved or exempted from the agreement

135 *Only* as a sole exception

136 *th'addition* the external honours

137 *Revenue* (accented on the second syllable)

139 *This coronet part between you.* They are to divide royal authority (symbolized by the coronet) between them. Perhaps one should imagine an appropriate stage action in which Gonerill and Regan touch or grasp the coronet.

Whom I have ever honoured as my king,   140
Loved as my father, as my master followed,
As my great patron thought on in my prayers –

LEAR

The bow is bent and drawn; make from the shaft.

KENT

Let it fall rather, though the fork invade
The region of my heart. Be Kent unmannerly
When Lear is mad. What wouldst thou do, old man?
Think'st thou that duty shall have dread to speak
When power to flattery bows? To plainness honour's
        bound
When majesty stoops to folly. Reserve thy state,
And in thy best consideration check   150

143 *The bow is bent and drawn; make from the shaft* you have wound up your speech in order to make some important point. Now let the point (barbed, no doubt) fly forward like an arrow. *Make from* is unknown to dictionaries, but must give some sense like 'let go'.

144–5 *Let it fall rather, though the fork invade | The region of my heart* I should prefer that my argumentative point should not hit you, even if the mis-shot arrow should kill me instead

145–6 *Be Kent unmannerly | When Lear is mad* my lack of manners could be justified only if you were mad

146 *thou.* The second-person singular, normally used to inferiors and intimates, is very extraordinary when applied to a king; Kent seems to be trying shock therapy in an attempt to bring Lear to his senses.

147–9 *duty ... power ... flattery ... honour ... majesty.* Kent presents an allegorical diagram of the relationships. *Duty* (Kent) must speak when *power* (Lear) bows to *flattery* (Gonerill and Regan); *honour* (Kent) must be plain-spoken when *majesty* (Lear) is foolish.

149 *stoops to folly.* The F reading, 'falls to folly', is easily explained by the conflation in the compositor's memory of the sound of *folly* and the idea of *stoops.*

Reserve thy state. Both this (the F reading) and Q's 'Reuerse thy doome' make reasonable sense. Q is not only, however, the weaker text in general; here it gives a more obvious sense, more likely to be the product of a vulgarizing and simplifying memory than the F reading, which has the sense 'Don't give away your power' (repeated in *Revoke thy gift* below – line 164). There would be little point in linking 'Reverse thy doom' ('Cancel your sentence on Cordelia') to *best consideration*; but *Reserve thy state* links well: 'Do not give your power away; hold back your decision and consider it carefully'.

150–51 *in thy best consideration check | This hideous rashness* restrain this terrible speed of abdication by pausing and considering it well

This hideous rashness. Answer my life my judgement,
Thy youngest daughter does not love thee least,
Nor are those empty-hearted whose low sounds
Reverb no hollowness.

LEAR   Kent, on thy life, no more!

KENT

My life I never held but as a pawn
To wage against thine enemies; nor fear to lose it,
Thy safety being motive.

LEAR   Out of my sight!

KENT

See better, Lear, and let me still remain
The true blank of thine eye.

LEAR

Now by Apollo –

160   KENT   Now by Apollo, King,
Thou swear'st thy gods in vain.

LEAR   O vassal, miscreant!

He makes to strike him

ALBANY *and* CORNWALL Dear sir, forbear!

KENT

Kill thy physician and thy fee bestow

---

151 *Answer my life my judgement* I will
stake my life on my opinion

153–4 *whose low sounds | Reverb no hollow-
ness.* 'Empty vessels sound most'; so,
by inversion, those who make little
noise may be thought to do so because they lack the hollow hearts of
hypocrites. *Reverb* seems to be a
Shakespearian coinage for 'reverber-
ate'.

157 *motive* that which promotes (my
action)

158–9 *let me still remain | The true blank
of thine eye* instead of ordering me out
of your sight, make me always the
means of point-blank true aim from
your eyes; looking through me you

will see things accurately. *Blank* has
usually been taken to mean 'the
bull's-eye of a target'; but the evidence suggests rather that *true blank*
means 'the direct line of sight', as of
an arrow or gun directed 'truly', that
is point-blank, at its target.

158 *still* always

160 *Apollo* (an appropriate god to
invoke at this point, as he was both
the archer-god (the god of straight
aiming at targets) and the sun-god
(the god of clear seeing))

161 *miscreant* unbeliever. Kent has
denied the gods.

163–4 *thy fee bestow | Upon the foul disease*
give the reward you should lavish

Upon the foul disease. Revoke thy gift,
Or whilst I can vent clamour from my throat
I'll tell thee thou dost evil.
LEAR   Hear me, recreant,
On thine allegiance hear me!
That thou hast sought to make us break our vow,
Which we durst never yet, and, with strained pride,
To come betwixt our sentence and our power,   170
Which nor our nature nor our place can bear,
Our potency made good, take thy reward.
Five days we do allot thee for provision
To shield thee from disasters of the world,
And on the sixth to turn thy hated back
Upon our kingdom. If on the tenth day following
Thy banished trunk be found in our dominions
The moment is thy death. Away! By Jupiter,
This shall not be revoked!
KENT

Fare thee well, King, sith thus thou wilt appear,   180
Freedom lives hence and banishment is here.
(*To Cordelia*)
The gods to their dear shelter take thee, maid,

on healthful advisers to those against whom they advise you, those who will be your death

168 *That* seeing that

169 *strained pride* pride that leads you to excess

170 *betwixt our sentence and our power* between my words and my deeds, my legal enactment and the fulfilment of it

171 *nor . . . nor* neither . . . nor

172 *Our potency made good* the potential of my power being fulfilled in execution. Lear says that since Kent has interposed himself between *sentence* and *power* he will find no gap between these two in his case: the sentence and power will appear together.

177 *trunk* body

179 *This shall not be revoked.* The emphasis is on *This*, with reference to line 164.

180–87 Kent's couplets, divided formally between the King, Cordelia, Gonerill and Regan, 'princes', mark the recession of the verse-level from immediate passion to sententious generality.

180–81 *sith thus thou wilt appear, | Freedom lives hence and banishment is here* since you are determined to act the tyrant, there can be no freedom in Britain

That justly think'st and hast most rightly said.
(*To Gonerill and Regan*)
And your large speeches may your deeds approve
That good effects may spring from words of love. –
Thus Kent, O princes, bids you all adieu;
He'll shape his old course in a country new.   *Exit*
        Flourish. Enter Gloucester with France and
        Burgundy, and attendants

GLOUCESTER
Here's France and Burgundy, my noble lord.

LEAR My lord of Burgundy,

190   We first address toward you, who with this king
        Hath rivalled for our daughter: what in the least
        Will you require in present dower with her
        Or cease your quest of love?

BURGUNDY   Most royal majesty,
        I crave no more than hath your highness offered,
        Nor will you tender less.

LEAR   Right noble Burgundy,
        When she was dear to us we did hold her so;
        But now her price is fallen. Sir, there she stands;
        If aught within that little-seeming substance,
        Or all of it, with our displeasure pieced,

200   And nothing more, may fitly like your grace,

184 *approve* confirm
185 *effects* results, realizations. The anti-
    thesis in lines 184 and 185 is, once
    again, that between *words* and *deeds*.
187 *shape his old course* 'continue to act
    upon the same principles' (Dr John-
    son) – of faithfulness, truth, and
    plain-speaking
(stage direction) *Flourish* a fanfare (used
    on stage to mark the ceremonial
    entry (or exit) of important persons)
191 *in the least* at the lowest
196 *so* dear, expensive, worth a large
    dowry

198 *little-seeming substance*. The phrase is
    difficult to disentangle (the hyphen
    is, of course, a modern addition).
    The charge can hardly be that Cord-
    elia is *little*; but it is likely to involve
    seeming (hypocrisy) – a Shakespearian
    obsession. Perhaps the best interpreta-
    tion is an ironic one, 'that girl so
    devoted to *substance* and fact, so *little*
    concerned with *seeming*'.
199 *pieced* augmented (here used
    ironically)
200 *fitly like* please by its fitness

She's there and she is yours.

BURGUNDY   I know no answer.

LEAR

Will you with those infirmities she owes,
Unfriended, new-adopted to our hate,
Dowered with our curse and strangered with our oath,
Take her or leave her?

BURGUNDY   Pardon me, royal sir,
Election makes not up in such conditions.

LEAR

Then leave her, sir, for, by the power that made me,
I tell you all her wealth. (*To France*) For you, great
          king,
I would not from your love make such a stray
To match you where I hate; therefore beseech you   210
T'avert your liking a more worthier way
Than on a wretch whom Nature is ashamed
Almost t'acknowledge hers.

FRANCE   This is most strange,
That she whom even but now was your best object,
The argument of your praise, balm of your age,
The best, the dearest, should in this trice of time

---

202 *those infirmities she owes* the disabilities she possesses. He proceeds to
enumerate them.
owes owns
204 *strangered with our oath* made a
stranger (to me) by my swearing to
sever our relationship (above, lines
113 ff.)
206 *Election makes not up in such conditions*
it is impossible to settle a choice
(*Take her or leave her*) when the condition of the lady is of the kind you
describe. This explains the *I know no
answer* at line 201.
208 *tell* (1) report to; (2) count

For you as for you
209 *make such a stray* stray so far
211 *T'avert your liking a more worthier way*
to turn your love in the direction of
some person more worth it
212-13 *Nature is ashamed | Almost t'ac-
knowledge hers.* Lear seems to be
denying Cordelia not only kinship to
him, but kinship to the human
species.
214 *your best object* the thing you best
liked to gaze upon
215 *The argument of your praise* the theme
you chose for praise

Commit a thing so monstrous to dismantle
So many folds of favour. Sure her offence
Must be of such unnatural degree
220 That monsters it; or your fore-vouched affection
Fall into taint; which to believe of her
Must be a faith that reason without miracle
Should never plant in me.

CORDELIA   I yet beseech your majesty –
If for I want that glib and oily art
To speak and purpose not, since what I well intend
I'll do't before I speak – that you make known
It is no vicious blot, murder or foulness,
No unchaste action or dishonoured step
That hath deprived me of your grace and favour,
230 But even for want of that for which I am richer:
A still-soliciting eye and such a tongue
That I am glad I have not, though not to have it
Hath lost me in your liking.

LEAR   Better thou
Hadst not been born than not t'have pleased me better.

---

217 *to* as to
217–18 *dismantle | So many folds of favour* strip away the protective clothing of your favour (the first appearance of the idea of stripping clothes, later so important in the play
219–20 *Must be of such unnatural degree | That monsters it* must be so far beyond ordinary human offences as to be monstrous
220–21 *or your fore-vouched affection | Fall into taint* if her offence is not monstrous then the alternative is for the affection for her you used to affirm to become suspect
221 *which to believe* to believe that her offence is so monstrous
221–3 *to believe ... Must be a faith that reason without miracle | Should never plant* to believe (in so impossible a thing) requires *faith*, and faith cannot be implanted by rational means, unaccompanied by the miraculous
224 *If for I want* if it is because I lack
225 *and purpose not* without intending to fulfil what I have spoken
227 *murder.* Critics have made the point that *murder* is a crime Cordelia need not clear herself of, for no one has accused her of it; but she is rehearsing here not her own real crimes, but the extremes that might be assumed of *a wretch whom Nature is ashamed | Almost t'acknowledge hers.*
228 *dishonoured* dishonourable
230 *for which* for want of which
231 *still-soliciting* always ogling for favours

FRANCE

    Is it but this, a tardiness in nature
    Which often leaves the history unspoke
    That it intends to do? My lord of Burgundy,
    What say you to the lady? Love's not love
    When it is mingled with regards that stands
    Aloof from th'entire point. Will you have her?   240
    She is herself a dowry.

BURGUNDY   Royal Lear,
    Give but that portion which yourself proposed
    And here I take Cordelia by the hand,
    Duchess of Burgundy.

LEAR

    Nothing! I have sworn; I am firm.

BURGUNDY (*to Cordelia*)

    I am sorry then you have so lost a father
    That you must lose a husband.

CORDELIA   Peace be with Burgundy!
    Since that respect and fortunes are his love,
    I shall not be his wife.

FRANCE

    Fairest Cordelia, that art most rich, being poor,   250
    Most choice, forsaken, and most loved, despised,

---

235 *tardiness in nature* natural reticence

236–7 *leaves the history unspoke | That it intends to do* does not speak out the inner thoughts which, none the less, it purposes to enact

239 *regards that stands.* The coupling of a plural subject with a singular verb was not a clear breach of grammar in Elizabethan English.

239–40 *regards that stands | Aloof from th'entire point* considerations (of dowry etc.) that stand quite apart from the single unqualified issue (love)

242 *portion* dowry

248 *Since that* since. Elizabethan English adds 'that' to several conjunctions and relative adverbs ('if that', 'when that', etc.) without altering sense, but giving added emphasis.

respect and fortunes are his love what he's in love with is worldly status and wealth

250–51 *art most rich, being poor, | Most choice, forsaken, and most loved, despised.* Some of the resonance of these lines no doubt comes from the reminiscence of 2 Corinthians 6.10, where Paul speaks of the ministry of Christ as 'poor, yet making many rich ... having nothing, and yet possessing all things'.

Thee and thy virtues here I seize upon.
Be it lawful I take up what's cast away.
Gods, gods! 'Tis strange that from their cold'st neglect
My love should kindle to inflamed respect.
Thy dowerless daughter, King, thrown to my chance,
Is queen of us, of ours, and our fair France.
Not all the dukes of waterish Burgundy
Can buy this unprized-precious maid of me.
260   Bid them farewell, Cordelia, though unkind.
Thou losest here, a better where to find.

LEAR

Thou hast her, France; let her be thine, for we
Have no such daughter, nor shall ever see
That face of hers again. Therefore begone,
Without our grace, our love, our benison!
Come, noble Burgundy.

> *Flourish. Exeunt Lear, Burgundy, Cornwall,*
> *Albany, Gloucester, and attendants*

FRANCE   Bid farewell to your sisters.

CORDELIA

The jewels of our father, with washed eyes
Cordelia leaves you. I know you what you are;
270   And, like a sister, am most loath to call
Your faults as they are named. Love well our father!

254–65 The couplets indicate (as usual) a formalization of the attitudes involved.

254–5 *from their cold'st neglect | My love should kindle.* He loves her because the gods seem to have abandoned her – the opposite process to that appearing in Burgundy.

258 *waterish Burgundy.* Burgundy is full of streams and rivers; but the principal implication of *water* here is of weakness, dilution (as against *wine*).

259 *unprized-precious* offered at no price at all by her father, but regarded as precious by me

260 *though unkind* though they have not acted like a family to you (yet you should preserve family decencies to them)

261 *Thou losest here, a better where to find. Here* and *where* are nouns: 'You are losing this place, in order to find a better place elsewhere'.

265 *benison* blessing

268 *washed* (1) washed with tears; (2) cleared, able to see you as you really are

271 *as they are named* by their true (unpleasant) names

To your professèd bosoms I commit him.
But yet, alas, stood I within his grace,
I would prefer him to a better place.
So farewell to you both.

REGAN
Prescribe not us our duty.

GONERILL   Let your study
Be to content your lord, who hath received you
At Fortune's alms. You have obedience scanted,
And well are worth the want that you have wanted.

CORDELIA
Time shall unfold what plighted cunning hides;   280
Who covers faults, at last with shame derides.
Well may you prosper!

FRANCE   Come, my fair Cordelia.

Exeunt France and Cordelia

GONERILL Sister, it is not little I have to say of what most
nearly appertains to us both. I think our father will
hence tonight.

REGAN That's most certain, and with you; next month
with us.

GONERILL You see how full of changes his age is. The
observation we have made of it hath not been little. He
always loved our sister most; and with what poor judge-   290
ment he hath now cast her off appears too grossly.

REGAN 'Tis the infirmity of his age. Yet he hath ever but
slenderly known himself

272 *To your professèd bosoms* to the tender
care you have alleged you felt
276 *study* effort, endeavour
278 *At Fortune's alms* as a charity give-
away
scanted stinted
279 *are worth the want that you have wanted*
deserve the want of that (affection)
which you have shown you lack (towards your father)

280 *plighted cunning* (the cunning that (1)
is pleated, plaited, folded under, concealed; (2) involves 'plighting', or
swearing as the truth, things that are
false)
281 *Who covers faults, at last with shame
derides* time begins by concealing
faults, but at last reveals them, to
the shame and derision of the
malefactors

GONERILL The best and soundest of his time hath been
but rash. Then must we look from his age to receive not
alone the imperfections of long-ingraffed condition, but
therewithal the unruly waywardness that infirm and
choleric years bring with them.

REGAN Such unconstant starts are we like to have from
300   him as this of Kent's banishment.

GONERILL There is further compliment of leave-taking
between France and him. Pray you, let us hit together.
If our father carry authority with such disposition as he
bears, this last surrender of his will but offend us.

REGAN We shall further think of it.

GONERILL We must do something, and i'th'heat.

                                  Exeunt

I.2   *Enter Edmund*

EDMUND
   Thou, Nature, art my goddess; to thy law

295 *look* expect
296 *imperfections of long-ingraffed condition*
faults firmly implanted (grafted) in
his character
297 *unruly waywardness* unpredictable
petulance
299 *unconstant starts* sudden jerks (as of a
frightened horse)
301 *compliment of leave-taking* ceremonious farewell
302 *hit together*. This probably means
'agree with one another', 'fit in with
one another', but 'aim together' is
also possible. In any case the sense
of physical violence cannot be wholly
discounted.
303–4 *If our father carry authority with
such disposition as he bears, this last
surrender of his will but offend us* if our
father persists in acting over our
heads, as he just has, this power that

he has just surrendered to us will
only do us harm
306 *We must do something.* The emphasis is
on *do* as against *think* in the line before.
and i'th'heat and strike while the
iron is hot

I.2 Edmund reveals that he is as evilly
calculating as Gonerill and Regan
(though more self-analytical). Gloucester
parallels Lear in folly, but on a lower
level of energy. Superstition makes him
a prey to ruthless intellectual exploitation
– as does the relaxed guilelessness of
Edgar.

1 *Nature* (a key-word in the play; see
Introduction, pages 524–5. What
seems to be meant here is a sanction
that precedes civilized law, the law
of nations, and lays stress on those
endowments that promote life in its

My services are bound. Wherefore should I
Stand in the plague of custom and permit
The curiosity of nations to deprive me,
For that I am some twelve or fourteen moonshines
Lag of a brother? Why bastard? Wherefore base?
When my dimensions are as well-compact,
My mind as generous, and my shape as true
As honest madam's issue? Why brand they us
With 'base'? with 'baseness'? 'bastardy'? 'base, base'?   10
Who in the lusty stealth of nature take
More composition and fierce quality
Than doth within a dull, stale, tired bed
Go to the creating a whole tribe of fops
Got 'tween asleep and wake? Well then,

most primitive conditions, nature red
in tooth and claw.)
goddess. Edmund must be thinking of
a mother-Nature goddess, a goddess
of fertility, whose rights precede
those of civilization.
law (the 'law', that is, of the jungle)
2 *services are bound.* Edmund sees his relation to his 'goddess' as a parody of
the feudal *service* owed to a liege
lord.
3 *Stand in the plague of custom* be subject
to the disabilities that customary law
imposes on younger sons. Edmund
might seem to be referring here to
his bastardy – the audience already
knows about this (1.1.12–15) – but it
emerges in line 5 that he is talking
about his status as a younger son.
4 *The curiosity of nations* the fine discriminations established by mere national
laws
deprive me (1) reduce my powers; (2)
disinherit me (younger sons did not,
bastards could not, inherit)
5 *For that* because
moonshines months
6 *Lag of* lagging behind

bastard . . . base. Edmund plays on *base*:
(1) ('baseborn') bastard; (2) low, vile,
despicable. He proceeds to prove *bastard* untrue as a description, because
he is not *base* in the second sense.
7 *my dimensions are as well-compact* I am as
well formed
8 *generous* gentleman-like
as true as truly stamped in my
father's image
9 *honest madam* the legitimate's married
mother
10–21 *base . . . legitimate.* 'Any word, if
repeated over and over in a mono-
tone, seems to lose its significance.
Edmund plays this trick with *base*
and *legitimate*, in order to prove that
they are meaningless terms' (G. L.
Kittredge).
11–12 *Who . . . take | More composition
and fierce quality* whose making requires more vigorous effort and
energy
11 *lusty stealth of nature. Lusty* involves
both vigour and lust: 'natural' love
(or lust) has to be vigorously taken,
or stolen.
14 *fops* fools

Legitimate Edgar, I must have your land.
Our father's love is to the bastard Edmund
As to the legitimate. Fine word 'legitimate'!
Well, my 'legitimate', if this letter speed
20   And my invention thrive, Edmund the base
Shall top the legitimate. I grow. I prosper.
Now gods stand up for bastards!

    Enter Gloucester

GLOUCESTER

Kent banished thus? and France in choler parted?
And the King gone tonight? prescribed his power?
Confined to exhibition? All this done
Upon the gad? Edmund, how now? What news?

EDMUND   So please your lordship, none.

GLOUCESTER   Why so earnestly seek you to put up that
letter?

30   EDMUND   I know no news, my lord.

GLOUCESTER   What paper were you reading?

EDMUND   Nothing, my lord.

GLOUCESTER   No? What needed then that terrible dispatch of it into your pocket? The quality of nothing
hath not such need to hide itself. Let's see! Come! If it
be nothing I shall not need spectacles.

17–18 *Our father's love ... legitimate* (recalling Gloucester's words at 1.1.19)

19 *speed* prosper

20 *invention* power of inventing (lies)

21 *top the*. This is an emendation from
Q's 'tooth' and F's 'to'th''. *Top* gives
excellent and Edmund-like extension
to the meanings of *base* in the preceding line: the *base* (low) will *top* (surpass, be higher than) the legitimate
Edgar.

23 *France in choler parted*. We have not
seen this; but the phrase serves as
convenient and dramatic shorthand
for the mode of relationship between
Cordelia and the rest of her family.

24 *prescribed his power* instructed about

what power he may possess. The Q
reading, 'subscribd his power', is
possible, but need not be preferred.

25 *Confined to exhibition* restricted to a
small allowance

26 *Upon the gad* suddenly (as a horse is
caused to bolt by a goad or *gad*)

28 *put up* pocket, conceal

33–4 *dispatch* (1) haste; (2) removal

34–5 *The quality of nothing hath not such
need to hide itself* if there was nothing
there, you wouldn't need to hide it;
it is not the nature of nothing to
require concealment

35–6 *If it be nothing I shall not need spectacles.* Note the anticipated irony:
here Gloucester is confident of the

EDMUND I beseech you, sir, pardon me. It is a letter from
my brother that I have not all o'er-read; and for so much
as I have perused, I find it not fit for your o'erlooking.

GLOUCESTER Give me the letter, sir.   40

EDMUND I shall offend either to detain or give it. The
contents, as in part I understand them, are to blame.

GLOUCESTER Let's see, let's see!

EDMUND I hope for my brother's justification he wrote
this but as an essay or taste of my virtue.

GLOUCESTER (*reading*) *This policy and reverence of age
makes the world bitter to the best of our times, keeps our
fortunes from us till our oldness cannot relish them. I begin
to find an idle and fond bondage in the oppression of aged
tyranny, who sways not as it hath power but as it is*   50
*suffered. Come to me that of this I may speak more. If our
father would sleep till I waked him, you should enjoy half
his revenue for ever, and live the beloved of your brother,*
                                                        Edgar.
Hum! Conspiracy! 'Sleep till I waked him, you should
enjoy half his revenue'. My son Edgar, had he a hand to
write this? a heart and brain to breed it in? When came
you to this? Who brought it?

power of his eyesight to distinguish
something from *nothing*; later he learns,
without eyes, the potentialities that
stem from deprivation, or *nothing*.

38–9 *for so much as I have perused* as far as
I have read it

39 *o'erlooking* perusal

42 *to blame* objectionable

45 *essay* (the same word as 'assay', a first
trial or sip – used technically of the
official 'tasting' of a great person's
food)

46 *policy and reverence* (hendiadys for
'policy of reverence') politic trick of
making us reverence

47 *to the best of our times* in the heyday of
our life

48 *our oldness cannot relish them* we are too
old to enjoy them

49–51 *an idle and fond bondage in the oppression of aged tyranny, who sways not as it
hath power but as it is suffered* the
tyrannical oppression of one's elders
(in withholding patrimonies etc.) is a
kind of slavery that it is needless and
foolish to submit to, for it operates
through our passivity, not because
of its strength

51–2 *If our father would sleep till I waked
him* if our father were put into my
power to decide his sleeping or
waking (that is, death or life)

53, 56 *revenue* (accented on the second
syllable)

EDMUND It was not brought me, my lord. There's the
60   cunning of it. I found it thrown in at the casement of my
closet.

GLOUCESTER You know the character to be your
brother's?

EDMUND If the matter were good, my lord, I durst swear
it were his; but in respect of that I would fain think it
were not.

GLOUCESTER It is his!

EDMUND It is his hand, my lord; but I hope his heart is
not in the contents.

70 GLOUCESTER Has he never before sounded you in this
business?

EDMUND Never, my lord. But I have heard him oft maintain it to be fit that, sons at perfect age and fathers
declined, the father should be as ward to the son, and
the son manage his revenue.

GLOUCESTER O villain, villain! His very opinion in the
letter! Abhorred villain! Unnatural, detested, brutish
villain! worse than brutish! Go, sirrah, seek him. I'll
apprehend him. Abominable villain! Where is he?

80 EDMUND I do not well know, my lord. If it shall please
you to suspend your indignation against my brother till
you can derive from him better testimony of his intent,
you should run a certain course; where, if you violently
proceed against him, mistaking his purpose, it would
make a great gap in your own honour and shake in
pieces the heart of his obedience. I dare pawn down my
life for him that he hath writ this to feel my affection to

61 *closet* study
62 *character* handwriting
65 *in respect of that* considering what the
    subject-matter really is
70 *sounded you* taken soundings or meas-
    urements of your depths
73 *fit* appropriate
    at perfect age being fully mature
    and adult

74 *ward* a minor, under protection of a
    guardian who managed his affairs
77 *detested* detestable
83 *run a certain course* proceed through
    certainties
    where whereas
86 *pawn down* stake
87 *feel* test

your honour and to no other pretence of danger.

GLOUCESTER Think you so?

EDMUND If your honour judge it meet I will place you   90
where you shall hear us confer of this and by an
auricular assurance have your satisfaction, and that
without any further delay than this very evening.

GLOUCESTER He cannot be such a monster –

EDMUND Nor is not, sure.

GLOUCESTER To his father that so tenderly and entirely
loves him. Heaven and earth! Edmund, seek him out.
Wind me into him, I pray you. Frame the business after
your own wisdom. I would unstate myself to be in a due
resolution.   100

EDMUND I will seek him, sir, presently, convey the business as I shall find means, and acquaint you withal.

GLOUCESTER These late eclipses in the sun and moon
portend no good to us. Though the wisdom of nature
can reason it thus and thus, yet nature finds itself
scourged by the sequent effects: love cools, friendship
falls off, brothers divide. In cities, mutinies; in countries,
discord; in palaces, treason; and the bond cracked 'twixt
son and father. This villain of mine comes under the

---

88 *pretence of danger* dangerous intention

90 *meet* proper

91–2 *by an auricular assurance have your satisfaction* satisfy yourself with certainties based on what you yourself hear

98 *Wind me into him* screw yourself into his inmost thoughts. *Me* is the so-called 'ethic dative' and need not be construed in a modern paraphrase. *Frame* organize

98–9 *after your own wisdom* as you think best

99 *unstate myself* give up my rank and fortune

99–100 *a due resolution* a state where my doubts were duly resolved

101 *presently* at once

convey manage

102 *withal* therewith

103 *late* recent (possibly remembering the eclipses of September and October 1605)

104–6 *Though the wisdom of nature can reason it thus and thus, yet nature finds itself scourged by the sequent effects* though science can explain natural events in rational terms, the results hurt us none the less for that

109, 114 *villain* (Edgar, who by the very breath of treachery has become ignoble, a *villain* (villein) in the sense of 'peasant')

109–10 *the prediction* (1) the prediction implied by the eclipses; (2) the prediction of the end of the world in the

110 prediction: there's son against father; the King falls
from bias of nature: there's father against child. We
have seen the best of our time. Machinations, hollowness, treachery, and all ruinous disorders follow us dis-
quietly to our graves – find out this villain, Edmund;
it shall lose thee nothing; do it carefully – and the noble
and true-hearted Kent banished! His offence, honesty!
'Tis strange.   *Exit*

EDMUND This is the excellent foppery of the world, that
when we are sick in fortune – often the surfeits of our
120 own behaviour – we make guilty of our disasters the sun,
the moon, and stars, as if we were villains on necessity,
fools by heavenly compulsion, knaves, thieves, and
treachers by spherical predominance, drunkards, liars,
and adulterers by an enforced obedience of planetary
influence; and all that we are evil in by a divine
thrusting-on. An admirable evasion of whoremaster
man, to lay his goatish disposition to the charge of a
star. My father compounded with my mother under the
Dragon's tail, and my nativity was under Ursa Major, so

New Testament, and especially the
signs of this described in Mark 13,
quoted in the Introduction, page
543.
111 *bias of nature* natural tendency (to
love one's children, etc.)
112–13 *hollowness* lack of inner substance
to support external appearance
115 *it shall lose thee nothing* ('a backhanded
promise to reward his detective
work' (G. L. Kittredge))
118 *excellent* (1) extreme; (2) splendid
(from Edmund's anti-human point
of view)
foppery folly
119–20 *sick in fortune – often the surfeits of
our own behaviour* reduced in fortune
as a result of our excesses (as overeat-
ing produces vomiting)

120 *guilty of* responsible for
123 *treachers* traitors
   by spherical predominance because
   certain planets (in their spheres) were
   ascendant at the time of our birth
126–8 *An admirable evasion of whoremaster
   man, to lay his goatish disposition to the
   charge of a star* it is strange that lecherous man should evade responsibility
   for his lechery by saying that a star
   made him like that
126 *admirable* truly strange and wonder-
   worthy. Compare *excellent* (line 118).
129 *Dragon's tail* (a name given to the
   intersection of the orbit of the descending moon with the line of the
   sun's orbit. Chaucer (*A Treatise on the
   Astrolabe* 11.4) names 'the Tail of the
   Dragon' among the 'wicked planets'.)

that it follows I am rough and lecherous. Fut! I should   130
have been that I am had the maidenliest star in the
firmament twinkled on my bastardizing. Edgar –
    (*Enter Edgar*)
pat he comes, like the catastrophe of the old comedy.
My cue is villainous melancholy, with a sigh like Tom
o'Bedlam. (*Aloud*) O these eclipses do portend these
divisions: (*he sings*) Fa, sol, la, mi.

EDGAR How now, brother Edmund! What serious contemplation are you in?

EDMUND I am thinking, brother, of a prediction I read
this other day, what should follow these eclipses.   140

EDGAR Do you busy yourself with that?

EDMUND I promise you, the effects he writes of succeed

Ursa Major the Great Bear. In astrological terms the horoscope is governed by Mars and Venus, producing a temperament not only daring and impetuous (*rough*) but also lascivious and adulterous (*lecherous*); but it may be that the Dragon and the Bear are mentioned only because of the associations with violence that these animals suggest.

130 *Fut!* (probably the same as "sfoot": by Christ's foot)

131 *that I am* what I am (that is, rough and lecherous)

132 *bastardizing* being conceived as a bastard

133 *pat* in the nick of time
like the catastrophe of the old comedy. Old-fashioned comedy, he implies, contrived the catastrophe (or ending) too mechanically, so that the required coincidence always turned up just when convenient.

134 *cue* (a theatrical word, fitting to *comedy* and *catastrophe*. Edmund tells us he is about to play a new role.)

134–5 *a sigh like Tom o'Bedlam.* It is not clear why Tom o'Bedlam –

the madman-beggar from the Bethlehem (*Bedlam*) or any other madhouse – should have a characteristic *sigh* – though he may well have *whined*.

136 *divisions* (1) conflicts – of father against son etc. as in lines 110–11; (2) musical 'divisions' – counterpoint against plainsong
Fa, sol, la, mi. Edmund sings (I assume) the notes F, G, A, B natural (using the names given to these notes in the C and G hexachords of the musical system pertaining in Shakespeare's day). He thus moves across the interval of the augmented fourth, called *diabolus in musica* (the devil in music) in the current musical mnemonic: *Mi contra Fa est diabolus in musica*. The phrase reflects the enmity between the tritone and the normal system of harmony. Shakespeare seems to be creating something like a musical emblem or 'motto theme' for the character of his discordant Bastard.

142 *the effects ... succeed* the results follow

unhappily, as of unnaturalness between the child and the
parent, death, dearth, dissolutions of ancient amities,
divisions in state, menaces and maledictions against king
and nobles, needless diffidences, banishment of friends,
dissipation of cohorts, nuptial breaches, and I know not
what.

EDGAR How long have you been a sectary astronomical?

EDMUND When saw you my father last?

EDGAR The night gone by.

EDMUND Spake you with him?

EDGAR Ay, two hours together.

EDMUND Parted you in good terms? Found you no displeasure in him by word nor countenance?

EDGAR None at all.

EDMUND Bethink yourself wherein you may have
offended him, and at my entreaty forbear his presence
until some little time hath qualified the heat of his displeasure, which at this instant so rageth in him that with
the mischief of your person it would scarcely allay.

EDGAR Some villain hath done me wrong.

EDMUND That's my fear. I pray you have a continent
forbearance till the speed of his rage goes slower; and,
as I say, retire with me to my lodging, from whence I
will fitly bring you to hear my lord speak. Pray ye, go!
There's my key. If you do stir abroad, go armed.

EDGAR Armed, brother?

EDMUND Brother, I advise you to the best. I am no honest
man if there be any good meaning toward you. I have

146 *diffidences* mistrustings
147 *dissipation of cohorts* break-up of military companies
149 *sectary astronomical* devotee of
astrology
158 *forbear his presence* avoid meeting
him
159 *qualified* reduced

160–61 *with the mischief of your person it
would scarcely allay* even if he did physical violence to you it would hardly
diminish
163–4 *have a continent forbearance* contain
your feelings (and keep away from
him)
166 *fitly* at the appropriate time

told you what I have seen and heard but faintly, nothing
like the image and horror of it. Pray you, away!

EDGAR Shall I hear from you anon?

EDMUND I do serve you in this business.

Exit Edgar

A credulous father and a brother noble,
Whose nature is so far from doing harms
That he suspects none; on whose foolish honesty
My practices ride easy – I see the business:
Let me, if not by birth, have lands by wit;
All with me's meet that I can fashion fit.   *Exit*   180

Enter Gonerill and Oswald, her steward   I.3

GONERILL Did my father strike my gentleman for chiding of his Fool?

OSWALD Ay, Madam.

GONERILL
By day and night he wrongs me; every hour

---

171 *told . . . but faintly* given only a faint
impression of
172 *the image and horror* the horrible picture that is true
173 *anon* soon
178 *practices* machinations
I see the business I understand how
my plot should advance
179 *if not by birth, have lands by wit* (because he is a bastard he cannot inherit
lands by *birth*, but he may be clever
enough to achieve them)
180 *All with me's meet that I can fashion
fit* whatever I can turn to my purposes I will regard as justified.

1.3 Time has elapsed since 1.1, and Lear
is now staying with Gonerill. This scene
prepares us for what we see in 1.4, and
allows us to understand the calculation

that lies behind the violences exposed
there.
(stage direction) *Oswald.* Q and F directions and prefixes call him '*Steward*'.
The use of the personal name in the
speech prefixes and stage directions
of modern editions derives from its
authentic use as a speech prefix in a
passage of the Q text which gives
two alternative perversions of 1.4.332
(given to '*Stew.*' in F). The name
Oswald also appears in the text, at
1.4.310, 324, and 330. It is probable
that Shakespeare used this name because he read that it was an Anglo-
Saxon name for a steward. The Steward's costume should be an important
facet of his character.
4 *By day and night.* This is sometimes
taken to be an oath; but it is more

He flashes into one gross crime or other
That sets us all at odds. I'll not endure it!
His knights grow riotous, and himself upbraids us
On every trifle. When he returns from hunting
I will not speak with him. Say I am sick.
10 If you come slack of former services
You shall do well; the fault of it I'll answer.

OSWALD He's coming, madam; I hear him.

GONERILL
Put on what weary negligence you please,
You and your fellows. I'd have it come to question.
If he distaste it let him to my sister,
Whose mind and mine I know in that are one,
Not to be overruled. Idle old man,
That still would manage those authorities
That he hath given away! Now, by my life,
20 Old fools are babes again, and must be used
With checks, as flatteries, when they are seen abused.
Remember what I have said.

OSWALD   Well, madam.

GONERILL
And let his knights have colder looks among you.
What grows of it, no matter. Advise your fellows so.
I would breed from hence occasions, and I shall,
That I may speak. I'll write straight to my sister
To hold my very course. Prepare for dinner.   *Exeunt*

likely, in the context of *every hour*, to
mean 'at all times'.
5 *flashes* breaks out suddenly
7 *upbraids us.* Note the transfer of the
royal plural from Lear to Gonerill.
10 *come slack of former services* are less
attentive in serving him than
previously
14 *come to question* be made an issue
15 *distaste it* find it offensive

21 *With checks, as flatteries, when they are
seen abused.* This has been interpreted
as 'with punishment instead of flattery when flattery becomes excessive'
and as 'with punishments as well as
flatteries when they (the old) are
misled'.
25 *occasions* opportunities, excuses
26 *speak* rebuke him
     straight at once

Enter Kent in disguise   1.4

KENT

If but as well I other accents borrow
That can my speech diffuse, my good intent
May carry through itself to that full issue
For which I razed my likeness. Now, banished Kent,
If thou canst serve where thou dost stand condemned,
So may it come thy master whom thou lovest
Shall find thee full of labours.

Horns within. Enter Lear and Knights

LEAR   Let me not stay a jot for dinner! Go, get it ready!

Exit First Knight

1.4 The conflict implicit in 1.1 and prepared for in 1.3 breaks out in action.
Bluntness in the disguised Kent and the
nagging truth of the Fool lead up to
Lear's violent repudiation of Gonerill
and her calculated insults. Varieties of
loyalty and respect for the past are opposed to icy and well-prepared control
of the present situation.

1 *as well* (in addition to the disguise he
  is wearing)

2 *my speech* my normal way of speaking
  diffuse confuse, obscure

3 *carry through itself to that full issue*
  achieve my aim completely

3–4 *that full issue | For which I razed my
  likeness.* Kent is the first of several in
  this play (Edgar, Lear, Gloucester)
  who 'die into life', become effective
  morally by losing their old social
  personality.

4 *razed my likeness* altered my appearance.
  If he did this by shaving off his
  beard the word *raze* would be particularly appropriate.
  banished Kent. In case the audience
  have not recognized his voice, he
  announces his identity.

5 *where thou dost stand condemned* (in the
  presence of Lear)

6 *come* come to pass that

7 *full of labours* hard-working

(stage direction) *Horns within* (to indicate
  the hunt that Lear returns from)
  Knights. F reads 'Enter Lear and Attendants' (Q: 'Enter Lear') but the speech
  prefixes below refer only to 'Knight'
  (Q: 'Seruant'). Some knights must be
  present if Gonerill's image of Lear's
  household is to make sense. The
  advice to the King in lines 63–5 suggests a rank above that of a common
  servant. On the other hand the im-
  periousness of Lear's commands
  would suggest that he is dealing with
  servants – though the orders given to
  the man who speaks in lines 63–5 are
  as imperious as any others in the
  scene. The usual modern stage direction gives 'Knights and Attendants',
  but I assume that knights are adequate to all the needs of the scene.
  Q keeps a '*Knight*' in 11.4 (F: '*Gentleman*'); but thereafter neither text
  mentions Knights.

How now? What art thou?

10   KENT   A man, sir.

LEAR   What dost thou profess? What wouldst thou with us?

KENT   I do profess to be no less than I seem: to serve him truly that will put me in trust, to love him that is honest, to converse with him that is wise and says little, to fear judgement, to fight when I cannot choose, and to eat no fish.

LEAR   What art thou?

KENT   A very honest-hearted fellow, and as poor as the

20   King.

LEAR   If thou be'st as poor for a subject as he's for a king thou art poor enough. What wouldst thou?

KENT   Service.

LEAR   Who wouldst thou serve?

KENT   You.

LEAR   Dost thou know me, fellow?

KENT   No, sir; but you have that in your countenance which I would fain call master.

LEAR   What's that?

30   KENT   Authority.

10 *A man* an ordinary human being (see lines 34–5; with a secondary sense of 'a servant')

11 *What dost thou profess?* Kent's point in *A man* – that he can offer only his basic humanity – is not understood by Lear. He asks 'What arts distinguish this man?', presuming that those who come to the King come because they have some special talent. Kent takes another sense of *profess*, and replies in his own terms: 'My art is to be myself – ordinary, decent, honest'.

13 *I do profess to be no less than I seem.* Kent's phrase has a second sense, aimed to remind the audience that

he is, in fact, much *more* than he seems.

16 *judgement*. The most plausible sense is 'the Last Judgement', giving moral meaning to the rest of life.

16–17 *eat no fish*. It is not clear what this means; but certainly it is a joke of the brusque kind that comes to characterize Kent in his Caius persona.

25 *You*. Notice the distinction between *thou* and *you* in this passage.

30 *Authority*. This, like *Service* (line 23), suggests the tendency of this exchange to turn the characters into personifications of abstract qualities such as were characteristic of Morality plays. Compare I.1.147–9.

LEAR What services canst thou do?

KENT I can keep honest counsel, ride, run, mar a curious
tale in telling it, and deliver a plain message bluntly.
That which ordinary men are fit for I am qualified in,
and the best of me is diligence.

LEAR How old art thou?

KENT Not so young, sir, to love a woman for singing, nor
so old to dote on her for anything. I have years on my
back forty-eight.

LEAR Follow me; thou shalt serve me if I like thee no   40
worse after dinner. I will not part from thee yet. Dinner,
ho, dinner! Where's my knave, my Fool? Go you and
call my Fool hither.   *Exit Second Knight*
    Enter Oswald
You! You, sirrah! Where's my daughter?

OSWALD So please you —   *Exit*

LEAR What says the fellow there? Call the clotpoll back.
                               Exit Third Knight
Where's my Fool? Ho, I think the world's asleep.
    Enter Third Knight
How now? Where's that mongrel?

THIRD KNIGHT He says, my lord, your daughter is not
well.   50

LEAR Why came not the slave back to me when I called
him?

THIRD KNIGHT Sir, he answered me in the roundest
manner he would not.

LEAR He would not!

THIRD KNIGHT My lord, I know not what the matter is,
but to my judgement your highness is not entertained

---

32 *curious* finely wrought. Kent implies
    that he is too blunt to be good at
    fine-spun rhetoric.
46 *clotpoll* one with a *clod* for his *poll*
(head), a fool
53 *roundest* most downright and uncom-
    promising

with that ceremonious affection as you were wont.
There's a great abatement of kindness appears as well
60   in the general dependants as in the Duke himself also
and your daughter.

LEAR Ha! Sayest thou so?

THIRD KNIGHT I beseech you pardon me, my lord, if I
be mistaken; for my duty cannot be silent when I think
your highness wronged.

LEAR Thou but rememberest me of mine own conception. I have perceived a most faint neglect of late,
which I have rather blamed as mine own jealous
curiosity than as a very pretence and purpose of un-
70   kindness. I will look further into't. But where's my
Fool? I have not seen him this two days.

THIRD KNIGHT Since my young lady's going into
France, sir, the Fool hath much pined away.

LEAR No more of that! I have noted it well. Go you and
tell my daughter I would speak with her.

                                         Exit Third Knight

Go you, call hither my Fool.   *Exit another Knight*
   Enter Oswald

O, you, sir, you! Come you hither, sir. Who am I, sir?

---

58 *ceremonious affection* (combination of
the affection due to a father and
the ceremony appropriate to a
king)

60 *the general dependants* the mass of
servants
the Duke himself. If one were to
examine dramatic evidence as if in a
court of law this would be found
unreliable. Albany later (line 270) is
ignorant of the situation, and the rest
of his conduct in the play confirms
the truth of this ignorance. The
speech of the Knight here marks
Shakespeare's anxiety to emphasize
the isolation of Lear.

66 *rememberest* remind

66–7 *mine own conception* what I have
thought

67 *faint* (not 'imperceptible', but
'languid')

68–9 *jealous curiosity* tendency to suspect
trifles as injuries to my dignity

69 *a very pretence* an actual intention

73 *the Fool hath much pined away*. The first
description of the Fool characterizes
him as delicate and sensitive. Coleridge remarked that he 'is no comic
buffoon ... Accordingly, he is prepared for – brought into living connexion with the pathos of the play,
with the sufferings' (*Coleridge on
Shakespeare*, edited by Terence
Hawkes (1969), page 204).

OSWALD My lady's father.

LEAR 'My lady's father', my lord's knave! You whoreson
dog! You slave! You cur! 80

OSWALD I am none of these, my lord, I beseech your
pardon.

LEAR Do you bandy looks with me, you rascal?
He strikes him

OSWALD I'll not be strucken, my lord.

KENT Nor tripped neither, you base football-player?
He trips him

LEAR I thank thee, fellow. Thou servest me and I'll love
thee.

KENT (*to Oswald*) Come, sir, arise, away! I'll teach you
differences. Away, away! If you will measure your
lubber's length again, tarry; but away, go to! Have you 90
wisdom?
He pushes Oswald out
So.

LEAR Now, my friendly knave, I thank thee. There's
earnest of thy service.
He gives him money
Enter the Fool

FOOL Let me hire him too. Here's my coxcomb.

LEAR How now, my pretty knave! How dost thou?

FOOL Sirrah, you were best take my coxcomb.

---

83 *bandy*. The technical term for a stroke
in tennis. The dialogue following
picks up the tennis metaphor; from
'bandying' looks, Lear turns to
blows. Oswald objects to being made
a tennis-ball; Kent trips him and says
that football, a plebeian game, is
more suitable for him than tennis, a
royal and noble game.

89 *differences* (the species or classes of
men, dividing a servant from a king,
and, incidentally, football from
tennis)

90 *lubber* clumsy fellow

90–92 *Have you wisdom? So.* The Steward
hesitates before accepting the push
through the door. Kent's phrase
means 'Surely you have more sense
than to resist'. The *So* marks the
Steward's 'wise' acceptance of the
situation, and his exit.

94 *earnest*. Lear hires Kent as his servant
with the usual initial token-payment,
a pledge of further payment to
come.

96 *pretty knave* dainty lad

97 *take my coxcomb* have my fool's cap

KENT Why, Fool?

FOOL Why? For taking one's part that's out of favour.
Nay, and thou canst not smile as the wind sits, thou'lt
catch cold shortly. There, take my coxcomb! Why, this
fellow has banished two on's daughters, and did the
third a blessing against his will. If thou follow him, thou
must needs wear my coxcomb. How now, nuncle!
Would I had two coxcombs and two daughters!

LEAR Why, my boy?

FOOL If I gave them all my living, I'd keep my coxcombs
myself. There's mine. Beg another of thy daughters.

LEAR Take heed, sirrah, the whip!

FOOL Truth's a dog must to kennel; he must be whipped
out when the Lady Brach may stand by the fire and
stink.

LEAR A pestilent gall to me!

(for your *earnest*, for you show yourself apt to act as a fool if you bind
yourself to one who's out of favour)

100 *and* if

smile as the wind sits adapt your behaviour to the currents of power

100–101 *thou'lt catch cold* (1) the *wind* of
power will make you suffer; (2)
you'll be turned out of doors (ironic
anticipation)

102–3 *banished two on's daughters, and did
the third a blessing* (a paradoxical inversion of the apparent situation. But
(the Fool implies) the values of 1.1
were inverted.)

102 *on's* of his

104 *nuncle*. 'Mine uncle' in childish talk
becomes transformed into 'my
nuncle'. Hence *nuncle* becomes the
word of a fool for his guardian or
superior.

107–8 *If I gave them ... thy daughters*
even if (like you) I had given away
all my possessions I should have
something left, good evidence of my

folly (in giving things away). I will
give you one coxcomb as a first sign
of folly; beg from your daughters if
you want a second sign

109 *the whip*. Domestic fools were (like
madmen) whipped into submission.

110 *must to kennel* must go out of doors
to the dog-house

110–12 *he must be whipped out when the
Lady Brach may stand by the fire and
stink* Truth is whipped out of doors
like a dog, but the falsely fawning
bitch-hound (*Brach*) is allowed to
remain comfortably indoors, however unpleasant the result

113 *A pestilent gall to me!* This may refer
to the Fool and his speeches – 'How
this fellow makes me wince!' – but is
more likely to pick up some inner
train of passion deriving from memory of Gonerill's household – 'How
intolerably bitter is the situation I'm
in!' *Gall* is both 'the bitter secretion
of the liver' and 'a sore place'.

FOOL   Sirrah, I'll teach thee a speech.

LEAR   Do.

FOOL   Mark it, nuncle:

> Have more than thou showest,
> Speak less than thou knowest,
> Lend less than thou owest,
> Ride more than thou goest,   120
> Learn more than thou trowest,
> Set less than thou throwest;
> Leave thy drink and thy whore
> And keep in-a-door,
> And thou shalt have more
> Than two tens to a score.

KENT   This is nothing, Fool.

FOOL   Then 'tis like the breath of an unfee'd lawyer: you gave me nothing for't. Can you make no use of nothing, nuncle?   130

LEAR   Why, no, boy. Nothing can be made out of nothing.

FOOL   (to Kent) Prithee tell him; so much the rent of his land comes to. He will not believe a fool.

LEAR   A bitter fool!

117–26 *Have more than thou showest ... two tens to a score* if you can be entirely prudent and self-concealing you will accumulate possessions

119 *thou owest* you own

120 *Ride more than thou goest* (that is, use your horse's legs rather than your own)
 goest walk

121 *Learn more than thou trowest* listen to much and believe little

122 *Set less than thou throwest* (not clear; possibly 'gamble small stakes for large winnings')

125–6 *more | Than two tens to a score.* This has been thought to refer to usurious increase; but it is probably only a riddling way of saying 'more than you would expect'.

127 *nothing* nonsense

128 *like the breath of an unfee'd lawyer* (following up the proverb: 'A lawyer will not plead but for a fee' – no fee, no breath, nothing)

129 *use* usury. Lear's reply recurs to the arithmetical point that nothing cannot be multiplied into something.

132–3 *so much the rent of his land comes to.* Dover Wilson suggests that the point being made is that all rent is 'something for nothing', a return without work done to earn it. More simply, Lear has now no land.

FOOL   Dost thou know the difference, my boy, between a
bitter fool and a sweet one?

LEAR   No, lad; teach me.

FOOL

That lord that counselled thee
　　To give away thy land,
140　　Come place him here by me;
　　Do thou for him stand.
The sweet and bitter fool
　　Will presently appear:
The one in motley here,
　　The other found out – there.

LEAR   Dost thou call me fool, boy?

FOOL   All thy other titles thou hast given away; that thou
wast born with.

KENT   This is not altogether fool, my lord.

150　FOOL   No, faith; lords and great men will not let me. If I
had a monopoly out they would have part on't; and
ladies too – they will not let me have all the fool to myself; they'll be snatching. Nuncle, give me an egg and
I'll give thee two crowns.

LEAR   What two crowns shall they be?

FOOL   Why, after I have cut the egg i'the middle and eat
up the meat, the two crowns of the egg. When thou

---

138 *That lord* (an oblique way of pointing to Lear himself, as is implied by
the following piece of play-acting)
141 *for him stand* impersonate him
143 *presently* immediately
145 *found out* discovered (in spite of his
'disguise' as a sane man)
there. He points to where Lear is
standing.
147–8 *that thou wast born with*. Probably
Shakespeare does not intend the Fool
to call Lear 'a born fool', but rather
to make the point that we are all
born with folly as a characteristic.

150 *No . . . will not let me*. Kent's *altogether fool* is taken by the Fool to
mean 'having all the folly there is'.
151 *a monopoly out* a right to sole possession granted by the sovereign. This
reference to a great abuse of the time
has been thought to account for the
omission of the whole passage (lines
138–53) from the Folio.
151–2 *and ladies too*. Presumably these
words should be illustrated by some
indecency with the Fool's bauble.
157 *the meat* the edible part

clovest thy crown i'the middle, and gavest away both
parts, thou borest thine ass on thy back o'er the dirt.
Thou hadst little wit in thy bald crown when thou   160
gavest thy golden one away. If I speak like myself in
this, let him be whipped that first finds it so.

> Fools had ne'er less grace in a year,
>> For wise men are grown foppish
> And know not how their wits to wear,
>> Their manners are so apish.

LEAR When were you wont to be so full of songs, sirrah?

FOOL I have used it, nuncle, e'er since thou madest thy
daughters thy mothers; for when thou gavest them the
rod and puttest down thine own breeches,   170

> (*sings*)
> Then they for sudden joy did weep,
>> And I for sorrow sung,
> That such a king should play bo-peep
>> And go the fools among.

Prithee, nuncle, keep a schoolmaster that can teach thy
fool to lie; I would fain learn to lie.

LEAR And you lie, sirrah, we'll have you whipped.

FOOL I marvel what kin thou and thy daughters are.
They'll have me whipped for speaking true; thou'lt
have me whipped for lying; and sometimes I am   180
whipped for holding my peace. I had rather be any kind

---

159 *borest thine ass on thy back o'er the dirt*
(like the old man in the fable who
did not wish to overload his ass, and
carried him to market (Poggio's *Face-
tiae* (1470), §24)

161-2 *If I speak like myself in this, let him
be whipped that first finds it so* let the
man who says that this is folly be
whipped, for he is the real fool

163 *grace* favour

164 *foppish* foolish. The wise men now
take the places of the fools, who in
consequence lose their popularity.

165 *know not how their wits to wear*. The
wise men, slavishly imitative of the
manners of the time, don't know
how to show their wisdom; in attempting to follow fashion they
become fools.

166 *apish* foolishly imitative

168-9 *madest thy daughters thy mothers*
gave your daughters the right to
chastise you

173 *play bo-peep* (behave with childish
folly)

177 *And* if

o'thing than a fool. And yet I would not be thee, nuncle.
Thou hast pared thy wit o'both sides and left nothing
i'the middle. Here comes one o'the parings.

Enter Gonerill

LEAR How now, daughter! What makes that frontlet on?
You are too much of late i'the frown.

FOOL Thou wast a pretty fellow when thou hadst no need
to care for her frowning. Now thou art an 0 without a
figure. I am better than thou art now; I am a fool; thou

190 art nothing. (*To Gonerill*) Yes, forsooth, I will hold my
tongue. So your face bids me, though you say nothing.
Mum, mum!
He that keeps nor crust nor crumb,
Weary of all, shall want some.

He points to Lear

That's a shelled peascod.

GONERILL
Not only, sir, this your all-licensed fool
But other of your insolent retinue
Do hourly carp and quarrel, breaking forth
In rank and not-to-be-endurèd riots. Sir,

200 I had thought by making this well known unto you
To have found a safe redress; but now grow fearful

185 *What makes that frontlet on?* what are
you doing, wearing that headband of
frowns?
188-9 *an 0 without a figure* a zero with no
other figure before it to give it value
193-4 *He that keeps nor crust nor crumb,* |
Weary of all, shall want some he
who (like Lear) in his weariness of
the world gives away everything will
come to want some of the things he
has given away
195 *a shelled peascod.* Since a peascod is
the *shell*, one that is *shelled* is nothing.
196-209 The rhetoric of Gonerill's
speech seems designed to convey an
impression of cold venom. Notice

the length of sentence (lines 199-209
form one sentence), the elaboration
of the subordinate clauses, the lack
of concrete imagery, the sharpness of
the alliteration (*found . . . safe . . . fearful; protect . . . put; 'scape censure . . .
redresses sleep*; etc.), the balance of
abstractions, the deviousness of the
rhythm.
196 *all-licensed* allowed to say and do
what he pleases
197 *insolent* contemptuous of rightful
authority
198 *carp* find fault, reprehend
199 *rank* gross
201 *safe redress* sure remedy

By what yourself too late have spoke and done
That you protect this course and put it on
By your allowance; which if you should, the fault
Would not 'scape censure, nor the redresses sleep;
Which in the tender of a wholesome weal
Might in their working do you that offence
Which else were shame, that then necessity
Will call discreet proceeding.

FOOL For you know, nuncle,   210

    The hedge-sparrow fed the cuckoo so long
    That it's had it head bit off by it young.

So out went the candle and we were left darkling.

LEAR Are you our daughter?

GONERILL

I would you would make use of your good wisdom,
Whereof I know you are fraught, and put away
These dispositions which of late transport you
From what you rightly are.

FOOL May not an ass know when the cart draws the
horse?   220

202 *too late* only too recently
203–4 *put it on | By your allowance* encourage it by your sanction
205 *nor the redresses sleep* and the remedies will not be slow
206–9 *Which in the tender of a wholesome weal . . . call discreet proceeding* the process of remedy, resulting from care (*tender*) for the health of the state (*weal*), might well harm you in a way that under normal circumstances would be called shameful; but the necessities of the state will then allow that it is *discreet proceeding* to prefer your harm to the state's
211 *The hedge-sparrow fed the cuckoo*. The *cuckoo* is (like Gonerill) an admirable example of 'necessities of state'; laid in the hedge-sparrow's nest, it grows so big from the hedge-sparrow's

(Lear's) nourishing that it becomes *discreet proceeding* for it to make room for itself by biting off its foster-parent's head.
212 *it's had* it has had. (Shakespeare is often careless of the sequence of tenses, as from the past (*fed*) above to the perfect tense here.)
it head . . . it young. The usual possessive of 'it' is 'his'; 'it' for 'its' seems especially common in 'baby talk'.
213 *So out went the candle*. Lear is presumably the candle of the state, whose extinction plunges the people into darkness.
216 *fraught* stored, loaded
217 *dispositions* states of mind
219–20 *May not an ass know when the cart draws the horse?* even a fool like me

Whoop, Jug, I love thee!

LEAR

Does any here know me? This is not Lear.
Does Lear walk thus, speak thus? Where are his eyes?
Either his notion weakens, his discernings
Are lethargied – Ha! Waking? 'Tis not so!
Who is it that can tell me who I am?

FOOL Lear's shadow.

LEAR I would learn that; for by the marks of sovereignty,
knowledge, and reason, I should be false persuaded I
230   had daughters.

FOOL Which they will make an obedient father.

LEAR Your name, fair gentlewoman?

GONERILL

This admiration, sir, is much o'the savour
Of other your new pranks. I do beseech you

can see that things are the wrong way round here (a daughter giving instructions to the King her father)

221 *Whoop, Jug, I love thee!* (perhaps the refrain from a lost song. Obviously it repudiates the involvement with others which appears in the preceding line.)
Jug Joan

224 *notion* power to understand

225 *Waking? 'Tis not so!* Lear assumes he must be dreaming (as later, with Cordelia, in IV.7).

228 *I would learn that* I seek an answer to the question 'Who am I?'

228–30 *for by the marks of sovereignty, knowledge, and reason, I should be false persuaded I had daughters.* An expanded paraphrase of this might read: 'When I look I see on myself the insignia of a king; and am not aware that in terms of knowledge and reason I have lost the right to rely on my assumptions; on these accounts I should suppose I was right in think-

ing I was King Lear, who had *daughters* (that is, children owing reverence and obedience). But no such *daughter* can be seen, so I cannot be King Lear.'

231 *Which*. This may (1) stand for 'whom', relating back to the *I* of Lear's speech, or (2) refer back to *Lear's shadow* in line 227. In the latter case we must suppose that the Fool is following his own uninterrupted train of thought, just as Lear is in lines 226 and 228.

233 *admiration* (perhaps 'astonishing behaviour'. G. L. Kittredge says 'Pretending to wonder who you are'.)
is much o'the savour has the same taste or characteristics

234 *pranks* childish or malicious games

234–45 *beseech . . . desired . . . A little . . .* In this speech words of humility alternate with words of insolent censure, creating a rhetorical effect of calculated venom.

To understand my purposes aright:
As you are old and reverend, should be wise.
Here do you keep a hundred knights and squires,
Men so disordered, so deboshed and bold,
That this our court, infected with their manners,
Shows like a riotous inn; epicurism and lust   240
Makes it more like a tavern or a brothel
Than a graced palace. The shame itself doth speak
For instant remedy. Be then desired,
By her that else will take the thing she begs,
A little to disquantity your train,
And the remainders that shall still depend
To be such men as may besort your age,
Which know themselves and you.

LEAR   Darkness and devils!
Saddle my horses! Call my train together!
Degenerate bastard, I'll not trouble thee.   250
Yet have I left a daughter.

GONERILL

You strike my people, and your disordered rabble
Make servants of their betters.

    Enter Albany

LEAR

Woe that too late repents! – O, sir, are you come?
Is it your will? Speak, sir! – Prepare my horses.
Ingratitude, thou marble-hearted fiend,
More hideous when thou showest thee in a child

---

238 *disordered* disorderly
    deboshed (a variant form of 'debauched')
    bold impudent
240 *Shows* appears
240–41 *epicurism and lust | Makes it more like a tavern or a brothel.* The *epicurism* (gluttony) belongs to the *tavern*, the *lust* to the *brothel*.
242 *a graced palace* a palace which his

grace, the King, graces
245 *disquantity your train* reduce the number of your followers
246 *the remainders that shall still depend* those who remain as your followers
247 *besort* be suitable for
248 *know . . . you.* Presumably she means 'know you to be a dangerous old man requiring restraint'.
254 *Woe that* woe to the person who

Than the sea-monster!

ALBANY   Pray, sir, be patient.

LEAR *(to Gonerill)*

Detested kite, thou liest!

260   My train are men of choice and rarest parts,
That all particulars of duty know
And in the most exact regard support
The worships of their name. O most small fault,
How ugly didst thou in Cordelia show!
Which, like an engine, wrenched my frame of nature
From the fixed place, drew from my heart all love,
And added to the gall. O Lear, Lear, Lear!
Beat at this gate that let thy folly in
              (he strikes his head)
And thy dear judgement out! Go, go, my people.

                                        Exeunt Kent and Knights

ALBANY

270   My lord, I am guiltless as I am ignorant
Of what hath moved you.

LEAR   It may be so, my lord.

              He kneels

Hear, Nature, hear! Dear goddess, hear!

---

258 *the sea-monster*. The sea was traditionally a home of horrors, and perhaps
sea-monster only means 'the kind of
monster that the sea traditionally produces'. If any specific sea-monster is
meant, that which destroyed Hip-
polytus probably fits best into the
context: as described in the 1581
translation of Seneca's *Phaedra* it is a
'monster' with a 'marble neck'; it is
sent as a punishment for filial
ingratitude.

259 *Detested kite* vile carrion-bird

260 *of choice and rarest parts* of carefully
selected, difficult-to-find qualities

262-3 *in the most exact regard support |
The worships of their name* are punctilious, even in details, to live up to
their honourable reputation

265 *engine* (usually said to be the rack,
but the rack does not seem like the
small fault, nor does it wrench the
frame *From the fixed place*. Some
device more like a lever or a crow-
bar seems to be intended.)

266 *the fixed place* (1) the foundations of
the *frame of nature*; (2) the natural
affection which supports human
existence

268 *this gate*. It is not clear which *gate* is
intended – the ears, the eyes, or the
mouth. It is very likely, however,
that Lear beats his head as the general
area of judgement and folly.

269 *dear* precious to me

Suspend thy purpose if thou didst intend
To make this creature fruitful.
Into her womb convey sterility,
Dry up in her the organs of increase,
And from her derogate body never spring
A babe to honour her. If she must teem,
Create her child of spleen, that it may live
And be a thwart disnatured torment to her.   280
Let it stamp wrinkles in her brow of youth,
With cadent tears fret channels in her cheeks,
Turn all her mother's pains and benefits
To laughter and contempt, that she may feel
How sharper than a serpent's tooth it is
To have a thankless child! Away, away!   *Exit*

ALBANY

Now gods that we adore, whereof comes this?

GONERILL

Never afflict yourself to know more of it;
But let his disposition have that scope
As dotage gives it.   290
        Enter Lear

LEAR

What, fifty of my followers at a clap?

275–8 *Into her womb . . . honour her*. Compare Deuteronomy 28.15, 18: '. . . if thou wilt not hearken unto the voice of the Lord thy God . . . cursed shall be the fruit of thy body.'

277 *derogate* degraded, dishonoured (in strong antithesis to *honour* below)

278 *teem* bear children

279 *Create her child of spleen* make her a child composed entirely of malice

280 *thwart disnatured* perverse and unnatural (that is, without filial affection)

282 *cadent* dropping
    fret wear away

283–4 *Turn all her mother's pains and benefits | To laughter and contempt* treat any

cares and pains of motherhood that Gonerill may experience with scornful laughter, and treat her joys in motherhood with contempt

289 *disposition* mood

289–90 *that scope | As dotage gives it* (meaning, presumably, violent talk and little action)

291 *fifty of my followers*. Editors have usually sought to explain this by realistic means: fifty followers must have been removed, without comment, at some earlier stage. I think that we should rather praise the bold foreshortening that makes the loss of fifty followers seem the consequence of an absence during which only four

Within a fortnight?

ALBANY   What's the matter, sir?

LEAR

I'll tell thee – (*to Gonerill*) life and death! I am
ashamed
That thou hast power to shake my manhood thus,
That these hot tears which break from me perforce
Should make thee worth them. Blasts and fogs upon
thee!
Th'untented woundings of a father's curse
Pierce every sense about thee! – Old fond eyes,
Beweep this cause again, I'll pluck ye out
300   And cast you with the waters that you loose
To temper clay. Yea, is't come to this?
Let it be so. I have another daughter,
Who, I am sure, is kind and comfortable.

---

lines are spoken. Certainly at line
320 there are *A hundred knights*, and
at lines 322 and 330 the same number
is repeated.
at a clap at one stroke
292 *a fortnight* (the length of time he has
been staying with Gonerill)
296 *Should make thee worth them* should
value you as if you were worth the
tears of a king
Blasts and fogs blighting influences
and disease-bearing fogs
297 *untented woundings* untentable wounds
(too deep to be probed with a *tent* or
roll of lint)
298 *fond* foolish
299 *Beweep this cause* if you shed tears
over this matter
300 *loose*. The F word may be the
common sixteenth-century spelling
of 'lose' (the eyes lose water when
they are plucked out), or it may be
the modern 'loose' (the eyes release
their water). It is probable that Shakespeare, given the overlap of spelling,

did not distinguish clearly between
the two words.
301 *To temper clay* to soften clay (a base
use, like the 'treading of mortar',
II.2.63–4)
301–2 *Yea, is't come to this?* | *Let it be so*. F
omits Q's 'yea . . . this?', and prints
instead 'Ha? let it be so'. Both versions are metrically defective, so it is
likely that the 'F' correction should
be added to the Q version, not
simply substituted for it. But there is
one word which the F corrector may
have meant actually to remove from
the text – the word 'yea', against
which F has, throughout its length,
a remarkable prejudice. If so, then
'Ha' should probably be regarded as
a substitute rather than an addition;
we cannot keep both exclamations,
and I prefer to retain the earlier one.
303 *kind and comfortable* like a true daughter, affectionate and ready to give
comfort

When she shall hear this of thee, with her nails
She'll flay thy wolvish visage. Thou shalt find
That I'll resume the shape which thou dost think
I have cast off for ever.   *Exit*

GONERILL   Do you mark that?

ALBANY

I cannot be so partial, Gonerill,
To the great love I bear you –

GONERILL

Pray you, content – What, Oswald, ho!   310
(*To the Fool*) You, sir, more knave than fool, after your
    master!

FOOL Nuncle Lear, nuncle Lear, tarry! Take the Fool
with thee.

> A fox, when one has caught her,
> And such a daughter
> Should sure to the slaughter,
> If my cap would buy a halter –
> So the fool follows after.   *Exit*

GONERILL

This man hath had good counsel! A hundred knights!
'Tis politic and safe to let him keep   320
At point a hundred knights! Yes, that on every dream,
Each buzz, each fancy, each complaint, dislike,
He may enguard his dotage with their powers
And hold our lives in mercy. – Oswald, I say!

304–5 *with her nails | She'll flay thy wolvish visage*. Ironically, Lear is made to describe Regan attacking Gonerill in the manner of one wolf attacking another.

307 *Do you mark that?* Gonerill urges Albany to note the treason implied in Lear's statement – as if he had said 'I shall take steps to recover the throne and so depose you'.

308–9 *partial . . . | To* biased because of

312–13 *Take the Fool with thee.* 'The literal sense is obvious; but the phrase was a regular farewell gibe: Take the epithet "fool" with you as you go' (G. L. Kittredge).

314–18 *caught her . . . daughter . . . slaughter . . . halter . . . after*. The rhymes seem to have been perfect in Elizabethan English: . . . 'hauter' . . . 'auter'.

321 *At point* armed ready for action

322 *buzz* whisper of rumour

324 *in mercy* at his mercy

ALBANY
    Well, you may fear too far.

GONERILL   Safer than trust too far.
    Let me still take away the harms I fear,
    Not fear still to be taken. I know his heart.
    What he hath uttered I have writ my sister;
    If she sustain him and his hundred knights
    When I have showed th'unfitness –
                Enter Oswald

330   How now, Oswald!
    What, have you writ that letter to my sister?

OSWALD Ay, madam.

GONERILL
    Take you some company and away to horse.
    Inform her full of my particular fear,
    And thereto add such reasons of your own
    As may compact it more. Get you gone,
    And hasten your return.   *Exit Oswald*
                No, no, my lord,
    This milky gentleness and course of yours,
    Though I condemn not, yet, under pardon,
340   You are much more a-taxed for want of wisdom
    Than praised for harmful mildness.

326 *still* always
327 *Not fear still to be taken* rather than
     live all the time in fear of being
     'taken away' myself
334 *my particular fear*. What this particu-
     lar (or 'personal') fear is does not
     appear.
336 *compact* confirm, strengthen
338 *milky gentleness and course* (hendiadys)
     effeminate and gentle course
340 *a-taxed for*. The various readings of
     the substantive texts are (1) Q uncor-
     rected: 'alapt'; (2) Q corrected: 'at-
     taskt for'; (3) F: 'at task for'. The

uncorrected Q reading is almost certainly a misreading of 'ataxt' ('t' and
'x' were often misread as 'l' and 'p').
The Q correction is a variant spelling
of this; and F is a 'regularization' of
Q corrected. An editor's reading
should be as close as it intelligibly
can to the original form, and in this
case an almost complete return is
possible; 'a-taxed' is a variant form
of 'taxed': 'complained of'.
341 *harmful mildness* gentleness that may
     harm the state

ALBANY
  How far your eyes may pierce I cannot tell;
  Striving to better, oft we mar what's well.
GONERILL Nay then –
ALBANY Well, well – th'event!   *Exeunt*

        Enter Lear, Kent, Knight, and the Fool   1.5
LEAR (*to Kent*) Go you before to Gloucester with these
  letters. Acquaint my daughter no further with anything
  you know than comes from her demand out of the letter.
  If your diligence be not speedy I shall be there afore
  you.
KENT I will not sleep, my lord, till I have delivered your
  letter.   *Exit*
FOOL If a man's brains were in's heels, were't not in
  danger of kibes?
LEAR Ay, boy.   10

342 *eyes may pierce*. Albany means 'into
  hidden events'; but we are powerfully reminded of the description of
  Gonerill in 11.4.167: *Her eyes are
  fierce.*
345 *Well, well – th'event!* Albany declines
  to continue the dispute, and puts the
  arbitration of their quarrel to the
  event – the outcome.

1.5 This scene follows straight after 1.4.
We are now outside Gonerill's castle.
Lear makes his old-fashioned attempts
to counter Gonerill's compact with
Regan, while the Fool bodingly prepares
us for disaster.
(stage direction) *Knight.* F reads '*Gentleman*' – no doubt one of the Knights
  of the previous scene.
1 *before* ahead of me
  Gloucester (the town, presumably,

rather than the Earl. But Shakespeare, no doubt, assumed that the
Earl lived in or near the town. Dover
Wilson prints 'Cornwall', on the
grounds that Lear could not know
that Regan, the recipient of the
letter, is at Gloucester. But Shakespeare often makes these 'errors' of
anticipation, not noticeable in the
theatre.)
2–3 *Acquaint my daughter no further . . .
  the letter*. Lear already distrusts
  Regan, and wishes not to give her
  any ammunition for an attack on his
  interpretation of the recent past.
8 *in's* in his
  were't. The 'it' is his 'brain' or
  (alternatively) (the same sense)
  brains.
9 *kibes* chilblains

FOOL Then I prithee be merry. Thy wit shall not go slipshod.

LEAR Ha, ha, ha!

FOOL Shalt see thy other daughter will use thee kindly;
for though she's as like this as a crab's like an apple, yet
I can tell what I can tell.

LEAR What canst tell, boy?

FOOL She will taste as like this as a crab does to a crab.
Thou canst tell why one's nose stands i'the middle on's
20 face?

LEAR No.

FOOL Why, to keep one's eyes of either side's nose; that
what a man cannot smell out he may spy into.

LEAR I did her wrong.

FOOL Canst tell how an oyster makes his shell?

LEAR No.

FOOL Nor I neither. But I can tell why a snail has a house.

LEAR Why?

FOOL Why, to put's head in; not to give it away to his
30 daughters, and leave his horns without a case.

11–12 *Thy wit shall not go slipshod* there is
no need for you to be shod in slip-
pers (because of the chilblains in your
wits), for your journey to Regan
shows you lack wits, even in your
heels. The train of thought is
started by the *diligence* promised by
Kent.

14 *use thee kindly*. As the next clause
shows, he really means 'treat you
according to her kind, or her nature',
but he allows the possible meaning
'be kind to you' to point to Lear's
expectation. Her 'kind' is as a sister
to Gonerill rather than a daughter to
Lear.

15 *she's as like this as a crab's like an apple*
Regan is as like Gonerill as a sour
apple is like an apple (that is, ident-
ical in *kind*)

18 *She will taste as like this as a crab does
to a crab* the experience of Regan will
be as sour and indigestible as the
experience of Gonerill

19 *on's* of his

22 *of either side's nose* on either side of his
nose

23 *what a man cannot smell out he may spy
into.* The Fool is picking up his *I can
tell what I can tell* (line 16). Man is
given organs of perception that, used
properly, may protect him from
folly.

24 *I did her wrong.* Presumably Cordelia
is meant. We recognize this immediately; but it is not clear *why* we do
so.

29 *put's* put his

LEAR I will forget my nature. So kind a father! – Be my
horses ready?

FOOL Thy asses are gone about 'em. The reason why the
seven stars are no more than seven is a pretty reason.

LEAR Because they are not eight?

FOOL Yes, indeed. Thou wouldst make a good fool.

LEAR To take't again perforce! Monster ingratitude!

FOOL If thou wert my fool, nuncle, I'd have thee beaten
for being old before thy time.

LEAR How's that?   40

FOOL Thou shouldst not have been old till thou hadst
been wise.

LEAR

O let me not be mad, not mad, sweet heaven!
Keep me in temper; I would not be mad!
How now! Are the horses ready?

KNIGHT Ready, my lord.

LEAR Come, boy.   *Exeunt all except the Fool*

FOOL

She that's a maid now, and laughs at my departure,
Shall not be a maid long, unless things be cut shorter.

                                                    Exit

---

31 *forget my nature* (that is, cease to be a
kind father)

37 *To take't again perforce!* 'He is meditat-
ing on his resumption of royalty'
(Dr Johnson).

perforce by violent means

Monster ingratitude! Compare
1.4.256–8.

43 *mad* (the first occasion when Lear
leads our thoughts in this direction;
no doubt he is picking up the *wise*
of the preceding line, in its meaning
'sane'. As Coleridge remarks, 'The
deepest tragic notes are often struck
by a half sense of an impending
blow' (*Coleridge on Shakespeare*,
edited by Terence Hawkes (1969),
page 205).)

48–9 *She that's a maid ... cut shorter.*
This couplet with its indecent pun
on *things* has been supposed to be
not Shakespeare's; but indecency and
authenticity are quite compatible.

48 *departure* (probably pronounced
'depart-er')

II.1   *Enter Edmund and Curan by opposite doors*

EDMUND Save thee, Curan.

CURAN And you, sir. I have been with your father and
given him notice that the Duke of Cornwall and Regan
his Duchess will be here with him this night.

EDMUND How comes that?

CURAN Nay, I know not. You have heard of the news
abroad – I mean the whispered ones, for they are yet but
ear-kissing arguments?

EDMUND Not I. Pray you what are they?

10   CURAN Have you heard of no likely wars toward 'twixt
the Dukes of Cornwall and Albany?

EDMUND Not a word.

CURAN You may do, then, in time. Fare you well, sir.

Exit

EDMUND

The Duke be here tonight! The better! best!
This weaves itself perforce into my business.
My father hath set guard to take my brother,

II.1 The parts of the plot begin to separate out into their constituent elements,
evil with evil, good with good. Edmund
completes his triumph over *A credulous
father and a brother noble*; Cornwall and
Regan move in to support him. Edgar,
now associated with Lear's knights (lines
93–4), is exiled (like Kent and Cordelia).
(stage direction) Here, and at II.2.0 and
III.1.0, I have substituted a modern
equivalent for the stage direction in F
('*Enter . . . seuerally*'). Entries and exits
'severally' – at opposite stage doors (compare III.1.55 and III.7.106) – are used by
Shakespeare to give visual effect to meet-
ings from far apart, or departures to
undertake different activities.

1 *Curan.* It is rare for Shakespeare to
give a proper name to a character as
little individualized as Curan is here

(his only appearance). It is not clear
why he does so at this point.

6 *news* (here takes a plural agreement)

8 *ear-kissing.* Most editors prefer Q's
'eare-bussing'. 'Bussing' is certainly
the more vivid word; but it is a
vulgar error to suppose that Shakespeare's vocabulary is characterized
principally by its use of quaint and
vivid elements.

arguments topics of conversation

10–11 *likely wars toward 'twixt the Dukes
of Cornwall and Albany* (the first of
frequent references to wars likely to
occur (*toward*) between the Dukes)

14 *The better! best!* so much the better!
In fact, nothing better could happen

15 *perforce* of necessity, without my seeking it

And I have one thing of a queasy question
Which I must act. Briefness and fortune work! –
Brother, a word! Descend! Brother, I say!
    Enter Edgar
My father watches. O, sir, fly this place;   20
Intelligence is given where you are hid.
You have now the good advantage of the night.
Have you not spoken 'gainst the Duke of Cornwall?
He's coming hither now i'the night, i'th'haste,
And Regan with him. Have you nothing said
Upon his party 'gainst the Duke of Albany?
Advise yourself.
EDGAR   I am sure on't, not a word.
EDMUND
    I hear my father coming. Pardon me;
In cunning I must draw my sword upon you.
Draw! Seem to defend yourself! Now quit you well.   30
(*Aloud*) Yield! Come before my father! Light, ho, here!
(*Aside*) Fly, brother! (*Aloud*) Torches, torches! (*Aside*)
    So farewell.   *Exit Edgar*
Some blood drawn on me would beget opinion

17 *one thing of a queasy question* a matter that requires delicate handling. He refers, presumably, to the disposing of Edgar.
   queasy (literally, 'liable to vomit')
18 *Briefness* speed of action
   Briefness and fortune work! I hope that quick action and good luck will help me
19 *Descend!* At 1.2.174 Edgar retired to Edmund's lodging. Presumably it is from this hiding place that he now *descends*.
23–6 *the Duke of Cornwall . . . the Duke of Albany*. Edmund was entirely ignorant of these matters only thirteen lines before. This is a good example of his quick-thinking opportunism.
26 *Upon his party 'gainst the Duke of Albany*. First Edmund suggested Edgar's peril from Cornwall; now he reverses the case and suggests that Edgar may have spoken too boldly on the side of Cornwall against Albany and so excited the latter's wrath. The prime object is to create a world teeming with dangers.
27 *Advise yourself* consider the matter
29 *In cunning* as a clever device
30 *quit you* defend yourself in the fight (with also, perhaps, a sense of *quit* meaning 'depart')

Of my more fierce endeavour. I have seen drunkards
Do more than this in sport.
> *He wounds himself in the arm*
> (*Aloud*)   Father, father! —
Stop, stop! — No help?
> *Enter Gloucester and servants with torches*

GLOUCESTER   Now, Edmund, where's the villain?

EDMUND

Here stood he in the dark, his sharp sword out,
Mumbling of wicked charms, conjuring the moon
To stand auspicious mistress.

GLOUCESTER   But where is he?

EDMUND

Look, sir, I bleed.

40 GLOUCESTER   Where is the villain, Edmund?

EDMUND

Fled this way, sir, when by no means he could —

GLOUCESTER

Pursue him, ho! Go after.   *Exeunt some servants*
                  'By no means' what?

EDMUND

Persuade me to the murder of your lordship;
But that I told him the revenging gods
'Gainst parricides did all the thunder bend,
Spoke with how manifold and strong a bond

34–5 *I have seen drunkards | Do more than this in sport.* 'Stabbing of arms', and mixing the blood with wine drunk to a mistress, was a practice of the gallants of Shakespeare's age.

37–9 *in the dark ... auspicious mistress.* Note Edmund's gift for theatrical invention — these details are well designed to affect the credulous Gloucester.

38–9 *Mumbling of wicked charms ... where is he?* Edmund appeals to Gloucester's tendency to superstition.

Gloucester's reply is, however, severely practical. There is some comedy in the cross-purposes of Edmund trying to get Edgar out of the way, and divert attention to himself, and Gloucester bent on the capture of his son.

41 *Fled this way.* As the eighteenth-century editor Capell said, Edmund should point in the wrong direction.

45 *bend* aim (like a bow). Compare II.4.222.

The child was bound to the father – sir, in fine,
Seeing how loathly opposite I stood
To his unnatural purpose, in fell motion
With his preparèd sword he charges home   50
My unprovided body, latched mine arm;
But when he saw my best alarumed spirits
Bold in the quarrel's right, roused to th'encounter,
Or whether gasted by the noise I made,
Full suddenly he fled.

GLOUCESTER   Let him fly far,
Not in this land shall he remain uncaught;
And found – dispatch. The noble Duke, my master,
My worthy arch and patron, comes tonight.
By his authority I will proclaim it
That he which finds him shall deserve our thanks,   60
Bringing the murderous coward to the stake;
He that conceals him, death.

EDMUND

When I dissuaded him from his intent,
And found him pight to do it, with curst speech
I threatened to discover him. He replied,

48–9 *how loathly opposite I stood* | *To* with
    what loathing I opposed
49 *fell motion* with a fierce thrust
50 *preparèd sword*. At 1.2.167 Edmund
    told Edgar to go armed. We may
    assume that Edgar has given sub-
    stance to the story by entering (line
    19) with his sword drawn (*preparèd*).
51 *unprovided* unprepared, unprotected
    latched. The F reading is less easy
    than Q's 'lanch'd' (or 'lanced'); but
    the fact that the change was made
    gives it a claim to credence. To
    latch is to 'catch' or 'nick', and this
    may seem more appropriate to the
    minor wound that Edmund has in-
    flicted on himself than the stronger
    'lanced'.

52 *my best alarumed spirits* my best
    energies called up by the *alarum* of
    battle
54 *gasted* terrified
55 *Let him fly far* however far he
    flies
57 *And found – dispatch*. Presumably the
    pause is filled in by some gesture,
    such as drawing his hand across his
    throat.
58 *arch and patron* (hendiadys) arch-
    patron
61 *to the stake* (metaphorically: 'to the
    place of final inescapable reckoning')
64 *pight* (past participle of 'pitch') firmly
    fixed (like tent-pegs)
    curst speech angry words
65 *discover* reveal

'Thou unpossessing bastard, dost thou think,
If I would stand against thee, would the reposal
Of any trust, virtue, or worth in thee
Make thy words faithed? No, what I should deny –

As this I would; ay, though thou didst produce
My very character – I'd turn it all
To thy suggestion, plot, and damnèd practice;
And thou must make a dullard of the world
If they not thought the profits of my death
Were very pregnant and potential spurs
To make thee seek it.'

GLOUCESTER   O strange and fastened villain!
Would he deny his letter, said he? I never got him.
        Tucket within
Hark, the Duke's trumpets! I know not why he comes. –
All ports I'll bar; the villain shall not 'scape.

The Duke must grant me that. Besides, his picture
I will send far and near, that all the kingdom
May have due note of him; and of my land,
Loyal and natural boy, I'll work the means

---

66 *unpossessing bastard*. Bastards were in law deemed incapable of inheriting land.

67–9 *would the reposal | Of any trust, virtue, or worth in thee | Make thy words faithed?* would the fact that trust has been placed in you, or any virtue or worth that you possess in yourself, make people believe what you say?

71 *character* handwriting (in the letter Edmund showed in 1.2)

71–2 *turn it all | To thy suggestion, plot, and damnèd practice* explain it as being due to your temptations, your plotting, and your wicked intriguing

73–6 *thou must make a dullard of the world . . . make thee seek it* you would have to make mankind very stupid to stop them thinking that you had full,

ready, and powerful motives to seek my death, given the advantages that would come to you if I were dead

76 *strange and fastened* fixed firm in his unnaturalness

77 *deny his letter* (in lines 70–71)
got begot
(stage direction) *Tucket* personal trumpet call

79 *ports* (probably 'seaports'; but it may mean the gates of walled towns)

80–81 *his picture | I will send far and near* (an early version of the 'wanted' poster outside police-stations)

83 *natural boy*. Gloucester means one who has expressed 'natural' loyalty to his father; but since a 'natural son' is a bastard, there is an ironic twist to the phrase.

To make thee capable.

Enter Cornwall, Regan, and attendants

CORNWALL

How now, my noble friend? Since I came hither –

Which I can call but now – I have heard strange news.

REGAN

If it be true, all vengeance comes too short

Which can pursue th'offender. How dost, my lord?

GLOUCESTER

O madam, my old heart is cracked; it's cracked.

REGAN

What, did my father's godson seek your life?   90

He whom my father named? your Edgar?

GLOUCESTER

O lady, lady, shame would have it hid!

REGAN

Was he not companion with the riotous knights

That tended upon my father?

GLOUCESTER

I know not, madam. 'Tis too bad, too bad!

EDMUND

Yes, madam, he was of that consort.

REGAN

No marvel then though he were ill affected.

---

84 *capable* (of inheriting land; that is, legitimized by process of law)

89 *my old heart is cracked; it's cracked.* The repetition suggests the sentimental self-pity that is a part of Gloucester's basic temperament. Compare *lady, lady* (line 92) and *too bad, too bad* (line 95).

90–91 *my father's godson . . . He whom my father named.* Regan immediately capitalizes on the new situation, to identify all wickedness with her father.

95–6 *I know not . . . Yes, madam . . .*

Gloucester's response to Regan's efforts to blame her father is not very satisfactory; he is too sunk in self-pity to catch her drift. It is Edmund, with his clear eye for the main chance, who gives her the reply she wants, thus establishing at first sight the natural rapport between them.

96 *consort* (accented on the second syllable). This is usually derogatory: 'gang, mob'.

97 *though* if

ill affected ill disposed

'Tis they have put him on the old man's death,
To have th'expense and waste of his revenues.
100   I have this present evening from my sister
Been well informed of them, and with such cautions
That if they come to sojourn at my house
I'll not be there.

CORNWALL   Nor I, assure thee, Regan.
Edmund, I hear that you have shown your father
A child-like office.

EDMUND   It was my duty, sir.

GLOUCESTER
He did bewray his practice, and received
This hurt you see, striving to apprehend him.

CORNWALL
Is he pursued?

GLOUCESTER   Ay, my good lord.

CORNWALL
If he be taken he shall never more
110   Be feared of doing harm. Make your own purpose
How in my strength you please. For you, Edmund,
Whose virtue and obedience doth this instant
So much commend itself, you shall be ours.
Natures of such deep trust we shall much need;

98 *put him on* urged him to undertake
99 *expense* spending
102 *my house.* Notice the mannish and
commanding air of Regan and the
merely confirmatory role of Cornwall
in this exchange.
105 *A child-like office* the duties that are
appropriate to a true son. Coming
from Cornwall the words have an
irony appropriate to Edmund.
106 *He did bewray his practice* Edmund
revealed Edgar's plot
110 *Be feared of doing harm* give rise to
the fear of his harmful deeds

110–11 *Make your own purpose | How in
my strength you please* fulfil your purpose (of capturing Edgar) by whatever means you like, drawing on my
resources as it suits you
113 *ours* one of my followers. Note the
royal plural.
114 *we shall much need* (with the implication: 'in the troubled times ahead of
us' – whether in wars with Lear or
wars with Albany is not certain)

You we first seize on.

EDMUND   I shall serve you, sir,
Truly, however else.

GLOUCESTER   For him I thank your grace.

CORNWALL
You know not why we came to visit you –

REGAN
Thus out of season, threading dark-eyed night –
Occasions, noble Gloucester, of some price,
Wherein we must have use of your advice.   120
Our father he hath writ, so hath our sister,
Of differences, which I best thought it fit
To answer from our home. The several messengers
From hence attend dispatch. Our good old friend,
Lay comforts to your bosom, and bestow
Your needful counsel to our businesses,
Which craves the instant use.

GLOUCESTER   I serve you, madam.
Your graces are right welcome.   *Exeunt. Flourish*

116 *Truly, however else* even if my imperfections prevent me from being as
efficient as I am true
118 *Thus out of season, threading dark-eyed
night.* Notice how imperiously Regan
takes over Cornwall's narrative and
makes it her own. *Out of season* may
imply that it is winter, a bad time for
travelling, or may only be repeating
the point that, in their haste to avoid
Lear, they have travelled all night.
The idea of threading the eye of a
needle in the dark, implicit in the
imagery used, conveys the sense of
effort and difficulty.
119 *Occasions . . . of some price* there are
reasons (or 'personal requirements')
of some importance. *Price* rather than

'prize' seems the most suitable modernization; see the note on 1.1.70.
122–3 *which I best thought it fit | To answer
from our home* which letters I thought
it best and most appropriate to reply
to away from home. Regan wishes
to delay receiving Lear till she has
consulted with Gonerill.
123–4 *The several messengers | From hence
attend dispatch* the men carrying the
respective letters are waiting here for
their dismissal
127 *Which craves the instant use* which requires to be dispatched at once. It is
not clear whether *Which* refers to
counsel or *businesses*. In Elizabethan
English the singular form *craves*
would be equally correct with either.

II.2   *Enter Kent and Oswald by opposite doors*

OSWALD

   Good dawning to thee, friend. Art of this house?

KENT Ay.

OSWALD Where may we set our horses?

KENT I'the mire.

OSWALD Prithee, if thou lovest me, tell me.

KENT I love thee not.

OSWALD Why then, I care not for thee.

KENT If I had thee in Lipsbury pinfold I would make thee
   care for me.

10   OSWALD Why dost thou use me thus? I know thee not.

KENT Fellow, I know thee.

OSWALD What dost thou know me for?

KENT A knave, a rascal, an eater of broken meats, a base,
   proud, shallow, beggarly, three-suited, hundred-pound,

II.2 The physical conflict between the two servants, Kent and Oswald the Steward, foreshadows in a semi-comic and pathetic vein the grander conflict to come. Gloucester and Cornwall move into sharper definition.

2 *Ay.* It is not clear why Kent says he is of Gloucester's household, unless it is to give occasion for further attacks on Oswald.

3 *we . . . our.* Presumably the plural refers to the attendants who accompany Oswald.

5 *if thou lovest me* (a conventional and rather affected phrase for 'please', which Kent chooses to take literally)

7, 9 *care . . . care.* Oswald says he does not *care for* ('like') Kent. Kent says he could make him *care* ('worry').

8 *Lipsbury pinfold.* No place called *Lipsbury* is known; so it is usually supposed to be an equivalent to 'lip-town', the space between the lips. A

pinfold is a pound for stray animals. The two words may well imply 'the strongly fenced area between the teeth', the whole phrase meaning 'If I had you between my teeth I would make you care'.

11 *I know thee* I can see through you. Notice the pejorative second-person singular throughout this dialogue.

13 *eater of broken meats.* After meals the scraps were collected into a basket, and these were the food of the lowest menials. Kent's general picture of Oswald is of a jumped-up menial pretending to be a gentleman – he is both *base* and *proud.*

14 *shallow* incapable of thought
three-suited (servant-like. Servants were allowed three suits a year. Compare III.4.129.)
hundred-pound (a great sum if the point is simply that Oswald is a menial. But about this time James I was

filthy-worsted-stocking knave; a lily-livered, action-taking, whoreson glass-gazing super-serviceable finical rogue, one-trunk-inheriting slave; one that wouldst be a bawd in way of good service, and art nothing but the composition of a knave, beggar, coward, pander, and the son and heir of a mongrel bitch; one whom I will beat into clamorous whining if thou deniest the least syllable of thy addition.

OSWALD Why, what a monstrous fellow art thou thus to rail on one that is neither known of thee nor knows thee!

KENT What a brazen-faced varlet art thou, to deny thou knowest me! Is it two days since I tripped up thy heels and beat thee before the King? Draw, you rogue! For though it be night, yet the moon shines. I'll make a sop o'the moonshine of you, you whoreson cullionly barber-monger! Draw!

He brandishes his sword

OSWALD Away! I have nothing to do with thee.

KENT Draw, you rascal! You come with letters against the King, and take Vanity the puppet's part against the

---

making knights for a hundred pounds; so that the phrase carries the idea of 'beggarly pretender to gentility'.)

15 *filthy-worsted-stocking knave.* Real gentlemen wore silk stockings.
lily-livered bloodless, cowardly

15–16 *action-taking* going to law (instead of fighting)

16 *super-serviceable.* This seems to be the only appearance of the word, so it is not clear exactly what it means – perhaps 'anxious to be of service in any way, however dishonourable'.
finical fussing about details

17 *one-trunk-inheriting* who inherited only as much as would go into one trunk

17–18 *wouldst be a bawd in way of good service* would do any service, however improper or disgusting, if that was required of you

19 *composition* compound

22 *addition* (something added to a man's name to denote his rank – here the names that Kent has 'added' to Oswald)

28–9 *make a sop o'the moonshine of you* make a mash of you, soak you in blood, while the moon shines (or 'while you talk "moonshine"' – nonsense)

29–30 *cullionly barbermonger* base fop, never out of the barber's shop

33 *Vanity the puppet* (Gonerill, seen as a Morality-play figure of Self-Regard, performed in a puppet play. There is also the sense of Gonerill as a puppet who should not speak except with her father's voice – the sense of the unnatural revolt of the puppet against the puppeteer.)

royalty of her father. Draw, you rogue! or I'll so
carbonado your shanks – Draw, you rascal! Come your
ways!

OSWALD   Help, ho! Murder! Help!

KENT   Strike, you slave!

     Oswald tries to escape

Stand, rogue! Stand, you neat slave! Strike!

     He beats him

40   OSWALD   Help, ho! Murder! Murder!

     Enter Edmund, Cornwall, Regan, Gloucester, and
     servants

EDMUND   How now! What's the matter? Part!

KENT   With you, goodman boy, and you please! Come, I'll
flesh ye; come on, young master.

GLOUCESTER   Weapons? Arms? What's the matter here?

CORNWALL

     Keep peace, upon your lives!

     He dies that strikes again. What is the matter?

REGAN

     The messengers from our sister and the King –

CORNWALL   What is your difference? Speak.

OSWALD   I am scarce in breath, my lord.

50   KENT   No marvel, you have so bestirred your valour. You
cowardly rascal, nature disclaims in thee; a tailor made
thee.

---

puppet. We should be aware of
not only the modern sense of 'mari-
onette', but also the earlier sense of
'doll' (poppet).

35 *carbonado your shanks* slash your legs
as if they were meat for broiling

35–6 *Come your ways* come on

39 *neat slave* elegant rascal

42 *With you* I'll fight with you
goodman boy master child, you who
have set yourself up with more authority than your years authorize
and you please if you like. For *and* F
prints 'if', which is probably a mod-

ernization. See the Account of the
Text, page 566.

43 *flesh ye* introduce you to bloodshed

48 *difference* dispute

51 *disclaims in thee* denies any part in
making you

51–2 *a tailor made thee.* The proverb is
that 'The tailor makes the man' –
with the sense that social status is
derived from clothes. Kent pushes
this one stage further: Oswald is
made, not simply socially but in
every sense, by his clothes.

CORNWALL Thou art a strange fellow. A tailor make a man?

KENT A tailor, sir. A stone-cutter or a painter could not have made him so ill, though they had been but two years o'the trade.

CORNWALL (*to Oswald*) Speak yet, how grew your quarrel?

OSWALD This ancient ruffian, sir, whose life I have   60
spared at suit of his grey beard –

KENT Thou whoreson zed, thou unnecessary letter! My lord, if you will give me leave, I will tread this unbolted villain into mortar and daub the wall of a jakes with him. 'Spare my grey beard', you wagtail!

CORNWALL Peace, sirrah!
You beastly knave, know you no reverence?

KENT
Yes, sir; but anger hath a privilege.

CORNWALL Why art thou angry?

KENT
That such a slave as this should wear a sword   70
Who wears no honesty. Such smiling rogues as these,
Like rats, oft bite the holy cords atwain,

55–6 *A tailor ... A stone-cutter or a painter could not have made him so ill* ... The tailor was one of the more despised of Elizabethan tradesmen, often thought of as cringing and effeminate.

62 *thou unnecessary letter.* Zed was thought *unnecessary* because most of its functions in English are taken over by 's', and because Latin manages without it. Similarly Oswald is a superfluous element in society.

63 *unbolted* unsifted, unkneaded; requiring to be trodden down (like lumpy mortar) before he can be useful

64 *jakes* lavatory

65 *wagtail.* G. L. Kittredge suggests that Oswald is too scared to stand still, and therefore reminds Kent of the uneasy tail-jerking of the wagtail. The word was often used in this period to mean 'wanton'.

67 *beastly* beast-like (not knowing the *reverence* etc. proper to human society)

68 *privilege* (to break the bounds of normal social decorum)

70–71 *should wear a sword | Who wears no honesty* carries the symbol of manhood, but lacks an honourable character

72 *the holy cords* the bonds of natural affection that bind the individual to society

Which are t' intrinse t'unloose; smooth every passion
That in the natures of their lords rebel,
Being oil to fire, snow to the colder moods,
Renege, affirm, and turn their halcyon beaks
With every gale and vary of their masters,
Knowing naught – like dogs – but following. –
A plague upon your epileptic visage!
80   Smile you my speeches as I were a fool?
Goose, if I had you upon Sarum Plain,
I'd drive ye cackling home to Camelot.

CORNWALL What, art thou mad, old fellow?

GLOUCESTER How fell you out? Say that.

KENT

No contraries hold more antipathy
Than I and such a knave.

CORNWALL

Why dost thou call him knave? What is his fault?

73 *t' intrinse t'unloose* too inward, secret, hidden (in their mode of tying) to be untied. Thus the bonds of matrimony or of filial obedience (or of royal duty) cannot be 'untied' (returned to their separate condition), but can be 'bitten' apart so that *love cools, friendship falls off*, etc. Oswald's nature is thus turned towards one of the central problems of the play.
smooth promote by flattery

74 *rebel.* In the typical image of man, passion can only emerge when it *rebels* against its overseer, reason.

75 *Being.* F's 'Being' and Q's 'Bring' seem equally good; and therefore, in the absence of other evidence, we must prefer the F reading.

76 *Renege* deny. Compare IV.6.98–100.
turn their halcyon beaks. The kingfisher (or *halcyon*) was supposed, if hung up, to vary direction with the wind. So flattering servants only possess opinions to point in whatever direc-

tion the passions of their masters require.

79 *epileptic visage.* Oswald is presumably trying to smile and at the same time twitching with terror.

80 *Smile.* F follows Q's unusual spelling 'Smoile'. Editors have sometimes thought that this reflected Kent's dialect disguise as Caius; but such an isolated expression of it would be pointless.

81-2 *Goose, if I had you . . . Camelot* (an obscure passage, which must have the general sense: 'If I had you at command I would make you add flight to your cackling laughter, like a goose being driven')

81 *Goose* foolish person
Sarum Plain Salisbury Plain

82 *Camelot* (the legendary capital of Arthur's kingdom; it is not known where it was situated; some Elizabethans believed it was at Winchester)

KENT His countenance likes me not.

CORNWALL

No more perchance does mine, nor his, nor hers.

KENT

Sir, 'tis my occupation to be plain.   90
I have seen better faces in my time
Than stands on any shoulder that I see
Before me at this instant.

CORNWALL   This is some fellow
Who, having been praised for bluntness, doth affect
A saucy roughness, and constrains the garb
Quite from his nature. He cannot flatter, he!
An honest mind and plain – he must speak truth!
And they will take it, so; if not, he's plain.
These kind of knaves I know, which in this plainness
Harbour more craft and more corrupter ends   100
Than twenty silly-ducking observants
That stretch their duties nicely.

KENT

Sir, in good faith, in sincere verity,
Under th'allowance of your great aspect,
Whose influence like the wreath of radiant fire
On flickering Phoebus' front –

CORNWALL   What mean'st by this?

88 *likes me not* does not please me

94–6 *doth affect . . . from his nature* pretends to a blunt rudeness of manner, and twists the habit (*garb*) of plain-speaking away from its (*his*) true nature (truth), turning it towards deception

98 *And they will take it, so; if not, he's plain* if people will swallow his rudeness, then that's all right; if they object, then he defends himself by the claim that this is just plain-speaking

100 *more corrupter.* The double comparative is a common Elizabethan usage.

101 *silly-ducking observants* obsequious attendants making themselves foolish with their low bows

102 *stretch their duties nicely* strain themselves to carry out their duties with the greatest finesse

104, 105 *aspect . . . influence* (astrological terms. Kent's parody of the *observants'* courtly dialect leads him to describe Cornwall as a planet.)

104 *aspect* (accented on the second syllable)

106 *flickering Phoebus' front* the fiery forehead of the sun

KENT To go out of my dialect which you discommend so
much. I know, sir, I am no flatterer. He that beguiled
you in a plain accent was a plain knave; which, for my
110 part, I will not be, though I should win your displeasure
to entreat me to't.

CORNWALL What was th'offence you gave him?

OSWALD I never gave him any.
It pleased the King his master very late
To strike at me upon his misconstruction,
When he, compact, and flattering his displeasure,
Tripped me behind; being down, insulted, railed,
And put upon him such a deal of man
That worthied him, got praises of the King
120 For him attempting who was self-subdued;
And in the fleshment of this dread exploit
Drew on me here again.

KENT   None of these rogues and cowards
But Ajax is their fool.

CORNWALL   Fetch forth the stocks!
You stubborn ancient knave, you reverend braggart,

---

107 *my dialect* (that of a plain-spoken
man)

110-11 *though I should win your displeasure
to entreat me to't.* It is difficult to
paraphrase this; perhaps the easiest
interpretation is: 'though I should
manage to overcome your displeasure to the extent that you would
entreat me to be a knave'.

115 *upon his misconstruction* as a result of
his (the King's) misunderstanding of
me

116 *he, compact* Kent, being in league
with the King
flattering his displeasure to gratify his
mood of anger

117 *being down, insulted* when I was down,
he abused me

118-19 *put upon him such a deal of man |
That worthied him* made himself out

to be such a hero that others thought
him worth something

120 *For him attempting who was self-subdued* for attacking a man who gave in
without a struggle

121 *fleshment* excitement of accomplishing. To *flesh* was to inflict injury in
warfare, especially for the first time.
dread exploit (ironical)

122-3 *None of these rogues and cowards | But
Ajax is their fool.* Either (1) 'To hear
people of his kind speak you would
think the great hero Ajax was a fool
beside them' or (2) 'Rogues and
cowards can deceive great men like
Cornwall (or Ajax)'.

124 *ancient knave ... reverend braggart.*
The same idea is repeated: Kent is
old and therefore should be revered;
but he is a knave and a braggart.

We'll teach you —

KENT   Sir, I am too old to learn.
Call not your stocks for me. I serve the King,
On whose employment I was sent to you.
You shall do small respect, show too bold malice
Against the grace and person of my master,
Stocking his messenger.   130

CORNWALL
Fetch forth the stocks! As I have life and honour,
There shall he sit till noon.

REGAN
Till noon? Till night, my lord, and all night too.

KENT
Why, madam, if I were your father's dog
You should not use me so.

REGAN   Sir, being his knave, I will.

CORNWALL
This is a fellow of the selfsame colour
Our sister speaks of. Come, bring away the stocks.
          Stocks brought out

GLOUCESTER
Let me beseech your grace not to do so.
His fault is much, and the good King, his master,
Will check him for't. Your purposed low correction   140
Is such as basest and contemned'st wretches
For pilferings and most common trespasses
Are punished with. The King must take it ill
That he, so slightly valued in his messenger,
Should have him thus restrained.

CORNWALL   I'll answer that.

REGAN
My sister may receive it much more worse

---

129 *grace and person* (both his mystical   135 *being* since you are
   body as King and his *person* as man)   136 *colour* character
132 *till noon*. The moon is still shining;   137 *bring away* bring along
   the sun begins to rise some thirty   140 *check* rebuke
   lines later (line 161).   141 *contemned'st* most despised

To have her gentleman abused, assaulted,
For following her affairs. – Put in his legs.
>   *Kent is put in the stocks*
Come, my lord, away.
>   *Exeunt all but Gloucester and Kent*

GLOUCESTER

150   I am sorry for thee, friend. 'Tis the Duke's pleasure,
Whose disposition all the world well knows
Will not be rubbed nor stopped. I'll entreat for thee.

KENT

Pray do not, sir. I have watched and travelled hard.
Some time I shall sleep out, the rest I'll whistle.
A good man's fortune may grow out at heels.
Give you good morrow!

GLOUCESTER   The Duke's to blame in this.
'Twill be ill taken.   *Exit*

KENT

Good King, that must approve the common saw,
Thou out of Heaven's benediction comest
160   To the warm sun.
Approach, thou beacon to this under globe,
That by thy comfortable beams I may
Peruse this letter. Nothing almost sees miracles
But misery. I know 'tis from Cordelia,
Who hath most fortunately been informed

---

152 *Will not be rubbed* cannot bear to be
hindered. A *rub* in bowls is anything
that impedes the bowl.
153 *watched ... hard* made myself stay
awake
158 *approve the common saw* prove the
truth of the well-known saying. The
particular *saw* is no doubt suggested
by the rising of the sun.
159–60 *out of Heaven's benediction comest |
To the warm sun* come from good to
bad
161 *beacon to this under globe* (the sun)

162 *comfortable* comforting
163–4 *Nothing almost sees miracles | But
misery* miracles (like this letter from
Cordelia) are especially likely to
occur to those in the lowest and
most depressed condition. Maynard
Mack thinks there is a reference to
Acts 16 where Paul and Silas, placed
in the stocks in Philippi, 'sang praises
unto God' and were released by an
earthquake (*King Lear in Our Time*
(1966), page 56).

Of my obscurèd course, and (*reading*) 'shall find time
From this enormous state, seeking to give
Losses their remedies'. All weary and o'erwatched,
Take vantage, heavy eyes, not to behold
This shameful lodging.   170
Fortune, good night; smile once more; turn thy wheel.

    He sleeps

    Enter Edgar   II.3

EDGAR
I heard myself proclaimed,
And by the happy hollow of a tree
Escaped the hunt. No port is free, no place
That guard and most unusual vigilance
Does not attend my taking. Whiles I may 'scape
I will preserve myself; and am bethought
To take the basest and most poorest shape

---

166 *my obscurèd course* my disguised way of life

166–8 *and 'shall find time ... their remedies'* (obscurely worded and perhaps corrupt. Some of the dislocation of sense may be due to Kent's reading out phrases from the letter. The general meaning must be that Cordelia will intervene and try to put things right.)

167 *this enormous state* this abnormal and wicked state of affairs

168–9 *o'erwatched . . . eyes* eyes made weary by being kept from sleep

171 (stage direction). *He sleeps.* I give no exit here. I believe that Kent remains on stage throughout the next scene and is discovered by Lear in II.4 still on stage. We may prefer to imagine that the stocks are set in a recess and are concealed by the drawing of a curtain.

II.3 This one-speech scene serves to give a short breathing-space in the effectively continuous action in the courtyard of Gloucester's castle which occupies II.2 and II.4. It also allows us to be aware of the transformation of Edgar into Poor Tom so that when we hear his name (III.4.37 and 41) and see him (III.4.43) we know with whom we are dealing.

1 *proclaimed* (as an outlaw. See II.1.59.)

2 *by the happy hollow of a tree* by the fortunate accident that there was a hollow tree in which I could hide

3 *No port is free.* See II.1.79.

6 *am bethought* have a mind

7 *most poorest.* The double superlative, like the double comparative (see II.2.100), is a means of giving emphasis.

That ever penury, in contempt of man,
Brought near to beast. My face I'll grime with filth,
10 Blanket my loins, elf all my hairs in knots,
And with presented nakedness outface
The winds and persecutions of the sky.
The country gives me proof and precedent
Of Bedlam beggars, who, with roaring voices,
Strike in their numbed and mortified bare arms
Pins, wooden pricks, nails, sprigs of rosemary;
And with this horrible object, from low farms,
Poor pelting villages, sheepcotes, and mills
Sometimes with lunatic bans, sometime with prayers,
20 Enforce their charity: 'Poor Turlygod! Poor Tom!'
That's something yet; Edgar I nothing am. *Exit*

8 *in contempt of man* despising the pretensions of humanity (to be superior to the beasts)
10 *Blanket my loins* (a useful indication of the stage appearance of the 'naked' Tom – he wore a piece of blanket as a loin-cloth)
   elf tangle into elf-locks. (Matted hair was thought to be the result of elvish malice.)
11 *with presented nakedness outface*. By persecuting himself, by *presenting* his nakedness to the storm, Edgar 'stares down' the hostile world.
14 *Bedlam beggars* beggars who claim they have been inmates of the Bethlehem (*Bedlam*) madhouse, and have licences to go about begging for their keep. 'This fellow . . . that sat half-naked . . . from the girdle upward . . . he swears he hath been in Bedlam and will talk franticly of purpose;

you see pins stuck in sundry places of his native flesh, especially in his arms, which pain he gladly puts himself to . . . only to make you believe he is out of his wits; he calls himself by the name of *Poor Tom* and, coming near anybody, cries out, *Poor Tom is a-cold*' (Thomas Dekker, *The Bellman of London*, 1608).
15 *mortified* dead to feeling (like *numbed*)
17 *object* spectacle
   low lowly, humble
18 *pelting* paltry
19 *bans* cursings
20 '*Poor Turlygod! Poor Tom!*'. Edgar enacts the role he must now fulfil. *Turlygod* is a word no one has explained.
21 *That's something yet; Edgar I nothing am* as Poor Tom there is some kind of existence for me; as Edgar I cannot exist

II.4

Kent still in the stocks
Enter Lear, the Fool, and a Gentleman

LEAR

'Tis strange that they should so depart from home
And not send back my messengers.

GENTLEMAN   As I learned,
The night before there was no purpose in them
Of this remove.

KENT   Hail to thee, noble master!

LEAR

Ha!
Makest thou this shame thy pastime?

KENT   No, my lord.

FOOL Ha, ha! He wears cruel garters. Horses are tied by
the heads, dogs and bears by the neck, monkeys by the
loins, and men by the legs. When a man's over-lusty at
legs, then he wears wooden nether-stocks.   10

LEAR

What's he that hath so much thy place mistook
To set thee here?

KENT   It is both he and she;
Your son and daughter.

LEAR No.

KENT Yes.

II.4 The climactic scene at the end of the
protasis or exposition of the play. Beginning at the level of the affront to Kent,
the tension mounts through Lear's dispute
with Regan and Cornwall – conducted
via Gloucester and so avoiding full-scale
confrontation – and reaches its first climax
when Gonerill arrives and we have the
full orchestration of 1.1 repeated, answering the 'I give you' of the opening
with a conclusive 'We take'. This dispute
only dies into another kind of climax as
Lear's speeches expand to prophetic
frenzy, as the storm thunders closer, and

as Lear rushes to join the cosmic furies,
and the wicked withdraw to safety.
3–4 *purpose ... Of this remove* intention
to move from one house to another
6 *Makest thou this shame thy pastime?* do
you sit in the stocks for fun?
7 *cruel garters* (1) the stocks; (2) crewel
(worsted) cross-garters
10 *wooden nether-stocks* stocks as
stockings
11 *place* (1) rank (as King's messenger);
(2) the place (where you sit) due to
you
13 *son* son-in-law

LEAR   No, I say.

KENT   I say yea.

LEAR   No, no, they would not.

KENT   Yes, they have.

20   LEAR   By Jupiter, I swear no!

KENT

     By Juno, I swear ay!

LEAR   They durst not do't;

     They could not, would not do't; 'tis worse than murder

     To do upon respect such violent outrage.

     Resolve me with all modest haste which way

     Thou mightst deserve or they impose this usage,

     Coming from us.

KENT   My lord, when at their home

     I did commend your highness' letters to them,

     Ere I was risen from the place that showed

     My duty kneeling, came there a reeking post,

30   Stewed in his haste, half breathless, panting forth

     From Gonerill his mistress salutations;

     Delivered letters, spite of intermission,

     Which presently they read; on whose contents

     They summoned up their meiny, straight took horse,

     Commanded me to follow and attend

     The leisure of their answer, gave me cold looks;

     And meeting here the other messenger,

     Whose welcome I perceived had poisoned mine –

---

19   *Yes.* Given the regular symmetry of this exchange one might expect 'Yes, yes' here; but one can hardly change the text for such a reason, even though the unreliable Quarto is the only authority for lines 18–19.

23   *upon respect* (either (1) 'against a man whose role required respect' or (2) 'deliberately')

24   *Resolve me with all modest haste* tell me with speed, but be temperate

26   *Coming from us* given that you came as a royal messenger

28–9   *from the place that showed | My duty kneeling* from the kneeling posture that showed my duty

29–30   *a reeking post, | Stewed in his haste* a sweating messenger, soaked in the sweat his haste had produced

32   *spite of intermission* in spite of the gasps and pauses that his breathless condition required

33   *presently* immediately
     on whose contents when they had read them

34   *meiny* household menials

Being the very fellow which of late
Displayed so saucily against your highness –   40
Having more man than wit about me, drew.
He raised the house with loud and coward cries.
Your son and daughter found this trespass worth
The shame which here it suffers.

FOOL Winter's not gone yet if the wild geese fly that way.

> Fathers that wear rags
>> Do make their children blind,
> But fathers that bear bags
>> Shall see their children kind.
> Fortune, that arrant whore,   50
>> Ne'er turns the key to the poor.

But for all this thou shalt have as many dolours for thy
daughters as thou canst tell in a year.

LEAR

O, how this mother swells up toward my heart!
Hysterica passio, down, thou climbing sorrow!
Thy element's below. Where is this daughter?

KENT With the Earl, sir, here within.

LEAR Follow me not; stay here.   *Exit*

GENTLEMAN

Made you no more offence but what you speak of?

KENT None.   60

---

40 *Displayed so saucily* acted in so obviously insolent a way
41 *man than wit* courage than discretion
45 *wild geese.* They fly south in the autumn. The events that Kent has described convey the same message as do wild geese seen flying south – the winter of displeasure and unkindness is to get worse.
47 *blind* (to the needs of their parents)
48 *bear bags* keep their money-bags
51 *turns the key* opens the door
52–3 *dolours for thy daughters* (1) griefs because of your daughters; (2) dollars in exchange for your daughters
53 *tell* (1) speak of; (2) count

54, 55 *mother . . . Hysterica passio* (a feeling of suffocation and giddiness thought to begin in the womb ('mother', *hystera* in Greek) and to affect the patient by climbing to the heart and then to the throat. One of the demoniacs in Harsnet's *A Declaration of Egregious Popish Impostures* (1603) suffered from the mother.)
56 *Thy element's below* your appropriate place is below. The 'mother' is not simply a medical condition appropriate to Lear; it is a visceral symbol of the breakdown in hierarchy, when the lower elements climb up to threaten or destroy the superior ones.

How chance the King comes with so small a number?

FOOL And thou hadst been set i'the stocks for that question, thou'dst well deserved it.

KENT Why, Fool?

FOOL We'll set thee to school to an ant to teach thee there's no labouring i'the winter. All that follow their noses are led by their eyes, but blind men; and there's not a nose among twenty but can smell him that's stinking. Let go thy hold when a great wheel runs down a hill, lest it break thy neck with following. But the great one that goes upward, let him draw thee after. When a wise man gives thee better counsel, give me mine again; I would ha' none but knaves use it, since a fool gives it.

> That sir which serves and seeks for gain,
>   And follows but for form,
> Will pack when it begins to rain,
>   And leave thee in the storm;
> But I will tarry, the fool will stay,
>   And let the wise man fly.
> The knave turns fool that runs away;
>   The fool no knave, perdy.

---

62 *And* if

62-3 *set i'the stocks for that question.* The question is subversive, for the answer must be that kings who lose their power also lose their followers.

65-6 *an ant . . . no labouring i'the winter.* Aesop's provident ant laboured when labour was profitable (in the summer); so Lear's followers stopped following when the winter of their master's fortune made following unprofitable.

66-9 *All that follow their noses . . . him that's stinking* those who go straight still follow what they see, and they can see Lear's downfall. Even the blind man who cannot *see* his downfall can smell the stink of failure

69 *a great wheel* (a great man)

73 *ha' . . . use.* This emendation assumes

that the F reading, 'I would hause none but knaues follow it' (where 'hause' replaces the Q 'haue'), derives from a correction 'ha use' written in the margin of Q. It is assumed that this was intended to replace Q's 'haue' by 'ha' and Q's 'follow' by 'use'. The F compositor, however, attributed both the corrections to 'haue' and left 'follow' intact.

74-7 *That sir . . . in the storm.* The servant's progress described here is very close to that which Iago praises in *Othello*, 1.1.49-54.

74 *sir* man (here specifically a servant)

75 *for form* out of habit or convention

76 *pack* depart

80-81 *The knave turns fool that runs away; | The fool no knave, perdy.* If this is textually correct it implies a sudden

KENT Where learned you this, Fool?

FOOL Not i'the stocks, fool.

Enter Lear and Gloucester

LEAR

Deny to speak with me? They are sick; they are weary?
They have travelled all the night? Mere fetches,
The images of revolt and flying-off.
Fetch me a better answer.

GLOUCESTER   My dear lord,
You know the fiery quality of the Duke,
How unremovable and fixed he is
In his own course.

LEAR   Vengeance, plague, death, confusion!   90
'Fiery'? What 'quality'? Why, Gloucester, Gloucester,
I'd speak with the Duke of Cornwall and his wife.

GLOUCESTER

Well, my good lord, I have informed them so.

LEAR

'Informed them'! Dost thou understand me, man?

GLOUCESTER Ay, my good lord.

LEAR

The King would speak with Cornwall, the dear father
Would with his daughter speak, commands, tends,
          service.

switch from worldly wisdom to spiritual truth: 'The knave (servant) who
deserts his master must eventually be
seen as a fool; but this fool will stay,
and so, in God's name, is no knave'.

83 *Not i'the stocks, fool.* In the context
this is equivalent to saying that Kent
is no knave.

85 *fetches* tricks

86 *images of revolt and flying-off* (representative of disobedience and desertion and the rejection of natural ties)

88 *quality* character

91 *What 'quality'?* Lear is still in the
world where individuality is far less

important than status and relationship. When king and father command, character is no excuse.

97 *commands, tends, service.* This is F's
reading. The text here is difficult if
not impossible to sort out. The Q
corrector's 'commands her seruice' is
probably mere tidying up without
authority. The original (uncorrected)
Quarto's 'come and tends seruice',
because it is nonsense, probably represents an honest attempt to read the
manuscript. If the Folio was printed
from the uncorrected form of the
Quarto page we could base little on

Are they 'informed' of this? My breath and blood!
'Fiery'? The 'fiery' Duke? Tell the hot Duke that –
100   No, but not yet! Maybe he is not well.
Infirmity doth still neglect all office
Whereto our health is bound; we are not ourselves
When nature, being oppressed, commands the mind
To suffer with the body. I'll forbear;
And am fallen out with my more headier will
To take the indisposed and sickly fit
For the sound man. – Death on my state! Wherefore
Should he sit here? This act persuades me
That this remotion of the Duke and her
110   Is practice only. Give me my servant forth.
Go tell the Duke and's wife I'd speak with them –
Now presently! Bid them come forth and hear me,
Or at their chamber door I'll beat the drum
Till it cry sleep to death.
    GLOUCESTER   I would have all well betwixt you.   *Exit*
    LEAR
O me, my heart, my rising heart! But down!

its preservation of the Q reading; on the other hand, if F was printed from the corrected page, its readings would imply a fresh look at the manuscript, and the coincidence with the uncorrected Q reading would prove authenticity. I think we must print either 'commands, tends' or something that looks like 'come and tends' in Elizabethan handwriting. The usual reading of modern editors, 'commands, tends', makes sense, but not good sense. Lear is making plain forceful demands, not complex or ironic ones like 'commands her service and tends his own'. 'True service' is a possible reading, and one easily misread in Elizabethan handwriting as 'tends service'.

101 *still* always

101–2 *neglect all office | Whereto our*

health is bound fail to fulfil the duties which are required of us when we are in health

105 *am fallen out with my more headier will* am no longer friendly to my more reckless impulse

107 *Death on my state!* (an oath – 'May my kingly power come to an end' – which is already fulfilled)

109 *remotion* (either (1) 'removal from one house to the other' or (2) 'holding themselves remote from me')

110 *practice* stratagem

111 *and's wife* (not 'my daughter')

112 *presently* at once

113 *chamber* bedroom

114 *cry sleep to death* kills off sleep by the noise it makes

116 *rising heart* (a further stage in the hysterica passio)

FOOL Cry to it, nuncle, as the cockney did to the eels
when she put 'em i'the paste alive. She knapped 'em
o'the coxcombs with a stick and cried 'Down, wantons,
down!' 'Twas her brother that in pure kindness to his   120
horse buttered his hay.

    Enter Cornwall, Regan, Gloucester, and servants

LEAR
Good morrow to you both.
CORNWALL   Hail to your grace.

    Kent is here set at liberty

REGAN
I am glad to see your highness.
LEAR
Regan, I think you are. I know what reason
I have to think so. If thou shouldst not be glad,
I would divorce me from thy mother's tomb,
Sepulchring an adult'ress. (*To Kent*) O, are you free?
Some other time for that. – Beloved Regan,
Thy sister's naught. O Regan, she hath tied
Sharp-toothed unkindness like a vulture here –   130
    (*laying his hand on his heart*)
I can scarce speak to thee – thou'lt not believe
With how depraved a quality – O Regan!

117–20 *as the cockney did . . . down!'* Cockney probably means here 'a pampered
and foolish person'. She had little
experience of making eel-pies, put
the eels in without killing them, and,
when they tried to wriggle out of
the pastry, rapped them on the
heads, crying 'Down, you roguish
creatures'. So Lear's heart tries to
rise out of the situation his folly has
created and must be *knapped*
('struck').

120–21 *'Twas her brother . . . buttered his
hay*. Cheating ostlers were said to
butter hay to stop the horses eating
it. The cockney's *brother* (that is, one

of the same breed of tender-hearted
fools) tries to be kind and succeeds
in being destructive (like Lear).

126–7 *divorce me from thy mother's tomb,* |
Sepulchring an adult'ress posthum-
ously divorce your mother, proved
unfaithful to me (by your unfilial
conduct)

127 It has been suggested that Kent
should exit here.

129 *naught* wicked

130 *like a vulture*. Shakespeare may be
remembering the torment of Prometheus, whose liver (believed to be
the seat of the passions) was endlessly
devoured by a vulture.

REGAN

    I pray you, sir, take patience. I have hope
    You less know how to value her desert
    Than she to scant her duty.

LEAR   Say? How is that?

REGAN

    I cannot think my sister in the least
    Would fail her obligation. If, sir, perchance,
    She have restrained the riots of your followers,
    'Tis on such ground and to such wholesome end
140   As clears her from all blame.

LEAR

    My curses on her.

REGAN   O sir, you are old.
    Nature in you stands on the very verge
    Of his confine. You should be ruled and led
    By some discretion that discerns your state
    Better than you yourself. Therefore I pray you
    That to our sister you do make return.
    Say you have wronged her.

LEAR   Ask her forgiveness?
    Do you but mark how this becomes the house:
        (*he kneels*)
    'Dear daughter, I confess that I am old;
150   Age is unnecessary; on my knees I beg

133–5 *I have hope . . . she to scant her duty.*
The sense is clear: 'I trust that she
does not know how to scant her
duty as well as you know how to
undervalue her'; but it is not easy to
make the words mean this. The most
probable explanation of the fact that
the literal sense seems opposite to
the required sense is that *scant* adds a
second negative idea to that in *less
know*; Shakespeare is anxious to stress
the negative, but fails to notice that
he has one too many, and that 'she
to do her duty' would be more

accurate.

138 *riots.* Regan and Gonerill use the
same vocabulary for the knights. See
I.3.7, I.4.199 and 240, and II.1.93.

144 *state* physical and mental condition
(but with an ironic echo of *state* meaning 'power, royalty')

148 *becomes the house* is appropriate to the
household (where the father is 'the
head of the house')

150 *Age is unnecessary.* In a survival-of-
the-fittest world (which Gonerill and
Regan are setting up) the aged
cannot be justified; no one needs

That you'll vouchsafe me raiment, bed, and food.'

REGAN

Good sir, no more! These are unsightly tricks.
Return you to my sister.

LEAR (*rising*)   Never, Regan.
She hath abated me of half my train,
Looked black upon me, struck me with her tongue,
Most serpent-like, upon the very heart.
All the stored vengeances of heaven fall
On her ingrateful top! Strike her young bones,
You taking airs, with lameness!

CORNWALL   Fie, sir, fie!

LEAR

You nimble lightnings, dart your blinding flames   160
Into her scornful eyes! Infect her beauty,
You fen-sucked fogs drawn by the powerful sun,
To fall and blister.

REGAN   O the blest gods!
So will you wish on me when the rash mood is on.

LEAR

No, Regan, thou shalt never have my curse.
Thy tender-hefted nature shall not give
Thee o'er to harshness. Her eyes are fierce; but thine
Do comfort, and not burn. 'Tis not in thee
To grudge my pleasures, to cut off my train,
To bandy hasty words, to scant my sizes,   170
And, in conclusion, to oppose the bolt
Against my coming in. Thou better knowest

them. If they are to be given *raiment,
bed, and food* it must be out of charity.
154 *abated* deprived
158-9 *Strike her young bones . . . with lameness* deform the bones of her unborn
child
159 *taking airs* infectious vapours
161-3 *Infect her beauty . . . blister* you noxious vapours that rise from bogs
when the sun shines on them, fall

down on her, blister her face and
mar her beauty
166 *tender-hefted* (literally, 'set into a delicate handle') endowed with a tender
sensibility
170 *sizes* allowances
171-2 *oppose the bolt | Against my coming
in.* The climax of these deprivations
is, ironically enough, the one which
Regan is shortly to put into practice.

The offices of nature, bond of childhood,
Effects of courtesy, dues of gratitude.
Thy half o'the kingdom hast thou not forgot,
Wherein I thee endowed.

REGAN   Good sir, to the purpose.

LEAR
Who put my man i'the stocks?
                    Tucket within

CORNWALL   What trumpet's that?

REGAN
I know't – my sister's. This approves her letter
That she would soon be here.
                    Enter Oswald

                                  Is your lady come?

LEAR
180   This is a slave whose easy-borrowed pride
Dwells in the fickle grace of her he follows.
Out, varlet, from my sight!

CORNWALL   What means your grace?

LEAR
Who stocked my servant? Regan, I have good hope
Thou didst not know on't.
                    Enter Gonerill

                                  Who comes here? O heavens!
If you do love old men, if your sweet sway
Allow obedience, if you yourselves are old,
Make it your cause! Send down and take my part!

---

173 *The offices of nature, bond of childhood*
the duties that are natural to our
state, such as the bond of affection
between child and parent

174 *Effects of courtesy* manifestations of a
courtly disposition

174–5 *gratitude.* | *Thy half o'the kingdom
...* It is worth noticing that Lear,
even at this point, climaxes his
arguments, not with the claims of
nature or courtesy, but with the eco-

nomic argument.

178 *approves* confirms

180 *easy-borrowed pride.* 'Pride' often
means 'ostentatious adornment'.
Oswald's splendid livery and his steward's chain (compare Malvolio) are
easy to put on and take off. What is
more, they depend on the whim of
'her grace'.

186 *Allow* approve

(*To Gonerill*) Art not ashamed to look upon this beard?
O Regan, will you take her by the hand?

GONERILL

Why not by th'hand, sir? How have I offended?   190
All's not offence that indiscretion finds
And dotage terms so.

LEAR   O sides, you are too tough!
Will you yet hold? – How came my man i'the stocks?

CORNWALL

I set him there, sir; but his own disorders
Deserved much less advancement.

LEAR   You? Did you?

REGAN

I pray you, father, being weak, seem so.
If till the expiration of your month
You will return and sojourn with my sister,
Dismissing half your train, come then to me.
I am now from home and out of that provision   200
Which shall be needful for your entertainment.

LEAR

Return to her, and fifty men dismissed!
No, rather I abjure all roofs and choose
To wage against the enmity o'th'air,
To be a comrade with the wolf and owl –
Necessity's sharp pinch! Return with her?

---

188 *beard* (an emblem of age, and therefore of authority and deserving)
191 *that indiscretion finds* that want of
judgement (like yours) discovers to
be so
192 *sides* (the sides of the chest, strained
by the swellings and passions of the
heart)
193 *hold* hold out, remain intact
195 *Deserved much less advancement.* The
stocks are a low seat, and a disgraceful punishment; but they are higher
than he deserves.

196 *being weak, seem so* don't act as if you
had strength you do not possess.
Shakespeare quickly transfers the contest from Cornwall to the daughters.
The central conflict must not be ob-
scured by subsidiary issues.
201 *entertainment* proper reception
204 *wage against the enmity o'th'air* struggle against the hostile environment
of the open air
205 *the wolf and owl* (solitary and rapa-
cious animals, hunting by night)
206 *Necessity's sharp pinch!* The phrase is

Why, the hot-blooded France that dowerless took
Our youngest born, I could as well be brought
To knee his throne and, squire-like, pension beg
To keep base life afoot. Return with her!
Persuade me rather to be slave and sumpter
To this detested groom.

      He points to Oswald

GONERILL   At your choice, sir.

LEAR

I prithee, daughter, do not make me mad.
I will not trouble thee, my child. Farewell.
We'll no more meet, no more see one another.
But yet thou art my flesh, my blood, my daughter –
Or rather a disease that's in my flesh,
Which I must needs call mine. Thou art a boil,
A plague-sore, or embossed carbuncle,
In my corrupted blood. But I'll not chide thee.
Let shame come when it will, I do not call it.
I do not bid the thunder-bearer shoot,
Nor tell tales of thee to high-judging Jove.
Mend when thou canst, be better at thy leisure;
I can be patient, I can stay with Regan,
I and my hundred knights.

REGAN   Not altogether so.

I looked not for you yet, nor am provided
For your fit welcome. Give ear, sir, to my sister;
For those that mingle reason with your passion

---

governed by *choose*, in apposition to *To be . . . owl. Necessity* is both 'poverty' and 'fate'.

207 *hot-blooded* passionate (supposed to be a French characteristic) and therefore likely to be violent

209 *knee* kneel before
squire-like like a body-servant

211 *sumpter* pack-horse, drudge

212 *groom* servant

219 *embossed* swollen (to a knob or boss)

220 *corrupted* (by the *disease . . . Which I must needs call mine*)

221 *come when it will.* Notice the confidence that shame is bound to be visited upon her, sooner or later.

222 *the thunder-bearer shoot* Jupiter aim his thunder-bolts (at you)

223 *high-judging* who judges from on high

229 *mingle reason with your passion* view your passionate outbursts with the cold eye of reason

Must be content to think you old, and so – 230
But she knows what she does.

LEAR   Is this well spoken?

REGAN

I dare avouch it, sir. What, fifty followers?
Is it not well? What should you need of more?
Yea, or so many, sith that both charge and danger
Speak 'gainst so great a number? How in one house
Should many people under two commands
Hold amity? 'Tis hard, almost impossible.

GONERILL

Why might not you, my lord, receive attendance
From those that she calls servants, or from mine?

REGAN

Why not, my lord? If then they chanced to slack ye, 240
We could control them. If you will come to me,
For now I spy a danger, I entreat you
To bring but five-and-twenty; to no more
Will I give place or notice.

LEAR

I gave you all –

REGAN   And in good time you gave it.

LEAR

Made you my guardians, my depositaries;
But kept a reservation to be followed
With such a number. What, must I come to you
With five-and-twenty – Regan, said you so?

---

230 *Must be content to think you old, and so* – have no choice but to see you as senile, with the result that ... Regan's contempt for his failure to accept his own senility chokes her utterance: the whole thing is so obvious that there is no point in speaking further.

234 *sith that* since. On *that*, see the note on 1.1.248.

charge expense

240 *slack ye* be negligent to you (as Oswald was commanded in 1.3.10)

241 *control them* call them to account

244 *place or notice* lodging or official recognition

246 *Made you my guardians, my depositaries* put you in charge of my estate, made you my trustees

REGAN

250   And speak't again, my lord. No more with me.

LEAR

Those wicked creatures yet do look well-favoured
When others are more wicked. Not being the worst
Stands in some rank of praise. (*To Gonerill*) I'll go
       with thee.
Thy fifty yet doth double five-and-twenty,
And thou art twice her love.

GONERILL   Hear me, my lord;
What need you five-and-twenty, ten, or five
To follow, in a house where twice so many
Have a command to tend you?

REGAN   What need one?

LEAR

O, reason not the need! Our basest beggars
260   Are in the poorest thing superfluous.
Allow not nature more than nature needs –
Man's life is cheap as beast's. Thou art a lady;
If only to go warm were gorgeous,
Why, nature needs not what thou gorgeous wear'st,
Which scarcely keeps thee warm. But for true need –

251 *well-favoured* fair of face
257 *To follow* to be your followers
259 *reason not the need!* don't try to apply
     rational calculation to *need* (as in line
     256)
259–60 *Our basest beggars | Are in the
     poorest thing superfluous* even the most
     deprived of men have among their
     few possessions something that is be-
     yond (*superfluous* to) their basic *needs*
261–2 *Allow not nature more than nature
     needs – | Man's life is cheap as beast's.*
     The usual punctuation of this in-
     volves a comma after *needs*, with the
     sense: 'If you do not allow nature
     more than is necessary, then man's
     life will have to be reckoned as cheap
     as a beast's'. This seems to me too

rational and hypothetical an argument for Lear at this point. He is (I
take it) angrily mimicking the compu-
tational arguments of his daughters:
'In your terms even the beggar's rags
are superfluous. Don't bother to believe that human nature has needs
greater than those of animal nature,
for it is as easy (or *cheap*) to buy a
human life as an animal life.'
263–5 *If only to go warm ... keeps thee
     warm* let us define 'the gorgeous' in
     dress as 'able to keep you warm'; yet
     nature does not need even that kind
     of gorgeousness in spite of the little
     warmth your gorgeous dresses do
     provide
265 *for* as for

You heavens, give me that patience, patience I need!
You see me here, you gods, a poor old man,
As full of grief as age, wretched in both;
If it be you that stirs these daughters' hearts
Against their father, fool me not so much   270
To bear it tamely; touch me with noble anger,
And let not women's weapons, water drops,
Stain my man's cheeks. No, you unnatural hags,
I will have such revenges on you both
That all the world shall – I will do such things –
What they are yet I know not; but they shall be
The terrors of the earth. You think I'll weep.
No, I'll not weep.
I have full cause of weeping;
     (*storm and tempest*)
                        but this heart
Shall break into a hundred thousand flaws   280
Or ere I'll weep. O Fool, I shall go mad!
Exeunt Lear, Gloucester, Kent, the Fool, and Gentleman
CORNWALL Let us withdraw; 'twill be a storm.
REGAN
    This house is little; the old man and's people
    Cannot be well bestowed.

---

268 *wretched in both*. This is the first time that Lear has described the wretchedness as against the dignity of age.

270 *fool me not so much* don't let me be such a fool. Realizing the wretched passivity of age, Lear prays to be given the *nobility* of manly anger, even of revenge.

276–7 *they shall be | The terrors of the earth*. Shakespeare does not hesitate to show Lear's alternative to weeping, his *noble anger*, as absurd boasting. Lear's nobility depends not on his power to terrorize the earth, but on his ability to assimilate into his passions those terrors of the earth which begin to make their sounds heard almost immediately.

280–81 *break into ... flaws | Or ere I'll weep. O Fool, I shall go mad!* The alternative to melting into tears (the woman's way) is to explode into fragments (*flaws*). And immediately Lear indicates the nature of this explosion, the fragmentation of sanity that is to ensue.

283 *and's* and his
284 *bestowed* accommodated

GONERILL

'Tis his own blame; hath put himself from rest
And must needs taste his folly.

REGAN

For his particular, I'll receive him gladly,
But not one follower.

GONERILL   So am I purposed.
Where is my lord of Gloucester?

CORNWALL

290   Followed the old man forth. He is returned.

                    Enter Gloucester

GLOUCESTER

The King is in high rage.

CORNWALL   Whither is he going?

GLOUCESTER

He calls to horse; but will I know not whither.

CORNWALL

'Tis best to give him way. He leads himself.

GONERILL

My lord, entreat him by no means to stay.

GLOUCESTER

Alack, the night comes on and the bleak winds
Do sorely ruffle. For many miles about
There's scarce a bush.

REGAN   O sir, to wilful men
The injuries that they themselves procure
Must be their schoolmasters. Shut up your doors.

300   He is attended with a desperate train,
And what they may incense him to, being apt

---

285 *from rest* from his bed
287 *For his particular* as far as he himself
     is concerned
293 *He leads himself* he is under no guid-
     ance but that of his own will
296 *ruffle* rage, brawl
298-9 *The injuries that they themselves pro-*

cure | Must be their schoolmasters they
have to learn their lesson in being
punished by the consequences of
their own wilful actions
300 *a desperate train* (the *riotous knights*
once again)
301-2 *apt | To have his ear abused.* This is

To have his ear abused, wisdom bids fear.

CORNWALL

Shut up your doors, my lord; 'tis a wild night.
My Regan counsels well. Come out o'the storm. *Exeunt*

Storm still. Enter Kent and a Gentleman by opposite   III.I
doors

KENT Who's there besides foul weather?

GENTLEMAN

One minded like the weather, most unquietly.

KENT I know you. Where's the King?

GENTLEMAN

Contending with the fretful elements:
Bids the wind blow the earth into the sea,
Or swell the curlèd waters 'bove the main,
That things might change or cease; tears his white hair,
Which the impetuous blasts with eyeless rage
Catch in their fury and make nothing of;

an example of a standard shift to which Regan and Gonerill resort: that their unkindness to their father is provoked by others, such as *riotous knights*, who mislead him ('abuse his ear'), and must therefore bear the responsibility for his suffering.

III.1 A bridge-passage between two scenes of higher dramatic tension. The narrative account of Lear's behaviour describes some of the meanings that we should attach to the *action* of III.2. Shakespeare gives here, at the very moment when evil has established its undisputed ascendancy, a glimpse of the counter-movement gathering momentum at Dover.

(stage direction) *still* (perhaps 'as before'

(at II.4.279), but more probably 'continuously')

2 *One minded like the weather* (the first statement of the equation between the inner world and the stormy weather which is so important in the next few scenes)

4 *Contending* (both (1) 'physically struggling against' and (2) 'competing in violence and anger')
the fretful elements the angry weather

5–6 *Bids the wind . . . 'bove the main.* Lear commands the earth to return to the state before creation separated water and earth.

6 *main* mainland

8 *eyeless rage* blind, indiscriminate wrath

9 *make nothing of* treat as worthless

10   Strives in his little world of man to out-storm
      The to-and-fro conflicting wind and rain.
      This night, wherein the cub-drawn bear would couch,
      The lion and the belly-pinchèd wolf
      Keep their fur dry, unbonneted he runs
      And bids what will take all.

KENT   But who is with him?

GENTLEMAN
      None but the Fool, who labours to out-jest
      His heart-struck injuries.

KENT   Sir, I do know you,
      And dare upon the warrant of my note
      Commend a dear thing to you. There is division –
20   Although as yet the face of it is covered
      With mutual cunning – 'twixt Albany and Cornwall;
      Who have – as who have not that their great stars
      Throned and set high – servants, who seem no less,
      Which are to France the spies and speculations

10 *his little world of man* (Lear as a microcosm or model of the external world) *out-storm*. The Q reading, 'out-scorne', is possible and therefore tempting (there is no F text at this point). But Elizabethan printers and transcribers frequently confused 'c' and 't', as well as 'm' and 'n'. *Out-storm* picks up and develops the important and central idea of the microcosm in a way which would be typically Shakespearian.

11 *to-and-fro conflicting* blowing now one way, now another

12 *the cub-drawn bear would couch* the bear, drained of her milk by her cubs and therefore ravenous, would lie in shelter

14 *unbonneted* not wearing a hat (a stronger idea then than now: totally abandoning self-respect as well as self-protection)

15 *bids what will take all* offers the world to any power which cares to have it. *Take all* is usually associated with the gambler's cry when he stakes everything on the last throw.

16 *out-jest* overcome by the force of his jokes

17 *heart-struck injuries* injuries that are like blows on the heart

18 *upon the warrant of my note* justified by my knowledge (of you)

19 *Commend ... to you* recommend to your care
   dear important

22 *their great stars* their fortune of being great

23 *who seem no less* who seem indeed to be real servants

24 *France* (the King of France)

24–5 *speculations* | *Intelligent of our state* observers collecting political intelligence

Intelligent of our state. What hath been seen,
Either in snuffs and packings of the Dukes,
Or the hard rein which both of them hath borne
Against the old kind King, or something deeper,
Whereof, perchance, these are but furnishings –
But true it is, from France there comes a power   30
Into this scattered kingdom, who already,
Wise in our negligence, have secret feet
In some of our best ports and are at point
To show their open banner. Now to you:
If on my credit you dare build so far
To make your speed to Dover, you shall find
Some that will thank you making just report
Of how unnatural and bemadding sorrow
The King hath cause to plain.
I am a gentleman of blood and breeding,   40
And from some knowledge and assurance offer

26–9 *Either in snuffs . . . but furnishings.*
Three things that the King of France
may have learned, and that may be
encouraging him to invade, are: (1)
the division between Albany and
Cornwall; (2) the harsh treatment of
King Lear, as if he were a horse
pulled back on a tight rein (a pun on
'reign'), given no freedom of movement; (3) *something deeper*, which explains both (1) and (2), making these
mere *furnishings* or accidentals. It
seems pointless to speculate on the
nature of this *something deeper*; it is
part of the deep shadow that belongs
to the picture.

26 *snuffs and packings* huffiness and secret
plots to secure revenge

29–30 *furnishings –* | *But true it is.* The
dash expresses a refusal by Kent to
speculate further; he returns to what
is known as a fact – the French
invasion.

30 *power* army

31 *scattered* (presumably refers to the dispersal of the royal power shown in
the first scene of the play)

32 *Wise in our negligence* taking advantage
of our neglect (*of national security*)
feet footholds

33–4 *are at point* | *To show their open
banner* are prepared to unfurl their
flag, and declare themselves

34 *Now to you* now I am going to suggest
what you can do

35 *my credit* your belief in me

35–6 *so far* | *To* so far as to

37 *making just report* for making an exact
report

38 *unnatural and bemadding sorrow* sorrow
caused (unnaturally) by his own flesh
and blood, so as to drive him mad

39 *plain* complain

This office to you.

GENTLEMAN

I will talk further with you.

KENT   No, do not.

For confirmation that I am much more
Than my out-wall, open this purse and take
What it contains. If you shall see Cordelia –
As fear not but you shall – show her this ring,
And she will tell you who that fellow is
That yet you do not know. Fie on this storm!
50   I will go seek the King.

GENTLEMAN

Give me your hand. Have you no more to say?

KENT

Few words, but to effect more than all yet:
That when we have found the King – in which your pain
That way, I'll this – he that first lights on him
Holla the other.   *Exeunt by opposite doors*

III.2   *Storm still. Enter Lear and the Fool*

LEAR

Blow, winds, and crack your cheeks! Rage! Blow!
You cataracts and hurricanoes, spout

---

42 *office* duty, function

45 *out-wall* outside appearance. Kent is
still dressed as Caius the servant.

46 *What it contains* (the *ring* mentioned
in the next line)

48 *fellow* (sometimes glossed 'companion'; but more likely to mean 'lower-
class person, servant')

52 *to effect* in their consequences

53–4 *in which your pain | That way* in
which matter I beg you to take pains
by searching in that direction

III.2 Lear and the Fool stumble across a

stage now representing 'the heath' where
man is fully exposed to the hostile physical world. Shakespeare uses the extension of this hostility in the storm to talk
about the storm of passions in Lear's
mind. Kent remains an emblem of loyal
endurance; but Lear is more and more
detached from any sense of an individual
self to which one may be usefully loyal.

1 *your cheeks*. The image is derived from
   the personifications of the winds
   shown puffing their cheeks at the
   corners of old maps.

2 *cataracts and hurricanoes* water from the

Till you have drenched our steeples, drowned the cocks!
You sulphurous and thought-executing fires,
Vaunt-curriers of oak-cleaving thunderbolts,
Singe my white head! And thou all-shaking thunder,
Strike flat the thick rotundity o'the world,
Crack Nature's moulds, all germens spill at once
That makes ingrateful man!

FOOL O nuncle, court holy-water in a dry house is better   10
than this rain-water out o'door. Good nuncle, in; ask thy
daughters' blessing. Here's a night pities neither wise
men nor fools.

LEAR

Rumble thy bellyful! Spit, fire! Spout, rain!
Nor rain, wind, thunder, fire are my daughters.
I tax not you, you elements, with unkindness;
I never gave you kingdom, called you children.
You owe me no subscription; then let fall
Your horrible pleasure. Here I stand, your slave,
A poor, infirm, weak, and despised old man.   20

heavens and from the seas. Here, as
in *Troilus and Cressida*, v.2.170 – the
only other occurrence of the word in
Shakespeare – *hurricano* is used to
mean 'waterspout'. Lear is asking for
a second deluge, or for a return to
the state before the creation of man.

3 *cocks* weathercocks (on the top of the
steeples)

4 *thought-executing* acting as fast as
thought

5 *Vaunt-curriers of oak-cleaving thunder-*
bolts. The *fires* of the lightning are
the advance guard of the thunder's
bolts or missiles, which are so powerful that they split the oak-tree.
Vaunt-curriers are those who run in
the 'van' of the main body. I have
avoided the usual modernization
'Vaunt-couriers' (F has 'Vaunt-
curriors', Q, 'vaunt-currers') because

it brings distracting associations into
the line.

7 *Strike flat the thick rotundity o'the world*
hit so hard that the roundness of the
world will be smashed flat. The suggestion of round-bellied fertility
being frustrated may also be present;
this would lead directly to the imagery of the following lines.

8 *Crack Nature's moulds* break the patterns by which all things are created
in their kinds
all germens spill destroy all the
seeds out of which all matter is
formed

10 *court holy-water* the flattery a man
must sprinkle to belong to the court

16 *I tax not you . . . with* I do not accuse
you of

18 *subscription* obedience, allegiance

But yet I call you servile ministers,
That will with two pernicious daughters join
Your high-engendered battles 'gainst a head
So old and white as this. O, ho! 'Tis foul!

FOOL   He that has a house to put's head in has a good head-
piece:

     The cod-piece that will house
       Before the head has any,
     The head and he shall louse;
30   So beggars marry many.
     The man that makes his toe
       What he his heart should make,
     Shall of a corn cry woe,
       And turn his sleep to wake.

For there was never yet fair woman but she made mouths
in a glass.

    Enter Kent

LEAR
No, I will be the pattern of all patience.
I will say nothing.

21–2 *yet I call you servile ministers,* | *That
will* I call you servile agents, in that
you are willing to
23 *high-engendered   battles* battalions
coming from the heavens
25–6 *a good head-piece* (1) a good head
covering; (2) good sense
27–9 *The cod-piece that will . . . shall louse*
the man who finds a home for his
penis before he has a roof over his
head is destined for lice-infested
beggary
27 *cod-piece* (a case for the male genitalia
('cods') attached to the breeches,
often, as Alexander Dyce says, 'osten-
tatiously indelicate' in this period.
Here (by metonymy of the covering
for the thing covered) the penis.)
30 *So beggars marry many* (obscure; does
many refer to the lice or the women?)

31–3 *The man that makes . . . cry woe* (another inversion of order; based on
the proverb 'Set not at thy heart
what should be at thy heel'. If you
lay your delight in what you should
spurn, you will be liable to suffer for
it, just as, if you valued your toe as
highly as you should value your
heart, its ailments would loom as
large.)
35–6 *For there was never yet fair woman but
she made mouths in a glass.* To 'make
mouths' carries, as well as the obvious meaning, the sense of 'treat with
contempt'. Apparently a foolish *non
sequitur*, the sentence may be a return
to the theme of the daughters:
'Women are by nature likely to despise what they see'.

KENT Who's there?

FOOL Marry, here's grace and a cod-piece – that's a wise   40
man and a fool.

KENT

Alas, sir, are you here? Things that love night
Love not such nights as these. The wrathful skies
Gallow the very wanderers of the dark
And make them keep their caves. Since I was man,
Such sheets of fire, such bursts of horrid thunder,
Such groans of roaring wind and rain I never
Remember to have heard. Man's nature cannot carry
Th'affliction nor the fear.

LEAR   Let the great gods
That keep this dreadful pudder o'er our heads   50
Find out their enemies now. Tremble, thou wretch
That hast within thee undivulgèd crimes
Unwhipped of justice. Hide thee, thou bloody hand,
Thou perjured, and thou simular of virtue
That art incestuous. Caitiff, to pieces shake,
That under covert and convenient seeming
Has practised on man's life. Close pent-up guilts,

---

40 *grace and a cod-piece* the spiritual and
the physical, the King (his grace)
and the fool. The idea of *a wise man*
is introduced to make the choice of
roles uncertain. The professional fool
often wore a particularly prominent
cod-piece; but Lear, like the cod-
piece above (line 27), had children
before he had wisdom.

44 *Gallow* (more properly 'gally')
frighten
wanderers of the dark nocturnal animals

48-9 *carry | Th'affliction nor the fear*
endure the physical affliction or the
terror it inspires

49-60 *Let the great gods ... than sinning.*
Lear's speech should be contrasted
with the preceding one by Kent.

Kent speaks of the physical effect of
the storm. Lear, careless of this, concentrates on its moral meaning.

50 *pudder* (a variant form of 'pother')
hubbub

51 *Find out their enemies now.* The *enemies*
(criminals), terrified by the storm,
will confess their crimes.

53 *bloody hand* (murderer. Compare
III.4.89.)

54 *simular of virtue* false claimant to
chastity

55 *Caitiff* base wretch

56 *under covert and convenient seeming*
behind a surface appearance that was
effective to conceal the truth and
fitting for the nefarious purposes
planned

57 *practised on* plotted against

Rive your concealing continents, and cry
These dreadful summoners grace. I am a man
More sinned against than sinning.

60   KENT   Alack, bare-headed?
Gracious my lord, hard by here is a hovel;
Some friendship will it lend you 'gainst the tempest.
Repose you there while I to this hard house –
More harder than the stones whereof 'tis raised;
Which even but now, demanding after you,
Denied me to come in – return and force
Their scanted courtesy.

LEAR   My wits begin to turn.
Come on, my boy. How dost my boy? Art cold?
I am cold myself. Where is this straw, my fellow?
70   The art of our necessities is strange
And can make vile things precious. Come, your hovel.
Poor fool and knave, I have one part in my heart
That's sorry yet for thee.

FOOL (sings)
He that has and a little tiny wit,

---

58 *Rive* break out
    continents hiding-places, bounds that
    hold you in
58–9 *cry | These dreadful summoners grace*
    cry for mercy to the elements that
    are sounding a summons to God's
    court (as the *summoners* call offenders
    before the ecclesiastical courts)
59–60 *I am a man | More sinned against
    than sinning. I* should be emphasized,
    in contrast to the *Close pent-up guilts*
    of other people.
60 *bare-headed.* See the note on III.1.14.
63, 64 *hard* unpitying
67 *scanted* limited
69 *my fellow* (Kent)
70–71 *The art of our necessities is strange |
    And can make vile things precious* neces-
    sity has a strange art (like that of the
    alchemist who turns base metal into

gold) which makes things that we
despised when we were prosperous
seem precious when we are in need
71 *vile.* Here and at III.4.138, III.7.82,
IV.2.38 and 47, and IV.6.278, Q and
F read 'vild' (or 'vilde'), common
alternative forms of the word in
Elizabethan English.
72–3 *I have one part in my heart | That's
    sorry yet for thee.* This may seem to
    imply a radical limitation on Lear's
    sympathy for a *fool and knave.* Perhaps
    we should read '. . . sorry yet – for
    thee' ('I have a part of me still cap-
    able of feeling sorrow, and that part
    is concerned with you').
74–7 *He that has . . . every day.* This is a
    stanza derived from the popular song
    that Feste sings at the end of *Twelfth
    Night.* Lear's mention of his *wits* (line

> With heigh-ho, the wind and the rain,
> Must make content with his fortunes fit,
> Though the rain it raineth every day.

LEAR True, boy. Come, bring us to this hovel.

Exeunt Lear and Kent

FOOL This is a brave night to cool a courtesan. I'll speak
a prophecy ere I go: 80

> When priests are more in word than matter,
> When brewers mar their malt with water,
> When nobles are their tailors' tutors,
> No heretics burned but wenches' suitors –
> Then shall the realm of Albion
> Come to great confusion.
>
> When every case in law is right,
> No squire in debt nor no poor knight,

---

67) reminds the Fool of the song, with its obviously appropriate refrain-line, and he uses it to enshrine the lesson that our wits must be adapted to our fortunes.

79 *a brave night to cool a courtesan.* It is not clear why the comment on the weather takes this form. Perhaps a pun is intended on 'night'/'knight'. If so, this would explain the sudden switch to medieval parody in the lines following.

81–94 *When priests . . . used with feet.* The *prophecy* begins as a parody of a passage attributed in the Elizabethan period to Chaucer:

> When faith faileth in priestès saws,
> And lordès hests are holden for
>   laws,
> And robbery is holden purchase,
> And lechery is holden solace,
> Then shall the land of Albion
> Be brought to great confusion.

Shakespeare turns this into a satiric statement of things that really do happen in his own day. The next 'stanza' involves a list of things not satirical and real, but utopian and ideal. In F this is followed by four lines of generalization (lines 85–6, 93–4), but as the passage is made up of two separate couplets saying different things, and as the first couplet completes the pseudo-Chaucerian matter of the first stanza, it seems best to follow the practice of those editors who have placed the couplets one at the end of each stanza.

81 *more in word than matter* better at talking about virtue than practising it

83 *nobles are their tailors' tutors* fashion-mad noblemen tell their tailors how to cut their elaborate clothes (as in Shakespeare's time)

84 *No heretics burned but wenches' suitors* when love is more important than religion. *Burned* may be a reference to the flames of love or to the physical effects of the pox.

86 *confusion* (four syllables: con-fu-si-on)

When slanders do not live in tongues,

90   Nor cutpurses come not to throngs,
When usurers tell their gold i'the field,
And bawds and whores do churches build –
Then comes the time, who lives to see't,
That going shall be used with feet.
This prophecy Merlin shall make; for I live before his
time.   *Exit*

III.3   *Enter Gloucester and Edmund with lights*
GLOUCESTER Alack, alack, Edmund, I like not this unnatural dealing. When I desired their leave that I might
pity him, they took from me the use of mine own house,
charged me on pain of perpetual displeasure neither to
speak of him, entreat for him, or any way sustain him.
EDMUND Most savage and unnatural!

90 *Nor . . . not.* In Elizabethan English two negatives do not necessarily make a positive.
cutpurses come not to throngs. The cutpurse, like his modern equivalent, the pickpocket, pushed in among large crowds, where he could cut and steal purses – commonly worn hanging from the belt – with greater ease.

91 *When usurers tell their gold i'the field.* Usurers were a part of city life, opposed to the traditional agricultural sources of wealth. Perhaps *gold i'the field* refers to grain, so that the phrase means 'when usurers turn farmers', or perhaps 'are willing to lend to farmers'.
tell count

92 *do churches build* (use their wealth for religious purposes)

94 *going shall be used with feet* feet will be

used for walking on ('an intentionally absurd truism', says G. L. Kittredge)

95–6 *Merlin . . . I live before his time.* According to Geoffrey of Monmouth, Lear lived during the eighth century B.C., and Arthur during the sixth century A.D.

III.3 In this prose scene, Gloucester's fate marches forward to the same betrayal as has already overtaken Lear. His pity for Lear keeps before us what is happening on the heath, but interrupts the lyrical passions of approaching madness with reminders of ordinary life.

1–2 *unnatural* (because it is their father that Gonerill and Regan have mistreated)

3 *pity* be merciful to (a use of the verb not elsewhere recorded, but cognate with 'have pity on' in the same sense)

GLOUCESTER Go to. Say you nothing. There is division
between the Dukes; and a worse matter than that. I
have received a letter this night; 'tis dangerous to be
spoken; I have locked the letter in my closet. These in-   10
juries the King now bears will be revenged home. There
is part of a power already footed. We must incline to the
King. I will look him and privily relieve him. Go you
and maintain talk with the Duke, that my charity be not
of him perceived. If he ask for me, I am ill and gone to
bed. If I die for it, as no less is threatened me, the King
my old master must be relieved. There is strange things
toward, Edmund. Pray you, be careful.   *Exit*

EDMUND

This courtesy forbid thee shall the Duke
Instantly know, and of that letter too.   20
This seems a fair deserving, and must draw me
That which my father loses – no less than all.
The younger rises when the old doth fall.   *Exit*

                Enter Lear, Kent, and the Fool   III.4
KENT

Here is the place, my lord; good my lord, enter.

7 *Go to* no more of that
8 *a worse matter.* Perhaps this refers to
the French invasion, which is what
the letter in fact describes (III.5.9–
10). But in lines 9–10 the invasion
seems a separate matter. Perhaps the
worse matter is yet another piece of
the 'shadow' in which Shakespeare
chooses to place the conflict of
Albany and Cornwall; compare *something deeper* (III.1.28, and the note on
III.1.26–9).
10 *closet* cabinet for private papers
11 *home* all the way, thoroughly
12 *footed* landed, got a foothold. The
same unusual word is used at III.7.45

of the French invasion (compare
III.1.32).
13 *look* seek
18 *toward* about to happen
19 *This courtesy forbid thee* (helping Lear,
which he was forbidden to do)
21 *a fair deserving* deserving of a fair
reward

III.4 A direct continuation of III.2.
Kent's concern for the physical well-
being of the King is frustrated finally by
the appearance of naked Tom, an apparition that releases Lear's last hold on his
own identity and submerges his sanity
in his sense of all the oppressed and

The tyranny of the open night's too rough
For nature to endure.

LEAR   Let me alone.

   Storm still

KENT
   Good my lord, enter here.

LEAR   Wilt break my heart?

KENT
   I had rather break mine own. Good my lord, enter.

LEAR
   Thou think'st 'tis much that this contentious storm
   Invades us to the skin; so 'tis to thee.
   But where the greater malady is fixed
   The lesser is scarce felt. Thou'dst shun a bear;
10 But if thy flight lay toward the roaring sea
   Thou'dst meet the bear i'the mouth. When the mind's
        free
   The body's delicate; this tempest in my mind
   Doth from my senses take all feeling else
   Save what beats there. – Filial ingratitude!
   Is it not as this mouth should tear this hand
   For lifting food to't? But I will punish home.
   No, I will weep no more! In such a night
   To shut me out! Pour on; I will endure.
   In such a night as this! O Regan, Gonerill!
20 Your old kind father, whose frank heart gave all!
   O, that way madness lies; let me shun that;

dispossessed of the world. Fool, King,
and Bedlam begin to forge a new dialect,
a rapt recitation of inner visions, compared to which the common-sense solici-
tudes of Kent and Gloucester seem external and superficial.

3 *nature* human nature
11-12 *When the mind's free | The body's
   delicate* when the mind is free of
   worry, it can afford to attend to the

body's petty complaints of
discomfort

15 *as this mouth should tear this hand* as if
   one part should harm another part
   of the same body (all of whose
   functions are for the united good
   of the whole). Lear sees himself
   and his daughters as part of such a
   body.

20 *frank heart* generous love

No more of that!

KENT   Good my lord, enter here.

LEAR

Prithee go in thyself; seek thine own ease.
This tempest will not give me leave to ponder
On things would hurt me more; but I'll go in.
(*To the Fool*) In, boy, go first. – You houseless
            poverty –
Nay, get thee in. I'll pray and then I'll sleep.

                              Exit the Fool

Poor naked wretches, wheresoe'er you are,
That bide the pelting of this pitiless storm,
How shall your houseless heads and unfed sides,   30
Your looped and windowed raggedness, defend you
From seasons such as these? O, I have ta'en
Too little care of this! Take physic, pomp;
Expose thyself to feel what wretches feel,
That thou mayst shake the superflux to them
And show the heavens more just.

EDGAR (*within*)

Fathom and half, fathom and half! Poor Tom!

            Enter the Fool from the hovel

 FOOL Come not in here, nuncle; here's a spirit. Help me,
help me!

25 *things would hurt me more* (the internal *tempest* of his thoughts of filial ingratitude)

26 *houseless poverty* (*Poor naked wretches* who have no covering from the storm)

27 *I'll pray.* The 'prayer' that Lear says before he goes to sleep is a highly unorthodox one, not for his own safety during the night, but for that of *wretches*; and not to the gods, but to the objects of their power.

31 *Your looped and windowed raggedness* your ragged clothes, full of 'windows' (which were normally un-glazed in Shakespeare's time) and loop-holes

32 *seasons* times, weather conditions

33 *Take physic, pomp* let the pompous man of authority learn how to be (morally) healthy

35 *shake the superflux* shake off superfluous possessions

37 *Fathom and half.* Edgar takes up the cry of the sailor singing out the depth of water his ship is passing through. The hovel is presumably half-submerged by the rainstorm. *Poor Tom.* See the note on II.3.14.

40   KENT Give me thy hand. Who's there?

FOOL A spirit, a spirit! He says his name's Poor Tom.

KENT What art thou that dost grumble there i'the straw?
Come forth.

Enter Edgar disguised as Poor Tom

EDGAR Away! The foul fiend follows me.
    Through the sharp hawthorn blow the cold winds.
    Humh! Go to thy bed and warm thee.

LEAR Didst thou give all to thy daughters? And art thou
come to this?

EDGAR Who gives anything to Poor Tom? whom the foul
50   fiend hath led through fire and through flame, through
ford and whirlpool, o'er bog and quagmire, that hath
laid knives under his pillow and halters in his pew, set
ratsbane by his porridge, made him proud of heart, to
ride on a bay trotting horse over four-inched bridges to

---

44 *Away!* keep away from me
   The foul fiend follows me. The mad
   were often supposed to be possessed
   or followed by devils.

45 *Through the sharp hawthorn blow the cold
   winds.* This has the air of a quotation
   from a song. Bishop Percy (1729–
   1811) has, in his *Reliques of Ancient
   English Poetry* (1765), a ballad ('The
   Friar of Orders Grey') with the line
   'See through the hawthorn blows the
   cold wind, and drizzly rain doth fall';
   but this ballad appears to be Percy's
   invention, patched together from
   scraps of Shakespeare. The Q reading, 'cold wind', is supported by the
   same song-fragment below (line 95).

46 *Humh!* Edgar shivers with cold.
   Go to thy bed and warm thee. The
   beggar Christopher Sly says something very similar in *The Taming of
   the Shrew*, Induction 1.7–8 – so it may
   well be another catch-phrase, possibly in reply to Jeronimo's famous

'What outcries pluck me from my
naked bed' (*The Spanish Tragedy*,
II.5.1).

47 *Didst thou give all to thy daughters?* (the
   first words that can be used to prove
   that Lear has finally lost his hold on
   external reality, is 'mad'. The appearance of 'Poor Tom' is undoubtedly
   intended to be the catalyst that releases the inner forces that have been
   beating in Lear's mind. Immediately after the *Poor naked wretches*
   speech he finds a figure with whom
   he can wholly identify himself and
   whose role (of madman) he can take
   over.)

52, 53 *knives ... halters ... ratsbane.*
   These are the traditional gifts (the
   poison is usually less specific) given
   by the Devil to the man who is in a
   state of despair, in the hope that he
   may kill himself and bring his soul
   into a state of perpetual damnation.

53 *porridge* soup

course his own shadow for a traitor. Bless thy five wits!
Tom's a-cold. O do, de, do, de, do, de. Bless thee from
whirlwinds, star-blasting, and taking! Do Poor Tom
some charity, whom the foul fiend vexes. There could I
have him now, and there, and there again, and there.
     Storm still

LEAR

What, has his daughters brought him to this pass?   60
Couldst thou save nothing? Wouldst thou give 'em all?

FOOL Nay, he reserved a blanket; else we had been all
shamed.

LEAR

Now all the plagues that in the pendulous air
Hang fated o'er men's faults light on thy daughters!

KENT He hath no daughters, sir.

LEAR

Death, traitor! Nothing could have subdued nature
To such a lowness but his unkind daughters.
Is it the fashion that discarded fathers
Should have thus little mercy on their flesh?   70

---

55 *course* hunt
  thy five wits. These were defined as
  'common wit, imagination, fantasy,
  estimation, memory'; or perhaps this
  is another way of saying 'your five
  senses' (taste, smell, sight, hearing,
  touch).
56 *O do, de, do, de, do, de.* This set of
  sounds is probably meant to represent Tom's teeth chattering with cold.
57 *star-blasting* being struck down by disease (disease was often supposed to
  be the result of the 'influence' of the
  stars)
  taking being 'taken' with an infection
58–9 *There could I have him now.* Tom
  searches for lice and devils at the
  same time.
64–5 *plagues that in the pendulous air
  Hang fated.* Like *star-blasting* (line 57),

this alludes to the idea that disease is
poured down by planetary influence
as a punishment on the wicked.
Stored up in the stars, it hangs (*pendulous*) like fate over the future of
wrong-doers.
65 *light* alight
67, 68 *subdued . . . unkind.* The accent in
  both cases falls on the first syllable.
67 *subdued nature* brought down the
  human state
70 *little mercy on their flesh* (referring to
  Edgar's nakedness, and to the thorns
  and sprigs (or splinters) stuck in his
  arms. When Edwin Booth was playing Lear he 'drew a thorn or wooden
  spike from Edgar's arm and thrust it
  into his own': A. C. Sprague, *Shakespeare and the Actors* (1944), page
  291.)

Judicious punishment! 'Twas this flesh begot
Those pelican daughters.

EDGAR

Pillicock sat on Pillicock Hill.
Alow, alow, loo, loo!

FOOL This cold night will turn us all to fools and madmen.

EDGAR Take heed o'the foul fiend, obey thy parents, keep
thy word's justice, swear not, commit not with man's
sworn spouse, set not thy sweet heart on proud array.
80   Tom's a-cold.

LEAR What hast thou been?

EDGAR A servingman, proud in heart and mind, that
curled my hair, wore gloves in my cap, served the lust of
my mistress' heart and did the act of darkness with her,
swore as many oaths as I spake words and broke them in
the sweet face of heaven; one that slept in the contriving
of lust and waked to do it. Wine loved I deeply, dice
dearly, and in woman out-paramoured the Turk – false

71 *Judicious* appropriate, fitting
72 *pelican daughters.* The pelican's young
(according to the medieval bestiaries)
smite their father and kill him. The
mother pelican first hits back, and
then revives the dead children by
shedding her own blood over them
– thus becoming the symbol of
Christ-like loving self-sacrifice. Lear
sees Gonerill and Regan as assaulting
him and also demanding that he sacrifice himself for them.
73 *Pillicock* (suggested by *pelican.* It
seems both to have meant a darling,
a beloved, and to have been a playful
word for penis (picking up the idea
from *flesh begot* in line 71).)
74 *Alow, alow, loo, loo!* Some sort of cry
of sporting encouragement seems to
be intended.
75 *This cold night will turn us all to fools.*
Note that as Edgar takes over the

role of the broken, rhapsodic, song-
singing madman, the Fool is reduced to the role of the balanced
observer.
77–9 *Take heed . . . proud array* (a crazy
parody of the Ten Commandments)
78–9 *commit not with man's sworn spouse*
do not commit adultery with one
who is sworn wife to another
79 *proud array* fine clothes. The idea of
clothes leads Tom naturally to his
next remark about the cold.
82 *servingman.* It is not clear whether this
refers to a servant in the ordinary
sense (with a *mistress* whose first role
is to command the household) or to
a 'servant' (that is, lover) with a
'mistress' (that is, a beloved).
83 *wore gloves in my cap.* Gallants wore
their mistress's gloves in their cap.
88 *the Turk* (the Grand Turk, the Sultan,
famous for his seraglio)

of heart, light of ear, bloody of hand; hog in sloth, fox in
stealth, wolf in greediness, dog in madness, lion in prey. 90
Let not the creaking of shoes nor the rustling of silks
betray thy poor heart to woman. Keep thy foot out of
brothels, thy hand out of plackets, thy pen from lenders'
books, and defy the foul fiend.
        Still through the hawthorn blows the cold wind,
        Says suum, mun, nonny.
Dolphin, my boy, boy, sesey! Let him trot by.
        Storm still
LEAR Thou wert better in a grave than to answer with thy
uncovered body this extremity of the skies. Is man no
more than this? Consider him well. Thou owest the 100
worm no silk, the beast no hide, the sheep no wool, the

89 *light of ear* 'credulous of evil' (Dr
Johnson)
89–90 *hog in sloth ... lion in prey*. The
seven deadly sins were often represented in art and literature by animals, illustrating the predominant
passion or the particular 'beast in
man' that was intended.
90 *stealth* (both 'stealing' and 'stealthi-
ness')
 dog in madness. The dog represents
madness because the transmission of
rabies to man makes the mad dog
particularly notable.
 prey the act of preying, pillage,
violence
93 *plackets* slits in the front of petticoats
95 *Still ... cold wind* (the same song-
fragment as in line 45)
96 *Says suum, mun, nonny*. Some kind of
refrain seems to be intended, and the
Q version, 'hay no on ny', is an
approximation to the traditional 'hey,
nonny, nonny'. The F reading, given
here, is likely to be nearer to the
original, because more difficult. Per-

haps it represents an imitation of the
cold wind whistling through the
hawthorn.
97 *Dolphin, my boy, boy, sesey! Let
him trot by*. Perhaps these are more
song-fragments – but, if so, the songs
have perished. *Dolphin* may be a
horse, *sesey* may be the French '*cessez*'
– but all this is merest conjecture.
98 *answer* encounter
99 *body ... skies* (the microcosm/macro-
cosm analogy once again)
99–100 *Is man no more than this? Consider
him well*. Shakespeare may have been
remembering Hebrews 2.6, 'What is
man, that thou shouldst be mindful
of him? Or the son of man, that thou
wouldst consider him?', or Florio's
Montaigne: '... miserable man;
whom if you consider well, what is
he?' ('An Apology of Raymond
Sebond', 'Tudor Translations'
(1893), Volume II, page 172).
100–101 *Thou owest ... no* you are not
indebted to ... for
101 *beast* (specifically 'cattle')

cat no perfume. Ha! Here's three on's are sophisticated.
Thou art the thing itself! Unaccommodated man is no
more but such a poor, bare, forked animal as thou art.
Off, off, you lendings! Come, unbutton here.

He tears off his clothes

FOOL Prithee, nuncle, be contented; 'tis a naughty night
to swim in. Now a little fire in a wild field were like an
old lecher's heart – a small spark, all the rest on's body
cold. Look, here comes a walking fire.

Enter Gloucester with a torch

110 EDGAR This is the foul fiend Flibberdigibbet. He begins
at curfew and walks till the first cock. He gives the web
and the pin, squenies the eye and makes the harelip,
mildews the white wheat, and hurts the poor creature of
earth.

102 *cat* civet cat (the source of some
perfumes)
sophisticated adulterated by the addition of clothes etc. away from the pure
(naked) state of man (*the thing itself*)
103 *Unaccommodated* unfurnished (with
clothes etc.), unsupported by a well-
fitting environment
104 *forked* having two legs
105 *lendings* (the clothes *lent* to man by
the *beast*, the *worm*, the *sheep*, etc.
Lear aims, by tearing off his clothes,
to identify himself with *the thing itself*,
with Poor Tom.)
unbutton. As a king he commands his
valet de chambre to undress him; as a
demented moralist he tears off his
clothes with his own hands.
(stage direction) *He tears off his clothes*.
Capell added '*Kent and the Fool strive
to hinder him*'.
106 *naughty* bad. The word was quite
without the childish connotations it
has since acquired.
107 *swim* (suggested both by the rain and
by Lear's stripping off his clothes)

a wild field a waste heath, a
wilderness
107–8 *an old lecher's heart*. This undoubtedly refers to Gloucester with his
torch, the lechery which begot
Edmund, and the evidence of *heart*
shown by his succouring of the
King. To secure a naturalistic explanation, we must suppose that the
Fool spies Gloucester after *swim in*,
though it is not clear how an actor
could convey this.
110 *Flibberdigibbet* (the name of one of
the devils who danced with a supposed demoniac in Harsnet's *Declaration*. See IV.1.60.)
111 *curfew . . . till the first cock* (said to be
from 9 p.m. till midnight; but may
have the more general sense of 'from
dusk till dawn' – when evil spirits
were most free)
111–12 *the web and the pin* cataract of the
eye
112 *squenies* causes to squint
113 *white* almost ripe

S'Withold footed thrice the 'old;
He met the nightmare and her nine-fold,
Bid her alight and her troth plight –
And aroint thee, witch, aroint thee!

KENT How fares your grace?

LEAR What's he?   120

KENT (to Gloucester) Who's there? What is't you seek?

GLOUCESTER What are you there? Your names?

EDGAR Poor Tom, that eats the swimming frog, the toad,
the todpole, the wall-newt and the water; that in the
fury of his heart, when the foul fiend rages, eats cow-
dung for sallets, swallows the old rat and the ditch-dog,
drinks the green mantle of the standing pool; who is
whipped from tithing to tithing and stock-punished and
imprisoned; who hath had three suits to his back, six
shirts to his body,   130
Horse to ride and weapon to wear –
But mice and rats and such small deer

115–18 *S'Withold ... aroint thee.* F's
'Swithold' presumably refers to Saint
Withold, elsewhere in Elizabethan
literature a defender against harms.
Here he is a defender against the
nightmare – the demon that descends
on people when they are asleep. The
saint paces the wold (*'old*) three times
(the magic number) and when he
meets the nightmare and her nine
(three times three) offspring he commands her to *alight* (get off the
sleeper's chest) and *plight her troth*
(swear – that she will do no harm).
And so he (Edgar) can bid all witches
aroint (begone!).

115 *'old* wold (rolling upland)

124 *todpole* (an alternative form of
'tadpole')
the wall-newt and the water the lizard
and the water-newt

124–5 *in the fury of his heart, when the foul*

fiend rages (when the fit of madness is
on him)

126 *sallets* salads, tasty morsels
the ditch-dog the dead dog thrown into
a ditch

127 *the green mantle of the standing pool* the
scum of the stagnant pond

128 *whipped from tithing to tithing.* Elizabethan law required vagabonds to be
whipped publicly and sent into another parish (*tithing*), where presumably the same thing happened again.
stock-punished set in the stocks

129–30 *three suits ... six shirts* (the allowance of a servingman, such as Edgar
alleges he has been (line 82))

132–3 *But mice ... seven long year.* This is
a version of a couplet from the popular medieval romance, *Bevis of
Hampton*. In the old-fashioned language of *Bevis, deer* means 'animals'.

Have been Tom's food for seven long year.
Beware my follower! Peace, Smulkin! Peace, thou fiend!

GLOUCESTER   What, hath your grace no better company?

EDGAR   The prince of darkness is a gentleman; Modo he's
called and Mahu.

GLOUCESTER
Our flesh and blood, my lord, is grown so vile
That it doth hate what gets it.

140   EDGAR   Poor Tom's a-cold.

GLOUCESTER
Go in with me. My duty cannot suffer
T'obey in all your daughters' hard commands;
Though their injunction be to bar my doors
And let this tyrannous night take hold upon you,
Yet have I ventured to come seek you out
And bring you where both fire and food is ready.

LEAR
First let me talk with this philosopher.
(*To Edgar*) What is the cause of thunder?

KENT   Good my lord,
Take his offer, go into the house.

---

134 *Beware my follower! Peace, Smulkin!*
Edgar warns them of the dangers of
his familiar spirit or devil, called
Smulkin after one of the devils in
Harsnet's *Declaration*. The name must
have been suggested by *mice*, since in
Harsnet Smulkin went out of the
possessed man's right ear 'in the
form of a mouse'.

136–7 *The prince of darkness is a gentleman;
Modo he's called and Mahu.* To Gloucester's complaint about the company,
Edgar replies that the devils he has
about him are noblemen. In Harsnet,
Modo and Mahu are grand command-
ers of legions of devils.

138–9 *Our flesh and blood ... doth hate*

what gets it our children hate their
parents

138 *vile*. See the note on III.2.71.

139 *gets* begets

140 *Poor Tom's a-cold.* Edgar fends off
the relevance of Gloucester's complaint about his son by retreating
into the role of the Bedlam beggar.

147 *philosopher* (expert in 'natural philosophy' or science. Perhaps it is
Edgar's 'philosophical approach'
(that is, acceptance of his hardships)
that gives Lear the idea that he is a
philosopher.)

148 *the cause of thunder* (one of the 'secrets
of nature' which a 'philosopher' or
professional wise man would be ex-

LEAR

    I'll talk a word with this same learnèd Theban.   150

    (*To Edgar*) What is your study?

EDGAR How to prevent the fiend and to kill vermin.

LEAR Let me ask you one word in private.

       Lear and Edgar talk apart

KENT

    Importune him once more to go, my lord.

    His wits begin t'unsettle.

GLOUCESTER   Canst thou blame him? –

      (*storm still*)

    His daughters seek his death. Ah, that good Kent,

    He said it would be thus, poor banished man!

    Thou sayest the King grows mad; I'll tell thee, friend,

    I am almost mad myself. I had a son,

    Now outlawed from my blood; he sought my life   160

    But lately, very late. I loved him, friend,

    No father his son dearer. True to tell thee,

    The grief hath crazed my wits. What a night's this! –

    I do beseech your grace –

LEAR   O, cry you mercy, sir.

    (*To Edgar*) Noble philosopher, your company.

EDGAR Tom's a-cold.

GLOUCESTER In, fellow, there, into th'hovel; keep thee warm.

---

pected to explain. It is apposite both to the immediate weather and to the larger questions of God's justice.)

150 *learnèd Theban* Greek sage

151 *What is your study?* in which branch of learning do you specialize? Edgar picks up *study* in the other sense: 'zealous endeavour'.

152 *prevent* forestall

154 *Importune* (accented on the second syllable)

160 *outlawed from my blood* (1) legally made an outlaw (as in II.1.59–62 and 109–10); (2) disowned as my son and heir (II.1.82–4)

164 *I do beseech your grace –*. Some action is clearly intended. The New Cambridge edition suggests: 'Gloucester takes his arm, trying to separate him from his "philosopher"; Lear refuses'.

cry you mercy I beg your pardon (I didn't notice you)

LEAR
Come, let's in all.
KENT   This way, my lord.
LEAR   With him!
170   I will keep still with my philosopher.
KENT Good my lord, soothe him: let him take the fellow.
GLOUCESTER Take him you on.
KENT Sirrah, come on. Go along with us.
LEAR Come, good Athenian.
GLOUCESTER No words, no words! Hush!
EDGAR
            Child Roland to the dark tower came;
            His word was still 'Fie, foh, and fum,
            I smell the blood of a British man.'   *Exeunt*

III.5   *Enter Cornwall and Edmund*
CORNWALL I will have my revenge ere I depart his house.
EDMUND How, my lord, I may be censured that nature

169 *With him!* Both words are heavily
     emphasized. Lear is impatient of the
     efforts to divert him from the confer-
     ence with his 'philosopher'.
170 *still* continuously
171 *soothe him* humour him
172 *Take him you on.* Kent should take
     ahead the 'philosopher' Edgar so that
     Lear can be persuaded to follow to
     the farmhouse.
175 *No words . . . Hush!* (presumably an
     indication (to the audience) that they
     are approaching the castle)
176 *Child Roland to the dark tower came*
     (perhaps another line from a ro-
     mance. *Child* is '*Infante*' ('Prince');
     Roland or Orlando is the most
     famous of Charlemagne's paladins.
     The *dark tower* is certainly Glouces-
     ter's castle in the immediate refer-
     ence, sinister enough in the *King Lear*

story, whatever it may have been in
the lost Roland story referred to here.)
177–8 '*Fie, foh, and fum, | I smell the blood
     of a British man*'. Here the Roland
     fragment seems to modulate into
     'Jack, the Giant-killer'. It may be no
     accident that Edgar, returning to his
     home, remembers the story of an-
     other son's triumphant return. The
     tower may have suggested the
     beanstalk.

III.5 The final fruits of Edmund's
'nature' are shown in the planned destruction of his natural father, his adoption
into the love of Cornwall, and his acquisi-
tion of the 'legitimate' title of Earl of
Gloucester.
2 *censured* judged
2, 3 *nature . . . loyalty* family affection . . .
     loyalty to the state

thus gives way to loyalty, something fears me to think of.

CORNWALL I now perceive it was not altogether your brother's evil disposition made him seek his death; but a provoking merit set a-work by a reprovable badness in himself.

EDMUND How malicious is my fortune that I must repent to be just! This is the letter he spoke of, which approves him an intelligent party to the advantages of France. O heavens! that this treason were not, or not I the detector.

CORNWALL Go with me to the Duchess.

EDMUND If the matter of this paper be certain, you have mighty business in hand.

CORNWALL True or false, it hath made thee Earl of Gloucester. Seek out where thy father is, that he may be ready for our apprehension.

EDMUND (aside) If I find him comforting the King it will stuff his suspicion more fully. (Aloud) I will persever in my course of loyalty, though the conflict be sore between that and my blood.

CORNWALL I will lay trust upon thee, and thou shalt find a dearer father in my love.   Exeunt

3 *something fears me* somewhat concerns me
6–7 *a provoking merit set a-work by a reprovable badness in himself.* This is puzzling, because it is not clear whether the reference is to Edgar or Gloucester. Most probably the meaning is: 'The fact that death was only Gloucester's due reward (*merit*) must also have provoked Edgar to act; but a man must be bad before he will allow himself to be provoked to parricide for such a reason'.
9 *to be* that I am
  just loyal to the state
9–10 *approves him an intelligent party to the*

advantages of France proves that he is a spy, seeking to give advantage to the French side
17–18 *that he may be ready for our apprehension* so that we may arrest him without any trouble
19 *comforting* giving aid to
20 *stuff his suspicion more fully* augment Cornwall's suspicion of Gloucester as a spy
  persever (equivalent to the modern 'persevere', but with the accent on the second syllable)
22 *my blood* my natural loyalty to my father

III.6   *Enter Kent and Gloucester*

GLOUCESTER Here is better than the open air. Take it thankfully; I will piece out the comfort with what addition I can. I will not be long from you.

KENT All the power of his wits have given way to his impatience. The gods reward your kindness!

Exit Gloucester

Enter Lear, Edgar, and the Fool

EDGAR Fraterretto calls me and tells me Nero is an angler in the lake of darkness. Pray, innocent, and beware the foul fiend.

FOOL Prithee, nuncle, tell me whether a madman be a
10   gentleman or a yeoman.

LEAR A king, a king!

FOOL No! He's a yeoman that has a gentleman to his son; for he's a mad yeoman that sees his son a gentleman before him.

LEAR

To have a thousand with red burning spits
Come hissing in upon 'em!

EDGAR The foul fiend bites my back.

FOOL He's mad that trusts in the tameness of a wolf, a horse's health, a boy's love, or a whore's oath.

III.6 The scene takes us inside the farm-house towards which Gloucester was conducting his companions at the end of III.4. The antiphonally placed voices of the three madmen – lunatic King, court fool, feigned Bedlam – weave the obsessive themes of betrayal, demoniac possession, and injustice into the most complex lyric structure in modern drama.

2 *piece out* augment

6 *Fraterretto* (one of the demonic names in Harsnet)

7 *Pray, innocent* (often thought to be addressed to the Fool (the *innocent*))

10 *yeoman* (a man who owns property but is not a gentleman, that is, does not have a coat-of-arms)

15–16 *To have a thousand ... upon 'em.* While Edgar and the Fool follow their separate trains of thought, Lear's mind is fixed on Gonerill and Regan; here he imagines them suffering the torments of Hell.

17 *bites* (the foul fiend in the form of a louse or flea; compare III.4.152)

18 *the tameness of a wolf.* The implication is that the wolf can never be tamed.

18–19 *a horse's health.* 'A horse is above all other animals subject to diseases' (Dr Johnson).

LEAR

It shall be done; I will arraign them straight.   20
(*To Edgar*)
Come, sit thou here, most learnèd justicer.
(*To the Fool*)
Thou sapient sir, sit here. No, you she-foxes –

EDGAR Look where he stands and glares! Want'st thou
eyes at trial, madam?
(*sings*) Come o'er the burn, Bessy, to me.

FOOL (*sings*) Her boat hath a leak
                And she must not speak
                Why she dares not come over to thee.

EDGAR The foul fiend haunts Poor Tom in the voice of a
nightingale. Hoppedance cries in Tom's belly for two   30
white herring. Croak not, black angel! I have no food for
thee.

KENT

How do you, sir? Stand you not so amazed.
Will you lie down and rest upon the cushings?

20 *arraign them*. Lear abandons the idea of the torments of Hell, and turns to the image of a trial for Gonerill and Regan.

21 *justicer* judge

23 *he* (possibly Lear, but probably 'the Fiend', with whom Edgar's speeches are continuously concerned)

23–4 *Want'st thou eyes at trial, madam?* The *madam at trial* must be Gonerill or Regan; but it is not clear what *Want'st thou eyes* means. It must connect with the glaring of the fiend in the previous sentence. Perhaps it means 'Can't you see who's looking at you?'

25–6 *Come o'er the burn ... hath a leak*. Edgar sings a snatch of popular song, which the Fool completes, providing a reason (doubtless obscene)

why Bessy should avoid having to do with her lover. See page 589.

29–30 *in the voice of a nightingale* (no doubt suggested by the Fool's singing)

30 *Hoppedance* (derived from Harsnet's 'Hoberdidance')

31 *white herring* unsmoked herring
Croak. The Elizabethans spoke of 'croaking guts' where we speak of 'rumbling tummies'. The noise is supposed to indicate hunger, which explains the next sentence. In Harsnet some 'croaking' was said to be the voice of a demon.
black angel. Black being the devil's colour, a *black angel* would be a demon.

33 *amazed* (stronger than the modern sense) in a maze, dumbfounded

34 *cushings* (an earlier form of 'cushions')

LEAR
I'll see their trial first; bring in their evidence.
(*To Edgar*)
Thou robed man of justice, take thy place.
(*To the Fool*)
And thou, his yokefellow of equity,
Bench by his side. (*To Kent*) You are o'the commission;
Sit you too.

40   EDGAR Let us deal justly.
Sleepest or wakest thou, jolly shepherd?
Thy sheep be in the corn,
And for one blast of thy minikin mouth
Thy sheep shall take no harm.
Pur, the cat is grey.

LEAR Arraign her first. 'Tis Gonerill! I here take my oath
before this honourable assembly she kicked the poor
King her father.

FOOL Come hither, mistress. Is your name Gonerill?

50   LEAR She cannot deny it.

FOOL Cry you mercy, I took you for a joint-stool.

35 *their evidence* the witnesses against them

36 *robed*. This no doubt refers to Tom's *Blanket* (II.3.10).
thy place (on the judges' bench)

37 *yokefellow* fellow
yokefellow of equity. The Courts of Justice and of Equity were the two main branches of the English legal system. In this trial, exceptionally, the two are combined (as at the trial of Mary, Queen of Scots).

38 *Bench by his side* join him on the judges' bench
commission (a body to whom power (in this case, judicial power) is delegated from the crown, specifically 'the commission of the peace', the body of justices of the peace)

41–4 *Sleepest or wakest ... no harm.* Dr

Johnson remarked: 'This seems to be a stanza of some pastoral song. A shepherd is desired to pipe, and the request is enforced by a promise that though his sheep be in the corn, i.e. committing trespass by his negligence, yet a single tune upon his pipe shall secure them from the pound'. The nursery rhyme of 'Little Boy Blue' is an obvious analogy.

43 *for one blast* as a result of even a single blast
minikin (either (1) shrill or (2) pretty, neat, fine)

45 *Pur, the cat is grey*. The cat may be another demon or familiar, as often in witchcraft. *Pur* may be the noise it makes, or its name ('Purre' is the name of a devil in Harsnet).

51 *I took you for a joint-stool* (a proverbial

LEAR

And here's another whose warped looks proclaim
What store her heart is made on. Stop her there!
Arms, arms, sword, fire! Corruption in the place!
False justicer, why hast thou let her 'scape?

EDGAR Bless thy five wits!

KENT

O pity! Sir, where is the patience now
That you so oft have boasted to retain?

EDGAR (*aside*)

My tears begin to take his part so much
They mar my counterfeiting.   60

LEAR

The little dogs and all –
Trey, Blanch, and Sweetheart – see, they bark at me.

EDGAR Tom will throw his head at them. Avaunt, you
curs!

Be thy mouth or black or white,
Tooth that poisons if it bite,
Mastiff, greyhound, mongrel grim,
Hound or spaniel, brach or lym,

insulting 'excuse' for not noticing
someone. A *joint-stool* is a stool made
by jointing together pieces of wood.)
52 *another* (Regan)
   warped looks twisted, distorted
   features
53 *What store her heart is made on* what
   kind of material her heart is made of.
   Compare lines 75–6.
54 *Arms, arms, sword, fire!* It is not clear
   what *fire* is doing in this list, which
   is concerned with means of stopping
   Regan's escape. If 'fire' could mean
   'fire your muskets', this would be
   acceptable; but there is no evidence
   that the word could be so used in
   1605.
   Corruption in the place! Even the court

of law is corrupt; the judge has con-
nived at the prisoner's escape.
56 *Bless thy five wits!* Edgar lapses into
   his jargon (compare III.4.55), unable,
   as his next utterance shows, to sustain his part in the charade.
61–2 *The little dogs and all . . . they bark at
   me* I am now so despicable that even
   the little lap-dogs (perhaps bitches,
   by their names) know they can bark
   at me
65 *or . . . or* either . . . or
66 *Tooth that poisons.* The only sense in
   which a dog's tooth *poisons* is
   through rabies.
68 *brach or lym* bitch-hound or blood-
   hound

> Or bobtail tike, or trundle-tail,
> 70   Tom will make him weep and wail;
> For, with throwing thus my head,
> Dogs leapt the hatch and all are fled.

Do, de, de, de. Sese! Come, march to wakes and fairs and market-towns. Poor Tom, thy horn is dry.

LEAR   Then let them anatomize Regan, see what breeds about her heart. Is there any cause in nature that makes these hard hearts? You, sir, I entertain for one of my hundred. Only I do not like the fashion of your garments. You will say they are Persian; but let them be changed.

KENT

80   Now, good my lord, lie here and rest awhile.

LEAR   Make no noise, make no noise; draw the curtains. So, so. We'll go to supper i'the morning.

---

69 *bobtail tike* cur with its tail 'bobbed' (cut short)
trundle-tail dog with a long drooping tail trundling (trailing) behind it

72 *leapt the hatch* jumped over the closed lower half of a divided door

73 *Do, de, de, de.* At III.4.56 a similar collection of syllables was supposed to represent Tom's teeth chattering.
Sese. Most editors change to 'Sessa', but one unexplained sound seems as good as another. Compare III.4.97.

73–4 *Come, march ... market-towns.* Tom addresses himself, to take his attention away from the painful scene before him. He resolves to set out for the places of resort most likely to yield good begging.

74 *thy horn is dry* (a formula used by the Bedlamites in begging for drink. It appears that they wore an ox-horn round their necks into which they poured the drink that was given them. In the present context it must also mean 'I have no more words for this situation'; in this scene Edgar says no more in his Tom persona.)

75 *anatomize* dissect

75–6 *what breeds about her heart* (as if some hard deposit was forming on it. Lear's mind may have moved in this direction because of Edgar's *dry* (line 74) and his reference to *horn*, which is formed by the process to which Lear alludes in reference to Regan's heart.)

76–7 *Is there any cause in nature that makes these hard hearts? Hard hearts* were well-known theological phenomena, caused by falling from grace. Despairing of supernatural causes, Lear asks for a natural, anatomical, reason.

77 *entertain* take into my service

78–9 *fashion of your garments ... Persian.* Tom's blanket now reminds Lear of the traditionally pompous garments of the Persians.

81–2 *draw the curtains. So, so.* Lear imagines himself on a luxurious bed, with his servant drawing the bed-curtains.

82 *We'll go to supper i'the morning.* Lear presumably remembers he has not had his supper. 'Never mind,' he

FOOL And I'll go to bed at noon.

> *Enter Gloucester*

GLOUCESTER

Come hither, friend. Where is the King my master?

KENT

Here, sir; but trouble him not; his wits are gone.

GLOUCESTER

Good friend, I prithee take him in thy arms;

I have o'erheard a plot of death upon him.

There is a litter ready; lay him in't

And drive toward Dover, friend, where thou shalt meet

Both welcome and protection. Take up thy master;   90

If thou shouldst dally half an hour, his life,

With thine and all that offer to defend him,

Stand in assurèd loss. Take up, take up,

And follow me, that will to some provision

Give thee quick conduct.

KENT   Oppressèd nature sleeps.

This rest might yet have balmed thy broken sinews

Which, if convenience will not allow,

Stand in hard cure. *(To the Fool)* Come, help to bear

thy master.

Thou must not stay behind.

GLOUCESTER   Come, come, away!

> *Exeunt Kent, Gloucester, and the Fool,*
> *bearing off the King*

---

says to himself, 'we can eat it at
breakfast time.'

83 *I'll go to bed at noon.* These are the last
words that the Fool speaks in the
play and they have been thought
(rather sentimentally) to refer to his
going to his grave in the prime of
life. But they are more likely to draw
on the proverbial sense of *going to bed
at noon*: that is, 'playing the fool'.

89 *drive.* The *litter* is presumably horse-
drawn.

94–5 *to some provision | Give thee . . . con-
duct* take you where you can get
supplies

96 *balmed thy broken sinews* healed your
shattered nerves. Shakespeare gives
to Lear the physical condition that
followed torture on the rack; but the
rack he has been on is a mental one.

98 *Stand in hard cure* will be hard to cure

EDGAR

100   When we our betters see bearing our woes,
        We scarcely think our miseries our foes.
        Who alone suffers, suffers most i'the mind,
        Leaving free things and happy shows behind;
        But then the mind much sufferance doth o'erskip
        When grief hath mates, and bearing fellowship.
        How light and portable my pain seems now,
        When that which makes me bend makes the King bow –
        He childed as I fathered. Tom, away!
        Mark the high noises, and thyself bewray
110   When false opinion, whose wrong thoughts defile thee,
        In thy just proof repeals and reconciles thee.
        What will hap more tonight, safe 'scape the King!
        Lurk, lurk!   *Exit*

100–101 *When we our betters see bearing our woes,* | *We scarcely think our miseries our foes* it is so disturbing to see our superiors oppressed by the same miseries as beset us that we almost cease to notice our own pains; we begin to think of these pains as not ours at all, but only levelled against the superior people

102–3 *Who alone suffers, suffers most i'the mind,* | *Leaving free things and happy shows behind* the principal suffering of the man who suffers on his own is the sense of having left behind him the whole world of carefree lives and joyful sights

104–5 *But then the mind much sufferance doth o'erskip* | *When grief hath mates, and bearing fellowship* we avoid much suffering when we know other people in the same plight who have to bear the same woes (a proverbial idea)

106 *portable* bearable

108 *He childed as I fathered* he with children who seek his life, as I have a father who seeks my life

109 *Mark the high noises* watch what's going on in the world of important people
thyself bewray reveal yourself (as Edgar)

110–11 *When false opinion, whose wrong thoughts defile thee,* | *In thy just proof repeals and reconciles thee* when the false story about you, which has made you seem morally corrupt, is proved wrong and you are shown to be just, so that you can be recalled to your true station and reconciled (with your father)

112 *What will hap more* whatever else happens

113 *Lurk* keep in hiding

Enter Cornwall, Regan, Gonerill, Edmund, and   III.7
servants

CORNWALL (*to Gonerill*) Post speedily to my lord your
husband, show him this letter. The army of France is
landed. – Seek out the traitor Gloucester.

Exeunt some servants

REGAN Hang him instantly!

GONERILL Pluck out his eyes!

CORNWALL Leave him to my displeasure. Edmund, keep
you our sister company; the revenges we are bound to
take upon your traitorous father are not fit for your be-
holding. Advise the Duke where you are going to a most
festinate preparation; we are bound to the like. Our   10
posts shall be swift and intelligent betwixt us. Farewell,
dear sister. Farewell, my lord of Gloucester.

Enter Oswald

How now? Where's the King?

OSWALD

My lord of Gloucester hath conveyed him hence.
Some five- or six-and-thirty of his knights,
Hot questrists after him, met him at gate,

III.7 The violent assaults on the mind
and dignity of Lear are now paralleled
by a physical assault on the eyes of
Gloucester. No counter-movement is
strong enough to stop this barbarism;
but the intervention of the servants
marks the beginning of an upswing of
the pendulum. A first defeat for wickedness appears in the death of Cornwall.

1 *Post speedily* hasten
  my lord (of Albany)

2 *this letter* (the letter about Cordelia's
  landing that Gloucester told
  Edmund about (III.3.9) and that
  Edmund conveyed to Cornwall
  (III.5.9))

7 *sister* sister-in-law (Gonerill, on her
  way to Albany)

9–10 *Advise the Duke where you are going
  to a most festinate preparation* advise
  the Duke of Albany, to whom you
  are going, to make speedy preparations (for war)

10–11 *Our posts shall be swift and intelligent*
  our couriers will move rapidly and
  convey full information

12 *my lord of Gloucester.* Edmund has
  already been promoted though
  his father is still alive. Compare line
  14.

16 *Hot questrists after him* eagerly searching for him. 'Questrist' seems to be

Who with some other of the lord's dependants
Are gone with him toward Dover, where they boast
To have well-armèd friends.

20   CORNWALL Get horses for your mistress.   *Exit Oswald*
GONERILL Farewell, sweet lord, and sister.
CORNWALL
Edmund, farewell.

> *Exeunt Gonerill and Edmund*

Go seek the traitor Gloucester.
Pinion him like a thief; bring him before us.

> *Exeunt servants*

Though well we may not pass upon his life
Without the form of justice, yet our power
Shall do a curtsy to our wrath, which men
May blame but not control.

> *Enter Gloucester, brought in by two or three servants*

Who's there? The traitor?

REGAN Ingrateful fox, 'tis he!
CORNWALL Bind fast his corky arms.
GLOUCESTER
30   What means your graces? Good my friends, consider
You are my guests. Do me no foul play, friends.
CORNWALL
Bind him, I say.

> *Servants tie his hands*

REGAN   Hard, hard! O filthy traitor!

Shakespeare's invention (from 'quest').

17 *the lord's* (Gloucester's)
24 *pass upon his life* pass a death sentence on him
25–6 *our power | Shall do a curtsy to our wrath* we will use our power (as co-sovereigns) in a way that gives precedence to our wrath
26 *curtsy*. I have modernized to the form that gives the better rhythm, and

(marginally) the better sense, but we should notice that 'courtesy' and 'curtsy' were not distinguished by the Elizabethans.

27 *control* curb, restrain
28 *Ingrateful fox*. He has shown ingratitude by failing in loyalty to his *arch and patron* Cornwall; he has been foxy in his sly and secretive dealing with Lear and his friends.
29 *corky* dry, withered

GLOUCESTER

Unmerciful lady as you are, I'm none.

CORNWALL

To this chair bind him. Villain, thou shalt find –

Regan plucks his beard

GLOUCESTER

By the kind gods, 'tis most ignobly done

To pluck me by the beard.

REGAN

So white, and such a traitor!

GLOUCESTER   Naughty lady,

These hairs which thou dost ravish from my chin

Will quicken and accuse thee. I am your host;

With robbers' hands my hospitable favours   40

You should not ruffle thus. What will you do?

CORNWALL

Come, sir; what letters had you late from France?

REGAN

Be simple-answered, for we know the truth.

CORNWALL

And what confederacy have you with the traitors

Late footed in the kingdom –

REGAN

To whose hands you have sent the lunatic King? Speak!

GLOUCESTER

I have a letter guessingly set down

Which came from one that's of a neutral heart

---

33 *none* no traitor

37 *Naughty* wicked

39 *quicken and accuse thee* come to life (as people) and speak against your actions

40 *hospitable favours*. This is usually said to mean 'the features (*favours*) of your host'; but perhaps 'the indulgences of my hospitality' is simpler.

41 *ruffle thus* treat with this outrage

42 *late* lately

43 *Be simple-answered* give us a straight answer

45 *footed* landed

46 *To whose hands you have sent the lunatic King?* This completes the question begun in line 44. *Lunatic King* is a good example of Shakespearian foreshortening: Regan has had no opportunity to learn about Lear's lunacy.

And not from one opposed.

CORNWALL   Cunning.

REGAN   And false.

CORNWALL

Where hast thou sent the King?

50 GLOUCESTER   To Dover.

REGAN

Wherefore to Dover? Wast thou not charged at peril –

CORNWALL

Wherefore to Dover? Let him answer that.

GLOUCESTER

I am tied to the stake, and I must stand the course.

REGAN Wherefore to Dover?

GLOUCESTER

Because I would not see thy cruel nails

Pluck out his poor old eyes; nor thy fierce sister

In his anointed flesh rash boarish fangs.

The sea, with such a storm as his bare head

In hell-black night endured, would have buoyed up

60 And quenched the stellèd fires;

Yet, poor old heart, he holp the heavens to rain.

---

51 *at peril* under the threat of punishment

53 *I am tied to the stake, and I must stand the course* like a bear in bear-baiting, I am tied to the stake, the dogs are attacking me, and I must endure it till the bout is ended

57 *anointed flesh.* The holy oil with which he was anointed at his coronation sanctified his person, and made physical assault on him a sacrilege.
rash boarish fangs. Rash, the Q reading for F's 'sticke', is not only more picturesque but also more accurate, since it is the hunting term for the slashing sideways movement of the boar's tusks. The three 'sh' sounds

in the line imply a slow deliberate delivery.

59–60 *would have buoyed up | And quenched the stellèd fires* would have risen up, like a buoy on the swell, high enough to extinguish the stars (with the implication of formlessness overcoming the pattern of order)

60 *stellèd fires.* The context shows that these must be the stars. 'Stelled' is not known elsewhere as an adjective. Shakespeare uses it as a participle, meaning 'delineated'; but it is easier to suppose that here he is making up a new word, meaning 'starry', from the Latin *stella*.

61 *holp* (old form of the past tense of 'help')

If wolves had at thy gate howled that dern time
Thou shouldst have said, 'Good porter, turn the key;
All cruels else subscribe'. But I shall see
The wingèd Vengeance overtake such children.

CORNWALL

See't shalt thou never. Fellows, hold the chair.
Upon these eyes of thine I'll set my foot.

GLOUCESTER

He that will think to live till he be old
Give me some help! – O, cruel! O, you gods!

REGAN

One side will mock another. Th'other too!   70

CORNWALL

If you see Vengeance –

FIRST SERVANT   Hold your hand, my lord!
I have served you ever since I was a child;
But better service have I never done you
Than now to bid you hold.

REGAN   How now, you dog!

FIRST SERVANT

If you did wear a beard upon your chin
I'd shake it on this quarrel.

          (*Cornwall draws his sword*)

                          What do you mean?

CORNWALL My villain!

---

62 *dern* dread, dark
64 *All cruels else subscribe*. This is a famous crux, for which any interpretation must be tentative. One problem is whether the clause belongs with what precedes or what follows. Supposing the former, I suggest 'Assent to any other cruel thing you like (but open the door to these poor creatures)'; the usual interpretation is: 'All other cruel creatures yield to pity (so you

should do so too, and turn the key)'.
65 *wingèd Vengeance*. Perhaps this means only 'swift vengeance'; but it is more likely to imply vengeance as an angel of divine wrath.
75–6 *If you did wear a beard upon your chin | I'd shake it* if you were a man I would attack you
77 *My villain!* my serf (daring to argue with me! – the same point as in line 79)

He lunges at him

FIRST SERVANT (*drawing his sword*)

Nay then, come on, and take the chance of anger.

He wounds Cornwall

REGAN

Give me thy sword. A peasant stand up thus!

She takes a sword and runs at him behind

FIRST SERVANT

80   O, I am slain! My lord, you have one eye left

To see some mischief on him. O!   *He dies*

CORNWALL

Lest it see more, prevent it. Out, vile jelly!

Where is thy lustre now?

GLOUCESTER

All dark and comfortless. Where's my son Edmund?

Edmund, enkindle all the sparks of nature

To quit this horrid act.

REGAN   Out, treacherous villain!

Thou call'st on him that hates thee. It was he

That made the overture of thy treasons to us;

Who is too good to pity thee.

GLOUCESTER

90   O my follies! Then Edgar was abused.

Kind gods, forgive me that and prosper him.

REGAN

Go thrust him out at gates and let him smell

---

78 *the chance of anger* the risk of what may happen when angry men fight

82 *Lest it see more, prevent it* so that your remaining eye shall not see any more mischief done to Cornwall, I will anticipate the mischief, on that very eye *vile*. See the note on III.2.71.

85 *enkindle all the sparks of nature* let your family loyalty blaze into anger

86 *quit* repay

88 *overture* (accented on the second syllable) revelation

90–91 *Edgar was abused.* | *Kind gods, forgive me that.* Gloucester's insight into moral and factual truth comes with great suddenness: 'So Edgar was slandered – forgive me for my part in that'. Note the absence of recrimination and the assumption that normal goodness still exists.

His way to Dover.   *Exit a servant with Gloucester*
                    How is't, my lord? How look you?

CORNWALL

I have received a hurt. Follow me, lady.
Turn out that eyeless villain. Throw this slave
Upon the dunghill. Regan, I bleed apace.
Untimely comes this hurt. Give me your arm.

                    Exit Cornwall, supported by Regan

SECOND SERVANT

I'll never care what wickedness I do
If this man come to good.

THIRD SERVANT   If she live long,
And in the end meet the old course of death,   100
Women will all turn monsters.

SECOND SERVANT

Let's follow the old Earl, and get the Bedlam
To lead him where he would; his roguish madness
Allows itself to anything.

THIRD SERVANT

Go thou. I'll fetch some flax and whites of eggs
To apply to his bleeding face. Now heaven help him!

                    Exeunt by opposite doors

---

93 *How look you?* how do you look on
yourself, how are you?

97 *Untimely.* Cornwall's one feeling
seems to be regret that the wound
will interfere with his schedule for
leading the army against Cordelia.

100 *meet the old course of death* die in the
normal way

101 *Women will all turn monsters* (a repetition of the point made about men in
lines 98–9: 'In that case women too

will lose their moral sense, and
behave monstrously')

103 *roguish madness.* This is the reading
of Q uncorrected; Q corrected omits
roguish. The epithet seems, however,
too Shakespearian to be accidental
and we must suppose that the corrector made a slip.

104 *Allows itself to anything* lends itself to
any task that may be imposed on him

IV.I   *Enter Edgar*

EDGAR

Yet better thus, and known to be contemned,
Than still contemned and flattered. To be worst,
The lowest and most dejected thing of fortune,
Stands still in esperance, lives not in fear.
The lamentable change is from the best;
The worst returns to laughter. Welcome, then,
Thou unsubstantial air that I embrace!
The wretch that thou hast blown unto the worst
Owes nothing to thy blasts.

Enter Gloucester, led by an Old Man

But who comes here?

10   My father, parti-eyed! World, world, O world!

IV.1 A scene showing the struggle to recover meaning and value in the world.
Edgar'sdeterminationtoendureandGlouc-
ester's determination to die counterpoint
one another in a tone moving between
the grotesque and the affectionate.

1–2 *better thus, and known to be contemned,*
| *Than still contemned and flattered* it is
better to be a beggar and know what
people think about you (contempt)
than to be despised (as at a court)
though flattered. The punctuation in
F and that in Q both allow the following phrase, *To be worst*, to be included
in the sentence; but it seems better to
attach it to the following lines, and F's
punctuation can be read in this way.

3 *most dejected thing of fortune* thing most
dejected (or cast down) by fortune

4 *Stands still in esperance* remains always
in possession of hope
fear (of something worse about
to happen)

6 *The worst returns to laughter* any change,
when you are at the worst, is bound
to be change for the better

7 *Thou unsubstantial air that I embrace*
(with my nakedness I embrace the
air, and I approve of it, even though
it is lacking in substance, in wealth,
in gifts, in comforts)

9 *Owes nothing to thy blasts.* Because the
wind's help led only to the worst,
Edgarisfreeofobligation,andtherefore
canembracehis'creditor'withoutfear.

10 *parti-eyed.* The uncorrected Q reading, 'poorlie, leed', was no doubt
responsible for the F reading,
'poorely led'; but since this gives a
modicum of sense it has been generally accepted. The Q correction,
'parti, eyd', on the other hand, must
be the result of a second attempt to
read the manuscript, and is the nearest to Shakespeare we can come. It is
usually supposed to be unintelligible
as it stands; but in F a comma is
often a substitute for a hyphen, and
may be so here. If we make this
substitution we then have *parti-eyed*,
a phrase like 'parti-coloured' or
'parti-coated' (*Love's Labour's Lost*,
v.2.754), 'party-bow' (the rainbow),

But that thy strange mutations make us hate thee
Life would not yield to age.

OLD MAN   O my good lord,
I have been your tenant and your father's tenant
These fourscore years!

GLOUCESTER
Away! Get thee away! Good friend, be gone.
Thy comforts can do me no good at all;
Thee they may hurt.

OLD MAN   You cannot see your way.

GLOUCESTER
I have no way and therefore want no eyes;
I stumbled when I saw. Full oft 'tis seen
Our means secure us, and our mere defects   20
Prove our commodities. O dear son Edgar,
The food of thy abusèd father's wrath!
Might I but live to see thee in my touch
I'd say I had eyes again.

OLD MAN   How now? Who's there?

EDGAR (aside)
O gods! Who is't can say 'I am at the worst'?

'party-flowers', or 'parti-membered' (having different members). *Parti-eyed* would mean 'having his eyes looking like a fool's coat in the red of blood and the white of eggs'. This provides a grotesque image, but there is no shortage of these in *King Lear*. Gloucester's eyes are the striking point about him, and Edgar would be expected to mention them. It may be better that he should refer to them as grotesque than dilute his response (and ours) by noticing only the social quality of his guide.

11-12 *But that thy strange mutations make us hate thee | Life would not yield to age* if it were not for these strange switches in fortune from good to bad, and the hatred of life that this generates, we would not be willing

to accept old age and death (or perhaps 'we would not age at all')

18 *I have no way* I have lost my path through life

19 *I stumbled when I saw* when I had my eyes I missed my moral footing, and tripped over false judgements

20-21 *Our means secure us, and our mere defects | Prove our commodities* our possessions (such as eyes) make us secure or over-confident, and total (*mere*) deprivation may prove an advantage

22 *The food of thy abusèd father's wrath* I used you to feed my anger on, when I was deceived (*abusèd*)

23 *in my touch* by touching you

25 *Who is't can say 'I am at the worst'?* The scene up to this point may be taken as an illustration of the folly of

I am worse than e'er I was.

OLD MAN   'Tis poor mad Tom.

EDGAR (aside)

And worse I may be yet. The worst is not,
So long as we can say 'This is the worst'.

OLD MAN

Fellow, where goest?

GLOUCESTER   Is it a beggar-man?

30   OLD MAN Madman and beggar too.

GLOUCESTER

He has some reason, else he could not beg.
I'the last night's storm I such a fellow saw
Which made me think a man a worm. My son
Came then into my mind; and yet my mind
Was then scarce friends with him. I have heard more
        since.
As flies to wanton boys are we to the gods;
They kill us for their sport.

EDGAR (aside)   How should this be?

Bad is the trade that must play fool to sorrow,
Angering itself and others. (Aloud) Bless thee, master!

Edgar's initial confidence in To be worst.

27–8 The worst is not, | So long as we can say 'This is the worst' the kind of consolation in which you say to yourself (as Edgar did in lines 1–6) 'I am now at the lowest point' is a sure indication of a buoyancy of hope that separates you from the real worst

33 think a man a worm (perhaps a reminiscence of Job 25.6: 'man a worm, even the son of man, which is but a worm')

36–7 As flies to wanton boys are we to the gods; | They kill us for their sport as playful and irresponsible boys make games out of the lives of flies, not really caring whether they live or die, so the gods (on this evidence) seem to be having fun with mankind's misery and death

37 How should this be? how can the mental even more than the physical condition of Gloucester have changed so radically?

38 Bad is the trade that must play fool to sorrow it is a bad business to have to spend your time uttering folly to a man (like my father) distressed by sorrow

39 Angering itself and others creating general anger, because of its inappropriateness

GLOUCESTER

Is that the naked fellow?

OLD MAN   Ay, my lord.   40

GLOUCESTER

Then prithee get thee away. If for my sake

Thou wilt o'ertake us hence a mile or twain

I'the way toward Dover, do it for ancient love,

And bring some covering for this naked soul,

Which I'll entreat to lead me.

OLD MAN   Alack, sir, he is mad.

GLOUCESTER

'Tis the time's plague when madmen lead the blind.

Do as I bid thee, or rather do thy pleasure.

Above the rest, begone.

OLD MAN

I'll bring him the best 'parel that I have,

Come on't what will.   *Exit*

GLOUCESTER   Sirrah naked fellow!   50

EDGAR

Poor Tom's a-cold. (*Aside*) I cannot daub it further.

GLOUCESTER Come hither, fellow.

EDGAR (*aside*)

And yet I must. (*Aloud*) Bless thy sweet eyes, they bleed.

GLOUCESTER Knowest thou the way to Dover?

EDGAR Both stile and gate, horse-way and footpath, Poor

Tom hath been scared out of his good wits. Bless thee,

good man's son, from the foul fiend. Five fiends have

---

43 *I'the way toward Dover* along the Dover road

46 *'Tis the time's plague* it is the kind of horror appropriate to our times

47 *or rather do thy pleasure.* Gloucester withdraws the command, remembering that it is quite inappropriate to his condition; 'Do what you wish' is the most he is entitled to say.

49 *'parel* apparel

50 *Come on't what will* whatever may happen (to me) as a result

51 *I cannot daub it further* that's the best I can do (in pretending to be Poor Tom)

55 *stile and gate, horse-way and footpath.* Each kind of path has its appropriate obstacle – the stile for the footpath, the gate for the horse-way (bridle-path).

56 *Tom hath been scared.* The landscape is for Tom a series of places to be scared in, where the foul fiend has appeared.

been in Poor Tom at once: of lust, as Obidicut; Hobbididence, prince of dumbness; Mahu, of stealing;
60   Modo, of murder; Flibberdigibbet, of mopping and
mowing, who since possesses chambermaids and
waiting-women. So bless thee, master!

GLOUCESTER

Here, take this purse, thou whom the heavens' plagues
Have humbled to all strokes. That I am wretched
Makes thee the happier. Heavens deal so still!
Let the superfluous and lust-dieted man
That slaves your ordinance, that will not see
Because he does not feel, feel your power quickly!
So distribution should undo excess

58–60 *Obidicut; Hobbididence ... Mahu
... Modo ... Flibberdigibbet.* Harsnet's forms are 'Hoberdicut', 'Hoberdidance', 'Maho', 'Modu', 'Fliberdigibbet', and, allowing for the probability that the Q reporters would
have difficulty in remembering these
outlandish names correctly, perhaps
we should prefer Harsnet's spellings.
Q's 'Stiberdigebit' is a clear compositor's misreading of a manuscript
form like Harsnet's (F is defective at
this point). Compare the Q form at
III.4.110: *'fliberdegibek'*. Above
(III.6.30) Shakespeare represents
Harsnet's 'Hoberdidance' as
Hoppedance.
60–62 *Flibberdigibbet, of mopping and
mowing, who since possesses chambermaids
and waiting-women.* 'Fliberdigibbet' is
a dancing devil in Harsnet, and a
'flibbertigibbet' is a flighty chattering
woman (hence, presumably, Harsnet's devil's name). The vices he represents here are in an appropriate
key: *mopping and mowing* – grimacing
and twisting the face, like chambermaids in their mistress's looking-
glass. There are three 'possessed'
chambermaids in Harsnet.

61 *since* (since they left Tom)
64 *Have humbled to all strokes* have
brought to the acceptance of every
kind of misery
64–5 *That I am wretched | Makes thee the
happier* (since (as in III.6.104–5)
misery loves company)
65 *Heavens deal so* (so that one man's
misery should be comforted by
another's)
still always
66 *the superfluous and lust-dieted man* the
man who has too much (compare
superflux, III.4.35) and who sates himself on his pleasures
67 *slaves your ordinance* does what he likes
with (makes a slave out of) the
divine rule (that one man should help
another)
67–8 *will not see | Because he does not feel.*
See means 'understand' and *feel* 'have
fellow-feeling with'; but Gloucester
is also thinking of his own condition,
brought to 'see' how things are when
he can only know them by touch.
Compare lines 23–4.
69 *So distribution should undo excess* (the
gods' powers would deprive the superfluous man of his excess and *shake
the superflux* to those in need)

And each man have enough. Dost thou know Dover?   70
EDGAR Ay, master.
GLOUCESTER
There is a cliff whose high and bending head
Looks fearfully in the confinèd deep;
Bring me but to the very brim of it
And I'll repair the misery thou dost bear
With something rich about me. From that place
I shall no leading need.
EDGAR   Give me thy arm;
Poor Tom shall lead thee.   *Exeunt*

Enter Gonerill and Edmund   IV.2
GONERILL
Welcome, my lord. I marvel our mild husband
Not met us on the way.
        Enter Oswald
                        Now, where's your master?
OSWALD
Madam, within; but never man so changed.
I told him of the army that was landed.
He smiled at it. I told him you were coming.
His answer was 'The worse'. Of Gloucester's treachery
And of the loyal service of his son
When I informed him, then he called me sot
And told me I had turned the wrong side out.

---

72 *bending* bending over, overhanging
73 *fearfully* frighteningly
   confinèd shut in (by the land on
   both sides of the English Channel)

IV.2 The upswing towards good is advanced by an extraordinary and unprepared volte-face. Albany has now become a man of clear moral commitment (though less clear in his commitment to action), opposed to the faction

of his wife Gonerill and her intended
paramour, Edmund.
1-2 *Welcome . . . way.* She welcomes him
   to her castle, where they have now
   arrived. She is surprised that her
   house-keeping husband has not
   come out of the castle to greet
   them.
8 *sot* fool
9 *turned the wrong side out* (that is, reversed
   the moral judgements – called

10   What most he should dislike seems pleasant to him;
        What like, offensive.

   GONERILL (*to Edmund*) Then shall you go no further.
        It is the cowish terror of his spirit
        That dares not undertake. He'll not feel wrongs
        Which tie him to an answer. Our wishes on the way
        May prove effects. Back, Edmund, to my brother!
        Hasten his musters and conduct his powers.
        I must change arms at home and give the distaff
        Into my husband's hands. This trusty servant
        Shall pass between us; ere long you are like to hear,

20   If you dare venture in your own behalf,
        A mistress's command. Wear this;
                (*giving a favour*)   spare speech.
        Decline your head; this kiss, if it durst speak,
        Would stretch thy spirits up into the air.
        Conceive; and fare thee well.

   EDMUND
        Yours in the ranks of death.

Gloucester's loyal service *treachery* and Edmund's treachery *loyal service*)

11 *What like* what he should like

12 *cowish* cowardly, effeminate

13 *undertake* take responsibility for any enterprise

13–14 *He'll not feel wrongs* | *Which tie him to an answer* he will ignore insults which require him to 'answer' them by challenging the wrong-doer to fight. It is for this reason he is ignoring the French invasion.

14–15 *Our wishes on the way* | *May prove effects* what we talked of and wished for as we came here together may well come to pass. Presumably the idea of Albany's cowardice gives Gonerill the further idea of getting rid of him, so making effective their ͡ish for union.

        ͡her   my   brother-in-law

16 *Hasten his musters* speed up his enlistment of soldiers
    powers troops

17 *I must change arms* . . . (1) I must change into military accoutrements; (2) my husband and I must exchange the work we do with our arms: he must take the distaff, and I will get the sword

20 *in your own behalf* thinking of yourself (and not of your loyalty to the cause)

21 *mistress* (with a *double-entendre*)

21–8 *mistress's command . . . bed.* The passage is full of sexual innuendoes stronger than anything said explicitly, as in *stretch thy spirits, Conceive, ranks of death, services, usurps my bed.*

24 *Conceive* think what this implies

25 *Yours in the ranks of death.* Edmund slightly over-acts the role of swashbuckling lover that has been foisted on him, though Gonerill does not seem to notice anything amiss.

GONERILL   My most dear Gloucester!
                                    Exit Edmund
O, the difference of man and man!
To thee a woman's services are due;
A fool usurps my bed.
OSWALD   Madam, here comes my lord.
                                            Exit
        Enter Albany
GONERILL
I have been worth the whistling.
ALBANY   O Gonerill,
You are not worth the dust which the rude wind   30
Blows in your face. I fear your disposition:
That nature which contemns its origin

---

death (often used as a metaphor for 'orgasm')

27 *a woman's services* (the service that a woman naturally gives to a real *man*)

28 *A fool usurps my bed* I am possessed by a fool (Albany) who does not know how to command. The uncorrected Q reading, 'My foote usurps my body', is the source of F's 'My Foole usurpes my body'; Q corrected reads 'A foole usurps my bed', which implies a second look at the manuscript, whereas the F reading need imply no more than an obvious correction of the copy-text (Q uncorrected). *Bed* seems better in meaning also, since it is the connubial possession of her she objects to rather than sexual possession. Compare IV.6.265–6, where in her letter of *mistress's command* she speaks of *his bed my gaol; from the loathed warmth whereof deliver me.*

29 *I have been worth the whistling.* This is based on the proverb 'It is a poor dog that is not worth the whistling'. The meaning is: 'So you have decided at last to come looking for me,

since even "a poor dog is worth whistling for"'.

30–31 *not worth the dust ... your face.* Albany picks up *worth the whistling* and twists it round so that the sarcasm rebounds: 'Even the wind that cares nothing for you whistles as it throws dust at you and that's too good for you; that's how much whistling you are worth'.

31 *I fear your disposition.* That Gonerill was worthless and neutral (like the *dust*) would not cause *fear*; but her *disposition*, the tendency of her character, is not neutral, but frighteningly destructive.

32 *contemns its origin* disdains the source from which it springs (Lear in this case)

its. Q uncorrected reads 'it', which could sometimes be used for 'its', but usually appears in Shakespeare in contexts of childish talk. The fact that the Q corrector changed 'it' to 'ith' implies either that he did not find the reading plausible or that it did not correspond to what he thought he saw in his copy.

Cannot be bordered certain in itself.
She that herself will sliver and disbranch
From her material sap perforce must wither
And come to deadly use.

GONERILL No more; the text is foolish.

ALBANY

Wisdom and goodness to the vile seem vile;
Filths savour but themselves. What have you done,
40   Tigers not daughters, what have you performed?
A father, and a gracious agèd man,
Whose reverence even the head-lugged bear would lick,
Most barbarous, most degenerate, have you madded.
Could my good brother suffer you to do it?
A man, a prince, by him so benefited?
If that the heavens do not their visible spirits
Send quickly down to tame these vile offences,
It will come –
Humanity must perforce prey on itself

'Ith' (that is, 'in the') does not make sense; but it would be easy to mistake 's' for 'h' in the manuscript.

33 *Cannot be bordered certain in itself* cannot be contained, or trusted to act in one way rather than another (and therefore must be *feared*)

34–5 *herself will sliver and disbranch | From her material sap* will tear herself from the stock on which she grew, as one tears a branch from a tree. *Material* means 'which gave her her (moral and physical) substance'.

36 *to deadly use* (a use proper to dead wood – to be burned. Compare Hebrews 6.8: 'But that which beareth thorns and briars is rejected and is nigh unto cursing; whose end is to be burned'. It may be that this is ⸱eferred to below in *text*.)

⸱ *the text is foolish* stop preach-
⸱ubject that makes no

38, 47 *vile*. See the note on III.2.71.

39 *Filths savour but themselves* filthy minds can only smell (and relish) their own odour

42 *head-lugged bear* bear pulled along by the ring in its nose (and therefore in no good temper)

44 *brother* brother-in-law (Cornwall)

45 *A man, a prince, by him so benefited* (a cumulative list of three reasons why Cornwall should not have acted thus: (1) he was a human being; (2) what is more, he was a prince, one with moral standards higher than those of mere humanity; (3) most of all, he was greatly in Lear's debt)

46 *their visible spirits* (not their invisible spirits (who are, presumably, all around us all the time) but manifest interventions, like those which will precede the Last Judgement)

49–50 *prey on itself | Like monsters of the deep.* The life of the sea creatures,

Like monsters of the deep.

GONERILL   Milk-livered man!   50
That bear'st a cheek for blows, a head for wrongs!
Who hast not in thy brows an eye discerning
Thine honour from thy suffering, that not knowest
Fools do those villains pity who are punished
Ere they have done their mischief. Where's thy drum?
France spreads his banners in our noiseless land,
With plumèd helm thy state begins to threat,
Whilst thou, a moral fool, sits still and cries
'Alack, why does he so?'

ALBANY   See thyself, devil!
Proper deformity shows not in the fiend   60
So horrid as in woman.

GONERILL   O vain fool!

where the big fishes eat up the little ones, was a common image of final moral disorder or chaos.

50 *Milk-livered man!* Gonerill can only see Albany's feverish moral vision as a result of lack of courage to seize the real situation, lack of blood in his liver, a substitution of female *Milk* for male blood. In this she resembles Lady Macbeth before the murder of Duncan.

51 *bear'st . . . a head for wrongs* your head is only an object for other people to rain their wrongful blows on

52–3 *an eye discerning | Thine honour from thy suffering* a capacity to see how far endurance is proper and how far suffering ought to be resented and revenged. Compare lines 13–14.

54–5 *Fools do those villains . . . their mischief* it is foolish to object to punishment which *precedes* crimes. Lear has not yet collaborated with the French, but he will; Gloucester's case must also be in the mind of Gonerill and of the audience, though

Albany has not yet heard of his punishment.

56 *noiseless land.* Noise is made equivalent to warlike preparation or resistance: Albany should beat his drum and march against the enemy.

57 *thy state begins to threat.* The Q corrector's change from 'slayer' to 'state' seems quite acceptable. A new grammatical subject in line 57 could only weaken the antithesis between *France* and *thou*. But the other change – 'begin threats' to 'begins thereat' – cannot be accepted as it stands, since it makes no sense. What would be ideal would be a relevant word easily mistaken for 'thereat', but none has been found; *to threat* makes good sense but it is not very like 'thereat'.

58 *a moral fool* foolish to sit and argue the moral pros and cons (instead of taking up arms)

59 *See thyself* contemplate your own condition (not mine)

60–61 *Proper deformity shows not in the fiend | So horrid as in woman* devilish

ALBANY
    Thou changèd and self-covered thing, for shame,
    Be-monster not thy feature. Were't my fitness
    To let these hands obey my blood,
    They are apt enough to dislocate and tear
    Thy flesh and bones. Howe'er thou art a fiend,
    A woman's shape doth shield thee.
GONERILL Marry, your manhood! Mew!
        Enter a Messenger
ALBANY What news?
MESSENGER
70   O, my good lord, the Duke of Cornwall's dead,
    Slain by his servant, going to put out
    The other eye of Gloucester.
ALBANY   Gloucester's eyes?
MESSENGER
    A servant that he bred, thrilled with remorse,
    Opposed against the act, bending his sword
    To his great master; who, thereat enraged,
    Flew on him and amongst them felled him dead,
    But not without that harmful stroke which since
    Hath plucked him after.
    ALBANY   This shows you are above,

grimaces are uglier in a woman than
they would be on the devil's face,
for they are appropriate (*Proper*) to
him
62 *changèd and self-covered thing* one who
has *changèd* her appearance so that it
no longer corresponds to her reality,
who has *covered* or concealed the fiend
within her behind the female graces
of her external self
63 *Be-monster not thy feature* don't show
in your external appearance the mon-
~~ster that~~ lives within you
        ~~fitness~~ if it were appro-

        ~~flesh~~ and bones

dislocate the bones and tear the flesh
66 *Howe'er thou art a fiend* however great
a fiend you are, in reality
68 *Marry, your manhood! Mew!* good heavens, you and your talk of your 'manhood' (in shielding my *woman's shape*)!
I'll show you what I think of it.
(*Mew* is a derisive cat-call.)
73 *that he bred* that he kept or supported
in his household
    thrilled with remorse pierced through
with feelings of compassion
76 *amongst them* (presumably 'amongst
the other servants')
78 *Hath plucked him after* has made him
follow his servant into death

You justicers, that these our nether crimes
So speedily can venge! But, O, poor Gloucester!   80
Lost he his other eye?
MESSENGER   Both, both, my lord.
This letter, madam, craves a speedy answer.
'Tis from your sister.
GONERILL (*aside*)   One way I like this well.
But being widow, and my Gloucester with her,
May all the building in my fancy pluck
Upon my hateful life. Another way
The news is not so tart. – (*Aloud*) I'll read and
        answer.   *Exit*
ALBANY
Where was his son when they did take his eyes?
MESSENGER
Come with my lady hither.
ALBANY   He is not here.
MESSENGER
No, my good lord; I met him back again.   90
ALBANY Knows he the wickedness?
MESSENGER
Ay, my good lord. 'Twas he informed against him,
And quit the house on purpose that their punishment
Might have the freer course.
ALBANY   Gloucester, I live
To thank thee for the love thou show'dst the King
And to revenge thine eyes. Come hither, friend;
Tell me what more thou knowest.   *Exeunt*

---

79 *justicers* (heavenly) judges
   nether crimes crimes committed down
   here on earth
83, 86–7 *One way I like this well . . . An-*
   other way | The news is not so tart.
   These both refer to the same
   thought: Cornwall's death brings
   one step nearer the possibility of

undivided rule over Britain.
85 *the building in my fancy* the dream of
   marrying Edmund that my amorous
   inclinations (*fancy*) have built up
86 *hateful* (because she will be left as
   Albany's wife, and will have to watch
   her sister enjoying Edmund)
90 *back* on his way back

IV.3   *Enter Kent and a Gentleman*

KENT Why the King of France is so suddenly gone back
      know you no reason?

GENTLEMAN Something he left imperfect in the state,
      which since his coming forth is thought of, which im-
      ports to the kingdom so much fear and danger that his
      personal return was most required and necessary.

KENT Who hath he left behind him general?

GENTLEMAN The Marshal of France, Monsieur La Far.

KENT Did your letters pierce the Queen to any demon-
10   stration of grief?

GENTLEMAN
      Ay, sir; she took them, read them in my presence,
      And now and then an ample tear trilled down
      Her delicate cheek. It seemed she was a queen
      Over her passion who, most rebel-like,
      Sought to be king o'er her.

KENT   O, then it moved her?

GENTLEMAN
      Not to a rage; patience and sorrow strove

IV.3 A series of short scenes (in or near
Dover) marks, as often at this point in a
Shakespearian tragedy, the alternate pos-
tures of the competing armies. But the
battle in *King Lear* is less important than
the moral attitudes of those involved. In
IV.3 Kent and a Gentleman narrate the
facts of the coming reunion between
Lear and Cordelia, and (more important)
the values that attach to Lear's shame
and to Cordelia's radiant and healing
beauty.

3 *imperfect* incomplete

9 *letters*. If the mission which the Gentleman undertakes to Cordelia in III.1
is the same one referred to here, the
verbal message has been transformed

into *letters*. This is understandable, as
the inconsistency would allow Shakespeare to make better dramatic effects
at both points.

12 *trilled*. The *Oxford English Dictionary*
says that 'trill' implies 'a more continuous motion than is expressed by
trickle'.

14 *her passion who* ... her emotion
which ...

16–17 *patience and sorrow strove | Who
should express her goodliest* her passions
and her power of control appeared
like competitors in her face and her
temper, each seeming to make her
more lovely than the other

Who should express her goodliest. You have seen
Sunshine and rain at once; her smiles and tears
Were like a better way; those happy smilets
That played on her ripe lip seem not to know   20
What guests were in her eyes, which parted thence
As pearls from diamonds dropped. In brief,
Sorrow would be a rarity most beloved
If all could so become it.

KENT   Made she no verbal question?

GENTLEMAN
Faith, once or twice she heaved the name of father
Pantingly forth, as if it pressed her heart,
Cried 'Sisters! Sisters! Shame of ladies! Sisters!
Kent! Father! Sisters! – What, i'the storm? i'the night?
Let pity not be believed!' There she shook
The holy water from her heavenly eyes,   30
And clamour moistened; then away she started
To deal with grief alone.

KENT   It is the stars,
The stars above us govern our conditions.

---

19 *Were like a better way*. This is difficult to construe, and so to punctuate: *like* may refer back to *Sunshine and rain* (the smiles and tears were like simultaneous sunshine and rain), or it may mean 'were like one another' (each resembled the other and in this relationship revealed *a better way*), or perhaps 'were like a vision of the way to Heaven'. In any case the meaning aimed at must be that she expressed a new mode of connexion, not found in nature and better than what is found there.

20 *seem* (historic present. Since the eighteenth century this has been regularized to the past 'seemed'; but Shakespeare's usage elsewhere justifies the original reading.)

23 *a rarity most beloved* (as much sought-after and precious as *pearls* and *diamonds* – or the beauty of Cordelia in her patience)

24 *become* adorn
verbal in words (beyond what was conveyed by her looks)

25–6 *heaved the name of father . . . as if it pressed her heart*. The use of *heave* and *heart* should remind us of *I cannot heave | My heart into my mouth* in 1.1.91–2. Cordelia is throughout the play characterized by a lack of fluent rhetoric.

29 *Let pity not be believed* let me believe (on this evidence) that pity does not exist

31 *clamour moistened* sprinkled with this *holy water* the outcry of her grief

Else one self mate and make could not beget
Such different issues. You spoke not with her since?
GENTLEMAN No.
KENT
Was this before the King returned?
GENTLEMAN   No, since.
KENT
Well, sir, the poor distressèd Lear's i'the town,
Who sometime in his better tune remembers
40   What we are come about, and by no means
Will yield to see his daughter.
GENTLEMAN   Why, good sir?
KENT
A sovereign shame so elbows him: his own unkindness
That stripped her from his benediction, turned her
To foreign casualties, gave her dear rights
To his dog-hearted daughters – these things sting
His mind so venomously that burning shame
Detains him from Cordelia.
GENTLEMAN   Alack, poor gentleman!
KENT
Of Albany's and Cornwall's powers you heard not?
GENTLEMAN 'Tis so. They are afoot.
KENT
50   Well, sir, I'll bring you to our master Lear
And leave you to attend him. Some dear cause
Will in concealment wrap me up awhile.
When I am known aright you shall not grieve
Lending me this acquaintance. I pray you
Go along with me.   *Exeunt*

34 *one self mate and make* one and the same husband and wife. ('Make' like 'mate' can apply to either spouse.)
37 *the King* (of France)
42 *A sovereign shame so elbows him* a dominating sense of shame so crowds and jostles him
44 *foreign casualties* the chances of existence in a foreign land
51 *Some dear cause* an important reason. The real reason is Shakespeare's desire to keep the revelation of Kent's identity till the last scene.

Enter, with drum and colours, Cordelia, Doctor, and   IV.4
soldiers

CORDELIA

Alack, 'tis he! Why, he was met even now
As mad as the vexed sea, singing aloud,
Crowned with rank fumiter and furrow-weeds,
With hardokes, hemlock, nettles, cuckoo-flowers,
Darnel, and all the idle weeds that grow
In our sustaining corn. (*To soldiers*) A century send
      forth;
Search every acre in the high-grown field
And bring him to our eye.   *Exeunt soldiers*
(*To Doctor*)   What can man's wisdom
In the restoring his bereavèd sense?

IV.4 Cordelia enacts the part the preceding scene described. The fertile English landscape is used to evoke both the
ungoverned wildness of the King (in
preparation for IV.6) and the natural
powers of restoration that Cordelia can
call up.

(stage direction) *with drum and colours*
with drums beating and flags waving
(indicative of battle order)

1 *he* (the one you have just been describing to me)

2 *mad as the vexed sea* tossed and turned
by his passions, as unpredictable as
the movement of a stormy sea

3-5 *rank fumiter . . . Darnel.* These
flowers seem, so far as they are identifiable, to be of bitter, pungent, or
poisonous kinds and therefore an
appropriate 'crown of thorns' for the
mad King; but they also reflect the
state of natural growth to which he
has allied himself.

3 *furrow-weeds* weeds that spring up in
the furrows of ploughed land

4 *hardokes* (F; Q: 'hor-docks'; not accurately identifiable; sometimes
equated with burdocks, hoar-docks,
harlocks (= charlocks), and other
possibilities)

5-6 *idle weeds that grow | In our sustaining
corn.* Lear is associated with the rank
and random uselessness of the
weeds, set in contrast to the planned
and useful grain which sustains life.
The *century* of soldiers, the organized life of Cordelia's army, is, on
the other hand, like the *sustaining
corn.*

6 *century.* Is it an accident that Cordelia
sends forth a hundred men to restore
the King who lost his 'hundred
knights'?

7 *the high-grown field.* It is now, for symbolic purposes, high summer at
Dover. The height of Lear's escape
into 'natural' chaos is supported by a
natural riot of vegetation.

8 *What can man's wisdom* what can human
science do

10   He that helps him, take all my outward worth.
      DOCTOR
            There is means, madam.
            Our foster-nurse of nature is repose,
            The which he lacks; that to provoke in him
            Are many simples operative, whose power
            Will close the eye of anguish.
      CORDELIA   All blest secrets,
            All you unpublished virtues of the earth,
            Spring with my tears! Be aidant and remediate
            In the good man's distress. Seek, seek for him,
            Lest his ungoverned rage dissolve the life
20   That wants the means to lead it.
                  Enter a Messenger
      MESSENGER   News, madam:
            The British powers are marching hitherward.
      CORDELIA
            'Tis known before. Our preparation stands
            In expectation of them. O dear father,
            It is thy business that I go about.
            Therefore great France
            My mourning and importuned tears hath pitied.

---

10 *outward worth* wealth. We should recognize the same Cordelia as in 1.1,
despising the outward shows that
others prize.

12 *foster-nurse* she who cherishes and
supports

13 *provoke* induce

14 *simples* herbs
operative effective

15–17 *blest secrets . . . unpublished virtues of
the earth,* | *Spring with my tears.* The
hidden or unknown recuperative
powers of herbs are to spring out of
the earth as the herbs themselves do
after a spring shower.

17 *aidant and remediate* (rare words, with
the sense of 'aiding and remedying',

used here to fit into the remote and
incantatory atmosphere of Cordelia's
prayer)

19 *ungoverned rage* violent and unchecked
temper

20 *means* (that is, his reason)

24 *It is thy business that I go about.* Cordelia
forswears personal political ambition
and proclaims Lear's restoration as
her only war-aim. But the echo of
Christ's answer when found by his
parents in the temple, 'I must go
about my father's business' (Luke
2.49), is presumably not accidental.

26 *importuned* importunate, beseeching.
The Q reading, 'important', has the
same meaning.

No blown ambition doth our arms incite
But love, dear love, and our aged father's right.
Soon may I hear and see him!   *Exeunt*

Enter Regan and Oswald   IV.5

REGAN
    But are my brother's powers set forth?
OSWALD   Ay, madam.
REGAN
    Himself in person there?
OSWALD   Madam, with much ado.
    Your sister is the better soldier.
REGAN
    Lord Edmund spake not with your lord at home?
OSWALD No, madam.
REGAN
    What might import my sister's letter to him?
OSWALD I know not, lady.
REGAN
    Faith, he is posted hence on serious matter.
    It was great ignorance, Gloucester's eyes being out,

27–8 *No blown ambition ... But love.* 1 Corinthians 13.4–5 seems to have been in Shakespeare's mind: 'Charity ... is not puffed up, is not ambitious, seeketh not her own' (Rheims version). In the Bishops' Bible it reads: 'Love ... swelleth not, dealeth not dishonestly, seeketh not her own'.

IV.5 The self-seeking wickedness of Gonerill and Regan has found out its own punishment in the desire that both feel for the person of Edmund. General destructive hate here is in strong contrast to the love and protectiveness that was the keynote of the preceding scene.
(stage direction) *Oswald.* Oswald has

delivered to Regan the letter that Gonerill promised to send at IV.2.87; and he has mentioned, it appears, that he is carrying another letter, from Gonerill to Edmund.

2 *with much ado* making a great fuss about it. This reflects Gonerill's view of Albany's moral scruples.

4 *Lord Edmund spake not with your lord at home?* Regan asks Oswald to confirm what he has already told her.

8 *Faith.* Regan's uncharacteristic oath is presumably designed to make palatable what may seem to Oswald to be a mere evasion.

9 *ignorance* lack of (political) understanding

10   To let him live. Where he arrives he moves
      All hearts against us. Edmund, I think, is gone,
      In pity of his misery, to dispatch
      His nighted life – moreover to descry
      The strength o'th'enemy.

OSWALD
      I must needs after him, madam, with my letter.

REGAN
      Our troops set forth tomorrow; stay with us.
      The ways are dangerous.

OSWALD   I may not, madam.
      My lady charged my duty in this business.

REGAN
      Why should she write to Edmund? Might not you
20   Transport her purposes by word? Belike –
      Some things – I know not what – I'll love thee much –
      Let me unseal the letter.

OSWALD   Madam, I had rather –

REGAN
      I know your lady does not love her husband –
      I am sure of that – and at her late being here
      She gave strange œillades and most speaking looks
      To noble Edmund. I know you are of her bosom.

OSWALD   I, madam?

13 *nighted* (1) benighted; (2) on which
(since he is blind) night has fallen
13–14 *moreover to descry | The strength o'th'
enemy*. The quick shift from moral
pretension – which she does not
properly understand – to practical
political realities is typical of Regan.
20–21 *Belike – | Some things – I know not
what* ... Regan's incoherence be-
tokens her attempt to think how she
can overcome her sister's advantage
with Edmund and Oswald's unco-
operativeness.
22 *I had rather –*. Presumably Oswald

wished to state (once again) his
loyalty to his mistress, in something
like 'I had rather die than disobey
my lady'.
25 *œillades*. This French word (defined
in Cotgrave's French dictionary of
1611 as 'an amorous look, affectionate wink ... passionate cast of the
eye, a sheep's eye') was almost nat-
uralized in the Elizabethan age (in
the pronunciation indicated by the
F spelling, 'Eliads'), but has now
reverted to foreignness.
26 *of her bosom* in her confidence

REGAN

I speak in understanding. Y'are; I know't.

Therefore I do advise you take this note:

My lord is dead; Edmund and I have talked,   30

And more convenient is he for my hand

Than for your lady's. You may gather more.

If you do find him, pray you give him this;

And when your mistress hears thus much from you,

I pray desire her call her wisdom to her.

So fare you well.

If you do chance to hear of that blind traitor,

Preferment falls on him that cuts him off.

OSWALD

Would I could meet him, madam! I should show

What party I do follow.

REGAN   Fare thee well.   *Exeunt*   40

Enter Gloucester and Edgar in peasant's clothes   IV.6

GLOUCESTER

When shall I come to the top of that same hill?

29 *I do advise you take this note* I recommend that you take note of what I am about to say

30 *talked* (here almost a technical term for the coming to agreement which preceded marriage)

31 *more convenient is he for my hand* it is more fitting that he should marry me. In normal parlance the lady's hand is *given* in marriage. Here, as elsewhere, Regan and Gonerill take the masculine role; their hands are not there to be given, but to seize on what they desire.

32 *You may gather more* I have left things unsaid, which you can well guess at

33 *give him this.* Some commentators assume that she gives a love-token rather than a letter. Certainly only one letter is clearly mentioned when Oswald dies – that from Gonerill; but it may be implied that he was carrying more than one (see the note on IV.6.248); one given by Regan at this point is not ruled out.

40 *What party I do follow.* Like a good politician Oswald seizes on the opportunity to conclude by expressing the solidarity of Gonerill and Regan.

IV.6 The expected reconciliation of Lear and Cordelia is postponed to allow the

EDGAR
You do climb up it now. Look how we labour.

GLOUCESTER
Methinks the ground is even.

EDGAR   Horrible steep.
Hark, do you hear the sea?

GLOUCESTER   No, truly.

EDGAR
Why then your other senses grow imperfect
By your eyes' anguish.

GLOUCESTER   So may it be indeed.
Methinks thy voice is altered, and thou speak'st
In better phrase and matter than thou didst.

EDGAR
Y'are much deceived. In nothing am I changed
10   But in my garments.

GLOUCESTER   Methinks y'are better spoken.

EDGAR
Come on, sir; here's the place. Stand still! How fearful

stories of the blind Gloucester and the
mad Lear to cross and reach a common
climax. This stupendous scene covers
three different actions: (1) Gloucester in
despair is brought to accept his lot by
the strange exercise of falling over an
imaginary Dover Cliff. This grotesque
and emblematic episode prepares us for
(2) the entry of Lear crowned with
flowers, now the master of a torrential
vein of mad moral eloquence. The
broken reverence of Gloucester, never
far from despair, and the free-wheeling
phantasmagoric energy of Lear point up
two opposite ways of reacting to oppression and impotence. But both are now
in the care of loving children. The 'capture' and cure of Lear belong to the next
scene; in the third part of this scene we
see Gloucester saved from the courtly
wickedness of Oswald by the cudgel of
Edgar (now *A most poor man*). The denouement of the Gloucester plot is prepared for by the time-honoured device
of an intercepted letter.

(stage direction) *in peasant's clothes*. This
    is added to show that the Old Man
    has kept the promise given at IV.1.49;
    Oswald below (line 231) calls Edgar
    a *peasant*.

1 *that same hill* the hill we talked about
    (Dover Cliff as described in IV.1.72–
    3)

7–8 *thou speak'st | In better phrase*. (Edgar
    now speaks in verse.)

11–24 *How fearful ... headlong*. Marshall
    McLuhan calls the Dover Cliff
    speech a 'Unique piece of three-

And dizzy 'tis to cast one's eyes so low!
The crows and choughs that wing the midway air
Show scarce so gross as beetles. Halfway down
Hangs one that gathers sampire – dreadful trade!
Methinks he seems no bigger than his head.
The fishermen that walk upon the beach
Appear like mice, and yon tall anchoring bark
Diminished to her cock; her cock, a buoy
Almost too small for sight. The murmuring surge   20
That on th'unnumbered idle pebble chafes
Cannot be heard so high. I'll look no more,
Lest my brain turn, and the deficient sight
Topple down headlong.

GLOUCESTER   Set me where you stand.

EDGAR
Give me your hand. You are now within a foot

dimensional verbal art ... What Shakespeare does here is to place five flat panels of two dimensions one behind the other. By giving these flat panels a diagonal twist they succeed each other, as it were, in a perspective from the "stand-still" point' (*The Gutenberg Galaxy* (1962), pages 16, 17). The set-piece description built up, layer by layer, by accumulation of small details is designed both to convey to the blind Gloucester the standards of measurement he should apply to the precipice and to convey to the audience the powerful and coherent nature of poetic illusion, by which Gloucester's 'cure' is to be effected.

13 *choughs* (pronounced 'chuffs'; members of the crow family)

15 *sampire* samphire (or 'Saint Pierre'; a maritime rock-herb, used in pickling,

and gathered on cliffs for this purpose)

18 *yon*. Here and at lines 118 and 152, F changed Q's 'yon' to 'yond'. This is a recurrent Folio mannerism, spread across several plays, and seems to reflect its modernizing tendencies (see the Account of the Text, page 566) rather than its concern for accuracy.

yon tall anchoring bark that sailing vessel there at anchor

19 *Diminished to her cock* looking as small as her cock-boat or dinghy

her cock, a buoy her cock-boat looks as small as a buoy

21 *th'unnumbered idle pebble* the innumerable loosely shifting pebbles. *Pebble* is the old collective plural.

23–4 *Lest my brain turn, and the deficient sight | Topple down* lest I lose my mental (and physical) balance, so that

Of th'extreme verge. For all beneath the moon
Would I not leap upright.

GLOUCESTER   Let go my hand.
Here, friend, 's another purse; in it a jewel
Well worth a poor man's taking. Fairies and gods
30   Prosper it with thee! Go thou further off.
Bid me farewell; and let me hear thee going.

EDGAR
Now fare ye well, good sir.

GLOUCESTER   With all my heart.

EDGAR (*aside*)
Why I do trifle thus with his despair
Is done to cure it.

GLOUCESTER (*kneeling*) O you mighty gods!
This world I do renounce, and in your sights
Shake patiently my great affliction off.
If I could bear it longer and not fall
To quarrel with your great opposeless wills,
My snuff and loathèd part of nature should
40   Burn itself out. If Edgar live, O bless him!
Now, fellow, fare thee well.

EDGAR   Gone, sir. Farewell.
            Gloucester throws himself forward
And yet I know not how conceit may rob

the eyes which have failed me fall
down with the rest of me
27 *Would I not leap upright* if I were as
close to the edge as you are I would
not dare even to jerk myself into an
upright position (or 'dare to jump
up vertically, so as to land on the
same spot')
28 *another purse* (in addition to the one
given at IV.1.63)
30 *Prosper it with thee* make it multiply
when in your possession
32 *With all my heart* I endorse heartily
what you have said; I am going to

fare well where I am going (to my
death)
36 *Shake patiently my great affliction off*
end my painful life, but not in passionate despair
38 *opposeless* that permit no opposition
39 *My snuff and loathèd part of nature* the
mere blackened wick of my senility,
with its offensive smell – all that
is left of the candle of my natural
life
41 *Gone* I have gone (as he was instructed
in line 30)
42–4 *I know not . . . to the theft* I think

The treasury of life, when life itself
Yields to the theft. Had he been where he thought,
By this had thought been past. – Alive or dead?
Ho, you, sir! Friend! Hear you, sir? Speak! –
Thus might he pass indeed. Yet he revives –
What are you, sir?

GLOUCESTER   Away, and let me die.

EDGAR

Hadst thou been aught but gossamer, feathers, air,
So many fathom down precipitating,   50
Thou'dst shivered like an egg; but thou dost breathe,
Hast heavy substance, bleed'st not, speak'st, art sound.
Ten masts at each make not the altitude
Which thou hast perpendicularly fell.
Thy life's a miracle. Speak yet again.

GLOUCESTER But have I fallen or no?

EDGAR

From the dread summit of this chalky bourn.
Look up a-height. The shrill-gorged lark so far
Cannot be seen or heard. Do but look up.

GLOUCESTER Alack, I have no eyes.   60
Is wretchedness deprived that benefit
To end itself by death? 'Twas yet some comfort
When misery could beguile the tyrant's rage
And frustrate his proud will.

EDGAR   Give me your arm.

that imagination may cause death when life gives itself up willingly
44 *Where he thought* (at the foot of the cliff)
47 *pass indeed* pass away, die, in reality
49 *gossamer*. The Q and F spellings – 'gosmore', 'Gozemore' – indicate the expected two-syllable pronunciation.
52 *Hast heavy substance* are made of flesh, are not a ghost
53 *at each* one on top of the other
57 *chalky bourn* chalk boundary (of England: Dover Cliff)
58 *The shrill-gorged lark* even the lark with its shrill, penetrating voice
63 *beguile* trick
beguile the tyrant's rage. Gloucester is thinking not of his own particular case, but of the traditional defence of suicide as it appeared among the Romans, and especially the

Up – so. How is't? Feel you your legs? You stand.

GLOUCESTER

Too well, too well.

EDGAR   This is above all strangeness.
Upon the crown o'the cliff what thing was that
Which parted from you?

GLOUCESTER   A poor unfortunate beggar.

EDGAR

As I stood here below methought his eyes
70   Were two full moons; he had a thousand noses,
Horns welked and waved like the enridgèd sea.
It was some fiend. Therefore, thou happy father,
Think that the clearest gods, who make them honours
Of men's impossibilities, have preserved thee.

GLOUCESTER

I do remember now. Henceforth I'll bear
Affliction till it do cry out itself
'Enough, enough', and die. That thing you speak of,
I took it for a man; often 'twould say
'The fiend, the fiend'; he led me to that place.

EDGAR

80   Bear free and patient thoughts.

Enter Lear fantastically dressed with wild flowers
But who comes here?

Roman Stoics under the tyranny
of such emperors as Nero or
Domitian.
65 *Feel you your legs?* have you any feeling
in your legs?
71 *welked and waved like the enridgèd sea*
twisted and ridged like the waves of
the sea. F's 'enraged' is an obvious
vulgarization.
72 *happy father* fortunate old man. Here,
as in lines 255 and 285, the true
relationship is expressed by Edgar in
a context which muffles its specific
meaning.
73 *the clearest gods* the spotless and most
pure gods

73–4 *make them honours | Of men's imposs-
ibilities* do things that are impossible
for men to do, and so make themselves to be honoured by men
75 *remember.* Perhaps he remembers the
fiend-like behaviour of the Bedlam-
ite; perhaps he remembers the morality of endurance proper to a religious
man.
76–7 *till it do cry out itself | 'Enough,
enough', and die* till affliction itself tire
of afflicting me and give up (as I
have been tempted to do)
80 *free* unburdened by guilt or self-
reproach. Typically, the moral poise
that Edgar achieves here is immedi-

The safer sense will ne'er accommodate
His master thus.

LEAR No, they cannot touch me for coining. I am the
King himself.

EDGAR O thou side-piercing sight!

LEAR Nature's above art in that respect. There's your
press-money. – That fellow handles his bow like a crow-
keeper. – Draw me a clothier's yard. – Look, look, a
mouse! – Peace, peace! this piece of toasted cheese will
do't. – There's my gauntlet; I'll prove it on a giant. –   90
Bring up the brown bills. – O, well flown, bird! I'the
clout, i'the clout! Hewgh! – Give the word.

ately subverted by the entry of
Lear.

81-2 *The safer sense will ne'er accommodate
| His master thus.* This is usually said
to refer to Lear's mad clothes
('Nobody sane would go around like
that'). I take Edgar to be saying:
'Sights like this cannot be accommodated inside a sane view of the
world', *His master* referring not to
Lear, but to the possessor of such a
safer sense ('saner view').

83-92 *they cannot touch . . . Give the word.*
Lear's madness expresses itself in a
string of commands and observations, entirely disjointed in content,
but linked by modulations of imagery. Thus *touch* – (1) arrest; (2) test
gold – leads to *coining*, which leads to
press-money; the idea of recruiting soldiers with *press-money* leads to images
of archery, of challenges, of *brown
bills* (halberdiers) and passwords – a
tissue of ideas interrupted only by
the *mouse* and the *toasted cheese.*

83 *they cannot touch me for coining.* Coining
lay within the royal prerogative.

85 *side-piercing* heart-rending (but with a
reminiscence of Christ on the Cross
(John 19.34))

86 *Nature's above art in that respect* (perhaps 'It is better to be the king who
creates the coinage than the image of
the king that the coin bears', for
only the latter can be counterfeited)

87 *press-money* (the sum paid to a recruit
when he was 'impressed', seized for
the army)

87-8 *a crow-keeper* (a farmer's boy, not a
military expert)

88 *Draw . . . a clothier's yard* extend the
bow for the full length of an arrow
(a cloth-yard long)

90 *do't* (catch the mouse)
*There's my gauntlet; I'll prove it on a
giant.* Lear throws down his 'gauntlet'
and challenges anyone (be he a giant)
to dispute his verdict.

91-2 *O, well flown, bird! I'the clout.* The
bird may be a falcon, or may refer to
the arrow which hits the *clout* (the
target).

92 *Hewgh!* (the noise made by the
arrow)
Give the word. For the first time in the
scene, Lear shows an awareness of
other people beside him; and his immediate impulse is to challenge them,
demand the password that distinguishes friend from foe.

EDGAR Sweet marjoram.

LEAR Pass.

GLOUCESTER I know that voice.

He falls to his knees

LEAR Ha! Gonerill with a white beard! They flattered me
like a dog and told me I had the white hairs in my beard
ere the black ones were there. To say 'ay' and 'no' to
everything that I said! 'Ay' and 'no' too was no good
100 divinity. When the rain came to wet me once and the
wind to make me chatter; when the thunder would not
peace at my bidding; there I found 'em, there I smelt
'em out. Go to, they are not men o'their words. They
told me I was everything. 'Tis a lie: I am not ague-
proof.

GLOUCESTER
The trick of that voice I do well remember.

93 *Sweet marjoram* (an appropriate pass-word, since the herb was used for diseases of the brain)

96 *Gonerill with a white beard.* It seems as if something in Gloucester's action or tone of voice suggests flattery. I have suggested that Gloucester, when he recognizes the King's voice, falls to his knees like a loyal servant. Lear's mind immediately harks back to Gonerill as archetype of flatterers – and *this* Gonerill has a white beard.

96–7 *They flattered me like a dog.* As always, Shakespeare sees the dog species as characterized by false fawning on its master.

97–8 *told me I had the white hairs in my beard ere the black ones were there.* Since this refers to flattery, the *white hairs* must be those of wisdom rather than age. The *I* must be emphasized, for he is reminded of all this by the sight of Gloucester's beard.

98–9 *To say 'ay' and 'no' to everything that I said* agreeing (or pretending to agree) with everything I said

99–100 *'Ay' and 'no' too was no good divinity.* Several passages in the New Testament might seem to supply the *divinity* that the flatterers erred against. Matthew 5.37 – 'But your communication shall be yea, yea; nay, nay. For whatsoever is added more than these, it cometh of evil' – is possible as a source; the actual injunction is against the oaths that may be added to 'yea, yea' or 'nay, nay', but it is preceded by 'Neither shalt thou swear by thy head, because thou canst not make one hair white or black', which might seem to have suggested lines 96–8 here. In 2 Corinthians 1.17–20 Paul defends himself against a charge of lightness by asserting that 'our preaching to you was not yea and nay' (was not ambiguous).

102–3 *there I found 'em, there I smelt 'em out* in these matters I was able to see through their lies and discover them for the flatterers they were

106 *trick* individual peculiarity

Is't not the King?

LEAR   Ay, every inch a king.
When I do stare see how the subject quakes.
I pardon that man's life. What was thy cause?
Adultery?   110
Thou shalt not die. Die for adultery? No.
The wren goes to't, and the small gilded fly
Does lecher in my sight.
Let copulation thrive; for Gloucester's bastard son
Was kinder to his father than my daughters
Got 'tween the lawful sheets.
To't, luxury, pell-mell, for I lack soldiers.
Behold yon simpering dame
Whose face between her forks presages snow,
That minces virtue and does shake the head   120
To hear of pleasure's name –
The fitchew nor the soilèd horse goes to't

---

107 *Is't not the King?* Nevill Coghill (*Shakespeare's Professional Skills* (1964), pages 25–6) says 'the act of homage that brings Gloucester to his knees, a loyal subject, leaves him there a seeming culprit, for that is how Lear interprets the ambiguity in kneeling; and now Gloucester's guilt is to be thrust home'.

109 *thy cause* your case; the charge against you

110 *Adultery.* The key distinction here and throughout the speech is between 'natural' or illegal sexuality, which gradually moves from *Adultery, lecher, copulation*, to the more violent representation of *luxury, pell-mell, riotous appetite*, and (on the other hand) the legal proprieties embodied in the *King*, the *lawful sheets*, the *women all above*. The process of the speech mimics the collapse of these legal safeguards into the horror of animal sexuality.

115 *kinder* (with the usual sense – 'more naturally childlike')

117 *luxury* lechery
pell-mell (as if in headlong, indiscriminate, and confused battle)
for I lack soldiers. Indiscriminate lechery is promoted by the King, for surplus population swells his army.

118 *yon.* See the note on line 18.

119 *Whose face between her forks presages snow.* Her *forks* are her legs. Her face *presages* or indicates that the other face *between her forks* is frigid or chaste.

120 *minces virtue* affects virtue by a show of squeamishness

120–21 *does shake the head | To hear of pleasure's name* shakes her head in disapproval at the very name of pleasure

122 *fitchew* polecat or weasel. 'Polecat' was a cant term for a prostitute.
soilèd full-fed with fresh grass (and

With a more riotous appetite.
Down from the waist they are centaurs,
Though women all above;
But to the girdle do the gods inherit,
Beneath is all the fiends' –
There's hell, there's darkness, there is the sulphurous
pit – burning, scalding, stench, consumption! Fie, fie,
fie! Pah, pah! Give me an ounce of civet; good apothe-
cary, sweeten my imagination. There's money for
thee.

He gives flowers

GLOUCESTER O, let me kiss that hand!

LEAR Let me wipe it first; it smells of mortality.

GLOUCESTER

O ruined piece of nature! This great world
Shall so wear out to naught. Dost thou know me?

LEAR I remember thine eyes well enough. Dost thou
squiny at me? No, do thy worst, blind Cupid; I'll not

therefore bursting with sexual
enthusiasm)

124 *Down from the waist they are centaurs.*
He means that, like centaurs, they
are bestial like horses (*soilèd horses*, as
above) below the waist. Centaurs
were from early times used as images
of man's lustful animal impulses.

126 *girdle* waist
inherit possess, hold power over

128–9 *hell . . . darkness . . . the sulphurous
pit – burning, scalding, stench, consumption.* The obvious sexual references
point to a climax of hysterical disgust
at female sexuality. At the same time
the fairly free verse form of the preceding lines breaks down into prose.

129 *consumption* destruction (especially
by fire)

130–31 *Give me an ounce of civet; good apothecary, sweeten my imagination.* The
imagination that has just conjured

up *stench* and *consumption* needs a perfume to sweeten its atmosphere. For
the purpose Lear will buy civet from
Gloucester, now imagined to be an
apothecary.

135 *piece of nature.* Probably *piece* has the
sense of 'masterpiece'; but the following phrase suggests a contrast between this *ruined piece* (portion) and
the *great world* or macrocosm also in
the process of being ruined.

137 *I remember thine eyes.* In Lear's un-
sweetened imagination the horror of
Gloucester's eyeless sockets provides
an image of the world he recognizes,
though he may not be able to recognize unmutilated forms.

138 *squiny* squint through half-shut eyes
blind Cupid. Cupid's traditional blindness and romantic associations give a
horrid appropriateness to the use of
his name for Edmund's progenitor.

love. Read thou this challenge; mark but the penning
of it.   140

GLOUCESTER

Were all thy letters suns, I could not see.

EDGAR *(aside)*

I would not take this from report. It is;

And my heart breaks at it.

LEAR Read.

GLOUCESTER What, with the case of eyes?

LEAR O, ho, are you there with me? No eyes in your head,
nor no money in your purse? Your eyes are in a heavy
case, your purse in a light; yet you see how this world
goes.

GLOUCESTER I see it feelingly.   150

LEAR What, art mad? A man may see how this world goes
with no eyes. Look with thine ears. See how yon justice
rails upon yon simple thief. Hark in thine ear – change
places and, handy-dandy, which is the justice, which is
the thief? Thou hast seen a farmer's dog bark at a
beggar?

GLOUCESTER Ay, sir.

---

139 *challenge.* Lear seems to revert to the
obsession of line 90.

142 *take this* accept this scene as real.
(The speech is an oblique Shakespearian defence of the non-realism of
what is before us.)

145 *the case of eyes* the sockets where the
eyes used to be

146 *are you there with me?* is that the
point you are making?

147-8 *in a heavy case* in a sad way (with a
pun on *case* meaning 'socket')

150 *I see it feelingly* (1) I recognize it with
keen feelings; (2) having no eyes, I
can only 'see' it by the feel of it

151 *What, art mad?* Lear takes Gloucester's *see it feelingly* in the sense of
'know it only imperfectly because I
know it only by feel'; and says 'You

must be mad to require eyes to know
the way of the world; all the senses
convey the same message, the same
image of the world as a place of
merely superficial social distinctions,
with no moral basis'.

152 *yon.* See the note on line 18.

153 *simple* of humble condition

153-5 *Hark in thine ear – change places
and, handy-dandy* . . . a whisper to the
justice of the peace bribes him to
reverse his decision. Then he is as
like the thief as one hand is like
another. Lear puts his hands behind
his back and pretends to shift an
object from one to the other. This is
the guessing-game of *handy-dandy*:
which hand holds the object? Here
the object is social status, and it is

the creature run from the cur? There thou
mightst behold the great image of authority: a dog's
160   obeyed in office.
Thou rascal beadle, hold thy bloody hand.
Why dost thou lash that whore? Strip thy own back.
Thou hotly lusts to use her in that kind
For which thou whipp'st her. The usurer hangs the
    cozener.
Thorough tattered clothes great vices do appear;
Robes and furred gowns hide all. Plate sins with gold,
And the strong lance of justice hurtless breaks;

mere luck to guess which thief is called to the dock and which to the bench.

    William R. Elton, in *King Lear and the Gods* (1966), page 86, note 24, quotes Thomas Powell's *The Attorney's Academy* (1623), page 217: '. . . and play at handy-dandy, which is the guardian, or which is the fool'.

158 *creature* man in his lowest state and therefore nearest to the animal. 'Creature' was often used of the animal in contradistinction to the human state. An ironic awareness of this may be intended.

159–60 *a dog's obeyed in office* (obedience is given not to intrinsic worth but to the accident of status)

161 *beadle* parish constable (charged with the duty of whipping offenders)
bloody (from the lashing)

164 *The usurer hangs the cozener* the big cheat is given the sanction of society and condemns the little cheat. In this period usurers or capitalists were acquiring respectability and were being appointed to offices such as that of magistrate, against the protests of preachers and poets.

165 *Thorough* (an alternative form of 'through')

great vices do appear. The Q reading, 'smal vices do appeare', makes perfect, if fairly trite, sense. But F corrected it to 'great Vices do appeare', for no reason that is discernible, unless the corrector found it in his 'copy'. We must either accept *great* or explain it away. The F reading can be defended in terms of sense as well as of text: it is not the smallness of their vices that distinguishes the poor, but the exposure to which they are subject. It must be allowed, however, that the antithesis is somewhat muffled by *great*. If the corrector's 'great', written in the margin, was inserted by the compositor of F in the wrong place, we might suppose that 'do great appear' was the original reading; the rhythmical emphasis in the line would then, however, seem to be in the wrong place.

166 *Robes and furred gowns* (the robes of the judges, and perhaps also of the usurers, as in *Measure for Measure*, III.2.7)
Plate arm in plate mail

167 *And the strong lance of justice hurtless breaks*. Notice the sense of effort conveyed by the sound of this line.
hurtless without hurting

Arm it in rags, a pygmy's straw does pierce it.
None does offend, none, I say none; I'll able 'em.
Take that of me, my friend, (*giving flowers*) who have   170
    the power
To seal th'accusers' lips. Get thee glass eyes,
And like a scurvy politician seem
To see the things thou dost not. Now, now, now, now!
Pull off my boots. Harder, harder – so.

EDGAR

O matter and impertinency mixed,
Reason in madness!

LEAR

If thou wilt weep my fortunes, take my eyes.
I know thee well enough; thy name is Gloucester.
Thou must be patient; we came crying hither.

---

168 *a pygmy's straw* (a weak weapon, opposite to a strong *lance* (compare *Othello*, v.2.268–9: 'Man but a rush against Othello's breast, | And he retires'). The frogs in the pseudo-Homeric *Battle of the Frogs and Mice* carried rushes for spears. The parallel mock-battle of the cranes and pygmies was also well known in Shakespeare's age, but had not been described in so much detail.)

169 *able* fortify, give power and capacity to

170 *Take that of me.* What we think the exact sense of *that* is depends on whether we suppose that Lear is more obsessed with kingship or with corruption at this point. If he is concerned with his kingship, what he gives Gloucester to *able* him will be some document of the royal prerogative. If corruption is uppermost in his mind (as I suppose) what he gives is 'money', and what *seals th'accusers' lips* is (as in lines 153–5) a bribe. In either case his flowers would seem the only things he can give.

171–3 *Get thee glass eyes . . . thou dost not.* Lear returns, at the end of his speech, to the subject with which he started it – Gloucester's failure to 'see' without eyes. You should be, he says, like a *politician*, one of those vile persons concerned to control affairs through 'policy' or trickery, who have the art of seeming to see what they cannot actually see (discovering, for example, imaginary plots so as to justify repression). You should be like them and conceal your blindness behind glass eyes.

171 *glass eyes* spectacles

173–4 *Now, now, now, now! | Pull off my boots. Harder, harder – so.* Exhausted by his speech, Lear sinks down and gives the command that might accompany such a feeling in ordinary life – on returning from hunting or a journey, for example. The *so* implies satisfaction when the job is done.

175 *matter and impertinency* relevant substance and irrelevancy

180   Thou knowest the first time that we smell the air
      We wawl and cry. I will preach to thee – Mark!

         He takes off his coronet of flowers

GLOUCESTER Alack, alack the day!

LEAR

      When we are born we cry that we are come
      To this great stage of fools. – This's a good block.
      It were a delicate stratagem to shoe
      A troop of horse with felt. I'll put't in proof;
      And when I have stolen upon these son-in-laws,
      Then kill, kill, kill, kill, kill, kill!

         He throws down his flowers and stamps on them
         Enter a Gentleman and two attendants.
         Gloucester and Edgar draw back

GENTLEMAN

      O, here he is. Lay hand upon him. – Sir,
190   Your most dear daughter –

LEAR

      No rescue? What, a prisoner? I am even
      The natural fool of fortune. Use me well;
      You shall have ransom. Let me have surgeons;
      I am cut to the brains.

GENTLEMAN   You shall have anything.

181 *wawl* cry out
184 *This's a good block.* It seems possible to detect a series of actions here. In accordance with good Anglican practice he takes off his 'hat' (his crown of flowers, I suppose) when he begins to 'preach' (line 181). His sermon has not, however, got beyond a line and a half when his attention is diverted to the hat he notices he is holding in his hand. *This's a good block*, he says: 'This is a well-made hat'.
185 *delicate stratagem* cunning trick
185–6 *to shoe | A troop of horse with felt.*

The idea of the *felt* no doubt comes from the hat-block mentioned before. The horsemen so shod could steal up on Albany and Cornwall (seen as responsible for their wives' crimes) and kill them.
186 *put't in proof* put it to the test
192 *The natural fool of fortune* born to be the plaything of fortune (just recently leading a charge against the sons-in-law, and now a prisoner)
194 *cut to the brains.* Notice how the expression combines both physical and mental wounding.

LEAR

No seconds? All myself?

Why, this would make a man a man of salt,

To use his eyes for garden water-pots,

Ay, and laying autumn's dust. I will die bravely,

Like a smug bridegroom. What! I will be jovial.

Come, come, I am a king; masters, know you that?   200

GENTLEMAN

You are a royal one, and we obey you.

LEAR Then there's life in't. Come, and you get it you shall get it by running. Sa, sa, sa, sa.

Exit running, followed by attendants

GENTLEMAN

A sight most pitiful in the meanest wretch,

Past speaking of in a king. – Thou hast one daughter

Who redeems nature from the general curse

Which twain have brought her to.

---

195 *seconds* supporters

196 *a man of salt* a man of tears

197–8 *To use . . . I will die.* The text is difficult to determine at this point. Q reads as here, except that after *dust* there is a new line and a new speech prefix: '*Lear.* I will . . .'. This suggests that something is missing, and the second Quarto (1619) supplies it: '*Gent.* Good Sir.' This is tempting, but there is no evidence that Q2's corrections of Q1 are the result of anything more than the compositor's ingenuity. F omits everything between *water-pots* and *I will die*, no doubt because the compositor's eye moved from 'I [Ay] and laying' to the 'I' in the same line.

198–9 *I will die bravely, | Like a smug bridegroom. Bravely* means not only 'with courage' but also 'in my fine attire' (flowers and all). It is this latter sense that leads to the image of the *smug* (neat, spruce) bridegroom.

202 *there's life in't* there's still a chance; at least I can make you run for your captive. Hearing them say that they obey him, he realizes that the captivity is not as absolute as he had supposed.

and if

203 *Sa, sa, sa, sa* (a cry of encouragement to the hounds in hunting)

206–7 *the general curse | Which twain have brought her to.* On the most factual level the *twain* are Gonerill and Regan, and the *general curse* brought about in nature is the current state of Britain, with brother against brother etc. (1.2.106–11). Behind this is the larger idea of the fallen condition of mankind caused by Adam and Eve (*twain*). On this level Cordelia is a Christ-like redeeming figure.

EDGAR (*coming forward*)
Hail, gentle sir.

GENTLEMAN   Sir, speed you; what's your will?

EDGAR
Do you hear aught, sir, of a battle toward?

GENTLEMAN
210   Most sure and vulgar. Everyone hears that
Which can distinguish sound.

EDGAR   But, by your favour,
How near's the other army?

GENTLEMAN
Near, and on speedy foot. The main descry
Stands on the hourly thought.

EDGAR   I thank you, sir; that's all.

GENTLEMAN
Though that the Queen on special cause is here,
Her army is moved on.

EDGAR   I thank you, sir.

Exit Gentleman

GLOUCESTER (*coming forward*)
You ever-gentle gods, take my breath from me.
Let not my worser spirit tempt me again
To die before you please.

EDGAR   Well pray you, father.

220   GLOUCESTER Now, good sir, what are you?

EDGAR
A most poor man made tame to fortune's blows,
Who, by the art of known and feeling sorrows,

---

208 *gentle* honourable
    speed you God speed you, God prosper
    you
210 *sure and vulgar* it's certain and every-
    body knows about it
210–11 *Everyone . . . Which can distinguish
    sound* everyone who has ears to hear
213 *on speedy foot* on foot, and advancing
    rapidly
213–14 *The main descry | Stands on the*

hourly thought a sighting of the main
    force of their army is expected from
    hour to hour
218 *my worser spirit* (usually taken to be
    'my evil angel'; but it may mean no
    more than 'my ill thoughts')
219 *Well pray you* that's a good thing to
    be praying for
221 *tame to* submissive, resigned to
222 *by the art of known and feeling sorrows*

Am pregnant to good pity. Give me your hand,
I'll lead you to some biding.

GLOUCESTER   Hearty thanks;
The bounty and the benison of heaven
To boot, and boot!

  Enter Oswald

OSWALD   A proclaimed prize! Most happy!
That eyeless head of thine was first framed flesh
To raise my fortunes. Thou old unhappy traitor,
Briefly thyself remember; the sword is out
That must destroy thee.

GLOUCESTER   Now let thy friendly hand 230
Put strength enough to't.

  Edgar intervenes

OSWALD   Wherefore, bold peasant,
Darest thou support a published traitor? Hence,
Lest that th'infection of his fortune take
Like hold on thee. Let go his arm!

EDGAR
'Chill not let go, zir, without vurther 'cagion.

---

as the result of the workings of sorrows that I have both felt in myself and known in others

223 *pregnant to* disposed to feel

224 *biding* place to stay

226 *To boot, and boot!* (probably means 'in addition', and may you make *boot* (profit) out of it')

proclaimed prize outlaw proclaimed as having a price on his head

Most happy! how lucky I am! The self-centred insensitivity of Oswald makes an effective contrast, set against the mutual support of the other characters in the scene.

229 *Briefly thyself remember* say your last prayer, and make it short

230 *friendly* (friendly to him, since he desires death more than anything else)

231 *bold peasant*. Oswald's words here,

as well as the general affectation of his language, give Edgar the idea of the vocabulary and the identity he can assume to answer him.

232 *published* proclaimed

233–4 *th'infection of his fortune take | Like hold on thee* his outlawry attach itself to you as well (for helping him)

235–40 *'Chill . . . 'choud . . . I'ce.* Edgar falls into the stage rustic (South-Western) of the time, in which 'I' is represented by 'Che' or 'Ich', so that 'I will' becomes *'Chill*; 'I should' becomes *'choud*; and 'I shall' becomes *I'ce*.

235 *vurther 'cagion* further occasion (in the sense of 'better cause'). *'Cagion* is stage rustic for 'occasion'; the F spelling 'casion' has some advantage for the mere reader, but the Q form may

OSWALD Let go, slave, or thou diest!

EDGAR Good gentleman, go your gate and let poor volk
pass. And 'choud ha' bin zwaggered out of my life,
'twould not ha' bin zo long as 'tis by a vortnight. Nay,
240   come not near th'old man; keep out, che vor' ye, or I'ce
try whether your costard or my ballow be the harder.
'Chill be plain with you.

OSWALD Out, dunghill!

EDGAR 'Chill pick your teeth, zir. Come; no matter vor
your foins.

They fight

OSWALD
Slave, thou hast slain me. Villain, take my purse.
If ever thou wilt thrive, bury my body
And give the letters which thou find'st about me
To Edmund, Earl of Gloucester. Seek him out
250   Upon the English party. O, untimely
Death! – Death –   *He dies*

EDGAR
I know thee well: a serviceable villain,
As duteous to the vices of thy mistress

---

well preserve the noise made on
Shakespeare's stage.

237 *go your gate* go your way

238 *And 'choud ha' bin zwaggered out of my
life* if fancy talk had been capable of
killing me

240 *che vor' ye* I warrant you

241 *costard* (literally, 'apple') head
ballow cudgel. The uncorrected form
in Q is 'battero', which the corrector,
obviously relying on native sense
rather than authority, changed to
'bat'. F reads 'Ballow', from which
word the uncorrected Q form must
derive. 'Ballow' is not common, but
J. Wright in his *English Dialect Dictionary* (6 volumes, 1898–1905) seems
to have found some examples.

244 *'Chill pick your teeth.* This suggests

that Edgar has now a sword or
dagger in his possession. If so he
must have acquired it from Oswald
– who has still a rapier with which
he makes *foins*. Perhaps in a first
bout (at line 242) Edgar has his
ballow, Oswald his sword and
dagger; Edgar beats down Oswald's
dagger and seizes it.

245 *foins* rapier thrusts (in the new Con-
tinental style)

248, 256 *letters.* Two letters may be
meant: (1) the one from Gonerill
read out below; (2) one from Regan,
perhaps given at IV.5.33 (see the
note). However, only one letter is
mentioned below; and 'letters' can
be used in the plural with only singular meaning.

As badness would desire.

GLOUCESTER   What, is he dead?

EDGAR

Sit you down, father; rest you. –
Let's see these pockets. The letters that he speaks of
May be my friends. He's dead. I am only sorry
He had no other deathsman. Let us see.
Leave, gentle wax; and manners blame us not;
To know our enemies' minds we rip their hearts;   260
Their papers is more lawful.

          (*He reads the letter*)
Let our reciprocal vows be remembered. You have many
opportunities to cut him off; if your will want not, time and
place will be fruitfully offered. There is nothing done if he
return the conqueror. Then am I the prisoner, and his bed
my gaol; from the loathed warmth whereof deliver me and
supply the place for your labour.

          Your – wife, so I would say – affectionate servant,

                                                  Gonerill.

O indistinguished space of woman's will!   270
A plot upon her virtuous husband's life,
And the exchange, my brother! Here in the sands
Thee I'll rake up, the post unsanctified

258 *deathsman* executioner
259 *Leave* grant us your leave
261 *Their papers* to rip their papers
263 *want* lack
264 *fruitfully offered* organized (by Gonerill) so that there will be results
There is nothing done. The victory will be meaningless.
267 *for your labour* (1) as a recompense for your labour; (2) as a place for your (amorous) labours
268 *servant.* This is usually glossed as 'lover', but it may be nothing more than conventional politeness. The strange addition of Q, 'and for you her owne for *Venter*', has not been

explained, and seems best left out of the text.
270 *indistinguished space of woman's will!* how far beyond apprehension is the range of woman's lust!
272–3 *Here in the sands | Thee I'll rake up.* It is not clear how this shallow burial of Oswald was accomplished on Shakespeare's stage. Presumably Edgar had to drag the body out of sight, either now (line 277) or at the end of the scene.
273 *unsanctified* (a curious way of saying 'wicked', suggested presumably by the thought that the sands in which he is proposing to bury Oswald –

Of murderous lechers; and in the mature time
With this ungracious paper strike the sight
Of the death-practised Duke. For him 'tis well
That of thy death and business I can tell.

GLOUCESTER

The King is mad; how stiff is my vile sense,
That I stand up and have ingenious feeling
280   Of my huge sorrows! Better I were distract;
So should my thoughts be severed from my griefs,
And woes by wrong imaginations lose
The knowledge of themselves.
      Drum afar off

EDGAR   Give me your hand.
Far off methinks I hear the beaten drum.
Come, father, I'll bestow you with a friend.   *Exeunt*

IV.7   *Enter Cordelia, Kent, and Doctor*

CORDELIA

O thou good Kent, how shall I live and work
To match thy goodness? My life will be too short
And every measure fail me.

unsanctified ground – are appropriate to the character of the man
buried)
274 *in the mature time* when the time is
ripe
275 *ungracious paper* wicked letter
276 *the death-practised Duke* (Albany,
whose death is being *practised* or
plotted)
278 *how stiff is my vile sense* how unrespon-
sive and unpliant my feelings are, *vile*
(basely physical) in this very incapa-
city to give way before *huge sorrows*
vile. See the note on III.2.71.
279 *ingenious* fully conscious
282–3 *woes by wrong imaginations lose | The
knowledge of themselves* woes would

cease to know their own pain by
entering into the illusions of the
insane

IV.7 The reunion of Cordelia and Kent
prepares the way for the reunion of Cordelia and Lear. The sense of awaking out
of a nightmare of cruelty into a world of
natural kindness makes this scene an
island of paradisal calm in a maelstrom
of horror.
3 *every measure fail me* no matter how
much I try to do, I will not be able
to do enough to recompense you.
Cordelia and Kent pick up the arithmetical ideas about desert which prevailed in I.1.

KENT

    To be acknowledged, madam, is o'er-paid.

    All my reports go with the modest truth,

    Nor more, nor clipped, but so.

CORDELIA   Be better suited.

    These weeds are memories of those worser hours.

    I prithee put them off.

KENT   Pardon, dear madam,

    Yet to be known shortens my made intent.

    My boon I make it that you know me not   10

    Till time and I think meet.

CORDELIA

    Then be't so, my good lord.

    (*To Doctor*)   How does the King?

DOCTOR Madam, sleeps still.

CORDELIA

    O you kind gods,

    Cure this great breach in his abusèd nature!

    Th'untuned and jarring senses O wind up

    Of this child-changèd father.

DOCTOR   So please your majesty,

    That we may wake the King. He hath slept long.

---

5 *All my reports go with the modest truth* let not what you say of me be excessive but merely report the truth

6 *Nor more, nor clipped, but so* neither exaggerated, nor cut short, but just as they happened. The word *clipped* picks up the coinage idea implicit in *paid* above (line 4).
suited clothed. Kent still wears the servant's livery he wore as Caius.

7 *weeds* clothes

9 *Yet to be known shortens my made intent* to reveal myself now would anticipate the plan I have made. It is not clear what Kent's *intent* could be – perhaps a last-minute climactic revelation. But it must be confessed that

this suits Shakespeare's interests more obviously than Kent's. It is a regular characteristic of Shakespeare's dramatic art that he delays the penetration of disguise till the final denouement.

10 *My boon I make it* the favour I beg is

16 *Th'untuned and jarring senses O wind up*. The slackened strings of his mind no longer yield sense or harmony (true relationships) but jar against one another. He needs the pegs screwed up and the harmony restored.

17 *child-changèd* (1) changed (to madness) by the cruelties of his children; (2) (less probably) changed into second childishness.

CORDELIA

Be governed by your knowledge and proceed
20   I'the sway of your own will. Is he arrayed?

DOCTOR

Ay, madam; in the heaviness of sleep
We put fresh garments on him.

> *Enter Gentleman ushering Lear in a chair carried by*
> *servants. All fall to their knees*

GENTLEMAN

Be by, good madam, when we do awake him;
I doubt not of his temperance.

CORDELIA   Very well.

> *Music sounds off stage*

DOCTOR

Please you draw near. – Louder the music there!

21, 23 DOCTOR ... GENTLEMAN.
These are the speech prefixes given
by Q. As F omits the Doctor from
this scene, it allots both speeches to
the Gentleman. All previous editors
transpose the speeches, giving the
first to the Gentleman and the second
to the Doctor. See the next note.

22 (stage direction) *Enter Gentleman.* F
has an entry for the Gentleman at
the beginning of the scene (substitut-
ing for the Doctor); Q has no entry
for him, but gives lines 23–4 as his
first speech. The addition of his entry
here restores Q's opening of the
scene and its distribution of speeches
at lines 21 and 23; and it explains
why, at line 91 below, the Gentleman
knows nothing of Kent's identity.
Enter ... Lear in a chair. This is the
F reading; Q has no entry for Lear.
In spite of some awkwardness there
can be little doubt that F is correct.
It restores Lear to his 'throne'; it
makes his falling to his knees a plausible action, which 'discovery' in a

bed (as indicated in many editions)
does not. The entry at this point
might seem too early; since Cordelia
is asked to *Be by* in the next line it
might be taken that her father is not
present. I suggest, however, that,
when Lear is carried on, Cordelia
falls to her knees, at that point of
the stage where she is standing. The
Gentleman says *Be by* and prepares
to wake him; Cordelia's *Very well* is
not, however, followed by any
immediate movement. The Doctor
repeats the request in a less indirect
form: *Please you draw near*, and only
now does Cordelia move forward
and kneel again by Lear's chair.

24 *temperance* calm behaviour
(stage diretion) Shakespeare and his
contemporaries often use music as
part of a process of mental healing,
or to represent dramatically the
magic power or healing force of
nature. Compare *Pericles*, III.2.93, *The
Tempest*, 1.2.392–4, and *Henry* VIII,
III.1.2–14.

CORDELIA (*kneeling by the chair and kissing his hand*)
>   O my dear father! Restoration hang
>   Thy medicine on my lips; and let this kiss
>   Repair those violent harms that my two sisters
>   Have in thy reverence made.

KENT   Kind and dear princess!

CORDELIA
>   Had you not been their father, these white flakes   30
>   Did challenge pity of them. Was this a face
>   To be opposed against the jarring winds?
>   To stand against the deep dread-bolted thunder,
>   In the most terrible and nimble stroke
>   Of quick cross lightning? To watch, poor perdu,
>   With this thin helm? Mine enemy's dog,
>   Though he had bit me, should have stood that night
>   Against my fire; and wast thou fain, poor father,
>   To hovel thee with swine and rogues forlorn
>   In short and musty straw? Alack, alack!   40
>   'Tis wonder that thy life and wits at once
>   Had not concluded all. – He wakes! Speak to him.

DOCTOR Madam, do you; 'tis fittest.

CORDELIA
>   How does my royal lord? How fares your majesty?

LEAR
>   You do me wrong to take me out o'the grave.

30 *white flakes* snow-white hair
31 *challenge* demand
33 *deep dread-bolted thunder* thunder with
   the thunderbolt that causes deep
   dread
35 *cross lightning* zigzag (fork) lightning
   perdu. A '*sentinelle perdue*' was an especially daring soldier who was
   placed (as a spy or a scout) so close
   to the enemy that he was considered
   virtually lost.
36 *this thin helm* (the thin hair of old
   age)
38 *fain* glad

39 *rogues forlorn* abandoned vagrants
40 *short and musty straw*. Long dry straw
   would make the best bed; short,
   broken-up straw, damp or mouldy,
   would not protect from the cold and
   wet.
42 *concluded all* come to an end
   altogether
   Speak to him. Cordelia's sense of
   shame and guilt, together with her
   temperament, so notably reticent in
   I.I, prompts her to retreat behind
   the Doctor.
45–8 *out o'the grave ... molten lead*. Lear

Thou art a soul in bliss; but I am bound
Upon a wheel of fire, that mine own tears
Do scald like molten lead.

CORDELIA   Sir, do you know me?

LEAR
You are a spirit, I know. Where did you die?

50   CORDELIA   Still, still far wide!

DOCTOR
He's scarce awake. Let him alone awhile.

LEAR
Where have I been? Where am I? Fair daylight?
I am mightily abused. I should even die with pity
To see another thus. I know not what to say.
I will not swear these are my hands. Let's see.
I feel this pin-prick. Would I were assured
Of my condition.

CORDELIA   O look upon me, sir,
And hold your hand in benediction o'er me.

        Lear falls to his knees
No, sir, you must not kneel.

LEAR   Pray do not mock me.

60   I am a very foolish fond old man,
Four score and upward, not an hour more nor less,
And, to deal plainly,
I fear I am not in my perfect mind.
Methinks I should know you, and know this man;
Yet I am doubtful; for I am mainly ignorant
What place this is; and all the skill I have

---

supposes that he is experiencing the
life after death (as in some sense he
is). He takes it that Cordelia is in
heaven and that he is in hell. The
wheel of fire was a common apocry-
phal appurtenance of the Christian
hell (as was *molten lead*). But these
images may have more force today
as expressions of the psychological

torments of guilt.
47 *that* so that
53 *abused* 'in a strange mist of uncer-
    tainty' (Dr Johnson)
54 *thus* (thus bewildered and lost)
60 *fond* silly
64 *this man* (Kent)
65 *mainly* very much

Remembers not these garments; nor I know not
Where I did lodge last night. Do not laugh at me,
For, as I am a man, I think this lady
To be my child Cordelia.

CORDELIA (*weeping*)   And so I am, I am.   70

LEAR

Be your tears wet? Yes, faith! I pray, weep not.
If you have poison for me I will drink it.
I know you do not love me, for your sisters
Have, as I do remember, done me wrong.
You have some cause; they have not.

CORDELIA   No cause, no cause.

LEAR

Am I in France?

KENT   In your own kingdom, sir.

LEAR Do not abuse me.

DOCTOR

Be comforted, good madam. The great rage,
You see, is killed in him; and yet it is danger
To make him even o'er the time he has lost.   80
Desire him to go in; trouble him no more
Till further settling.

CORDELIA   Will't please your highness walk?

LEAR You must bear with me. Pray you now, forget and
forgive. I am old and foolish.

Exeunt all but Kent and Gentleman

GENTLEMAN Holds it true, sir, that the Duke of Cornwall
was so slain?

KENT Most certain, sir.

---

71 *Be your tears wet?* (are your tears real,
   or am I still snared in illusion?)
76 *your own kingdom* the kingdom which
   is (still) yours
80 *even o'er the time* fill up the gap in
   time (by reliving the experience he
   has passed through)
82 *Till further settling* till he is better

settled in his mind
83 *You must bear with me.* Presumably he
   leans on her as he leaves, so that the
   verb has both a physical and a mental
   reference.
85 *Holds it true* does it continue to be
   accepted as true

GENTLEMAN Who is conductor of his people?

KENT As 'tis said, the bastard son of Gloucester.

90   GENTLEMAN They say Edgar, his banished son, is with
the Earl of Kent in Germany.

KENT Report is changeable. 'Tis time to look about. The
powers of the kingdom approach apace.

GENTLEMAN The arbitrament is like to be bloody. Fare
you well, sir.   *Exit*

KENT

My point and period will be throughly wrought,
Or well or ill, as this day's battle's fought.   *Exit*

V. I   *Enter, with drum and colours, Edmund, Regan,*
gentlemen, and soldiers

EDMUND (*to a gentleman*)

Know of the Duke if his last purpose hold
Or whether since he is advised by aught
To change the course. (*To Regan*) He's full of alteration
And self-reproving. (*To gentleman*) Bring his constant
pleasure.

Exit gentleman

92 *look about* be wary

92–3 *The powers of the kingdom* the British
forces (as against Cordelia's French
ones)

94 *arbitrament* deciding of the dispute

96–7 *My point and period will be throughly*
wrought, | Or well or ill the sentence
of my life and my purpose will be
brought to a fully worked-out conclusion or full stop, and it will be clear
whether it has been for good or for
ill

96 *throughly*. This, the Q reading – F

omits the passage – is a common
Elizabethan   alternative   for
'thoroughly'.

v.i The snare of jealous lust draws more
tightly around Regan, Gonerill, and
Edmund. Meantime the preparations for
the battle go ahead; but a further reckoning, beyond the battle, is prepared
for.

1 *his last purpose* (to fight with Regan
and Edmund against Cordelia)

4 *constant pleasure* settled resolution

REGAN

    Our sister's man is certainly miscarried.

EDMUND

    'Tis to be doubted, madam.

REGAN   Now, sweet lord,

    You know the goodness I intend upon you.

    Tell me but truly – but then speak the truth –

    Do you not love my sister?

EDMUND   In honoured love.

REGAN

    But have you never found my brother's way   10

    To the forfended place?

EDMUND   That thought abuses you.

REGAN

    I am doubtful that you have been conjunct

    And bosomed with her, as far as we call hers.

EDMUND No, by mine honour, madam.

REGAN

    I never shall endure her; dear my lord,

    Be not familiar with her.

EDMUND   Fear not.

    She and the Duke her husband!

        Enter, with drum and colours, Albany, Gonerill, and
        soldiers

GONERILL *(aside)*

    I had rather lose the battle than that sister

    Should loosen him and me.

---

5 *Our sister's man is certainly miscarried.* When Regan parted with Oswald (in IV.5) he was on his way to Edmund. She assumes that something has happened to him.

6 *doubted* feared

9 *In honoured love* in an honourable way. Edmund has become a (verbal) devotee to the idea of honour.

10–11 *found my brother's way | To the for-* *fended place* played her husband's role in that part of her body *forfended* ('forbidden') to you (by the commandment against adultery)

12–13 *conjunct | And bosomed with her, as far as we call hers* coupled and intimate with her, to the fullest extent

15 *I never shall endure her* (that is, if the two of you become too intimate)

16 *familiar* unduly intimate

ALBANY
20   Our very loving sister, well be-met.
Sir, this I heard; the King is come to his daughter,
With others whom the rigour of our state
Forced to cry out. Where I could not be honest,
I never yet was valiant. For this business,
It touches us as France invades our land,
Not bolds the King, with others – whom, I fear,
Most just and heavy causes make oppose.

EDMUND
Sir, you speak nobly.

REGAN   Why is this reasoned?

GONERILL
Combine together 'gainst the enemy.
30   For these domestic and particular broils
Are not the question here.

ALBANY   Let's then determine
With th'ancient of war on our proceeding.

EDMUND
I shall attend you presently at your tent.

REGAN Sister, you'll go with us?

GONERILL No.

REGAN
'Tis most convenient. Pray go with us.

---

22 *the rigour of our state* the harshness of
our administration
25–7 *It touches us . . . oppose* I am moved
(to be *valiant* and fight) because this
is a French invasion of Britain; but
in so far as France's purpose is to
embolden the King (and others with
just cause of complaint) I am not
touched. Albany's language is exces-
sively harsh; the fact that Q is our
only text at this point makes corruption a real possibility.

28 *you speak nobly.* See the note on line 9.
Why is this reasoned? (what is the point
of this academic talk about reasons
for fighting? The important thing is
to fight.)
30 *domestic and particular broils* family and
individual quarrels
32 *th'ancient of war* the most experienced
warriors
33 *presently* immediately

GONERILL (*aside*)
    O, ho, I know the riddle. (*Aloud*) I will go.
                          Exeunt both the armies
        As Albany is going out, enter Edgar

EDGAR
    If e'er your grace had speech with man so poor,
    Hear me one word.

ALBANY (*to his captains*) I'll overtake you.
                  (*To Edgar*) Speak.

EDGAR
    Before you fight the battle, ope this letter.   40
    If you have victory, let the trumpet sound
    For him that brought it. Wretched though I seem,
    I can produce a champion that will prove
    What is avouchèd there. If you miscarry,
    Your business of the world hath so an end,
    And machination ceases. Fortune love you.

ALBANY
    Stay till I have read the letter.

EDGAR   I was forbid it.
    When time shall serve, let but the herald cry
    And I'll appear again.   *Exit*

ALBANY
    Why, fare thee well. I will o'erlook thy paper.   50
    Enter Edmund

EDMUND
    The enemy's in view; draw up your powers.
    Here is the guess of their true strength and forces

---

37 *the riddle*. Gonerill detects behind Regan's words the fear of leaving her with Edmund while she goes with Albany to the council of war.

40 *this letter* (the letter from Gonerill to Edmund which Edgar took from Oswald's dead body)

44 *avouchèd* guaranteed

46 *machination* (the plots and counter-plots that belong to the *business of the world*)

47 *I was forbid it* (by Shakespeare, who does not wish any anticipation here of the denouement in v.3)

52 *Here*. Edmund hands Albany a paper.

By diligent discovery; but your haste
Is now urged on you.

ALBANY   We will greet the time.   *Exit*

EDMUND

To both these sisters have I sworn my love;
Each jealous of the other as the stung
Are of the adder. Which of them shall I take?
Both? One? Or neither? Neither can be enjoyed
If both remain alive. To take the widow
60   Exasperates, makes mad, her sister Gonerill,
And hardly shall I carry out my side,
Her husband being alive. Now then, we'll use
His countenance for the battle, which being done,
Let her who would be rid of him devise
His speedy taking off. As for the mercy
Which he intends to Lear and to Cordelia,
The battle done and they within our power,
Shall never see his pardon; for my state
Stands on me to defend, not to debate.   *Exit*

---

53 *diligent discovery* careful reconnais-
    sance
54 *greet the time* go forward to welcome
    the occasion
56 *jealous* suspicious, watchful
61–2 *And hardly shall I carry out my side,* |
    Her husband being alive. The emphasis
    falls on *Her.* He is now talking about
    enjoying Gonerill. He cannot *take*
    Regan because of Gonerill's opposi-
    tion; it is difficult to fulfil his side of

the bargain with Gonerill (that is,
satisfy her lust) because her husband
is alive.
62 *Now then* let me see, let me think it
    out
63 *countenance for the battle* authority, sup-
    port, while the battle is in progress
65 *taking off* killing
68 *Shall* they shall
69 *Stands* depends

Alarum within. Enter, with drum and colours, Lear,   V.2
Cordelia holding his hand, and soldiers, over the
stage, and exeunt
Enter Edgar and Gloucester

EDGAR
Here, father, take the shadow of this tree
For your good host. Pray that the right may thrive.
If ever I return to you again
I'll bring you comfort.
GLOUCESTER   Grace go with you, sir!

Exit Edgar

Alarum and retreat within. Enter Edgar

EDGAR
Away, old man! Give me thy hand; away!
King Lear hath lost; he and his daughter ta'en.
Give me thy hand; come on.
GLOUCESTER
No further, sir; a man may rot even here.
EDGAR
What, in ill thoughts again? Men must endure
Their going hence even as their coming hither;   10
Ripeness is all. Come on.
GLOUCESTER   And that's true too.   *Exeunt*

---

v.2 Gloucester, still guided by Edgar, waits while Lear and Cordelia lose the battle.
1 *father* (as at IV.6.72, a general word of respect rather than a revelation of the particular relationship)
2 *host* shelterer
4 (stage direction) *Alarum and retreat within.* The climactic battle of *King Lear* is treated very cursorily. Shakespeare is interested in motives and in results, but the actual process of the battle is unimportant to him. The

real battle between good and evil must be fought out elsewhere.
9–10 *Men must endure | Their going hence even as their coming hither* just as childbirth involves pain and trouble, so death is not just a matter of sitting and rotting, but a painful process that has to be struggled through till it be granted from above
11 *Ripeness is all* (man's duty is not to wait to *rot*, but to await the time of *Ripeness*, which is the time appointed for death. That is all that matters.)

V.3   *Enter in conquest with drum and colours Edmund;*
                    Lear and Cordelia as prisoners; soldiers, Captain

EDMUND
    Some officers take them away. Good guard,
    Until their greater pleasures first be known
    That are to censure them.

CORDELIA   We are not the first
    Who with best meaning have incurred the worst.
    For thee, oppressèd King, I am cast down;
    Myself could else out-frown false Fortune's frown.
    (*To Edmund*)
    Shall we not see these daughters and these sisters?

LEAR
    No, no, no! Come, let's away to prison.
    We two alone will sing like birds i'the cage;
10   When thou dost ask me blessing I'll kneel down
    And ask of thee forgiveness; so we'll live,
    And pray, and sing, and tell old tales, and laugh
    At gilded butterflies, and hear poor rogues
    Talk of court news; and we'll talk with them too –
    Who loses and who wins, who's in, who's out –
    And take upon's the mystery of things
    As if we were God's spies; and we'll wear out
    In a walled prison, packs and sects of great ones
    That ebb and flow by the moon.

EDMUND   Take them away.

v.3 In the chaos following the battle a still moment of resignation is achieved by the captive Lear and Cordelia. Albany strives to organize justice, and Edgar appears like a *deus ex machina* to defeat Edmund. The lust of the sisters destroys both of them. But the turn towards justice, which seems to be confirmed by the deaths of the wicked, is suddenly halted and even reversed by the entry of Lear with Cordelia dead from prison. His own death follows as a corollary on this; Albany and Edgar are left to bear *The weight of this sad time*.

1 *Good guard* keep a strict guard on them

2–3 *their greater pleasures ... That* the more explicit decisions of those who

16 *take upon's* assume the burden of

17 *God's*. I assume that only one God is meant, even though this requires a monotheistic faith from the pagan Lear.

wear out survive beyond

LEAR

Upon such sacrifices, my Cordelia,   20
The gods themselves throw incense. Have I caught
   thee?
    (*He embraces her*)
He that parts us shall bring a brand from heaven
And fire us hence like foxes. Wipe thine eyes;
The good-years shall devour them, flesh and fell,
Ere they shall make us weep. We'll see 'em starved first.
Come.   *Exeunt Lear and Cordelia, guarded*

EDMUND

Come hither, captain. Hark.
Take thou this note; go follow them to prison.
One step I have advanced thee; if thou dost
As this instructs thee, thou dost make thy way   30
To noble fortunes. Know thou this, that men
Are as the time is; to be tender-minded
Does not become a sword; thy great employment
Will not bear question; either say thou'lt do't
Or thrive by other means.

CAPTAIN   I'll do't, my lord.

EDMUND

About it; and write happy when th' hast done.
Mark, I say 'instantly'; and carry it so
As I have set it down.

22–3 *He that parts us shall bring a brand
from heaven | And fire us hence like
foxes.* Foxes are driven out of their
holes by fire and smoke (and then
killed). But the fire that parts Lear
and Cordelia will have to be more
than human. Perhaps Lear is thinking
of the final conflagration, at the Last
Judgement.

24 *The good-years shall devour them.* It is
not clear what kind of bogey-men
are meant by *The good-years*. But the
tone of the statement seems to be

that of a father's homely reassurance
to a frightened child.
fell skin

30–31 *make thy way | To noble fortunes*
become a nobleman

31–2 *men | Are as the time is* moral prin-
ciples change according to circumstances

33 *Does not become a sword* is not appropriate for a soldier

36 *write happy* call yourself a fortunate
man

37 *carry it* arrange it

CAPTAIN

I cannot draw a cart nor eat dried oats;

40   If it be man's work, I'll do't.   *Exit*

> *Flourish. Enter Albany, Gonerill, Regan, and officers*

ALBANY

·   Sir, you have showed today your valiant strain,

And Fortune led you well. You have the captives

Who were the opposites of this day's strife;

I do require them of you, so to use them

As we shall find their merits and our safety

May equally determine.

EDMUND   Sir, I thought it fit

To send the old and miserable King

To some retention and appointed guard;

Whose age had charms in it, whose title more,

50   To pluck the common bosom on his side

And turn our impressed lances in our eyes

Which do command them. With him I sent the Queen,

My reason all the same; and they are ready

Tomorrow or at further space t'appear

Where you shall hold your session. At this time

We sweat and bleed; the friend hath lost his friend,

And the best quarrels in the heat are cursed

By those that feel their sharpness.

---

41 *your valiant strain* the valour that you
have derived from your ancestors.
Note the implicit denial, in this, of
Edmund's bastardy speech, 1.2.1–22.
46 *equally* with justice
49 *title* (1) kingship; (2) legal right to
the possession of the land
51 *impressed lances* conscript pikemen
(but the reverberations of the
strongly physical side of the image
should also be noted: common humanity might turn back on us, and
press their points into the very eye-

balls which should control them in a
commanding vision of how things
must be)
57–8 *And the best quarrels in the heat are
cursed | By those that feel their sharpness*
even good arguments are hateful at
this moment of passionate involvement, when we are all suffering the
pains and losses of battle. Edmund
stalls for time to get Lear and Cordelia killed, pretending that they
would not, at the moment, get a fair
hearing at their trial.

The question of Cordelia and her father
Requires a fitter place.

ALBANY   Sir, by your patience,   60
I hold you but a subject of this war,
Not as a brother

REGAN   That's as we list to grace him.
Methinks our pleasure might have been demanded
Ere you had spoke so far. He led our powers,
Bore the commission of my place and person,
The which immediacy may well stand up
And call itself your brother.

GONERILL   Not so hot!
In his own grace he doth exalt himself
More than in your addition.

REGAN   In my rights,
By me invested, he compeers the best.   70

ALBANY
That were the most if he should husband you.

REGAN
Jesters do oft prove prophets.

GONERILL   Holla, holla!
That eye that told you so looked but asquint.

REGAN
Lady, I am not well; else I should answer
From a full-flowing stomach. (*To Edmund*) General,
Take thou my soldiers, prisoners, patrimony,
Dispose of them, of me; the walls is thine.
Witness the world that I create thee here

---

62 *we*. Regan has assumed the plural of
  royalty.
66 *immediacy* the condition of being 'immediate' to my sovereignty, next in
  line
69 *your addition* the title you have given
  him
70 *compeers* equals

75–9 *General . . . master*. Regan creates
  Edmund *General* of the city (herself)
  which she surrenders. He has conquered her *walls* (her 'resistance') and
  now has the right to dispose of her
  soldiers etc. She gives in
  unconditionally.

My lord and master.

GONERILL   Mean you to enjoy him?

ALBANY

80   The let-alone lies not in your good will.

EDMUND

Nor in thine, lord.

ALBANY   Half-blooded fellow, yes.

REGAN (*to Edmund*)

Let the drum strike and prove my title thine.

ALBANY

Stay yet; hear reason. Edmund, I arrest thee
On capital treason, and, in thy attaint,
          (*he points to Gonerill*)
This gilded serpent. For your claim, fair sister,
I bar it in the interest of my wife.
'Tis she is sub-contracted to this lord,
And I her husband contradict your banns.
If you will marry, make your loves to me;
My lady is bespoke.

90   GONERILL   An interlude!

ALBANY

Thou art armed, Gloucester; let the trumpet sound.

---

79 *enjoy him.* By linguistic convention, men 'enjoy' women, not vice versa. The application to Regan marks her masculine and commanding nature.

80 *The let-alone lies not in your good will* the power to hinder it does not lie within the scope of your consent

83 *hear reason.* Albany does not seem to be arguing for talk rather than action, since almost immediately he calls for the trumpet to sound. His speech contains the details of the complex situation, the 'reasons' which will be needed to *prove title.*

84–5 *and, in thy attaint, | This gilded serpent* and I also arrest Gonerill who has provided the *attaint* or accusation against you. The F word, 'arrest', is

clearly a mistaken repetition of the word in the line above. Note the style of this whole speech: Albany slips into the quasi-legal formality and paradox of the *deus ex machina.*

85 *sister* sister-in-law

87 *sub-contracted* (only *sub*-contracted because she is already contracted to Albany)

89 *If you will marry, make your loves to me.* If Gonerill and Edmund are contracted to one another, then Albany is the only man free to enter into a new relationship.

90 *An interlude!* what an old-fashioned little farce! 'Interludes' were short, often humorous, plays of the pre-Shakespearian period.

If none appear to prove upon thy person
Thy heinous, manifest, and many treasons,
There is my pledge.

    He throws down his glove

                  I'll make it on thy heart,
Ere I taste bread, thou art in nothing less
Than I have here proclaimed thee.

REGAN   Sick, O sick!

GONERILL (*aside*)
    If not, I'll ne'er trust medicine.

EDMUND (*throwing down his glove*)
    There's my exchange. What in the world he is
    That names me traitor, villain-like he lies.
    Call by the trumpet. He that dares approach,   100
    On him, on you – who not? – I will maintain
    My truth and honour firmly.

ALBANY   A herald, ho!

    Enter a Herald

Trust to thy single virtue; for thy soldiers,
All levied in my name, have in my name
Took their discharge.

REGAN   My sickness grows upon me.

ALBANY
    She is not well. Convey her to my tent.

                  Exit Regan, supported

Come hither, herald; let the trumpet sound,
And read out this.

    A trumpet sounds

94 *make it* (perhaps equivalent to 'make it good', fulfil it)
95 *in nothing* in no point
97 *medicine* poison
98–9 *What in the world he is | That* whatever the rank of the person who
99 *villain-like* like a slave
103 *thy single virtue* your unaided valour
108–15 (stage directions) *A trumpet sounds* ... Considerable textual confusion surrounds this heraldic occasion. The text (line 112) speaks of three trumpet calls. F in fact has four, one before the reading of the challenge and three after; Albany commands the first and the Herald the other three. Q has three trumpet calls, the first commanded by a *Captain*, the second and the third by *Bastard* (that is, Edmund). Editors

HERALD (*reading*) *If any man of quality or degree within the*
lists of the army will maintain upon Edmund, supposed
Earl of Gloucester, that he is a manifold traitor, let him
appear by the third sound of the trumpet. He is bold in his
defence.

(*First trumpet*)

Again!

(*Second trumpet*)

Again!

Third trumpet
Trumpet answers within. Enter Edgar armed, a
trumpet before him

ALBANY
Ask him his purposes, why he appears
Upon this call o'the trumpet.

HERALD   What are you?
Your name, your quality, and why you answer
This present summons?

EDGAR   Know, my name is lost,
By treason's tooth bare-gnawn and canker-bit;
Yet am I noble as the adversary
I come to cope.

ALBANY   Which is that adversary?

EDGAR
What's he that speaks for Edmund, Earl of Gloucester?

EDMUND
Himself. What sayest thou to him?

EDGAR   Draw thy sword,
That if my speech offend a noble heart
Thy arm may do thee justice. Here is mine.

often try to compromise between the
two versions, but since they are alternative organizations of the same
thing it seems best to stick to one –
F's in this case.

115 (stage direction) *a trumpet* a trum-
     peter
120 *canker-bit* worm-eaten
122 *cope* match

He draws his sword
Behold; it is the privilege of mine honours,
My oath, and my profession. I protest,
Maugre thy strength, place, youth, and eminence,
Despite thy victor sword and fire-new fortune,   130
Thy valour and thy heart, thou art a traitor,
False to thy gods, thy brother, and thy father,
Conspirant 'gainst this high illustrious prince,
And, from th'extremest upward of thy head
To the descent and dust below thy foot,
A most toad-spotted traitor. Say thou 'no',
This sword, this arm, and my best spirits are bent
To prove upon thy heart, whereto I speak,
Thou liest.
EDMUND   In wisdom I should ask thy name;
But since thy outside looks so fair and warlike   140
And that thy tongue some 'say of breeding breathes,
What safe and nicely I might well delay
By rule of knighthood, I disdain and spurn.
Back do I toss these treasons to thy head,
With the hell-hated lie o'erwhelm thy heart,
Which, for they yet glance by and scarcely bruise,
This sword of mine shall give them instant way

127–8 *Behold; it is the privilege of mine honours, | My oath, and my profession* see my sword; the right to draw it is the privilege conferred on me by my honour, by my oath of knighthood, and my religious vows (*professions*)

129 *Maugre* in spite of

130 *thy . . . fire-new fortune* your new-minted rank as military leader and earl

134 *extremest upward* topmost part

136 *toad-spotted traitor* spotted (stained) with treason as the toad is spotted (allegedly with venom)

141 *thy tongue some 'say of breeding breathes* the way you speak gives some *assay* or proof of the quality of your up-bringing. But perhaps F's 'say' only means 'speech'.

142 *nicely* by being meticulous

145 *the hell-hated lie* the lie (that I am a traitor) which I hate as I hate hell

146–8 *Which, for they yet . . . rest for ever* the mere return of accusations to your head and heart glances off your armour; but my sword will push them straight into your heart, and there they will remain. *Which* probably refers back both to *treasons* and to *heart* ('into which').

146 *for* because

Where they shall rest for ever. Trumpets, speak!

Alarums. Fights. Edmund falls

ALBANY (*to Edgar, about to kill Edmund*)

Save him, save him!

GONERILL   This is practice, Gloucester.

150 By the law of war thou wast not bound to answer.

An unknown opposite. Thou art not vanquished,

But cozened and beguiled.

ALBANY   Shut your mouth, dame,

Or with this paper shall I stop it. – Hold, sir!

(*To Gonerill*)

Thou worse than any name, read thine own evil.

No tearing, lady! I perceive you know it.

GONERILL

Say if I do; the laws are mine, not thine.

Who can arraign me for't?

ALBANY   Most monstrous! O!

(*To Edmund*)

Knowest thou this paper?

EDMUND   Ask me not what I know.

Exit Gonerill

ALBANY

Go after her. She's desperate. Govern her.

Exit First Officer

148, 149 (stage directions) *Edmund falls ... to Edgar, about to kill Edmund.* I have inserted these stage directions to explain Albany's words, which are not clearly directed in the text. Some supposed that it is Gonerill who says *Save him, save him!*, which solves the problem in another way.

149 *practice* plotting

152 *cozened and beguiled* tricked and deceived

153 *this paper* (the letter from Gonerill to Edmund which passed through the hands of Oswald and Edgar. It is

not clear if the 'stopping' is to be physical or mental.)

Hold, sir! It is not clear to whom this is addressed. Perhaps it is to Edgar, with his sword once again at Edmund's throat.

156 *the laws are mine, not thine* (presumably because she is the daughter of the sovereign (the source of legality), and Albany only the consort)

157 *Who can arraign me* (as sovereign she cannot be brought to trial)

159 *desperate* (in the state of despair, theologically defined as 'having lost any

EDMUND

What you have charged me with, that have I done,   160
And more, much more; the time will bring it out.
'Tis past; and so am I. But what art thou
That hast this fortune on me? If thou'rt noble,
I do forgive thee.

EDGAR   Let's exchange charity.

I am no less in blood than thou art, Edmund;
If more, the more th' hast wronged me.
My name is Edgar, and thy father's son.
The gods are just, and of our pleasant vices
Make instruments to plague us:
The dark and vicious place where thee he got   170
Cost him his eyes.

EDMUND   Th' hast spoken right. 'Tis true.

The wheel is come full circle; I am here.

ALBANY

Methought thy very gait did prophesy
A royal nobleness. I must embrace thee.
Let sorrow split my heart if ever I
Did hate thee or thy father.

EDGAR   Worthy prince,
I know't.

---

sense of Divine Grace', and therefore
liable to commit suicide. This is
why she has to be 'governed' or
restrained.)

163 *noble* of good breeding. The same
idea is picked up in Edgar's *no less in
blood* ('of no worse breeding') in line
165. Edmund has relapsed from the
revolutionary posture of his I.2 soliloquy into traditional conceptions of
nobility and breeding.

166 *If more* if legitimacy confers more
nobility than illegitimacy does

168 *our pleasant vices* the vicious acts
which give us pleasure

170-71 *The dark and vicious place where*

thee he got | Cost him his eyes (the
darkness of sin resulted in the physical darkness of his blind state)

171-2 *'Tis true. | The wheel is come full
circle.* Edmund picks up Edgar's
point about the poetic justice of
Destiny (*'Tis true*), and applies it to
himself. He made Edgar his enemy,
he embraced force and deceit as
methods; and now the disguised
Edgar has conquered him by force.
We should remember how he alleged
Edgar's sword had wounded him in
II.1. Now he is killed by the method
he used to start his career.

ALBANY   Where have you hid yourself?

How have you known the miseries of your father?

EDGAR

By nursing them, my lord. List a brief tale;

180   And when 'tis told, O that my heart would burst!

The bloody proclamation to escape

That followed me so near – O, our life's sweetness,

That we the pain of death would hourly die

Rather than die at once – taught me to shift

Into a madman's rags, t'assume a semblance

That very dogs disdained; and in this habit

Met I my father with his bleeding rings,

Their precious stones new lost; became his guide,

Led him, begged for him, saved him from despair,

190   Never – O fault! – revealed myself unto him

Until some half hour past, when I was armed,

Not sure, though hoping, of this good success,

I asked his blessing, and from first to last

Told him my pilgrimage; but his flawed heart –

Alack, too weak the conflict to support –

'Twixt two extremes of passion, joy and grief,

Burst smilingly.

EDMUND   This speech of yours hath moved me,

And shall perchance do good. But speak you on;

You look as you had something more to say.

181–97 *The bloody proclamation ... Burst smilingly.* The narrative of important and moving events off-stage, told by a messenger, traditionally makes its effect by a more rhetorical, more statuesque mode than is usual in dramatic poetry. The example here (properly called a *period* – a classical paragraph – in line 202) involves continuously suspended syntax carrying the narration forward without a single full-stop.

181 *The bloody proclamation* (the proclamation (see II.3.1) that he should be put to death if found)

183–4 *we the pain of death would hourly die | Rather than die at once* we prefer to suffer the pain of death every hour of our life rather than die quickly and get it over with

194, 196–7 *his flawed heart ... smilingly* his cracked (*flawed*) heart burst under the contrary pressures of joy and grief; but this was not a death in despair; at the moment of death he knew joy

ALBANY

If there be more, more woeful, hold it in;   200
For I am almost ready to dissolve,
Hearing of this.

EDGAR   This would have seemed a period
To such as love not sorrow; but another
To amplify too much would make much more
And top extremity.
Whilst I was big in clamour, came there in a man,
Who, having seen me in my worst estate,
Shunned my abhorred society; but then finding
Who 'twas that so endured, with his strong arms
He fastened on my neck and bellowed out   210
As he'd burst heaven, threw him on my father,
Told the most piteous tale of Lear and him
That ever ear received; which in recounting
His grief grew puissant, and the strings of life
Began to crack. Twice then the trumpets sounded,
And there I left him tranced.

ALBANY   But who was this?

EDGAR
Kent, sir, the banished Kent, who, in disguise,
Followed his enemy king and did him service
Improper for a slave.

201 *dissolve* weep myself into liquid
202 *a period* a complete sentence, with
    its own consummation and final
    point of punctuation
203–5 *but another . . . And top extremity.*
    The first *period* was an 'amplification'
    (in the language of rhetoric) of one
    sorrow (Gloucester's); to amplify
    another sorrow (Kent's) in the same
    way would take one beyond the
    period (limit) of what one can stand.
    Kent's *period* is in fact shorter than
    Gloucester's.
206 *big* ready to burst forth

207 *worst estate* poorest condition (when
    he was Poor Tom)
209 *so endured* lived as Poor Tom
211 *threw him on my father* threw himself
    on the body of the dead Gloucester
214 *puissant* overpowering
    the strings of life the heart-strings (but
    I think the vocal cords are also in
    Shakespeare's mind: the violence of
    his outcry cracked both vocal cords
    and heart-strings)
216 *tranced* in a trance, unconscious
218 *his enemy king* (King Lear, who had
    (I.I.178) declared himself his enemy)

Enter a Gentleman with a bloody knife

GENTLEMAN
Help, help! O, help!

EDGAR   What kind of help?

220 ALBANY   Speak, man.

EDGAR
What means this bloody knife?

GENTLEMAN   'Tis hot; it smokes!
It came even from the heart of – O, she's dead!

ALBANY Who dead? Speak, man.

GENTLEMAN
Your lady, sir; your lady! And her sister
By her is poisoned; she confesses it.

EDMUND
I was contracted to them both. All three
Now marry in an instant.

EDGAR   Here comes Kent.

Enter Kent

ALBANY
Produce the bodies, be they alive or dead.

Exit Gentleman

This judgement of the heavens that makes us tremble

230 Touches us not with pity. (*To Kent*) O, is this he?
The time will not allow the compliment
Which very manners urges.

KENT   I am come
To bid my King and master aye good night.

---

221 *smokes* steams
222 *from the heart of –*. The failure to
    complete the statement allows the
    coup de théâtre of suggesting for a
    moment that it is Cordelia who is
    killed.
227 *marry* join together
231–2 *the compliment | Which very manners
    urges* the formal courtesies which
    good manners alone would cause us

to observe
233 *aye good night* farewell for ever. We
    are not told, and need not know,
    whether Kent has a premonition of
    Lear's death or assumes that his own
    death is imminent, as may be sug-
    gested by *the strings of life | Began to
    crack* (lines 214–15). In either case,
    his dramatic task is done.

Is he not here?

ALBANY   Great thing of us forgot.
    Speak, Edmund, where's the King? and where's
        Cordelia?
        Gonerill's and Regan's bodies are brought out
    See'st thou this object, Kent?

KENT
    Alack, why thus?

EDMUND   Yet Edmund was beloved.
    The one the other poisoned for my sake
    And after slew herself.

ALBANY Even so. Cover their faces.   240

EDMUND
    I pant for life; some good I mean to do
    Despite of mine own nature. Quickly send –
    Be brief in it – to the castle, for my writ
    Is on the life of Lear and on Cordelia.
    Nay, send in time!

ALBANY   Run, run, O run!

EDGAR
    To who, my lord? Who has the office? Send
    Thy token of reprieve.

EDMUND
    Well thought on. (*To Second Officer*) Take my sword,
    Give it the captain.

EDGAR   Haste thee for thy life.

---

235 (stage direction) *brought out. Out*, in
the theatrical sense being used here,
means 'out, on to the stage'; in these
terms 'in' means 'inside the stage-
façade, behind the stage'. F's '*brought
out*' implies a theatrical origin for the
'copy' behind it, just as Q's '*brought
in*' implies a literary 'copy' not used
for stage purposes. The dead daughters are all brought back on to the
stage to reassemble there the cast of
I.I.

236 *object* spectacle of pity or horror
243 *brief* quick
249 EDGAR *Haste thee for thy life*. I
follow F here (Q, followed by many
editors, gives the speech to '*Duke*' –
that is, Albany – and makes Edgar
exit, bringing him on stage again
with Lear). Edgar must be placed on
the stage beside Edmund; he takes
the sword from him and gives it,
with his instructions, to the Officer.

Exit Second Officer

EDMUND

250   He hath commission from thy wife and me
             To hang Cordelia in the prison, and
             To lay the blame upon her own despair,
             That she fordid herself.

ALBANY

             The gods defend her. Bear him hence awhile.

Edmund is borne off.

Enter Lear with Cordelia in his arms,
followed by Second Officer and others

LEAR

             Howl, howl, howl! O, you are men of stones!
             Had I your tongues and eyes I'd use them so
             That heaven's vault should crack. She's gone for ever.
             I know when one is dead and when one lives;
             She's dead as earth. Lend me a looking-glass;
260   If that her breath will mist or stain the stone,

252–3 *blame upon her own despair,* | *That she fordid herself.* If we compare the language applied in lines 289–90 to the deaths of Gonerill and Regan (*fordone themselves,* | *And desperately are dead*) we can see the ironic repetition of the first Act here: there is an attempt to make Cordelia seem to behave in the same way as her sisters, but it does not succeed.

254 *The gods defend her.* A. C. Bradley and others have seen an ironic relationship between this and the stage direction immediately following: *Enter Lear with Cordelia in his arms.*

255 *O, you are men of stones.* I think that the primary idea here is of statues, silent, frozen-still (in horror), and impermeable by grief. The over-all image governing the following lines may be that of a funerary chapel or pantheon with statues and a vault: but as this is *heaven's vault* an intentional confusion between the living and the dead is created.

256 *Had I your tongues and eyes.* It is not clear how they could use their *eyes* to make *heaven's vault crack,* except that tongues used for outcry and eyes used for weeping come irresistibly together. Perhaps the only point made is that Lear's eyes are failing him (as in line 280). *Tongues* and *eyes* represent within the human microcosm the sources of thunder and lightning in the macrocosm – the vault of heaven. Thus the tempest is recalled.

260 *stone* mirror (perhaps short for 'specular stone', a species of mica, selenite, or talc)

Why then she lives.

KENT   Is this the promised end?

EDGAR

Or image of that horror?

ALBANY   Fall and cease!

LEAR

This feather stirs – she lives! If it be so,
It is a chance which does redeem all sorrows
That ever I have felt.

KENT   O my good master!

LEAR

Prithee away.

EDGAR   'Tis noble Kent, your friend.

LEAR

A plague upon you, murderers, traitors all!
I might have saved her; now she's gone for ever.
Cordelia, Cordelia, stay a little. Ha!
What is't thou sayest? Her voice was ever soft,   270
Gentle and low – an excellent thing in woman.
I killed the slave that was a-hanging thee.

SECOND OFFICER

'Tis true, my lords; he did.

LEAR   Did I not, fellow?
I have seen the day, with my good biting falchion
I would have made him skip. I am old now

261 *the promised end* the end of the world (as foretold in Mark 13). Kent may also mean 'the end that Lear promised himself when he divided the kingdom'.

262 *image* representation. Similarly, Macduff calls the death of Duncan 'The Great Doom's image' (*Macbeth*, II.3.75).
Fall and cease let the heavens fall and life on earth cease

269 *stay a little*. We should notice the

ironic relation of this second (permanent) exile to the first.

272 *I killed the slave.* So much for the *noble fortunes* promised at line 31.

274 *falchion* (an old-fashioned word for sword, appropriate to the memory of Lear's youth, as is the 'long sword' that Justice Shallow (in *The Merry Wives of Windsor*, II.1.203) remembers from *his* youth)

275 *him*. This is F's reading; Q has 'them'. In meaning they seem to be

And these same crosses spoil me. – Who are you?
Mine eyes are not o'the best, I'll tell you straight.

KENT

If Fortune brag of two she loved and hated
One of them we behold.

LEAR

This is a dull sight. Are you not Kent?

280   KENT   The same –
Your servant Kent. Where is your servant Caius?

LEAR

He's a good fellow, I can tell you that;
He'll strike, and quickly too. He's dead and rotten.

KENT

No, my good lord; I am the very man –

LEAR   I'll see that straight.

KENT

That from your first of difference and decay
Have followed your sad steps –

LEAR   You are welcome hither.

KENT

Nor no man else. All's cheerless, dark, and deadly.
Your eldest daughters have fordone themselves,

---

indifferent – which gives F, the better text, the preference.

276 *these same crosses spoil me* these troubles of my old age have spoiled me (as a swordsman)

278–9 *If Fortune brag of two she loved and hated | One of them we behold.* The two people are clearly Lear and Kent, both fortunate and unfortunate in extreme degrees. Each beholds *One* – they are looking at one another.

280 *This is a dull sight* (often thought to be a complaint about his fading eyesight rather than a comment on what he sees before him)

285 *I'll see that straight* I'll attend to that

immediately. Lear copes with the tedium of people who try to distract him from Cordelia by promising to attend to them later.

286 *your first of difference and decay* from the beginning of your change and decline of fortune

288 *Nor no man else.* This completes his preceding sentence (*I am the very man . . . Nor no man else*), but also begins his reply to Lear's *Welcome* ('I am not welcome, nor is anyone else – *All's . . . deadly*').
deadly death-like

289 *fordone themselves* destroyed themselves

And desperately are dead.

LEAR   Ay, so I think.   290

ALBANY

He knows not what he sees, and vain is it
That we present us to him.

EDGAR   Very bootless.

        Enter a Messenger

MESSENGER

Edmund is dead, my lord.

ALBANY   That's but a trifle here.

You lords and noble friends, know our intent:
What comfort to this great decay may come
Shall be applied. For us, we will resign
During the life of this old majesty
To him our absolute power.
(*To Edgar and Kent*)   You to your rights
With boot, and such addition as your honours
Have more than merited. All friends shall taste   300
The wages of their virtue, and all foes
The cup of their deservings. – O, see, see!

LEAR

And my poor fool is hanged! No, no, no life!

---

290 *desperately are dead* have died in a
   state of despair. This suggests an
   assumption that they both committed
   suicide (even though we know that
   Regan was poisoned by Gonerill),
   thus bringing the moral pattern to a
   neat conclusion.

291 *He knows not what he sees.* The point
   seems to be that Lear's sight, rather
   than his utterance, has become imperfect. This ties in with *present us to him*
   in the next line and with the references above to failing sight (lines
   256 and 280) – which do not fit with
   F's 'He knowes not what he saies'.

292 *bootless* useless, profitless

295 *this great decay* (Lear himself, and the
   situation which surrounds him)

296 *us, we.* Albany, as sovereign ruler of
   Britain, assumes the royal plural

299 *With boot, and . . . addition* with something extra (presumably new titles of
   honour)

302 *O, see, see!* What exactly draws their
   attention is not clear, but it must
   be some new posture of Lear as he
   cradles Cordelia in his arms, or
   picks her up again, or kneels at her
   side.

303 *my poor fool.* Presumably Cordelia is

Why should a dog, a horse, a rat have life,
And thou no breath at all? Thou'lt come no more;
Never, never, never, never, never.
Pray you undo this button. Thank you, sir.
Do you see this? Look on her! Look, her lips!
Look there! Look there!   *He dies*

EDGAR   He faints. My lord, my lord!

KENT

Break, heart; I prithee break.

310   EDGAR   Look up, my lord.

KENT

Vex not his ghost. O, let him pass. He hates him
That would upon the rack of this tough world
Stretch him out longer.

EDGAR   He is gone indeed.

KENT

The wonder is he hath endured so long.
He but usurped his life.

ALBANY

Bear them from hence. Our present business

---

meant (since she is the centre of his attention, and was hanged), 'poor fool' being a common Shakespearian form of parental endearment. It is impossible to know if the reminiscence of the Fool's title is accidental or intentional. It has been suggested that the same boy actor played both parts; but the Fool is likely to have been played by Robert Armin (see Introduction, page 518).

no life. I take it that Lear is making a general point ('Let all life cease') rather than the particular one: 'There is no life left in Cordelia'.

307   *this button* (presumably the button at his own throat, which seems to be causing his feeling of suffocation.

But it could equally well be a button on Cordelia's garment.)

308   *Do you see this? Look on her! Look, her lips!* Clearly Lear imagines he sees Cordelia coming to life again. Whether this means that 'Lear dies of joy' (as A. C. Bradley suggested) or that he is in a mere delirium is more doubtful, and not very important for the play as a whole. It would be difficult for any actor to project a precise interpretation.

312   *the rack of this tough world* the torture-machine that stretches a man between hope and despair. The *tough* suggests that it is the body that is referred to, as the rack of the spirit.

Is general woe.

(*To Kent and Edgar*)

                Friends of my soul, you twain,
Rule in this realm, and the gored state sustain.

KENT

I have a journey, sir, shortly to go.
My master calls me, I must not say no.   320

EDGAR

The weight of this sad time we must obey;
Speak what we feel, not what we ought to say.
The oldest hath borne most; we that are young
Shall never see so much nor live so long.

               Exeunt with a dead march

321–4 *The weight . . . live so long.* Q gives the final speech to Albany ('Duke'). Tragedies commonly end with a generalizing speech from the most senior survivor, and this may have been in the Q pirates' minds. F corrects to 'Edgar', and certainly the *we that are young* sounds better in the mouth of Edgar. We may also notice that Albany in line 317 addresses both Kent and Edgar, and that (apart from this speech) Edgar has no reply.

321 *weight* sadness. The use of the word may imply that Edgar is already carrying Lear (or Cordelia) from the stage.

322 *Speak what we feel, not what we ought to say.* Regal formality has broken down into individual feelings. There may be in this an element of apology for taking the last speech from Albany.

MACBETH

Introduction

THE SENSE OF THE PLAY

Reduced to its plot-line, *Macbeth* sounds like a crime-does-not-pay melodrama. The lady who, in the Thurber story, saw it in Penguin Books and supposed that it must be a whodunit, need not have been so violently disillusioned: 'I got real comfy in bed that night and all ready to read a good mystery story, and here I had *The Tragedy of Macbeth* – a book for high-school students, like *Ivanhoe*.' *Macbeth* is in fact far more a crime story than a costume melodrama like *Ivanhoe*. But as a crime-does-not-pay story it is less concerned with the uncovering of the crime to others than with the uncovering of the criminal *to himself*. The play spreads out from our interest in the hero; and the hero is here a criminal, or rather a man obsessed by his relation to those criminal tendencies that are so universal that we best describe them by speaking of 'evil'. The play is a discovery or anatomy of evil. Of all Shakespeare's plays *Macbeth* is the one most obsessively concerned with evil. Of course, evil men had appeared in Shakespeare's plays before 1606 – Aaron the Moor, for example, Don John, Shylock, Claudius, Iago, Edmund – but in each of these cases the evil was a shadow placed amid sunlight, beside the radiance of Desdemona, Cordelia, Beatrice or the suffering-for-good of Titus and Othello. Here the evil is, for once and without doubt, larger, more fascinating, more effective than the pallid representation of good (III.2.52–3):

> *Good things of day begin to droop and drowse,*
> *Whiles night's black agents to their preys do rouse.*

Macbeth falls, but does not do so primarily because of the

processes or power of his enemies. His black tyranny produces the engines of its own destruction; the movement that carries Malcolm, Macduff and Seyward above him is generated first by his own downward tendency and only secondarily by their efforts.

The pallid quality of Malcolm and the other 'good' men of this play is not, however, to be seen simply as Shakespeare's failure to produce radiance. Humility and self-distrust – even self-effacement – are necessary antitheses to the qualities of evil, as this work displays them. E. M. W. Tillyard puts this effectively: Malcolm is 'the ideal ruler who has subordinated all personal pleasures, and with them all personal charm, to his political obligations' (*Shakespeare's History Plays*, p. 317). Good struggles forward in the world of *Macbeth*; but evil is all-pervasive. The whole land lies under its interdict; good men die or fly; but even in flight they cannot escape from its power. They are walled up in the suspiciousness of the isolated individual. They do not know what other men may mean, or what is true or false; 'fair' may be 'foul'; they must guard their own tongues.

Act IV, scene 3 (the long scene of testing in the English court), can be viewed, in this respect, as the turning-point of the play, since there the suspiciousness, the sense that the individual cannot move directly, gradually gives way before the knowledge of mutual dependence, of national identity, and of divine blessing. Sharing comes as a kind of holy cure for suffering. The *malaise* that has spread from Macbeth into his subjects and even into his enemies, the inability to trust another, the need to conceal thoughts, to

> *look like the innocent flower,*
> *But be the serpent under't . . .*

as Lady Macbeth says (1.5.63–4), is checked here; and in the following scenes the plague is gradually driven back to the single castle and the single man. Only when he is dead, his head on a pole, is 'The time . . . free'.

If Malcolm is 'the medicine of the sickly weal' Macbeth is its disease – a point the imagery is constantly making. One of the difficulties of approaching Macbeth is that he is seen so roundedly and so simultaneously as a social and a psychological disease. His infection spreads outside his own mind and into the minds of others. At the same time, he is himself the first victim, though thereafter (like the werewolf) the victimizer.

If we call Macbeth a victim we will wish to know how he was first infected; and this is one of the crucial questions of the play. This question also requires to be tackled on the social no less than the psychological plane. When we first hear of Macbeth he is a great warrior, marvellously steeped in blood (1.2.40–42):

> *Except they meant to bathe in reeking wounds . . .*
> *I cannot tell.*

The stage-horror of the messenger's account of the extraordinarily bloody series of battles in Act I is being used at the explicit level to suggest that Macbeth is a hero. But I think that we are also aware (and meant to be aware) that this horrifying potentiality (even *penchant*) for destruction is held inside human morality only by bonds of loyalty that are easy to snap – witness the exemplary first Thane of Cawdor, whose inheritor Macbeth becomes (1.2.70):

> *What he hath lost, noble Macbeth hath won.*

Macbeth begins in frightening loyalty (like a wild animal on a lead). Shakespeare makes nothing of his genuine and legal claim to the throne (as it appears in Holinshed's *Chronicles*, where he found the story) – an explanation if not an excuse for his action; but he does seem to suggest that the succession was not finally settled when Macbeth arrived back in court in Act I, scene 4. And it is only then that Duncan announces (lines 38–40):

> *We will establish our estate upon*
> *Our eldest, Malcolm, whom we name hereafter*
> *The Prince of Cumberland . . .*

Duncan's sudden act here (it was not expected by 'cousin' Macbeth) has something of the same wilful arbitrariness as Lear's division of his kingdom. But one must not make this point to 'excuse' Macbeth's subsequent actions. I take it that the function of these early hints is to stress the uncertainty of loyalty as a controlling counterweight to violence and blood-thirstiness. Once loose this man on society, the early scenes seem to be saying, and he will not stop 'Even till destruction sicken'.

We must add to the uncertainty of the social sanctions that hold Macbeth in place a corresponding uncertainty about psychological restraint. The wife who knows him best tells us (I.5.19–23) that he is one who

> *wouldst not play false,*
> *And yet wouldst wrongly win. Thou'dst have, great Glamis,*
> *That which cries, 'Thus thou must do' if thou have it,*
> *And that which rather thou dost fear to do*
> *Than wishest should be undone.*

That is, Macbeth *fears* to do evil; but what he fears is the image of himself committing the evil deed, rather than the evil deed itself. What is startling by its absence from this moral landscape is any sense of positive *love* for good, any sense of personal involvement in virtue, loyalty, restraint. Here, as on the social plane, the power of Macbeth (*ambition* here rather than blood-thirstiness) is presented as free-floating, with only the weakest of psychological restraints attached, and with powerful enemies of restraint (like Lady Macbeth) dedicated (quite literally) to its destruction. And in such a miasma of undirected power, free-floating will-lessness, 'Fair is foul', 'the battle's lost and won', indecision has the only decisive victory.

But *Macbeth* does not finally chronicle the triumphs of indecision. Evil does not become alive or actual until it is endorsed by the *will*, say the moral theologians, and so it is in *Macbeth*. The play begins with the Witches, and the Witches must be supposed to be evil; but the mode of evil they can create is potential only, not actual, till the human agent takes it inside his mind and makes it his own by a motion of the will. This is demonstrated in the play in two ways; firstly by the tale the First Witch tells of her utmost malice – the tale of the 'master o'the *Tiger*' (1.3.18–25):

> *I'll drain him dry as hay;*
> *Sleep shall neither night nor day*
> *Hang upon his penthouse lid.*
> *He shall live a man forbid.*
> *Weary sev'n-nights nine times nine*
> *Shall he dwindle, peak, and pine.*
> *Though his bark cannot be lost,*
> *Yet it shall be tempest-tossed.*

The history of the 'master o'the *Tiger*' is a preview of the history of another 'pilot ... | Wracked as homeward he did come' – of Macbeth. Macbeth too will be drained as dry as hay (morally rather than physically) but his bark *will* be lost, because he scuttles it himself.

The other, and far more important, demonstration of the Witches' evil as potential rather than actual appears in the contrast of Macbeth and Banquo. 'Our captains, Macbeth and Banquo' are coupled in the King's mouth as approximate equals, and there is no suggestion that one is superior in rank to the other. They are alike in dignity and in bravery; the Witches salute both of them. The essential difference appears in response to the salute.

> *... why do you start, and seem to fear*
> *Things that do sound so fair?*

says Banquo to his partner (1.3.50–51). Thus Innocence greets Guilt. It is not that Banquo is innocent of the knowledge of

Evil: he recognizes the Witches for what they are – 'The instruments of darkness' – but he sees his own role as requiring him to combat this something external, since (lines 122–5)

> *oftentimes, to win us to our harm,*
> *The instruments of darkness tell us truths;*
> *Win us with honest trifles, to betray's*
> *In deepest consequence.*

Banquo recognizes the evil and sees it as something threatening, but outside himself. Macbeth, as soon as he can speak apart from his fellows, unfolds a different reaction (1.3. 133–41):

> *why do I yield to that suggestion*
> *Whose horrid image doth unfix my hair,*
> *And make my seated heart knock at my ribs*
> *Against the use of nature? Present fears*
> *Are less than horrible imaginings.*
> *My thought, whose murder yet is but fantastical,*
> *Shakes so my single state of man*
> *That function is smothered in surmise,*
> *And nothing is but what is not.*

'Suggestion' is a technical term of theology, meaning 'a prompting or incitement to evil; a temptation of the Evil One'; it is a thing in itself external; but Macbeth finds the stability of his moral nature already yielding, already 'moved'. In terms of his physical nature, his 'fixed' hair and his 'seated' heart leave their appointed places; his 'single state of man', his little kingdom of human faculties, finds its functioning 'smothered' by the tingling horror-pleasure of anticipated evil. The suggestion of the Witches 'starts' Macbeth (in more senses than one) because it finds an answering image inside his own mind. 'Macbeth has already contemplated the murder,' say literal-minded critics. Whether or not this is so seems not to be a crucial point in terms of the view of evil that the play contains; for (as Milton later announces)

> *Evil into the mind of God or Man*
> *May come and go, so unapprov'd, and leave*
> *No spot or blame behind . . .*

Adam is here speaking of Eve's dream, and he goes on

> *Which gives me hope*
> *That what in sleep thou didst abhor to dream*
> *Waking thou never wilt consent to do.*
>
> *Paradise Lost*, v.117–21

This view of evil is precisely endorsed later in *Macbeth* (ii.i.-8–9) when Banquo begs the 'Merciful powers' to

> *Restrain in me the cursèd thoughts that nature*
> *Gives way to in repose.*

Banquo, no less than Macbeth, may have contemplated murder in this 'natural' way of allowing the thought to pass through his mind. But he recognizes such 'cursèd thoughts' for what they are, as he recognized the 'instruments of darkness' – and not simply in terms of intellectual recognition, but by a positive and almost sensory reaction to the 'smell' of evil. Macbeth's sensory reactions, on the other hand, point not to a direct and uncompromising rejection of evil, but to a paralysis of the moral powers.

I spoke earlier of Macbeth's gift for bloodshed, and his ambition, as 'free-floating' qualities which were, in themselves, neither good nor bad, but as the direction of their use made them so. Ambition to excel as an obedient general, blood-thirstiness in the destruction of national foes – these are in-sulated from evil by loyal intent. But the Witches hold up a mirror in which Macbeth sees his powers fulfilled in a quite contrary way, and the fear-and-joy that this evokes in him is such that he cannot wrench his will into a denial. He is 'pos-sessed' by the image of himself that the Witches show; and though he can respond to Banquo's description of the external appearance created by this 'possession' ('Look how

our partner's rapt') with the commonplaces of external morality
(1.3.143–4):

> *If chance will have me king, why chance may crown me*
> *Without my stir*

and

> *Come what come may,*
> *Time and the hour runs through the roughest day,*

nevertheless the effect is that of a man gradually waking out of
a dream, a dream that turns the 'reality' of social obligations
and social chat into a rigmarole of play-acting. His life hereafter
is increasingly to be eaten up by this dream-self, by this 'new'
Macbeth springing up within him and making the normal
motions of his conventional self sound like 'a tale | Told by an
idiot . . . Signifying nothing'.

   Macbeth, coming out of the dream of fulfilled ambition that
the Witches show him, comes back into a world of shared
responsibilities and paternal affection, so luminously benevolent, so joyfully held together – even at the point of the traitor
Cawdor's execution – that the dream seems impossible even to
speak about (and Macbeth and his Lady speak about it, in fact,
only by periphrasis or euphemism). His real affection for his
King and for his wife intertwine in his journey to prepare a
welcome in Inverness. The individual will-to-good is paralysed
(or anaesthetized) inside him; but the sense of social obligations
and virtues seems to remain entire – like a rotten apple with an
unblemished skin. Inverness Castle still looks like 'a pleasant
seat', Lady Macbeth like a 'most kind hostess', Macbeth like a
'worthiest cousin' and, strangest of all (1.7.17–20), Duncan like
a king who

> *hath been*
> *So clear in his great office, that his virtues*
> *Will plead like angels, trumpet-tongued against*
> *The deep damnation of his taking-off.*

Lady Macbeth's function in the destruction of Macbeth is (ironically enough) to push the 'new' Macbeth that the Witches' 'suggestion' has tempted Macbeth into accepting, right through the smiling surface of the social scene (to which she belongs), to translate the anaesthetized lack of will-to-good into a positive (and fatal) evil action (1.7.35–6, 39–41).

> *Was the hope drunk*
> *Wherein you dressed yourself? . . . Art thou afeard*
> *To be the same in thine own act and valour*
> *As thou art in desire?*

Macbeth knows that he can give no reasons for acting in the way thus proposed (1.7.25–8):

> *I have no spur*
> *To prick the sides of my intent but only*
> *Vaulting ambition which o'erleaps itself*
> *And falls on the other.*

But in *his* sleep-walking scene (Act II, scene 1) he needs no more than her impulsion (weak in itself) to move the whole passive weight of his will-less power into frightening action. As the visionary dagger moves without force towards Duncan's bedchamber, so does the envisioning Macbeth.

The impulse comes from Lady Macbeth, I have said, and the actual performance is Macbeth's; but in no real sense is this a shared action. Lady Macbeth is willing to make it so: her 'Consider it not so deeply', her 'My husband!', her

> *Why, worthy thane,*
> *You do unbend your noble strength*

for example, are direct invitations to shared guilt; but Macbeth's replies, his 'Methought I heard a voice cry, "Sleep no more!"', his 'There's one did laugh in's sleep', his 'But wherefore could not I pronounce "Amen"?' and so on are like cries of terror from one half of his nature to the other, from the new Macbeth to the old, for reassurance:

To know my deed 'twere best not know myself.

The essential dialogue here is with himself; and Lady Macbeth, like other people in the play, remains accessory merely. The deed is done, for reasons that he does not understand; the rest of his life is the attempt to live with the deed as well as the self that his social existence might seem to imply. The deed itself is a denial of all social obligations, all sharing, all community of feeling, even with his wife; but it is only gradually that the complete divorce between self and society is realized and accepted, where realization means total sterility, and acceptance requires moral death.

Macbeth's bringing of his world into conformity with the man that he has become is the process I described at the beginning of this Introduction in terms of a social disease. It is not a process that he self-consciously undertakes as a practical programme. He thinks of himself as a part of the social order, as a man married, ruling, leading those willing to be led; but the hollowness of the order that he can encompass forces him backwards all the time into the total isolation that is his 'natural' milieu.

Thus in the banquet scene (Act III, scene 4) and in the scenes associated with it (Act III, scenes 1 and 2) Macbeth acts as a man still seeking a social good, a good that only needs the deaths of Banquo and Fleance to make it click into place. In fact, the death of Banquo alters nothing important, and the escape of Fleance is seen not as the one chance that spoils an otherwise perfect piece of kingship, but rather as a type of the future that always eludes (and must elude) the grasp of the tyrannical present. Macbeth operates throughout all these scenes by incessant falsehood or prevarication. With considerable skill he extracts from Banquo, in the stream of his false flattery, the basic facts necessary for the murder. He lies to the assembled Lords when he welcomes them and pretends hospitality. There is no reason to suppose he is not lying to the Murderers when he tells them that Banquo is their enemy.

He certainly lies in his pretence of trusting them; for why else does he plant the Third Murderer in their midst? He will not even trust his wife, as he makes clear with grim joviality (III.2.45–6):

> *Be innocent of the knowledge, dearest chuck,*
> *Till thou applaud the deed.*

The gap that the deed has made, even between its two accomplices, is obvious here. Lady Macbeth's

> *Why do you keep alone . . .?*
> *Things without all remedy*
> *Should be without regard; what's done is done*

(III.2.8–12) is painfully irrelevant to the real situation of Macbeth's mind. It may be true that what's done is done; but the man new-made by the deed is still alive, and cannot be 'without regard'. This is Macbeth's problem; he cannot forget the deed; for that would be to forget himself. He has become 'the deed's creature' so completely that the only movement he can make is towards the sterility of total identification with his deed (III.4.135–7):

> *I am in blood*
> *Stepped in so far, that, should I wade no more,*
> *Returning were as tedious as go o'er.*

But in the banquet scene itself the first thing that must impress us is the skill with which host and hostess can collaborate to establish a show of order and conviviality. It is impressive, but, as Murderer and Ghost indicate, far from reality. Moreover, the banquet here is bound to remind us of the earlier banquet, in Act I, scene 7, where a real order still existed, surrounding the benevolent Duncan

> *shut up*
> *In measureless content,*

where Macbeth himself, skulking outside the door, was the

only breach in nature. And we should also be reminded of Duncan's lines about Macbeth (1.4.55–7):

> *he is full so valiant,*
> *And in his commendations I am fed;*
> *It is a banquet to me.*

Our sense of 'banqueting' in the play has moved a long way from this.

The bloodstained Murderer should also cast his shadow backwards – to the bleeding Captain in Act 1, scene 2. But the bleeding Captain brought news of the deaths of enemies; the bloodshed then was open and honourable; and treachery (that of Cawdor) was remote (and past). Now the bloodstained messenger cannot be openly acknowledged; for the blood upon his face is that of Banquo, the 'chief guest', whose absence from the feast is being deplored; treachery is no longer external; indeed it is now the principle by which the court operates.

The banquet scene establishes itself, with dramatic tentacles reaching back to earlier scenes, as a phoney show of order, in which Macbeth's 'real' life of bloodshed and treachery seeks to hide behind 'mouth-honour, breath | Which the poor heart would fain deny'. This is a climactic scene because it also establishes, once and for all, that the real world of Macbeth's bloodshed and treachery *cannot* be repressed, nor its dreadful burgeoning halted; it erupts to the surface inconveniently enough in the First Murderer; but catastrophically when the Ghost of Banquo enters to claim the royal seat that his children are going to inherit. The surface of mutual congratulation is shattered. The scene may begin with: 'You know your own degrees, sit down' – a paradigm of order – but it soon emerges (III.4.108–9) that

> *You have displaced the mirth, broke the good meeting*
> *With most admired disorder.*

And it ends (lines 118–19) with something like a rout of the social virtues:

> *Stand not upon the order of your going;*
> *But go at once.*

One of the most effective theatrical points in the whole play occurs here. The coda of the scene shows us the King and Queen, now alone, slumped in their finery amid the debris of the 'great feast', while guilt, horror and relentless resolution pass before their minds. Lady Macbeth, exhausted by the terrible events just passed and by the effort to cover up for her husband, never really re-establishes herself. She is never again to be capable of the resolution that we have seen here and heretofore; she has drawn out all the stops that she knows; she has used again the supreme taunt of effeminacy, which was so effective before the murder; but here it has had only limited success. True, Macbeth has recovered his poise, and the Ghost has vanished; but the recovery has been in terms that establish his psychological power over himself only at the expense of his social ruin. Her success excludes herself from the recovery, for Macbeth no longer needs her. He climbs out of his abyss by planning new exploits, by action which needs no pondering (III.4.138–9):

> *Strange things I have in head, that will to hand;*
> *Which must be acted ere they may be scanned.*

Life still offers a future, for there are still people to be murdered – Macduff for example – and this is enough to keep him going. With appalling clarity he now accepts the Witches for what they are – 'the worst' – and knows the course that lies in front of him (lines 134–5):

> *For mine own good*
> *All causes shall give way.*

Having faced up to, and named, his fate, he is ready to face the Witches again.

Act IV, scene 1, differs from the earlier Witch-scenes in a number of ways. Macbeth now seeks out the Witches on his

own account; and he is now an adept seeking physical details of
the future rather than the innocent, susceptible of moral shock,
that rode across the heath in Act 1, scene 3. He knows that his
success is being bought by damnation, and he does not care.
All he cares about is 'security' in what he does; in that case
moral status becomes irrelevant; for then (III.4.20–22) he is

> perfect,
> *Whole as the marble, founded as the rock,*
> *As broad and general as the casing air . . .*

But what is 'security'? Hecat reminds us (III.5.32–3) that

> *you all know security*
> *Is mortals' chiefest enemy.*

This is a useful reminder, for the word is one that has lost its
relevant meaning. The *Oxford English Dictionary* tells us that it
is '*archaic*: a culpable absence of anxiety'. The absence of
anxiety was conceived to be culpable, because man may not be
confident or 'secure' about the most important thing in life –
his salvation. If he is 'secure', then it must be because the Devil
has closed up his senses to the obvious and omnipresent
dangers that everyone knew to lurk around the living – because
he is in that state of sadness that theologians called 'despair'.
An Elizabethan Morality play makes these points abundantly
clear to us, and throws a flood of light on the second half of
Macbeth. It is called *The Cradle of Security*. The text has perished,
but the preacher R. Willis recalled, towards the end of his life,
having seen a performance of it in Gloucester, in some year
around 1570:

My father took me with him and made me stand between his legs, as he
sat upon one of the benches where we saw and heard very well. The play
was called 'The Cradle of Security', wherein was personated a king or
some great prince, with his courtiers of several kinds, amongst which
three ladies were in special grace with him; and they, keeping him in
delights and pleasures, drew him from his graver counsellors, hearing of

sermons, and listening to good counsel and admonitions, that in the end they got him to lie down in a cradle upon the stage, where these three ladies, joining in a sweet song, rocked him asleep, that he snorted again; and in the meantime closely conveyed under the clothes wherewithal he was covered a vizard like a swine's snout upon his face, with three wire chains fastened thereunto, the other end whereof being holden severally by those three ladies, who fall to singing again, and then discovered his face, that the spectators might see how they had transformed him, going on with their singing. Whilst all this was acting, there came forth of another door at the farthest end of the stage two old men, the one in blue with a sergeant-at-arms's mace on his shoulder, the other in red with a drawn sword in his hand, and leaning with the other hand upon the other's shoulder. And so they two went along in a soft pace round about by the skirt of the stage, till at last they came to the cradle, when all the court was in greatest jollity; and then the foremost old man with his mace struck a fearful blow upon the cradle, whereat all the courtiers, with the three ladies and the vizard all vanished; and the desolate prince, starting up bare-faced, and finding himself thus sent for to judgement, made a lamentable complaint of his miserable case, and so was carried away by wicked spirits. This prince did personate in the moral, the wicked of the world; the three ladies, Pride, Covetousness, and Luxury; the two old men, the end of the world and the Last Judgement. This sight took such impression in me, that when I came towards man's estate, it was as fresh in my memory as if I had seen it newly acted.

It is in such a cradle that the Witches rock Macbeth in the second half of the play. They assure him that whatever he does, he has nothing to fear (IV.1.78–80):

> *Be bloody, bold, and resolute; laugh to scorn*
> *The power of man; for none of woman born*
> *Shall harm Macbeth.*

A man less desperately secure than Macbeth might question that 'power of *man*', for the evil-doer had, traditionally, more to fear from God than from man; but the desperate man is in no condition to make moral discriminations. He grasps at

every straw: he knows that the future can hold nothing for
him; but he must act as if he could plan ahead meaningfully.
And murder remains a meaningful activity even when other
human possibilities have faded away (IV.1.149–52):

> *The castle of Macduff I will surprise,*
> *Seize upon Fife, give to the edge o' the sword*
> *His wife, his babes, and all unfortunate souls*
> *That trace him in his line.*

Act IV is made up of two contrasting glimpses into the future
and two contrary journeys in search of security or reassurance.
Macbeth journeys to the hovel of the Witches for assurance
that he need not fear the future. Macduff travels to the
English court to find hope, to seek a cure for the horror of the
recent past. The 'testing' of Macduff is in contrast to Macbeth's
attempt to question the powers that speak to him: in one case
the mistrust that separates men is removed by the testing; in
the other case, the questions lead only further into the fog of
self-deception; and at the end of Act IV, scene 1, when the
Witches vanish, Macbeth is more alone than ever:

> *Where are they? Gone! Let this pernicious hour*
> *Stand aye accursèd in the calendar . . .*
> *Infected be the air whereon they ride,*
> *And damned all those that trust them.*

He is left clutching the Witches' promise – his 'charm' as
Macduff calls it – and (in spite of himself) depending on it; for
he has nothing else to depend on. The court of Edward the
Confessor, in contrast to the Witches' hovel, is a place of holy
arts. The only charms used are 'holy prayers', and the effect is
to cure

> *strangely visited people,*
> *All swollen and ulcerous, pitiful to the eye . . .*

The Witches 'infect' where they ride, but King Edward disin-
fects. Macbeth promises evil, and performs it before the promise

is well out of his mouth: Malcolm promises evil, but never even dreams of performing it. King Edward has a 'heavenly gift of prophecy'; the prophetic powers of the Witches come from hell. Macduff's suffering for the loss of his children is a measure of his true humanity, measured by his involvement in the sufferings of others (IV.3.220–26):

> *I must also feel it as a man.*
> *I cannot but remember such things were*
> *That were most precious to me . . . Sinful Macduff!*
> *They were all struck for thee. Naught that I am,*
> *Not for their own demerits, but for mine,*
> *Fell slaughter on their souls.*

Macbeth, on the other hand, has come to measure 'manliness' by the absence of feelings, as his wife had earlier instructed him to; and when his wife dies he can neither remember with gratitude nor look forward to 'things . . . | That were most precious to me.' Throughout the last Act, up to the episode of his death, he has his 'security', his assurance that he will not die by 'one of woman born'. But the enemies that he has to contend with are not ones that can be dealt with by arms or by the strength of a fortress. He puts his armour on long before it is required; but within his impregnable fortress we see his wife fall, before a foe that cannot be resisted – her own conscience; he cannot put an armour on her heart. Despair, which has turned him to stone, has turned her to water, imprisoned her forever in the horror of the past; with the only obvious escape-route running through suicide. Death walks the battlements of Dunsinane in many forms, and few of them involve the official enemy from England. The castle, whose stony strength resembles that of Macbeth himself, immobile in despair, is (like his 'sere [and] yellow leaf') in clear contrast to the 'leavy screen' from Birnan Wood which Malcolm's soldiers take up to protect them as they travel through the country, and then throw down again; just as his fixed posture of 'valiant fury' contrasts with the humility and tentativeness

of their hold on the future: 'Let our just censures,' says
Macduff, 'Attend the true event'; and Seyward takes up the
same point (v.4.19–20):

> *Thoughts speculative their unsure hopes relate,*
> *But certain issue strokes must arbitrate . . .*

They rely on the future to fulfil their hopes; he knows that the
future cannot differ from the present: 'I have lived long enough
. . . Life's but a walking shadow . . . I 'gin to be aweary of the
sun.'

It is interesting to note that in the last Act-and-a-half the
name 'Macbeth' is little used; he is 'the tyrant', 'the confident
tyrant'; this loss of personal identity and assimilation to the
type of 'the tyrant' is in keeping with the general movement of
the play. Within the castle we witness the atrophy of hope, of
the sense of a personal future. Macbeth here is like those
'betrayers of their lords' that Dante finds frozen in the rigid
silence of the bottom of Hell, iced-up in despair. Outside, in
the army of Malcolm, we see the same facts from a more social
point of view: a disease has to be plucked out of the body
politic. And this is certainly one of the leading effects made at
the end of the play. 'The time is free', the 'dead butcher and his
fiend-like queen' have been properly disposed of. Yet the
ending is not couched simply in these social terms. The final
exchange between Macbeth and Macduff points at a more
complex valuation. Macbeth's refusal to fight with Macduff
because

> *my soul is too much charged*
> *With blood of thine already*

(v.6.44–5) is unexpected and (no doubt) implausible in terms of
real-life psychology. But the idea of a 'good' Macbeth, buried
somewhere beneath the activities of a will dedicated to evil,
has not been allowed to perish altogether at any point in the
play. The fact that 'the tyrant' can describe, so movingly
(v.3.24–5),

> *that which should accompany old age,*
> *As honour, love, obedience, troops of friends*

while stressing that he cannot have these things, is sufficient to point to us the wasted potentialities behind the wicked actuality. And so with the final unwillingness to fight Macduff. Macbeth is a man, not a fiend. Motions of the will tending to good still fluctuate round the hardened heart, though they are powerless to affect the general disposition of his will, or to undo what has been done. The same may be said of the brief *anagnorisis*, the sudden moment of total recognition of what the 'juggling fiends' have done – when he draws back from Macduff and says 'I'll not fight with thee.' It is not a moment that can be expanded: time is irreversible; Macbeth has become 'the tyrant' and his fate in life is to be exhibited as 'the tyrant'. What the force of his vitality (that *sine qua non* of heroism) has turned into is a power to accept whatever is necessary, to die with harness on his back; and so he dies, as he began the play, fighting manfully. But without the flinching, without the moment of *anagnorisis*, the final heroic resistance would not be fully human, and if Macbeth was not fully human we would not be interested enough to do more than detest him. As it is, we detest not so much what he *is*, as what he has become, the *process* of damnation.

The same point might be made, in rather more conventional terms, by pointing out that 'Macbeth is a poet'. This is, of course, a dangerous over-simplification. It is Shakespeare who is the poet, and any assumption that Macbeth himself has 'a poetic temperament' (whatever that may be) would be notable false psychology. But it is true that the play's poetic energy contrives to centre on Macbeth, right to the end. And the poetic temper of the play is one that is particularly appropriate to Macbeth. The rhythms have a new fluency for Shakespearian verse, suitable to the rapid and violent change of focus and interest that characterizes his thought. There is a sense of barely suppressed impatience or violence in the disjunction of image from image, thought from thought, phrase from phrase as may be seen in the following (III.2.45–55):

> *Be innocent of the knowledge, dearest chuck,*
> *Till thou applaud the deed. Come, seeling night,*
> *Scarf up the tender eye of pitiful day,*
> *And with thy bloody and invisible hand*
> *Cancel and tear to pieces that great bond*
> *Which keeps me pale. Light thickens*
> *And the crow makes wing to the rooky wood;*
> *Good things of day begin to droop and drowse,*
> *Whiles night's black agents to their preys do rouse.*
> *Thou marvell'st at my words; but hold thee still.*
> *Things bad begun make strong themselves by ill.*

The imagery of the play is very notable and has often been commented upon; it, likewise, is lurid and violent – 'shapes of horror, dimly seen in the murky air or revealed by the glare of the cauldron' (as Bradley says). Darkness, blood, fire, the reverberation of noise like thunder, the world of the actor, of the man wearing clothes that are too grand for him – these are continuously invoked to give us (once again) the sense of an inferno barely controlled beneath the surface crust.

The poetic impression is of a hold on coherence which is tossed and distorted by inner violence and destructiveness, nearly broken up by the pressures upon it, but which survives, however narrowly; and this spills over to affect our impression of Macbeth himself. His mind, likewise, is distorted by violence and terror; and though there is nothing morally admirable about the capacity to speak well, we are in fact held sympathetically by a sense of surviving significance in his rhythms, even in those final speeches whose content is devoted to the meaninglessness of existence.

The poetry, in short, carries our sympathy beyond the point where ordinary human identification can expect to operate. We continue to respond to the rhythms of the human heart even when the lives before us are, as Dr Johnson pointed out, 'merely detested'.

THE PLAY IN PERFORMANCE

It is usually supposed today that *Macbeth* was first performed before James I and his royal guest, King Christian IV of Denmark, some time during the latter's visit to England – 17 July to 11 August 1606. It has been argued that the performance took place at Hampton Court on 7 August 1606, one of the three occasions when Shakespeare's company acted before the kings, and this is perfectly possible.

It can also be argued, over and above this, that the play was *written* with James's tastes in mind (see 'Background of the Play', below). If so, it was also (presumably) written with indoor performance in mind; and this would link up with some features of its theatrical technique. A play designed specifically for the afternoon daylight of The Globe might find it hard to give a visual equivalent to the verbal atmosphere of darkness and murk that characterizes *Macbeth*. But a courtly 'nocturnal' could very well project the sense of gloom that the play requires. The play may also have been designed to be spectacular – many court plays were. Apparitions, and such sound effects as thunder, owls, bells, oboes, and trumpets, abound. It is a moot point how the Witches made their exits and entrances. Some kind of 'disappearing trick' seems to be implied for the exit at 1.3.77. 'Whither are they vanished?' asks Banquo. Macbeth answers:

> *Into the air; and what seemed corporal*
> *Melted, as breath into the wind.*

Again, Macbeth says in Act IV, scene 1:

> *Infected be the air whereon they ride*

– which may be taken to imply flying witches. The Jacobean court masque used elaborate stage-machinery and it may be that *Macbeth* did likewise.

It has been supposed that the last figure in the dumb-show

of kings in Act IV, scene 1, who is said in the text to have 'a glass in his hand', represented Mary, Queen of Scots; and used the glass to reflect the figure of James himself, the principal spectator of the play. No doubt it would have been improper to represent James in any other way; but it is difficult to see how the glass operated, or how the audience knew it was operating. Certainly the performances at The Globe must have used a different technique.

Elizabethan and Jacobean court plays were seldom designed only for the court; and *Macbeth*, if the company followed the normal practice, would be played at The Globe soon afterwards. We know that it *was* played at the public theatre, for a record of one such early performance – on 20 April 1611 – has survived among the papers of Dr Simon Forman, an astrologer who kept notes of plays seen, 'for policy': that is, in order to record moral or social lessons that he had learned (the textual implications of Forman's note are discussed on page 817):

In Macbeth, at the Globe, 1610 [mistake for 1611], *the 20th of April* [Saturday], *there was to be observed first how Macbeth and Banquo two noblemen of Scotland, riding through a wood, there stood before them three women fairies or nymphs, and saluted Macbeth, saying three times unto him, Hail, Macbeth, king of Codon, for thou shalt be a king, but shalt beget no kings, &c. Then said Banquo What, all to Macbeth and nothing to me? Yes, said the nymphs, Hail, to thee, Banquo; thou shalt beget kings, yet be no king. And so they departed, and came to the Court of Scotland, to Duncan king of Scots, and it was in the days of Edward the Confessor. And Duncan bade them both kindly welcome, and made Macbeth [sic] forthwith Prince of Northumberland, and sent him home to his own castle, and appointed Macbeth to provide for him, for he would sup with him the next day at night, and did so. And Macbeth contrived to kill Duncan, and through the persuasion of his wife did that night murder the king in his own castle, being his guest. And there were many prodigies seen that night and the day before. And when Macbeth had murdered the king, the blood on his hands could not be washed off by any means, nor from his wife's hands, which handled the bloody daggers in hiding them, by which means they became both much amazed and affronted. The murder being known, Duncan's two sons fled, the one to England, the [other to] Wales, to save themselves; they being fled, they were supposed guilty of the murder of their father, which was nothing so. Then was Macbeth crowned king, and then he for fear of Banquo, his old companion, that he should beget kings but be no king himself, he contrived the death of Banquo, and caused him to be murdered on the way as he rode. The next night, being at supper with his noblemen, whom he had bid to a feast, to the which also Banquo should have come, he began to speak of noble Banquo, and to wish that he were there. And as he thus did, standing up to drink a carouse to him, the ghost of Banquo came and sat down in his chair behind him. And he, turning about to sit down again, saw the ghost of Banquo which fronted him so, that he fell into a great passion of fear and fury, uttering many words about his murder, by which, when they heard that Banquo was murdered, they suspected Macbeth. Then Macduff fled to England to the king's son, and so they raised an army and came into Scotland, and at Dunston Anyse overthrew Macbeth. In the mean time, while Macduff was in England, Macbeth slew Macduff's wife and children, and after, in the battle, Macduff slew Macbeth. Observe also how Macbeth's queen did rise in the night in her sleep, and walked, and talked and confessed all, and the Doctor noted her words.*

We can know little for certain about the nature of these Jacobean performances. Presumably the part of Macbeth was played originally by Richard Burbage, who created the title-roles of all the great Shakespeare tragedies. Presumably the parts of Lady Macbeth and Lady Macduff were played by boys; and it is likely that men played the Witches' parts, as they did other crone-roles of the Elizabethan stage.

Presumably the play was costumed in contemporary style; but IV.3.160, where Malcolm seems to recognize Ross as a Scotsman by his clothes, suggests that touches of 'Scottishness' appeared. Certainly the costuming stayed contemporary up to and beyond the time of Garrick, who played the hero in the scarlet coat of an eighteenth-century general. But in 1772 Macklin adopted the tartan and the kilt as more appropriate to the primitive nature of the action; and from that time forward barbaric clothing has prevailed, reaching a climax (one trusts) in the Orson Welles film of 1948 which set the play (evidently) in the sartorial reign of Genghis Khan.

Sir William Davenant refashioned the play, about 1663, into something much more 'regular' or neo-classical; scansion and vocabulary were pruned into line with neo-classical tastes, so that

> *What bloody man is that? He can report,*
> *As seemeth by his plight, of the revolt*
> *The newest state*

becomes

> *What aged man is that? If we may guess*
> *His message by his looks, he can relate*
> *The issue of the battle.*

'Superfluous' or eccentric characters, like the Old Man, the bleeding Captain, and the Porter disappear, or turn into Seyton – here the universal factotum and confidant. I shall discuss later (pages 820/21) the textual problems raised by the *Macbeth* songs in the Davenant version. The point to make here is their appropriateness to a new conception of the play. Davenant introduces a completely new Witch-scene, after Act II, scene 4. On the blasted heath Lady Macduff meets Macduff in flight from Inverness, and the Witches prophesy to them, as earlier to Banquo and Macbeth, and entertain them with a couple of new songs. Davenant's version of *Macbeth* is not only more 'regular' but also more obviously spectacular than Shakespeare's. A contemporary refers to 'The tragedy of *Macbeth*, altered by Sir William Davenant, being dressed in all its finery, as new clothes, new scenes, machines, as flyings for the Witches, with all the singing and dancing in it . . . all excellently performed, being in the nature of an opera.' Presumably it was this version that Pepys saw in 1667, when he referred to *Macbeth* as 'a most excellent play in all respects, especially in divertissement, though it be a deep tragedy; which is a strange perfection in a tragedy, it being most proper here and suitable'. What the discerning Pepys enjoyed, English theatre-goers went on enjoying for more than a century, while the original *Macbeth* vanished. The traditional operatic conception of *Macbeth* continued to hold the stage even after Garrick had (in 1744) deleted most of Davenant's changes. (The same weakening in the sense of supernatural evil is evident in the Verdi *Macbeth* no less than in the Davenant one. Singing witches are likely to be too tuneful to be terrifying, however good the tunes.) The Witches' divertissements continued to be staged into Irving's time: that is, till 1888.

Garrick's *Macbeth* deleted much of Davenant's rewriting, but was by no means a purely Shakespearian text. The most famous Garrick addition was the speech he gave to the dying Macbeth:

> *'Tis done! The scene of life will quickly close.*
> *Ambition's vain delusive dreams are fled,*
> *And now I wake to darkness, guilt and horror.*
> *I cannot bear it! Let me shake it off —*
> *It will not be; my soul is clogged with blood —*
> *I cannot rise! I dare not ask for mercy —*
> *It is too late; hell drags me down; I sink,*
> *I sink — my soul is fled for ever! O – O –*   Dies

The stage-history of *Macbeth* requires, as I have suggested, that we notice the diversion of Shakespeare's play towards external spectacle. When we notice this movement, however, we should also observe that the natural and (as it were) internal spectacle of *Macbeth* was, at the same time, being reduced. The appearance of Banquo's ghost in the banqueting scene (Act III, scene 4) was a famous moment in the Jacobean theatre (as contemporary witness attests). But no one in the scene except Macbeth sees the Ghost; and the rationalizing mind of the eighteenth century was bound to be attracted by the possibility that the Ghost was a figment of Macbeth's imagination. The solitary reader's perception of the inner mind of the hero was assuming precedence over the external and theatrical signs of that mind. The physical presence of one of the race of stage ghosts, with 'their mealy faces, white shirts and red rags stuck on in imitation of blood' was finally dispelled in J. P. Kemble's production of 1794 – a production, be it noted, that introduced new splendours into the Hecat scenes. The learned approved the innovation; but the populace wanted to see the Ghost, and producers were obliged to restore him. Since that time various learned hands have sought to expunge the ghost from this scene, but none has succeeded in affecting the theatrical tradition.

J. P. Kemble's Macbeth was concerned with psychological nuance, as the business of the Ghost may suggest, but we are still, in his reign, in the period of the *noble* Macbeth, projected through a classical mode of acting as slow-moving, dignified, suffering. Kemble's sister, Mrs Siddons, was the most famous of all Lady Macbeths; and it is obvious, from the great wealth of eye-witness accounts, that she contrived to be at once more attractive, more courteous, more forceful, more terrifying than any ordinary human being. The 'statue-like solemnity' of her movements and of her utterance allowed her to convey an impression of the 'giants before the Flood', of grandly primitive simplicity. Later critics, however, complained that she was too overbearing and too scornful of her husband's weakness to provide a truthful image of Shakespeare's Lady – of the wavering and deeply divided nature of one who destroys her own finer self in order to satisfy her husband's ambitions.

The Romantic sense of greatness of spirit as naturally a prey to Childe-Harold-like alternations of extremes – this was better served by the Macbeth of Edmund Kean; for Kean seems to have brought out particularly the terror and dismay that shadow the King's nobility. The movement from noble to ignoble Macbeth was a fairly continuous nineteenth-century movement, and was taken an obvious stage further by Irving at the end of the century. Macbeth, in Irving's interpretation, was obviously unmanned by guilt. A contemporary noted that 'Mr Irving's Macbeth, as he becomes unscrupulous and reckless, becomes also abject.' In the encounter with Banquo's ghost, Macready (in the middle of the nineteenth century) had thrown his cloak over his face ('Hence, horrible shadow') and sunk back into his chair. Irving not only threw his cloak over his face but fell down at the foot of the throne.

Most modern Macbeths are of this breed – anxious, dismayed, hysterical, but lacking in the stature that would terrify us. It is worth noticing that the final duologue of Act III, scene 4, which is the emotional highlight of many modern productions, was hardly mentioned in the accounts of eighteenth-century and nineteenth-century productions.

The obviously primitive setting of *Macbeth*, and the remoteness of its manners from those of modern times, make it a difficult play to modernize. Sir Barry Jackson produced a *Macbeth* in modern dress, in London in 1928, but this was generally disliked. A review noted that 'if conditions and costumes are made modern, criminology must be also'. The Macbeth, who reminded a critic of 'a Scottish gentleman in considerable difficulties', would have been discovered, the same review continued, 'and arrested in a few hours, by the village constable'.

On the other hand the plot of *Macbeth* is clearly strong enough and archetypal enough to survive transposition into quite remote media. The American film *Joe Macbeth* (1955) translated the play into Chicago gang terms. Joe Macbeth, the lieutenant of 'king-pin Duca', the Chicago number one, has future greatness foretold him by Rosie cutting the cards; urged on by his newly wed and ambitious wife, he kills Duca on a lakeshore diving-raft ('the knife knows where to go, Joe. Just follow it'); and later has also to kill Bankie, his former friend.

The Chicago inter-gang bloodbath provides a convincing translation of the final scenes of the play.

The Japanese film *Throne of Blood* (1957) makes an even more radical transmutation. Not only is the dialogue in Japanese, but it seems to have little to do with Shakespeare's text. The director's effort has been to externalize Macbeth's mind in terms of visual images rather than words. Hence the importance of the forest, which is here at once an impediment in the way of Washizu's (Macbeth's) conquest of the castle (the kingdom) and a symbol of the natural barbarity of his mind.

Both these adaptations stress the point that, by conquering, Macbeth becomes what Duncan was – the object (rather than the subject) of ambition and treachery. In these terms the plot can be endlessly fertile of imitation.

BACKGROUND OF THE PLAY

Shakespeare found the story of *Macbeth* in two separate sections of Holinshed's *Chronicles* (1587). One section is concerned with the secret murder of King Duff and the other with Macbeth's killing of Duncan (in battle) and his subsequent reign. This was legendary rather than historical material – though something resembling it may well have occurred in the middle of the eleventh century – and Shakespeare (as in the parallel instances of *King Lear* and *Cymbeline*) treated his source with a degree of liberty that was not possible in the Histories. The 'history' of *Macbeth* is, in fact, moral rather than factual history; just as the 'Scotland' of *Macbeth* is a country of the mind rather than a real geographical location. Those who bring to the play experience of the country or the century, beyond what the play provides, are in danger of distorting what is really there. More relevant is the image of Scottish history that appeared on Shakespeare's horizon via the mind of the new King of England – James I.

As noted above, *Macbeth* is generally supposed to have been

written in 1606 for performance before James I and his royal
guest, King Christian IV of Denmark. The play seems designed
to catch at several of James's obsessive interests: first of all at
his interest in his native country and its past, and in particular
at his pride in his own lineage. The unhistorical figure of
Banquo, and the unbroken fertility of the Stuarts, descending
directly through nine generations – both of these are made
much of in the play, particularly in the dumb-show of Act IV,
scene 1, where Stuart monarchs pass before Macbeth's stupefied
gaze –

> *What, will the line stretch out to the crack of doom?*

Furthermore, James had written learnedly on witches and
was known to have a powerful interest in this subject. In 1605,
when he visited Oxford (Shakespeare may have been present),
Dr Matthew Gwinn, a Fellow of St John's College, welcomed
him with a show of Three Sibyls, much approved by James.
The three quasi-sibyls of Dr Gwinn's show are derived from
the 'three women in strange and wild apparel ... either the
Weird Sisters, that is (as ye would say) the goddesses of destiny
or else some nymphs or fairies' who accost Macbeth and
Banquo in Holinshed's *Chronicles of Scotland*. In Gwinn's entertainment they remind James of the prophecies to Banquo (his
supposed ancestor) and then hail the King himself, as (firstly)
King of Scotland, (secondly) King of England, and (thirdly)
King of Ireland.

In spite of Gwinn's usage, and of Holinshed's description of
the ladies as 'goddesses ... nymphs or fairies', Shakespeare
represents *his* Weird Sisters, however, as traditional Scottish
witches, with withered skin, beards, and a native love of
mischief – witches such as had appeared in Forres, and were
described by Holinshed as depriving the monarch of sleep and
health, in an episode that forms part of the primary material of
the *Macbeth* story. Moreover, Shakespeare uses the same witches
again in Act IV, where Holinshed speaks of 'certain wizards, in
whose words he put great confidence', and of 'Witches', quite

distinct from the nymphs or fairies of the earlier episode. Thus Shakespeare centres the play on a struggle between the individual and the recurrent forces of demonic possession, where his source does not.

But the struggle is not simply between an individual (any individual) and the powers of darkness. The play offers a continuous study of modes of kingship. Duncan, Macbeth, Malcolm, and Edward the Confessor reveal complementary insights into the nature of that connexion between Divinity and royal position that James was so concerned about. Act IV, scene 3, is largely concerned with definition of 'the king-becoming graces', and its report of Edward the Confessor's virtues is used to establish the potency of virtuous kingship in our minds before the play plunges onward to demonstrate the fate of vicious kingship (and queenship). The episode of Edward's 'touching' for 'the Evil' (scrofula) seems to have been written, indeed, to link the play's sense of royal virtue with James. As the text tells us (IV.3.155):

> To the succeeding royalty he leaves
> The healing benediction.

By the date of the play James had begun, after some hesitation, to 'touch' for the King's Evil.

We should also notice that the opponents of Divine Kingship are not simply the diabolical forces of evil; they are also traitors and weaklings, equivocators and false believers, such as had been plentifully apparent in the most dramatic antimonarchical episode of James's reign – the Gunpowder Plot of 1605 – and in the subsequent treason trials, especially that of the Provincial of the Jesuit Order in England, Father Garnet. Garnet's trial had excited great detestation because, when he was discovered in lies told to his examiners, he alleged that he had done so in accordance with the doctrine of 'Equivocation', which allowed the faithful to say one thing while holding (but not uttering) mental reservations. This is usually thought to be referred to directly in the Porter's 'Faith, here's an equivocator that could swear in both the scales against either scale, who committed treason enough for God's sake, yet could not equivocate to heaven' (II.3.8–11). Equivocation, the 'double sense' of Macbeth, the swearing and lying that young Macduff refers to in Act IV, scene 2, is indeed a principal mode of the operation of evil forces throughout the play.

Whether the play as we have it in the only surviving authentic text – that of the first Folio (1623) – is the play that was performed at Hampton Court, or the play as seen at The Globe – this has been considered to be another real problem. Simon Forman's account, cited above (pages 808–9), diverges from the play we can read. But should we suppose that there was ever a play corresponding exactly to Forman's account? It seems fairly clear from his wording that he has remembered or consulted Holinshed's chronicle of the reign; which implies uncertainty of memory and contamination from an outside source – both suspicious qualities in a witness. In any case Forman was not writing as a theatrical reporter; he was writing notes on matters that might be useful to remember. Can we blame him, or be surprised, if he did not write down what did not seem worth memorializing?

The shortness of our text (about 2,100 lines) may be thought to point to court origin – James was bored by long performances. On the other hand, the text that reached the printing-house in 1622 (and emerged in the first Folio) is very unlikely to have come from the court, and very likely to have come from the public theatre. The concentration of the action (notice the absence of any sub-plot) is in fact a quality close to the essential life of the play; it is hard to imagine any addition that would not be a dilution. It has sometimes been argued that matters are left unexplained (whether Macbeth had discussed the murder with his wife; whether or not he knew of Cawdor's treachery), but what Shakespeare play does not give rise to such complaints? Nothing essential to *Macbeth* is left in doubt; and the art of chiaroscuro, of leaving the inessential in richly suggestive shadow, is no strange element in Shakespeare's art.

Macbeth is a play of stark disjunctions (murders amid feastings, the laughing Porter at the gate of hell, the whitest innocence beside the blackest treachery, femininity coupled with violence), and the tersest of narrative methods is required. It is hard to imagine that either the Globe *Macbeth* or the court *Macbeth* could have differed in any important respects from the *Macbeth* we have today.

Of course the 'steep tragic contrasts' which I have been describing as essential to the play have often been thought to be the result of corruption rather than design; and it has been assumed, from time to time, that the bleeding Captain, the Old Man of Act II, scene 4, the Porter, young Macduff, and even the last hundred lines of the play, are non-Shakespearian. These are, however, fairly generally accepted nowadays. The only parts of the play to excite general suspicion today are those involving Hecat, and these deserve fuller discussion.

Hecat appears twice (III.5.1–35, and IV.1.38–43), though she is mentioned on several other occasions, and in both these appearances (as in one other passage, IV.1.124–31, when she seems to be absent) we have recurrent features different from anything else in the Witch-scenes of *Macbeth*. The poetry of the *Macbeth* Witches is characterized by a four-beat trochaic rhythm:

> *Liver of blaspheming Jew,*
> *Gall of goat, and slips of yew . . .*
> *Finger of birth-strangled babe,*
> *Ditch-delivered by a drab,*
> *Make the gruel thick and slab.*

This rhythm is not simply the literary mode that Shakespeare chose, but is rather an essential part of the creation; it is the tone of voice that we must think of as 'natural' to these creatures. It holds, in its drumming insistence, in its obsessively narrow range of effects (hovering between threat and ritual), the key to the quality of their natures. And the rhythm (and so the nature) of Hecat is quite different:

> *And, which is worse, all you have done*
> *Hath been but for a wayward son,*
> *Spiteful and wrathful, who, as others do,*
> *Loves for his own ends, not for you.*

The basic beat here is iambic, and a much greater degree of freedom from steady recurrence seems to be permissible. The difference that the change from trochaic to iambic metre causes can be seen from a simple rephrasing of the Witches' lines given above. If we had read (with Davenant)

> *The liver of blaspheming Jew,*
> *With gall of goats and slips of yew,*
> *Plucked when the moon was in eclipse,*
> *With a Turk's nose and Tartar's lips;*
> *The finger of a strangled babe*
> *Born of a ditch-delivered drab,*
> *Shall make the gruel thick and slab,*

I suggest that we would have found the passage less terrifying, more 'normal', more acceptable. But not only do the Hecat lines *sound* different; they refer to a different relationship between Macbeth and the Witches. In Act III, scene 5, Hecat rebukes the Witches for unauthorized dealings with Macbeth who

> *Loves for his own ends, not for you.*

The suggestion of *love* between the Witches and any human being is ludicrously unlike anything that we have been led to expect. Moreover the Witches here seem concerned (self-consciously) with entertainment, in a way utterly remote from their characters as earlier established. They dance and sing; and at the end of Act IV, scene 1, they do this specifically to 'cheer up' Macbeth:

FIRST WITCH

> *But why*
> *Stands Macbeth thus amazedly?*
> *Come, sisters, cheer we up his sprites*
> *And show the best of our delights.*
> *I'll charm the air to give a sound,*
> *While you perform your antic round,*
> *That this great King may kindly say*
> *Our duties did his welcome pay.*

Music. The Witches dance; and vanish

MACBETH

> *Where are they? Gone! Let this pernicious hour*
> *Stand aye accursèd in the calendar.*

The discontinuity here between the Witches' efforts and Macbeth's response seems more than another effect of contrast. It is as if the two sides were on totally different wavelengths, or speaking out of different plays.

Mention of the music brings us to the most obvious and perhaps the most misleading elements in this whole tangled situation. The two songs named in the Folio text – 'Black spirits etc.' (IV.I.43) and 'Come away, come away etc.' (III.5.35) – appear (in full) in Sir William Davenant's rewriting of *Macbeth* for Restoration tastes (*c.* 1663) and (earlier) in a manuscript play by Thomas Middleton, *The Witch* – dated between 1609 and 1616. (They are printed on pages 837-9.) The Middleton play provides the natural setting for these songs, and there can be little doubt that they were written by Middleton for his own play. The obvious explanation must be that they were inserted into *Macbeth* at some point between 1609 and the publication of *Macbeth* in the first Folio (1623), presumably as part of an expanded version, used in a revival.

Songs are regular centres of corruption and textual uncertainties in the printed plays of this period. The conditions of their preservation differed in some important ways from those of the play-texts themselves. They were very often omitted from the printed texts, and were liable to be interpolated into plays some time after the first edition. Presumably, fashions in song-style and in lyric altered more rapidly than fashions in spoken verse; and the commercial consequence was that theatrical managers required changes here more frequently than in other respects.

We do not have in *Macbeth*, however, the whole texts of the songs that appear in *The Witch*, only the first lines. The reference by catch-lines appears in other plays, it is true, but then the title normally refers to a well-known tune. I believe that *Macbeth* is unique in using catch-lines to refer to songs that are only known from a single dramatic text, and obviously written for that text. It is possible indeed that full texts of the Middleton songs did not appear in any *Macbeth* before the Quarto of 1673 – where they are, presumably, derived from Davenant's version. It is even possible, indeed, that it is the music (probably written by Robert Johnson, musician to the King's Men, in the first decade of the seventeenth century) that is referred to in the Folio *Macbeth*, rather than any particular set of words.

Moreover, even if the full Middleton texts were used in the Jacobean performances of *Macbeth*, it does not follow that the words of Act III, scene 5, or of the two iambic passages in Act IV, scene 1, were also written by Middleton. They are not in the least like the witch-rhetoric of *The Witch*. They exist to introduce the balletic and operatic elements in *Macbeth*, but since songs were regarded as general (and detachable) playhouse property, there is no particular necessity to suppose that Middleton wrote the introductory lines. Their author could well be Shakespeare himself.

Further Reading

Among single-volume editions, Kenneth Muir's Arden edition (1951; last revised 1984) remains the most useful. There is an interestingly argued Oxford edition (1990), with elaborate apparatus, edited by Nicholas Brooke; among paperbacks, one should mention the revised Bantam, edited by David Bevington (1988); G. L. Kittredge's edition (1936) is worth consulting for the well-focused fullness of its annotations. The Harrow edition of Watkins and Lemmon (1964) concentrates on the theatrical possibilities of the play, illustrated by line drawings of Globe-type performances. A comprehensive account of scholarship and criticism is to be found in *Macbeth: An Annotated Bibliography* by Thomas Wheeler (The Garland Shakespeare Biographies, 1990).

Sources

The relevant passages from Holinshed's *Chronicle*, the principal source, are printed in Furness's New Variorum edition (1873), in Kenneth Muir's and in Nicholas Brooke's. Geoffrey Bullough's *Narrative and Dramatic Sources of Shakespeare*, Volume VII (1973), discusses and prints all known sources and anologues.

The Play

(1) *Classic Criticism*
Brian Vickers' *Shakespeare: The Cultural Heritage*, six volumes (1974–81), presents substantial extracts from theatrical and literary comments up to 1801. The most famous literary essay on *Macbeth* – De Quincey's 'On the Knocking on the Gate in *Macbeth*' – is available (slightly abbreviated) in Furness. R. G.

Moulton's *Shakespeare as a Dramatic Artist* (1885) remains the most pertinently accessible of Victorian treatments. Moulton's 'arrangement' of *Macbeth* as a Greek tragedy (in *The Ancient Classical Drama*, 1890) is a stimulating exercise in comparative criticism. Scholarship that opens up the background of the play can be sampled in Walter Clyde Curry's essay on 'Demonic Metaphysics' in his *Shakespeare's Philosophical Patterns* (1937), in Willard Farnham's *Shakespeare's Tragic Frontier* (1950) and in H. N. Paul, *The Royal Play of Macbeth* (1950) – but see the comments on Paul in Muir's Appendix D and in the Appendix to Chapter 8 in J. R. Brown's *Focus on 'Macbeth'* (1981). A. C. Bradley's chapter in *Shakespearean Tragedy* (1904) remains unsurpassed in its accurate attention to detail coupled with a coherent and lucid theoretical basis. But, in so far as this coherence depends on a subordination of the poetry spoken to the person speaking, it has excited rejection, first in L. C. Knights' 1933 essay 'How Many Children Had Lady Macbeth?' – reprinted in *Explorations* (1946) – and subsequently in many works concerned to validate the images in the play as the source of its inner meaning, as in Cleanth Brooks' 'The Naked Babe and the Cloak of Manliness' in *The Well-Wrought Urn* (1942) and in G. Wilson Knight's *The Wheel of Fire* (1930) and *The Imperial Theme* (1931). E. M. W. Tillyard pointed out *Macbeth*'s relation to the History Plays in his *Shakespeare's History Plays* (1944).

(2) *Modernist Criticism*

Judged by the size of the bibliography, *Macbeth* seems in the last three decades to have attracted less critical interest than the other 'Bradleian' tragedies – *Othello*, *King Lear* and *Hamlet*. The classical simplicity of the plot, what Emrys Jones (*Scenic Form in Shakespeare*, 1971) has called the 'elegance' and 'formal coherence' of its plotting and the apparent determinism of its moral structure, with good and evil placed at opposite poles, may have discouraged further essays in description. Modernist criticism has chosen to go behind the apparently tidy coherence that classic criticism described, concentrating, like the New

Critics of the thirties, on the disruptive energy that emerges in the poetry of the play. But the modernists are less interested in describing this as part of a moral pattern than as an indicator of the suppressed energies of political groups opposed to the Stuart kings. Feminism and radical politics (not always separable) have provided the principal vocabularies for this enterprise.

The feminist mode finds an obvious justification in the play's recurrent interest in 'manliness' (violent soldiership) and in its exploration of the consequences of this in the contrasting fates of husband and wife. Freud had given his blessing to this enquiry in a brief discussion on the effect of 'success' in fragmenting character (a point taken up again in Barbara Everett's *Young Hamlet* (1989)). Freud is particularly concerned with the incoherence of the victim-wife, Lady Macbeth (see *The Standard Edition of the Complete Works*, Vol 4 (1957), pp. 318–24). Janet Adelman – in *Cannibals, Witches and Divorce*, ed. Marjorie Garber (1987) – replaces Bradley's moral universals with Freud's psychological ones and sees Macbeth's career as a history of psychic disorientation, requiring him to take refuge in the fantasy of total maleness in order to cope with female domination (appearing in both the Witches and Lady Macbeth).

The disruption of 'conformist' views produced by reading the play from the point of view of gender politics can also be achieved in more purely historical terms. The recentness of the Gunpowder Plot of 1605 and the trials of Jesuit 'traitors' (referred to in the Porter's speech) have suggested to some that the play has a hidden political agenda. See Stephen Mullaney's article in *ELH* 47 (1980), 32–47. David Norbrook's essay on *Macbeth*, printed in Sharpe and Zwicker, *Politics of Discourse* (1987), argues against the classic position that the play turns on an absolute contrast between the tyrant Macbeth and the good king Duncan. He finds in the background of the play and in Scottish history (drawing on Arthur M. Clark's *Murder under Trust*, 1981) evidence of anti-monarchical currents of thought and deduces Shakespeare's imaginative sympathy with such thoughts. Alan Sinfield in *Faultlines* (1992) offers a very similar view (Duncan is delegitimized by the violence needed to sustain him; in a world sustained by violence Macbeth has no other way of expressing political opposition.) Compare also the essay by Michael Hawkins in John R. Brown's *Focus on Macbeth* (1981).

Brown's collection concentrates mainly on what may be called 'the psychology of performance'. Sinfield's more recent collection of essays (1992) focuses on modernist positions. *Shakespeare Survey 19* (1966) is devoted to *Macbeth* and contains a survey of critical studies; many of the essays in the volume are reprinted in *Aspects of 'Macbeth'*, edited by Kenneth Muir and Philip Edwards (1977). R. A. Foakes has an excellent bibliographical essay in Stanley Wells's *Shakespeare: A Bibliographical Guide* (1990).

Stage History

Stage history has occupied more space than usual in recent writings on *Macbeth*, perhaps because theatre allows more scope for a free play of interpretation. Stage history is discussed in the New Cambridge edition by J. Dover Wilson (1947), in Brooke's Oxford edition and in A. C. Sprague's *Shakespeare and the Actors* (1944). Dennis Bartholomeusz's *Macbeth and the Players* (1969) gives an illuminating account of stage actions from 1610 to 1964. Marvin Rosenberg, *The Masks of Macbeth* (1978), takes the reader through the play and at each point describes various theatrical realizations. Gordon Williams, in *Macbeth: Text and Performance* (1985), offers a useful set of summary points. The Cornmarket Press has issued facsimiles of playhouse texts for 1671, 1673, 1674, 1753, 1761 and 1794. The manuscript of Middleton's *The Witch* is printed as a Malone Society Reprint (eds. Greg and Wilson, 1948–50). The Witch-scenes from *The Witch* are printed in Furness. Davenant's operatic version (written before 1668, published in 1674) appears in Furness, in Christopher Spencer's *Five Restoration Adaptations of Shakespeare* (1965) and in a full scholarly edition by the same author in 1961. The Orson Welles and Polanski films, the BBC Shakespeare Series production and the Royal Shakespeare Theatre version with Ian McKellen and Judi Dench are available in video cassette.

An Account of the Text

The Names of the Characters

Some of the character-names printed in this text may seem strange to readers, and some of the characters mentioned in the list do not usually appear in such lists. A few words should be said about the principles and about individual cases.

The names of characters in *Macbeth* are very consistent, and need no altering from the usage of the first Folio to make them intelligible; but editors have normally altered some names, in the interest of modernity, or historical accuracy. The Folio always refers to Lady Macbeth as *Lady*, to Duncan as *King* and to Lady Macduff as *Wife* ('Macduff's Wife'), and these I have preserved, as marking important and potentially authorial observations about these characters. Names like *Seyton* and *Seyward* have been presented in this form, as indicating their Shakespearian pronunciation. The fact that modern historians call the historical characters on whom these are based *Seaton* and *Siward* seems beside the point. We should not correct Shakespeare's historical knowledge for him, change *Berowne* (in *Love's Labour's Lost*) into 'Biron', or correct the spelling *Banquo* (= Banquho) into 'Banwho' – no doubt the accurate modern notation; for Shakespeare's world is not that of the modern historian, but one created to stand by itself. His *Hecat* (two syllables) is not the classical Hecate (three syllables) but a creative variation upon that original; his *Birnan* is not the geographically precise modern Birnam, his *Cathness* and *Menteth* are not the modern Caithness and Menteith but names he found in Holinshed. On the other hand there is no point in preserving old *spellings* of modern names, where pronunciation is not in question: 'Lenox' for Lennox, or 'Rosse' for Ross.

The 'Other Murderers' who appear in the list are those who murder Lady Macduff and her son in Act IV, scene 2. These are distinct from the 'Three Murderers' with whom Macbeth arranges the murder of Banquo.

The 'Three other Witches' are those who enter with Hecat at IV.I.38, and who seem to be distinct from the Weird Sisters of the rest of the play.

The Sources of the Text

Macbeth was never printed in Shakespeare's lifetime, no doubt because his company – The King's Men – was able to keep the manuscript from the printers, so preserving the appeal of the play in the theatre. It first appeared in Shakespeare's *Comedies, Histories, Tragedies* (1623) – the so-called first Folio (hereafter referred to as 'F'). The text there has been the subject of much suspicion (like almost everything in that famous volume); it is true that the play is shorter than any other tragedy (about 2,100 lines), but it is difficult to prove anything by this, apart from shortness. The text as we have it is intelligible throughout, orderly and coherent – Acts and scenes are regularly marked. These qualities are usually taken to imply that the printed version is at some distance from the author's manuscript; for authors are less likely to be consistent and orderly than are the hacks who prepare manuscripts for specific occasions; and in the theatrical world of Shakespeare, this hack was most likely to be the bookkeeper or prompter, whose business it was to transform the author's creative act into a programme of stage activity, a prompt-book and a set of parts. It is usually supposed that the printers of F had the prompt-book (or a transcript of it) in the printing-house, and from this set up the *Macbeth* pages in F.

The editor's duty is, in this case, to follow the F text, except where manifest printing errors have occurred (not collated below), or where Shakespeare's intention seems to be misrepresented by the printing. A list of these latter cases is given

below. Unless otherwise stated, the alternative version given is
that of F, except that the 'long s' [ʃ] is not used.

COLLATIONS

1.1.	8–9	I come, *Gray-Malkin.* *All. Padock* calls anon: faire is foule, and foule is faire
1.2.	0	(stage direction) *King Duncan, Malcolm*] *King Malcome*
	14	quarrel] Quarry
	45	(stage direction) *Exit Captain with Attendants*] not in F
	58	point-rebellious,] Point, rebellious (most editors: point rebellious,)
1.3.	96–7	as hail | Came] as Tale | Can (Johnson: as tale | Came)
	126	(stage direction) *They walk apart*] not in F
1.4.	0	(stage direction) *King Duncan, Lennox*] *King, Lenox*
	2	Are] Or
1.5.	15	human-kindness] humane kindnesse
1.6.	0	(stage direction) *King Duncan, Malcolm*] *King, Malcolme*
	9	most] must
	10	(stage direction) *Enter Lady Macbeth*] *Enter Lady*
	31	(stage direction) *He kisses her*] not in F
1.7.	6	shoal] Schoole
	28	(stage direction) *Enter Lady Macbeth*] *Enter Lady*
	66	a-fume] a Fume (other editors follow this F reading)
11.1.	30	(stage direction) *Exit Banquo and Fleance*] *Exit Banquo*
	55	strides] sides
	56	sure] sowre
	57	way they] they may
11.2.	0	(stage direction) *Enter Lady Macbeth*] *Enter Lady*

	8	(stage direction) MACBETH (*within*)] *Enter Macbeth*
	13	(stage direction) *Enter Macbeth, carrying two blood-stained daggers*] not in F
	63	green one red] Greene one, Red
		(stage direction) *Enter Lady Macbeth*] *Enter Lady*
II.3.	19	(stage direction) *He opens the gate*] not in F
	39	(stage direction) *Enter Macbeth*] F places after line 38
	70	(stage direction) *Exeunt Macbeth and Lennox*] F places after *awake* (line 70)
	77	(stage direction) *Enter Lady Macbeth*] *Enter Lady*
	122	(stage direction) *Lady Macbeth is taken out*] not in F
	131	(stage direction) *Exeunt all but Malcolm and Donalbain*] *Exeunt*
III.1.	11	(stage direction) *Lady Macbeth, Lennox*] *Lady Lenox*
	44	(stage direction) *Exeunt Lords and Lady Macbeth*] *Exeunt Lords*
	69	seeds] as in F (most editors: seed)
	139	(stage direction) *Exeunt Murderers*] not in F
	141	(stage direction) *Exit*] *Exeunt*
III.3.	16	(stage direction) *They attack Banquo*] not in F
	18	(stage direction) *Banquo falls. Fleance escapes*] not in F
III.4.	0	(stage direction) *Lady Macbeth, Ross*] *Lady, Rosse*
	4	(stage direction) *He walks around the tables*] not in F
	12	(stage direction) *He rises and goes to the Murderer*] not in F
	38	(stage direction) *Enter the Ghost of Banquo and sits in Macbeth's place*] F places after 'it' (line 36)
	72	(stage direction) *Exit Ghost*] not in F
	106	(stage direction) *Exit Ghost*] not in F
	143	in deed] indeed
III.6.	24	son] Sonnes
	38	the] their
IV.1.	43	(stage direction) *Exeunt Hecat and the other three*

Witches] not in F

	58	germens] Germaine
	92	Birnan] Byrnam
	96	Rebellious dead] as in F (most editors: Rebellion's head)
	105	(stage direction) *Hautboys*] F places after 'this' (line 105)
	110	(stage direction) *and Banquo; the last king*] *and Banquo last,*
IV.2.	79	(stage direction) *Enter Murderers*] F places after 'faces' (line 79)
	83	shag-haired] shagge-ear'd
	84	(stage direction) *He stabs him*] not in F
	85	(stage direction) *Son dies. Exit Wife crying 'Murder'*] *Exit crying Murther*
IV.3.	4	down-fallen] downfall
	15	deserve] discerne
	133	thy] they
	145	(stage direction) *Exit Doctor*] F places after 'amend' (line 145)
	234	tune] time
V.1.	18	(stage direction) *Enter Lady Macbeth*] *Enter Lady*
V.3.	19	(stage direction) *Exit Servant*] not in F
	21	chair . . . dis-seat] cheere . . . dis-eate
	39	Cure her] Cure
	55	senna] Cyme
	60	(stage direction) *Exit*] not in F
	62	(stage direction) *Exit*] *Exeunt*
V.5.	5	farced] *forc'd*
	7	(stage direction) *A cry within of women*] F places after *noise* (line 7)
	8	(stage direction) *Exit*] not in F
	15	(stage direction) *Enter Seyton*] not in F
V.6.	10	F marks a new scene at this point
	73	(stage direction) *Exit Macduff*] not in F

'*Mislineation*' *in* Macbeth

'Mislineation' is the name given by textual scholars to a presentation of verse which seems to the best modern readers to run counter to the author's presumed intention; and which therefore requires the editor to redivide lines, so as to approach more nearly the presumed original intention. A fairly obvious example occurs in *Macbeth* 1.4.23–8, which appears in the Folio as follows:

Macb. The seruice, and the loyaltie I owe,/
In doing it, payes it selfe.
Your Highnesse part,/is to receiue our Duties:
And our Duties/are to your Throne, and State,
Children, and Seruants;/which doe but what they should,
By doing euery thing/safe toward your Loue
And Honor.
King. Welcome hither:/

Editors normally reline this, the new line-ends coming at the points where I have inserted the oblique strokes. The reasons which lie behind their efforts are both aesthetic and arithmetical. The lines as printed run oddly and clumsily; the sense rhythms contradict the verse-rhythms quite arbitrarily. Moreover, it can be noticed that the completion of the half-line, with subsequent division into full lines, produces a neat metrical ending (a single and complete line of verse). The sum adds up. But no more than arithmetical regularity would have been achieved, if the sense-rhythms had not also been made to run more easily; since they do so here, this may be taken as a confirmation of the propriety of the relineation.

The difficulty of recognizing mislineation in Shakespeare is usually greater than this. There is no necessity for Shakespeare's lines to scan absolutely; and certainly there is no rule that interjections or new speeches should complete incomplete lines of verse. He thought of his plays as spoken rather than written and no doubt thought of his rhythmic units in terms of the voice rather than the page. The editor is not dealing with material which aspires towards any single and definite printed form. This is particularly obvious when the editor has to deal with problems of verse or prose. It hardly helps here to know that Shakespeare did not think in terms of 'Now I'll write in prose', 'I think I'll write a few lines in verse here', but moved effortlessly all the way along a scale from the most rhythmical to the least rhythmical units. Conversations like that between young Macduff and his mother (Act IV, scene 2), mainly in short units, raise really insoluble editorial problems when lines of the conversation fall into fairly obvious blank-verse units: 'Thou speak'st with all thy wit', says Macduff's wife, 'And yet, i'faith, with wit enough for thee.' Is this verse or prose? The proper answer is 'Neither; it is speech'. The Folio prints this example as verse, perhaps for no very good reason; and I have been content to follow it; but most editors have changed it to prose.

Macbeth is a play with a great deal of mislineation; and it is often suggested that this proves that it was rewritten or otherwise cut about. A number of reasons for this emerge, however, which have nothing to do with revision or rewriting. The Folio is printed in double columns, on a narrower allowance of space for long lines than in modern reprints. This leads to a number of what may be called 'normal' mislineations. The end of Act II, scene 2, is printed in two passages of half-lines instead of whole lines (lines 65-9 and 73, 74) partly to leave space for the *Knock* and *Exeunt* stage-directions on the right-hand side of the column. 1.3.77 is similarly divided into two, to allow space for the stage-direction *Witches vanish*.

These are considerations which apply to all the plays; but there are further considerations which narrow the field of inquiry. The plays which W. W. Greg's *The Shakespeare First Folio* mentions as posing particular problems of lineation are *Antony and Cleopatra*, *Timon of Athens*, and *Coriolanus*. Add *Macbeth* to these and we have a probably complete list of the plays that Shakespeare wrote between 1606 and 1608. The verse of these plays has in common a new looseness of structure or fluidity of movement, and this may have imposed on either Shakespeare *or* the transcriber *or* the compositors (or all three) problems of conveying the 'feel' of the verse on to the page. Certainly there is evidence that the Folio compositors found it difficult to handle their material. The rhetoric of reported action, as it appears in *Macbeth*, has an individual rhythmic character, including a formal use of quasi-Virgilian short lines ('Till he faced the slave'; 'I cannot tell'; 'And fan our people cold'; 'Craves composition'; 'My liege') which seems to have confused the compositor of Act I, scene 2, and Act I, scene 4, as it confuses modern editors. Again the fragmentary whispered conversation of Act II, scene 2, in the style of

LADY
   Did not you speak?
MACBETH   When?
LADY   Now.
MACBETH   As I descended?

imposed its own problems, and produced its own crop of irregularities. It is worth noticing that the Witch-scenes, with their clearly marked short lines, yield hardly any examples of mislineation.

But the difficulties of the compositors printing *Macbeth* did not arise solely from the rhetorical complexities of the verse. They arose also from the technique of printing they employed – no doubt aggravated in this instance by complex line-structure. We now know that the Folio was not printed in simple sequence (page one first, followed by page two, followed by page three, etc.) but simultaneously at divergent parts of the book. In order to achieve this, the 'copy' which the printers used had to be marked off in approximate page-lengths, so that when printer A met up with printer B the material would join neatly without gaps or overlaps. The printed form had to be manipulated to fill the space of a page even if the material turned out to be too great or too little. When there was too little material, the compositor would take to 'losing space' by printing in short lines. When he was 'saving space' he joined up lines. Several examples of this seem to be shown in *Macbeth*. The second column of page 136 in the Folio, containing the first forty-seven lines of Act II, scene 2, is jammed full of type. Lines like 'I had most need of Blessing, and Amen stuck in my throat' are pushed right up to the edge of the page. It seems obvious that the compositor is saving space. The same seems to be true on the first page of *Macbeth* in the Folio (1.1 and 1.2.1–65).

On the other hand the first column of page 133 (1.3.105–56) is very spaciously laid-out, partly by the device of printing several of the lines in two parts. The compositor clearly was arranging to have the heading for scene 4 at the head of his second column and was prepared to 'misline' to get it there. Other fairly clear examples of 'space-losing' occur on Folio page 138 (II.3.70–II.4.19) and in the second column of page 145 (IV.2.31–85).

I give below a full list of mislineations which have been emended in this edition. The alternative version comes from the Folio. The end of the line in the Folio version is marked by a vertical stroke preceded by the last word of the line; the spelling of the Folio has been preserved; but Elizabethan typographical conventions have been normalized to accord with modern practice. The lay-out is necessarily curt and even cryptic, but the interested reader should be able to reconstruct what has happened in each case and see how far the mislineations fit into the categories outlined above.

1.2.	33–5	Dismayed ... lion] ... *Banquoh* | ... Eagles | ... Lyon |
	38, 39	So ... foe] *One line*
	42, 43	I cannot ... help] ... faint | ... helpe |
1.3.	5	And ... I] And mouncht, & mouncht, and mouncht | ... I |
	77	With ... you] ... greeting | ... you |

	81	Melted . . . stayed] . . . Winde | . . . stay'd |
	107, 108	The Thane . . . robes] . . . lives | . . . Robes |
	110–13	Which he . . . know not] . . . loose | . . . Norway | . . . helpe | . . . labour'd | . . . not |
	130, 131	Cannot . . . success] . . . good | . . . successe |
	143	If . . . crown me] . . . King | . . . Crowne me |
	149–53	Give . . . time] . . . favour | . . . forgotten | . . . registred | . . . Leafe | . . . them | . . . upon | . . . time |
	156	Till . . . friends] . . . enough | . . . friends |
I.4.	3–9	My liege . . . died] | . . . back | . . . die | . . . hee | . . . Pardon | . . . Repentance | . . . him | . . . dy'de |
	24–8	In doing . . . honour] | . . . selfe | . . . Duties | . . . State | . . . should | . . . Love | . . . Honor |
I.5.	20, 21	And yet . . . have it] . . . winne | . . . cryes | . . . have it |
I.6.	1, 2	This . . . itself] . . . seat | . . . it selfe |
	17–20	Against . . . hermits] . . . broad | . . . House | . . . Dignities | . . . Ermites |
II.1.	4	Hold . . . heaven] . . . Sword | . . . Heaven |
	7–9	And yet . . . repose] . . . sleepe | . . . thoughts | . . . repose |
	16, 17	By . . . content] . . . Hostesse | . . . content |
	25, 26	If you . . . for you] . . . consent | . . . for you |
II.2.	2–6	What . . . possets] . . . fire | . . . shriek'd | . . . good-night | . . . open | . . . charge | . . . Possets |
	14	I . . . noise] . . . deed | . . . noyse |
	18, 19	Hark . . . chamber] *One line*
	22–5	There's . . . to sleep] . . . sleepe | . . . other | . . . Prayers | . . . to sleepe |
	32, 33	I had . . . throat] *One line*
	65–9	To wear . . . more knocking] . . . white | . . . entry | . . . Chamber | . . . deed | . . . Constancie | . . . unattended | . . . more knocking |
	73, 74	To know . . . couldst] . . . deed | . . . my selfe | . . . knocking | . . . could'st |

II.3.	22, 23	Faith ... things] *Two lines of verse*: ... Cock | ... things |
	48, 49	I'll ... service] *One line*
	51–3	The night ... death] ... unruly | ... downe | ... Ayre | ... Death |
	56–8	New-hatched ... shake] ... time | ... Night ... fevorous | ... shake |
	83, 84	O Banquo ... murdered] *One line*
	118–20	What ... brewed] ... here | ... hole | ... away | ... brew'd |
	132	What ... them] ... doe |. ... them |
	134–8	Which ... shot] ... easie | ... England | ... I | ... safer | ... Smiles | ... bloody | ... shot |
II.4.	14	And ... certain] ... Horses | ... certaine |
	19, 20	They ... Macduff] ... did so | ... upon't | ... good *Macduffe* |
III.1.	34, 35	Craving ... with you] ... Horse | ... Night | ... with you |
	41–5	Till ... pleasure] ... societie | ... welcome | ... alone | ... with you | ... men | ... pleasure |
	47–50	Bring ... dares] ... us | ... thus | ... deepe | ... that | ... dares |
	71	And ... there] ... th'utterance | ... there |
	74–81	Well then ... might] ... then | ... speeches | ... past | ... fortune | ... selfe | ... conference | ... you | ... crost | ... them | ... might |
	84–90	I did ... ever] ... so | ... now | ... meeting | ... predominant | ... goe | ... man | ... hand | ... begger'd | ... ever |
	113, 114	Both ... enemy] *One line*
	127	Your ... most] ... you | ... most |
III.2.	16	But ... suffer] ... dis-joynt | ... suffer |
	22	In ... grave] ... extasie | ... Grave |
	32, 33	Unsafe ... streams] ... lave | ... streames |
	43, 44	Hath ... note] ... Peale | ... note |
III.3.	17	O ... fly, fly, fly] ... Trecherie | ... flye, flye,

flye |

III.4.	1, 2	You . . . welcome] . . . downe	. . . welcome	
	12, 13	The table . . . face] *One line*
	15, 16	My lord . . . him] *One line*
	19, 20	Most . . . perfect] . . . Sir	. . . scap'd	. . . againe	. . . perfect	
	47	Here . . . highness] . . . Lord	. . . Highnesse	
	108, 109	You have . . . disorder] . . . mirth	. . . disorder	
	121	It . . . blood will have blood] . . . say	Blood will have Blood	
III.5.	36	Come . . . again] . . . be	. . . againe	
III.6.	1	My . . . thoughts] . . . Speeches	. . . Thoughts	
IV.1.	70	Macbeth, Macbeth, Macbeth . . . Macduff] *Macbeth, Macbeth, Macbeth*	. . . *Macduffe*	
	78	Be . . . scorn] . . . resolute	. . . scorne	
	85, 86	What . . . king] *One line*
IV.2.	27	Fathered he is . . . fatherless] Father'd he is	. . . Father-lesse	
	35, 36	Poor . . . gin] . . . Bird	. . . Lime	. . . Gin	
	37	Why . . . set for] . . . Mother	. . . set for	
	39	Yes . . . father] . . . dead	. . . Father	
	59, 60	Now . . . father] *Verse:* . . . Monkie	. . . Father	
	79	To say . . . faces] . . . harme	. . . faces	
IV.3.	25	Perchance . . . doubts] . . . there	. . . doubts	
	102, 103	Fit . . . miserable] *One line*
	173, 174	Dying . . . grief] . . . sicken	. . . true	. . . griefe	
	211–13	My children . . . killed too] . . . Children too	. . . found	. . . kil'd too	
V.1.	44, 45	Go to, go to . . . not] Go too, go too	. . . not	
V.6.	1	Now . . . down] . . . enough	. . . downe	
	93	Hail . . . stands] . . . art	. . . stands	

Words for the Songs in *Macbeth*

1. 'Come away, come away' (III.5.35)
The full text of a song with this first line is found in the MS
play *The Witch*, by Middleton, and in Davenant's version of
Macbeth. The Davenant text of the song is far from clear, and I
have been obliged to seek for light in the Middleton text. The
essential matter seems to be that it is a *divided* song, with 'voices
off' calling on Hecat to join them in their aerial exercises.
Music in the air must be heard before Hecat says 'Hark! I am
called.' Shakespeare's *Macbeth*, indeed, needs no more than the
first two lines of the song, to be followed by Hecat's flying
exit. The text of the full song given here is conflated from the
Middleton and Davenant versions:

> *Song in the air*
> Come away, come away;
> Hecat, Hecat, come away.

HECAT
> I come, I come, I come, I come,
> With all the speed I may,
> With all the speed I may.
> Where's Stadlin?

(IN THE AIR)
> Here.

HECAT
> Where's Puckle?

(IN THE AIR)
> Here.
> And Hoppo too, and Helwaine too.

We lack but you, we lack but you.
Come away, make up the count.

HECAT

I will but 'noint, and then I mount.

(IN THE AIR)

Here comes down one to fetch his dues,
A kiss, a coll, a sip of blood;
And why thou stay'st so long I muse,
Since the air's so sweet and good.

A spirit like a cat descends

HECAT

O, art thou come?
What news, what news?

SPIRIT

All goes still to our delight:
Either come, or else
Refuse, refuse.

HECAT

Now I am furnished for the flight.
(*going up*).
Now I go, now I fly,
Malkin my sweet spirit, and I.
O what a dainty pleasure 'tis
To ride in the air
When the moon shines fair,
And sing, and dance, and toy, and kiss,
Over woods, high rocks, and mountains,
Over seas, our mistress' fountains,
Over steeples, towers, and turrets,
We fly by night 'mong troops of spirits.
No ring of bells to our ears sounds,
No howls of wolves, no yelps of hounds,
No, not the noise of water's breach,
Or cannon's throat, our height can reach.

(IN THE AIR)

No ring of bells etc.

2. 'Black spirits' (IV.1.43)

The full text of a song with this first line is found in the MS play *The Witch*, by Middleton, and in Davenant's printed version of *Macbeth*; I quote the latter version, in which particular references to the plot of *The Witch* have been deleted:

HECATE

Black spirits, and white,
Red spirits, and grey,
Mingle, mingle, mingle,
You that mingle may.

FIRST WITCH

Tiffin, Tiffin, keep it stiff in;
Firedrake, Puckey, make it lucky;
Liar Robin, you must bob in.

CHORUS

Around, around, about, about;
All ill come running in, all good keep out.

FIRST WITCH

Here's the blood of a bat.

HECATE

O, put in that, put in that.

SECOND WITCH

Here's lizard's brain.

HECATE

Put in a grain.

FIRST WITCH

Here's juice of toad, here's oil of adder;
That will make the charm grow madder.

SECOND WITCH

Put in all these, 'twill raise the stench.

HECATE

Nay, here's three ounces of a red-haired wench.

CHORUS

Around, around, about, about;
All ill come running in, all good keep out.

MACBETH

The Characters in the Play

DUNCAN, King of Scotland
MALCOLM
DONALBAIN } his sons
MACBETH, Thane of Glamis, later of Cawdor, later King of Scotland
BANQUO
MACDUFF
LENNOX
ROSS } Thanes of Scotland
MENTETH
ANGUS
CATHNESS

FLEANCE, Banquo's son
SEYWARD, Earl of Northumberland
YOUNG SEYWARD, his son
SEYTON, Macbeth's armour-bearer
SON OF MACDUFF
A Captain
An English Doctor
A Scottish Doctor
A Porter
An Old Man

LADY MACBETH
WIFE OF MACDUFF

Throughout the notes, 'F' refers to the text contained in the first Folio of Shakespeare's works (1623).

Gentlewoman attendant on Lady Macbeth
Three Weird Sisters
Three other Witches

HECAT
Apparitions

Three Murderers
Other Murderers

Lords, Gentlemen, Officers, Soldiers
Attendants, Messengers

Thunder and lightning. Enter three Witches

FIRST WITCH

When shall we three meet again?
In thunder, lightning, or in rain?

SECOND WITCH

When the hurly-burly's done,
When the battle's lost and won.

THIRD WITCH

That will be ere the set of sun.

FIRST WITCH

Where the place?

SECOND WITCH   Upon the heath.

THIRD WITCH

There to meet with Macbeth.

FIRST WITCH

I come, Grey-Malkin.

SECOND WITCH   Padock calls!

THIRD WITCH   Anon!

ALL

Fair is foul, and foul is fair.

I.I 'The true reason for the first appearance of the witches is to strike the keynote of the character of the whole drama' (Coleridge).

3 *hurly-burly* confused turmoil

4 *lost and won.* This is purposefully equivocal. When 'Fair is foul' (line 9), losing may count as winning.

8 *Grey-Malkin, Padock.* These are the 'familiars' or demon-companions of the witches. The usual identification of the first and second familiars with a cat and a toad is not fully confirmed by IV.1.1–3, and must be left undecided.

Anon soon. The Third Witch replies to her (unnamed) familiar.

10   Hover through the fog and filthy air.   *Exeunt*

I.2   *Alarum within*
             Enter King Duncan, Malcolm, Donalbain, Lennox,
             with Attendants, meeting a bleeding Captain

KING
     What bloody man is that? He can report,
     As seemeth by his plight, of the revolt
     The newest state.

MALCOLM   This is the sergeant
     Who like a good and hardy soldier fought
     'Gainst my captivity. Hail, brave friend!
     Say to the King the knowledge of the broil
     As thou didst leave it.

CAPTAIN   Doubtful it stood,
     As two spent swimmers that do cling together
     And choke their art. The merciless Macdonwald –
10   Worthy to be a rebel, for to that
     The multiplying villainies of nature
     Do swarm upon him – from the Western Isles
     Of kerns and galloglasses is supplied,
     And fortune on his damnèd quarrel smiling
     Showed like a rebel's whore. But all's too weak:

10 *Hover*. This may be taken to imply that the witches depart by flying.

I.2 The bleeding sergeant – himself an effective symbol of the battle he describes, and of Macbeth's part therein – speaks the inflated language suitable to his function as a passionate and weighty messenger. The *Alarum* at the beginning of the scene should form a natural bridge between the 'filthy air' of the witches' exit and the blood-daubed human being who staggers in from their 'hurly-burly'.

3 *sergeant* (a word of three syllables). The rank is not that of the modern N.C.O. but of an officer who is called '*Captain*' in the stage direction.

9 *choke their art* make impossible the art of swimming

10 *to that* as if to that end

11–12 *multiplying villainies of nature | Do swarm upon him* hosts of rebels join him like noxious insects swarming

12 *Western Isles* Hebrides

13 *kerns and galloglasses* light and heavy-armed Celtic levies

For brave Macbeth – well he deserves that name –
Disdaining fortune, with his brandished steel,
Which smoked with bloody execution,
Like valour's minion carvèd out his passage
Till he faced the slave –   20
Which ne'er shook hands nor bade farewell to him
Till he unseamed him from the nave to the chops,
And fixed his head upon our battlements.

KING

O valiant cousin! Worthy gentleman!

CAPTAIN

As, whence the sun 'gins his reflection,
Shipwracking storms and direful thunders;
So, from that spring whence comfort seemed to come,
Discomfort swells. Mark, King of Scotland, mark!
No sooner justice had, with valour armed,
Compelled these skipping kerns to trust their heels   30
But the Norweyan lord, surveying vantage,
With furbished arms and new supplies of men,
Began a fresh assault.

KING   Dismayed not this
Our captains, Macbeth and Banquo?

CAPTAIN   Yes –
As sparrows, eagles, or the hare, the lion.
If I say sooth I must report they were

---

16 *that name* (brave)
20 *the slave* Macdonwald
21 *ne'er shook hands nor bade farewell to
him* engaged in none of the courtesies
(or decencies) of war
22 *nave to the chops* navel to the jaws
24 *cousin*. This is a general term of kinship; but accurate (in the modern
sense) here.
25 *reflection* turning-back at the vernal
equinox
26 *thunders*. The rhythm of the line is
very often pieced-out by adding a
verb ('break' is the favourite). But

both rhythm and syntax work by
suspension; the discord is not resolved till we reach *come* in the following line.
30 *skipping* lightly armed (perhaps also
with the sense of 'foot-loose', 'light
in allegiance')
31 *Norweyan*. The sources say 'Danish'.
It has been suggested that Shakespeare changed this to avoid giving
offence to Christian IV. See Introduction, p. 807.
   surveying vantage seeing his chance
36 *say sooth* tell the truth

As cannons overcharged with double cracks;
So they
Doubly redoubled strokes upon the foe.
40   Except they meant to bathe in reeking wounds
Or memorize another Golgotha
I cannot tell.
– But I am faint; my gashes cry for help.

KING

So well thy words become thee as thy wounds,
They smack of honour both. Go get him surgeons.

Exit Captain with Attendants

Enter Ross and Angus

Who comes here?

MALCOLM   The worthy Thane of Ross.

LENNOX

What a haste looks through his eyes!
So should he look that seems to speak things strange.

ROSS

God save the King!

KING

Whence cam'st thou, worthy thane?

50   ROSS   From Fife, great King,
And fan our people cold.
Norway himself, with terrible numbers,
Assisted by that most disloyal traitor,
The Thane of Cawdor, began a dismal conflict,
Till that Bellona's bridegroom, lapped in proof,
Confronted him with self-comparisons,

---

38 *So they*. This short line, in the manner
of Virgil, is used (like the epic simile)
to mark the heroic technique of the
messenger's speech.

41 *memorize another Golgotha* make another field of the dead as memorable
as Calvary

48 *seems to* shows he is going to

53 *Norway* the King of Norway

56 *Bellona's bridegroom* (Macbeth, fit husband for the goddess of war)
lapped in proof clad in tested armour

57 *him* the King of Norway
self-comparisons (1) in terms of bravery;
(2) (ironically) in terms of treason

Point against point-rebellious, arm 'gainst arm,
Curbing his lavish spirit; and to conclude,
The victory fell on us —

KING   Great happiness!   60

ROSS
— That now Sweno, the Norways' king,
Craves composition;
Nor would we deign him burial of his men
Till he disbursèd at Saint Colm's Inch
Ten thousand dollars to our general use.

KING
No more that Thane of Cawdor shall deceive
Our bosom interest. Go pronounce his present death,
And with his former title greet Macbeth.

ROSS
I'll see it done.

KING
What he hath lost, noble Macbeth hath won.   *Exeunt*   70

Thunder. Enter the three Witches   I.3
FIRST WITCH Where hast thou been, sister?
SECOND WITCH Killing swine.
THIRD WITCH Sister, where thou?

58 *Point against point-rebellious, arm . . .* F reads 'Point, rebellious'; most editors suppose that this makes *rebellious* qualify *arm*. I take the comma to be here (as often) equivalent to the modern hyphen, so that the first phrase means 'sword raised against rebellious sword'.
59 *lavish* excessive, ill-disciplined
62 *composition* truce, agreement
64 *Saint Colm's Inch* Inchcolm (in the Firth of Forth)
70 *What he hath lost, noble Macbeth hath*

won. Note the ironic assimilation of the past traitor, Cawdor, and the future traitor, Macbeth.

1.3 This climactic scene brings together the thesis and antithesis of the first two scenes — the withered sisters and the blood-soaked soldiers. It reveals the quality of Macbeth's nature and contrasts that of Banquo; but it leaves the future open and ambiguous.
2 *Killing swine* (the bloodiest of domestic slaughterings)

FIRST WITCH

A sailor's wife had chestnuts in her lap,
And munched and munched and munched. 'Give me,'
        quoth I.
'Aroint thee, witch!' the rump-fed ronyon cries.
Her husband's to Aleppo gone, master o'the *Tiger*.
        But in a sieve I'll thither sail
        And like a rat without a tail
10   I'll do, I'll do, and I'll do.

SECOND WITCH

        I'll give thee a wind.

FIRST WITCH

        Th'art kind.

THIRD WITCH

        And I another.

FIRST WITCH

        I myself have all the other.
        And the very ports they blow
        All the quarters that they know
        I'the shipman's card.
        I'll drain him dry as hay;
        Sleep shall neither night nor day
20   Hang upon his penthouse lid.

6 *Aroint thee* begone
  ronyon (term of abuse)
7 *Tiger*. This was an actual ship that
  sailed to Aleppo in 1583; it was in
  the London news in 1606. It sailed
  from England on 5 December 1604
  and arrived back after fearful experiences on 27 June 1606. If we call the
  time away 568 days, this would be
  close enough to the 'Weary sev'n-
  nights nine times nine' that the
  witches calculate (567 days).
9 *without a tail*. Impersonation by witchcraft was liable to deficiencies of this
  kind.
10 *do* (as in the modern vague abusive

'I'll do him' = 'I'll cause him harm')
15 *the very ports they blow*. The winds
  blow *from* the ports, so that it is
  impossible to enter them.
16 *quarters* directions
17 *card* compass
18–23 *I'll drain him dry as hay ... peak,
  and pine*. Though ostensibly about
  the master of the *Tiger*, this serves as
  an accurate forecast of the fate of
  Macbeth. But lines 24–5 indicate an
  alternative ending to the story.
20 *penthouse* a lean-to shed (his eyelids,
  oppressed by sleep, will slope over
  his eyes like the roof of a penthouse)

He shall live a man forbid.
Weary sev'n-nights nine times nine
Shall he dwindle, peak, and pine.
Though his bark cannot be lost,
Yet it shall be tempest-tossed.
Look what I have!

SECOND WITCH   Show me, show me!

FIRST WITCH

Here I have a pilot's thumb,
Wracked as homeward he did come.

Drum within

THIRD WITCH

A drum! a drum!
Macbeth doth come.   30

ALL

The Weird Sisters, hand in hand,
Posters of the sea and land,
Thus do go, about, about;
Thrice to thine, and thrice to mine,
And thrice again, to make up nine.
Peace! The charm's wound up.

Enter Macbeth and Banquo

MACBETH

So foul and fair a day I have not seen.

BANQUO

How far is't called to Forres? What are these,
So withered and so wild in their attire,

---

23 *peak* grow thin and sharp-featured
31 *Weird Sisters. Wyrd* is the Anglo-Saxon word for fate and *Weird* (noun) is the medieval and (later) northern form for one of the three Fates or Destinies – sometimes called the *Weird Sisters*. This was the nomenclature that Shakespeare inherited, but subsequent use of the phrase has been largely affected by *Macbeth*. The F spelling *weyard* gives a necessary clue to Shakespeare's pronunciation.
32 *Posters* travellers
37 *So foul and fair a day* (catching up the 'Fair is foul' exit of the witches in 1.1; so that, on entering, Macbeth seems to be entering into *their* world, in mind as well as body)
38 *is't called* is it said to be; is it

40   That look not like the inhabitants o'the earth,
        And yet are on't? Live you? Or are you aught
        That man may question? You seem to understand me
        By each at once her choppy finger laying
        Upon her skinny lips. You should be women;
        And yet your beards forbid me to interpret
        That you are so.

MACBETH   Speak if you can! What are you?

FIRST WITCH
        All hail, Macbeth! Hail to thee, Thane of Glamis!

SECOND WITCH
        All hail, Macbeth! Hail to thee, Thane of Cawdor!

THIRD WITCH
        All hail, Macbeth, that shalt be king hereafter!

BANQUO
50   Good sir, why do you start, and seem to fear
        Things that do sound so fair? – I'the name of truth,
        Are ye fantastical, or that indeed
        Which outwardly ye show? My noble partner
        You greet with present grace, and great prediction
        Of noble having and of royal hope
        That he seems rapt withal. To me you speak not.
        If you can look into the seeds of time
        And say which grain will grow and which will not,
        Speak then to me who neither beg nor fear
60   Your favours nor your hate.

FIRST WITCH
        Hail!

43 *choppy* chapped, and so rough. The
Witches lay their fingers to their lips,
presumably to indicate the secret or
forbidden nature of their
communication.

47–9 *All hail*. It is worth noticing that
Shakespeare elsewhere (*Richard II*,
IV.1.169) associates this phrase with
Judas's betrayal of Christ.

47 *Glamis*. It appears (1.5.13 and elsewhere) that Shakespeare used a two-
syllable pronunciation of this word,
'Gla-miss', rather than the modern
'Glams'.

50–51 Note the pun on *fear* and *fair*
(pronounced alike in Shakespeare's
day).

52 *fantastical* imaginary

SECOND WITCH

Hail!

THIRD WITCH

Hail!

FIRST WITCH

Lesser than Macbeth, and greater.

SECOND WITCH

Not so happy, yet much happier.

THIRD WITCH

Thou shalt get kings, though thou be none.
So all hail, Macbeth and Banquo!

FIRST WITCH

Banquo and Macbeth, all hail!

MACBETH

Stay, you imperfect speakers! Tell me more!
By Sinell's death I know I am Thane of Glamis;   70
But how of Cawdor? The Thane of Cawdor lives
A prosperous gentleman. And to be king
Stands not within the prospect of belief –
No more than to be Cawdor. Say from whence
You owe this strange intelligence; or why
Upon this blasted heath you stop our way
With such prophetic greeting? Speak, I charge you!

Witches vanish

BANQUO

The earth hath bubbles as the water has,
And these are of them. Whither are they vanished?

MACBETH

Into the air; and what seemed corporal   80
Melted, as breath into the wind. Would they had stayed!

BANQUO

Were such things here as we do speak about?

69 *imperfect* insufficiently explicit
70 *Sinell* (a name for Macbeth's father)
71 *The Thane of Cawdor lives.* Evidently

Macbeth does not know that the
Thane of Cawdor has been assisting
Norway.

Or have we eaten on the insane root
That takes the reason prisoner?

MACBETH
Your children shall be kings.

BANQUO   You shall be king.

MACBETH
And Thane of Cawdor too, went it not so?

BANQUO
To the selfsame tune and words. Who's here?

Enter Ross and Angus

ROSS
The King hath happily received, Macbeth,
The news of thy success; and when he reads
90   Thy personal venture in the rebels' fight
His wonders and his praises do contend
Which should be thine, or his. Silenced with that,
In viewing o'er the rest o'the selfsame day
He finds thee in the stout Norweyan ranks,
Nothing afeard of what thyself didst make,
Strange images of death. As thick as hail
Came post with post; and every one did bear
Thy praises, in his kingdom's great defence,
And poured them down before him.

ANGUS   We are sent
100   To give thee from our royal master thanks;
Only to herald thee into his sight,
Not pay thee.

ROSS
And, for an earnest of a greater honour,

---

83 *the insane root* any root that makes
insane those who eat it
91-2 *His wonders and his praises do contend*
| *Which should be thine, or his.* If he
expresses his wonder (is dumbfounded) he cannot convey your
praises. If he praises you he cannot
express his own wonder (by being

dumb)
103 *earnest* pledge
a greater honour. Presumably Ross
is only trying to convey Duncan's
hyperbolic promises. But Macbeth
(and the audience) are bound to think
of the third prophecy.

He bade me from him call thee Thane of Cawdor
In which addition, hail, most worthy thane,
For it is thine.

BANQUO   What! Can the devil speak true?

MACBETH

The Thane of Cawdor lives. Why do you dress me
In borrowed robes?

ANGUS   Who was the Thane lives yet;
But under heavy judgement bears that life
Which he deserves to lose. Whether he was combined   110
With those of Norway, or did line the rebel
With hidden help and vantage, or that with both
He laboured in his country's wrack, I know not;
But treasons capital, confessed, and proved
Have overthrown him.

MACBETH (*aside*)   Glamis, and Thane of Cawdor!
The greatest is behind. – Thanks for your pains.
(*to Banquo*) Do you not hope your children shall be kings,
When those that gave the Thane of Cawdor to me
Promised no less to them?

BANQUO   That trusted home
Might yet enkindle you unto the crown   120
Besides the Thane of Cawdor. But 'tis strange;
And oftentimes, to win us to our harm,
The instruments of darkness tell us truths;
Win us with honest trifles, to betray's
In deepest consequence.
Cousins, a word, I pray you.
        They walk apart

MACBETH (*aside*)   Two truths are told
As happy prologues to the swelling Act
Of the imperial theme. – I thank you, gentlemen.

---

111 *line* support
    rebel Macdonwald
119 *home* all the way

127 *swelling Act* magnificent theatrical
    experience

(*aside*) This supernatural soliciting
130 Cannot be ill, cannot be good. If ill,
Why hath it given me earnest of success
Commencing in a truth? I am Thane of Cawdor.
If good, why do I yield to that suggestion
Whose horrid image doth unfix my hair,
And make my seated heart knock at my ribs
Against the use of nature? Present fears
Are less than horrible imaginings.
My thought, whose murder yet is but fantastical,
Shakes so my single state of man
140 That function is smothered in surmise,
And nothing is but what is not.
BANQUO Look how our partner's rapt.
MACBETH (*aside*)
    If chance will have me king, why chance may crown me
    Without my stir.
BANQUO   New honours come upon him
    Like our strange garments, cleave not to their mould
    But with the aid of use.
MACBETH (*aside*)   Come what come may,
    Time and the hour runs through the roughest day.
BANQUO
    Worthy Macbeth, we stay upon your leisure.

---

129 *soliciting* allurement. (This is not
really true; the witches do not allure;
they simply present; but Macbeth's
mind sees their words as allurement.)

130 *Cannot be ill, cannot be good* (a subjec-
tive equivalent to 'Fair is foul')

133 *suggestion* prompting or incitement
to evil

134 *horrid* literally 'bristling' (like the
hair)

136–7 *Present fears | Are less than horrible
imaginings*. Frightful things in the
present have less effect on us than
imagined horrors.

138 *fantastical* imaginary

139 *single* individual (sometimes taken to
mean 'weak')

140–41 *function is smothered in surmise, |
And nothing is but what is not* the
power to act is annihilated by my
speculations; so that the only thing
that exists in the present is what
does not really exist in the present –
thoughts of the future

146 *Come what come may* whatever
happens

147 *Time and the hour runs through the
roughest day.* Whatever is going to
happen *will* happen, inevitably.

MACBETH

Give me your favour. My dull brain was wrought
With things forgotten. Kind gentlemen, your pains   150
Are registered where every day I turn
The leaf to read them. Let us toward the King.
(*to Banquo*) Think upon what hath chanced, and at more
        time,
The interim having weighed it, let us speak
Our free hearts each to other.

BANQUO   Very gladly.

MACBETH

Till then, enough! – Come, friends.   *Exeunt*

Flourish. Enter King Duncan, Lennox, Malcolm,   1.4
Donalbain, and Attendants

KING

Is execution done on Cawdor?
Are not those in commission yet returned?

MALCOLM

My liege,
They are not yet come back. But I have spoke
With one that saw him die, who did report
That very frankly he confessed his treasons,
Implored your highness' pardon, and set forth
A deep repentance. Nothing in his life
Became him like the leaving it. He died

149–50 *My dull brain was wrought | With things forgotten.* Macbeth excuses his inattention by the lie that his mind is caught up in things of the past. In fact, it is caught up in the future.

155 *free hearts* open feelings

1.4 The first Cawdor's good end is played against the second Cawdor's bad beginning. The court of Duncan is revealed as a family unit, bound by natural ties of trust and loyalty. The naming of the heir, which might have given the historical Macbeth a legitimate cause to supplant the King, is here brought forward without this political consequence; it merely isolates Macbeth from the national life, drives him further into the world of his imagination.

10   As one that had been studied in his death
     To throw away the dearest thing he owed
     As 'twere a careless trifle.

    KING   There's no art
     To find the mind's construction in the face.
     He was a gentleman on whom I built
     An absolute trust.
              Enter Macbeth, Banquo, Ross, and Angus
                              O worthiest cousin!
     The sin of my ingratitude even now
     Was heavy on me. Thou art so far before,
     That swiftest wing of recompense is slow
     To overtake thee. Would thou hadst less deserved,
20   That the proportion both of thanks and payment
     Might have been mine. Only I have left to say,
     'More is thy due than more than all can pay.'

    MACBETH
     The service and the loyalty I owe,
     In doing it, pays itself. Your highness' part
     Is to receive our duties; and our duties
     Are to your throne and state, children and servants,
     Which do but what they should by doing everything
     Safe toward your love and honour.

    KING   Welcome hither.
     I have begun to plant thee, and will labour

10 *had been studied* had learned his part in
   the play
11 *owed* owned
15 *O worthiest cousin!* Note the ironic
   turn from Cawdor, as a traitorous
   hypocrite, to Macbeth.
17 *before* in advance of my power of
   repayment
20 *proportion both of thanks and payment*
   the weighing up how much was due
   and how much should be paid
21-2 *Only I have left to say,* | '*More is thy
   due than more than all can pay*' all that I

have to pay you with is the statement
that I cannot repay you
23-4 *The service and the loyalty I owe,* | *In
   doing it, pays itself* the reward for
   service and loyalty is found in the
   joy of doing loyal acts of service
25-8 *and our duties . . . to your throne . . .
   do but what they should by doing everything
   | Safe toward your love and honour* our
   duties to your throne only express
   their nature as absolute dependants
   when they are doing everything possible to protect you

To make thee full of growing. – Noble Banquo,   30
That hast no less deserved, nor must be known
No less to have done so, let me enfold thee
And hold thee to my heart.

BANQUO   There if I grow,
The harvest is your own.

KING   My plenteous joys,
Wanton in fulness, seek to hide themselves
In drops of sorrow. Sons, kinsmen, thanes,
And you whose places are the nearest, know
We will establish our estate upon
Our eldest, Malcolm, whom we name hereafter
The Prince of Cumberland: which honour must   40
Not unaccompanied invest him only,
But signs of nobleness, like stars, shall shine
On all deservers. From hence to Inverness,
And bind us further to you.

MACBETH
The rest is labour, which is not used for you.
I'll be myself the harbinger and make joyful
The hearing of my wife with your approach;
So humbly take my leave.

KING   My worthy Cawdor!

MACBETH (*aside*)
The Prince of Cumberland! That is a step
On which I must fall down, or else o'erleap,   50
For in my way it lies. Stars, hide your fires,
Let not light see my black and deep desires.
The eye wink at the hand; yet let that be
Which the eye fears, when it is done, to see.   *Exit*

---

37 *you whose places are the nearest* the next nearest to the throne (after the *Sons, kinsmen, thanes*)

38 *estate* state, kingdom

45 *The rest is labour, which is not used for you* it is wearisome to be inactive, when we know we ought to be doing some-thing to serve you

46 *harbinger* officer sent ahead of the king to arrange his lodgings

53 *wink* keep shut
let that be may the action come into being

KING
  True, worthy Banquo; he is full so valiant,
  And in his commendations I am fed;
  It is a banquet to me. Let's after him
  Whose care is gone before to bid us welcome.
  It is a peerless kinsman.   *Flourish. Exeunt*

I.5   *Enter Macbeth's Wife alone with a letter*
  LADY *They met me in the day of success, and I have learned*
    by the perfectest report they have more in them than mortal
    knowledge. When I burned in desire to question them fur-
    ther, they made themselves air, into which they vanished.
    Whiles I stood rapt in the wonder of it, came missives from
    the King, who all-hailed me Thane of Cawdor; by which
    title before these Weird Sisters saluted me, and referred me
    to the coming on of time with, 'Hail, king that shalt be.'
    This have I thought good to deliver thee, my dearest partner
10 *of greatness, that thou mightest not lose the dues of re-*
    joicing by being ignorant of what greatness is promised thee.
    Lay it to thy heart, and farewell.
  Glamis thou art, and Cawdor, and shalt be
  What thou art promised. Yet do I fear thy nature:
  It is too full o'the milk of human-kindness
  To catch the nearest way. Thou wouldst be great,
  Art not without ambition, but without
  The illness should attend it. What thou wouldst highly
  That wouldst thou holily, wouldst not play false,

I.5 The violent certainty of Lady Macbeth acts as a catalyst to crystallize a
mode of action and of character-develop-
ment out of the uncertainties of previous
scenes. At the same time a new and
more intimate image of Macbeth
emerges to complicate what we have
known and guessed at.
15 *human-kindness* the quality of creature-

liness, or humanity, that he sucked
from his mother; what binds the individual to the social order of Man.
(There is no evidence that Lady
Macbeth has to fear the *kindness* – in
the ordinary modern sense – of
Macbeth's nature.)
18 *illness* wickedness
    highly greatly

And yet wouldst wrongly win. Thou'dst have, great
    Glamis,   20
That which cries, 'Thus thou must do' if thou have it,
And that which rather thou dost fear to do
Than wishest should be undone. Hie thee hither
That I may pour my spirits in thine ear,
And chastise with the valour of my tongue
All that impedes thee from the golden round
Which fate and metaphysical aid doth seem
To have thee crowned withal.
        Enter Messenger

                           What is your tidings?

MESSENGER
The King comes here tonight.
LADY   Thou'rt mad to say it!
Is not thy master with him? Who, were't so,   30
Would have informed for preparation.
MESSENGER
So please you, it is true. Our Thane is coming;
One of my fellows had the speed of him,
Who, almost dead for breath, had scarcely more
Than would make up his message.
LADY   Give him tending:
He brings great news.   *Exit Messenger*
              The raven himself is hoarse
That croaks the fatal entrance of Duncan
Under my battlements. Come, you spirits
That tend on mortal thoughts, unsex me here
And fill me from the crown to the toe top-full   40

---

21 *That which cries, 'Thus thou must do' if*
thou have it. The ambitious ends proposed cry out for immoral action on
the part of anyone who hopes to
achieve them.
22 *that* (the end which Macbeth 'wouldst
. . . have')
24 *That I may pour my spirits in thine ear*

(as Claudius poisoned the elder
Hamlet)
27 *metaphysical* supernatural
35 *tending* attendance
36 *raven* (messenger of death)
37 *fatal* (to Duncan)
39 *mortal thoughts* murderous designs
unsex take away my feminine qualities

Of direst cruelty. Make thick my blood;
Stop up the access and passage to remorse,
That no compunctious visitings of nature
Shake my fell purpose, nor keep peace between
The effect and it. Come to my woman's breasts
And take my milk for gall, you murdering ministers,
Wherever, in your sightless substances,
You wait on nature's mischief. Come, thick night,
And pall thee in the dunnest smoke of hell,
50 That my keen knife see not the wound it makes,
Nor heaven peep through the blanket of the dark
To cry, 'Hold, hold!'
   Enter Macbeth
      Great Glamis, worthy Cawdor!
Greater than both by the all-hail hereafter!
Thy letters have transported me beyond
This ignorant present, and I feel now
The future in the instant.
MACBETH   My dearest love,
Duncan comes here tonight.
LADY   And when goes hence?
MACBETH
Tomorrow, as he purposes.
LADY   O never
Shall sun that morrow see!
60 Your face, my thane, is as a book where men

---

41 *Make thick my blood* ('so that pity cannot flow along her veins and reach her heart' – Bradley)

44-5 *keep peace between | The effect and it* act as a restraining influence, and so impede the translation of purpose into effect

46 *take my milk for gall* 'take away my milk and put gall into the place' (Dr Johnson)
murdering ministers agents of murder (the 'spirits' of line 38)

47 *sightless* invisible

48 *wait on nature's mischief* accompany natural disasters

49 *pall thee* wrap yourself

53 *the all-hail hereafter*. The third 'All hail' with which the Witches greeted Macbeth (1.3.49) prophesied that he should become King. Lady Macbeth refers to this future state.

May read strange matters. To beguile the time
Look like the time, bear welcome in your eye,
Your hand, your tongue; look like the innocent flower,
But be the serpent under't. He that's coming
Must be provided for; and you shall put
This night's great business into my dispatch,
Which shall to all our nights and days to come
Give solely sovereign sway and masterdom.

MACBETH
We will speak further.

LADY   Only look up clear:
To alter favour ever is to fear.   70
Leave all the rest to me.   *Exeunt*

Hautboys and torches. Enter King Duncan, Malcolm,   I.6
Donalbain, Banquo, Lennox, Macduff, Ross, Angus,
and Attendants

KING
This castle hath a pleasant seat; the air
Nimbly and sweetly recommends itself
Unto our gentle senses.

BANQUO   This guest of summer,
The temple-haunting martlet, does approve
By his loved mansionry that the heaven's breath

61–2 *To beguile the time | Look like the time*
  to deceive people look as they expect
  you to look
70 *favour* face, appearance

I.6 The final calm before the storm. In
immediate contrast to the enclosed darkness of the previous scene is the open,
light naturalness of this one. The elaboration of Lady Macbeth's rhetoric is a
symptom of her falsity.
(stage direction) *Hautboys and torches.* Are
these needed in this daylight scene?
Perhaps the attendants who normally

perform these functions are meant.
1 *seat* situation
1–3 *the air | Nimbly and sweetly recommends
  itself | Unto our gentle senses* the air is
  prompt to come forward and show
  its merits
3 *gentle senses* (perhaps 'the senses which
  the air greets like gentlemen' or
  simply 'our refined sensibilities')
4 *temple-haunting martlet* the martin, commonly building its nest in churches
  approve prove
5 *his loved mansionry* his love of building
  here

Smells wooingly here; no jutty, frieze,
Buttress, nor coign of vantage, but this bird
Hath made his pendent bed and procreant cradle;
Where they most breed and haunt I have observed
The air is delicate.

Enter Lady Macbeth

10   KING   See, see, our honoured hostess –
The love that follows us sometime is our trouble,
Which still we thank as love. Herein I teach you
How you shall bid 'God 'ield us' for your pains,
And thank us for your trouble.

LADY   All our service
In every point twice done and then done double
Were poor and single business to contend
Against those honours deep and broad wherewith
Your majesty loads our house. For those of old,
And the late dignities heaped up to them,
We rest your hermits.

20   KING   Where's the Thane of Cawdor?
We coursed him at the heels and had a purpose
To be his purveyor; but he rides well,
And his great love, sharp as his spur, hath holp him
To his home before us. Fair and noble hostess,
We are your guest tonight.

LADY   Your servants ever
Have theirs, themselves, and what is theirs, in compt,

---

6 *jutty* projection
7 *coign of vantage* advantageous corner
9 *haunt* frequent
11–14 *The love that follows us sometime is our trouble, | Which still we thank as love. Herein I teach you | How you shall bid 'God 'ield us' for your pains, | And thank us for your trouble* I have followed you to Inverness. This indicates my love; yet it is also troublesome. However in such situations we tend to think of the love and ignore the trouble. By saying this I have taught you how to pray for the good of those who trouble you
13 *bid* pray
16 *single* slight, trivial
20 *We rest your hermits* we remain bound to pray for you
22 *purveyor* officer sent in advance, to obtain food for the main party
26–8 *in compt, | To make their audit at your highness' pleasure, | Still to return your own.* Macbeth and his Lady are only the *stewards* of their possessions; they are ready to account for them and render them up whenever Duncan, the real owner, requires.

To make their audit at your highness' pleasure,
Still to return your own.

KING   Give me your hand;
Conduct me to mine host. We love him highly,
And shall continue our graces towards him.   30
By your leave, hostess.   *He kisses her. Exeunt*

Hautboys. Torches. Enter a Sewer and divers Servants   1.7
with dishes and service over the stage. Then enter
Macbeth

MACBETH
If it were done when 'tis done, then 'twere well
It were done quickly. If the assassination
Could trammel up the consequence, and catch
With his surcease success – that but this blow
Might be the be-all and the end-all! – here,
But here, upon this bank and shoal of time,
We'd jump the life to come. But in these cases
We still have judgement here – that we but teach
Bloody instructions, which, being taught, return

1.7 This scene is the climax of Act 1, with the order and the disorder themes brought into sharpest opposition. The opening dumb-show of feasting must create a context of trust and benevolence around Macbeth's soliloquy and the dialogue that follows, so as to keep the argument for society before our eyes while (with our minds) we see the individual move towards his great betrayal.

(stage direction) *Sewer* superintendent of the feast

1 *If it were done when 'tis done* if the doing of the deed were the end of it

3 *trammel up the consequence* catch up (as in a net) the trail of consequences that follows any action. (The metaphor is continued in *catch | With his surcease success.*)

4 *With his surcease.* Either (1) by Duncan's death or (2) by putting an end to the consequences. Shakespeare regularly uses *his* for modern 'its'.

that but so that only

6 *bank and shoal.* The F 'Banke and Schoole' can be seen simply as an older spelling of the version printed here – the sense being that time is only an isthmus between two eternities. On the other hand, *bank* often means *bench*, and the train of words 'bank ... school ... judgement ... teach' seems significant.

7 *jump the life to come* hazard things outside the scope of here-and-now

8 *that* in that

10 　　To plague the inventor. This even-handed justice
　　　Commends the ingredience of our poisoned chalice
　　　To our own lips. He's here in double trust:
　　　First, as I am his kinsman and his subject,
　　　Strong both against the deed; then, as his host,
　　　Who should against his murderer shut the door,
　　　Not bear the knife myself. Besides, this Duncan
　　　Hath borne his faculties so meek, hath been
　　　So clear in his great office, that his virtues
　　　Will plead like angels, trumpet-tongued against
20 　　The deep damnation of his taking-off;
　　　And Pity, like a naked new-born babe
　　　Striding the blast, or heaven's cherubin, horsed
　　　Upon the sightless curriers of the air,
　　　Shall blow the horrid deed in every eye,
　　　That tears shall drown the wind. I have no spur

10 *even-handed justice* precise retribution. The lines which follow forecast the exact nature of Macbeth's fate – by destroying trust he destroys his own capacity for trust.

11 *ingredience* composition
poisoned chalice. The chalice is a particularly treacherous vehicle of murder, being (like Macbeth's castle) the vessel of sacredness and trust.

17 *faculties* powers

18 *clear* spotless

22 *Striding the blast* astride the storm (of indignation)

22-3 *heaven's cherubin, horsed | Upon the sightless curriers of the air*. Probably suggested by the 18th Psalm: 'He rid upon the Cherub [A.V. *Cherubins*] and he did fly; he came fleeing upon the wings of the wind.' The *sightless* (invisible) *curriers* (runners) are the winds in motion. The baby Pity, and the baby-like cherubin (Shakespearian form of Hebrew *Cherubim*), will ride on the winds and blow the deed like dust into every eye, so that

everyone will know it, and weep (1) because of the dust; (2) because of pity.

23 *curriers*. I have preserved this form (1) to avoid the inappropriate connotations of the modern *courier*; (2) to keep the short vowel-sound of the Elizabethan form, in a line requiring (because of the sense) to be made up of short sounds. F reads 'Curriors'.

25 *That tears shall drown the wind* ('alluding to the remission of the wind in a shower' – Johnson)

25-8 *I have no spur | To prick the sides of my intent but only | Vaulting ambition which o'erleaps itself | And falls on the other*. The horse imagery of 'Striding' and 'horsed' leads now (1) to a view of Macbeth's intention to murder as a horse that must be spurred, and (2) to a view of ambition (which could be a spur or stimulus) as a rider vaulting into his saddle, but overshooting the mark and falling on the other side.

To prick the sides of my intent but only
Vaulting ambition which o'erleaps itself
And falls on the other.
    Enter Lady Macbeth
                    How now? What news?

LADY
    He has almost supped. Why have you left the chamber?

MACBETH
    Hath he asked for me?

LADY   Know you not he has?   30

MACBETH
    We will proceed no further in this business.
    He hath honoured me of late, and I have bought
    Golden opinions from all sorts of people
    Which would be worn now in their newest gloss,
    Not cast aside so soon.

LADY   Was the hope drunk
    Wherein you dressed yourself? Hath it slept since?
    And wakes it now to look so green and pale
    At what it did so freely? From this time
    Such I account thy love. Art thou afeard
    To be the same in thine own act and valour   40
    As thou art in desire? Wouldst thou have that
    Which thou esteem'st the ornament of life,
    And live a coward in thine own esteem,
    Letting 'I dare not' wait upon 'I would',
    Like the poor cat i'the adage?

MACBETH   Prithee peace.
    I dare do all that may become a man;

---

28 *the other* (side)

(stage direction) *Enter Lady Macbeth* (sometimes seen as an ironic answer to Macbeth's *I have no spur*)

32 *bought* (by his bravery in battle)

34 *in their newest gloss.* The 'Golden opinions' are seen as new suits of clothes.

37 *green and pale* nauseated, as in the morning after drunkenness

39 *Such* (as drunken lechery)

41–2 *that | Which thou esteem'st the ornament of life* (greatness, the crown)

44 *wait upon* accompany

45 *the adage* (the proverb: 'the cat wanted to eat fish, but would not wet her feet')

46–7 *I dare do all that may become a man; | Who dares do more is none* to be daring

Who dares do more is none.

LADY   What beast was't then
That made you break this enterprise to me?
When you durst do it, then you were a man;
50   And to be more than what you were, you would
Be so much more the man. Nor time nor place
Did then adhere, and yet you would make both.
They have made themselves, and that their fitness now
Does unmake you. I have given suck, and know
How tender 'tis to love the babe that milks me;
I would while it was smiling in my face
Have plucked my nipple from his boneless gums
And dashed the brains out, had I so sworn as you
Have done to this.

MACBETH   If we should fail?

LADY   We fail!
60   But screw your courage to the sticking place,
And we'll not fail. When Duncan is asleep –
Whereto the rather shall his day's hard journey
Soundly invite him – his two chamberlains

is manly; but to be too daring may carry one right outside the limits proper to human (and humane) activity. Lady Macbeth's reply is that a man deficient in continued daring is a *beast*. To exceed in daring is to exceed in *manliness*. She chooses to ignore the question of *humanity*

48 *break this enterprise to me.* Presumably she refers to the letter she reads above, so that what she says is not literally true; but Lady Macbeth is persuading, not recounting, and neither she nor Shakespeare is bound to literal truth.

53 *They have made themselves* (Duncan is now in our power)
that their fitness that fitness of theirs (fitness of time and place for the murder)

54 *unmake you* make you incapable

59–61 *We fail! | But screw your courage to the sticking place, | And we'll not fail.* Lady Macbeth's reply is printed in F as a question – but the question-mark then served also for the exclamation-mark. If she scornfully repeats Macbeth's question, then *But* must mean 'only'. If (with an exclamation-mark) she accepts the possibility of failure, *But* is the usual disjunctive. I have preferred the latter interpretation.

60 *screw your courage to the sticking place.* The metaphor is from the cross-bow, in which the 'sticking place' was the notch into which the string fitted when sufficiently 'screwed up'.

63 *chamberlains* attendants on the bed-chamber

Will I with wine and wassail so convince
That memory, the warder of the brain,
Shall be a-fume, and the receipt of reason
A limbeck only. When in swinish sleep
Their drenchèd natures lies as in a death,
What cannot you and I perform upon
The unguarded Duncan? What not put upon   70
His spongy officers, who shall bear the guilt
Of our great quell?
MACBETH   Bring forth men-children only!
For thy undaunted mettle should compose
Nothing but males. Will it not be received,
When we have marked with blood those sleepy two
Of his own chamber, and used their very daggers,
That they have done't?
LADY   Who dares receive it other,
As we shall make our griefs and clamour roar
Upon his death?
MACBETH   I am settled; and bend up
Each corporal agent to this terrible feat.   80
Away, and mock the time with fairest show:
False face must hide what the false heart doth know.
                              Exeunt

---

64 *wassail* festivity
   convince overcome
65 *the warder of the brain* (memory
   guards us against the performance of
   deeds that proved shameful in the
   past)
66–7 *receipt of reason | A limbeck only.*
   The part of the brain where reasons
   are received or collected will be a
   retort or alembic, full of the fumes
   that accompany distillation.
68 *drenchèd* (with drink)
71 *spongy officers* (the drink-sodden

chamberlains)
72 *quell* murder
72–4 *Bring forth men-children only! | For
   thy undaunted mettled should compose |
   Nothing but males.* Macbeth accepts
   and endorses his wife's version of
   'manliness'.
74 *received* (by the minds of observers)
79–80 *bend up | Each corporal agent* strain
   every muscle
81 *mock the time.* Macbeth repeats his
   wife's advice to 'beguile the time'
   (1.5.61).

II.1   *Enter Banquo, and Fleance with a torch before him*

BANQUO
How goes the night, boy?

FLEANCE
The moon is down; I have not heard the clock.

BANQUO
And she goes down at twelve.

FLEANCE   I take't 'tis later, sir.

BANQUO
Hold, take my sword. There's husbandry in heaven:
Their candles are all out. Take thee that too.
A heavy summons lies like lead upon me
And yet I would not sleep. Merciful powers,
Restrain in me the cursèd thoughts that nature
Gives way to in repose.
                    Enter Macbeth and a Servant with a torch
                                Give me my sword!
10   Who's there?

MACBETH
A friend.

BANQUO
What, sir, not yet at rest? The King's a-bed.
He hath been in unusual pleasure,
And sent forth great largess to your offices.
This diamond he greets your wife withal
By the name of most kind hostess, and shut up
In measureless content.

MACBETH   Being unprepared

II.1 Just before the fatal deed Banquo is reintroduced beside Macbeth to highlight the central distinction between a moral will and a moralizing imagination.

4 *husbandry* thrift (the heavens are *husbanding* their resources)

5 *Take thee that too.* 'That is precisely

what the actor who plays Banquo hands to the actor (or actress) who plays Fleance — "his dagger" in Booth's production; "his hat" in Phelps's' (Sprague).

14 *offices* servants' quarters

16 *shut up* concluded his speech

Our will became the servant to defect,
Which else should free have wrought.

BANQUO   All's well.
I dreamt last night of the three Weird Sisters.   20
To you they have showed some truth.

MACBETH   I think not of them.
Yet, when we can entreat an hour to serve,
We would spend it in some words upon that business,
If you would grant the time.

BANQUO   At your kind'st leisure.

MACBETH
If you shall cleave to my consent when 'tis,
It shall make honour for you.

BANQUO   So I lose none
In seeking to augment it, but still keep
My bosom franchised and allegiance clear,
I shall be counselled.

MACBETH   Good repose the while.

BANQUO
Thanks, sir; the like to you.   *Exit Banquo and Fleance*   30

MACBETH
Go bid thy mistress, when my drink is ready
She strike upon the bell. Get thee to bed.

                                Exit Servant

Is this a dagger which I see before me,
The handle toward my hand? Come, let me clutch thee –
I have thee not and yet I see thee still!
Art thou not, fatal vision, sensible
To feeling as to sight? Or art thou but
A dagger of the mind, a false creation,

---

18 *Our will became the servant to defect* our
desire (to be hospitable) was bound
in by the limitations imposed by our
unpreparedness

25 *cleave to my consent when 'tis* adhere to
my opinion when we discuss the
matter

27–8 *keep | My bosom franchised and alle-
giance clear* keep my heart free from
evil, and my allegiance to the King
untainted

36 *fatal* ominous
sensible open to sensory apprehension

Proceeding from the heat-oppressèd brain?
40 I see thee yet, in form as palpable
As this which now I draw.
Thou marshall'st me the way that I was going,
And such an instrument I was to use. —
Mine eyes are made the fools o'the other senses,
Or else worth all the rest. — I see thee still;
And, on thy blade and dudgeon, gouts of blood,
Which was not so before. There's no such thing.
It is the bloody business which informs
Thus to mine eyes. Now o'er the one half-world
50 Nature seems dead, and wicked dreams abuse
The curtained sleep. Witchcraft celebrates
Pale Hecat's offerings; and withered Murder,
Alarumed by his sentinel the wolf,
Whose howl's his watch, thus with his stealthy pace,
With Tarquin's ravishing strides, towards his design
Moves like a ghost. Thou sure and firm-set earth,
Hear not my steps, which way they walk, for fear
Thy very stones prate of my whereabout
And take the present horror from the time
60 Which now suits with it. — Whiles I threat, he lives:

---

42 *Thou marshall'st me the way that I was going.* The visionary dagger seems to float before him and lead him (like a *marshal* or usher) to the door of Duncan's bedchamber.

44–5 *Mine eyes are made the fools o'the other senses, | Or else worth all the rest.* Either the dagger does not exist, in which case the sight of it is false; or else the vision is of a higher truth than that of normal sense-experience.

46 *dudgeon* handle
gouts drops

48 *informs* makes shapes

49 *half-world* hemisphere

51 *curtained* (1) behind bed-curtains; (2)

hidden from conscious control

51–2 *Witchcraft celebrates | Pale Hecat's offerings.* Witchcraft celebrates its sacrificial rites to Hecat (goddess of the moon as well as of witches, and therefore 'Pale').

53 *Alarumed* aroused

55 *Tarquin's ravishing strides* the stealthy steps that Tarquin took while moving towards his rape of Lucrece

58 *Thy very stones prate of my whereabout.* This is probably from Luke 19.40: 'if these hold their peace, then shall the stones cry'.

59 *take the present horror from the time* break the ghastly silence

Words to the heat of deeds too cold breath gives.
  A bell rings
I go, and it is done; the bell invites me.
Hear it not, Duncan, for it is a knell
That summons thee to heaven or to hell.   *Exit*

          Enter Lady Macbeth   II.2
LADY
  That which hath made them drunk hath made me bold;
  What hath quenched them hath given me fire. – Hark! –
      Peace!
  It was the owl that shrieked, the fatal bellman
  Which gives the stern'st good-night. He is about it.
  The doors are open, and the surfeited grooms
  Do mock their charge with snores; I have drugged their
      possets
  That death and nature do contend about them
  Whether they live or die.
MACBETH (*within*)   Who's there? What, ho!
LADY
  Alack, I am afraid they have awaked,
  And 'tis not done. The attempt and not the deed   10
  Confounds us. – Hark! – I laid their daggers ready;
  He could not miss 'em. Had he not resembled

II.2 An ecstasy of moral hysteria follows
the murder. The disjointed language suggests both guilt and terror, in a kind of
hell cut off from humanity, till reawak-
ened by the 'knocking' at the end of the
scene.
2 *quenched* made unconscious (by drink)
3 *fatal bellman*. The owl, as the bird of
   death, is compared to the bellman
   sent to give 'stern'st good-night' to
   condemned prisoners the night

before their execution.
5 *The doors are open* (1) the physical impediments have been overcome; (2)
   moral restraints have been abolished
   grooms royal servants with specific
   household duties
6 *mock their charge* make a mockery of
   their duty to guard the King
   possets restorative night-drinks
7 *nature* the forces of life

My father as he slept, I had done't.

Enter Macbeth, carrying two bloodstained daggers

My husband!

MACBETH

I have done the deed. Didst thou not hear a noise?

LADY

I heard the owl-scream and the cricket's cry.

Did not you speak?

MACBETH   When?

LADY   Now.

MACBETH   As I descended?

LADY

Ay.

MACBETH

Hark!

Who lies i'the second chamber?

LADY   Donalbain.

MACBETH (*looks at his hands*)

20   This is a sorry sight.

LADY

A foolish thought, to say a sorry sight.

MACBETH

There's one did laugh in's sleep, and one cried 'Murder!'

That they did wake each other. I stood and heard them.

But they did say their prayers and addressed them

Again to sleep.

LADY   There are two lodged together.

---

13 *My husband* (the only time she uses this term throughout the play)

20 *sorry sight.* We heard much about the loyally blood-stained Macbeth in 1.2. The first time we *see* him blood-stained it is with the blood of his rightful King.

21 *A foolish thought, to say a sorry sight.* Lady Macbeth attempts a comforting jocularity: 'It would be foolish (or "sorry") of you to feel sorrow for such a deed.'

22 *one did laugh in's sleep, and one cried 'Murder!'* Presumably Donalbain and his companion (Malcolm?) in the second chamber (also the *one* and *other* of line 26).

MACBETH

    One cried 'God bless us' and 'Amen' the other,
    As they had seen me with these hangman's hands.
    Listening their fear I could not say 'Amen'
    When they did say 'God bless us.'

LADY

    Consider it not so deeply.   30

MACBETH

    But wherefore could not I pronounce 'Amen'?
    I had most need of blessing, and 'Amen'
    Stuck in my throat.

LADY   These deeds must not be thought
    After these ways; so, it will make us mad.

MACBETH

    Methought I heard a voice cry, 'Sleep no more!
    Macbeth does murder sleep – the innocent sleep,
    Sleep that knits up the ravelled sleave of care,
    The death of each day's life, sore labour's bath,
    Balm of hurt minds, great nature's second course,
    Chief nourisher in life's feast.'

LADY   What do you mean?   40

MACBETH

    Still it cried 'Sleep no more' to all the house;
    'Glamis hath murdered sleep, and therefore Cawdor
    Shall sleep no more, Macbeth shall sleep no more.'

LADY

    Who was it that thus cried? Why, worthy thane,
    You do unbend your noble strength, to think
    So brain-sickly of things. Go, get some water,

27 *hangman's* bloody (because he dismembered as well as hanged)

30 *Consider* contemplate

32 *most need of blessing* (because he was falling into sin). Notice the avoidance of responsibility for his action.

34 *so* if you do so

37 *ravelled sleave* tangled skein

38 *bath* (that which eases the hurt)

39 *second course* (1) the most sustaining dish in the feast – the 'Chief nourisher' (anciently, meat came in the second course); (2) the second mode of existence

45 *unbend* dismantle

And wash this filthy witness from your hand.
Why did you bring these daggers from the place?
They must lie there. Go, carry them and smear
The sleepy grooms with blood.

50 MACBETH   I'll go no more.
I am afraid to think what I have done;
Look on't again I dare not.

LADY   Infirm of purpose!
Give me the daggers. The sleeping and the dead
Are but as pictures. 'Tis the eye of childhood
That fears a painted devil. If he do bleed,
I'll gild the faces of the grooms withal,
For it must seem their guilt.   *Exit*
    Knock within

MACBETH   Whence is that knocking?
How is't with me when every noise appals me?
What hands are here! Ha – they pluck out mine eyes!
60 Will all great Neptune's ocean wash this blood
Clean from my hand? No, this my hand will rather
The multitudinous seas incarnadine,
Making the green one red.
    Enter Lady Macbeth
LADY My hands are of your colour; but I shame
    To wear a heart so white.
        Knock
                                I hear a knocking
At the south entry. Retire we to our chamber.

---

47 *filthy witness* (the tell-tale blood)
54–5 *pictures . . . bleed.* Notice the stark
contrast between these words. Lady
Macbeth must be seen to be falsifying.
56–7 . *I'll gild the faces of the grooms withal,*
| *For it must seem their guilt.* The
pun marks the tension of the
moment: moreover, to Lady Mac-
beth '*guilt* is something like *gilt* – one
can wash it off or paint it on'
(Cleanth Brooks).

62 *multitudinous* 'multiform'; or 'teeming
with multitudes of creatures'
incarnadine turn red
63 *green one red* either 'green-one red' or
'green, one red'. Compare Revelation
16.3: 'And the second angel shed his
vial upon the sea, and it turned as it
were into the blood of a dead man.'
64 *My hands are of your colour* (from 'gild-
ing' the faces of the chamberlains)

A little water clears us of this deed;
How easy is it then! Your constancy
Hath left you unattended.

    Knock

                      Hark! more knocking.
Get on your nightgown, lest occasion call us   70
And show us to be watchers. Be not lost
So poorly in your thoughts.

MACBETH

To know my deed 'twere best not know myself.

    Knock

Wake Duncan with thy knocking! I would thou couldst!

                             Exeunt

    Enter a Porter. Knocking within   II.3

PORTER Here's a knocking indeed! If a man were porter of
hell-gate he should have old turning the key.

    Knock

Knock, knock, knock! Who's there i'the name of
Belzebub? Here's a farmer that hanged himself on the

---

67 *A little water* (in strong contrast to
multitudinous seas above)

71 *watchers* awake (*watch* is a variant
form of 'wake')

73 *To know my deed 'twere best not know
myself.* If I am to think about the
murder I must stop being conscious
of the man I have been.

II.3 This scene is sometimes thought
un-Shakespearian because 'low'. But the
Porter scene is a typically Elizabethan
'double-take' of damnation and its pre-
cedents, based on the tradition of
'Estates-Satire', in which 'some of all
professions' (line 17) were surveyed and
condemned. The Porter of hell-gate was
a figure in the medieval drama, an oppo-

site to St Peter, and opponent of Christ
in 'the harrowing of Hell'. The faked
business of the following 'council scene'
(undercut by the asides of Malcolm and
Donalbain) points forward to the empti-
ness of social gatherings under Macbeth.
(stage direction) *within* behind the stage
    façade (meaning *outside* in terms of
    stage illusion)

2 *old* plenty of (colloquial intensive)

4–5 *Here's a farmer that hanged himself on
the expectation of plenty.* The farmer
stored his crops, hoping that prices
would rise; when the next season
produced an expectation of plentiful
crops, prices fell and he hanged himself (the traditional expression of
religious despair).

expectation of plenty. Come in time! Have napkins enow about you; here you'll sweat for't.

Knock

Knock, knock! Who's there in the other devil's name? Faith, here's an equivocator that could swear in both the scales against either scale, who committed treason enough for God's sake, yet could not equivocate to heaven. O, come in, equivocator.

Knock

Knock, knock, knock! Who's there? Faith, here's an English tailor come hither for stealing out of a French hose. Come in, tailor; here you may roast your goose.

Knock

Knock, knock! Never at quiet! What are you? – But this place is too cold for hell. I'll devil-porter it no further. I had thought to have let in some of all professions that go the primrose way to the everlasting bonfire.

Knock

Anon, anon! I pray you remember the porter.

He opens the gate. Enter Macduff and Lennox

5 *Come in time.* This, the F reading, makes a weak kind of sense: 'Come in good time.' Dover Wilson's emendation to 'time-server' is attractive and apposite, but not necessary.
napkins (to mop up the sweat. Did the farmer hang himself in his napkin?)

7 *the other devil.* The Porter wishes to mention some devil other than Belzebub (line 4), but cannot remember the name of any.

8 *equivocator.* Usually taken as a reference to the Jesuits, and especially to Father Garnet who, in the Gunpowder Plot trial, 'equivocated', swore evidence with mental reservation that it was not true. But equivocation (by Witches, by Macbeth) runs through-

out the whole play. See Introduction (p. 816).

9–10 *treason enough for God's sake* (presumably another reference to the Jesuit)

13–14 *stealing out of a French hose.* 'Hose' were breeches, which about the time of *Macbeth* changed fashion from wide to narrow ('French') fitting. The tailor had been accustomed to steal cloth from the baggy breeches, but was detected in the closer-fitting ones.

14 *roast your goose* (1) heat your smoothing iron (goose); (2) ?'cook your goose' (undo yourself)

19 *I pray you remember the porter.* Returning to his role as the company clown, the Porter begs for a tip.

MACDUFF

Was it so late, friend, ere you went to bed,   20
That you do lie so late?

PORTER Faith, sir, we were carousing till the second
cock; and drink, sir, is a great provoker of three things.

MACDUFF What three things does drink especially provoke?

PORTER Marry, sir, nose-painting, sleep, and urine.
Lechery, sir, it provokes and unprovokes: it provokes
the desire but it takes away the performance. Therefore
much drink may be said to be an equivocator with
lechery: it makes him and it mars him; it sets him on and   30
it takes him off; it persuades him and disheartens him,
makes him stand to and not stand to; in conclusion, equivocates him in a sleep and giving him the lie, leaves him.

MACDUFF I believe drink gave thee the lie last night.

PORTER That it did, sir, i'the very throat on me. But I
requited him for his lie and, I think, being too strong
for him, though he took up my legs sometime, yet I
made a shift to cast him.

MACDUFF Is thy master stirring?

Enter Macbeth

Our knocking has awaked him; here he comes.   40

LENNOX

Good morrow, noble sir.

MACBETH   Good morrow both.

MACDUFF

Is the King stirring, worthy thane?

MACBETH   Not yet.

22-3 *second cock* three o'clock in the
morning. (It is now daybreak.)
32-3 *equivocates him in a sleep* fulfils his
lechery only in a dream
33 *giving him the lie* (1) deceives him; (2)
floors him; (3) makes him urinate
(lie = lye)

37 *took up my legs* (as a wrestler lifts his
opponent)
38 *cast* (1) throw (as in wrestling); (2)
vomit

MACDUFF

He did command me to call timely on him.

I have almost slipped the hour.

MACBETH   I'll bring you to him.

MACDUFF

I know this is a joyful trouble to you,

But yet 'tis one.

MACBETH

The labour we delight in physics pain.

This is the door.

MACDUFF   I'll make so bold to call,

For 'tis my limited service.   *Exit*

LENNOX

Goes the King hence today?

50   MACBETH   He does; he did appoint so.

LENNOX

The night has been unruly. Where we lay,

Our chimneys were blown down, and, as they say,

Lamentings heard i'the air, strange screams of death,

And prophesying, with accents terrible,

Of dire combustion and confused events

New-hatched to the woeful time. The obscure bird

Clamoured the live-long night. Some say the earth

Was feverous and did shake.

MACBETH   'Twas a rough night.

LENNOX

My young remembrance cannot parallel

A fellow to it.

        Enter Macduff

---

43 *timely* early
47 *The labour we delight in physics pain*
    when we enjoy doing something,
    the enjoyment counters the labori-
    ousness
49 *limited* appointed
52–6 *Our chimneys were blown down . . .*

woeful time. Nature expresses the
breach of natural order by 'natural'
convulsions.
56 *New-hatched to the woeful time* newly
    emerged to make the time woeful
    obscure bird (the owl, bird of darkness,
    thought to portend death)

MACDUFF   O horror, horror, horror!   60
  Tongue nor heart cannot conceive nor name thee!
MACBETH *and* LENNOX
  What's the matter?
MACDUFF
  Confusion now hath made his masterpiece;
  Most sacrilegious murder hath broke ope
  The Lord's anointed temple and stole thence
  The life o'the building.
MACBETH   What is't you say? The life?
LENNOX
  Mean you his majesty?
MACDUFF
  Approach the chamber and destroy your sight
  With a new Gorgon. Do not bid me speak.
  See, and then speak yourselves.
                    Exeunt Macbeth and Lennox
                    Awake, awake!   70
  Ring the alarum bell! Murder and treason!
  Banquo and Donalbain, Malcolm, awake!
  Shake off this downy sleep, death's counterfeit,
  And look on death itself! Up, up, and see
  The Great Doom's image! Malcolm, Banquo,
  As from your graves rise up and walk like sprites
  To countenance this horror. Ring the bell!

61 *Tongue nor heart cannot conceive nor name thee!* Note the chiastic order: it is the heart which conceives, the tongue which names.

63 *Confusion* destruction

65 *The Lord's anointed temple* the temple (body) of the Lord's anointed (combining 2 Corinthians 6.16: 'Ye [Christians] are the temple of the living God' and 1 Samuel 24.10: 'the Lord's anointed'. Note the context of this latter passage).

69 *Gorgon.* She turned to stone those who looked on her.

75 *Great Doom's image* a replica of the Last Judgement

76 *As from your graves rise up* act as if at the Last Judgement itself, to fit in with the present horror ('countenance' is also used in the sense of 'behold')

77 *Ring the bell!* This is sometimes supposed to be a stage direction added by the prompter, and accidentally printed as part of the text.

Bell rings
Enter Lady Macbeth

LADY
What's the business,
That such a hideous trumpet calls to parley
The sleepers of the house? Speak, speak!

80 MACDUFF   O gentle lady,
'Tis not for you to hear what I can speak.
The repetition in a woman's ear
Would murder as it fell.
            Enter Banquo
                              O Banquo, Banquo!
Our royal master's murdered.

LADY   Woe, alas!
What, in our house!

BANQUO   Too cruel, anywhere.
Dear Duff, I prithee contradict thyself
And say it is not so.
            Enter Macbeth, Lennox, and Ross

MACBETH
Had I but died an hour before this chance
I had lived a blessèd time; for from this instant
90 There's nothing serious in mortality.
All is but toys, renown and grace is dead,
The wine of life is drawn, and the mere lees
Is left this vault to brag of.
            Enter Malcolm and Donalbain

DONALBAIN
What is amiss?

MACBETH   You are, and do not know't.
The spring, the head, the fountain of your blood
Is stopped, the very source of it is stopped.

79 *trumpet*. The trumpet is an appropriate metaphor for the bell, because of
the Last Judgement atmosphere.
90 *mortality* human life
92 *lees* dregs
93 *vault* (1) wine vault; (2) sky
94 *You are* (you are *amiss*, since you
have lost your father)

MACDUFF

Your royal father's murdered.

MALCOLM   O, by whom?

LENNOX

Those of his chamber, as it seemed, had done't:
Their hands and faces were all badged with blood,
So were their daggers, which, unwiped, we found   100
Upon their pillows; they stared and were distracted;
No man's life was to be trusted with them.

MACBETH

O yet I do repent me of my fury,
That I did kill them.

MACDUFF   Wherefore did you so?

MACBETH

Who can be wise, amazed, temperate and furious,
Loyal and neutral, in a moment? No man.
The expedition of my violent love
Outrun the pauser reason. Here lay Duncan,
His silver skin laced with his golden blood,
And his gashed stabs looked like a breach in nature   110
For ruin's wasteful entrance; there the murderers,
Steeped in the colours of their trade, their daggers
Unmannerly breeched with gore. Who could refrain,
That had a heart to love, and in that heart
Courage to make's love known?

LADY (swooning)   Help me hence, ho!

MACDUFF

Look to the lady!

MALCOLM (to Donalbain) Why do we hold our tongues,

99 *badged* marked
107 *expedition* haste
108 *pauser* that should make one pause
109 *His silver skin laced with his golden blood* ('dressed in the most precious of garments, the royal blood itself' – Cleanth Brooks)
113 *Unmannerly breeched* wearing an im-

proper (? inhuman) kind of breeches (the blood of the King, the man they should defend)
115 (stage direction) *swooning*. Critics dispute whether this is a genuine swoon (due to womanly exhaustion) or a ruse (designed to distract attention from her husband).

That most may claim this argument for ours?

DONALBAIN (*to Malcolm*)
What should be spoken here where our fate,
Hid in an auger-hole, may rush and seize us?
120 Let's away. Our tears are not yet brewed.

MALCOLM (*to Donalbain*)
Nor our strong sorrow upon the foot of motion.

BANQUO
Look to the lady!

> *Lady Macbeth is taken out*

And when we have our naked frailties hid
That suffer in exposure, let us meet
And question this most bloody piece of work
To know it further. Fears and scruples shake us.
In the great hand of God I stand, and thence
Against the undivulged pretence I fight
Of treasonous malice.

MACDUFF   And so do I.

ALL   So all.

MACBETH
130 Let's briefly put on manly readiness,
And meet i'the hall together.

ALL   Well contented.

> *Exeunt all but Malcolm and Donalbain*

MALCOLM
What will you do? Let's not consort with them.

---

117 *argument* theme of discourse (here, the horror of Duncan's death)
119 *Hid in an auger-hole* concealed, by treachery, in the smallest crevice
120 *brewed* matured
121 *strong sorrow upon the foot of motion.* Our sorrow is stronger than shows at the moment; it has not yet begun to move, to take action.
123 *our naked frailties hid* clothed our poor, half-naked bodies – with a side-glance at the frailty of the whole

human condition
126 *scruples* doubts
127 *In the great hand of God I stand* I put myself at God's disposal (to be compared with Macbeth's appeal for 'manly' readiness' below)
thence relying on God
128 *undivulged pretence* purpose as yet unrevealed
130 *put on manly readiness* put on clothes *and* resolute minds

To show an unfelt sorrow is an office
Which the false man does easy. I'll to England.

DONALBAIN

To Ireland, I. Our separated fortune
Shall keep us both the safer. Where we are
There's daggers in men's smiles. The nea'er in blood
The nearer bloody.

MALCOLM   This murderous shaft that's shot
Hath not yet lighted; and our safest way
Is to avoid the aim. Therefore to horse,   140
And let us not be dainty of leave-taking
But shift away. There's warrant in that theft
Which steals itself when there's no mercy left.   *Exeunt*

          Enter Ross with an Old Man   II.4

OLD MAN

Threescore and ten I can remember well;
Within the volume of which time I have seen
Hours dreadful and things strange; but this sore night
Hath trifled former knowings.

ROSS   Ha, good father,
Thou seest the heavens, as troubled with man's act,
Threatens his bloody stage. By the clock 'tis day,

137–8 *The nea'er in blood | The nearer
bloody* the more closely related
people are, the more likely they are
to try to murder us
140 *the aim* the beginning of the
purpose
141 *dainty of* particular about
142–3 *There's warrant in that theft | Which
steals itself when there's no mercy
left* in these circumstances to steal
away is a justified kind of stealing

II.4 This scene serves to slow down the

time movement and to withdraw the
camera from the agonizing close-ups of
the preceding episodes. The Old Man
here is a choric figure, imported to give
a view of the action from outside, and to
show it in large-scale perspective. The
natural 'portents' take their place in this
perspective as expressing heaven's view
of what has happened.
4 *trifled* made trivial
   father old man
5–6 *heavens . . . act . . . stage* (all theatrical
   terms)

And yet dark night strangles the travelling lamp;
Is't night's predominance or the day's shame
That darkness does the face of earth entomb
When living light should kiss it?

10 OLD MAN   'Tis unnatural,
Even like the deed that's done. On Tuesday last,
A falcon towering in her pride of place
Was by a mousing owl hawked at and killed.

ROSS

And Duncan's horses – a thing most strange and cer-
    tain –
Beauteous and swift, the minions of their race,
Turned wild in nature, broke their stalls, flung out,
Contending 'gainst obedience, as they would
Make war with mankind.

OLD MAN   'Tis said they ate each other.

ROSS

They did so, to the amazement of mine eyes
That looked upon't.
            Enter Macduff
20   Here comes the good Macduff.
How goes the world, sir, now?

MACDUFF   Why, see you not?

ROSS

Is't known who did this more than bloody deed?

MACDUFF

Those that Macbeth hath slain.

ROSS   Alas the day!
What good could they pretend?

MACDUFF   They were suborned.
Malcolm and Donalbain, the King's two sons,

---

7 *travelling lamp* the sun
12 *towering in her pride of place* circling to
   reach her highest pitch (technical
   terms of falconry)
13 *a mousing owl* (an owl whose nature it
   is to hunt close to the ground for

mice, not for falcons)
15 *minions of their race* the darlings of
   horse-breeding
24 *pretend* intend
   suborned bribed to do evil

Are stolen away and fled, which puts upon them
Suspicion of the deed.

ROSS   'Gainst nature still!
Thriftless ambition that will raven up
Thine own life's means! — Then 'tis most like
The sovereignty will fall upon Macbeth?   30

MACDUFF
He is already named and gone to Scone
To be invested.

ROSS   Where is Duncan's body?

MACDUFF
Carried to Colmekill,
The sacred storehouse of his predecessors
And guardian of their bones.

ROSS   Will you to Scone?

MACDUFF
No, cousin, I'll to Fife.

ROSS   Well, I will thither.

MACDUFF
Well, may you see things well done there — Adieu! —
Lest our old robes sit easier than our new.

ROSS
Farewell, father.

OLD MAN
God's benison go with you, and with those   40
That would make good of bad, and friends of foes!

                                        Exeunt

28–9 *raven up | Thine own life's means*
devour improvidently the sustenance
(lineal respect, paternal love) on
which their life and their own succession depended

30 *sovereignty will fall upon Macbeth*. Macbeth was the next heir, Duncan and
Macbeth both being grandsons, of
the older and younger branches respectively, of Malcolm II, the previous king.

33 *Colmekill* Iona (the burial-place of
Scottish kings from 973 to 1040)

36 *Fife* (Macduff's own territory)

38 *Lest our old robes sit easier than our
new* (the new monarch is likely to
be more severe than the former
one)

40–41 *God's benison go with you, and with
those | That would make good of bad, and
friends of foes!* Blessed be the
peacemakers.

III.1   *Enter Banquo*

BANQUO

Thou hast it now: King, Cawdor, Glamis, all
As the weird women promised; and I fear
Thou playedst most foully for't. Yet it was said
It should not stand in thy posterity
But that myself should be the root and father
Of many kings. If there come truth from them,
As upon thee, Macbeth, their speeches shine,
Why by the verities on thee made good
May they not be my oracles as well

10   And set me up in hope? But hush! No more.

*Sennet sounded. Enter Macbeth as King, Lady
Macbeth, Lennox, Ross, Lords, and Attendants*

MACBETH

Here's our chief guest.

LADY   If he had been forgotten
It had been as a gap in our great feast
And all-thing unbecoming.

MACBETH

Tonight we hold a solemn supper, sir,
And I'll request your presence.

BANQUO   Let your highness
Command upon me, to the which my duties
Are with a most indissoluble tie
Forever knit.

III.1 After some time has elapsed we
meet Macbeth again and note that he has
developed into a very poised tyrant. The
contrast with Banquo is one which he
cannot now bear, and his new skill is
shown in his organizing the means to
remove his 'enemy'.

4 *stand in thy posterity* remain in your
   family

7 *shine* are glowingly fulfilled

10 (stage direction) *Sennet* flourish of
   trumpets to announce important
   entry

15 *I'll* (condescension from the royal *we*
   to the personal *I* to indicate special
   affability – shown also by *request*)

16 *to the which*. The antecedent to *which*
   is the idea of 'your commandment'.

17 *indissoluble* (main stress on second
   syllable)

MACBETH
   Ride you this afternoon?
BANQUO   Ay, my good lord.
MACBETH
   We should have else desired your good advice,   20
   Which still hath been both grave and prosperous,
   In this day's council; but we'll take tomorrow.
   Is't far you ride?
BANQUO
   As far, my lord, as will fill up the time
   'Twixt this and supper. Go not my horse the better,
   I must become a borrower of the night
   For a dark hour or twain.
MACBETH   Fail not our feast.
BANQUO
   My lord, I will not.
MACBETH
   We hear our bloody cousins are bestowed
   In England and in Ireland, not confessing   30
   Their cruel parricide, filling their hearers
   With strange invention. But of that tomorrow,
   When therewithal we shall have cause of state
   Craving us jointly. Hie you to horse. Adieu
   Till you return at night. Goes Fleance with you?
BANQUO
   Ay, my good lord; our time does call upon's.
MACBETH
   I wish your horses swift and sure of foot;
   And so I do commend you to their backs.
   Farewell.   *Exit Banquo*
   Let every man be master of his time   40
   Till seven at night.

21 *still* always
25 *the better* better than that
32 *strange invention* (that Macbeth was the
   murderer)
33 *therewithal* besides that
   cause of state state business

To make society the sweeter welcome,
We will keep ourself till supper-time alone.
While then, God be with you!

> *Exeunt Lords and Lady Macbeth*
> Sirrah!

A word with you. Attend those men our pleasure?

SERVANT

They are, my lord, without the palace gate.

MACBETH

Bring them before us.   *Exit Servant*
                    To be thus is nothing;
But to be safely thus! – Our fears in Banquo
Stick deep; and in his royalty of nature
50   Reigns that which would be feared. 'Tis much he dares,
And to that dauntless temper of his mind
He hath a wisdom that doth guide his valour
To act in safety. There is none but he
Whose being I do fear; and under him
My genius is rebuked as, it is said,
Mark Antony's was by Caesar. He chid the sisters
When first they put the name of king upon me,
And bade them speak to him. Then, prophet-like,
They hailed him father to a line of kings.
60   Upon my head they placed a fruitless crown
And put a barren sceptre in my grip,

42-3 *To make society the sweeter welcome,* |
We will keep ourself till supper-time
alone I will avoid company now so
that it may be more pleasant when
we meet again at supper
47 *To be thus* to be King
48-9 *Our fears in Banquo* | *Stick deep* our
fear of Banquo is like a thorn in our
flesh
49 *royalty of nature* natural regality of
temper
50 *that* the 'royalty', a quality loftily
independent of Macbeth's interests.
Compare Iago's 'He hath a daily

beauty in his life | That makes me
ugly' in *Othello*, v.i.19-20.
55 *genius* guardian spirit
it is said (by Plutarch, in the *Life of*
Antony). Compare *Antony and Cleo-*
patra, ii.3.29-31: 'thy spirit | Is all
afraid to govern thee near him; |
But, he away, 'tis noble.'
61 *grip*. Editors usually print 'gripe', the
F form. But there seems no case
against modernizing; in this sense,
the two forms of the word are
indistinguishable.

Thence to be wrenched with an unlineal hand,
No son of mine succeeding. If it be so,
For Banquo's issue have I filed my mind,
For them the gracious Duncan have I murdered,
Put rancours in the vessel of my peace,
Only for them; and mine eternal jewel
Given to the common enemy of man,
To make them kings, the seeds of Banquo kings!
Rather than so, come fate into the list   70
And champion me to the utterance! Who's there?

    Enter Servant and two Murderers

Now go to the door, and stay there till we call.

                   Exit Servant

Was it not yesterday we spoke together?

MURDERERS

It was, so please your highness.

MACBETH   Well then now,
Have you considered of my speeches? Know
That it was he in the times past which held you
So under fortune, which you thought had been
Our innocent self. This I made good to you
In our last conference; passed in probation with you
How you were borne in hand, how crossed, the
    instruments,   80
Who wrought with them, and all things else that might
To half a soul and to a notion crazed

62 *unlineal* not of my family
64 *filed* defiled
65 *gracious* filled with (religious) grace
66 *Put rancours in the vessel of my peace*
    put irritants where there used to be
    peace. In view of the prevailingly
    religious tone of the context *vessel*
    may be the chalice and the whole
    phrase mean 'took me out of the
    state of grace'.
67 *eternal jewel* immortal soul
68 *the common enemy of man* the devil

70–71 *come fate into the list | And champion
    me to the utterance!* Let fate enter the
    tournament and face me in a duel *à
    outrance*, that is, to the death
76–7 *held you | So under fortune* kept you
    in a lowly condition
79 *passed in probation* went over the
    proofs
80 *borne in hand* kept in delusion
    instruments agents
82 *half a soul* a halfwit

Say, 'Thus did Banquo.'

FIRST MURDERER   You made it known to us.

MACBETH

I did so; and went further, which is now
Our point of second meeting. Do you find
Your patience so predominant in your nature
That you can let this go? Are you so gospelled,
To pray for this good man and for his issue,
Whose heavy hand hath bowed you to the grave,
And beggared yours for ever?

90   FIRST MURDERER   We are men, my liege.

MACBETH

Ay, in the catalogue ye go for men,
As hounds and greyhounds, mongrels, spaniels, curs,
Shoughs, water-rugs, and demi-wolves are clept
All by the name of dogs. The valued file
Distinguishes the swift, the slow, the subtle,
The house-keeper, the hunter, every one,
According to the gift which bounteous nature
Hath in him closed; whereby he does receive
Particular addition from the bill

100   That writes them all alike. And so of men.

---

83 *Banquo*. Notice how this essential information about the name of the
person being discussed is delayed to
the end of the speech.

87 *so gospelled* so meekly Christian (as to
'love your enemies . . . pray for them
which hurt you and persecute you' –
Matthew 5.44)

90 *yours* (your family, your issue)

91–107 *Ay, in the catalogue ye go for men*
. . . Macbeth now uses the taunt of
unmanliness which was so effective
when used against him.

91 *catalogue* an undiscriminating list (set
in contrast to the *valued file*)

93 *Shoughs* shaggy Icelandic dogs (probably pronounced to rhyme with *lochs*)
water-rugs. The name suggests that
these are rough-haired water-dogs.
demi-wolves cross-bred from dog and
wolf

94 *valued file* the catalogue re-arranged
to show the prices

96 *house-keeper* domestic watchdog

99–100 *Particular addition from the bill* |
That writes them all alike. The *valued
file* gives back an individual title to
each item, to discriminate it from the
sameness of mere species, found in
the *bill*.

Now, if you have a station in the file,
Not i'the worst rank of manhood, say't,
And I will put that business in your bosoms,
Whose execution takes your enemy off,
Grapples you to the heart and love of us,
Who wear our health but sickly in his life,
Which in his death were perfect.

SECOND MURDERER   I am one, my liege,
Whom the vile blows and buffets of the world
Hath so incensed that I am reckless what I do
To spite the world.

FIRST MURDERER   And I another,   110
So weary with disasters, tugged with fortune,
That I would set my life on any chance
To mend it or be rid on't.

MACBETH   Both of you
Know Banquo was your enemy.

MURDERERS   True, my lord.

MACBETH
So is he mine, and in such bloody distance
That every minute of his being thrusts
Against my near'st of life; and though I could
With bare-faced power sweep him from my sight
And bid my will avouch it, yet I must not,
For certain friends that are both his and mine,   120
Whose loves I may not drop, but wail his fall
Who I myself struck down. And thence it is
That I to your assistance do make love,

101–2 *file ... rank* (moving from the sense of *file* in line 94 above to the military sense)
106 *in his life* while he lives
111 *tugged with* knocked about by
112 *set* gamble
115 *distance* (1) dissension; (2) space between combatants in fencing
116–17 *every minute of his being thrusts | Against my near'st of life* his very

existence is like a sword thrusting against my vitals (picking up second sense in *distance* above, line 115)
118 *With bare-faced power* using my power as King quite openly
119 *bid my will avouch it* justify it by my impulse
120 *For* for the sake of; on account of
123 *I to your assistance do make love* I woo your power to come to my aid

Masking the business from the common eye
For sundry weighty reasons.

SECOND MURDERER   We shall, my lord,
Perform what you command us.

FIRST MURDERER   Though our lives –

MACBETH
Your spirits shine through you. Within this hour, at
        most,
I will advise you where to plant yourselves,
Acquaint you with the perfect spy o'the time,
130 The moment on't; for't must be done tonight;
And something from the palace; always thought
That I require a clearness; and with him,
To leave no rubs nor botches in the work,
Fleance his son, that keeps him company,
Whose absence is no less material to me
Than is his father's, must embrace the fate
Of that dark hour. Resolve yourselves apart;
I'll come to you anon.

MURDERERS   We are resolved, my lord.

MACBETH
I'll call upon you straight. Abide within.

                                        Exeunt Murderers
140 It is concluded! Banquo, thy soul's flight,
If it find heaven, must find it out tonight.   *Exit*

---

127 *Your spirits shine through you.* Say no
    more; I see your resolution in your
    eyes.
129 *the perfect spy o'the time* perhaps the
    Third Murderer (who appears in III.3);
    but may simply mean 'the perfect
    report (espial) on the time (to
    commit the murder)'

131 *something* somewhat; some distance
    thought be it understood
132 *I require a clearness* I must be able to
    clear myself of any suspicion
133 *rubs nor botches* unevennesses, clumsy
    work
137 *Resolve yourselves apart* go away and
    make up your minds

Enter Macbeth's Lady and a Servant III.2

LADY

Is Banquo gone from court?

SERVANT

Ay, madam, but returns again tonight.

LADY

Say to the King I would attend his leisure
For a few words.

SERVANT · Madam, I will. *Exit*

LADY Naught's had, all's spent,

Where our desire is got without content.
'Tis safer to be that which we destroy
Than by destruction dwell in doubtful joy.

Enter Macbeth

How now, my lord? Why do you keep alone,
Of sorriest fancies your companions making,
Using those thoughts which should indeed have died   10
With them they think on? Things without all remedy
Should be without regard; what's done is done.

MACBETH

We have scorched the snake, not killed it;
She'll close and be herself, whilst our poor malice
Remains in danger of her former tooth.
But let the frame of things disjoint, both the worlds
        suffer
Ere we will eat our meal in fear, and sleep

III.2 The development in Macbeth is
shown in domestic as well as political relationship. He dominates his wife's conduct
with eloquent restlessness. Note also the
corresponding change in Lady Macbeth.
4 *Naught's had, all's spent* we have given
    everything, and achieved nothing
7 *by destruction dwell in doubtful joy*
    achieve, by destroying, only an appre-
    hensive joy
9 *sorriest* most wretched

10 *Using* keeping company with
11 *them* (may imply a number of
    murders)
13 *scorched* slashed, as with a knife
14 *close* join up again (as a worm does)
15 *former tooth* her fangs, as dangerous
    as they were before the 'scorching'
16 *frame of things disjoint* the whole struc-
    ture of the universe go to pieces
    both the worlds suffer terrestrial and
    celestial worlds perish

In the affliction of these terrible dreams
That shake us nightly; better be with the dead
20   Whom we, to gain our peace, have sent to peace,
Than on the torture of the mind to lie
In restless ecstasy. Duncan is in his grave;
After life's fitful fever he sleeps well;
Treason has done his worst. Nor steel, nor poison,
Malice domestic, foreign levy, nothing
Can touch him further.

LADY   Come on,
Gentle my lord, sleek o'er your rugged looks,
Be bright and jovial among your guests tonight.

MACBETH
So shall I, love; and so I pray be you.
30   Let your remembrance apply to Banquo,
Present him eminence both with eye and tongue.
Unsafe the while that we
Must lave our honours in these flattering streams,
And make our faces vizards to our hearts,
Disguising what they are.

LADY   You must leave this.

MACBETH
O, full of scorpions is my mind, dear wife!
Thou know'st that Banquo and his Fleance lives.

LADY
But in them nature's copy's not eterne.

---

20 *to gain our peace, have sent to peace* (we killed to gain peace of mind, but have only managed to give peace to our victims)
21 *the torture of the mind* (the bed is a rack)
22 *In restless ecstasy* in a frenzy of delirium
23 *fitful* marked by paroxysms or fits
25 *foreign levy* an army levied abroad
27 *rugged* (monosyllabic here)
30 *Let your remembrance apply* remember to pay special attention (*remembrance* has four syllables)

31 *Present him eminence* give him special honour
32-3 *Unsafe the while that we | Must lave our honours in these flattering streams.* The time is so unsafe for us that we can only keep our honours clean by washing them in flattery. ('A grotesque and violent figure which shows the impatient self-contempt of the speaker' – Kittredge.)
33 *vizards* false faces
38 *nature's copy* (1) the form that Nature has given them by copying the first

MACBETH

There's comfort yet! They are assailable.
Then be thou jocund. Ere the bat hath flown   40
His cloistered flight, ere to black Hecat's summons
The shard-borne beetle, with his drowsy hums,
Hath rung night's yawning peal, there shall be done
A deed of dreadful note.

LADY   What's to be done?

MACBETH

Be innocent of the knowledge, dearest chuck,
Till thou applaud the deed. Come, seeling night,
Scarf up the tender eye of pitiful day,
And with thy bloody and invisible hand
Cancel and tear to pieces that great bond
Which keeps me pale. Light thickens   50
And the crow makes wing to the rooky wood;
Good things of day begin to droop and drowse,
Whiles night's black agents to their preys do rouse.
Thou marvell'st at my words; but hold thee still.
Things bad begun make strong themselves by ill.
So, prithee, go with me.   *Exeunt*

creation: 'particular casts from Nature's mould'; (2) copyhold – a lease that can be broken

40 *jocund*. Note how joy is associated with death.

41 *cloistered*. The bat flies in and around buildings rather than in the open air.

42 *shard-borne* (1) born (sic) in dung; (2) borne aloft by its wing-cases

44 *note* (1) memory; (2) sound

45 *dearest chuck* (a grim intimacy)

46–7 *Come, seeling night,* | *Scarf up the tender eye of pitiful day*. Night is to hide the dreadful deed from daylight as the falconer *seels* or sews up the eyes of the hawk.

47 *Scarf up* blindfold

48 *bloody and invisible*. The falconer's hand *is bloody* (from the *seeling*) and *is invisible* to the hawk, now effectively blinded.

49 *that great bond* the moral law; or perhaps the sixth commandment, against killing. (Perhaps *bond* should be pronounced *band*, to rhyme with *hand*.)

50 *pale* (1) paled, fenced-in – following a secondary sense in *bond* (= bondage); (2) tender-hearted, a creature seeing through the 'tender eye of pitiful day'
thickens grows dense, opaque, dim

53 *to their preys do rouse* bestir themselves to hunt their prey

III.3   *Enter three Murderers*

FIRST MURDERER
But who did bid thee join with us?

THIRD MURDERER   Macbeth.

SECOND MURDERER
He needs not our mistrust, since he delivers
Our offices and what we have to do
To the direction just.

FIRST MURDERER   Then stand with us;
The west yet glimmers with some streaks of day.
Now spurs the lated traveller apace
To gain the timely inn; and near approaches
The subject of our watch.

THIRD MURDERER   Hark, I hear horses!

BANQUO (*within*)
Give us a light there, ho!

SECOND MURDERER   Then 'tis he.
10   The rest that are within the note of expectation,
Already are i'the court.

FIRST MURDERER   His horses go about.

THIRD MURDERER
Almost a mile; but he does usually.
So all men do, from hence to the palace gate
Make it their walk.

            Enter Banquo and Fleance, with a torch

SECOND MURDERER
A light, a light!

III.3 The altercation between the Third
Murderer and the other two is a nice
illustration of the dependence of tyranny
on mistrust.

3 *offices* duties
4 *To the direction just* exactly as required
    stand 'wait here'; or 'join our side'
6 *lated* belated; overtaken by the night

10 *within the note of expectation* in the list
    of expected guests
12–14 *but he does usually.* | *So all men do,*
    from hence to the palace gate | *Make it*
    their walk. F has a comma after 'usu-
    ally', allowing one to phrase it: 'he
    does . . . (so all men . . .) make it
    their walk'.

THIRD MURDERER
    'Tis he.

FIRST MURDERER   Stand to't!

BANQUO
  It will be rain tonight.

FIRST MURDERER   Let it come down!
      They attack Banquo

BANQUO
  O treachery! Fly, good Fleance, fly, fly, fly!
  Thou mayst revenge – O slave!
      Banquo falls. Fleance escapes

THIRD MURDERER
  Who did strike out the light?

FIRST MURDERER   Was't not the way?

THIRD MURDERER
  There's but one down; the son is fled.

SECOND MURDERER   We have lost   20
  Best half of our affair.

FIRST MURDERER
  Well, let's away and say how much is done.   *Exeunt*

      Banquet prepared. Enter Macbeth, Lady Macbeth,   III.4
      Ross, Lennox, Lords, and Attendants

MACBETH
  You know your own degrees, sit down. At first

---

16 *Let it come down* let 'the rain of blood'
  come down

III.4 This scene gives the success and
failure of Macbeth's assault on 'royalty'
its climactic expression, and makes the
contrast between false order and true
order quite explicit. It should recall the
earlier banquet which welcomed Duncan
to Inverness (1.7) – a true image of kingly

content; and it also looks forward to the
inhuman banquet of the Witches in IV.1.
The final episode, with the King and
Queen abandoned and guilt-oppressed
amid the relics of their feasting, gives
eloquent visual expression to the meaning of their fates.

1 *degrees* rank, position at table. The feast
  is a symbol of order.

1–2 *At first | And last* once and for all

And last, the hearty welcome.

LORDS   Thanks to your majesty.

MACBETH

Ourself will mingle with society
And play the humble host.

    He walks around the tables

Our hostess keeps her state; but in best time
We will require her welcome.

LADY

Pronounce it for me, sir, to all our friends,
For my heart speaks they are welcome.

    Enter First Murderer

MACBETH

See, they encounter thee with their hearts' thanks;
10   Both sides are even. Here I'll sit i'the midst.
Be large in mirth. Anon we'll drink a measure
The table round.

    He rises and goes to the Murderer

There's blood upon thy face!

FIRST MURDERER

                'Tis Banquo's then.

MACBETH

'Tis better thee without than he within.
Is he dispatched?

FIRST MURDERER My lord, his throat is cut;
That I did for him.

MACBETH   Thou art the best o'the cut-throats.
Yet he's good that did the like for Fleance.

2, 6, 8 *welcome*. 'The first three speeches
of the King and Queen end with the
word "welcome"' (Kittredge).

3 *mingle with society* leave the dais; move
round among the guests

5 *state* canopied throne
  in best time when it is most
appropriate

9–10 *See, they encounter thee with their*

hearts' thanks; | *Both sides are even.*
Perhaps some stage direction is necessary here to indicate the mode by
which the guests show their *even*
(equivalent) response to the Queen.
On the other hand, the *even* is often
taken to refer to the table: both
sides are full, so *Here I'll sit i'the
midst.*

If thou didst it, thou art the nonpareil.

FIRST MURDERER

Most royal sir – Fleance is scaped.

MACBETH

Then comes my fit again. I had else been perfect,   20
Whole as the marble, founded as the rock,
As broad and general as the casing air;
But now I am cabined, cribbed, confined, bound in
To saucy doubts and fears. – But Banquo's safe?

FIRST MURDERER

Ay, my good lord; safe in a ditch he bides,
With twenty trenchèd gashes on his head,
The least a death to nature.

MACBETH   Thanks for that.
There the grown serpent lies. The worm that's fled
Hath nature that in time will venom breed,
No teeth for the present. Get thee gone. Tomorrow   30
We'll hear ourselves again.   *Exit Murderer*

LADY   My royal lord,
You do not give the cheer. The feast is sold
That is not often vouched, while 'tis a-making,
'Tis given with welcome. To feed were best at home;

---

18 *the nonpareil* without an equal
20 *fit* fever of anxiety
    perfect completely secure, healthy
21 *Whole* unbroken (in surface)
    founded secure
22 *As broad and general* as wide-
    embracing
    casing enveloping
23 *cabined, cribbed, confined, bound in* impris-
    oned (the 'damnable iteration' con-
    veys Macbeth's hysterical intensity)
24 *saucy* importunate
24, 25 *safe* (heavily ironic)
28 *worm* little serpent
31 *hear ourselves* hear one another.
    (Notice the assimilation of the King
    and the murderer.)

32 *give the cheer* welcome your guests
32–4 *The feast is sold* | *That is not often
vouched, while 'tis a-making,* | *'Tis given
with welcome.* It is merely a commercial affair if the hosts do not punctuate the feast with assertions of
welcome.
34–5 *To feed were best at home;* | *From
thence, the sauce to meat is ceremony.* If
feeding is the sole concern, home is
the best place for it; away from
home it is ceremony that makes a
feast worthwhile. (*Ceremony*, pronounced 'seer-money', seems to
have been trisyllabic in Shakespeare's day.)

From thence, the sauce to meat is ceremony;
Meeting were bare without it.

MACBETH   Sweet remembrancer!
Now good digestion wait on appetite,
And health on both!

LENNOX   May't please your highness sit.

Enter the Ghost of Banquo and sits in Macbeth's place

MACBETH
Here had we now our country's honour roofed,
40 Were the graced person of our Banquo present;
Who may I rather challenge for unkindness
Than pity for mischance.

ROSS   His absence, sir,
Lays blame upon his promise. Please't your highness
To grace us with your royal company?

MACBETH
The table's full.

LENNOX   Here is a place reserved, sir.

MACBETH
Where?

LENNOX
Here, my good lord. What is't that moves your highness?

MACBETH
Which of you have done this?

LORDS   What, my good lord?

MACBETH
Thou canst not say I did it; never shake
50 Thy gory locks at me.

ROSS
Gentlemen, rise. His highness is not well.

---

36 *remembrancer* an officer whose original function was to remind his superior of his duties
37 *good digestion wait on appetite* enjoy whatever you eat
39 *our country's honour* all the nobility of Scotland
40 *graced* (1) our guest of honour; (2) full of grace
41 *challenge for* reproach with
48 *done this* (1) killed Banquo; (2) filled up the seat
49 *Thou canst not say I did it*. He defends himself by saying that he did not strike the actual blow against Banquo.

LADY (*descends from her throne*)
>Sit, worthy friends. My lord is often thus;
>And hath been from his youth. Pray you keep seat.
>The fit is momentary; upon a thought
>He will again be well. If much you note him,
>You shall offend him and extend his passion.
>Feed, and regard him not. – Are you a man?

MACBETH
>Ay, and a bold one, that dare look on that
>Which might appal the devil.

LADY   O proper stuff!
>This is the very painting of your fear.   60
>This is the air-drawn dagger which you said
>Led you to Duncan. O, these flaws and starts,
>Impostors to true fear, would well become
>A woman's story at a winter's fire,
>Authorized by her grandam. Shame itself!
>Why do you make such faces? When all's done
>You look but on a stool.

MACBETH   Prithee, see there!
>Behold! Look! Lo! – How say you?
>Why, what care I if thou canst nod! Speak, too!
>If charnel-houses and our graves must send   70
>Those that we bury, back, our monuments
>Shall be the maws of kites.   *Exit Ghost*

LADY   What, quite unmanned in folly?

54 *upon a thought* in a moment
59 *proper stuff* stuff and nonsense
61 *air-drawn* sketched out of air; pulled through air
62 *flaws* sudden gusts (of passion)
63–5 *Impostors to true fear, would well become | A woman's story at a winter's fire, | Authorized by her grandam.* These are not concerned with reality, but are simply passions such as would be appropriate to a dramatic rendering of a ghost-story – one whose credibility rests on the authority of an old woman.
65 *Authorized* (accent on second syllable)
70–72 *If charnel-houses and our graves must send | Those that we bury, back, our monuments | Shall be the maws of kites* if the dead return from normal burial-places, we will have to throw their bodies for birds of prey to eat
70 *charnel-houses* bone-stores

MACBETH
If I stand here, I saw him.

LADY   Fie, for shame!

MACBETH
Blood hath been shed ere now, i'the olden time,
Ere humane statute purged the gentle weal;
Ay, and since too, murders have been performed
Too terrible for the ear. The times has been
That, when the brains were out, the man would die,
And there an end. But now they rise again
80   With twenty mortal murders on their crowns,
And push us from our stools. This is more strange
Than such a murder is.

LADY   My worthy lord,
Your noble friends do lack you.

MACBETH   I do forget.
Do not muse at me, my most worthy friends:
I have a strange infirmity, which is nothing
To those that know me. Come, love and health to all!
Then I'll sit down. Give me some wine; fill full!
        Enter Ghost
I drink to the general joy o'the whole table,
And to our dear friend Banquo, whom we miss.
90   Would he were here! To all – and him – we thirst,
And all to all.

LORDS   Our duties and the pledge!

MACBETH (*sees the Ghost*)
Avaunt, and quit my sight! Let the earth hide thee!
Thy bones are marrowless, thy blood is cold.

---

75 *Ere humane statute purged the gentle weal*
before the benevolence of law
cleansed society and made it gentle
80 *mortal murders* fatal wounds
81 *push us from our stools* (1) occupy the
seat at the feast; (2) take over the
succession to the throne

90 *we thirst* we are anxious to drink
91 *And all to all* let all men drink to
everyone
Our duties and the pledge! We drink
our homage to you, and the toast
you have just proposed.

Thou hast no speculation in those eyes
Which thou dost glare with.

LADY   Think of this, good peers,
But as a thing of custom; 'tis no other;
Only it spoils the pleasure of the time.

MACBETH
What man dare, I dare.
Approach thou like the rugged Russian bear,
The armed rhinoceros, or the Hyrcan tiger,   100
Take any shape but that, and my firm nerves
Shall never tremble. Or be alive again,
And dare me to the desert with thy sword:
If trembling I inhabit then, protest me
The baby of a girl. Hence, horrible shadow!
Unreal mockery, hence!   *Exit Ghost*
                        Why, so; being gone,
I am a man again. – Pray you sit still.

LADY
You have displaced the mirth, broke the good meeting
With most admired disorder.

MACBETH   Can such things be,
And overcome us like a summer's cloud,   110
Without our special wonder? You make me strange
Even to the disposition that I owe
When now I think you can behold such sights
And keep the natural ruby of your cheeks,

---

94 *speculation* power of knowing what
you see
100 *armed* armour-plated
Hyrcan. Tigers in Latin literature
were often said to come from Hyr-
cania, by the Caspian Sea.
101 *nerves* sinews
104 *If trembling I inhabit then* if I live
in a trembling body, if I harbour
trembling
105 *The baby of a girl* (a multiplication of

unmanly types; *baby* is sometimes
thought to refer to a doll)
108 *displaced* removed
109 *With most admired disorder* with this
strange disordering of your wits
110 *overcome us like a summer's cloud* bring
sudden gloom over us, as a cloud
may do in a sunlit day
111–12 *strange | Even to the disposition that
I owe* seem unlike the brave person I
have supposed myself to be

When mine is blanched with fear.

ROSS   What sights, my lord?

LADY

I pray you speak not; he grows worse and worse.
Question enrages him. At once, good night.
Stand not upon the order of your going;
But go at once.

LENNOX   Good night; and better health
Attend his majesty!

120   LADY   A kind good-night to all!

Exeunt Lords

MACBETH

It will have blood, they say; blood will have blood.
Stones have been known to move and trees to speak;
Augurs and understood relations have
By maggot-pies, and choughs, and rooks brought forth
The secret'st man of blood. What is the night?

LADY

Almost at odds with morning, which is which.

MACBETH

How sayst thou, that Macduff denies his person
At our great bidding?

LADY   Did you send to him, sir?

MACBETH

I hear it by the way. But I will send.

---

118 *Stand not upon the order of your going*
(an exit in strong contrast to the
entrance, III.4.1). The *disorder* in Macbeth's mind has produced social
disorder.

121 *It will have blood, they say; blood will
have blood*. The F punctuation (followed here – most editors put the
semi-colon before *they*) can be interpreted as an initial, half-reverie, statement of the proverb (from Genesis
9.6) followed by a more complete
repetition and explanation of it.

122–5 *Stones have been known to move and
trees to speak . . .* (the whole of nature
conspires to reveal the unnatural sin
of murder)

123 *Augurs* prophecies
understood relations either (1) reports properly comprehended; or (2)
connexions elucidated

124 *maggot-pies, and choughs* magpies and
crows

127 *How sayst thou, that* what do you say
to the fact that

There's not a one of them, but in his house 130
I keep a servant fee'd. I will tomorrow –
And betimes I will – to the Weird Sisters.
More shall they speak; for now I am bent to know
By the worst means the worst. For mine own good
All causes shall give way. I am in blood
Stepped in so far, that, should I wade no more,
Returning were as tedious as go o'er.
Strange things I have in head, that will to hand;
Which must be acted ere they may be scanned.

LADY

You lack the season of all natures, sleep. 140

MACBETH

Come, we'll to sleep. My strange and self-abuse
Is the initiate fear that wants hard use.
We are yet but young in deed.   *Exeunt*

Thunder. Enter the three Witches, meeting Hecat   III.5

FIRST WITCH

Why, how now, Hecat? You look angerly.

130–31 *There's not a one of them, but in his house* | *I keep a servant fee'd* (an explanation of how he heard 'by the way')

132 *betimes* either (1) early in the morning; or (2) while there is yet time

139 *Which must be acted ere they may be scanned.* There is not time to con the part, it must be put into performance at once.

140 *season* preservative

141–2 *My strange and self-abuse* | *Is the initiate fear that wants hard use* my strange self-deception (seeing Banquo's ghost) is only due to the terror of the beginner who lacks toughening experience

143 *young in deed* novices in crime

III.5 One of the scenes most regularly suspected of being interpolations. Hecat is a new and hitherto unannounced character, and the nature of the Witches seems to have been changed; Macbeth is now viewed as an *adept* or disciple of the Witches, not a victim. On the other hand, the end of Hecat's speech catches at a principal theme of the whole play (see Introduction, pp. 799–800) and her speech, though distinguished from the Witch-utterances by its iambic (rather than trochaic) rhymes, is poetically very accomplished.

HECAT

Have I not reason, beldams, as you are
Saucy and over-bold? How did you dare
To trade and traffic with Macbeth
In riddles and affairs of death,
And I, the mistress of your charms,
The close contriver of all harms,
Was never called to bear my part,
Or show the glory of our art?

10 And, which is worse, all you have done
Hath been but for a wayward son,
Spiteful and wrathful, who, as others do,
Loves for his own ends, not for you.
But make amends now: get you gone,
And at the pit of Acheron
Meet me i'the morning. Thither he
Will come, to know his destiny.
Your vessels and your spells provide,
Your charms and everything beside.

20 I am for the air; this night I'll spend
Unto a dismal and a fatal end.
Great business must be wrought ere noon
Upon the corner of the moon:
There, hangs a vaporous drop profound;
I'll catch it ere it come to ground;
And that distilled by magic sleights
Shall raise such artificial sprites
As by the strength of their illusion
Shall draw him on to his confusion.

30 He shall spurn fate, scorn death, and bear
His hopes 'bove wisdom, grace, and fear.

---

2 *beldams* hags
7 *close* secret
15 *Acheron* hell
21 *Unto a dismal and a fatal end* with a

view to a disastrous and fatal
conclusion
24 *profound* with deep or powerful
qualities

And you all know security
Is mortals' chiefest enemy.
Music and a song
Hark! I am called. My little spirit, see,
Sits in a foggy cloud and stays for me.
Sing within: 'Come away, come away,' etc.

FIRST WITCH
Come, let's make haste; she'll soon be back again.

Exeunt

Enter Lennox and another Lord   III.6

LENNOX
My former speeches have but hit your thoughts,
Which can interpret further. Only I say
Things have been strangely borne. The gracious Duncan
Was pitied of Macbeth: marry, he was dead!
And the right valiant Banquo walked too late;
Whom you may say, if 't please you, Fleance killed,
For Fleance fled. Men must not walk too late.
Who cannot want the thought how monstrous
It was for Malcolm and for Donalbain
To kill their gracious father? Damnèd fact,   10

32 *security* culpable absence of anxiety (it is a key word in the play; see Introduction, p. 800)

35 (stage direction) *Sing*. See p. 837.

III.6 In terms of the intrigue, this scene exists to tell us that Macbeth's purpose of sending to Macduff, mentioned in III.4.129, has now been fulfilled; and that Macduff has fled to England. But the speech of Lennox serves further – as an exposé of the mind under tyranny, reduced to irony as its sole mode of opposition – to present the claustrophobic atmosphere of Scotland and the scent of freedom (in the downright refusal of Macduff).

1-2 *My former speeches have but hit your thoughts,* | *Which can interpret further.* What I have already said to you has matched what you think; and you must draw your own conclusions. (The whole conversation is an example of the reserve that must accompany tyranny.)

2 *Only I say* I only say

3, 5 *gracious Duncan ... right valiant Banquo*. No doubt these are Macbeth's phrases.

10 *fact* crime

How it did grieve Macbeth! Did he not straight –
In pious rage – the two delinquents tear,
That were the slaves of drink, and thralls of sleep?
Was not that nobly done? Ay, and wisely too;
For 'twould have angered any heart alive
To hear the men deny't. So that I say
He has borne all things well; and I do think
That had he Duncan's sons under his key –
As, an't please heaven, he shall not – they should find
20   What 'twere to kill a father – so should Fleance.
But, peace! For from broad words, and 'cause he failed
His presence at the tyrant's feast, I hear
Macduff lives in disgrace. Sir, can you tell
Where he bestows himself?

LORD   The son of Duncan,
From whom this tyrant holds the due of birth,
Lives in the English court, and is received
Of the most pious Edward with such grace
That the malevolence of fortune nothing
Takes from his high respect. Thither Macduff
30   Is gone to pray the holy king, upon his aid,
To wake Northumberland and warlike Seyward,
That by the help of these – with Him above
To ratify the work – we may again
Give to our tables meat, sleep to our nights,
Free from our feasts and banquets bloody knives,
Do faithful homage and receive free honours –

12 *pious* (1) religious; (2) son-like
15–16 *For 'twould have angered any heart
     alive | To hear the men deny't.* He
     killed them so that men should not
     be angered by hearing them deny it.
21 *broad words* unrestrained talk
22 *tyrant's* (Lennox is now talking
     'broad' himself)
27 *the most pious Edward* (Edward the
     Confessor)

28 *malevolence of fortune* his loss of his
     throne
30 *to pray the holy king, upon his aid* to beg
     Edward for assistance
34 *Give to our tables meat* hold open feasts
36 *Do faithful homage and receive free hon-
     ours.* The implication is that under
     Macbeth the homage paid to the sov-
     ereign is hypocritical, the honours
     not *free*, but bought by servility.

All which we pine for now. And this report
Hath so exasperate the King that he
Prepares for some attempt of war.

LENNOX   Sent he to Macduff?

LORD

He did. And with an absolute 'Sir, not I!'   40
The cloudy messenger turns me his back
And hums, as who should say 'You'll rue the time
That clogs me with this answer.'

LENNOX   And that well might
Advise him to a caution to hold what distance
His wisdom can provide. Some holy angel
Fly to the court of England and unfold
His message ere he come, that a swift blessing
May soon return to this our suffering country,
Under a hand accursed!

LORD   I'll send my prayers with him.

                                    Exeunt

37 *this report.* If the *King* in line 38 is Macbeth (see note on that line) then the report might be (a) that of Macduff's flight or (b) that of Malcolm's reception in England. The syntax would suggest (a); but this has the disadvantage of contradicting IV.1.141 (where Macbeth appears ignorant of Macduff's flight) and it seems preferable to understand (b) here. We may, if we wish, imagine that Shakespeare's original draft ran straight on from *respect* (line 29) to *And* (line 37).

38 *the.* The F reading *their* suggests that the king is Edward; and this would make perfect sense as far as the Lord's speech is concerned. But the

he of Lennox's reply must be Macbeth; and if this is so, the *King* of line 38 must also be Macbeth.

40–41 *And with an absolute 'Sir, not I!' | The cloudy messenger turns me his back.* The messenger turns back towards his master, bearing Macduff's absolute 'Not I' answer.

41 *cloudy* lowering, scowling
me (ethic dative; only present to give emphasis)

42 *hums* says 'hum' ('um', 'umph')

43 *clogs* impedes my advancement. (Messengers bearing bad news did not recommend themselves to tyrants.)

44 *him* Macduff
distance (between himself and Macbeth)

IV.1   *Thunder. Enter the three Witches*

FIRST WITCH
                 Thrice the brinded cat hath mewed.

SECOND WITCH
                 Thrice, and once the hedge-pig whined.

THIRD WITCH
                 Harpier cries! 'Tis time, 'tis time!

FIRST WITCH
                 Round about the cauldron go;
                 In the poisoned entrails throw:
                 Toad that under cold stone
                 Days and nights has thirty-one.
                 Sweltered venom, sleeping got,
                 Boil thou first i'the charmèd pot.

ALL
10   Double, double, toil and trouble;
                 Fire burn, and cauldron bubble.

SECOND WITCH
                 Fillet of a fenny snake
                 In the cauldron boil and bake;
                 Eye of newt, and toe of frog,
                 Wool of bat, and tongue of dog,
                 Adder's fork, and blind-worm's sting,

IV.1 Usually set in a cavern, because of the 'pit of Acheron' reference in III.5; but line 46 seems to imply a building with a door. The scene bears the same (generative) relationship to the second half of the play as do the prophecies of 1.3 to the first half. The iambic speeches, 39–43, 124–31, are often thought interpolated; they exist to justify the song and dance, and obviously differ in their tone – more delicate and pleasant – from the rest of the Witch material.

1 *brinded cat* streaked cat (the First Witch's familiar)

2 *hedge-pig* hedgehog

3 *Harpier* (the third familiar – a word formed from *Harpy*)

7 *thirty-one* (meaning, I suppose, 'one full month')

8 *Sweltered venom, sleeping got* venom sweated out during sleep

10, 20 etc. *Double, double, toil and trouble* let toil and trouble be doubled in the world

12 *fenny* living in fen or marshland

15 *tongue of dog* (appears in this sinister catalogue because of Shakespeare's abhorrence of canine fawning)

16 *fork* forked tongue

Lizard's leg and howlet's wing,
For a charm of powerful trouble,
Like a hell-broth, boil and bubble.

ALL

Double, double, toil and trouble;   20
Fire burn, and cauldron bubble.

THIRD WITCH

Scale of dragon, tooth of wolf,
Witch's mummy, maw and gulf
Of the ravined salt sea shark,
Root of hemlock digged i'the dark,
Liver of blaspheming Jew,
Gall of goat, and slips of yew
Slivered in the moon's eclipse,
Nose of Turk, and Tartar's lips,
Finger of birth-strangled babe,   30
Ditch-delivered by a drab,
Make the gruel thick and slab.
Add thereto a tiger's chaudron
For the ingredience of our cauldron.

ALL

Double, double, toil and trouble;
Fire burn, and cauldron bubble.

---

blind-worm slow-worm (now known to be venom-less)

17 *howlet* young owl

18 *For* in order to produce

19 *boil and bubble* (imperatives)

23 *Witch's mummy* mummified fragments of a witch
maw and gulf gullet and stomach

24 *ravined* having finished devouring his prey

25 *digged i'the dark* (at the time when it was most noxious)

26 *Liver* (supposed to be the seat of the passions) *of blaspheming Jew* ('blaspheming' because he denies Christ's divinity)

27 *Gall* secretion of the liver; rancour
slips seedlings
yew (because poisonous)

28 *Slivered in the moon's eclipse* torn from the tree at a particularly baneful time

29 *Turk ... Tartar's* (like *Jew*, line 26, and *babe*, line 30, attractive to witches because unchristened)

31 *Ditch-delivered by a drab* born in a ditch, the child of a harlot

32 *slab* viscous

33 *chaudron* entrails

34 *cauldron.* The Elizabethan pronunciation of *cauldron* (as of *vault*, *falcon*, *caulk* etc.) kept the 'l' silent, so that the rhyme with *chaudron* was perfect.

SECOND WITCH

Cool it with a baboon's blood;
Then the charm is firm and good.

Enter Hecat and the other three Witches

HECAT

O well done! I commend your pains;
40   And everyone shall share i'the gains.
And now about the cauldron sing
Like elves and fairies in a ring,
Enchanting all that you put in.

Music and a song: 'Black spirits' etc.

        Exeunt Hecat and the other three Witches

SECOND WITCH

By the pricking of my thumbs,
Something wicked this way comes.
Open, locks, whoever knocks!

Enter Macbeth

MACBETH

How now, you secret, black, and midnight hags!
What is't you do?

ALL   A deed without a name.

MACBETH

I conjure you, by that which you profess,
50   Howe'er you come to know it, answer me –
Though you untie the winds and let them fight

---

37 *baboon's blood.* Hot and lustful; and therefore only cooling to the unnaturally fiery. *Baboon* has accent on first syllable.

38 (stage direction) *Enter Hecat and the other three Witches.* The song 'Black Spirits' (as it appears in Middleton's *The Witch*) does not require more than three performers; though the refrain might be thought to deserve a larger body. If a chorus of six Witches seems offensive we can read (as is sometimes done): 'Enter Hecat [to] the other three Witches', and so

avoid increasing the Witch population.

43 (stage direction) *song.* See p. 839.

47 *secret, black, and midnight hags* wicked practitioners of 'black' magic

51–9 *Though you untie the winds and let them fight* ⌊ ... *Even till destruction sicken* though order, civilization and the cosmos itself be destroyed

51 *Though you untie the winds.* Compare Revelation 7.1: 'I saw four Angels stand on the four corners of the earth, holding the four winds of the earth.'

Against the churches; though the yesty waves
Confound and swallow navigation up;
Though bladed corn be lodged and trees blown down;
Though castles topple on their warders' heads;
Though palaces and pyramids do slope
Their heads to their foundations; though the treasure
Of nature's germens tumble all together
Even till destruction sicken – answer me
To what I ask you.

FIRST WITCH   Speak.

SECOND WITCH   Demand.

THIRD WITCH   We'll answer.   60

FIRST WITCH

Say if thou'dst rather hear it from our mouths
Or from our masters.

MACBETH   Call 'em. Let me see 'em.

FIRST WITCH

Pour in sow's blood that hath eaten
Her nine farrow; grease that's sweaten
From the murderer's gibbet, throw
Into the flame.

ALL   Come high or low,
Thyself and office deftly show.

Thunder. First Apparition, an Armed Head

MACBETH

Tell me, thou unknown power –

FIRST WITCH   He knows thy thought.
Hear his speech, but say thou naught.

52 *yesty* foaming
54 *Though bladed corn be lodged* though new corn be beaten flat
57–8 *the treasure | Of nature's germens tumble all together* the patterns of creation fall into confusion
58 *nature's germens* the seeds or material essences of things
59 *Even till destruction sicken* (through over-eating)
62 *masters* the powers of Fate
67 *Thyself and office* thyself performing thy function
(stage direction) *an Armed Head* (presumably that of Macbeth himself, cut off by Macduff. The same property head would suffice for both occasions.)

FIRST APPARITION

70   Macbeth, Macbeth, Macbeth, beware Macduff!
Beware the Thane of Fife! Dismiss me. Enough.

He descends

MACBETH

Whate'er thou art, for thy good caution, thanks;
Thou hast harped my fear aright. But one word more –

FIRST WITCH

He will not be commanded. Here's another
More potent than the first.

Thunder. Second Apparition, a Bloody Child

SECOND APPARITION

Macbeth, Macbeth, Macbeth!

MACBETH

Had I three ears, I'd hear thee.

SECOND APPARITION

Be bloody, bold, and resolute; laugh to scorn
The power of man; for none of woman born

80   Shall harm Macbeth.   *He descends*

MACBETH

Then live Macduff; what need I fear of thee?
But yet I'll make assurance double sure,
And take a bond of fate. Thou shalt not live;
That I may tell pale-hearted fear it lies,
And sleep in spite of thunder.

*Thunder. Third Apparition, a Child crowned, with a
tree in his hand*

What is this
That rises like the issue of a king,
And wears upon his baby brow the round

---

73 *harped* guessed
75 (stage direction) *a Bloody Child* (presumably Macduff, 'from his mother's
womb untimely ripped')
83 *take a bond of fate* (a *bond* to 'make
assurance double sure' – by disposing
of Macduff (and the First Appari-

tion's warning) *and* relying on 'none
of woman born')
85 *thunder* (traditionally the expression
of God's anger)
(stage direction) *a Child crowned, with a
tree in his hand* (Malcolm, advancing
with a branch of Birnan Wood)

And top of sovereignty?

ALL   Listen, but speak not to't.

THIRD APPARITION

Be lion-mettled, proud, and take no care

Who chafes, who frets, or where conspirers are;   90

Macbeth shall never vanquished be, until

Great Birnan Wood to high Dunsinane Hill

Shall come against him.   *He descends*

MACBETH   That will never be.

Who can impress the forest, bid the tree

Unfix his earth-bound root? Sweet bodements! Good!

Rebellious dead rise never till the wood

Of Birnan rise, and our high-placed Macbeth

Shall live the lease of nature, pay his breath

To time and mortal custom. Yet my heart

Throbs to know one thing: tell me, if your art   100

Can tell so much, shall Banquo's issue ever

Reign in this kingdom?

ALL   Seek to know no more.

MACBETH

I will be satisfied! Deny me this

---

92 *Birnan.* F has 'Byrnam' here; the correct form in modern geography is *Birnam*. But Elizabethan authorities spell the word with an *n* ('Bernane' in Holinshed; 'Brynnane' in Wintoun's *Original Chronicle*); and this is the form the Folio uses on every other occasion when the name appears (IV.1.97; v.3.2 and 60; v.4.3; v.5.34 and 44; v.6.69). We must assume that the *m* is an error here, and that *Birnan* is the correct Shakespearian form.

93–101 *That will never be . . . | Can tell so much.* As Kittredge notes, Macbeth's continuation of the rhymed speech-form of the Apparition implies his absorption into that world of false 'security'. Note also his third-person reference to himself in line 97.

94 *impress* conscript

95 *bodements* auguries

96 *Rebellious dead.* Theobald's emendation 'Rebellion's head' has been generally accepted. It takes up, very neatly, the idea of 'where conspirers are' above. But the idea of *dead* is much closer to 'Unfix . . . root', which can be seen to resurrect, in Macbeth's mind, the obsession with Banquo that runs through the scene. Banquo's ghost is a type of the rebellious – 'But now they rise . . . and push us from our stools.'

99 *mortal custom* the custom of dying

And an eternal curse fall on you! Let me know.
Why sinks that cauldron?

Hautboys

And what noise is this?

FIRST WITCH
Show!

SECOND WITCH
Show!

THIRD WITCH
Show!

ALL

Show his eyes and grieve his heart;
110   Come like shadows, so depart.

*A show of eight kings, and Banquo; the last king with
a glass in his hand*

MACBETH

Thou art too like the spirit of Banquo. Down!
Thy crown does sear mine eye-balls. And thy hair,
Thou other gold-bound brow, is like the first.
A third is like the former. – Filthy hags,
Why do you show me this? – A fourth? Start, eyes!
What, will the line stretch out to the crack of doom?
Another yet? A seventh? I'll see no more!
And yet the eighth appears, who bears a glass
Which shows me many more. And some I see
120   That two-fold balls and treble sceptres carry.
Horrible sight! Now I see 'tis true,
For the blood-boltered Banquo smiles upon me,

110 (stage direction) *eight kings, and Banquo.* Banquo was supposed to be the ancestor of the Stuart line. The eight kings would be Robert II, Robert III, James I, James II, James III, James IV, James V, Mary Queen of Scots. If we exclude Mary we have to include Walter Stewart (preceding Robert II).

116 *What, will the line stretch out to the crack of doom?* The Stuarts were proud of their unbroken lineal descent.

118 *a glass.* See Introduction, pp. 807–8.

120 *That two-fold balls and treble sceptres carry* unite the crowns of England and Scotland (two-fold) and rule over Scotland, England, and Ireland (treble) – as did James I

122 *blood-boltered* his hair matted with blood

And points at them for his. What! Is this so?

FIRST WITCH

      Ay, sir, all this is so. But why
      Stands Macbeth thus amazedly?
      Come, sisters, cheer we up his sprites
      And show the best of our delights.
      I'll charm the air to give a sound,
      While you perform your antic round,
      That this great king may kindly say   130
      Our duties did his welcome pay.
      Music. The Witches dance; and vanish

MACBETH

Where are they? Gone! Let this pernicious hour
Stand aye accursèd in the calendar.
Come in, without there.

      Enter Lennox

LENNOX   What's your grace's will?

MACBETH

Saw you the Weird Sisters?

LENNOX   No, my lord.

MACBETH

Came they not by you?

LENNOX   No, indeed, my lord.

MACBETH

Infected be the air whereon they ride,
And damned all those that trust them. I did hear
The galloping of horse. Who was't came by?

LENNOX

'Tis two or three, my lord, that bring you word   140
Macduff is fled to England.

MACBETH   Fled to England!

---

123 *for his* (claiming them as his descendants)

131 (stage direction) *The Witches dance.* This has been thought to be a further borrowing of music from *The Witch*, where we read 'here they dance the Witches' dance, and Exit'.

LENNOX

Ay, my good lord.

MACBETH

Time, thou anticipat'st my dread exploits.
The flighty purpose never is o'ertook
Unless the deed go with it. From this moment
The very firstlings of my heart shall be
The firstlings of my hand. And even now,
To crown my thoughts with acts, be it thought and done:
The castle of Macduff I will surprise,
150   Seize upon Fife, give to the edge o'the sword
His wife, his babes, and all unfortunate souls
That trace him in his line. No boasting, like a fool;
This deed I'll do before this purpose cool.
But no more sights! – Where are these gentlemen?
Come, bring me where they are.   *Exeunt*

IV.2   *Enter Macduff's Wife, her Son, and Ross*

WIFE

What had he done to make him fly the land?

ROSS

You must have patience, madam.

WIFE   He had none.

144–5 *The flighty purpose never is o'ertook |
Unless the deed go with it.* We never
realize our quickly vanishing purposes, unless we act at the very
moment when we form these
purposes.
148 *it* (what follows)
152 *trace* follow his tracks
154 *these gentlemen* (the 'two or three' of
line 140)

IV.2 The scene breaks the grim descent

of Macbeth by an interlude of domestic
pathos. Both Ross and the nameless Messenger represent the natural sympathy of
the oppressed under devilish pressure;
their flight catches the weakness of any
amiable ordinary individual under these
circumstances and mirrors that of
Macduff himself. Notice the descent
from the 'honourable' murderers of
Banquo to the brutish ruffians of this
scene.

His flight was madness; when our actions do not,
Our fears do make us traitors.

ROSS   You know not
Whether it was his wisdom or his fear.

WIFE

Wisdom! To leave his wife, to leave his babes,
His mansion and his titles, in a place
From whence himself does fly? He loves us not.
He wants the natural touch; for the poor wren,
The most diminutive of birds, will fight,   10
Her young ones in her nest, against the owl.
All is the fear and nothing is the love,
As little is the wisdom, where the flight
So runs against all reason.

ROSS   My dearest cuz,
I pray you school yourself. But, for your husband,
He is noble, wise, judicious, and best knows
The fits o'the season. I dare not speak much further,
But cruel are the times when we are traitors
And do not know, ourselves; when we hold rumour
From what we fear, yet know not what we fear,   20
But float upon a wild and violent sea,
Each way and move. I take my leave of you;
Shall not be long but I'll be here again.

3-4 *when our actions do not,* | *Our fears do
make us traitors.* Macduff had *done*
nothing traitorous; but his fear made
him fly, and that is treachery.

10 *diminutive.* F uses the alternative form
'diminitive', the sound of which may
be thought more appropriate to the
meaning of the line.

11 *Her young ones in her nest* when her
young ones are in the nest

14 *cuz* cousin, relative

15 *school yourself* teach yourself wisdom

17 *The fits o'the season* the unexpected
convulsions of this time; ? what is
fitting

18-19 *when we are traitors* | *And do not
know, ourselves* when we are proclaimed as traitors and ourselves do
not know that we are

19-20 *when we hold rumour* | *From what we
fear* when all we have to hold on to
are rumours, based on what we fear
might be

22 *Each way and move.* The sense must be
that the ignorantly fearful are at the
mercy of the sea of fear; and are
moved whatever way the sea moves.
The language is not easy to fit into
this; nor is the favourite emendation,
'Each way and none'.

> Things at the worst will cease or else climb upward
> To what they were before. – My pretty cousin,
> Blessing upon you!

WIFE

> Fathered he is, and yet he's fatherless.

ROSS

> I am so much a fool, should I stay longer
> It would be my disgrace and your discomfort.
30   I take my leave at once.   *Exit*

WIFE

> Sirrah, your father's dead.
> And what will you do now? How will you live?

SON

> As birds do, mother.

WIFE   What, with worms and flies?

SON

> With what I get, I mean; and so do they.

WIFE

> Poor bird, thou'dst never fear
> The net nor lime, the pitfall nor the gin!

SON

> Why should I, mother? Poor birds they are not set for.
> My father is not dead, for all your saying.

WIFE

> Yes, he is dead. How wilt thou do for a father?
40 SON Nay, how will you do for a husband?
WIFE Why, I can buy me twenty at any market.
SON Then you'll buy 'em to sell again.

---

29 *It would be my disgrace and your discomfort.* I should weep and so disgrace
my manhood and distress you.

31 *Sirrah* (playful and affectionate address here)

36 *lime* birdlime (a sticky substance
spread on branches, etc., to catch
birds)

gin snare

37 *Poor birds they are not set for* traps etc.
are not set for a *poor* bird (as you call
me – line 35)

42 *Then you'll buy 'em to sell again* you
can't want all that number for your
own consumption

WIFE
    Thou speak'st with all thy wit;
    And yet, i'faith, with wit enough for thee.

SON Was my father a traitor, mother?

WIFE Ay, that he was.

SON What is a traitor?

WIFE Why, one that swears and lies.

SON And be all traitors that do so?

WIFE
    Every one that does so is a traitor,   50
    And must be hanged.

SON
    And must they all be hanged that swear and lie?

WIFE Every one.

SON Who must hang them?

WIFE Why, the honest men.

SON Then the liars and swearers are fools; for there are
liars and swearers enow to beat the honest men and hang
up them.

WIFE Now God help thee, poor monkey! But how wilt
thou do for a father?   60

SON If he were dead, you'd weep for him; if you would
not, it were a good sign that I should quickly have a new
father.

WIFE Poor prattler, how thou talk'st!
    Enter a Messenger

MESSENGER
    Bless you, fair dame! I am not to you known,
    Though in your state of honour I am perfect.

43-4 *Thou speak'st with all thy wit;* | *And yet, i'faith, with wit enough for thee* you're not being very sensible; but sensible enough, I suppose, considering your age

48 *swears and lies* takes an oath and breaks it. (Lady Macduff is thinking of the marriage-oath to cherish the wife, as well as the oath to the King.)

59 *monkey* ('used tenderly, in the fantasticality of affection' – Kittredge)

66 *Though in your state of honour I am perfect* though I am perfectly acquainted with your honourable condition

I doubt some danger does approach you nearly.
If you will take a homely man's advice,
Be not found here. Hence with your little ones!
To fright you thus methinks I am too savage;
To do worse to you were fell cruelty,
Which is too nigh your person. Heaven preserve you!
I dare abide no longer.   *Exit*

WIFE   Whither should I fly?
I have done no harm. But I remember now
I am in this earthly world, where to do harm
Is often laudable, to do good sometime
Accounted dangerous folly. Why then, alas,
Do I put up that womanly defence
To say I have done no harm?
        Enter Murderers

MURDERER   What are these faces?
Where is your husband?

WIFE
I hope in no place so unsanctified
Where such as thou mayst find him.

MURDERER   He's a traitor.

SON
Thou liest, thou shag-haired villain!

MURDERER   What, you egg,
Young fry of treachery!
       He stabs him

SON   He has killed me, mother!
Run away, I pray you.
      Son dies. Exit Wife crying 'Murder'

71–2 *To do worse to you were fell cruelty,* |
Which is too nigh your person it would
be cruel to do more than frighten
(i.e. harm) you, but such cruelty is
close at hand
78 *womanly* womanish, feeble
80 *Where is your husband?* Coming from

Macbeth, they must know that he is
fled; but the Gestapo-type question
may serve to incriminate Lady
Macduff.
82, 83 *thou* (pejorative use of second
person singular)
84 *fry* fish-spawn

Enter Malcolm and Macduff IV.3

MALCOLM

Let us seek out some desolate shade, and there
Weep our sad bosoms empty.

MACDUFF   Let us rather

Hold fast the mortal sword; and like good men
Bestride our down-fallen birthdom. Each new morn
New widows howl, new orphans cry, new sorrows
Strike heaven on the face, that it resounds
As if it felt with Scotland, and yelled out
Like syllable of dolour.

MALCOLM   What I believe, I'll wail;

What know, believe; and what I can redress,
As I shall find the time to friend, I will.   10
What you have spoke, it may be so perchance.
This tyrant, whose sole name blisters our tongues,
Was once thought honest; you have loved him well;
He hath not touched you yet. I am young; but something
You may deserve of him, through me; and wisdom

IV.3 This, the longest scene in the play, performs a number of important structural functions. Of the three sections: (a) Malcolm's testing of Macduff, (b) the description of Edward the Confessor, and (c) the announcement of the slaughter of Macduff's family, the first is the most elaborate. It adds a further strand to the image of wariness and suspiciousness that characterizes tyranny. Malcolm's self-accusations describe the contrast between virtue and vice in kingship and Macduff's reactions are those of the ideal subject. Pious Edward touching for 'the Evil' is directly antithetical to Macbeth, and the doctor here should be contrasted with that in V.1. Macduff's reaction to Ross's bitter news exhibits full human range of feeling, of understanding and resolve to act. With piety to crown the effort, and with resolve to carry it forward, the counter-move against Macbeth is fully launched.

3 *mortal* deadly

4 *Bestride our down-fallen birthdom* stand over and defend the fallen body of the kingdom of our birth

6 *Strike heaven on the face* are as a slap in the face of goodness

6–8 *that it resounds | As if it felt with Scotland, and yelled out | Like syllable of dolour.* The noise of the blow against heaven echoes as if heaven were wailing for sorrow, like Scotland.

10 *to friend* favourable

14 *I am young; but* ... (1) although I am unimportant; (2) although I may seem innocent, I can understand that ...

15 *wisdom* it is wisdom

To offer up a weak poor innocent lamb
T'appease an angry god.

MACDUFF
I am not treacherous.

MALCOLM   But Macbeth is.
A good and virtuous nature may recoil
20 In an imperial charge. But I shall crave your pardon:
That which you are my thoughts cannot transpose;
Angels are bright still though the brightest fell.
Though all things foul would wear the brows of grace,
Yet grace must still look so.

MACDUFF   I have lost my hopes.

MALCOLM
Perchance even there where I did find my doubts.
Why in that rawness left you wife and child,
Those precious motives, those strong knots of love,
Without leave-taking? I pray you,
Let not my jealousies be your dishonours
30 But mine own safeties. You may be rightly just,
Whatever I shall think.

MACDUFF   Bleed, bleed, poor country!
Great tyranny, lay thou thy basis sure,
For goodness dare not check thee; wear thou thy wrongs,
The title is affeered. Fare thee well, lord!
I would not be the villain that thou think'st
For the whole space that's in the tyrant's grasp,

19–20 *recoil | In an imperial charge* be pushed backwards (morally) by the force of a royal command (image from gunnery)

21 *transpose* change (suspicion cannot make Macduff evil)

22 *the brightest* Lucifer

24 *so* (like grace)

25 *Perchance even there where I did find my doubts.* Macduff left his family in Macbeth's power. Was the betrayal of Malcolm to be the price of their safety? It was this thought that alerted Malcolm's *doubts*; and so Macduff will have to give up the *hope* of recovering his family.

26 *rawness* unprotected condition

27 *motives* (1) incentives to action; (2) objects *moving* one's emotions

29 *jealousies* suspicions

32–3 *tyranny . . . thou . . . thou* (Macbeth)

34 *affeered* legally confirmed

And the rich East to boot.

MALCOLM   Be not offended;
I speak not as in absolute fear of you.
I think our country sinks beneath the yoke,
It weeps, it bleeds, and each new day a gash   40
Is added to her wounds. I think withal
There would be hands uplifted in my right;
And here from gracious England have I offer
Of goodly thousands. But for all this,
When I shall tread upon the tyrant's head
Or wear it on my sword, yet my poor country
Shall have more vices than it had before,
More suffer, and more sundry ways, than ever,
By him that shall succeed.

MACDUFF   What should he be?

MALCOLM
It is myself I mean; in whom I know   50
All the particulars of vice so grafted
That, when they shall be opened, black Macbeth
Will seem as pure as snow and the poor state
Esteem him as a lamb, being compared
With my confineless harms.

MACDUFF   Not in the legions
Of horrid hell can come a devil more damned
In evils to top Macbeth.

MALCOLM   I grant him bloody,
Luxurious, avaricious, false, deceitful,
Sudden, malicious, smacking of every sin
That has a name. But there's no bottom, none,   60
In my voluptuousness. Your wives, your daughters,
Your matrons, and your maids, could not fill up

---

37 *to boot* as well
43 *gracious England* (Edward the Confessor, full of God's grace)
52 *opened* (as a bud opens – after *grafted*)
56, 57 *devil* ... *evils* (both monosyllables)
57 *top* surpass
58 *Luxurious* lustful
59 *Sudden* violent

The cistern of my lust; and my desire
All continent impediments would o'erbear
That did oppose my will. Better Macbeth
Than such a one to reign.

MACDUFF   Boundless intemperance
In nature is a tyranny. It hath been
The untimely emptying of the happy throne,
And fall of many kings. But fear not yet
70   To take upon you what is yours. You may
Convey your pleasures in a spacious plenty
And yet seem cold; the time you may so hoodwink.
We have willing dames enough. There cannot be
That vulture in you to devour so many
As will to greatness dedicate themselves,
Finding it so inclined.

MALCOLM   With this there grows
In my most ill-composed affection such
A staunchless avarice that, were I king,
I should cut off the nobles for their lands,
80   Desire his jewels and this other's house,
And my more-having would be as a sauce
To make me hunger more, that I should forge
Quarrels unjust against the good and loyal,
Destroying them for wealth.

MACDUFF   This avarice
Sticks deeper, grows with more pernicious root
Than summer-seeming lust; and it hath been

---

64 *continent* (1) chaste; (2) restraining
65 *will* lust
67 *nature* human nature
71 *Convey* manage secretly
72 *hoodwink* blindfold
75 *greatness* (the great man, King
     Malcolm)
76 *so* (lustfully)
77 *ill-composed affection* disposition com-
     posed of evil elements

78 *staunchless* unquenchable
80 *his* (one man's)
81–2 *And my more-having would be as a
      sauce | To make me hunger more* the
      more I swallowed up, the sharper
      my appetite should be
82 *that* so that
86 *summer-seeming* that beseems or befits
      the summer of life (early manhood)

The sword of our slain kings. Yet do not fear:
Scotland hath foisons to fill up your will
Of your mere own. All these are portable,
With other graces weighed.

MALCOLM   But I have none.   90
The king-becoming graces,
As justice, verity, temperance, stableness,
Bounty, perseverance, mercy, lowliness,
Devotion, patience, courage, fortitude,
I have no relish of them, but abound
In the division of each several crime,
Acting it many ways. Nay, had I power, I should
Pour the sweet milk of concord into hell,
Uproar the universal peace, confound
All unity on earth.

MACDUFF   O Scotland, Scotland!   100

MALCOLM
If such a one be fit to govern, speak.
I am as I have spoken.

MACDUFF   Fit to govern!
No, not to live! O nation miserable,
With an untitled tyrant, bloody-sceptred,
When shalt thou see thy wholesome days again,
Since that the truest issue of thy throne
By his own interdiction stands accused
And does blaspheme his breed? Thy royal father

88 *foisons* abundance
   will passion
89 *Of your mere own* out of your own
   royal possessions
   portable bearable
93 *perseverance* (accented on the second
   syllable)
95–6 *abound | In the division of each several
   crime* I am fertile in the variations
   that can be produced in each separate
   (*several*) crime

98 *milk* (symbolizing, as already in the
   play, the innocence of natural
   relationships)
99 *Uproar* reduce to confusion
104 *untitled* with no legal right
107 *accused*. F *accust* may also be modernized as 'accursed'.
108 *does blaspheme his breed* is a slander to
   his family

Was a most sainted king; the queen that bore thee,

110   Oftener upon her knees than on her feet,
Died every day she lived. Fare thee well!
These evils thou repeat'st upon thyself
Hath banished me from Scotland. O my breast,
Thy hope ends here!

MALCOLM   Macduff, this noble passion,
Child of integrity, hath from my soul
Wiped the black scruples, reconciled my thoughts
To thy good truth and honour. Devilish Macbeth
By many of these trains hath sought to win me
Into his power, and modest wisdom plucks me

120   From over-credulous haste. But God above
Deal between thee and me; for even now
I put myself to thy direction, and
Unspeak mine own detraction, here abjure
The taints and blames I laid upon myself
For strangers to my nature. I am yet
Unknown to woman, never was forsworn,
Scarcely have coveted what was mine own,
At no time broke my faith, would not betray
The devil to his fellow, and delight

130   No less in truth than life. My first false speaking
Was this upon myself. What I am truly
Is thine and my poor country's to command;
Whither indeed, before thy here-approach,
Old Seyward with ten thousand warlike men,
Already at a point, was setting forth.
Now we'll together; and the chance of goodness

---

111 *Died every day she lived* mortified herself daily (by religious exercises)
113 *breast* heart
115 *Child of integrity* produced by the
integrity of your spirit
116 *black scruples* wicked suspicions
118 *trains* lures

126 *Unknown to woman* a virgin
131 *upon* against
135 *at a point* fully prepared
136–7 *and the chance of goodness | Be like our
warranted quarrel!* May the chance of
good success be proportionate to the
justness of our cause

Be like our warranted quarrel! Why are you silent?

MACDUFF

Such welcome and unwelcome things at once
'Tis hard to reconcile.

Enter a Doctor

MALCOLM   Well, more anon. —
Comes the King forth, I pray you?   140

DOCTOR

Ay, sir. There are a crew of wretched souls
That stay his cure. Their malady convinces
The great assay of art; but at his touch,
Such sanctity hath heaven given his hand,
They presently amend.

MALCOLM   I thank you, doctor.

Exit Doctor

MACDUFF

What's the disease he means?

MALCOLM   'Tis called the Evil —
A most miraculous work in this good king,
Which often since my here-remain in England
I have seen him do. How he solicits heaven
Himself best knows: but strangely visited people,   150
All swollen and ulcerous, pitiful to the eye,
The mere despair of surgery, he cures,
Hanging a golden stamp about their necks
Put on with holy prayers; and 'tis spoken,
To the succeeding royalty he leaves
The healing benediction. With this strange virtue
He hath a heavenly gift of prophecy,

142–3 *convinces | The great assay of art* defeats the greatest efforts of medical skill

143–5 *but at his touch, | Such sanctity hath heaven given his hand, | They presently amend.* This is 'touching' for scrofula or 'the King's Evil', which began with Edward the Confessor and remained a prerogative of the English crown.

145 *presently* immediately

152 *mere* complete

153 *stamp* coin

And sundry blessings hang about his throne
That speak him full of grace.

       Enter Ross

MACDUFF   See who comes here.

MALCOLM

160   My countryman; but yet I know him not.

MACDUFF

My ever gentle cousin, welcome hither.

MALCOLM

I know him now. Good God betimes remove
The means that makes us strangers!

ROSS   Sir, amen.

MACDUFF

Stands Scotland where it did?

ROSS   Alas, poor country,
Almost afraid to know itself! It cannot
Be called our mother, but our grave; where nothing
But who knows nothing is once seen to smile;
Where sighs and groans and shrieks that rent the air
Are made, not marked; where violent sorrow seems
170   A modern ecstasy. The dead man's knell
Is there scarce asked for who, and good men's lives
Expire before the flowers in their caps,
Dying or ere they sicken.

MACDUFF   O relation
Too nice and yet too true.

MALCOLM   What's the newest grief?

ROSS

That of an hour's age doth hiss the speaker;

---

160 *My countryman; but yet I know him not.*
   Malcolm presumably recognizes the
   'Scottish' costume Ross is wearing.
162 *betimes* speedily
166–7 *nothing | But who knows nothing* no
   one except a person totally ignorant
169 *not marked* not noticed, because they
   are everywhere

170 *A modern ecstasy* a commonplace
   passion
173 *or ere they sicken* before they have time
   to fall ill
174 *Too nice* over-delicately phrased
175 *doth hiss the speaker* causes him to be
   hissed (because the news is out of
   date)

Each minute teems a new one.

MACDUFF   How does my wife?

ROSS

Why, well.

MACDUFF

And all my children?

ROSS   Well too.

MACDUFF

The tyrant has not battered at their peace?

ROSS

No. They were well at peace when I did leave 'em.

MACDUFF

Be not a niggard of your speech. How goes't?   180

ROSS

When I came hither to transport the tidings
Which I have heavily borne, there ran a rumour
Of many worthy fellows that were out,
Which was to my belief witnessed the rather
For that I saw the tyrant's power afoot.
Now is the time of help. (*To Malcolm*) Your eye in Scotland
Would create soldiers, make our women fight
To doff their dire distresses.

MALCOLM   Be't their comfort
We are coming thither. Gracious England hath
Lent us good Seyward and ten thousand men –   190
An older and a better soldier none
That Christendom gives out.

ROSS   Would I could answer
This comfort with the like. But I have words
That would be howled out in the desert air,

176 *teems* brings forth plenteously
177 *well . . . well* (because 'we use | To say the dead are well' (*Antony and Cleopatra*, II.5.33–4))
181–2 *the tidings* | *Which I have heavily borne.* Is this the *heavy* (sad) news of Macduff's family?
183 *out* in arms
188 *doff* take off
189 *Gracious England* (Edward the Confessor)
191 *none* there are none
192 *gives out* proclaims

Where hearing should not latch them.

MACDUFF   What concern they?
The general cause, or is it a fee-grief
Due to some single breast?

ROSS   No mind that's honest
But in it shares some woe, though the main part
Pertains to you alone.

MACDUFF   If it be mine,
200   Keep it not from me; quickly let me have it.

ROSS
Let not your ears despise my tongue for ever,
Which shall possess them with the heaviest sound
That ever yet they heard.

MACDUFF   Humh! I guess at it.

ROSS
Your castle is surprised, your wife and babes
Savagely slaughtered. To relate the manner
Were on the quarry of these murdered deer
To add the death of you.

MALCOLM   Merciful heaven!
What, man! Ne'er pull your hat upon your brows.
Give sorrow words: the grief that does not speak
210   Whispers the o'erfraught heart and bids it break.

MACDUFF
My children too?

ROSS   Wife, children, servants, all
That could be found.

MACDUFF   And I must be from thence!
My wife killed too?

ROSS   I have said.

MALCOLM   Be comforted.
Let's make us medicines of our great revenge

---

195 *latch* catch
196–7 *a fee-grief | Due to some single breast*
   a grief with a single owner

206 *quarry* heap of dead animals
208 *pull your hat* (a conventional sign of
   grief)

To cure this deadly grief.

MACDUFF   He has no children.
All my pretty ones? Did you say all?
O hell-kite! All? What, all my pretty chickens
And their dam, at one fell swoop?

MALCOLM
Dispute it like a man.

MACDUFF   I shall do so;
But I must also feel it as a man.   220
I cannot but remember such things were
That were most precious to me. Did heaven look on
And would not take their part? Sinful Macduff!
They were all struck for thee. Naught that I am,
Not for their own demerits, but for mine,
Fell slaughter on their souls. Heaven rest them now!

MALCOLM
Be this the whetstone of your sword; let grief
Convert to anger; blunt not the heart, enrage it.

MACDUFF
O, I could play the woman with mine eyes
And braggart with my tongue! But, gentle heavens,   230
Cut short all intermission. Front to front
Bring thou this fiend of Scotland and myself.
Within my sword's length set him; if he scape,
Heaven forgive him too.

MALCOLM   This tune goes manly.
Come, go we to the King; our power is ready;
Our lack is nothing but our leave. Macbeth
Is ripe for shaking, and the powers above

215 *deadly* which would otherwise be
  fatal
217 *hell-kite* (that swooped on his chickens like a bird from hell)
219 *Dispute* struggle against
224 *for thee* because of thee. (Heaven
  would have intervened if Macduff's
  wickedness had not dissuaded it.)
  Naught wicked

231 *intermission* interval of time
236 *Our lack is nothing but our leave* we
  lack nothing but leave-taking
237 *ripe for shaking.* Perhaps a reminiscence from Nahum's prophecy of the
  fall of Nineveh: 'All thy strong aids
  are as fig trees with the first ripe
  figs: if they be stirred they fall into
  the mouth of the eater' (Nahum 3.12).

Put on their instruments. Receive what cheer you may:
The night is long that never finds the day.   *Exeunt*

V.I   *Enter a Doctor of Physic and a Waiting-Gentlewoman*

DOCTOR I have two nights watched with you, but can
perceive no truth in your report. When was it she last
walked?

GENTLEWOMAN Since his majesty went into the field I
have seen her rise from her bed, throw her nightgown
upon her, unlock her closet, take forth paper, fold it,
write upon't, read it, afterwards seal it, and again return
to bed; yet all this while in a most fast sleep.

DOCTOR A great perturbation in nature, to receive at once
10   the benefit of sleep and do the effects of watching. In
this slumbery agitation, besides her walking and other
actual performances, what, at any time, have you heard
her say?

GENTLEWOMAN That, sir, which I will not report after
her.

DOCTOR You may to me; and 'tis most meet you should.

238 *Put on their instruments* (1) put on
their weapons; (2) thrust us forward,
as their agents

v.1 The scene re-enacts the life of bloodshed in terms of dream and hallucination
(like a Noh play). It is the climax of
Shakespeare's exploration of individual
psychological secrets. The broken prose
fragments of Lady Macbeth's speech
measure the collapse of the human mind
under inhuman pressures, while the
Gentlewoman and the Doctor represent
a choric norm. The Doctor (probably
played by the same actor as the Doctor

in IV.3) serves to focus the contrast between the English throne with its
heaven-given medical powers, and the
Scottish with its disease 'beyond my
practice'.

5 *nightgown*. The Elizabethans slept without garments; the *nightgown* was
equivalent to today's 'dressing-
gown'. Re-enacts II.2.70.

8 *while* time

9–10 *A great perturbation in nature, to re-*
ceive at once the benefit of sleep and do the
effects of watching. Lady Macbeth
'equivocates' with sleep.

10 *watching* waking

GENTLEWOMAN Neither to you nor anyone, having no witness to confirm my speech.

Enter Lady Macbeth with a taper

Lo you! Here she comes. This is her very guise; and, upon my life, fast asleep. Observe her; stand close.   20

DOCTOR How came she by that light?

GENTLEWOMAN Why, it stood by her. She has light by her continually; 'tis her command.

DOCTOR You see her eyes are open.

GENTLEWOMAN Ay, but their sense are shut.

DOCTOR What is it she does now? Look how she rubs her hands.

GENTLEWOMAN It is an accustomed action with her to seem thus washing her hands. I have known her continue in this a quarter of an hour.   30

LADY Yet here's a spot.

DOCTOR Hark! She speaks. I will set down what comes from her, to satisfy my remembrance the more strongly.

LADY Out, damned spot! Out, I say! – One: two: why then, 'tis time to do't. – Hell is murky! – Fie, my lord, fie! A soldier and afeard? – What need we fear who knows it, when none can call our power to accompt? – Yet who would have thought the old man to have had so much blood in him?

DOCTOR Do you mark that?   40

LADY The Thane of Fife had a wife; where is she now? – What, will these hands ne'er be clean? – No more o'that, my lord, no more o'that. You mar all with this starting.

17–18 *having no witness to confirm my speech.* The Waiting-Gentlewoman is as suspicious as other subjects of tyranny.

31 *Yet* ('after all this washing' – Kittredge)

34 *One: two.* She recalls the timing of Duncan's murder.

35 *do't* murder Duncan

Hell is murky ('a sudden glimpse into the abyss at her feet' – Dover Wilson)

42 *will these hands ne'er be clean?* This recalls (as so much of this scene does): 'A little water clears us of this deed; | How easy is it then!' (II.2.67–8).

DOCTOR Go to, go to: you have known what you should
not.

GENTLEWOMAN She has spoke what she should not, I am
sure of that. Heaven knows what she has known.

LADY Here's the smell of the blood still. All the perfumes
of Arabia will not sweeten this little hand. Oh! Oh! Oh!

50 DOCTOR What a sigh is there! The heart is sorely charged.

GENTLEWOMAN I would not have such a heart in my
bosom for the dignity of the whole body.

DOCTOR Well, well, well.

GENTLEWOMAN Pray God it be, sir.

DOCTOR This disease is beyond my practice; yet I have
known those which have walked in their sleep who have
died holily in their beds.

LADY Wash your hands; put on your nightgown; look not
so pale. I tell you yet again, Banquo's buried; he cannot

60 come out on's grave.

DOCTOR Even so?

LADY To bed, to bed! There's knocking at the gate.
Come, come, come, come, give me your hand. What's
done cannot be undone. To bed, to bed, to bed.

Exit

DOCTOR Will she go now to bed?

GENTLEWOMAN Directly.

DOCTOR

Foul whisperings are abroad, unnatural deeds
Do breed unnatural troubles; infected minds
To their deaf pillows will discharge their secrets.

70 More needs she the divine than the physician.
God, God forgive us all! Look after her,
Remove from her the means of all annoyance

---

50 *charged* burdened

63–4 *What's done cannot be undone* (a tragically ironic echo of III.2.12: 'what's
done is done')

66 *Directly* immediately

67–8 *unnatural deeds | Do breed unnatural*

troubles. Rebellion is 'unnatural', but
is naturally produced when sover-
eigns commit unnatural deeds.

72 *Remove from her the means of all annoyance.* She is in a state of Despair
(religiously conceived), and therefore

And still keep eyes upon her. So, good night.
My mind she has mated, and amazed my sight.
I think, but dare not speak.

GENTLEWOMAN   Good night, good doctor.

Exeunt

Drum and colours. Enter Menteth, Cathness, Angus,   V.2
Lennox, Soldiers

MENTETH
The English power is near, led on by Malcolm,
His uncle Seyward and the good Macduff.
Revenges burn in them; for their dear causes
Would to the bleeding and the grim alarm
Excite the mortified man.

ANGUS   Near Birnan Wood
Shall we well meet them; that way are they coming.

CATHNESS
Who knows if Donalbain be with his brother?

LENNOX
For certain, sir, he is not. I have a file
Of all the gentry: there is Seyward's son
And many unrough youths that even now   10
Protest their first of manhood.

MENTETH   What does the tyrant?

CATHNESS
Great Dunsinane he strongly fortifies.
Some say he's mad. Others, that lesser hate him,
Do call it valiant fury; but for certain
He cannot buckle his distempered cause
Within the belt of rule.

ANGUS   Now does he feel

must be considered a potential
suicide.
74 *mated* confounded

v.2.4 *alarm* the call to battle
10 *unrough* beardless

11 *Protest their first of manhood* proclaim
that they are now (for the first time)
acting as men

15 *distempered* diseased; perhaps 'swollen
with dropsy'

His secret murders sticking on his hands;
Now minutely revolts upbraid his faith-breach.
Those he commands move only in command,
20   Nothing in love. Now does he feel his title
Hang loose about him like a giant's robe
Upon a dwarfish thief.
MENTETH   Who then shall blame
His pestered senses to recoil and start,
When all that is within him does condemn
Itself for being there?
CATHNESS   Well, march we on
To give obedience where 'tis truly owed.
Meet we the medicine of the sickly weal,
And with him pour we in our country's purge
Each drop of us.
LENNOX   Or so much as it needs
30   To dew the sovereign flower and drown the weeds.
Make we our march towards Birnan.   *Exeunt, marching*

V.3   *Enter Macbeth, Doctor, and Attendants*
MACBETH
Bring me no more reports; let them fly all.

---

17 *sticking* (like dried blood)
18 *minutely* occurring every minute (accented on first syllable)
19 *in* because of
22-3 *blame | His pestered senses to recoil
and start* blame his afflicted nerves
for jumping back and quivering
24-5 *When all that is within him does con-
demn | Itself for being there* when his
whole nature revolts against his
existence
27 *medicine* (1) drug; or more probably
(2) physician (i.e. Malcolm)
sickly weal the diseased commonwealth
28-9 *And with him pour we in our country's*

purge | Each drop of us as men *purge*
their disorders by bloodletting, so let
us pour out our blood (in battle) to
purge *the sickly weal*
30 *sovereign* (1) royal; (2) powerfully
medicinal

v.3 The desperate 'security' of Macbeth,
without hope, without companionship
and therefore without meaning in his
life — this is represented externally by
the siege and internally by his despair.
The Doctor serves, once again, to link
the state of the mind with the state of
the land, psychology with politics.
1 *them* (the thanes)

Till Birnan Wood remove to Dunsinane
I cannot taint with fear. What's the boy Malcolm?
Was he not born of woman? The spirits that know
All mortal consequences have pronounced me thus:
'Fear not, Macbeth; no man that's born of woman
Shall e'er have power upon thee.' Then fly, false thanes,
And mingle with the English epicures.
The mind I sway by and the heart I bear
Shall never sag with doubt nor shake with fear.   10
            Enter Servant
The devil damn thee black, thou cream-faced loon!
Where got'st thou that goose look?

SERVANT

There is ten thousand –

MACBETH   Geese, villain?

SERVANT   Soldiers, sir.

MACBETH

Go prick thy face and over-red thy fear,
Thou lily-livered boy. What soldiers, patch?
Death of thy soul! Those linen cheeks of thine
Are counsellors to fear. What soldiers, whey-face?

SERVANT

The English force, so please you.

MACBETH

Take thy face hence.   *Exit Servant*
            Seyton! – I am sick at heart
When I behold – Seyton, I say! – This push   20
Will chair me ever or dis-seat me now.

8 *English epicures.* From the traditional
Scottish point of view the English are
characterized by luxurious softness.
9 *sway* rule myself
11 *damn thee black.* Damned souls were
thought to be black in colour.
12 *goose look* look of cowardly folly
14 *prick thy face and over-red thy fear* stick
pins in your face and let the blood
hide your pallor

15 *lily-livered* lacking in red-blooded
bravery
patch fool
16 *linen* bleached
20 *push* crisis
21 *chair.* Printed in F as *cheer*; the two
words were pronounced alike; but
chair seems the more apposite word
to keep in line with *push* and *dis-seat.*

I have lived long enough: my way of life
Is fallen into the sere, the yellow leaf;
And that which should accompany old age,
As honour, love, obedience, troops of friends,
I must not look to have; but, in their stead,
Curses, not loud, but deep, mouth-honour, breath
Which the poor heart would fain deny and dare not.
Seyton!

Enter Seyton

SEYTON
What's your gracious pleasure?

30   MACBETH   What news more?

SEYTON
All is confirmed, my lord, which was reported.

MACBETH
I'll fight till from my bones my flesh be hacked.
Give me my armour.

SEYTON   'Tis not needed yet.

MACBETH
I'll put it on.
Send out more horses, skirr the country round,
Hang those that talk of fear. – Give me mine armour. –
How does your patient, doctor?

DOCTOR   Not so sick, my lord,
As she is troubled with thick-coming fancies
That keep her from her rest.

MACBETH   Cure her of that.

23 *sere, the yellow leaf* (a withered condition)
27–8 *breath | Which the poor heart would fain deny* words of allegiance which the emotions cannot accept as true – as in 'equivocation'. Compare Isaiah 29.13: 'This people when they be in trouble do honour me with their mouth and with their lips, but their heart is far from me.'

35 *more*. F prints the alternative Elizabethan form 'moe'.
skirr scour
37 *your patient*. The *your* is emphatic, to make the contrast between Macbeth's treatment of the realm and the doctor's of Lady Macbeth – a contrast that recurs at lines 47–8 and 50–54.
38 *thick-coming* frequently appearing

Canst thou not minister to a mind diseased,   40
Pluck from the memory a rooted sorrow,
Raze out the written troubles of the brain,
And with some sweet oblivious antidote
Cleanse the stuffed bosom of that perilous stuff
Which weighs upon the heart?
DOCTOR   Therein the patient
Must minister to himself.

MACBETH
Throw physic to the dogs! I'll none of it. –
Come, put mine armour on, give me my staff.
Seyton, send out. – Doctor, the thanes fly from me. –
Come, sir, dispatch. – If thou couldst, doctor, cast   50
The water of my land, find her disease
And purge it to a sound and pristine health,
I would applaud thee to the very echo
That should applaud again. – Pull't off, I say. –
What rhubarb, senna, or what purgative drug
Would scour these English hence? Hear'st thou of them?

DOCTOR
Ay, my good lord; your royal preparation
Makes us hear something.

MACBETH   – Bring it after me.
I will not be afraid of death and bane
Till Birnan forest come to Dunsinane.   *Exit*   60

---

42 *written* engraved
44 *stuffed* clogged (Kittredge notes the clogged movement of the line)
48 *staff* baton of office
50–51 *cast | The water* examine the urine
55 *senna.* F reads *cyme*; and this has been found in English, as an Anglicization of Greek/Latin *cyma*: the tender shoots of plants. But I suspect that the appearance of this rare word in

the F text is an accident; and that Shakespeare's word was *cynne* – a variant spelling of *senna* – which has the right meaning and the right value for scansion.
56 *scour* (1) remove rapidly (as *skirr* above); (2) cleanse the body by purgatives; (3) also used of cleaning armour
58 *it* (the piece of armour)

DOCTOR

> Were I from Dunsinane away and clear,
> Profit again should hardly draw me here.   *Exit*

V.4   *Drum and colours. Enter Malcolm, Seyward, Macduff,*
             Seyward's Son, Menteth, Cathness, Angus, and Soldiers
             marching

MALCOLM

> Cousins, I hope the days are near at hand
> That chambers will be safe.

MENTETH   We doubt it nothing.

SEYWARD

> What wood is this before us?

MENTETH   The wood of Birnan.

MALCOLM

> Let every soldier hew him down a bough
> And bear't before him; thereby shall we shadow
> The numbers of our host and make discovery
> Err in report of us.

SOLDIERS   It shall be done.

SEYWARD

> We learn no other but the confident tyrant
> ‚Keeps still in Dunsinane and will endure
> Our setting down before't.

10 MALCOLM   'Tis his main hope.

> For where there is advantage to be given,
> Both more and less have given him the revolt,
> And none serve with him but constrainèd things

---

62 *Profit* (the traditional motive of
doctors)

v.4 Now all the nobles we have known
from earlier in the play have joined Malcolm's army. Notice the humility of their
grasp on the future, to be compared
with Macbeth's furious indifference.

2 *chambers* (perhaps bedchambers – they
were not safe for Duncan)
5 *shadow* conceal
6 *discovery* spying
10 *setting down before't* besieging it
11 *there is advantage to be given* opportunity (to escape) is afforded them
12 *more and less* great men and humble men

Whose hearts are absent too.

MACDUFF   Let our just censures
Attend the true event, and put we on
Industrious soldiership.

SEYWARD   The time approaches
That will with due decision make us know
What we shall say we have, and what we owe.
Thoughts speculative their unsure hopes relate,
But certain issue strokes must arbitrate;   20
Towards which, advance the war.   *Exeunt, marching*

Enter Macbeth, Seyton, and Soldiers, with drum and   V.5
colours

MACBETH
Hang out our banners on the outward walls.
The cry is still, 'They come.' Our castle's strength
Will laugh a siege to scorn. Here let them lie
Till famine and the ague eat them up.
Were they not farced with those that should be ours
We might have met them dareful, beard to beard,
And beat them backward home.
        A cry within of women
                              What is that noise?

SEYTON
It is the cry of women, my good lord.   *Exit*

14–15 *Let our just censures | Attend the
  true event* if our judgements are to be
  accurate they must wait to know the
  true end of the affair
18 *What we shall say we have, and what we
  owe* (the difference between talk and
  true possession – *owe* = own)
20 *But certain issue strokes must arbitrate*
  only blows decide the real future

v.5 The alternation of scenes in Act v
makes this a natural extension of v.3.
The supreme horror of the heart numbed

by despair appears in the reaction to
Lady Macbeth's death. From this time
forth Macbeth's life is a waiting for the
end.
5 *farced* stuffed. The F word 'forc'd' is
  sometimes defended as having the
  sense of 'reinforced'; but this meaning is only doubtfully attested. In
  view of the food images in the line
  before it seems best to take 'forc'd'
  as the common Elizabethan variant
  of *farced*.
6 *dareful* in open battle

MACBETH

I have almost forgot the taste of fears.

10   The time has been my senses would have cooled

To hear a night-shriek, and my fell of hair

Would at a dismal treatise rouse and stir

As life were in't. I have supped full with horrors:

Direness, familiar to my slaughterous thoughts,

Cannot once start me.

     Enter Seyton

                  Wherefore was that cry?

SEYTON

The queen, my lord, is dead.

MACBETH

She should have died hereafter.

There would have been a time for such a word –

Tomorrow, and tomorrow, and tomorrow,

20   Creeps in this petty pace from day to day

To the last syllable of recorded time;

And all our yesterdays have lighted fools

The way to dusty death. Out, out, brief candle!

Life's but a walking shadow, a poor player

---

10 *cooled* chilled with terror

11 *my fell of hair* the hair on my skin

12 *dismal treatise* a story of disaster

13 *supped full with* had my fill of. The metaphor takes us back to III.4.

14 *familiar*. Is there a reminiscence here of the Witches' *familiars*?

17 *should*. I think this means 'certainly would' rather than 'ought to have'.
hereafter at some time – what does the actual moment matter?

18 *There would have been a time for such a word*. His mind moves back from the meaninglessness of any future to the meaningfulness of the past. 'At one time I could have responded to such a word (announcement).' The transition to the following line implies the

transition from that past to this present.

20 *in this petty pace* in the petty manner of this pace. I assume that he paces as he speaks.

21 *To the last syllable of recorded time* till time reaches the last recorded word

23 *dusty death* death, which is a matter of 'dust to dust'

24 *shadow*. Suggested by *lighted . . . candle* and suggesting *player* in its turn. Compare Job 8.9: 'We are but of yesterday . . . our days upon earth are but a shadow.'
a poor player. The actor is *poor* (i.e. worthy of pity) because his voice soon ceases to be heard.

That struts and frets his hour upon the stage
And then is heard no more. It is a tale
Told by an idiot, full of sound and fury,
Signifying nothing.
>   *Enter a Messenger*
Thou com'st to use thy tongue: thy story quickly!

MESSENGER

Gracious my lord,   30
I should report that which I say I saw,
But know not how to do't.

MACBETH   Well, say, sir.

MESSENGER

As I did stand my watch upon the hill
I looked toward Birnan and anon methought
The wood began to move.

MACBETH   Liar and slave!

MESSENGER

Let me endure your wrath if't be not so.
Within this three mile may you see it coming.
I say, a moving grove.

MACBETH   If thou speak'st false,
Upon the next tree shall thou hang alive
Till famine cling thee. If thy speech be sooth,   40
I care not if thou dost for me as much.
I pull in resolution, and begin
To doubt the equivocation of the fiend
That lies like truth. 'Fear not till Birnan Wood
Do come to Dunsinane' – and now a wood
Comes toward Dunsinane. Arm, arm, and out!
If this which he avouches does appear,
There is nor flying hence nor tarrying here.
I 'gin to be aweary of the sun,
And wish the estate o'the world were now undone. –   50

25 *frets* expresses discontent and disdain   42 *pull in* rein in. (Many editors have
40 *cling* shrink up, wither   preferred to emend to 'pall in'.)
   sooth true

Ring the alarum bell! – Blow wind, come wrack,
At least we'll die with harness on our back.   *Exeunt*

V.6   *Drum and colours. Enter Malcolm, Seyward, Macduff,*
           and their army, with boughs

MALCOLM
        Now near enough. Your leavy screens throw down,
        And show like those you are. You, worthy uncle,
        Shall with my cousin, your right noble son,
        Lead our first battle. Worthy Macduff and we
        Shall take upon's what else remains to do,
        According to our order.
SEYWARD   Fare you well.
        Do we but find the tyrant's power tonight,
        Let us be beaten if we cannot fight.
MACDUFF
        Make all our trumpets speak, give them all breath,
10   Those clamorous harbingers of blood and death.
                                                Exeunt

            Alarums continued
            Enter Macbeth
MACBETH
        They have tied me to a stake, I cannot fly,
        But bear-like I must fight the course. What's he
        That was not born of woman? Such a one
        Am I to fear, or none.
                Enter Young Seyward

v.6 Usually printed as four separate scenes, but logic would demand either more divisions (e.g. at lines 23 and 73) or none at all. The battle is a series of spotlights but the action must be continuous. The alternation between sides that has marked Act v so far now speeds up, till the two blur into one victory and one defeat.

2 *uncle* (Seyward)
4 *battle* battalion
   we. Malcolm now assumes the royal *we*.
10 *harbingers* forerunners
11 *They have tied me to a stake* (like a bear being baited)
12 *the course* (one round of dogs versus bear)

YOUNG SEYWARD

What is thy name?

MACBETH   Thou'lt be afraid to hear it.

YOUNG SEYWARD

No, though thou call'st thyself a hotter name
Than any is in hell.

MACBETH   My name's Macbeth.

YOUNG SEYWARD

The devil himself could not pronounce a title
More hateful to mine ear.

MACBETH   No, nor more fearful.

YOUNG SEYWARD

Thou liest, abhorrèd tyrant! With my sword   20
I'll prove the lie thou speak'st.

    Fight, and Young Seyward slain

MACBETH   Thou wast born of woman.
But swords I smile at, weapons laugh to scorn,
Brandished by man that's of a woman born.   *Exit*

    Alarums. Enter Macduff

MACDUFF

That way the noise is. Tyrant, show thy face.
If thou be'st slain, and with no stroke of mine,
My wife and children's ghosts will haunt me still.
I cannot strike at wretched kerns, whose arms
Are hired to bear their staves. Either thou, Macbeth,
Or else my sword with an unbattered edge
I sheathe again undeeded. There thou shouldst be: 30
By this great clatter one of greatest note
Seems bruited. Let me find him, fortune!
And more I beg not.   *Exit*

    Alarums. Enter Malcolm and Seyward

SEYWARD

This way, my lord. The castle's gently rendered.
The tyrant's people on both sides do fight;

---

30 *undeeded* without   any   deeds 34 *gently rendered* surrendered without
performed   fighting

The noble thanes do bravely in the war;
The day almost itself professes yours,
And little is to do.

MALCOLM   We have met with foes
That strike beside us.

SEYWARD   Enter, sir, the castle.   *Exeunt*

Alarum. Enter Macbeth

MACBETH

40   Why should I play the Roman fool and die
On mine own sword? Whiles I see lives, the gashes
Do better upon them.

Enter Macduff

MACDUFF   Turn, hellhound, turn!

MACBETH

Of all men else I have avoided thee.
But get thee back; my soul is too much charged
With blood of thine already.

MACDUFF   I have no words;
My voice is in my sword, thou bloodier villain
Than terms can give thee out.

Fight. Alarum

MACBETH   Thou losest labour.
As easy mayst thou the intrenchant air
With thy keen sword impress, as make me bleed.

50   Let fall thy blade on vulnerable crests,
I bear a charmèd life which must not yield
To one of woman born.

MACDUFF   Despair thy charm,
And let the angel whom thou still hast served
Tell thee Macduff was from his mother's womb
Untimely ripped.

MACBETH

Accursèd be that tongue that tells me so;

---

39 *strike beside us* miss intentionally   48 *intrenchant* that cannot be gashed
40 *the Roman fool* (some Stoic suicide –   53 *angel* demon
   e.g. Brutus)   *still* always

For it hath cowed my better part of man;
And be these juggling fiends no more believed
That palter with us in a double sense,
That keep the word of promise to our ear   60
And break it to our hope. I'll not fight with thee.

MACDUFF
Then yield thee, coward;
And live to be the show and gaze o'the time.
We'll have thee, as our rarer monsters are,
Painted upon a pole, and underwrit,
'Here may you see the tyrant.'

MACBETH   I will not yield
To kiss the ground before young Malcolm's feet
And to be baited with the rabble's curse.
Though Birnan Wood be come to Dunsinane
And thou opposed, being of no woman born,   70
Yet I will try the last. Before my body
I throw my warlike shield. Lay on, Macduff;
And damned be him that first cries, 'Hold, enough!'

Exeunt fighting

Alarums. Enter fighting, and Macbeth slain

Exit Macduff

Retreat and flourish. Enter with drum and colours
Malcolm, Seyward, Ross, Thanes, and Soldiers

MALCOLM
I would the friends we miss were safe arrived.

SEYWARD
Some must go off; and yet, by these I see

---

58 *juggling* deceiving, cheating
59 *palter with us in a double sense* equivocate by double meanings
64 *monsters* prodigies, marvels
65 *Painted upon a pole* on a painted cloth set up on a pole (in front of the booth)
71 *try the last* make the final test (of fate)
73 (stage direction) *Exeunt fighting. Alarums. Enter fighting, and Macbeth*

slain. It is not clear why F has these two contradictory directions. Perhaps they *Exeunt* from the main stage and then *Enter* on the inner stage (or balcony) where a curtain can be drawn to conceal Macbeth's body.
(stage direction) *Retreat* the trumpet-call for the end of the fighting
75 *go off* die (perhaps a stage metaphor = exit)

So great a day as this is cheaply bought.

MALCOLM

Macduff is missing and your noble son.

ROSS

Your son, my lord, has paid a soldier's debt.
He only lived but till he was a man;
80   The which no sooner had his prowess confirmed
In the unshrinking station where he fought
But, like a man, he died.

SEYWARD   Then he is dead?

ROSS

Ay, and brought off the field. Your cause of sorrow
Must not be measured by his worth, for then
It hath no end.

SEYWARD   Had he his hurts before?

ROSS

Ay, on the front.

SEYWARD   Why then, God's soldier be he.
Had I as many sons as I have hairs
I would not wish them to a fairer death.
And so his knell is knolled.

MALCOLM   He's worth more sorrow;
And that I'll spend for him.

90 SEYWARD   He's worth no more:
They say he parted well, and paid his score.
And so God be with him. – Here comes newer comfort.

Enter Macduff with Macbeth's head

MACDUFF

Hail, King! For so thou art. Behold where stands
The usurper's cursèd head. The time is free.
I see thee compassed with thy kingdom's pearl

---

87 *hairs* (with pun on *heirs*)
91 *parted* departed
   score reckoning, account
93 *stands* (presumably the head is on a
   pole)

95 *pearl* (suggested probably by the idea
   of 'peers' and by the pearls which
   surround a crown)

That speak my salutation in their minds,
Whose voices I desire aloud with mine. –
Hail, King of Scotland!

ALL   Hail, King of Scotland!
    Flourish

MALCOLM
We shall not spend a large expense of time
Before we reckon with your several loves,   100
And make us even with you. My thanes and kinsmen,
Henceforth be earls, the first that ever Scotland
In such an honour named. What's more to do,
Which would be planted newly with the time,
As calling home our exiled friends abroad
That fled the snares of watchful tyranny,
Producing forth the cruel ministers
Of this dead butcher and his fiend-like queen –
Who, as 'tis thought, by self and violent hands
Took off her life – this, and what needful else   110
That calls upon us, by the grace of Grace
We will perform in measure, time, and place.
So thanks to all at once, and to each one,
Whom we invite to see us crowned at Scone.

                       Flourish. Exeunt

100 *reckon with your several loves* add up
what we owe to each individual
102 *Scotland* (? the King of Scotland)
104 *Which would be planted newly with the
time* which ought to be given a new
beginning in a new age

107 *ministers* agents
109 *by self and violent hands* by her own
violent hands
111 *by the grace of Grace* with God's help
112 *measure, time, and place* with due
order in every dimension

READ MORE IN PENGUIN

In every corner of the world, on every subject under the sun, Penguin represents quality and variety – the very best in publishing today.

For complete information about books available from Penguin – including Puffins, Penguin Classics and Arkana – and how to order them, write to us at the appropriate address below. Please note that for copyright reasons the selection of books varies from country to country.

In the United Kingdom: Please write to *Dept. EP, Penguin Books Ltd, Bath Road, Harmondsworth, West Drayton, Middlesex UB7 ODA*

In the United States: Please write to *Consumer Sales, Penguin USA, P.O. Box 999, Dept. 17109, Bergenfield, New Jersey 07621-0120*. VISA and MasterCard holders call 1-800-253-6476 to order Penguin titles

In Canada: Please write to *Penguin Books Canada Ltd, 10 Alcorn Avenue, Suite 300, Toronto, Ontario M4V 3B2*

In Australia: Please write to *Penguin Books Australia Ltd, P.O. Box 257, Ringwood, Victoria 3134*

In New Zealand: Please write to *Penguin Books (NZ) Ltd, Private Bag 102902, North Shore Mail Centre, Auckland 10*

In India: Please write to *Penguin Books India Pvt Ltd, 706 Eros Apartments, 56 Nehru Place, New Delhi 110 019*

In the Netherlands: Please write to *Penguin Books Netherlands bv, Postbus 3507, NL-1001 AH Amsterdam*

In Germany: Please write to *Penguin Books Deutschland GmbH, Metzlerstrasse 26, 60594 Frankfurt am Main*

In Spain: Please write to *Penguin Books S. A., Bravo Murillo 19, 1° B, 28015 Madrid*

In Italy: Please write to *Penguin Italia s.r.l., Via Felice Casati 20, I–20124 Milano*

In France: Please write to *Penguin France S. A., 17 rue Lejeune, F–31000 Toulouse*

In Japan: Please write to *Penguin Books Japan, Ishikiribashi Building, 2–5–4, Suido, Bunkyo-ku, Tokyo 112*

In South Africa: Please write to *Longman Penguin Southern Africa (Pty) Ltd, Private Bag X08, Bertsham 2013*

BY THE SAME AUTHOR

The plays in these collections are accompanied by notes and an introduction to each text, making them of particular value to students,
scholars and theatre-goers.

Four Histories
Richard II · Henry IV Part I · Henry IV Part II · Henry V

This tetralogy of plays inhabits the turbulent period of change from
the usurpation of the throne of Richard II by Bolingbroke to the
triumph – some would say triumphalism – of heroic kingship under
Henry V. Walter Pater found the central idea of the *Histories* to be
'the irony of kingship – average human nature, flung with wonderfully pathetic effect into the vortex of great events'.

Four Comedies
*The Taming of the Shrew · A Midsummer Night's Dream ·
As You Like It · Twelfth Night*

Shakespearian comedy has as much to do with the structure and
movement of the drama as with the wit of its dialogue or the humour
of its characters. In these four comedies there is a near-tragic crisis at
which disaster or happiness may ensue, but the overriding force of
goodwill and the power of understanding, love and generosity brings
us through to a joyful conclusion.

and

Three Roman Plays
Julius Caesar · Antony and Cleopatra · Coriolanus